ויקרא

LEVITICUS

ויקרא

LEVITICUS

Commentary by

BERNARD J. BAMBERGER

THE TORAH

*A
Modern
Commentary*

III

Union of American Hebrew Congregations

NEW YORK

LIBRARY OF CONGRESS CATALOGING IN PUBLICATION DATA

BAMBERGER, BERNARD JACOB, 1904–

THE TORAH: *A Modern Commentary*

LEVITICUS.
    Includes Hebrew text with English translation by the
Jewish Publication Society.

    Includes bibliographical references.
    1. Bible. O.T. Leviticus—Commentaries.
    I. Jewish Publication Society of America.
    II. Bible. O.T. Leviticus. Hebrew. 1978.
    III. Bible. O.T. Leviticus. English. Jewish Publication
        Society. 1978.
    IV. Title.

BS1255.3.B35   222'.13'077   78–16998
ISBN 0–8074–0011–4

TO THE MEMORY OF

Dr. William Rosenau

1865-1943

RABBI SCHOLAR TEACHER FRIEND

PUBLICATION OF
THIS VOLUME OF

The Torah: A Modern Commentary

has been made possible
by the generosity of the

MIRIAM STERN FOX FUND

Other volumes in this series
have been made possible by the
generosity of the
Falk Foundation, Kivie Kaplan,
and Maurice Saltzman

Preface

BEFORE I UNDERTOOK to write this commentary, I had the enormous privilege of serving on the committee which prepared the present Torah translation. I profited immeasurably in understanding the text, through involvement in the labor of translation and especially through the insights received from my learned colleagues. I acknowledge my indebtedness to them all: to Dr. Harry Freedman, Dr. Solomon Grayzel, and the late Dr. Max Arzt, and above all to our three distinguished professional Bible scholars, Dr. Harry M. Orlinsky, Dr. H. L. Ginsberg, and the late Dr. Ephraim A. Speiser.

In preparing the present work, I had the constant help and guidance of three erudite consultants, Dr. Alexander Guttmann, Dr. William W. Hallo, and Dr. Matitiahu Tsevat. Their vast knowledge was always at my disposal, correcting many errors and directing me to materials of which I was not aware. They were invariably gracious, whether their suggestions were adopted—as was usually the case—or whether they were modified or even rejected, perhaps unwisely. I am most grateful to all three.

This volume has been greatly enriched by the inclusion of Dr. Hallo's authoritative essay on *Leviticus and Ancient Near Eastern Literature*. The agreement between his statements and many passages of the commentary is by no means accidental: I made abundant use of materials he supplied. His essay elaborates more fully and systematically many points touched on in the commentary; he has, moreover, presented a general approach to Leviticus which is somewhat different from my own.

I likewise thank Dr. Robert I. Kahn, chairman of the Advisory Committee, Dr. Leonard S. Kravitz, and Dr. Bernard H. Mehlman, for a number of highly useful suggestions.

During the period of composition, I had occasion to work successively with Rabbi Alexander M. Schindler, Rabbi Jack D. Spiro, Mr. Abraham Segal, of blessed memory, and Rabbi Leonard A. Schoolman who dealt with the administrative aspects of the commentary project. I thank them all for many courtesies.

The manuscript was first edited by Mrs. Louise B. Stern, whose keen eye detected a number of fuzzy passages that required clarification. The final editing, which involved some rearrangement of material, was done by Mrs. Josette Knight. I want to acknowledge my great good fortune in having two such skilled and conscientious editors. My thanks also to Mrs. Annette Abramson for her careful assistance. Mr. Ralph Davis has handled the technical aspects of producing the book with his usual expertise and taste.

Lastly, when I used the resources of the New York library of the Hebrew Union College - Jewish Institute of Religion, my work was made easier and more pleasant by the kindness of Dr. I. Edward Kiev, of blessed memory, of his two charming assistants, Mrs. Susan Tabor and Mrs. Catherine Markush, and more recently of his successor, Mr. Philip E. Miller.

B. J. B.

CONTENTS

PREFACE   ix

INTRODUCING LEVITICUS   xv

    The character of the book and the commentary
    The name of the book
    The contents of the book
    Priestly writing and holiness writing
    Interpreters of Leviticus
    Some suggestions to the reader

LEVITICUS AND ANCIENT NEAR EASTERN   xxiii
    LITERATURE   William W. Hallo

PART I   Laws of Sacrifice

INTRODUCTION   3

    Ancient concepts of sacrifice · Ancient sacrifices 3 · Sacrifice in the Bible 4 ·
    Talmudic views 6 · Medieval views · Modern attitudes 7 · The sacrificial
    legislation of the Torah 8

The Olah–Burnt Offering [1:1-17]   9

The Minchah–Meal Offering [2:1-16]   15

Zevach Shelamim–Sacrifice of Well-Being [3:1-17]   21

Chatat–Sin Offering [4:1-35]   27

Chatat–Sin Offering; Asham–Guilt Offering [5:1-26]   37

Laws of Sacrifice–Olah, Minchah, Chatat [6:1-23]   47

Laws of Sacrifice–Zevach Shelamim [7:1-38]   53

PART II   The Dedication of the Tabernacle
and
The Ordination of the Priests

The Divine Presence in the Sanctuary [8:1- 10:20]   65

    The prohibition of intoxicants 66 · Priestly perquisites 67

PART III   Permitted and Forbidden Foods

The Dietary Laws [11:1-23]   89

    *A few definitions 89 · The scope of the dietary laws · The reason for the
dietary laws 90 · The dietary laws in Jewish history 91 · Some modern
problems 92 · Reform Judaism and the dietary laws 93*

PART IV   Defilement and Purification

Defilement from Animal Carcasses [11:24-47]   103

Defilement through Childbirth [12:1-8]   113

Defilement from Tzara'at [13:1-46]   117

    A note on Judaism and medicine 118

Tzara'at of Garments [13:47-59]   129

Purification from Tzara'at [14:1-32]   133

Tzara'at of Houses [14:33-57]   143

Defilement by Discharge from the Sex Organs [15:1-33]   149

PART V   The Day of Atonement

Yom Kippur [16:1-34]   159

> *The message of the Day of Atonement 159 · The origins of Yom Kippur ·*
> *Azazel 160 · The hazards of the Yom Kippur service 161 · Atonement*
> *and return 162 · Some problems of the biblical material 163*

PART VI   The Law of Holiness

Further Laws about Sacrifice and Food [17:1-16]   177

> *Secular slaughtering prohibited 177 · The prohibition of blood 179*

Sex Offenses [18:1-30]   185

> *Biblical attitudes toward sex 185 · Postbiblical Jewish attitudes 186 ·*
> *Modesty 187 · Incest 188 · Homosexual behavior 189 · Bestiality · Molech*
> *worship 191*

The Life of Holiness [19:1-37]   201

> *Holiness 201 · Sanctifying and profaning the name · The golden rule 204*

Punishment of Sex Offenses [20:1-27]   219

Laws concerning the Priests [21:1-22:33]   227

> *The priestly role · Israelite priesthood 227 · During the Second Temple 228 ·*
> *In later centuries · The laws in chapters 21 and 22*

The Festival Calendar [23:1-44]   243

I CALENDAR RECKONING   243

> *The day · The week · Months and years · The names of the months · Changes*
> *and controversies · Eras*

II THE BIBLICAL HOLY DAYS   247

> *Sabbath · Passover/Feast of Unleavened Bread · The offering of the omer ·*
> *The omer period · The Feast of Weeks (Shavuot) · Festival of the New*
> *Year (Rosh Hashanah) · The Day of Atonement · The Feast of Booths*
> *(Sukot) · Shemini Atzeret · New moon*

Oil, Bread, and the Blasphemer [24:1-23]   263

    Oil for the Temple lamps · The bread of display · The blasphemer 263

Sabbatical Year and Jubilee [25:1-55]   271

  I THE SABBATICAL YEAR   271

  II THE JUBILEE YEAR   272

    *The law · Was the law ever practiced? · The Book of Jubilees · The influence
    of the jubilee law*

III SLAVERY   276

Blessings and Curses [26:1-46]   289

    Tochechah 289 · The problem of retribution 290 · The sources of hope 292

PART VII   Supplementary Laws

Vows, Gifts, and Dues [27:1-34]   305

    Erech, Erkecha 305 · Hekdesh · Cherem 306

APPENDIX I (to Chapter 11) [The Dietary Laws]   317

APPENDIX II (to Chapter 16) [Order of Service for the High Priest on   319
    the Day of Atonement]

APPENDIX III (to Chapter 18) [Prohibited Degrees of Relationship for   321
    Marriage]

REFERENCE NOTES   325

BIBLIOGRAPHY   343

HAFTAROT   349

Introducing Leviticus

The Character of the Book and the Commentary

The third book of the Torah, Leviticus, contains some of the loftiest passages found in the Bible. It is in this book that we read, "Love thy neighbor as thyself" and "Proclaim liberty throughout the land."

But much of the book is devoted to matters completely remote from our present-day life—directions for sacrifice and rules of ritual defilement and purification. Nearly all these laws ceased to function when the Temple was destroyed in 70 C.E. They have no relevance to the conduct of even the most strictly Orthodox Jew, and they are omitted from such standard codes as the *Shulchan Aruch*. Orthodox belief, indeed, holds that this is only a temporary interruption: When the Messiah comes, the Temple will be rebuilt and the sacrificial cult resumed. Prayers for this restoration are included in the Orthodox prayer book. But most modern Jews—not only those committed to Reform Judaism—regard these sacrificial practices as completely out of date; they do not expect or want them to be revived.

This commentary is intended for the general reader who is not concerned with antiquarian research and who wants to know what message Scripture has for him now. It is written on the assumption that there is much in the Torah that is meaningful for the contemporary human being and, especially, for the contemporary Jew; and it attempts to reveal enduring values in the ancient text.

But the first half of the Book of Leviticus contains much that is not relevant to our times. The philosopher Philo (who lived in Alexandria at the beginning of the Christian era) found all sorts of spiritual meanings in the sacrificial cult; explaining the laws symbolically and allegorically, he honestly believed he had penetrated to their deepest and truest intent. This method is not possible for us. Our only honest approach is the historical approach, understanding the material in the light of the time when it was composed, against the background of ancient Near Eastern culture.

Such an enterprise is not entirely unprofitable even for the general reader. It reveals a dramatic development in concepts of religion and morality within the Bible itself. In this one book of Leviticus, there are a few passages where the word *kadosh* (usually rendered "holy") has the force of "taboo," and there are others where it designates the highest level of ethical and spiritual aspiration.

We shall find, moreover, that, while the ritual procedures here described resembled in some ways those of other ancient peoples, they also display significant differences. The distinctive outlook of developing Judaism made itself felt even in an area resistant to change—that of custom and ceremony administered by a hereditary, and therefore generally conservative, priesthood.

Most important, perhaps, is the fact that these materials were made accessible to all the people. Other Near Eastern nations had myths and legends that occasionally remind us of the stories of the Pentateuch. They also had bodies of civil and criminal law, such as the Code of Hammurabi which was inscribed on a monument set up in a public place. But their ritual and liturgical texts were generally kept in temples for the exclusive use of the priests. Only in the Torah do we find stories, laws, and rituals combined into an inclusive document available to everyone.

The Book of Deuteronomy commands that parents shall teach its contents diligently to their children and provides that the entire book shall be read publicly every seven years. But even Deuteronomy left priestly matters entirely in the hands of the priests. It does not describe the procedures of sacrifice, and it refers the people to the priests for guidance regarding "leprosy" (Deut. 24:8). It was therefore something of a revolution when the priestly laws were included in a work designed for the entire population. These laws were not to be professional secrets any longer. A number of sections begin, "Speak to the priests, the sons of Aaron," or "Speak to Aaron and his sons," but others—among them the very first section on sacrifice— begin, "Speak to the Israelite people." The concept of a complete Torah, which all may study who have the will to do so, expresses a new democratic spirit.

In addition, the seemingly unpromising ritual sections have at times called forth by the talmudic rabbis comments that are worth noting for their beauty and profound insight.

There are other subjects treated in Leviticus that are still operative in the lives of many Jews. The dietary laws are a notable instance. Even those Jews who do not observe *kashrut* should know something of the character and spirit of the rules of food, which have often been misunderstood and misrepresented by well-meaning but uninformed amateurs.

Still other sections deal with topics that are of concern to all committed Jews. Examples are the chapters on permitted and forbidden sex relations and the detailed account of holy days and festivals. Our treatment of such passages will assume that we have much to learn from the Torah, even though we do not accept its authority blindly and without question. And in the great Law of Holiness and the section on the jubilee year we shall find ourselves challenged by the noblest and most exacting of ethical and religious ideals.

Our presentation will often refer to the origins and the primary intent of ancient observances. The reader, however, should bear in mind that a custom may continue long after its original meaning has been discarded and forgotten. We should not assume, for example, that the generations of Jews who brought sacrifices to the Temple, or the writers who compiled the sacrificial laws in Leviticus, still believed that God is literally in need of food.

Nor is the value of a living custom necessarily impaired because it originated in superstition. A simple instance (not related to the Book of Leviticus) will make this plain. Rites of burial and mourning are incredibly ancient; they were originally intended to protect the survivors from the spirits of the dead. The latter were deemed to be resentful at being deprived of the comforts and associations they had enjoyed in life. To keep the departed one from returning and injuring his family, a pile of stones was heaped over his grave. Our custom of erecting a tombstone derives ultimately from that ancient fear; but obviously that is not the reason that we today mark the graves of our departed.

Unlike the first two books of the Bible, the third contains only a few bits of narrative. It is essentially a compendium of law. It has seemed desirable, therefore, to provide a fairly extended introduction to each section of the text before expounding it verse by verse.

The Name of the Book

At the beginning of the Christian era, or perhaps earlier, the name *Torat Kohanim*, "The Priestly Torah," was applied to our book. It is also usually referred to in Hebrew by its first word, *Vayikra*, "And He called." The Greek translators called it *to Leuitikon*, "the Levitical book," and the Latin version of this name—Leviticus—has been generally adopted. Oddly, the Levites are mentioned in this book only in chapter 25, verses 32 through 34, though of course the priests were members of the tribe of Levi.

The Contents of the Book

Laws of sacrifice: chapters 1 through 7.

The dedication of the Tabernacle and the ordination of the priests, with certain attendant events: chapters 8 through 10.

Dietary laws: chapter 11, verses 1 through 23.

Laws of defilement and purification: chapter 11, verse 24 through chapter 15, verse 33.

The Day of Atonement: chapter 16.

Additional laws about sacrifice and food: chapter 17.

Permitted and forbidden sex relations: chapters 18 and 20.

The Law of Holiness—ethical and ritual: chapter 19.

Laws for the priesthood: chapters 21 and 22.

The Sabbath and festival calendar: chapter 23.

Two laws and an incident involving blasphemy: chapter 24.

The sabbatical and jubilee years: chapter 25.

An exhortation, containing blessings for the observance of the law and curses for its violation: chapter 26.

Laws concerning vows, gifts, and dues: chapter 27.

Priestly Writing and Holiness Writing

The reader has already been made aware of the view that the Torah is a composite work. Though many conclusions of nineteenth-century biblical criticism have been challenged, it is hardly possible to deny the existence of three principal elements in the Pentateuch.[1] One is the Book of Deuteronomy, distinctive in viewpoint, contents, and style; it is referred to by scholars as D. The second comprises the vivid, dramatic, and moving narratives in Genesis, Exodus, and Numbers and is called JE.[2] These books also contain extensive sections comprising a priestly document, P; and Leviticus consists altogether of priestly material. P includes a considerable amount of narrative, but it is primarily concerned with law and ritual. It is somewhat more systematic in outlook than the other documents, and its style is more precise and detailed. It can be dignified and impressive, as in the opening chapter of Genesis; but the modern reader may find

---

[1] In addition, there are a number of poetic passages and three short codes of law: Exod. 20; 21–23; 34:10–26.

[2] JE is supposed to be drawn from two separate sources, designated J and E. J is so called because it regularly calls God by the name JHWH (or YHWH) and also because it was probably composed in the Kingdom of Judah. E, which originated in the Northern Kingdom, ordinarily uses the name *Elohim*, the Hebrew word for "God." But the separation of these two elements is often difficult and uncertain.

tedious its concern for genealogies, the details of the structure and furnishings of the Tabernacle, and fine points of ritual law.

Though the entire Book of Leviticus is drawn from priestly sources, it is not a completely unified and ordered code. For example, it treats at length of sacrifices, but other important regulations on the subject—also from P—are found in Exodus and Numbers. The chapters on ritual defilement (11–15) do not mention the most severe type of defilement, contact with a corpse. This matter is alluded to briefly in chapter 21, verses 1 through 4, but a full exposition appears only in Numbers, chapter 19.

Even within the Book of Leviticus there is a certain lack of system. The section on sacrifice consists of two parts, chapters 6 and 7 providing additional rules for the various types of offering already discussed in chapters 1 through 5. (Chapter 17 offers still further material on sacrifice.) Chapter 20 is largely a repetition of the laws in chapter 18.

Clearly, P is not a single seamless whole, written by one author. It is a compilation of priestly traditions drawn from various sources and, no doubt, from various periods. There are numerous discrepancies of detail; and there is some indication that, after the basic compilation was finished, additions and editorial changes were made. But the attempts of some scholars to analyze P into its component documents and establish the date of each are far from convincing.[3] Moreover, study has increasingly revealed that there was a long oral tradition behind many of the written documents. A given law may have existed for centuries before it was embodied in one of our present texts.

But, even in translation, one can detect a marked change in content, style, and mood in the second half of the book. Chapters 1 through 16 and chapter 27 are similar in matter and manner to P materials found in other books of the Torah. But chapters 17

through 26 have many distinctive characteristics. They frequently explain the purpose and intent of the laws, something rare in P. In addition to stating the reasons for individual provisions, these chapters constantly refer to their overall purpose—to maintain the holiness of the Israelite people. And holiness is understood not only in terms of ceremonial purity but especially in terms of personal and social righteousness. The divine source and sanction of all these rules is constantly emphasized by such phrases as "I the Lord am your God" after a given commandment. In their combination of moral and ritual elements and in their hortatory tone, these chapters remind us of D.[4] In short, they are a distinctive component of P, or else an entirely separate document, called by scholars the Holiness Code, H; it contains most of the Leviticus passages that appeal to the contemporary reader.

Though H is different from the other parts of the Torah, it shows many points of resemblance to the prose writings of the prophet Ezekiel. Scholars have compiled long lists of phrases that occur frequently in Ezekiel and H and seldom, if ever, in other biblical texts. It has even been suggested that Ezekiel was the author of the Holiness Code; but in fact Ezekiel's program of religious observance contradicts some regulations of Leviticus, and some of his theological ideas are also at variance with those of H. It seems, however, quite possible that H dates from the time of the prophet's activity—that is, the years following the downfall of Judah, in the sixth century B.C.E.

[3] A recent commentary on Leviticus by Karl Elliger (Tübingen: Mohr, 1966) goes to extremes in that sort of analysis and has been disregarded in the preparation of this book.

[4] Not that the P writers were indifferent to ethical considerations: see Lev. 1:10, 14; 5:20 ff., etc. But P was intended to provide a guide for ritual, not for moral conduct.

When did the main body of the priestly writing originate? Tradition, of course, held that the entire Torah was given to Moses at Sinai. The nineteenth-century Bible critics considered P the latest part of the Torah, composed during or after the Babylonian exile (approximately 597 to 516 B.C.E.). It was intended as a sort of constitution for the Second Commonwealth, when the Jews had no king and the High Priest was leader and spokesman of the nation. According to this theory, P was the framework into which JE and D were fitted, in the fifth century B.C.E.

This once widely accepted view has been challenged in various ways by many twentieth-century Bible scholars, among whom Yehezkel Kaufmann has been one of the boldest and most original.[5] He held that P is not the latest, but the earliest, of the sources incorporated in the Torah. It contains primitive elements, such as the rite of the scapegoat (Lev. 16:8–10, 20–22), which could not have originated after the period of the great prophets. Moreover, P often reflects conditions very different from those of the exile and its aftermath.

The newer critics are in many ways persuasive. But it is always easier to demolish old views than to construct viable new ones. The earlier critics proved conclusively that the Torah is not a unit and that it does not date as a whole from the time of Moses; but their reconstruction of early Israelite history was far from definitive. A host of difficulties has been marshaled against it in recent decades; but the newer attempts at synthesis, such as Kaufmann's, are also open to question.

The present writer believes that there is a measure of truth in both positions. The written documents of the Pentateuch, as we have seen, are a crystallization of many traditions, some of them very ancient. This is also true of P. Despite a certain uniformity of style and outlook, it contains many discrepancies that indicate it is a composite of various sources. The substance of P was not created in the fifth century B.C.E., but it seems probable that the priestly materials were given their present form at that time. The editors preserved without change much that was ancient, but they also made modifications and additions to meet new needs. The scapegoat law is only one of the genuinely archaic elements in P; but the priestly writing also contains passages where we meet a contrived and artificial "antiquity"—especially, the account of an elaborate shrine with a highly organized sacrificial system, completely inappropriate to desert conditions. The advanced, almost philosophic monotheism of the Creation story in Genesis chapter 1[6] is also suggestive of a relatively late date. So is the sharp distinction in P between priests and Levites—whereas in D these two terms are synonymous.[7] The Book of Leviticus as we have it is the end product of a long and complex evolution.

Interpreters of Leviticus

For centuries Jewish children began their Bible studies with the Book of Leviticus. This strange choice was justified by the contention that pure young children should first learn about the sacrifices which were brought in purity.[8]

But adults also studied the work intensively. The rabbinic commentaries to biblical

[5] Y. Kaufmann, *The Religion of Israel* (abridged English translation by M. Greenberg, Chicago: University of Chicago Press, 1966).
[6] This enlightened spirit is the more remarkable when we consider that this chapter contains vestigial allusions to the polytheistic Babylonian creation-myth.
[7] See Introduction to Lev. 21.
[8] H. Schauss, *The Lifetime of the Jew* (Cincinnati: Union of American Hebrew Congregations, 1950), p. 100 and n. 114.

books are known as *midrashim*, and of these the one to Leviticus is among the longest and most detailed. It is called *Torat Kohanim* and also *Sifra* (*the* Book). The material is drawn largely from the expositions of the second-century Rabbi Akiba and his disciples.

The word *midrash* means "search," "interpretation"; and *midrashim* often draw inferences from the biblical text that go far beyond its plain sense. But the midrashic method of Rabbi Akiba was particularly intensive. He was convinced that every word and every letter of the Pentateuch is charged with rich and varied meaning. In *Sifra*, a legal ruling may be deduced from an "and" or a "but," thus providing biblical support for regulations hitherto known only by tradition. *Sifra* comments on nearly every verse of Leviticus in terms of both halachah, law, and haggadah, moral and religious edification.

It is probable that *Sifra* was compiled in the third century C.E. Later on, other midrashim to Leviticus were edited, perhaps in the sixth or seventh century. These works are almost exclusively haggadic, consisting of sermons attached to the opening sentences of different sections of the biblical book. They deal with themes of interest to the average listener who might find the details of sacrifice, and the like, rather dull and dry. Thus the sermon on the opening verse, "The LORD called to Moses," treats of prophecy and revelation; that on chapter 2, verse 1, "When a person [*nefesh*] presents," understands *nefesh* as "soul" and discusses the relation of soul and body. Though chapter 10, verse 9, prohibits the use of wine only to a priest who is about to officiate, the midrashim use it for a general homily on the evils of drink, containing some humorous touches. The verse, "If your brother, being in straits" (25:35), calls forth a lengthy and magnificent sermon on charity. These materials are found in a work called *Vayikra*

Rabbah (roughly, "The Big Midrash to Leviticus") and in *Midrash Tanchuma* which extends over the entire Torah and exists in at least two versions. Many comments on Leviticus are also found in other *midrashim* and in the two Talmuds. Much of this material was assembled in medieval compilations, the *Yalkut Shimoni* and the *Midrash Hagadol*.

Our volume draws upon these sources as well as upon the great medieval Jewish commentators, Rashi, Ibn Ezra, and others. From *Sifra* down, they often give sound explanations of the biblical text. But, even when we find their interpretations incorrect or fanciful, they have something to teach us. We learn from them how the Torah was understood by earlier generations, who sometimes found in the text new and elevating thoughts.

We owe a great deal to the critical studies of Christian biblical scholars of the last hundred and fifty years. Their commentaries on Leviticus, however, are not among their most successful achievements—perhaps because it was difficult for them to relate to the contents of this book. A recent commentary from which I profited is that of N. H. Snaith[9] who made extensive use of Jewish sources.

Two modern Jewish commentaries on Leviticus deserve special mention. One is the *Critical and Historical Commentary* of M. M. Kalisch[10] who was among the first Jewish scholars to utilize critical methods for the study of the Bible. Even for his age, he was too much inclined to explain age-old rites in rationalistic and moralistic terms; and his work is now largely out of date. But it is a mine of information on the history of biblical

---

[9] N. H. Snaith, *Leviticus and Numbers, The Century Bible* (new edition, London: Nelson, 1967).
[10] M. M. Kalisch, *A Critical and Historical Commentary on the Old Testament: Leviticus*, 2 vols. (London: Longmans Green, Reader and Dyer, 1867–1872).

exegesis, and it contains many penetrating remarks.

The massive German commentary of David Hoffmann[11] was written from an uncompromisingly Orthodox viewpoint. But he was well acquainted with the work of the nineteenth-century Christian biblical critics, and he was frequently successful in turning their critical weapons against them. A review of this learned work was published by the Christian Bruno Baentsch, whose own commentary on Leviticus we shall cite occasionally.[12] Baentsch admitted that he had learned much from Hoffmann, despite his Orthodox approach.

Mention should also be made of two modern Hebrew commentaries on the entire Torah, including Leviticus. That of Samuel David Luzzatto[13] combines a strong commitment to tradition with considerable originality. The other, by Arnold B. Ehrlich,[14] is one of the most brilliant works of modern biblical science. Though sometimes erratic, and now partly outdated, Ehrlich's work had considerable influence on the present Torah translation.[15]

Some Suggestions to the Reader

This commentary is based on the translation of the Torah published by the Jewish Publication Society of America in 1963 and

revised in 1967 (NJPS). The translators provided a number of marginal notes to the translation, and they are here incorporated in the commentary and marked "T.N." for "Translator's Note." It should be observed that alternate renderings given in these notes and introduced by "Or" were considered by the Translation Committee almost as acceptable as those adopted in the text; those introduced by "Others" are well-known translations, usually found in the 1917 translation of the Jewish Publication Society (OJPS), which the committee did not find acceptable.

Much of the material in Leviticus is technical, and we do not always have exact equivalents in English for the Hebrew terms. It has therefore seemed desirable to use in this commentary these Hebrew terms (after defining them) rather than the more or less approximate English renderings.

We shall also frequently employ the word "halachah," which is derived not from the Bible but from rabbinic literature. It comes from a root meaning "to go" and designates the concretely legal elements in Judaism, including civil, criminal, family, procedural, and ritual law—in contrast to matters of belief, aspiration, and idealism which cannot be formulated into specific, enforceable duties. The word "halachah" can mean the entire corpus of Jewish law or a ruling on a single question.

The accepted halachah is often at variance with what seems to be the literal sense of the biblical verse on which the halachah is based. Often, indeed, there is no conflict; but frequently the rabbis go far beyond the plain intent of the text in the far-reaching and fanciful inferences they draw, and occasionally the halachah flatly negates the simple meaning of the scriptural words. (This was fully recognized by the traditional commentators. They assumed in all such cases that authentic tradition going back to Moses at Sinai required them to accept as

[11] D. Hoffmann, *Das Buch Leviticus*, 2 vols. (Berlin: M. Poppelauer, Vol. I, 1905; Vol. II, 1906).

[12] B. Baentsch, *Exodus-Leviticus-Numeri* (Nowack's *Handkommentar*, Göttingen: Vandenboeck und Ruprecht, 1903).

[13] *Perush Shadal al Chamishah Chumshei Torah* (new edition, Tel Aviv: Devir, 1965).

[14] *Mikra Kifeshuto* (reprinted in *The Library of Biblical Studies*, 3 vols., New York: Ktav Publishing House, 1969).

[15] All the commentators mentioned in this section will be cited in the notes simply by name, it being understood that the reference is to their comment on the passage under discussion; a page reference is occasionally added.

normative an explanation that was not in accord with the usual rules of grammar and philology.)[16]

The Jewish reader needs to know not only the probable original meaning of a Bible verse but also how that verse has been understood in Jewish tradition, especially in regard to religious practice and observance. These divergent viewpoints are frequently explained in the introductions to the various sections of the ensuing commentary. Individual items are treated as follows:

The commentary proper cites *Sifra* and other rabbinic sources, as well as the great medieval commentaries, when these writings appear to give a correct, or at least plausible, explanation of the biblical text. Where, however, the halachah appears to go beyond or against the plain sense of Scripture, it is summarized in the section headed "Gleanings." (As a rule, such halachic summaries are not direct quotations from the sources.) The references provided in the notes are in no way exhaustive; they sometimes cite primary sources and sometimes the codification of the halachah by Maimonides and his successors. Most often, however, we rely on the explanation of a given verse in *Sifra*, in which case the reference is simply "Sifra" or is omitted altogether.

It will be seen further that the "Gleanings" are usually divided into two sections, the first containing the halachic materials, the second headed by the Hebrew term "Haggadah." This word, from a root meaning "to tell," refers to all nonlegal elements in talmudic and midrashic literature, especially those concerned with belief and with moral edification. In these sections there are more direct quotations, but often it was necessary to summarize and to explain for clarity and brevity. Included also are some selections from later Jewish literature which is not properly haggadic but is likewise edifying.

[16] See Ibn Ezra's introduction to his Torah commentary and below, pp. 56, 61, 117.

Leviticus
and Ancient Near Eastern Literature

WILLIAM W. HALLO

In the primeval garden of Genesis stood the tree of life. Man was bidden to eat of it, along with all the other trees of the garden, excepting only one, the tree of death. He did eat of it and this, "man's first disobedience," created a logical contradiction which even God could not have tolerated. Having tasted of the tree of mortality, man could not now also redeem the promise of immortality or, as the text puts it, "stretch out his hand and take also from the tree of life and eat [of it] and so live forever." Therefore he was permanently banned from the garden and destined forever after to wring a hard-earned subsistence from the soil by the sweat of his brow. The offer of sustenance without toil was withdrawn together with the promise of immortality.

But the concept of the tree of life was not abandoned; it reemerged in the Book of Proverbs as the symbol of wisdom (3:18) and justice (11:30) and in postbiblical theology as the symbol of the Bible itself. The Torah became a tree of life to those who lay hold of it, as we are reminded in the liturgy whenever the Torah scroll is returned to the Ark. What this signifies (in rabbinic exegesis) is that fear of the Lord and obedience to the

Torah can still redeem a part of the primeval promise: not eternal life, but length of days; not sustenance without toil, but toil rewarded by subsistence. These reformulations are most explicit in Deuteronomy, with its almost simplistic system of rewards and punishments. But they inform the entire Torah and offer a special clue to the literary character of Leviticus.

Leviticus is the shortest of the Five Books of Moses. It is also the middle book, and its centrality in the Pentateuch is more than a mere matter of position. (It was typically the first text of the traditional *cheder*.) For all its apparent attention to archaic and obsolete priestly concerns, a far different focus emerges when the book is set against the Torah as a whole and against the literature of the surrounding Near East. Then we see that its real concern is with consumption of food (chs. 1–11) and with the related requirements of purification (chs. 12–16) and sanctification (chs. 17–27). These three broad topics provide, as it were, the warp of the book, while the woof is based on another triad: God, priests, and laity. To each are assigned very specific portions of all edibles, each receive distinct roles in purification and discrete levels of holiness. Thus Leviticus can be regarded as a homogeneous literary work, even though we cannot prove that it ever existed as a separate book in its own right, and even though the critics differ widely in their hypotheses about the various documents and traditions that may have gone into its composition.

The Comparative Approach

After a century and more of "biblical archeology," a comparative approach to Leviticus may well begin with an appeal to those concrete material remains recovered in the excavations which throw welcome light on customs and ceremonies previously preserved only in the verbal descriptions of the biblical book. Thus, for example, the laws of the ritual bath which the Mishnah developed from the prescriptions in Leviticus 15 were found to apply to the disposition and measurements of the *mikvaot* unearthed at Masada from the time of the Second Temple (see Gleanings to 15:5 with note 12). This is startling confirmation, albeit mute. More often, the architectural and other remains are further illuminated by epigraphic finds, i.e., by monumental or archival inscriptions. Arad, for example, served as a border fortress for the Kingdom of Judah in the time of the First Temple; as such, it was privileged to have its own sanctuary (prior to the centralization of the cult at Jerusalem) complete with altar. Not only do some of its measurements and other dispositions correspond to those prescribed for the Jerusalem temple, but in or around it were found ostraca (potsherds) inscribed with names of priestly families (e.g., Keros, Meremoth, Pashhur) known from the later books of the Bible (see note 3 to chs. 21 and 22).[1] Better even than the laconic ostraca is the evidence of literary texts. When the text (16:12) details the rules regarding the censer, it is easy to picture this cultic instrument in light, not only of the many actual censers (often in the form of a hand) excavated all over the Near East, but also of the parallel wording of texts such as the daily ritual of the Egyptian temple of Amon-Re at Karnak, which included instructions for taking the censer, laying its bowl upon its arm, and putting the incense on the fire.[2]

A word of caution is nonetheless in order before proceeding to utilize the extensive literary parallels from the Near Eastern environment. Responsible comparison must beware of false analogies by imposing the restraint of sound philology. Thus, e.g., the twelve loaves of 24:5 have long been compared to the "sweet bread" offering (*akal mutqi*) in dozens or multiples of dozens in Late Babylonian rituals. But, when the Akkadian adjective for sweet (*matqu*) was found in a lexical text as an explanation of *a-kal pa-nu*, the conclusion was hastily drawn that here was the Babylonian original of the biblical "bread of display" (the traditional "shewbread," i.e., *lechem pānîm*, Exod. 25:30; etc.). And, just as the twelve loaves of Leviticus 24 equalled the shewbread of Exodus 25, so, it was argued, the "sweet bread" of Babylonia was also called "shewbread." In fact, however, the Akkadian term must be read *a-lap-pa-nu*; it refers to a bittersweet taste; a beer of such taste; and the barley from which this beer is made. In short, there is no shewbread in Akkadian. And, if the number twelve has any significance, it should be sought, not in the Babylonian evidence which is actually later, but in the Israelite system of twelve tribes.

[1] Yochanan Aharoni, "The Israelite Sanctuary at Arad" in *New Directions in Biblical Archaeology*, eds. D. N. Freedman and J. C. Greenfield (Garden City: Doubleday, 1969), pp. 25–39.
[2] James B. Pritchard, ed., *Ancient Near Eastern Texts* (Princeton: Princeton University Press, 2nd ed., 1955), p. 325, n. 3. [Hereafter cited as Pritchard, *ANET*.]

The Concept of Consumption

We turn then to the main concerns of Leviticus, beginning with the "concept of consumption" as it is reflected in the cult (chs. 1–11) and epitomized in the dictum about the Aaronide priests: "For they offer the Lord's offerings by fire, the food of their God, and so must be holy" (21:6; cf. 21:8). The basic conception underlying this dictum is a widely held one in the ancient Near East: the gods, like men, need to eat in order to live, and men are there to provide for them. Already some of the oldest Mesopotamian myths justify the creation of man in these terms: the great gods, weary of the task of furnishing their own sustenance, initially force the lesser gods to labor for them, but these rebel and mankind is created to relieve them of their labors.[3] Pale reflections of the same conception linger in the mythical version of Creation in Genesis (2:4–7, 15). But when it comes to the cultic expression of this conception, Israel parts company with its Near Eastern heritage. The polytheistic cult was firmly rooted in and centered around the physical image of the deity—anthropomorphic in Mesopotamia and Syria, in Egypt theriomorphic (animal-shaped) as well. Much of the cult was devoted to what, in a pregnant phrase, has been called "the care and feeding of the gods."[4] It involved the physical presentation, to the cult statue of the deity, of real victuals twice daily and in added amounts on special days of the cultic calendar. The victuals included meat, fowl, and fish, as well as cereals, oils, and other vegetarian items, as is clear from countless records of offerings carefully drawn up by the clergy responsible for the temple accounts. Each kind of food demanded its own ceremonial, such as sprinkling for cereals and libation for oils. It was most elaborate for meats. The living animal was slaughtered and its inedible portions carefully set aside for such uses as leather-making (from the skin). The entrails, which were not considered fit for consumption, were minutely inspected for their ominous significance, and a whole "science" of divination (extispicy) developed around the interpretation of the precise configuration of lungs, intestines, and especially the liver (hepatoscopy). The edible portions were then offered to the divine statue at a table set behind drawn curtains. After the proper time had elapsed, the table was cleared and what the statue had graciously deigned to leave over was eaten by the king. The balance of the enormous daily deliveries to the temples was then distributed to the clergy for their consumption. On special festive occasions the laity too was victualled from these deliveries; they, or at least the leavings, were considered sanctified by their prior contact with the deity.

Clearly, the cultic pattern is totally different in ancient Israel, and Leviticus reflects the difference. There is no statue or other physical image of the deity and no need to "feed" it. Equally important, "there is no augury in Jacob, no divining in Israel" (Num. 23:23; cf. Lev. 19:26), hence no need to inspect the entrails of the slaughtered animal. Finally, though the priesthood was maintained by tithes and other means and received a share of the regular offerings (a practice sometimes abused as in I Samuel 2:13–16), the king was neither the principal ministrant nor the designated beneficiary of the cult which, in keeping with the emerging Israelite doctrine of collective responsibility, was an obligation on the population as a whole, or at least on all adult males. The rationale for sacrifice was correspondingly

---

[3] Cf. W. G. Lambert and A. R. Millard, *Atra-ḫasīs: The Babylonian Story of the Flood* (Oxford: Oxford University Press, 1969).

[4] A. Leo Oppenheim, *Ancient Mesopotamia* (Chicago: University of Chicago Press, 1964), pp. 183–198.

different. Let us begin with the meat offering.

Israelite belief involved a strict hierarchy of God, man, and world in which man ranked midway between the divine realm and the material world of nature, including plants and animals and the things made from them. The law distinguished clearly among these realms, and this was equally true of cultic as of civil legislation. Offenses against God could only be pardoned by God, offenses against human life could not be absolved by material compensation. But offenses against nature also were subject to retaliation, for it was recognized that nature had its own defenses. The spilling of animal blood was in some sense an offense against nature and courted the risk of punishment, although never on the level of human bloodshed. It was to obviate such punishment that successive provisions were made to invest the act of animal slaughtering with a measure of divine sanction (see commentary to ch. 17). The common denominator of these provisions was to turn mere slaughter into sanctification. The "sacrifice" was a sacred-making of the consumption that followed.

The levitical legislation enshrined this principle in a painstaking distribution of consumption among deity, priesthood, and laity. Repeatedly, the first eleven chapters of the book specify which parts of the animal belonged to God and which to the priests; only the balance, if any, was available to the Israelite who brought the sacrifice. This principle, once formulated, was extended to meal offerings as well, and beyond that to the secondary functions of sacrifice: though in origin designed to sanctify the very act of consumption, sacrifice ultimately served as well to sanctify other human activities and to atone for other human transgressions. While deriving many of its mechanics from ancient Near Eastern models, it thus evolved a distinctive rationale.

The Requirements of Purification

The laws of kashrut (ch. 11) form a logical conclusion to the legislation on consumption and are quite without parallel in the ancient Near East. They cover only foods of animal origin and form a suitable transition to the second major concern of Leviticus, namely purification (chs. 12–16). Having concluded the "instructions concerning animals" (11:46) with a short section on defilement from animal carcasses and the like, the text begins the laws of purification with a short section on defilement by the "blood of parturition" before moving on to its main concern, defilement by various biological phenomena such as skin diseases, fungus, menstruation, and genital discharges (chs. 12–15). The priestly prescriptions covering these conditions are fully analyzed in the commentary; what the modern reader most often asks is why such unsavory matters are taken up by Leviticus at all. The comparative approach supplies a suggestive answer: the ancient Near Eastern milieu was acutely sensitive to the conditions described in these chapters—not, however, primarily as a hygienic or medical problem, but for their ominous significance. Fungus-like growths in houses, for example, were interpreted in elaborate cuneiform handbooks of prognostication. Other handbooks provided appropriate rituals, not so much for treating the symptom, but for averting the (usually evil) consequences it portended. One example out of many will have to suffice. A fungus called *katarru* is treated at length in chapter 12 of *šumma ālu*, the "terrestrial omen series" (so called to distinguish it from the series devoted to astrological omens and to freak births respectively). If such a fungus is found "in a man's house, on the outer north wall, the owner of the house will die and his house will be scattered. To avert the evil, you make six axes of tamarisk and scrape away some of the fungus with them. . . . You recite: 'Ea performed (the incantation), Ea undid (the evil).' On that day the owner of the house slaughters a red male sheep before Ishum. . . . You throw that holy water over him, and its (the portent's) evil will be dissipated."[5] Even without studying all the possible permutations on the nature, location, and significance of each fungus, or the entire ritual (including both symbolic acts and conjurational formulas) prescribed for each individual case, one can readily see that the Mesopotamian concern was rooted in the mantic world view. That is, natural (or "unnatural") phenomena were signals vouchsafed to men by the gods, an "early warning system" of evils to come. Ritual was needed to dissipate, not the fungus, but the (greater) evil that it portended. The levitical legislation was therefore perhaps a reaction to a very deep-seated popular prejudice, shared to some extent by the Israelites. Without attempting to eradicate such fear at one stroke, it wisely instituted a systematic set of rules for dealing with the symptoms that inspired it.

The legislation about the day of atonement which follows (ch. 16) would seem like an unwarranted intrusion at this point, for in its historical dimension it links up with the narrative of ch. 10, while in its legal dimension it belongs with the festal calendar of ch. 23. It should therefore probably be re-garded as a special instance of defilement (in this case the forbidden encroachment by the priesthood into the sphere of the divine). To this is added the central role played by an animal in the ritual absolving the priest. From the point of view of literary structure, it thus combines the emphasis on animals in the first section of the book with that on defilements in the second and provides a fitting literary conclusion to both. Seen in this light, the central emphasis is not on the festival but on the "scapegoat." The evident "primitive" character of this ritual figure is confirmed by folkloristic parallels from all over the world, and the sophisticated cultures of the ancient Near East are conspicuously missing from these parallels.[6] True, "when the ancient Egyptians sacrificed a bull, they invoked upon its head all the evils that might otherwise befall themselves" and then "either sold the bull's head to the Greeks or cast it into the river."[7] But this is already a far cry from the physical transfer of men's sins to an animal, still preserved in a late Assyrian incantation where we read: "Take the scapegoat (mašhuldubbû), place its head upon his (the afflicted king's) head. . . . Let that spittle fall (from his mouth) into its mouth. May that king be pure, may he be clean."[8]

Possibly the earliest evidence for the institution of the scapegoat comes from the Hittite texts of Anatolia, where a sacrificial animal described as nakkuššiš is loaded with the impurities of the penitent and sent on its way.[9] The Hittite technical term was borrowed from Hurrian and appears in earlier Hurro-Akkadian texts from Nuzi and Alalakh in the more general meaning of "substitute." Etymologically, it appears to be composed of "to let go" (nakk-) and the abstract suffix (-ši), providing an interesting parallel to one of the proposed etymologies for azāzēl, the "goat that departs" (see commentary to ch. 16 with note 4) which, by

[5] Richard I. Caplice, *The Akkadian Namburbi Texts: An Introduction* (Sources from the Ancient Near East, Vol. 1, No. 1, 1974), p. 18. Cf. *idem, Journal of Near Eastern Studies,* 33, 1974, pp. 345–349. [Hereafter cited as *JNES.*]

[6] Cf., e. g., James G. Frazer, "Public Scapegoats," *The Golden Bough* (New York: Macmillan, abridged ed., 1960), ch. LVII, pp. 651–679.

[7] *Ibid.,* p. 661.

[8] Caplice, "Namburbi Texts in the British Museum, III," *Orientalia,* 36 (1967), pp. 293 f.

[9] O. R. Gurney, "Magic Rituals: The Scapegoat," in *Some Aspects of Hittite Religion* (The Schweich Lectures of the British Academy, 1976, 1977), Lecture III, pp. 47–52. Cf. Jim Hicks, *The Empire Builders* (New York: Time-Life Books, 1974), pp. 105–113.

"loan-translation," became *caper emissarius* in the Vulgate and "scape-goat" in English. (The latter term was apparently coined by William Tyndale, the first great English Bible translator, in 1530).

The Laws of Sanctification

The balance of Leviticus (chs. 17–26; for 27 see below) is devoted to the laws of sanctification and may well have once constituted a discrete literary entity (see commentary). But it is artfully woven into the book almost from its opening verse (17:11), whose key verb "atone" (*kappēr*) links it to the laws of atonement in ch. 16. The verb is attested also in other Semitic languages, but only in biblical Hebrew is it so central to the cult.[10] Rites of expiation are relatively rare in older Egyptian and Mesopotamian religion which centered most of its attention on the person of the king. In Old Kingdom Egypt, the king was himself a god and the object of worship; in Mesopotamia, he was the deputy of the local or imperial deity, and it was only or largely *his* ethical conduct and cultic meticulousness that served as warrant for the common weal. With the rise of a more "personal religion" in the second millennium, the common man began to adopt the royal belief in a kind of filial relationship to his personal god or to a divine pair conceived of as his heavenly parents.[11] But the idea of a collective, national responsibility, so intimately woven into the cult of expiation in Leviticus (e.g., 4:13), reached little further than the bland platitudes of the so-called wisdom literature in hieroglyphic and cuneiform. The contrast may best be illustrated in connection with ch. 19, "the decalogue of the Holiness Code" (see commentary to 19:3 with note 16). Although most often quoted for its lofty ethical prescriptions, the chapter nevertheless shares with the rest of Leviticus a primary preoccupation with cult and consumption. Many of its individual provisions can be closely paralleled from the ancient Near East, but in significantly different literary contexts. In New Kingdom Egypt, for example, the deceased individual was accompanied to his grave by the so-called "Book of the Dead" which replaced the earlier mortuary texts known as Pyramid Texts (Old Kingdom) and Coffin Texts (Middle Kingdom) and extended their benefits from the king and the nobility to the private individual. A standard element of these later mortuary texts was the "protestation of guiltlessness," a kind of "negative confession" with many parallels to Leviticus 19. Compare, for instance, "I have neither increased nor diminished the grain measure. . . . I have not added to the weight of the balance. I have not weakened the plummet of the scales"[12] with Lev. 19:35 f. In Mesopotamia, similar sentiments are embedded in the "Wisdom" literature, a miscellaneous category of genres addressed to and concerned with the common man. Thus the great preceptive hymn to the sun-god Shamash, patron of justice and righteousness, contrasts "the merchant who practices trickery as he holds the balances, who uses two sets of weights" with "the honest merchant who holds the balances and gives good weight" or "the merchant . . . who weighs out loans (of corn) by the minimum standard but requires a large quantity in repayment"

[10] B. A. Levine, *In the Presence of the Lord: A Study of Cult and Some Cultic Terms in Ancient Israel* (Leiden, Holland: E. J. Brill, 1974), Pt. Two and App. III, pp. 56–77, 123–127.

[11] Thorkild Jacobsen, *The Treasures of Darkness: A History of Mesopotamian Religion* (New Haven: Yale University Press, 1976), Ch. 5, pp. 145–164.

[12] Pritchard, *ANET*, p. 34.

[13] *Ibid.*, p. 388; the translation follows Lambert, *Babylonian Wisdom Literature* (Oxford: Clarendon Press, 1960), p. 133. Cf. *idem*, "Morals in Ancient Mesopotamia," *Jaarbericht van het Voorasiatisch-Egyptisch Genootschap Ex Oriente Lux*, 15 (1957–1958), pp. 184–196, for an authoritative synthesis.

with "the honest merchant who weighs out loans (of corn) by the maximum standard, thus multiplying kindness."[13] The traditional rendering of 19:16 (see commentary) finds some support in the Akkadian "Counsels of Wisdom" with its many strictures against talebearing or unnecessary involvement in the disputes of others.[14] Such advice, usually addressed to princes and courtiers, is also characteristic of Egyptian "Instructions" of all periods,[15] which share with the "Counsels" a secular setting; they are pragmatic admonitions justified by long experience rather than cultic injunctions sanctioned by divine command. Nowhere is the contrast more explicit, perhaps, than in 19:23–25 which echoes paragraph 60 of the Laws of Hammurabi[16]—only that there the tenant farmer shares the yield of the fifth year, not with God, but with the human lessor!

Having thus arrived at the sphere of Near Eastern law, one might expect to find more parallels in it to the legislation of Leviticus. Such parallels do, after all, abound with the legislation of Exodus and Deuteronomy—but only its casuistic legislation, i.e., that phrased in the typical "conditional" form of precedent- (or case-) law. That phrasing characterizes civil and criminal legislation and is largely absent in Leviticus, whose laws are mostly cultic in content (or at least in context) and apodictic (or "unconditional")

in form. A good illustration is provided by the laws on sexual conduct (chs. 18 and 20), for such conduct was also a major concern of all Near Eastern case-law. On the surface there appear to be striking similarities. Cases of adultery with a consenting married woman, for example, demand that both "the adulterer and the adulteress shall be put to death" in Leviticus (20:10); in the Sumerian laws of Ur-Nammu (§ 4), the laws of Eshnunna (§ 28), Hammurabi (§§ 129, 133), the Assyrian laws (§§ 13–16, 23), and the Hittite laws (§§ 197 f.), they are likewise "treated with the utmost gravity, the death penalty being often faced by the adulteress, her lover, or both, depending on the circumstances."[17] Forbidden marriages and incestuous relationships (Lev. 20:11–21; cf. 18:6–18) are dealt with in the laws of Hammurabi (§§ 154–158) and the Hittite laws (§§ 189–195), homosexuality (Lev. 18:22, 20:13) in the Assyrian laws (§ 20), and bestiality (Lev. 18:23, 20:15–16) in the Hittite laws (§§ 199–200A). The Hittites condemned both incest and bestiality as ḫurkel, i.e., "illicit sex," though they provided a purification ritual and ultimately the payment of a fine to mitigate the capital punishment ordinarily mandated by the laws.[18]

In spite of their common concerns, however, the levitical and Near Eastern laws differ widely. The latter were promulgated by kings as integral parts of civil and criminal law. They formed part of the foundation of royal authority, as is clear from the repeated provision for royal intervention. In case of adultery, for example, if the aggrieved husband chooses to spare his wife, the king may spare his subject (laws of Hammurabi § 129; cf. Assyrian laws § 15, Hittite laws § 198). The levitical laws, on the other hand, are part and parcel of the Holiness Code and, especially if considered in conjunction with ch. 19, repeatedly invoke the formulas that base the human and social relations in ques-

[14] Pritchard, ANET, pp. 426 f.; Lambert, Babylonian Wisdom Literature, pp. 96–107.
[15] Pritchard, ANET, pp. 412–425.
[16] Ibid., p. 169.
[17] J. J. Finkelstein, "Sex Offenses in Sumerian Laws," Journal of the American Oriental Society, 86 (1966), p. 366. [Hereafter cited as JAOS.] For the passages in question see Pritchard, ANET, pp. 161 ff.; ANET (3rd. ed., 1969), p. 523.
[18] H. A. Hoffner, Jr., "Incest, Sodomy, and Bestiality in the Ancient Near East," in Orient and Occident: Essays Presented to Cyrus H. Gordon (Alter Orient und Altes Testament, Vol. 22, 1973), pp. 81–90.

tion on the authority and holiness of God. The conclusion of the pericope, moreover, proclaims in connection with one of these formulas the very same contrast to the existing mores that is here averred: "You shall be holy to Me, for I the Lord am holy, and I have set you apart from the other peoples to be Mine" (20:26).

The next pericope (21–22) provides additional legislation for the priesthood, this time from the point of view of the Holiness Code. Only two provisions can be singled out here by way of example. The Aaronides (priestly descendants of Aaron) are to "do guard duty" for the Lord on pain of death by divine agency. This is the technical meaning of 22:9, a provision elaborated and "reformed" in Numbers 18 (see "Numbers and Ancient Near Eastern Literature" in the forthcoming Numbers volume of this Commentary series). Hittite instructions similarly hold the armed guardians of the sanctuary personally liable for various encroachments on the *sancta* within—but here their delinquencies are punished by human agency.[19]

In connection with sacrificial animals, the practice of castration is categorically prohibited (see commentary to 22:24). It may be worth noting that the evidence for castration of domesticated animals is abundant in the cuneiform sources. A recent summary of this evidence suggests that it may throw some light on the cultic terminology of the Israelites. The oft-repeated injunction that sacrificial animals be males "without blemish" (*tāmîm*; females only in Lev. 3:1, 6 and 4:28) may involve a euphemism for non-castrated in light of the Akkadian *šuklulu*, like the Hebrew word applied to sacrificial animals and meaning literally "perfect, complete." Similarly, "mutilated" in the next verse (22:25) may be a euphemism for castrated, with the further specification "they have a defect" (*mûm bām*) being a later gloss that obscured the original meaning.[20]

The cultic calendar of Leviticus has innumerable points of contact with the ancient Near East (see in detail the commentary to ch. 23). Suffice it here to emphasize the single most conspicuous point of contrast: the biblical week. True, occasional seven-day periods were observed on special occasions like the dedication of Gudea's temple at Lagash in Sumer or of Solomon's in Jerusalem (I Kings 8:65 f., reading with Septuagint).[21] But no other calendar insists on the eternal and unalterable succession of seven-day periods, independent of all earthly or astronomical considerations. Originally perhaps conceived as an expression of God's sovereignty over time,[22] the Sabbath day became an inalienable rest-day and therefore a uniquely Israelite contribution to the social legislation of the world. The concept was so deeply embedded in the Israelite frame of reference that it was (secondarily) superimposed on the very notion of Creation itself, which in other respects borrowed much from Near Eastern models. Moreover, it was extended from the week to the year in the concepts of the sabbatical year and the jubilee (ch. 25). Every seventh year the land is to enjoy a Sabbath (25:2) and after "seven sabbaths of years"

[19] Jacob Milgrom, *Studies in Levitical Terminology* I (University of California Publications [in] Near Eastern Studies, Vol. 14, 1970), Ch. II; *idem*, "The Shared Custody of the Tabernacle and a Hittite Analogy," *JAOS*, 90 (1970), pp. 204–209.

[20] B. Landsberger, *The Fauna of Ancient Mesopotamia: First Part* (Materialien zum Sumerischen Lexikon, Vol. 8, No. 1, 1960), pp. 66–75. In postexilic times, the priestly author of Isaiah 56:1–8 may have relaxed some of these restrictions; see Harry M. Orlinsky, *Essays in Biblical Culture* (New York: Ktav, 1974), pp. 94–98.

[21] Cf. E. C. Kingsbury, "A Seven-Day Ritual in the Old Babylonian Cult at Larsa," *Hebrew Union College Annual*, 34 (1963), pp. 1–34, esp. p. 27. [Hereafter cited as *HUCA*.]

[22] M. Tsevat, "The Basic Meaning of the Biblical Sabbath," *Zeitschrift für die Alttestamentliche Wissenschaft*, 84 (1972), pp. 447–459.

(25:8; NJPS version: "seven weeks of years") a jubilee. Here, too, biblical law instituted a novel social reform, albeit not destined to spread over the world like the Sabbath itself.[23] The weekly Sabbath and the sabbatical year were wholly Israelite innovations, and, while the jubilee year may have owed something to Near Eastern precedent, this precedent was restructured (like the biblical version of Creation) by means of the sabbatical idea. Both the *(an)durāru* of the Akkadians[24] and their so-called *mīšarum*-edicts[25] provide precedents of sorts. The latter, in particular, seems to have evolved under the Hammurabi dynasty into a periodic remission of debts and freeing of debt-slaves. But this was again strictly under royal auspices and at the royal whim. It was proclaimed in the first or second year of each king's reign, and sometimes at uncertain intervals thereafter. Only the biblical legislation provided divine sanction for the institution and, at least in theory, for its predictable periodicity.[26]

Conclusion

The Holiness Code concludes (ch. 26) with a catalog of blessings as at the end of the Covenant Code (Exod. 23:20–33) and of sanctions in the time-honored manner of the Mesopotamian law codes. An appendix on vows and related matters (ch. 27) serves to round out the book. Leviticus emerges from the structural and comparative analysis outlined above as a coherent literary work divided (like other books of the Pentateuch) into some three sections discrete in content, but unified in its insistence on the theocratic basis of its legislation. God, priesthood, and laity—the three subjects of its concern—all replace the royal focus of the Near Eastern sources with which comparisons are possible. Not the king but God is the source of law and the agency of its enforcement; not the king but the priest is the chief cultic ministrant; not the king but the "whole community of Israel" is to obey the cultic instructions and thus earn the right to consume the fat of the land.

[23] Cf. E. Neufeld, "Socio-Economic Background of Yobel and Šemiṭṭa," *Rivista degli Studi Orientali*, 33 (1958), pp. 53–124.

[24] J. Lewy, "The Biblical Institution of Derôr in the Light of Akkadian Documents," *Eretz-Israel*, 5, 1958 (Jerusalem: Israel Exploration Society), pp. 21 ff.

[25] Finkelstein, "Some New *Misharum* Material and Its Implications," in *Studies in Honor of Benno Landsberger*, eds. Hans G. Güterbock and Thorkild Jacobsen (Assyriological Studies, Vol. 16, 1965), pp. 233–246.

[26] William W. Hallo, "New Moons and Sabbaths: A Case-Study in the Contrastive Approach," *HUCA*, 48 (1977), pp. 1–18.

PART I

Laws of Sacrifice

Introduction

Today the word "sacrifice" means an act of self-deprivation. We give up something of value for the sake of a greater value: we may sacrifice a vacation to make more money, or sacrifice luxuries in order to educate our children, or sacrifice life for nation or faith. Such a sacrifice is deemed regrettable, even though necessary; if we could attain the larger end without the sacrifice, we should do so. Prudence therefore counsels us to make a sacrifice only after careful deliberation and to sacrifice no more than is needed to attain our goal.

1. Ancient Concepts of Sacrifice

That is not what the ancients meant by sacrifice. To them it was a religious rite, most often a joyous one. The offering was as large and choice as the worshiper could afford to make it. It was always a sacrifice *to* some deity or power, not—as in our usage—a sacrifice *for* some end. The sacrifice might indeed be offered in the hope of obtaining a favor, of warding off disaster, or of achieving purification from ritual defilement or sin. But just as often, perhaps more often, it was an expression of reverence and thanksgiving.

We should note that the term "sacrifice" comes from a Latin word meaning "to make something holy." The most common Hebrew equivalent is *korban*, "something brought near," i.e., to the altar [1].

2. Ancient Sacrifices

The institution of sacrifice was virtually universal among ancient peoples, going back far beyond recorded history; it still survives in some primitive cultures. Scholars have propounded various theories as to its origin: some have found the beginnings in totemism, some in ancestor worship, and so on. All such opinions are highly speculative. Sacrifice took many forms, which may have arisen separately and out of different motives. There were communal, family, and individual sacrifices; some were mandatory and offered at regular intervals, others were voluntary. Often the sacrifice took the form of a communal meal. A portion of the animal was offered to the deity, the remainder was cooked and eaten by the sacrificer and his guests who thus felt themselves in literal communion with their god.

The sacrifice was usually of food and drink, though other items, such as perfumes and incense, were sometimes offered. Bread, milk, grain, fruit, beer, wine, and other items of diet were offered by various peoples. But the most usual object of sacrifice was an animal.

It was generally believed that the supernatural powers—whether spirits of the dead, demons, or gods—have the same material needs as we and can be propitiated by satisfying those needs. An ancient Hittite text

3

requires priests to be neat in appearance and conscientious in practice when serving the gods, and it continues: "Are the minds of men and of the gods generally different? No! With regard to the matter with which we are dealing? No! Their minds are exactly alike" [2]. And in warning the priest not to appropriate for his own use a sheep designated for sacrifice, this text says: "Just think how the man reacts who sees his most valued possession snatched away from before his eyes" [3]. A Babylonian document gives instruction that the gods of a certain temple should be served an evening meal, a main morning meal, and a second morning meal [4]. In the Babylonian flood story, the interruption of sacrifice seems to have reduced the gods to a state of starvation for, when the survivors of the flood offered sacrifice, "the gods crowded like flies about the sacrificer" [5].

Originally, offerings were simply left at tombs, or at places regarded as haunts of the gods. In Egypt and Mesopotamia, sacrifices were usually presented to the images of the gods, later they were removed and eaten by the king or the priests. But many peoples adopted the practice of burning sacrifices, or a portion of them, on an altar. This procedure was followed in India, among the Greeks and Romans, and among some peoples of western Asia, including Israel. It suggests that the gods are sustained by inhaling the odor of the burning food. Survivals of such thinking appear in the Torah. A few passages speak of sacrifices as "the food of God" (Lev. 21:16–23; Num. 28:2); more often, they are described as providing a "pleasing odor to the Lord" (Lev. 1:9 and elsewhere).

3. Sacrifice in the Bible

Did the biblical authors intend such expressions to be taken literally? A positive answer is not easy to give. No doubt some simpleminded worshipers believed that God requires food, yet the Bible contains protests against such a notion. Psalm 50, which was presumably sung in the Temple and which commends the sacrifice of thanksgiving (v. 14), represents God as saying: "Were I hungry, I would not tell you, / for Mine is the world and all it holds. / Do I eat the flesh of bulls, / or drink the blood of he-goats?" (Ps. 50:12, 13).

Probably old forms and phraseology were retained without a clear consciousness of their original meanings. We today continue to practice ancient customs in connection with marriage, death, and mourning, and we are unaware of the primitive concepts that generated these customs. Many public ceremonies in Great Britain retain the forms and language of the period when the sovereign was an absolute monarch, though the crown today has no direct political power. Very likely the authors of Leviticus regarded sacrifice as simply an act of homage to God and not as a means of satisfying His hunger.

Israelite sacrifice, though it resembled other ancient cults in various ways, also presents striking contrasts to them. Many peoples believed that sacrifice was not merely a method of obtaining divine favor but an indispensable means of maintaining the god's vitality. The Bible, despite a few allusions to the food of God, nowhere suggests that God needs sacrifices, and it repeatedly asserts the opposite [6].

It was a common practice to connect divination with sacrifice. Omens of good or ill fortune were derived from the appearance of the organs of a sacrificed beast. The Babylonians had a whole "science" of predicting the future from such omens, especially from the size and shape of the liver [7]. Before an important undertaking, especially a battle, the Greeks and Romans would sacrifice and would inspect the entrails of the victim, to determine whether or not a happy outcome might be expected. Nothing of this sort was found in Israelite practice.

It appears, too, that the sacrificial cult in Mesopotamia was basically a matter for the king and priests and that the common people had little to do with it. Israelite sacrifice was a more democratic affair. Provision was made for inexpensive offerings which even the poor could afford. And one of the most familiar types of sacrifice had the form of a festive meal of which the worshipers partook—a form of sacrifice unknown in Babylonia. But the more democratic tendencies are also to be found in Greek and Carthaginian practices [8].

Egyptian and Babylonian documents contain liturgical texts that had to be recited as the sacrifices were performed [9]. Biblical law makes no mention of such prescribed prayers. But we know that sacrificial rites were often accompanied by vocal and instrumental music; and many of the psalms were composed for use in the Temple [10].

Only the priestly writings provide detailed instructions for the various kinds of sacrifices [11]. But throughout the Bible sacrifice was regarded as a normal element of personal, family, and civic life. The first instance of sacrifice in the Bible is in the story of Cain and Abel; and from that point on there are constant references to the practice.

Biblical sacrifices were both communal and individual. The communal sacrifices were almost all mandatory: the burnt offerings brought daily at morning and evening and the additional sacrifices for Sabbath and holy days [12]. Some individual sacrifices were also obligatory: the paschal lamb and various sacrifices of purification. Most of the individual offerings were voluntary.

One group of biblical utterances requires special notice: the prophetic sermons that contrast the demands of ethical religion with the formal cult of sacrifice and insist on the primacy of moral conduct in individual and social life. Some of these statements are quite extreme:

"Though you offer Me burnt offerings and meal offerings, / I will not accept them, / And I will not notice your sacrifices of fat beasts.... But let justice roll down like water, / And righteousness like a perennial stream. Did you bring Me sacrifices and offerings in the wilderness for forty years, O people of Israel?" (Amos 5:22–25. Cf. Jer. 7:22, "When I freed your fathers from the land of Egypt, I did not speak with them nor command them concerning burnt offering or sacrifice"; see also I Sam. 15:22–23; Isa. 1:11–13; Hos. 6:6; Mic. 6:6–8.)

Some modern scholars have therefore concluded that the preexilic prophets rejected all formal worship and called for a religion of ethical conduct only.

Jewish tradition understood these utterances to be directed not against sacrifice as such, but against the substitution of ritual for morality. Sacrifice *is* acceptable, according to this view, but only when it is offered with clean hands and a pure heart. The traditional expositors were indeed compelled to interpret the prophetic teaching thus, in order to harmonize it with the authoritative requirements of the Torah. Many modern scholars regard this explanation as historically correct. The prophets, these scholars argue, could not have advocated a cultless religion; that would have been a contradiction in terms for ancient man, and perhaps for modern man as well. It is clear that many prophets, especially during and after the exile, were strongly committed to the Temple and its worship, at the same time championing ethical values.

The critics of the sacrificial system were not advocating a new *form* of worship. Isaiah and Amos spoke with strong disapproval also of the prayers and religious music of their time. Whatever their intent may have been, their critique of formal worship was not understood as an absolute rejection.

Throughout the biblical period, and for centuries thereafter, sacrifice was considered proper and necessary, when performed with sincerity and with proper regard for the other requirements of the Torah.

It requires an enormous effort of imagination on our part to understand how untold generations found the sacrificial rites inspiring. We eat much more meat than our biblical ancestors did; but it comes to us neatly prepared and packaged, and many of us do not even see it till it is ready for the table. The sights, sounds, and smells of the slaughterhouse would be very upsetting to our squeamish generation. Ancient man was not so sheltered. He lived closer to the realities of birth, life, and death. He was not unfamiliar with the slaughtering of animals and their preparation for food; and, when these activities were performed in a sacred place as part of a solemn ritual, he found them dignified and meaningful.

It was of the Temple with its sacrificial cult that the Psalmist exclaimed: "O Lord, I love Your Temple abode,/the dwelling-place of Your presence" (Ps. 26:8).

It is to this Temple and cult that many of our favorite psalms allude (read Ps. 4, 27, 84—and 23!).

4. Talmudic Views

In the century before the Christian era, religious leadership in Palestine passed largely from the hereditary priests to a group of learned laymen known as the Pharisees. The latter had widespread popular support, and so they were able to make certain changes in Temple procedure, expressive of a more progressive religious outlook and of a democratic spirit.

But in 70 C.E. the Romans burned the Temple, and they never permitted it to be rebuilt. The sacrificial cult came to an end [13]. By that time a new institution for prayer and study, the synagogue, was fully developed, and was meeting effectively the religious needs of the Jewish people in the homeland and the Diaspora. But still the loss of the Temple was felt keenly. It was the national Shrine; and sacrifices could be performed nowhere else. Petitions for the rebuilding of the Temple and the restoration of the cult were soon added to the regular synagogue prayers.

The Rabbis, the successors of the Pharisees, introduced into the synagogue a number of practices formerly associated with the Temple. But they made no provision for "interim" sacrifices. They could have found some precedents for sacrifice outside Jerusalem despite the prohibitions of Deuteronomy (12:5–6). In the fifth century B.C.E., a Jewish military colony in Egypt had a temple of sorts. More important was the temple at Leontopolis (also in Egypt), established about 170 B.C.E. by the High Priest Onias IV whose father had been deprived of his office by the Syrian tyrant Antiochus IV. This temple remained in existence till the Romans closed it after the fall of Jerusalem. The Rabbis never acknowledged its legitimacy, but they never denounced it as wholly sinful. But when the Temple in Jerusalem was destroyed, they did not choose to follow such precedents and set up a substitute form of sacrifice.

Not that they ever consciously questioned the value of the cult. They prayed for its restoration; and they discussed the Temple ritual in fullest detail. The study of the sacrificial laws, they declared, was as acceptable to God as the actual performance of the rites [14]. When Rabbi Sheshet fasted, he prayed that the diminution of blood and fat in his body, due to the fast, might be accepted by God as equivalent to sacrificial blood and fat [15]. Rabbinic preachers depicted a heavenly temple, in which the angel Michael officiated as High Priest [16].

But some of the scholars may have felt that the day of sacrifice had passed. Perhaps this is implicit in the notion that study about sacrifice is as efficacious as bringing sacrifice. Shortly after the Temple was destroyed, it is said, the aged Rabban Johanan ben Zakkai visited its ruins in the company of his pupils. One of them bewailed the cessation of the rites that provided atonement for sin. The old sage replied, "Do not grieve, my son. We have a means of atonement that is equal to sacrifice—the doing of kind deeds. For it is said, 'I desire mercy, and not sacrifice'" (Hos. 6:6) [17]. A few centuries later, Rabbi Isaac declared that prayer takes precedence over sacrifice [18].

Still more remarkable is a parable of Rabbi Levi, a contemporary of Rabbi Isaac: The son of a king became mentally confused and fell into the habit of eating carrion. Thereupon the king ordered his servants to serve kosher meat from the same kinds of animals at his own table so that the son might regain the habit of eating proper food. Similarly, said Rabbi Levi, Israel became addicted to idolatry while in Egypt; and in the desert they still brought offerings to the goat-demons. Thereupon God said, "Let them bring regular sacrifices to Me, and they will be protected from the tendency to idolatry" [19].

5. Medieval Views

Rabbi Levi's parable may have suggested the rationalistic explanation of sacrifice offered by the philosopher Moses Maimonides (1135–1204) [20]. That famous thinker held that the sacrificial legislation was a concession to human frailty. In ancient times, sacrifice was the universal practice; the Hebrews who left Egypt could not imagine a religion without it. Had they not been permitted to bring offerings to the true God, they would inevitably have sacrificed to other deities. Biblical sacrifice was the means by which they were weaned away from heathenism and instructed in true beliefs [21]. Moreover, the animals designated for sacrifice were those held sacred by the Hindus, Egyptians, and Sabeans, which were never slaughtered by those peoples. Thus Israelite sacrifices were a repudiation of pagan superstition [22].

Such reasoning might seem to suggest that sacrifice was a temporary expedient, no longer of any value. But Maimonides drew no such conclusion. His monumental code of Jewish law includes a full exposition of the sacrificial rites, ready for use when the Messiah should arrive and the Temple be rebuilt.

Nevertheless, his explanation of sacrifice was severely criticized by the more traditionally minded. Nachmanides (on Lev. 1:9) noted that Abel and Noah brought sacrifices at a time when idolatry had not yet appeared. Basically, he objected to treating so important an element of the Torah as a mere pedagogic device. The traditionalists insisted that sacrifice must have a positive value, even though our reason is inadequate to explain it. The Kabalists found mystical, even cosmic, implications in sacrifice. And the philosopher poet, Judah Halevi, had argued, nearly a century before Maimonides, that Temple and sacrifice are indispensable for the reestablishment of a perfect relationship between God and Israel—and, through Israel, between God and mankind [23].

6. Modern Attitudes

It was only with the rise of Reform Judaism at the end of the eighteenth century that believing Jews renounced the hope of restoring sacrifice [24]. The Reformers said plainly that, whatever purpose sacrifice may have served in ancient times, it is now obsolete and without meaning for the future. They therefore eliminated from the synagogue service the traditional prayers for the restoration of Temple and cult. Today the Conservative and Reconstructionist groups have also explicitly renounced the hope of returning to the sacrificial system; and, tacitly, so have large masses of Jews not affiliated with these modernist movements.

Even among the Orthodox, allegiance to the cult seems to be chiefly verbal, consisting of reminiscences of a distant past and hopes for a vague and distant future. Some fifty years ago, Rabbi Abraham I. Kook, the saintly leader of the Orthodox Ashkenazim of Palestine, anticipating the speedy coming of the Messiah, attempted to found a school for the practical training of priests. But the project attracted little support.

In Christianity, on the other hand, the idea of sacrifice was reinterpreted and given central importance. The death of Jesus was explained as the true sacrifice which had been foreshadowed by the animal sacrifices of the "Old Testament"; and the mass is regarded as the regular repetition of that sacrifice [25].

7. The Sacrificial Legislation of the Torah

Chapters 1 through 7 of Leviticus contain extended, but not entirely complete, instruction for the different types of sacrifice brought by individuals. (In 4:13–22, an offering for the entire community is treated.) Additional directions concerning sacrifice appear in other parts of the book as well as in priestly sections of Exodus and Numbers [26].

The present section consists of two parts. The first five chapters explain the procedures for five different kinds of offerings; then these same offerings are treated a second time in chapters 6 and 7. Characteristic of the latter section is the introductory formula, "This is the ritual of . . . ." There is some repetition in the second section, but not much; the two expositions generally supplement each other. Plainly, the editor or editors of Leviticus drew on several sources and copied down what they thought important, without recasting the material into a unified whole.

The Olah—Burnt Offering

The first type of sacrifice discussed is called *olah*, "what goes up," i.e., goes up in smoke, because the entire animal, except for its hide, was burned on the altar. Other types of sacrifice were consumed in part by fire, and the rest was eaten by the priests, or by the priests and worshipers. In English, *olah* has for centuries been translated "burnt offering."

The *olah* had a high degree of sanctity, and it was regarded as the "standard" sacri-fice. Most required communal sacrifices were *olot*. In contrast, sacrifices made by the Greeks to the Olympian gods were always shared by the worshipers; only sacrifices made to the dread underground deities to ward off evil were presented as *holocausts*, i.e., completely burned [1].

The present chapter deals with the *olah* brought by an individual as a voluntary offering.

א וַיִּקְרָא* אֶל־מֹשֶׁה וַיְדַבֵּר יְהוָה אֵלָיו מֵאֹהֶל מוֹעֵד

ב לֵאמֹר: דַּבֵּר אֶל־בְּנֵי יִשְׂרָאֵל וְאָמַרְתָּ אֲלֵהֶם אָדָם כִּי־יַקְרִיב מִכֶּם קָרְבָּן לַיהוָה מִן־הַבְּהֵמָה מִן־הַבָּקָר

ג וּמִן־הַצֹּאן תַּקְרִיבוּ אֶת־קָרְבַּנְכֶם: אִם־עֹלָה קָרְבָּנוֹ מִן־הַבָּקָר זָכָר תָּמִים יַקְרִיבֶנּוּ אֶל־פֶּתַח אֹהֶל מוֹעֵד

ד יַקְרִיב אֹתוֹ לִרְצֹנוֹ לִפְנֵי יְהוָה: וְסָמַךְ יָדוֹ עַל רֹאשׁ

* א א' זעירא.

1] The LORD called to Moses and spoke to him from the Tent of Meeting, saying:

2] Speak to the Israelite people, and say to them:

When any of you presents an offering of cattle to the LORD, he shall choose his offering from the herd or from the flock.

3] If his offering is a burnt offering from the herd, he shall make his offering a male without blemish. He shall bring it to the entrance of the Tent of Meeting, for acceptance in his behalf before the LORD. 4] He shall lay his hand upon the head

---

1:1] *The Lord called to Moses and spoke to him.* The Hebrew order is "And He called to Moses. And the LORD said to him." This may be because this sentence continues the narrative at the end of Exodus: the divine Presence filled the Tabernacle, and so Moses would not venture to enter the Tent until God summoned him (Palestinian Targums).

From the Tent of Meeting. God called to him from the Tent and spoke to him after he entered (Rashbam).

2] *He shall choose his.* Literally, "you shall offer your" (T.N.).

From the herd. Beef cattle.

From the flock. Sheep or goats.

3] *Without blemish.* Only a healthy, normal animal was fit for sacrifice. The prophet Malachi denounced those who brought to the Temple sick, blind, or lame animals which they would not have dared present to a political ruler (Mal. 1:8).

Before the Lord. The translation follows the Targum in connecting this phrase with "acceptance in his behalf." But in chapter 1, verse 5, "before the LORD" plainly means "in the Tent, in front of the inner Shrine."

4] *Lay his hand upon the head of the burnt offering.* Thus formally designating the animal as *his* sacrifice. This ceremony was required for all quadrupeds offered by an individual, but not for communal sacrifices, and not for fowl.

In expiation for him. Other types of sacrifices are prescribed as atonement for sin (chapters 4 and 5); this is the only passage that speaks of an *olah* expiating guilt. It may preserve an old tradition otherwise unknown to us (see Gleanings).

הָעֹלָה וְנִרְצָה לוֹ לְכַפֵּר עָלָיו: וְשָׁחַט אֶת־בֶּן הַבָּקָר ה

לִפְנֵי יְהוָה וְהִקְרִיבוּ בְּנֵי אַהֲרֹן הַכֹּהֲנִים אֶת־הַדָּם

וְזָרְקוּ אֶת־הַדָּם עַל־הַמִּזְבֵּחַ סָבִיב אֲשֶׁר־פֶּתַח אֹהֶל

מוֹעֵד: וְהִפְשִׁיט אֶת־הָעֹלָה וְנִתַּח אֹתָהּ לִנְתָחֶיהָ: וְנָתְנוּ ו

בְּנֵי אַהֲרֹן הַכֹּהֵן אֵשׁ עַל־הַמִּזְבֵּחַ וְעָרְכוּ עֵצִים עַל־

הָאֵשׁ: וְעָרְכוּ בְּנֵי אַהֲרֹן הַכֹּהֲנִים אֵת הַנְּתָחִים אֶת־ ח

of the burnt offering, that it may be acceptable in his behalf, in expiation for him.
5] The bull shall be slaughtered before the LORD; and Aaron's sons, the priests,
shall offer the blood, dashing the blood against all sides of the altar which is at the
entrance of the Tent of Meeting.   **6]** The burnt offering shall be flayed and cut
up into sections.   **7]** The sons of Aaron the priest shall put fire on the altar and
lay out wood upon the fire;   **8]** and Aaron's sons, the priests, shall lay out the sec-

---

5] *Shall be slaughtered.* Or, "he [i.e., the donor] shall slaughter." Slaughtering did not have to be performed by priests though, no doubt, the latter frequently killed the animals because of their experience in such matters. (Ezek. 44:11 assigns this duty to the Levites.) But the text explicitly requires the priests to handle the blood.

Shall offer the blood. According to tradition, they received the blood in bowls as it welled from the animal's throat; they brought it to the altar and dashed it against two opposite corners so that it spattered on all four sides [2]. This blood ceremony was regarded as the act of atonement [3].

6] *Shall be flayed.* Some ancient pictures of sacrifice show an animal being burned whole on the altar [4]. But Israelite practice required the removal of the hide, the washing of the entrails, and the disjointing of the carcass before it was placed on the altar. This was also the practice of many other peoples [5]. Here, too, we could translate "he shall flay" (cf.

commentary on 1:5); the work might be done by non-priests [6].

The hide became the property of the officiating priest (7:8). It was his only compensation for offering an *olah*. Of most other sacrifices, the priest received at least a portion of the meat. Israelite priests were not usually paid for their services in money. But a Phoenician temple in Marseilles had a regular schedule of tariffs posted, stating the fee in cash and in meat for each kind of animal. The priests were, however, required to forego payment if the sacrificer was poor [7].

7] *Shall put fire on the altar.* According to chapter 6, verse 6, the fire was always to be kept burning; according to chapter 9, verse 24, it was of heavenly origin. Such discrepancies show that Leviticus was put together from a variety of sources.

8] *Shall lay out the sections.* Previous to this, the meat was salted (2:13); along with it, meal and drink offerings were placed on the altar (Num. 15:1ff.).

הָרֹאשׁ וְאֶת־הַפֶּדֶר עַל־הָעֵצִים אֲשֶׁר עַל־הָאֵשׁ אֲשֶׁר

ט עַל־הַמִּזְבֵּחַ: וְקִרְבּוֹ וּכְרָעָיו יִרְחַץ בַּמָּיִם וְהִקְטִיר

הַכֹּהֵן אֶת־הַכֹּל הַמִּזְבֵּחָה עֹלָה אִשֵּׁה רֵיחַ־נִיחוֹחַ

י לַיהוָה: ס וְאִם־מִן־הַצֹּאן קָרְבָּנוֹ מִן־הַכְּשָׂבִים אוֹ

יא מִן־הָעִזִּים לְעֹלָה זָכָר תָּמִים יַקְרִיבֶנּוּ: וְשָׁחַט אֹתוֹ

עַל יֶרֶךְ הַמִּזְבֵּחַ צָפֹנָה לִפְנֵי יְהוָה וְזָרְקוּ בְּנֵי אַהֲרֹן

יב הַכֹּהֲנִים אֶת־דָּמוֹ עַל־הַמִּזְבֵּחַ סָבִיב: וְנִתַּח אֹתוֹ לִנְתָחָיו

וְאֶת־רֹאשׁוֹ וְאֶת־פִּדְרוֹ וְעָרַךְ הַכֹּהֵן אֹתָם עַל־הָעֵצִים

יג אֲשֶׁר עַל־הָאֵשׁ אֲשֶׁר עַל־הַמִּזְבֵּחַ: וְהַקֶּרֶב וְהַכְּרָעַיִם

יִרְחַץ בַּמָּיִם וְהִקְרִיב הַכֹּהֵן אֶת־הַכֹּל וְהִקְטִיר

tions, with the head and the suet, on the wood that is on the fire upon the altar.
9] Its entrails and legs shall be washed with water, and the priest shall turn the whole into smoke on the altar as a burnt offering, an offering by fire of pleasing odor to the LORD.

10] If his offering for a burnt offering is from the flock, of sheep or of goats, he shall make his offering a male without blemish. **11]** It shall be slaughtered before the LORD on the north side of the altar, and Aaron's sons, the priests, shall dash its blood against all sides of the altar. **12]** When it has been cut up into sections, the priest shall lay them out, with the head and the suet, on the wood that is on the fire upon the altar. **13]** The entrails and the legs shall be washed with water;

9] *Turn the whole into smoke.* Make sure it catches fire and is consumed.

An offering by fire. This phrase renders the Hebrew *isheh*, related to *esh*, "fire." It is a general term for all the usual forms of sacrifice.

Of pleasing odor to the Lord. See p. 4 and cf. Gen. 8:21.

10] *From the flock.* One who cannot afford a bull may offer a less costly animal. The procedure is the same and the sacrifice is just as valid.

11] *On the north side of the altar.* This detail is not mentioned in the preceding instructions for the bull; it is understood by *Sifra* to apply to both—no doubt correctly.

הַמִּזְבֵּחָה עֹלָה הוּא אִשֵּׁה רֵיחַ נִיחֹחַ לַיהֹוָה: פ

יד וְאִם מִן־הָעוֹף עֹלָה קָרְבָּנוֹ לַיהֹוָה וְהִקְרִיב מִן־

טו הַתֹּרִים אוֹ מִן־בְּנֵי הַיּוֹנָה אֶת־קָרְבָּנוֹ: וְהִקְרִיבוֹ הַכֹּהֵן

אֶל־הַמִּזְבֵּחַ וּמָלַק אֶת־רֹאשׁוֹ וְהִקְטִיר הַמִּזְבֵּחָה

טז וְנִמְצָה דָמוֹ עַל קִיר הַמִּזְבֵּחַ: וְהֵסִיר אֶת־מֻרְאָתוֹ

בְּנֹצָתָהּ וְהִשְׁלִיךְ אֹתָהּ אֵצֶל הַמִּזְבֵּחַ קֵדְמָה אֶל־מְקוֹם

יז הַדָּשֶׁן: וְשִׁסַּע אֹתוֹ בִכְנָפָיו לֹא יַבְדִּיל וְהִקְטִיר אֹתוֹ

הַכֹּהֵן הַמִּזְבֵּחָה עַל־הָעֵצִים אֲשֶׁר עַל־הָאֵשׁ עֹלָה הוּא

אִשֵּׁה רֵיחַ נִיחֹחַ לַיהֹוָה: ס

Leviticus 1

14–17

the priest shall offer up and turn the whole into smoke on the altar. It is a burnt offering, an offering by fire, of pleasing odor to the LORD.

14] If his offering to the LORD is a burnt offering of birds, he shall choose his offering from turtledoves or pigeons.   15] The priest shall bring it to the altar, pinch off its head, and turn it into smoke on the altar; and its blood shall be drained out against the side of the altar.   16] He shall remove its crop with its contents, and cast it into the place of the ashes, at the east side of the altar.   17] The priest shall tear it open by its wings, without severing it, and turn it into smoke on the altar, upon the wood that is on the fire. It is a burnt offering, an offering by fire, of pleasing odor to the LORD.

14] *A burnt offering of birds.* The poor worshiper was also to have the opportunity to bring an *olah*.

Pigeons. Literally, "children of a pigeon," which tradition understood as "young pigeon." This may well have been the original intent. The adult turtledove is about the same size as the young pigeon; thus, in either case, the offering would be plump and delicate-looking.

15] *Pinch off its head.* With his fingers.

And turn it into smoke. After performing the actions detailed in the ensuing clauses.

Its blood shall be drained out. The small quantity of blood made the procedure of chapter 1, verse 5, unnecessary in the case of fowl.

16] *He shall remove its crop with its contents.* Others, "with its feathers" (T.N.). The word *notzah* is here rendered "contents" because it makes good sense in this context (so Targums) [8]. Ordinarily *notzah* means "feather." Accordingly, Rabbi Ishmael explained that an incision was to be made in the body and the crop removed with the skin and feathers covering it [9].

And cast it into the place of the ashes. The place where ashes from the altar fire were piled before removal (Lev. 6:3).

13

GLEANINGS

Where no reference is provided, or there is only the word Sifra, the passage is found in Sifra to the verse.

Halachah

1:2] *Any of You*

Literally, "a man of you." The word "man" implies that burnt offerings may be accepted from Gentiles [10]. The phrase "of you" forbids accepting an offering from an apostate Jew.   SIFRA

4] *Lay His Hand*

The Targums also render "hand" singular. But the Talmud inferred from Leviticus, chapter 16, verse 21, that the sacrificer must place both hands on the animal's head [11].

6] *Shall Be Flayed*

The head was not to be skinned; wool on the head of a sheep and the whiskers of a goat were to be left intact. Suet was laid over the throat to conceal the bloody cut.

7] *Shall Put Fire on the Altar*

Even though the fire was of heavenly origin,

additional wood was to be placed on it before the *olah* was brought up.

11] *On the North Side of the Altar*

This instruction is repeated several times in these chapters. The halachah generalizes: All the "most holy" sacrifices—*olah, chatat, asham*—were to be slaughtered on the north side of the altar. *Shelamim*, which were of lesser holiness, might be slaughtered anywhere in the court of the Tabernacle/Temple.

15] *Pinch Off Its Head*

This operation was performed at the back of the neck, breaking the bone and severing the windpipe. For human consumption the fowl must be slaughtered by cutting the throat with a knife.

Haggadah

1:1] *The Lord Called to Moses*

Before every act of revelation, God would call, "Moses, Moses!" as at the burning bush. It was an expression of affection and of urgency. And each time Moses would respond, "Here I am."

4] *In Expiation for Him*

For what sins does the *olah* atone? For neglect of positive commandments (*Sifra*). According to another opinion, for sinful thoughts [12]. But there is a widely accepted view that a sinful intention is not accounted a sin if it is not carried out, although credit is given for good intentions that are not fulfilled [13].

16] *He Shall Remove Its Crop with Its Contents*

Birds fly about and eat seed from other men's

land. Therefore the crop that held stolen food must be discarded before the fowl is offered to God. But animals eat fodder supplied by their owners, and so their inwards may be burned on the altar after they are washed.   SIFRA

Fowls are offered unplucked. Nothing is more repulsive than the smell of burning feathers; yet God commanded that the birds be offered with feathers intact so that the poor man's offering might look more impressive. A plucked bird would be small and scrawny looking [14].

17] *Pleasing Odor*

"Whether one offers much or little makes no difference. if only his heart is directed to God."

The Minchah—Meal Offering

The term *minchah* is used in the Bible for "gift" (Gen. 32:14), for "tribute" (I Kings 5:1), and for "sacrifice" in general (Gen. 4:3ff.). But in Leviticus, and elsewhere in P, it means specifically an offering prepared from grain. (In postbiblical Hebrew, *minchah* came to mean "the afternoon prayer" and, more generally, "afternoon" [1].)

This chapter deals with cereal offerings brought as separate voluntary gifts (except perhaps those treated in verses 13 through 16). Frankincense was regularly placed on such offerings. Animal sacrifices were accompanied by mandatory meal offerings—bread along with meat—for which frankincense was not required (Num. 15:1ff.) [2].

Flour and oil were the ingredients of the *minchah*. It might be uncooked, or prepared in an oven, griddle, or pan, as the donor chose. The frankincense was placed on top just before the offering was brought to the altar.

א וְנֶ֗פֶשׁ כִּֽי־תַקְרִ֞יב קׇרְבַּ֤ן מִנְחָה֙ לַֽיהֹוָ֔ה סֹ֖לֶת יִהְיֶ֣ה
ב קׇרְבָּנ֑וֹ וְיָצַ֤ק עָלֶ֙יהָ֙ שֶׁ֔מֶן וְנָתַ֥ן עָלֶ֖יהָ לְבֹנָֽה׃ וֶהֱבִיאָ֗הּ
אֶל־בְּנֵ֣י אַהֲרֹן֮ הַכֹּהֲנִים֒ וְקָמַ֨ץ מִשָּׁ֜ם מְלֹ֣א קֻמְצ֗וֹ
מִסׇּלְתָּהּ֙ וּמִשַּׁמְנָ֔הּ עַ֖ל כׇּל־לְבֹנָתָ֑הּ וְהִקְטִ֨יר הַכֹּהֵ֜ן
אֶת־אַזְכָּרָתָהּ֙ הַמִּזְבֵּ֔חָה אִשֵּׁ֛ה רֵ֥יחַ נִיחֹ֖חַ לַֽיהֹוָֽה׃
ג וְהַנּוֹתֶ֙רֶת֙ מִן־הַמִּנְחָ֔ה לְאַהֲרֹ֖ן וּלְבָנָ֑יו קֹ֥דֶשׁ קׇֽדָשִׁ֖ים
ד מֵֽאִשֵּׁ֥י יְהֹוָֽה׃ ס וְכִ֤י תַקְרִב֙ קׇרְבַּ֣ן מִנְחָ֔ה מַאֲפֵ֖ה
תַנּ֑וּר סֹ֣לֶת חַלּ֤וֹת מַצֹּת֙ בְּלוּלֹ֣ת בַּשֶּׁ֔מֶן וּרְקִיקֵ֥י מַצּ֖וֹת

1] When a person presents an offering of meal to the Lord, his offering shall be of choice flour; he shall pour oil upon it, lay frankincense on it,   2] and present it to Aaron's sons, the priests. The priest shall scoop out of it a handful of its choice flour and oil, as well as all of its frankincense; and this token portion he shall turn into smoke on the altar, as an offering by fire, of pleasing odor to the Lord.   3] And the remainder of the meal offering shall be for Aaron and his sons, a most holy portion from the Lord's offerings by fire.

4] When you present an offering of meal baked in the oven, [it shall be of] choice flour: unleavened cakes with oil mixed in, or unleavened wafers spread with oil.

2:2] *Choice flour.* Hebrew *solet*—not "fine flour," as in earlier translations. *Solet* is meal made from the hard kernels of wheat (semolina) as is clear from Avot 5:15, "a sieve lets through the *kemach* [ordinary flour] but retains the *solet*" [3].

Frankincense. An aromatic gum obtained from Arabia (Jer. 6:20).

Token portion. Hebrew *azkarah*, from a root meaning "remember, take thought of." This portion, burned on the altar, is to bring the worshiper to mind before God.

3] *Shall be for Aaron and his sons.* Shall be eaten by the priests.

A most holy portion. Food designated as "most holy" had to be consumed inside the sacred area by priests. Food that was holy in a lesser degree (below, 7:11ff.) could be eaten outside the sacred precincts by priests and their families, as well as by lay persons who were properly purified.

4] *Oven.* Hebrew *tanur*, a cylindrical vessel of clay in which fire was kindled on a bed of pebbles. When it was well heated, the ashes were swept out and the dough was pressed against the walls of the *tanur*.

ה מְשֻׁחִים בַּשָּׁמֶן: ס וְאִם־מִנְחָה עַל־הַמַּחֲבַת קָרְבָּנֶךְ

ו סֹלֶת בְּלוּלָה בַשֶּׁמֶן מַצָּה תִהְיֶה: פָּתוֹת אֹתָהּ פִּתִּים

ז וְיָצַקְתָּ עָלֶיהָ שָׁמֶן מִנְחָה הִוא: ס וְאִם־מִנְחַת

ח מַרְחֶשֶׁת קָרְבָּנֶךָ סֹלֶת בַּשֶּׁמֶן תֵּעָשֶׂה: וְהֵבֵאתָ אֶת־

הַמִּנְחָה אֲשֶׁר יֵעָשֶׂה מֵאֵלֶּה לַיהוָה וְהִקְרִיבָהּ אֶל־

ט הַכֹּהֵן וְהִגִּישָׁהּ אֶל־הַמִּזְבֵּחַ: וְהֵרִים הַכֹּהֵן מִן־הַמִּנְחָה

אֶת־אַזְכָּרָתָהּ וְהִקְטִיר הַמִּזְבֵּחָה אִשֵּׁה רֵיחַ נִיחֹחַ

י לַיהוָה: וְהַנּוֹתֶרֶת מִן־הַמִּנְחָה לְאַהֲרֹן וּלְבָנָיו קֹדֶשׁ

יא קָדָשִׁים מֵאִשֵּׁי יְהוָה: כָּל־הַמִּנְחָה אֲשֶׁר תַּקְרִיבוּ

Leviticus 2

5–11

5] If your offering is a meal offering on a griddle, it shall be of choice flour with oil mixed in, unleavened.   6] Break it into bits and pour oil on it; it is a meal offering.

7] If your offering is a meal offering in a pan, it shall be made of choice flour in oil.

8] When you present to the LORD a meal offering that is made in any of these ways, it shall be brought to the priest who shall take it up to the altar.   9] The priest shall remove the token portion from the meal offering and turn it into smoke on the altar as an offering by fire, of pleasing odor to the LORD.   10]   And the remainder of the meal offering shall be for Aaron and his sons, a most holy portion from the LORD's offerings by fire.

11] No meal offering that you offer to the LORD shall be made with leaven, for

---

5] *Griddle.* Yielding a crisp wafer.

7] *Pan.* Yielding a soft, moist bread.

11] *No meal offering . . . shall be made with leaven.* This may be a survival of old desert practice; the nomads generally baked their bread unleavened. Ancient customs are often retained in religious rites after they have been otherwise discarded. (For example, the Torah is read in the synagogue from a handwritten parchment scroll.) In later Jewish literature, leaven is sometimes a symbol of moral corruption or religious rebellion, but such a notion was hardly in the mind of the biblical author. Some of the cakes used in the thanksgiving sacrifice were leavened, some were not (7:12, 13). Two leavened loaves were to be offered on the Feast of Weeks (23:17). Of course, this leavened bread was not burned on the altar.

לַיהוָה לֹא תַעֲשֶׂה חָמֵץ כִּי כָל־שְׂאֹר וְכָל־דְּבַשׁ לֹא־
יב תַקְטִירוּ מִמֶּנּוּ אִשֶּׁה לַיהוָה: קָרְבַּן רֵאשִׁית תַּקְרִיבוּ
יג אֹתָם לַיהוָה וְאֶל־הַמִּזְבֵּחַ לֹא־יַעֲלוּ לְרֵיחַ נִיחֹחַ: וְכָל־
קָרְבַּן מִנְחָתְךָ בַּמֶּלַח תִּמְלָח וְלֹא תַשְׁבִּית מֶלַח בְּרִית
אֱלֹהֶיךָ מֵעַל מִנְחָתֶךָ עַל כָּל־קָרְבָּנְךָ תַּקְרִיב
יד מֶלַח: ס וְאִם־תַּקְרִיב מִנְחַת בִּכּוּרִים לַיהוָה אָבִיב
קָלוּי בָּאֵשׁ גֶּרֶשׂ כַּרְמֶל תַּקְרִיב אֵת מִנְחַת בִּכּוּרֶיךָ:

you must not turn into smoke any leaven or any honey as an offering by fire to the
LORD.   12] You may bring them to the LORD as an offering of choice products;
but they shall not be offered up on the altar for a pleasing odor.   13] You shall
season your every offering of meal with salt; you shall not omit from your meal
offering the salt of your covenant with God; with all your offerings you must offer
salt.

14] If you bring a meal offering of first fruits to the LORD, you shall bring grain
in season parched with fire, grits of the fresh ear, as your meal offering of first fruits.

Honey. Honey is often mentioned in the Bible, especially in the familiar phrase "a land flowing with milk and honey." Many ancient peoples used it for sacrifice, and we do not know why the Torah barred it from the altar. In rabbinic literature, and possibly in some Bible passages, Hebrew *devash* designates not only bee honey but also a man-made preparation of mashed fruit. (Arabic *dibs* has the latter meaning.)

12] *An offering of choice products.* Exact meaning of Hebrew uncertain (T.N.). The obscure phrase (literally, "an offering of beginning") may allude to the first-fruit ceremony of Deuteronomy 26.

13] *Salt.* Salt, which gives flavor to food and acts as a preservative, was required not only for the *minchah* but, as the end of the verse makes plain, for all sacrifices.

The salt of your covenant with God. In ancient times, as often today, agreements were sealed with a formal meal. For men to take salt together was a symbolic way of concluding a pact. The Bible therefore describes a solemn covenant as a "covenant of salt" (Num. 18:19; II Chron. 13:5).

14] *A meal offering of first fruits.* Exactly what ceremony is meant is uncertain. Commentators have often taken this as a supplement to the law of Deuteronomy, chapter 26 (above, 2:12; see also Num. 18:13). But the halachah understood it as a reference to the new grain offering (*omer*) of Leviticus, chapter 23, verses 10 through 13.

טו וְנָתַתָּ עָלֶיהָ שֶׁמֶן וְשַׂמְתָּ עָלֶיהָ לְבֹנָה מִנְחָה הִוא:

טז וְהִקְטִיר הַכֹּהֵן אֶת־אַזְכָּרָתָהּ מִגִּרְשָׂהּ וּמִשַּׁמְנָהּ עַל

כָּל־לְבֹנָתָהּ אִשֶּׁה לַיהֹוָה: פ

Leviticus 2:15–16

15] You shall add oil to it and lay frankincense on it; it is a meal offering.   16] And the priest shall turn a token portion of it into smoke: some of the grits and oil, with all of the frankincense, as an offering by fire to the LORD.

GLEANINGS

Haggadah

2:1] *When a Person Presents*

"Person" renders Hebrew *nefesh*, often translated "soul." A voluntary *minchah* was likely to be the gift of a poor person who could not afford anything else; all the more must we value it aright. Once, says the Midrash, a priest expressed contempt for the handful of flour a woman brought to the Temple. God rebuked him in a dream: "She offered her very soul"[4].

13] *The Salt of Your Covenant with God*

A fanciful midrash understands the verse to mean "the covenant your God made about salt." At creation, God separated the waters above the expanse of heaven from those below it (Gen. 1:7); and the waters relegated to the lower level grieved at being so far from God's abode. So God comforted them with the promise that their briny oceans would one day provide the salt to be used on His altar [5].

Zevach Shelamim—Sacrifice of Well-Being

We come now to the sacrifice whose distinctive feature was the festive meal eaten by the sacrificer and his guests after the prescribed portions had been offered on the altar and a share had been given to the priests. But this characteristic procedure is explained only in chapter 7, verses 11ff. The present chapter deals only with the rites at the altar.

The word *zevach*, from a root meaning "to slaughter" [1], is sometimes used for sacrifice in general (Ps. 4:6, 51:19). Frequently, however, it means *zevach shelamim*, especially when it is joined with *olah* (Exod. 18:12; Deut. 12:6; Jer. 7:21). P most often uses the full term *zevach shelamim*.

The second part of the term has been traditionally associated with *shalom*, "peace," and the whole phrase has been translated "peace offering." But in colloquial English that expression means a gift to appease someone who has been offended—and such was not the intent of *shelamim*. Others have connected the word with another meaning of the root *shlm*, "to repay, make good," with reference to the payment of a vow (7:16). But, though some *shelamim* were brought to fulfill a vow, many were not. The rendering "sacrifice of well-being" is an educated guess: it too connects the term with *shalom* in the broader sense of "wholeness, happiness, health." In the Bible, the word has these meanings more often than that of "peace"—and it fits the festive character of the sacrifice.

וְאִם־זֶבַח שְׁלָמִים קָרְבָּנוֹ אִם מִן־הַבָּקָר הוּא מַקְרִיב

א

אִם־זָכָר אִם־נְקֵבָה תָּמִים יַקְרִיבֶנּוּ לִפְנֵי יְהוָה: וְסָמַךְ

ב

יָדוֹ עַל־רֹאשׁ קָרְבָּנוֹ וּשְׁחָטוֹ פֶּתַח אֹהֶל מוֹעֵד וְזָרְקוּ

בְּנֵי אַהֲרֹן הַכֹּהֲנִים אֶת־הַדָּם עַל־הַמִּזְבֵּחַ סָבִיב:

וְהִקְרִיב מִזֶּבַח הַשְּׁלָמִים אִשֶּׁה לַיהוָה אֶת־הַחֵלֶב

ג

הַמְכַסֶּה אֶת־הַקֶּרֶב וְאֵת כָּל־הַחֵלֶב אֲשֶׁר עַל־הַקֶּרֶב:

וְאֵת שְׁתֵּי הַכְּלָיֹת וְאֶת־הַחֵלֶב אֲשֶׁר עֲלֵהֶן אֲשֶׁר עַל־

ד

הַכְּסָלִים וְאֶת־הַיֹּתֶרֶת עַל־הַכָּבֵד עַל־הַכְּלָיוֹת

יְסִירֶנָּה: וְהִקְטִירוּ אֹתוֹ בְנֵי־אַהֲרֹן הַמִּזְבֵּחָה עַל־

ה

1] If his offering is a sacrifice of well-being—

If he offers of the herd, whether a male or a female, he shall bring before the LORD one without blemish.   2] He shall lay his hand upon the head of his offering and slaughter it at the entrance of the Tent of Meeting; and Aaron's sons, the priests, shall dash the blood against all sides of the altar.   3] He shall then present from the sacrifice of well-being, as an offering by fire to the LORD, the fat that covers the entrails and all the fat that is about the entrails;   4] the two kidneys and the fat that is on them, that is at the loins; and the protuberance on the liver, which he shall remove with the kidneys.   5] Aaron's sons shall turn these into smoke on

3:1]   *A sacrifice of well-being.* Others, "peace offering." Exact meaning of *shelamim* uncertain (T.N.).

3–4]   *He shall present . . . the fat . . . with the kidneys.* These parts (plus the broad tail in the case of sheep, verse 9) are the ones burned on the altar, not only in the case of *shelamim*, but of all sacrifices except the *olah*—of which everything but the hide is consumed on the altar.

4]   *The protuberance [yoteret] on the liver.* The meaning of *yoteret* has been debated. Rashi thought it was the diaphragm; but several ancient sources support the view that it was a projecting lobe of the liver [2]. Our translation follows this opinion.

הָעֹלָה אֲשֶׁר עַל־הָעֵצִים אֲשֶׁר עַל־הָאֵשׁ אִשֵּׁה רֵיחַ
נִיחֹחַ לַיהוָה: פ

ו וְאִם־מִן־הַצֹּאן קָרְבָּנוֹ לְזֶבַח שְׁלָמִים לַיהוָה זָכָר אוֹ
ז נְקֵבָה תָּמִים יַקְרִיבֶנּוּ: אִם־כֶּשֶׂב הוּא־מַקְרִיב אֶת־
ח קָרְבָּנוֹ וְהִקְרִיב אֹתוֹ לִפְנֵי יְהוָה: וְסָמַךְ אֶת־יָדוֹ עַל־
רֹאשׁ קָרְבָּנוֹ וְשָׁחַט אֹתוֹ לִפְנֵי אֹהֶל מוֹעֵד וְזָרְקוּ בְּנֵי
ט אַהֲרֹן אֶת־דָּמוֹ עַל־הַמִּזְבֵּחַ סָבִיב: וְהִקְרִיב מִזֶּבַח
הַשְּׁלָמִים אִשֶּׁה לַיהוָה חֶלְבּוֹ הָאַלְיָה תְמִימָה לְעֻמַּת
הֶעָצֶה יְסִירֶנָּה וְאֶת־הַחֵלֶב הַמְכַסֶּה אֶת־הַקֶּרֶב וְאֵת

Leviticus 3
6–9

the altar, with the burnt offering which is upon the wood that is on the fire, as an offering by fire, of pleasing odor to the LORD.

6] And if his offering for a sacrifice of well-being to the LORD is from the flock, whether a male or a female, he shall offer one without blemish.   **7]** If he presents a sheep as his offering, he shall bring it before the LORD   **8]** and lay his hand upon the head of his offering. It shall be slaughtered before the Tent of Meeting, and Aaron's sons shall dash its blood against all sides of the altar.   **9]** He shall then present, as an offering by fire to the LORD, the fat from the sacrifice of well-being: the whole broad tail, which shall be removed close to the backbone; the fat that

9] *The whole broad tail.* In the Near East, sheep were and are of a variety having a heavy tail; it weighs ten pounds or more, and it is considered a delicacy. Herodotus (fifth century B.C.E.) tells of little carts used by the shepherds to support the tails of their sheep and prevent them from being broken; the same device is mentioned in the Mishnah some six centuries later [3].

The punctuation of the English rendering implies that the tail was among the fat portions reserved for the altar and so, by implication, forbidden as human food. This conclusion was actually drawn by the Karaite sect; but rabbinic tradition permitted the fat tail of nonsacrificial sheep to be eaten.

כָּל־הַחֵלֶב אֲשֶׁר עַל־הַקֶּרֶב: וְאֵת שְׁתֵּי הַכְּלָיֹת וְאֶת־
הַחֵלֶב אֲשֶׁר עֲלֵהֶן אֲשֶׁר עַל־הַכְּסָלִים וְאֶת־הַיֹּתֶרֶת
עַל־הַכָּבֵד עַל־הַכְּלָיֹת יְסִירֶנָּה: וְהִקְטִירוֹ הַכֹּהֵן
הַמִּזְבֵּחָה לֶחֶם אִשֶּׁה לַיהֹוָה: פ

וְאִם־עֵז קָרְבָּנוֹ וְהִקְרִיבוֹ לִפְנֵי יְהֹוָה: וְסָמַךְ אֶת־יָדוֹ
עַל־רֹאשׁוֹ וְשָׁחַט אֹתוֹ לִפְנֵי אֹהֶל מוֹעֵד וְזָרְקוּ בְּנֵי
אַהֲרֹן אֶת־דָּמוֹ עַל־הַמִּזְבֵּחַ סָבִיב: וְהִקְרִיב מִמֶּנּוּ
קָרְבָּנוֹ אִשֶּׁה לַיהֹוָה אֶת־הַחֵלֶב הַמְכַסֶּה אֶת־הַקֶּרֶב
וְאֵת כָּל־הַחֵלֶב אֲשֶׁר עַל־הַקֶּרֶב: וְאֵת שְׁתֵּי הַכְּלָיֹת
וְאֶת־הַחֵלֶב אֲשֶׁר עֲלֵהֶן אֲשֶׁר עַל־הַכְּסָלִים וְאֶת־
הַיֹּתֶרֶת עַל־הַכָּבֵד עַל־הַכְּלָיֹת יְסִירֶנָּה: וְהִקְטִירָם
הַכֹּהֵן הַמִּזְבֵּחָה לֶחֶם אִשֶּׁה לְרֵיחַ נִיחֹחַ כָּל־חֵלֶב

covers the entrails and all the fat that is about the entrails; 10] the two kidneys and the fat that is on them, that is at the loins; and the protuberance on the liver, which he shall remove with the kidneys. 11] The priest shall turn these into smoke on the altar as food, an offering by fire to the LORD.

12] And if his offering is a goat, he shall bring it before the LORD 13] and lay his hand upon its head. It shall be slaughtered before the Tent of Meeting, and Aaron's sons shall dash its blood against all sides of the altar. 14] He shall then present as his offering from it, as an offering by fire to the LORD, the fat that covers the entrails and all the fat that is about the entrails; 15] the two kidneys and the fat that is on them, that is at the loins; and the protuberance on the liver, which he shall remove with the kidneys. 16] The priest shall turn these into smoke on the altar as food, an offering by fire, of pleasing odor.

ויקרא ג:יז   יז   לַיהֹוָה: חֻקַּת עוֹלָם לְדֹרֹתֵיכֶם בְּכֹל מוֹשְׁבֹתֵיכֶם

Leviticus 3:17   כָּל־חֵלֶב וְכָל־דָּם לֹא תֹאכֵלוּ:   פ

All fat is the LORD's.   **17]** It is a law for all time throughout the ages, in all your settlements: you must not eat any fat or any blood.

17] *You must not eat any fat.* This categorical language could not be taken with absolute literalness. One cannot eat meat without getting some of the fat that is mixed in with the muscle. Tradition sensibly understood *chelev* in the technical sense of "prohibited fat." It is hard fat—according to Rabbi Akiba, that which is layered, covered by a membrane, and capable of being peeled off [4]. Permitted fat is called *shuman.* Present-day Orthodox usage requires the slaughterer or butcher to remove all *chelev* from meat that is offered for sale. The fat of game and fowl is not forbidden.

Or any blood. See p. 179.

Chatat—Sin Offering

The previous chapters concerned sacrifices brought voluntarily. We now come to offerings that were obligatory on those who had incurred guilt. They served chiefly to expiate unintentional sins. (There are a few exceptions in chapter 5.) The law did not permit one to do a deliberate wrong and then square the account with a sacrifice. "The sacrifice of the wicked is an abomination to the Lord" (Prov. 15:8).

Ceremonial atonement for unwitting violations of the law was a psychologically sound procedure. People are often deeply disturbed if they cause harm by accident, ignorance, or oversight. The sacrifice relieved the troubled conscience. To this day, in the Yom Kippur confession, we ask forgiveness "for the sins we have sinned before You under duress or through choice . . . unwittingly or defiantly." Implicit in such a prayer is the acknowledgment that we should have shown greater care and foresight. Modern law too operates with the concepts of contributory negligence and criminal negligence.

The sacrifice prescribed in this chapter is called *chatat*, usually translated "sin offering." The translators' footnote to these words in verse 3 reads, "So traditionally; more precisely, 'offering of purgation' " [1]. Actually, the one word conveys both meanings.

The verb *chata* meant primarily "to miss the mark" [2]. The sinner is one who misses the proper objective; hence, *chata* in Scripture usually means "to commit a sin or crime." The noun *chet* means "sin" or "guilt"; the noun *chatat*, likewise meaning "sin" or "guilt," also refers to the offering that cancels out sin. Further, some forms of the verb *chata* are used for the ritual acts (especially sprinkling, Num. 19:19) which remove defilement.

In form, the *chatat* differs from other sacrifices in the special treatment of the blood of the animal. This ritual takes two forms. If the sinner is the "anointed priest," or if the offering expiates an offense of the entire community, the blood is taken into the "holy place"; some of it is sprinkled toward the inner Shrine, and some is placed on the horns of the incense altar. In such cases, the carcass of the animal is burned outside the camp. But, if the sinner is a secular ruler or a commoner, the blood is put on the horns of the main altar and the meat is eaten by the priests. In either case, the usual fat parts are burned on the altar [3].

27

א וַיְדַבֵּר יְהֹוָה אֶל־מֹשֶׁה לֵּאמֹר: דַּבֵּר אֶל־בְּנֵי יִשְׂרָאֵל
לֵאמֹר נֶפֶשׁ כִּי־תֶחֱטָא בִשְׁגָגָה מִכֹּל מִצְוֹת יְהֹוָה אֲשֶׁר
ג לֹא תֵעָשֶׂינָה וְעָשָׂה מֵאַחַת מֵהֵנָּה: אִם הַכֹּהֵן הַמָּשִׁיחַ
יֶחֱטָא לְאַשְׁמַת הָעָם וְהִקְרִיב עַל חַטָּאתוֹ אֲשֶׁר חָטָא
ד פַּר בֶּן־בָּקָר תָּמִים לַיהֹוָה לְחַטָּאת: וְהֵבִיא אֶת־הַפָּר
אֶל־פֶּתַח אֹהֶל מוֹעֵד לִפְנֵי יְהֹוָה וְסָמַךְ אֶת־יָדוֹ עַל־
ה רֹאשׁ הַפָּר וְשָׁחַט אֶת־הַפָּר לִפְנֵי יְהֹוָה: וְלָקַח הַכֹּהֵן

Leviticus 4
1–5

* ד סבירין אשר לפני.

1] The LORD spoke to Moses, saying: 2] Speak to the Israelite people thus:

When a person unwittingly incurs guilt in regard to any of the LORD's commandments about things not to be done, and does one of them—

3] If it is the anointed priest who has incurred guilt, so that blame falls upon the people, he shall offer for the sin of which he is guilty a bull of the herd without blemish as a sin offering to the LORD.   4] He shall bring the bull to the entrance of the Tent of Meeting, before the LORD, and lay his hand upon the head of the bull. The bull shall be slaughtered before the LORD,   5] and the anointed priest

---

4:2] *Person.* Hebrew *nefesh*, often rendered "soul." Some commentators remark that the soul is involved in every transgression, but Bachya notes that *nefesh* sometimes means the combination of soul and body, sometimes body alone (e.g., Lev. 21:1).

Incurs guilt. These words render a form of the verb *chata*, "to sin."

3] *The anointed priest.* Aaron or his successors, "the priest who is exalted [literally, great] above his fellows" (21:10). In later usage he was called *Kohen Gadol*, "High Priest." (This title appears a few times

in the Bible.) Because he was the spiritual leader, his offense brought blame upon the people; because of his eminence, his offering was the largest and most costly.

As a sin offering. So traditionally; more precisely, "offering of purgation" (T.N.).

4] *Before the Lord.* See commentary on 1:3.

5] *The anointed priest.* He performed the rite on his own behalf.

הַמָּשִׁיחַ מִדַּם הַפָּר וְהֵבִיא אֹתוֹ אֶל־אֹהֶל מוֹעֵד:

ו וְטָבַל הַכֹּהֵן אֶת־אֶצְבָּעוֹ בַּדָּם וְהִזָּה מִן־הַדָּם שֶׁבַע

פְּעָמִים לִפְנֵי יְהֹוָה אֶת־פְּנֵי פָּרֹכֶת הַקֹּדֶשׁ: ז וְנָתַן הַכֹּהֵן

מִן־הַדָּם עַל־קַרְנוֹת מִזְבַּח קְטֹרֶת הַסַּמִּים לִפְנֵי יְהֹוָה

אֲשֶׁר בְּאֹהֶל מוֹעֵד וְאֵת כָּל־דַּם הַפָּר יִשְׁפֹּךְ אֶל־

ח יְסוֹד מִזְבַּח הָעֹלָה אֲשֶׁר־פֶּתַח אֹהֶל מוֹעֵד: וְאֶת־כָּל־

חֵלֶב פַּר הַחַטָּאת יָרִים מִמֶּנּוּ אֶת־הַחֵלֶב הַמְכַסֶּה

ט עַל־הַקֶּרֶב וְאֵת כָּל־הַחֵלֶב אֲשֶׁר עַל־הַקֶּרֶב: וְאֵת

שְׁתֵּי הַכְּלָיֹת וְאֶת־הַחֵלֶב אֲשֶׁר עֲלֵיהֶן אֲשֶׁר עַל־

---

shall take some of the bull's blood and bring it into the Tent of Meeting.   6] The priest shall dip his finger in the blood, and sprinkle of the blood seven times before the LORD, in front of the curtain of the Shrine.   7] The priest shall put some of the blood on the horns of the altar of aromatic incense, which is in the Tent of Meeting, before the LORD; and all the rest of the bull's blood he shall pour out at the base of the altar of burnt offering, which is at the entrance of the Tent of Meeting. 8] He shall remove all the fat from the bull of sin offering: the fat that covers the entrails and all the fat that is about the entrails;   9] the two kidneys and the fat

---

Into the Tent of Meeting. Beyond the court, with its large altar, into the "holy place," containing the altar of incense, the lamp stand, and the table for shewbread.

6] *Sprinkle.* Hebrew *hizah,* an entirely different procedure than that for other sacrifices, the blood of which was dashed (Hebrew *zarak*) from bowls against the sides of the outer altar.

In front of the curtain of the Shrine. The curtain separated the "holy place" from the "Holy of Holies" containing the ark. The priest stood some distance away and sprinkled blood in the direction of the

inner Shrine; the curtain would not be stained, except by accident.

7] *On the horns of the altar.* See Exodus, chapter 30, verse 2. These four projections on the corners of an altar are mentioned in several biblical passages. (See especially I Kings 2:28, where Joab takes sanctuary by clinging to the horns of the altar.) They are also found on some ancient altars unearthed by archeologists. Their meaning is uncertain.

And all the rest of the bull's blood.... The blood ritual having been completed, the remaining blood is disposed of decently.

הַכְּסָלִים וְאֶת־הַיֹּתֶרֶת עַל־הַכָּבֵד עַל־הַכְּלָיוֹת
יְסִירֶנָּה: כַּאֲשֶׁר יוּרַם מִשּׁוֹר זֶבַח הַשְּׁלָמִים וְהִקְטִירָם
הַכֹּהֵן עַל מִזְבַּח הָעֹלָה: וְאֶת־עוֹר הַפָּר וְאֶת־כָּל־
בְּשָׂרוֹ עַל־רֹאשׁוֹ וְעַל־כְּרָעָיו וְקִרְבּוֹ וּפִרְשׁוֹ: וְהוֹצִיא
אֶת־כָּל־הַפָּר אֶל־מִחוּץ לַמַּחֲנֶה אֶל־מָקוֹם טָהוֹר אֶל־
שֶׁפֶךְ הַדֶּשֶׁן וְשָׂרַף אֹתוֹ עַל־עֵצִים בָּאֵשׁ עַל־שֶׁפֶךְ
הַדֶּשֶׁן יִשָּׂרֵף: פ

Leviticus 4

10–13

וְאִם כָּל־עֲדַת יִשְׂרָאֵל יִשְׁגּוּ וְנֶעְלַם דָּבָר מֵעֵינֵי הַקָּהָל
וְעָשׂוּ אַחַת מִכָּל־מִצְוֹת יְהֹוָה אֲשֶׁר לֹא־תֵעָשֶׂינָה

that is on them, that is at the loins; and the protuberance on the liver, which he shall remove with the kidneys— 10] just as it is removed from the ox of the sacrifice of well-being. The priest shall turn them into smoke on the altar of burnt offering. 11] But the hide of the bull, and all its flesh, as well as its head and legs, its entrails and its dung— 12] all the rest of the bull—he shall carry to a clean place outside the camp, to the ash heap, and burn it up with wood; it shall be burned on the ash heap.

13] If it is the whole community of Israel that has erred and the matter escapes the notice of the congregation, so that they do any of the things which by the LORD's commandments ought not to be done, and thus find themselves culpable—

11–12] Usually the meat of the *chatat* was consumed by the priests who performed the sacrifice (6:19ff.). But obviously the High Priest should not eat of the sacrifice he brought for his own sin; so, when the blood and fat had been offered, the rest of the carcass had to be removed and burned that it might not be misused or defiled. Similarly with the *chatat* brought for the sin of all the people (4:21) [4].

12] *The ash heap.* See 6:4.

13] *The whole community of Israel.* The ancient Israelites had a strong sense of communal solidarity; they believed that the misdeeds of some members of the group, especially the leaders, could bring guilt upon all. (See especially Josh. 7; I Sam. 14:24–45.) Certainly, it was not necessary for every member of the community to violate the law before a *chatat* was required.

יד וְאָשֵׁמוּ: וְנוֹדְעָה הַחַטָּאת אֲשֶׁר חָטְאוּ עָלֶיהָ וְהִקְרִיבוּ
הַקָּהָל פַּר בֶּן־בָּקָר לְחַטָּאת וְהֵבִיאוּ אֹתוֹ לִפְנֵי אֹהֶל
טו מוֹעֵד: וְסָמְכוּ זִקְנֵי הָעֵדָה אֶת־יְדֵיהֶם עַל־רֹאשׁ הַפָּר
טז לִפְנֵי יְהֹוָה וְשָׁחַט אֶת־הַפָּר לִפְנֵי יְהֹוָה: וְהֵבִיא הַכֹּהֵן
יז הַמָּשִׁיחַ מִדַּם הַפָּר אֶל־אֹהֶל מוֹעֵד: וְטָבַל הַכֹּהֵן
אֶצְבָּעוֹ מִן־הַדָּם וְהִזָּה שֶׁבַע פְּעָמִים לִפְנֵי יְהֹוָה אֵת־
יח פְּנֵי הַפָּרֹכֶת: וּמִן־הַדָּם יִתֵּן עַל־קַרְנֹת הַמִּזְבֵּחַ אֲשֶׁר
לִפְנֵי יְהֹוָה אֲשֶׁר בְּאֹהֶל מוֹעֵד וְאֵת כָּל־הַדָּם יִשְׁפֹּךְ
יט אֶל־יְסוֹד מִזְבַּח הָעֹלָה אֲשֶׁר־פֶּתַח אֹהֶל מוֹעֵד: וְאֵת
כ כָּל־חֶלְבּוֹ יָרִים מִמֶּנּוּ וְהִקְטִיר הַמִּזְבֵּחָה: וְעָשָׂה לַפָּר
כַּאֲשֶׁר עָשָׂה לְפַר הַחַטָּאת כֵּן יַעֲשֶׂה־לּוֹ וְכִפֶּר עֲלֵהֶם

Leviticus 4

14–20

14] when the sin through which they incurred guilt becomes known, the congregation shall offer a bull of the herd as a sin offering, and bring it before the Tent of Meeting.   15] The elders of the community shall lay their hands upon the head of the bull before the LORD, and the bull shall be slaughtered before the LORD. 16] The anointed priest shall bring some of the blood of the bull into the Tent of Meeting,   17] and the priest shall dip his finger in the blood and sprinkle of it seven times before the LORD, in front of the curtain.   18] Some of the blood he shall put on the horns of the altar which is before the LORD in the Tent of Meeting, and all the rest of the blood he shall pour out at the base of the altar of burnt offering, which is at the entrance of the Tent of Meeting.   19] He shall remove all its fat from it and turn it into smoke on the altar.   20] He shall do with this bull just as is done with the [priest's] bull of sin offering; he shall do the same with

15] *The elders . . . shall lay their hands upon the head of the bull.* As representatives of the community, they designate the sacrifice as that of the entire people. (Most communal sacrifices were offered without this ceremony.) Otherwise, this sacrifice was performed exactly like that of the High Priest.

כא הַכֹּהֵן וְנִסְלַח לָהֶם: וְהוֹצִיא אֶת־הַפָּר אֶל־מִחוּץ
לַמַּחֲנֶה וְשָׂרַף אֹתוֹ כַּאֲשֶׁר שָׂרַף אֵת הַפָּר הָרִאשׁוֹן
חַטַּאת הַקָּהָל הוּא: פ

כב אֲשֶׁר נָשִׂיא יֶחֱטָא וְעָשָׂה אַחַת מִכָּל־מִצְוֹת יְהוָה
כג אֱלֹהָיו אֲשֶׁר לֹא־תֵעָשֶׂינָה בִּשְׁגָגָה וְאָשֵׁם: אוֹ־הוֹדַע
אֵלָיו חַטָּאתוֹ אֲשֶׁר חָטָא בָּהּ וְהֵבִיא אֶת־קָרְבָּנוֹ שְׂעִיר
כד עִזִּים זָכָר תָּמִים: וְסָמַךְ יָדוֹ עַל־רֹאשׁ הַשָּׂעִיר וְשָׁחַט
אֹתוֹ בִּמְקוֹם אֲשֶׁר־יִשְׁחַט אֶת־הָעֹלָה לִפְנֵי יְהוָה
כה חַטָּאת הוּא: וְלָקַח הַכֹּהֵן מִדַּם הַחַטָּאת בְּאֶצְבָּעוֹ

Leviticus 4

21–25

it. Thus the priest shall make expiation for them, and they shall be forgiven. **21]** He shall carry the bull outside the camp and burn it as he burned the first bull; it is the sin offering of the congregation.

22] In case it is a chieftain who incurs guilt by doing unwittingly any of the things which by the commandment of the LORD his God ought not to be done, and finds himself culpable— **23]** once the sin of which he is guilty is brought to his knowledge, he shall bring as his offering a male goat without blemish. **24]** He shall lay his hand upon the goat's head, and it shall be slaughtered at the spot where the burnt offering is slaughtered before the LORD; it is a sin offering. **25]** The priest shall

20] *Shall make expiation.* Hebrew *kipper.* For the meaning of this term, see the introduction to chapter 16, p. 162.

They shall be forgiven. From Hebrew *salach.* This verb is used in the Bible for divine forgiveness only. But, in modern Hebrew, *selichah* is the idiom for "Excuse me!"

22] *A chieftain.* Hebrew *nasi.* This term is often used for the tribal leaders (Exod. 35:27; Num. 1:10) and could refer to them here. But we should then expect a phrase like "chieftain of a tribe," or "one of the chieftains." Ezekiel, moreover, applies the word *nasi*

to rulers of the Davidic family. He calls King Zedekiah "*Nasi* of Israel" (Ezek. 21:30) and foretells the day when "My servant David shall be *nasi* in their midst" (34:24). The word here may therefore mean "king" and was so understood by *Sifra.*

Note that procedure for the *chatat* of the *nasi* and of the private citizen is markedly different from that of verses 1 through 21, aside from the lesser value of the animals offered.

24] *Where the burnt offering is slaughtered.* Cf. 1:11 (T.N.).

וְנָתַן עַל־קַרְנֹת מִזְבַּח הָעֹלָה וְאֶת־דָּמוֹ יִשְׁפֹּךְ אֶל־
כו יְסוֹד מִזְבַּח הָעֹלָה: וְאֶת־כָּל־חֶלְבּוֹ יַקְטִיר הַמִּזְבֵּחָה
כְּחֵלֶב זֶבַח הַשְּׁלָמִים וְכִפֶּר עָלָיו הַכֹּהֵן מֵחַטָּאתוֹ
וְנִסְלַח לוֹ: פ

כז וְאִם־נֶפֶשׁ אַחַת תֶּחֱטָא בִשְׁגָגָה מֵעַם הָאָרֶץ בַּעֲשֹׂתָהּ
כח אַחַת מִמִּצְוֹת יְהוָה אֲשֶׁר לֹא־תֵעָשֶׂינָה וְאָשֵׁם: אוֹ
הוֹדַע אֵלָיו חַטָּאתוֹ אֲשֶׁר חָטָא וְהֵבִיא קָרְבָּנוֹ שְׂעִירַת
כט עִזִּים תְּמִימָה נְקֵבָה עַל־חַטָּאתוֹ אֲשֶׁר חָטָא: וְסָמַךְ
אֶת־יָדוֹ עַל רֹאשׁ הַחַטָּאת וְשָׁחַט אֶת־הַחַטָּאת בִּמְקוֹם
ל הָעֹלָה: וְלָקַח הַכֹּהֵן מִדָּמָהּ בְּאֶצְבָּעוֹ וְנָתַן עַל־קַרְנֹת
מִזְבַּח הָעֹלָה וְאֶת־כָּל־דָּמָהּ יִשְׁפֹּךְ אֶל־יְסוֹד הַמִּזְבֵּחַ:

Leviticus 4
26—30

take with his finger some of the blood of the sin offering and put it on the horns of the altar of burnt offering; and the rest of its blood he shall pour out at the base of the altar of burnt offering.   26] All its fat he shall turn into smoke on the altar, like the fat of the sacrifice of well-being. Thus the priest shall make expiation on his behalf for his sin, and he shall be forgiven.

27] If any person from among the populace unwittingly incurs guilt by doing any of the things which by the LORD's commandments ought not to be done, and finds himself culpable—   28] once the sin of which he is guilty is brought to his knowledge, he shall bring a female goat without blemish as his offering for the sin of which he is guilty.   29] He shall lay his hand upon the head of the sin offering, and the sin offering shall be slaughtered at the place of the burnt offering.   30] The priest shall take with his finger some of its blood and put it on the horns of the altar of burnt offering; and all the rest of its blood he shall pour out at the base of the altar.

27] *Populace.* Literally, "people of the country" (T.N.).

33

לא וְאֶת־כָּל־חֶלְבָּהּ יָסִיר כַּאֲשֶׁר הוּסַר חֵלֶב מֵעַל זֶבַח
הַשְּׁלָמִים וְהִקְטִיר הַכֹּהֵן הַמִּזְבֵּחָה לְרֵיחַ נִיחֹחַ לַיהוָה
וְכִפֶּר עָלָיו הַכֹּהֵן וְנִסְלַח לוֹ: פ

לב וְאִם־כֶּבֶשׂ יָבִיא קָרְבָּנוֹ לְחַטָּאת נְקֵבָה תְמִימָה

לג יְבִיאֶנָּה: וְסָמַךְ אֶת־יָדוֹ עַל רֹאשׁ הַחַטָּאת וְשָׁחַט אֹתָהּ

לד לְחַטָּאת בִּמְקוֹם אֲשֶׁר יִשְׁחַט אֶת־הָעֹלָה: וְלָקַח הַכֹּהֵן
מִדַּם הַחַטָּאת בְּאֶצְבָּעוֹ וְנָתַן עַל־קַרְנֹת מִזְבַּח הָעֹלָה

לה וְאֶת־כָּל־דָּמָהּ יִשְׁפֹּךְ אֶל־יְסוֹד הַמִּזְבֵּחַ: וְאֶת־כָּל־
חֶלְבָּהּ יָסִיר כַּאֲשֶׁר יוּסַר חֵלֶב הַכֶּשֶׂב מִזֶּבַח
הַשְּׁלָמִים וְהִקְטִיר הַכֹּהֵן אֹתָם הַמִּזְבֵּחָה עַל אִשֵּׁי
יְהוָה וְכִפֶּר עָלָיו הַכֹּהֵן עַל־חַטָּאתוֹ אֲשֶׁר־חָטָא
וְנִסְלַח לוֹ: פ

Leviticus 4
31–35

31] He shall remove all its fat, just as the fat is removed from the sacrifice of well-being; and the priest shall turn it into smoke on the altar, for a pleasing odor to the LORD. Thus the priest shall make expiation for him, and he shall be forgiven.

32] If the offering he brings as a sin offering is a sheep, he shall bring a female without blemish.   **33]** He shall lay his hand upon the head of the sin offering, and it shall be slaughtered as a sin offering at the spot where the burnt offering is slaughtered.   **34]** The priest shall take with his finger some of the blood of the sin offering and put it on the horns of the altar of burnt offering, and all the rest of its blood he shall pour out at the base of the altar.   **35]** And all its fat he shall remove just as the fat of the sheep of the sacrifice of well-being is removed; and this the priest shall turn into smoke on the altar, over the LORD's offerings by fire. Thus the priest shall make expiation on his behalf for the sin of which he is guilty, and he shall be forgiven.

31] *For a pleasing odor to the Lord.* This formula was needed to indicate that these offerings too, though occasioned by sin, are dear to God, who welcomes the repentant (Luzzatto).

GLEANINGS

Halachah

A sin offering was required for inadvertent commission of an act forbidden by the Torah which, if deliberate, would have been punished by being "cut off from one's kin" (see commentary on 7:21). A *chatat* was not required for omission of a positive commandment. One who defiantly violated a negative law was exempt from sacrifice, for such a sacrifice would have been unavailing. His guilt could be purged away in time only by continued repentance, observance of the Day of Atonement, and the acceptance of punitive suffering, or by death [5].

4:2] And Does One of Them

If one committed several offenses, or repeated the same offense several times, he had to bring a *chatat* for each violation.

3] So That Blame Falls upon the People

Targum Pseudo-Jonathan understands: He made a mistake while bringing an offering for the people's guilt.

Bull of the Herd
A three-year-old.

12] Outside the Camp

In later centuries, outside the city of Jerusalem.

13] The Whole Community of Israel

The Rabbis, with their more developed sense of individual responsibility, were reluctant to accept the notion that the whole community must shoulder the guilt for the unknown misdeeds of a few. They therefore explained this law as referring to a case in which the Sanhedrin, the highest court, gave an erroneous legal ruling, and the people consequently violated the law without intention. The clause, *the matter escapes the notice of the congregation*, is literally "the matter is hidden from the eyes of the congregation"; and the eyes of the congregation, says *Sifra*, are the judges of the Sanhedrin. (Isa. 29:10 calls the prophets the eyes of the people.) They explained in the same way the guilt of the anointed priest (4:3) who was also authorized to issue ritual decisions and, so by an error, could lead the people to unwitting sin.

Haggadah

4:1] When a Person Unwittingly Incurs Guilt

Scripture says: "Whatever is in your power to do, do with all your might" (Eccles. 9:10). While you have the strength, fulfill the commandments, do charity, turn back to God. While the lamp is still burning, replenish the oil so that it does not go out. If you have sinned, do not persist in defiance; repent, and the Holy One (blessed be He) will accept you. If you have sinned a little, let it seem much to you—even if the fault was unwitting [6].

22] In Case [Asher] . . . a Chieftain . . . Incurs Guilt

Rabban Johanan ben Zakkai punned: Happy

(*ashre*) is the generation whose leader is manly enough to admit his sins! SIFRA

27] If Any Person from among the Populace . . . Incurs Guilt

The patriarchs were able to rejoice in all the sufferings You brought upon them: for every dispensation they praised Your name. But we lack the strength to stand up under trial. When You become angry, we sin; and, when we sin, You grow angry. Do wonders for us, as You did for the patriarchs, and then we will be able to endure [7].

35

Chatat—Sin Offering; Asham—Guilt Offering

This chapter begins with four special cases that require a *chatat* (verses 1–13). Then we are introduced (verses 14–16) to another kind of sacrifice called *asham*, "guilt offering" or "penalty offering." In form, this sacrifice is identical with the *chatat* except that for the *asham* a ram is mandatory whereas, under varying circumstances, the *chatat* may be a bull, sheep, goat, fowl, or even a meal offering. In intent, however, the two sacrifices seem different. The *asham* is brought chiefly by one who has misappropriated property. He must restore what he has taken plus a 20 per cent indemnity; then by bringing an *asham* he is fully restored to divine favor.

It would be convenient if we could say that the *chatat* was brought for inadvertent offenses and the *asham* for deliberate misappropriation of property. But, in fact, this chapter requires a *chatat* for withholding legal testimony, no doubt deliberately (verses 1 and 5), and an *asham* for certain unwitting transgressions (verses 17–19). These seeming inconsistencies cannot readily be brought into a coherent system, and the talmudic Rabbis had trouble with them (see Gleanings). Apparently the chapter is composed of traditions, reflecting different periods or different priestly groups, which were assembled but not thoroughly edited.

The word *asham*, be it noted, conveys the ideas both of guilt and of punishment. The expressions "finds himself culpable," "realized his guilt," and "his penalty" are all forms of the same word.

א וְנֶ֣פֶשׁ כִּֽי־תֶחֱטָ֗א וְשָֽׁמְעָה֙ ק֣וֹל אָלָ֔ה וְה֣וּא עֵ֔ד א֥וֹ רָאָ֖ה

ב א֣וֹ יָדָ֑ע אִם־ל֥וֹא יַגִּ֖יד וְנָשָׂ֥א עֲוֺנֽוֹ: א֣וֹ נֶ֗פֶשׁ אֲשֶׁ֣ר תִּגַּע֮
   בְּכׇל־דָּבָ֣ר טָמֵא֒ א֤וֹ בְנִבְלַת֙ חַיָּ֣ה טְמֵאָ֔ה א֚וֹ בְּנִבְלַת֙
   בְּהֵמָ֣ה טְמֵאָ֔ה א֕וֹ בְּנִבְלַ֖ת שֶׁ֣רֶץ טָמֵ֑א וְנֶעְלַ֣ם מִמֶּ֔נּוּ

ג וְה֥וּא טָמֵ֖א וְאָשֵֽׁם: א֣וֹ כִ֤י יִגַּע֙ בְּטֻמְאַ֣ת אָדָ֔ם לְכֹל֙
   טֻמְאָת֔וֹ אֲשֶׁ֥ר יִטְמָ֖א בָּ֑הּ וְנֶעְלַ֣ם מִמֶּ֔נּוּ וְה֥וּא יָדַ֖ע

ד וְאָשֵֽׁם: א֣וֹ נֶ֡פֶשׁ כִּ֣י תִשָּׁבַע֩ לְבַטֵּ֨א בִשְׂפָתַ֜יִם לְהָרַ֣ע

1] If a person incurs guilt:

When he has heard a public imprecation and—although able to testify as one who has either seen or learned of the matter—he does not give information, so that he is subject to punishment;

2] Or when a person touches any unclean thing—be it the carcass of an unclean beast or the carcass of unclean cattle or the carcass of an unclean creeping thing—and the fact has escaped him, and then, being unclean, he finds himself culpable;

3] Or when he touches human uncleanness—any such uncleanness whereby one becomes unclean—and, though he has known it, the fact has escaped him, but later he finds himself culpable;

4] Or when a person utters an oath to bad or good purpose—whatever a man

---

5:1] *When he has heard a public imprecation.* Namely, against one who withholds testimony (T.N.). Someone engaged in a lawsuit (or perhaps the court) publicly calls on those who have information about the case to appear and testify; and a curse is invoked on anyone who fails to respond. A person who withholds evidence thereby becomes a sinner and is subject to the curse. Later he has a change of heart and confesses. He must then expiate the offense with a *chatat.* "Because many decent people avoid giving testimony for fear of hurting others or of making enemies, the Torah must state plainly that failure to testify makes one liable to divine punishment" (Luzzatto).

2] *Any unclean thing . . . carcass of an unclean beast. . . .* Ritual defilement from animals is explained in 11:29ff.

3] *. . . Human uncleanness* is treated in chapters 12 through 15 and in Num. 19:11ff.

Finds himself culpable. It is not sinful to become ritually unclean; such defilement is inevitable in the ordinary course of living. Sin occurs only if one who has been defiled enters the sanctuary or eats consecrated meat without having been purified [1].

4] *Utters.* Literally, "utters with his lips" (T.N.).

An oath. Violation of oaths regarding civil claims

אוֹ לְהֵיטִיב לְכֹל אֲשֶׁר יְבַטֵּא הָאָדָם בִּשְׁבֻעָה וְנֶעְלַם
מִמֶּנּוּ וְהוּא־יָדַע וְאָשֵׁם לְאַחַת מֵאֵלֶּה: וְהָיָה כִי־יֶאְשַׁם
לְאַחַת מֵאֵלֶּה וְהִתְוַדָּה אֲשֶׁר חָטָא עָלֶיהָ: וְהֵבִיא
אֶת־אֲשָׁמוֹ לַיהוָה עַל חַטָּאתוֹ אֲשֶׁר חָטָא נְקֵבָה מִן־
הַצֹּאן כִּשְׂבָּה אוֹ־שְׂעִירַת עִזִּים לְחַטָּאת וְכִפֶּר עָלָיו
הַכֹּהֵן מֵחַטָּאתוֹ: וְאִם־לֹא תַגִּיעַ יָדוֹ דֵּי שֶׂה וְהֵבִיא
אֶת־אֲשָׁמוֹ אֲשֶׁר חָטָא שְׁתֵּי תֹרִים אוֹ־שְׁנֵי בְנֵי־יוֹנָה
לַיהוָה אֶחָד לְחַטָּאת וְאֶחָד לְעֹלָה: וְהֵבִיא אֹתָם
אֶל־הַכֹּהֵן וְהִקְרִיב אֶת־אֲשֶׁר לַחַטָּאת רִאשׁוֹנָה וּמָלַק

ה

ו

ז

ח

Leviticus 5
5–8

may utter in an oath—and, though he has known it, the fact has escaped him, but later he finds himself culpable in any of these matters—

5] when he realizes his guilt in any of these matters, he shall confess that wherein he has sinned. 6] And he shall bring as his penalty to the LORD, for the sin of which he is guilty, a female from the flock, sheep or goat, as a sin offering; and the priest shall make expiation on his behalf for his sin.

7] But if his means do not suffice for a sheep, he shall bring to the LORD, as his penalty for that of which he is guilty, two turtledoves or two pigeons, one for a sin offering and the other for a burnt offering. 8] He shall bring them to the priest, who shall offer first the one for the sin offering, pinching its head at the nape without

---

is treated below, 5:20ff. *Sifra* therefore takes this passage, perhaps correctly, as referring to oaths of a religious character ("I swear I will fast today!") which are violated by oversight.

5–6] These verses summarize the law of chapter 4, verses 27ff., adding the requirement of a confession.

7] *But if his means do not suffice for a sheep....* This section, which permits the offender to bring a less

expensive *chatat* if he cannot afford the standard sacrifice, may be the direct continuation of chapter 4, verse 35, and so it applies to all sin offerings. Tradition, however, limited the concession to the cases cited in chapter 5, verses 1 through 6.

8–10] If a pair of birds is substituted, the first only is presented as a *chatat* and the procedure is a little different from that of the *olah* of fowl (1:15ff.). The latter procedure is followed for the second bird.

ט אֶת־רֹאשׁוֹ מִמּוּל עָרְפּוֹ וְלֹא יַבְדִּיל: וְהִזָּה מִדַּם
הַחַטָּאת עַל־קִיר הַמִּזְבֵּחַ וְהַנִּשְׁאָר בַּדָּם יִמָּצֵה אֶל־
י יְסוֹד הַמִּזְבֵּחַ חַטָּאת הוּא: וְאֶת־הַשֵּׁנִי יַעֲשֶׂה עֹלָה
כַּמִּשְׁפָּט וְכִפֶּר עָלָיו הַכֹּהֵן מֵחַטָּאתוֹ אֲשֶׁר־חָטָא
יא וְנִסְלַח לוֹ: ס וְאִם־לֹא תַשִּׂיג יָדוֹ לִשְׁתֵּי תֹרִים אוֹ
לִשְׁנֵי בְנֵי־יוֹנָה וְהֵבִיא אֶת־קָרְבָּנוֹ אֲשֶׁר חָטָא עֲשִׂירִת
הָאֵפָה סֹלֶת לְחַטָּאת לֹא־יָשִׂים עָלֶיהָ שֶׁמֶן וְלֹא־יִתֵּן
יב עָלֶיהָ לְבֹנָה כִּי חַטָּאת הִוא: וֶהֱבִיאָהּ אֶל־הַכֹּהֵן
וְקָמַץ הַכֹּהֵן מִמֶּנָּה מְלוֹא קֻמְצוֹ אֶת־אַזְכָּרָתָהּ
יג וְהִקְטִיר הַמִּזְבֵּחָה עַל אִשֵּׁי יְהֹוָה חַטָּאת הִוא: וְכִפֶּר
עָלָיו הַכֹּהֵן עַל־חַטָּאתוֹ אֲשֶׁר־חָטָא מֵאַחַת מֵאֵלֶּה

severing it.   9] He shall sprinkle some of the blood of the sin offering on the side
of the altar, and what remains of the blood shall be drained out at the base of the
altar; it is a sin offering.   10] And the second he shall prepare as a burnt offering,
according to regulation. Thus the priest shall make expiation on his behalf for the
sin of which he is guilty, and he shall be forgiven.

11] And if his means do not suffice for two turtledoves or two pigeons, he shall
bring as his offering for that of which he is guilty a tenth of an *ephah* of choice flour
for a sin offering; he shall not add oil to it or lay frankincense on it, for it is a sin
offering.   12] He shall bring it to the priest, and the priest shall scoop out of it a
handful as a token portion of it and turn it into smoke on the altar, with the Lord's
offerings by fire; it is a sin offering.   13] Thus the priest shall make expiation on
his behalf for whichever of these sins he is guilty, and he shall be forgiven. It shall
belong to the priest, like the meal offering.

11] If a cereal offering is substituted, it must not
have a festive character; oil and frankincense are
therefore to be omitted.

13] *It shall belong to the priest, like the meal offering.*
I.e., the normal *minchah* of chapter 2; after the token

וְנִסְלַח לוֹ וְהָיְתָה לַכֹּהֵן כַּמִּנְחָה: ס וַיְדַבֵּר יְהוָה

אֶל־מֹשֶׁה לֵּאמֹר: נֶפֶשׁ כִּי־תִמְעֹל מַעַל וְחָטְאָה בִּשְׁגָגָה

מִקָּדְשֵׁי יְהוָה וְהֵבִיא אֶת־אֲשָׁמוֹ לַיהוָה אַיִל תָּמִים

מִן־הַצֹּאן בְּעֶרְכְּךָ כֶּסֶף־שְׁקָלִים בְּשֶׁקֶל־הַקֹּדֶשׁ

לְאָשָׁם: וְאֵת אֲשֶׁר חָטָא מִן־הַקֹּדֶשׁ יְשַׁלֵּם וְאֶת־

חֲמִישִׁתוֹ יוֹסֵף עָלָיו וְנָתַן אֹתוֹ לַכֹּהֵן וְהַכֹּהֵן יְכַפֵּר

עָלָיו בְּאֵיל הָאָשָׁם וְנִסְלַח לוֹ: פ

וְאִם־נֶפֶשׁ כִּי תֶחֱטָא וְעָשְׂתָה אַחַת מִכָּל־מִצְוֹת יְהוָה

Leviticus 5

14–17

14] And the LORD spoke to Moses, saying:

15] When a person commits a trespass, being unwittingly remiss about any of the LORD's sacred things, he shall bring as his penalty to the LORD a ram without blemish from the flock, convertible into payment in silver by the sanctuary weight, as a guilt offering.   **16]** He shall make restitution for that wherein he was remiss about the sacred things, and he shall add a fifth part to it and give it to the priest. The priest shall make expiation on his behalf with the ram of the guilt offering, and he shall be forgiven.

17] And when a person, without knowing it, sins in regard to any of the LORD's

portion is burned, the remainder is to be eaten by the priest.

14-16] The first example of the *asham* concerns an offense which was deemed especially grave, even if unwittingly committed; the profane use of food, money, or other objects belonging to the sanctuary. Such misappropriation was called *meilah*, "trespass." An entire treatise of the Mishnah and Talmud, named *Meilah*, is based on these few verses.

15] *A ram . . . convertible into payment in silver by the sanctuary weight.* Older translations render "according to thy valuation in silver by shekels, after the shekel

of the sanctuary." (On "thy valuation," see commentary on 27:2.) The present rendering reflects the fact, known from cuneiform sources, that in ancient Near Eastern practice a money payment could be substituted for a sacrificial animal [2]. Money, of course, meant a specified weight of metal; coinage did not begin in Palestine before the fourth century B.C.E.

17-19] This paragraph is vague and perplexing. It seems to require an *asham* for inadvertent offenses, such as chapter 4 proposes to expiate with a *chatat*. The Rabbis gave a forced explanation: These verses, they say, apply to the individual who suspects,

יח אֲשֶׁר לֹא־תֵעָשֶׂינָה וְלֹא־יָדַע וְאָשֵׁם וְנָשָׂא עֲוֺנוֹ: וְהֵבִיא
אַיִל תָּמִים מִן־הַצֹּאן בְּעֶרְכְּךָ לְאָשָׁם אֶל־הַכֹּהֵן וְכִפֶּר
עָלָיו הַכֹּהֵן עַל שִׁגְגָתוֹ אֲשֶׁר־שָׁגָג וְהוּא לֹא־יָדַע וְנִסְלַח
יט לוֹ: אָשָׁם הוּא אָשֹׁם אָשַׁם לַיהוָה: פ

כא וַיְדַבֵּר יְהוָה אֶל־מֹשֶׁה לֵּאמֹר: נֶפֶשׁ כִּי תֶחֱטָא וּמָעֲלָה
מַעַל בַּיהוָה וְכִחֵשׁ בַּעֲמִיתוֹ בְּפִקָּדוֹן אוֹ־בִתְשׂוּמֶת
כב יָד אוֹ בְגָזֵל אוֹ עָשַׁק אֶת־עֲמִיתוֹ: אוֹ־מָצָא אֲבֵדָה

commandments about things not to be done, and then realizes his guilt, he shall be subject to punishment.   18] He shall bring to the priest a ram without blemish from the flock, or the equivalent, as a guilt offering. The priest shall make expiation on his behalf for the error that he committed unwittingly, and he shall be forgiven. 19] It is a guilt offering; he has incurred guilt before the LORD.

20] The LORD spoke to Moses, saying: 21] When a person sins and commits a trespass against the LORD by dealing deceitfully with his fellow in the matter of a deposit or a pledge, or through robbery, or by defrauding his fellow,   22] or by

but is not sure, that he has violated a law [3] (see Gleanings).

18] *The equivalent.* I.e., in currency; cf. 5:15 (T.N.).

20–26] If by dishonest conduct one person causes financial loss to another, he must restore the full amount and pay a substantial penalty sum; then only may he bring the *asham* (cf. the similar law in Num. 5:5ff.).

21] *Sins and commits a trespass against the Lord.* To injure one's fellow man is to commit trespass against God; and "trespass" (5:15) is taking something holy for one's own use.

A pledge. Meaning of Hebrew uncertain (T.N.).

The expression *tesumet yad*, "placing in [or of] the hand," occurs nowhere else in the Bible. It must refer to something entrusted to the man's care— according to Ibn Ezra, to jointly owned property.

Robbery. Hebrew *gazel*, taking something by force or threat of force.

Defrauding. Hebrew *ashak*. In this case the culprit denies wrongdoing.

22] *If he swears falsely.* This seems to mean that, had he not perjured himself, he would be obligated only to return the misappropriated property and would be exempt from the indemnity and sacrifice. But Rashi and Ibn Ezra understand this clause as enumerating still another category of sin—denying falsely on oath a money debt he has incurred.

וְכִחֶשׁ בָּהּ וְנִשְׁבַּע עַל־שָׁקֶר עַל־אַחַת מִכֹּל אֲשֶׁר־
כג יַעֲשֶׂה הָאָדָם לַחֲטֹא בָהֵנָּה: וְהָיָה כִּי־יֶחֱטָא וְאָשֵׁם
וְהֵשִׁיב אֶת־הַגְּזֵלָה אֲשֶׁר גָּזָל אוֹ אֶת־הָעֹשֶׁק אֲשֶׁר עָשָׁק
אוֹ אֶת־הַפִּקָּדוֹן אֲשֶׁר הָפְקַד אִתּוֹ אוֹ אֶת־הָאֲבֵדָה
כד אֲשֶׁר מָצָא: אוֹ מִכֹּל אֲשֶׁר־יִשָּׁבַע עָלָיו לַשֶּׁקֶר וְשִׁלַּם
אֹתוֹ בְּרֹאשׁוֹ וַחֲמִשִׁתָיו יֹסֵף עָלָיו לַאֲשֶׁר הוּא לוֹ יִתְּנֶנּוּ
כה בְּיוֹם אַשְׁמָתוֹ: וְאֶת־אֲשָׁמוֹ יָבִיא לַיהוָה אַיִל תָּמִים
כו מִן־הַצֹּאן בְּעֶרְכְּךָ לְאָשָׁם אֶל־הַכֹּהֵן: וְכִפֶּר עָלָיו
הַכֹּהֵן לִפְנֵי יְהוָה וְנִסְלַח לוֹ עַל־אַחַת מִכֹּל אֲשֶׁר־
יַעֲשֶׂה לְאַשְׁמָה בָהּ:

Leviticus 5
23—26

Haftarah Vayikra, p. 349

finding something lost and lying about it; if he swears falsely regarding any one of the various things that one may do and sin thereby— **23]** when one has thus sinned and, realizing his guilt, would restore that which he got through robbery or fraud, or the deposit that was entrusted to him, or the lost thing that he found, **24]** or anything else about which he swore falsely, he shall repay the principal amount and add a fifth part to it. He shall pay it to its owner when he realizes his guilt. **25]** Then he shall bring to the priest, as his penalty to the LORD, a ram without blemish from the flock, or the equivalent, as a guilt offering. **26]** The priest shall make expiation on his behalf before the LORD, and he shall be forgiven for whatever he may have done to draw blame thereby.

25] *The equivalent.* See note on verse 18.

GLEANINGS

Halachah

The uncertainties of chapters 4 and 5 were resolved thus:

4:1] The *chatat* of chapter 4 was to be brought for inadvertent violations of negative laws, of which the deliberate violation would have entailed being "cut off from one's kin" (p. 51).

2] The sins enumerated in chapter 5, verses 1 through 4, entail a *chatat*, normally a sheep; but an impecunious sinner may bring an offering of lesser value. This offering is therefore traditionally called *korban oleh veyored*, "an offering that may go up or down."

3] One who is uncertain whether or not he has broken a law brings the "doubtful *asham*" of verses 17 through 19. If later he discovers that he actually did commit the offense, he must also bring a standard *chatat*.

4] The regular *asham* is brought for the cases in chapter 5, verses 15 and 16 and verses 20 through 26 also in Numbers, chapter 5, verses 5 through 9.

5:1] *When He Has Heard a Public Imprecation*
The halachah limited the penalty to those who were individually approached by the litigant and adjured to give evidence and whose failure to respond caused the litigant financial loss.

7] *But if His Means Do Not Suffice for a Sheep*
Even if he has a sheep, but needs it for his own support, he should bring a lesser offering.

16] *A Fifth Part*
According to the halachah, the indemnity is to be one-fifth, not of the principal sum, but of the total amount to be repaid. Put the other way, the principal sum is to be four-fifths of the total repaid. Thus, if the property misappropriated is worth one hundred shekels, the indemnity would be twenty-five shekels—one-fifth of the total sum (one hundred twenty-five) due the sanctuary.

Haggadah

5:16] *He Shall Make Restitution*
When the nations of the world heard this law, they said: "According to our laws, one who takes so much as a hook belonging to Caesar is to be lacerated with a plowshare; but this God is placated by a simple act of restitution. Moreover, He is more lenient about the misappropriation of what is His (He designates this as an "error," verse 15) than about robbing a human being [4].

17–19] Why should the "doubtful *asham*," brought when possibly no offense has been committed, be the costly ram while for an undoubted transgression one may offer a ewe or even fowls or flour? Because, a man might not take seriously the mere possibility of having sinned, if the Torah had not thus shown the gravity of the matter.   NACHMANIDES

21] *Commits a Sin against the Lord*
God is more concerned about the wrong done by man to his fellow than about offenses directed at Him alone. Said Rabbi Akiba: "Loans and other

transactions are ordinarily consummated in the presence of witnesses; one who denies the transaction thereby denies the testimony of the witnesses. But, when one entrusts something privately to another, he wants the matter to be known only to the Third Party. And, should the recipient deny the deposit, he denies that the Third Party was present with them." SIFRA

Said Rabbi Jose: See the blindness of him who robs or defrauds! For a trifling sum he is called sinner, liar, thief, defrauder. He must bring a costly *asham* and is forgiven only through confession and repentance. Moreover Scripture accounts him as having taken a life. Whose life? According to one opinion, that of his victim; according to another opinion, his own life. But the righteous, who are generous and give to others, are accounted as having acquired lives. They become like their Creator who revives the spirit of the lowly and oppressed [5].

Laws of Sacrifice—Olah, Minchah, Chatat

The offerings discussed in the first five chapters are now treated a second time, in the same order as before. Most of the material in this chapter and the next is new, some of it essential. See p. 8.

1. *The Olah—Burnt Offering*

See chapter 1 which describes the procedure for the various types of *olot* in full detail. These directions are now supplemented by instructions for the care of the altar fire.

2. *The Minchah—Meal Offering*

Verses 7 through 11 of chapter 6 repeat the content of chapter 2, verse 11, but they spell out more fully the rules for the consumption of the *minchah* as well as the other "most holy offerings," the *chatat* and *asham*. They were to be eaten by male members of the priestly order, within the precincts of the sanctuary. (*Shelamim*, which were of lesser sanctity, could be eaten by men and women, priests and non-priests, anywhere within the camp.) Moreover, the priests' portion of the *minchah* had to be prepared without leavening.

Verses 9 through 11, which indicate that the meal offerings were to be divided among the priests, appear to contradict chapter 7, verses 9 and 10 which limit this rule to uncooked offerings, while assigning the cooked ones to the priest who presents them. Here too we see the combination of variant traditions (cf. Gleanings on 6:9).

Verses 12 through 16 introduce a new subject—the *minchah* as inaugural offering. The plain sense seems to be that the "anointed priest," i.e., High Priest, had to bring this offering when he first assumed his duties. But, from the word "regular" (Hebrew *tamid*), *Sifra* infers that the High Priest must offer this *minchah* daily. And, from the words "his sons," the conclusion was drawn that ordinary priests must bring the inaugural *minchah* once before officiating at the altar.

3. *The Chatat—Sin Offering*

Verses 17 through 23 give us essential information about the *chatat*. Chapter 4 had dealt only with those portions of the sacrifice that were to be burned on the altar. Now we learn that the meat was to be eaten by the priests as a "most holy" portion, except in the cases treated in chapter 4, verses 3 through 21.

צו
ויקרא ו
א–ה

א וַיְדַבֵּר יְהֹוָה אֶל־מֹשֶׁה לֵּאמֹר: צַו אֶת־אַהֲרֹן וְאֶת־
בָּנָיו לֵאמֹר זֹאת תּוֹרַת הָעֹלָה הִוא הָעֹלָה עַל
מֹוקְדָה עַל־הַמִּזְבֵּחַ כָּל־הַלַּיְלָה עַד־הַבֹּקֶר וְאֵשׁ
ג הַמִּזְבֵּחַ תּוּקַד בּוֹ: וְלָבַשׁ הַכֹּהֵן מִדּוֹ בַד וּמִכְנְסֵי־בַד
יִלְבַּשׁ עַל־בְּשָׂרוֹ וְהֵרִים אֶת־הַדֶּשֶׁן אֲשֶׁר תֹּאכַל הָאֵשׁ
ד אֶת־הָעֹלָה עַל־הַמִּזְבֵּחַ וְשָׂמוֹ אֵצֶל הַמִּזְבֵּחַ: וּפָשַׁט
אֶת־בְּגָדָיו וְלָבַשׁ בְּגָדִים אֲחֵרִים וְהוֹצִיא אֶת־הַדֶּשֶׁן
ה אֶל־מִחוּץ לַמַּחֲנֶה אֶל־מָקוֹם טָהוֹר: וְהָאֵשׁ עַל־
הַמִּזְבֵּחַ תּוּקַד־בּוֹ לֹא תִכְבֶּה וּבִעֵר עָלֶיהָ הַכֹּהֵן

* ב מ' זעירא.

Tzav

Leviticus 6

1–5

1] The LORD spoke to Moses, saying: 2] Command Aaron and his sons thus: This is the ritual of the burnt offering: The burnt offering itself shall remain where it is burned upon the altar all night until morning, while the fire on the altar is kept going on it. 3] The priest shall dress in linen raiment, with linen breeches next to his body; and he shall take up the ashes to which the fire has reduced the burnt offering on the altar and place them beside the altar. 4] He shall then take off his vestments and put on other vestments, and carry the ashes outside the camp to a clean place. 5] The fire on the altar shall be kept burning, not to go out: every

6:2] *The ritual.* Hebrew *Torah.* The older translations regularly translated this word as "law," which is often inaccurate and misleading. The present translation attempts to indicate some of the various shades of meaning; most often it renders *Torah* by "instruction."

The burnt offering itself shall remain. . . . The sacrifices were all performed during daylight hours. The altar portions of *shelamim, chatat,* and *asham,* consisting chiefly of fat, burned rapidly. It would take longer to consume the entire fleshy carcass of the *olah,* so these portions were left on the altar to burn through the night.

3] Each morning a priest was to clear away the debris and ashes from the altar hearth and to mend the fire.

In linen raiment. The usual four priestly vestments, tunic, sash, turban, and breeches, enumerated in Exodus 28:40–42 (*Sifra*).

עֵצִים בַּבֹּקֶר בַּבֹּקֶר וְעָרַךְ עָלֶיהָ הָעֹלָה וְהִקְטִיר

עָלֶיהָ חֶלְבֵי הַשְּׁלָמִים: אֵשׁ תָּמִיד תּוּקַד עַל־הַמִּזְבֵּחַ

לֹא תִכְבֶּה: ס וְזֹאת תּוֹרַת הַמִּנְחָה הַקְרֵב אֹתָהּ

בְּנֵי־אַהֲרֹן לִפְנֵי יְהוָה אֶל־פְּנֵי הַמִּזְבֵּחַ: וְהֵרִים מִמֶּנּוּ

בְּקֻמְצוֹ מִסֹּלֶת הַמִּנְחָה וּמִשַּׁמְנָהּ וְאֵת כָּל־הַלְּבֹנָה

אֲשֶׁר עַל־הַמִּנְחָה וְהִקְטִיר הַמִּזְבֵּחַ רֵיחַ נִיחֹחַ

אַזְכָּרָתָהּ לַיהוָה: וְהַנּוֹתֶרֶת מִמֶּנָּה יֹאכְלוּ אַהֲרֹן וּבָנָיו

מַצּוֹת תֵּאָכֵל בְּמָקוֹם קָדֹשׁ בַּחֲצַר אֹהֶל־מוֹעֵד

יֹאכְלוּהָ: לֹא תֵאָפֶה חָמֵץ חֶלְקָם נָתַתִּי אֹתָהּ מֵאִשָּׁי

קֹדֶשׁ קָדָשִׁים הוּא כַּחַטָּאת וְכָאָשָׁם: כָּל־זָכָר בִּבְנֵי

Leviticus 6

6–11

* ח סבירין ממנה.

morning the priest shall feed wood to it, lay out the burnt offering on it, and turn into smoke the fat parts of the offerings of well-being.   6] A perpetual fire shall be kept burning on the altar, not to go out.

7] And this is the ritual of the meal offering: Aaron's sons shall present it before the LORD, in front of the altar.   8] A handful of the choice flour and oil of the meal offering shall be taken from it, with all the frankincense that is on the meal offering, and this token portion shall be turned into smoke on the altar as a pleasing odor to the LORD.   9] What is left of it shall be eaten by Aaron and his sons; it shall be eaten as unleavened cakes, in the sacred precinct; they shall eat it in the enclosure of the Tent of Meeting.   10] It shall not be baked with leaven; I have given it as their portion from My offerings by fire; it is most holy, like the sin offering and the penalty offering.   11] Only the males among Aaron's descendants may eat of it, as

6] *A perpetual fire . . . not to go out.* Such regulations were well known in Greek and Roman practice. A famous instance was the hearth in Rome tended by the vestal virgins.

11] *Anything that touches these shall become holy.* The translation follows the talmudic authorities and Rashi. The quality of "holiness" was thought to be transmitted by contact as an electrical charge passes

49

אַהֲרֹן יֹאכְלֶ֫נָּה חָק־עוֹלָם לְדֹרֹתֵיכֶם מֵאִשֵּׁי יְהוָֹה
כֹּל אֲשֶׁר־יִגַּע בָּהֶם יִקְדָּשׁ: פ

יב וַיְדַבֵּ֣ר יְהוָֹה אֶל־מֹשֶׁה לֵּאמֹר: זֶה קָרְבַּן אַהֲרֹן וּבָנָיו
אֲשֶׁר־יַקְרִ֣יבוּ לַיהוָֹה בְּיוֹם הִמָּשַׁח אֹתוֹ עֲשִׂירִת הָאֵפָה
סֹלֶת מִנְחָה תָּמִיד מַחֲצִיתָהּ בַּבֹּקֶר וּמַחֲצִיתָהּ בָּעָרֶב:

יד עַל־מַחֲבַת בַּשֶּׁמֶן תֵּעָשֶׂה מֻרְבֶּכֶת תְּבִיאֶנָּה תֻּפִינֵי מִנְחַת

טו פִּתִּים תַּקְרִיב רֵיחַ־נִיחֹחַ לַיהוָֹה: וְהַכֹּהֵן הַמָּשִׁיחַ תַּחְתָּיו
מִבָּנָיו יַעֲשֶׂה אֹתָהּ חָק־עוֹלָם לַיהוָֹה כָּלִיל תָּקְטָר:

טז וְכָל־מִנְחַת כֹּהֵן כָּלִיל תִּהְיֶה לֹא תֵאָכֵל: פ

יז וַיְדַבֵּ֣ר יְהוָֹה אֶל־מֹשֶׁה לֵּאמֹר: דַּבֵּר אֶל־אַהֲרֹן וְאֶל־
יח בָּנָיו לֵאמֹר זֹאת תּוֹרַת הַחַטָּאת בִּמְקוֹם אֲשֶׁר תִּשָּׁחֵט

their due for all time throughout the ages from the LORD's offerings by fire. Anything that touches these shall become holy.

12] The LORD spoke to Moses, saying: 13] This is the offering that Aaron and his sons shall offer to the LORD on the occasion of his anointment: a tenth of an *ephah* of choice flour as a regular meal offering, half of it in the morning and half of it in the evening,   14] shall be prepared with oil on a griddle. You shall bring it well soaked, and offer it as a meal offering of baked slices, of pleasing odor to the LORD. 15] And so shall the priest, anointed from among his sons to succeed him, prepare it; it is the LORD's—a law for all time—to be turned entirely into smoke.   16] So, too, every meal offering of a priest shall be a whole offering: it shall not be eaten.

17] The LORD spoke to Moses, saying: 18] Speak to Aaron and his sons thus: This is the ritual of the sin offering: the sin offering shall be slaughtered before the

from one conductor to another. Thus, if meat from a *shelamim* sacrifice came into contact with a *minchah*, it would become "most holy" and could then be eaten only by priests in the sanctuary [1].

13] *His anointment.* Or, "their anointment" (T.N.).

14] *Baked slices.* Meaning of Hebrew *tufiné* uncertain (T.N.).

הָעֹלָה תִּשָּׁחֵט הַחַטָּאת לִפְנֵי יְהֹוָה קֹדֶשׁ קָדָשִׁים הוּא:

יט הַכֹּהֵן הַמְחַטֵּא אֹתָהּ יֹאכְלֶנָּה בְּמָקוֹם קָדֹשׁ תֵּאָכֵל

כ בַּחֲצַר אֹהֶל מוֹעֵד: כֹּל אֲשֶׁר־יִגַּע בִּבְשָׂרָהּ יִקְדָּשׁ

וַאֲשֶׁר יִזֶּה מִדָּמָהּ עַל־הַבֶּגֶד אֲשֶׁר יִזֶּה עָלֶיהָ תְּכַבֵּס

כא בְּמָקוֹם קָדֹשׁ: וּכְלִי־חֶרֶשׂ אֲשֶׁר תְּבֻשַּׁל־בּוֹ יִשָּׁבֵר וְאִם־

כב בִּכְלִי נְחֹשֶׁת בֻּשָּׁלָה וּמֹרַק וְשֻׁטַּף בַּמָּיִם: כָּל־זָכָר

כג בַּכֹּהֲנִים יֹאכַל אֹתָהּ קֹדֶשׁ קָדָשִׁים הוּא: וְכָל־חַטָּאת

אֲשֶׁר יוּבָא מִדָּמָהּ אֶל־אֹהֶל מוֹעֵד לְכַפֵּר בַּקֹּדֶשׁ לֹא

תֵאָכֵל בָּאֵשׁ תִּשָּׂרֵף: פ

Leviticus 6
19–23

LORD, at the spot where the burnt offering is slaughtered: it is most holy. **19]** The priest who offers it as a sin offering shall eat of it; it shall be eaten in the sacred precinct, in the enclosure of the Tent of Meeting. **20]** Anything that touches its flesh shall become holy; and if any of its blood is spattered upon a garment, you shall wash the bespattered part in the sacred precinct. **21]** An earthen vessel in which it was boiled shall be broken; if it was boiled in a copper vessel, [the vessel] shall be scoured and rinsed with water. **22]** Only the males in the priestly line may eat of it: it is most holy. **23]** But no sin offering may be eaten from which any blood is brought into the Tent of Meeting for expiation in the sanctuary; any such shall be consumed in fire.

18] *At the spot.* Cf. 1:11 (T.N.).

19] *The priest who offers it as a sin offering shall eat of it.* I.e., is obligated to eat of it, as the eating is apparently part of the expiatory process. But the priests in general *may eat of it* (6:22). So Hoffmann.

20] *Anything that touches its flesh.* See commentary on 6:11.

And if any of its blood is spattered. . . . The blood had such a high degree of "holiness" that a garment on which a drop had fallen might not be taken out of the sanctuary until it had been washed.

21] *An earthen vessel . . . shall be broken.* The porous earthenware would absorb juices of the meat and, thus, part of a most holy sacrifice would be left over, violating the rule that it be eaten promptly [2]. The only remedy was to break the pottery vessel. This act, and the scouring of metal pots, had to be done inside the sacred precinct.

23] This verse sums up chapter 4, verses 3 through 21.

GLEANINGS

Halachah

6:3] *He Shall Take Up the Ashes . . . and Place Them beside the Altar*

This removal of ashes from the altar was the first item in the daily schedule of the sanctuary [3]. According to tradition, it was a formality, only one scoopful of ashes being placed beside the altar [4]. Most of the ashes were heaped up in a pile in the center of the altar; when it grew too high to manage, one of the priests would carry the ashes out of the city [5]. This tradition is in apparent contradiction with verse 4 which seems to require the priest who removes the ashes from the altar to carry them promptly outside the camp.

19] *The Priest Who Offers It as a Sin Offering Shall Eat of It*

During the period of the Second Temple, the priests were organized in twenty-four divisions, called *mishmarot*. (I Chron. 24 ascribes this arrangement to David.) Each *mishmar* served for a week at a time, and each of its subdivisions, called a *bet av*, "father's house," served one day of that week. Against the plain sense of this and other verses, *Sifra* [6] assigns these perquisites to the entire *bet av* on duty the day the sacrifice is presented.

Haggadah

6:3] *The Priest Shall Dress in Linen Raiment*

He wore his sacred robes even to remove the ashes from the altar, to indicate his complete dedication. Not even this menial labor could impair his priestly dignity, since it was performed as a ministry to God.   BACHYA

6] *A Perpetual Fire Shall Be Kept Burning on the Altar, Not to Go Out*

This perpetual fire has served generations of Jewish preachers as a symbol of unquenchable devotion. Marvels were related concerning it. It came forth from God's presence (9:24), and it burned continuously for 116 years, yet the thin copper sheathing of the altar never melted, and its wooden core was not charred [7]. It crouched on the altar in the shape of a lion, and it blazed as brilliantly as the sun [8].

Laws of Sacrifice — Zevach Shelamim

This far from orderly chapter is notable chiefly for basic material concerning the *shelamim* sacrifice (7:11–18, 28–34). It also contains directions, mostly repetitive, about the *asham* (7:1–10); the obligation of ritual purity for those who handle or consume sacrificial meats (7:19–21); renewed prohibition of blood and fat (7:22–26); combined with these items, more material on the perquisites of the priests; and the first references in Leviticus to the penalty of being "cut off from one's kin" (7:20 and elsewhere).

In chapter 3, directions for the *shelamim* were limited to the procedures at the altar. Here the sacrifice of well-being is treated in its essential character of a sacred meal. Two forms are distinguished: (1) the offering of thanksgiving (or acknowledgment), *todah*, and (2) the sacrifice brought in fulfillment of a vow, *neder*, or as a freewill offering, *nedavah*.

The *todah* differs from the other *shelamim* in two ways: (1) It is accompanied by an elaborate offering of bread and (2) it must be eaten on one day and the ensuing night while the other *shelamim* may be eaten over two days. No doubt other ancient peoples brought sacrifices in a spirit of gratitude, but a special category of thanksgiving offerings appears only in Israel. Great merit was attached to this sacrifice which seeks neither material nor spiritual benefit. A psalm which denies that God needs sacrifice still asserts, "He who sacrifices a thank offering honors Me" (Ps. 50:23).

Many ancient peoples were accustomed to make vows, especially in conditional form ("If I receive such-and-such a benefit, I will bring such-and-such an offering"). The vow might be the promise of a sacrifice; it is such vows that biblical authors urge us to pay promptly (Deut. 23:22ff.; Eccles. 5:3ff.) and which are mentioned in various psalms (22:26, 116:18, and others). But the Torah also deals at length with vows of abstinence in the Book of Numbers, chapters 6 and 30.

וְזֹאת תּוֹרַת הָאָשָׁם קֹדֶשׁ קָדָשִׁים הוּא: בִּמְקוֹם אֲשֶׁר

יִשְׁחֲטוּ אֶת־הָעֹלָה יִשְׁחֲטוּ אֶת־הָאָשָׁם וְאֶת־דָּמוֹ יִזְרֹק

עַל־הַמִּזְבֵּחַ סָבִיב: וְאֵת כָּל־חֶלְבּוֹ יַקְרִיב מִמֶּנּוּ אֵת

הָאַלְיָה וְאֶת־הַחֵלֶב הַמְכַסֶּה אֶת־הַקֶּרֶב: וְאֵת שְׁתֵּי

הַכְּלָיֹת וְאֶת־הַחֵלֶב אֲשֶׁר עֲלֵיהֶן אֲשֶׁר עַל־הַכְּסָלִים

וְאֶת־הַיֹּתֶרֶת עַל־הַכָּבֵד עַל־הַכְּלָיֹת יְסִירֶנָּה: וְהִקְטִיר

אֹתָם הַכֹּהֵן הַמִּזְבֵּחָה אִשֶּׁה לַיהֹוָה אָשָׁם הוּא: כָּל־

זָכָר בַּכֹּהֲנִים יֹאכְלֶנּוּ בְּמָקוֹם קָדוֹשׁ יֵאָכֵל קֹדֶשׁ

קָדָשִׁים הוּא: כַּחַטָּאת כָּאָשָׁם תּוֹרָה אַחַת לָהֶם

הַכֹּהֵן אֲשֶׁר יְכַפֶּר־בּוֹ לוֹ יִהְיֶה: וְהַכֹּהֵן הַמַּקְרִיב אֶת־

עֹלַת אִישׁ עוֹר הָעֹלָה אֲשֶׁר הִקְרִיב לַכֹּהֵן לוֹ יִהְיֶה:

וְכָל־מִנְחָה אֲשֶׁר תֵּאָפֶה בַּתַּנּוּר וְכָל־נַעֲשָׂה בַמַּרְחֶשֶׁת

Leviticus 7
1–9

1] This is the ritual of the guilt offering: it is most holy. 2] The guilt offering shall be slaughtered at the spot where the burnt offering is slaughtered, and the blood shall be dashed on all sides of the altar. 3] All its fat shall be offered: the broad tail; the fat that covers the entrails; 4] the two kidneys and the fat that is on them at the loins; and the protuberance on the liver, which shall be removed with the kidneys. 5] The priest shall turn them into smoke on the altar as an offering by fire to the Lord; it is a guilt offering. 6] Only the males in the priestly line may eat of it; it shall be eaten in the sacred precinct: it is most holy.

7] The guilt offering is like the sin offering. The same rule applies to both: it shall belong to the priest who makes expiation thereby. 8] So, too, the priest who offers a man's burnt offering shall keep the skin of the burnt offering that he offered. 9] Further, any meal offering that is baked in an oven, and any that is prepared in

7:1] *Most holy.* Therefore the rules in verse 6 apply to it.   7] *It shall belong.* I.e., the meat and the hide.

וְעַל־מַחֲבַת לַכֹּהֵן הַמַּקְרִיב אֹתָהּ לוֹ תִהְיֶה: וְכָל־
מִנְחָה בְלוּלָה־בַשֶּׁמֶן וַחֲרֵבָה לְכָל־בְּנֵי אַהֲרֹן תִּהְיֶה
אִישׁ כְּאָחִיו: פ

יא וְזֹאת תּוֹרַת זֶבַח הַשְּׁלָמִים אֲשֶׁר יַקְרִיב לַיהוָה: אִם
יב עַל־תּוֹדָה יַקְרִיבֶנּוּ וְהִקְרִיב עַל־זֶבַח הַתּוֹדָה חַלּוֹת
מַצּוֹת בְּלוּלֹת בַּשֶּׁמֶן וּרְקִיקֵי מַצּוֹת מְשֻׁחִים בַּשָּׁמֶן
יג וְסֹלֶת מֻרְבֶּכֶת חַלֹּת בְּלוּלֹת בַּשָּׁמֶן: עַל־חַלֹּת לֶחֶם
יד חָמֵץ יַקְרִיב קָרְבָּנוֹ עַל־זֶבַח תּוֹדַת שְׁלָמָיו: וְהִקְרִיב
מִמֶּנּוּ אֶחָד מִכָּל־קָרְבָּן תְּרוּמָה לַיהוָה לַכֹּהֵן הַזֹּרֵק
טו אֶת־דַּם הַשְּׁלָמִים לוֹ יִהְיֶה: וּבְשַׂר זֶבַח תּוֹדַת שְׁלָמָיו

Leviticus 7
10–15

a pan or on a griddle, shall belong to the priest who offers it.   10] But every other meal offering, with oil mixed in or dry, shall go to the sons of Aaron all alike.

11] This is the ritual of the sacrifice of well-being that one may offer to the LORD:

12] If he offers it for thanksgiving, he shall offer together with the sacrifice of thanksgiving unleavened cakes with oil mixed in, unleavened wafers spread with oil, and cakes of choice flour with oil mixed in, well soaked.   13] This offering with cakes of leavened bread added, he shall offer along with his thanksgiving sacrifice of well-being.   14] Out of this he shall offer one of each kind as a gift to the LORD; it shall go to the priest who dashes the blood of the offering of well-being. 15] And the flesh of his thanksgiving sacrifice of well-being shall be eaten on the day that it is offered; none of it shall be set aside until morning.

12] *If he offers it for thanksgiving.* . . . Three kinds of unleavened bread, plus an exceptional offering of leavened bread, accompanied the *todah*. This does not contradict the prohibition of leaven in chapter 2, verse 11, since the bread was not placed on the altar.

14] *Kind.* Literally, "offering" (T.N.).

Gift. Hebrew *terumah*, "something lifted up." *Terumah* as a technical term is rendered "heave offering" in verse 34 and frequently.

15] *Shall be eaten on the day that it is offered.* Whereas other *shelamim* could still be eaten on the second day (7:16f.).

55

בְּיוֹם קָרְבָּנוֹ יֵאָכֵל לֹא־יַנִּיחַ מִמֶּנּוּ עַד־בֹּקֶר: וְאִם־ טז

נֶדֶר אוֹ נְדָבָה זֶבַח קָרְבָּנוֹ בְּיוֹם הַקְרִיבוֹ אֶת־זִבְחוֹ

יֵאָכֵל וּמִמָּחֳרָת וְהַנּוֹתָר מִמֶּנּוּ יֵאָכֵל: וְהַנּוֹתָר מִבְּשַׂר יז יח

הַזֶּבַח בַּיּוֹם הַשְּׁלִישִׁי בָּאֵשׁ יִשָּׂרֵף: וְאִם הֵאָכֹל יֵאָכֵל

מִבְּשַׂר־זֶבַח שְׁלָמָיו בַּיּוֹם הַשְּׁלִישִׁי לֹא יֵרָצֶה הַמַּקְרִיב

אֹתוֹ לֹא יֵחָשֵׁב לוֹ פִּגּוּל יִהְיֶה וְהַנֶּפֶשׁ הָאֹכֶלֶת מִמֶּנּוּ

עֲוֹנָהּ תִּשָּׂא: וְהַבָּשָׂר אֲשֶׁר יִגַּע בְּכָל־טָמֵא לֹא יֵאָכֵל יט

בָּאֵשׁ יִשָּׂרֵף וְהַבָּשָׂר כָּל־טָהוֹר יֹאכַל בָּשָׂר: וְהַנֶּפֶשׁ כ

16] If, however, the sacrifice he offers is a votive or a freewill offering, it shall be eaten on the day that he offers his sacrifice, and what is left of it shall be eaten on the morrow.   17] What is then left of the flesh of the sacrifice shall be consumed in fire on the third day.   18] If any of the flesh of his sacrifice of well-being is eaten on the third day, it shall not be acceptable; it shall not count for him who offered it. It is an offensive thing, and the person who eats of it shall bear his guilt.

19] Flesh that touches anything unclean shall not be eaten; it shall be consumed in fire. As for other flesh, only he who is clean may eat such flesh.   20] But the per-

---

16] *Votive.* Brought for a vow, whether conditional or outright. The freewill offering was presumably brought without prior commitment (but see Gleanings).

17] *Shall be consumed in fire on the third day.* This rendering (instead of "What is left ... on the third day shall be consumed in fire") follows Nachmanides who explains: The meat may be eaten during two days and the night between them. On the second night it may not be eaten, but disposal by fire does not take place till next morning.

18] *It shall not count.* I.e., improper treatment of the sacrificial meat nullifies the sacrifice. Presumably, if the offering had been brought to fulfill a vow, the worshiper would have to bring a substitute.

An offensive thing. Hebrew *pigul.* The plain sense is that eating the meat after the second day renders it *pigul* and thereby invalidates the entire sacrifice. The halachah departs completely from this plain sense (see Gleanings).

Shall bear his guilt. The expression is clarified in verses 20 and 21 as well as in chapter 19, verse 8: the offender will be "cut off from his kin."

19-21] Like ritual holiness (6:11), ritual uncleanness is transmitted by physical contact [1]. Sacred food which is accidentally defiled may not be eaten; it must be burned without ceremony. A ritually unclean person who eats consecrated food is guilty of sacrilege and subject to severe penalties. The rules stated here for *shelamim* apply to all types of consecrated food.

אֲשֶׁר־תֹּאכַל בָּשָׂר מִזֶּבַח הַשְּׁלָמִים אֲשֶׁר לַיהֹוָה

כא וְטֻמְאָתוֹ עָלָיו וְנִכְרְתָה הַנֶּפֶשׁ הַהִוא מֵעַמֶּיהָ: וְנֶפֶשׁ

כִּי־תִגַּע בְּכָל־טָמֵא בְּטֻמְאַת אָדָם אוֹ בִּבְהֵמָה

טְמֵאָה אוֹ בְּכָל־שֶׁקֶץ טָמֵא וְאָכַל מִבְּשַׂר־זֶבַח

הַשְּׁלָמִים אֲשֶׁר לַיהֹוָה וְנִכְרְתָה הַנֶּפֶשׁ הַהִוא מֵעַמֶּיהָ:

כב וַיְדַבֵּר יְהֹוָה אֶל־מֹשֶׁה לֵּאמֹר: דַּבֵּר אֶל־בְּנֵי יִשְׂרָאֵל

כד לֵאמֹר כָּל־חֵלֶב שׁוֹר וְכֶשֶׂב וָעֵז לֹא תֹאכֵלוּ: וְחֵלֶב

נְבֵלָה וְחֵלֶב טְרֵפָה יֵעָשֶׂה לְכָל־מְלָאכָה וְאָכֹל לֹא

כה תֹאכְלֻהוּ: כִּי כָּל־אֹכֵל חֵלֶב מִן־הַבְּהֵמָה אֲשֶׁר יַקְרִיב

מִמֶּנָּה אִשֶּׁה לַיהֹוָה וְנִכְרְתָה הַנֶּפֶשׁ הָאֹכֶלֶת מֵעַמֶּיהָ:

Leviticus 7
21–25

son who, in a state of uncleanness, eats flesh from the LORD's sacrifices of well-being, that person shall be cut off from his kin.   **21]** When a person touches anything unclean, be it human uncleanness or an unclean animal or any unclean creature, and eats flesh from the LORD's sacrifices of well-being, that person shall be cut off from his kin.

22] And the LORD spoke to Moses, saying: **23]** Speak to the Israelite people thus: You shall eat no fat of ox or sheep or goat.   **24]** Fat from animals that died or were torn by beasts may be put to any use, but you must not eat it.   **25]** If anyone eats the fat of animals from which offerings by fire may be made to the LORD,

---

20] *Shall be cut off from his kin.* This expression, with variations, is found also in earlier books of the Torah, always in priestly writings [2]. Some scholars have explained the penalty as ostracism from the community, others as capital punishment [3]. But several related passages make clear that it is God who cuts off the offender from his kin (Lev. 17:10, 20:3-6). The term then refers to divine rather than human punishment, most probably premature death [4].

21] *Unclean creature.* Hebrew *sheketz*, literally, "abomination"; several manuscripts and ancient versions read *sheretz*, "swarming things" (T.N.).

23] *Fat.* I.e., hard, coarse fat (suet). Cf. 3:3-5 (T.N.). On the prohibition of fat, see commentary on 3:17. The present paragraph exempts the fat of game animals from the rule.

24] *Animals that died.* Hebrew *nevelah*, "carcass," i.e., that died a natural death. (Cf. Deut. 14:21.)

Or were torn by beasts. Hebrew *terefah.* In current usage, any nonkosher food is referred to as *terefah* (see p. 90; cf. Exod. 22:30).

May be put to any use. E.g., to lubricate hides.

כו וְכָל־דָּם לֹא תֹאכְלוּ בְּכֹל מוֹשְׁבֹתֵיכֶם לָעוֹף

כז וְלַבְּהֵמָה: כָּל־נֶפֶשׁ אֲשֶׁר־תֹּאכַל כָּל־דָּם וְנִכְרְתָה

הַנֶּפֶשׁ הַהִוא מֵעַמֶּיהָ: פ

כט וַיְדַבֵּר יְהוָה אֶל־מֹשֶׁה לֵּאמֹר: דַּבֵּר אֶל־בְּנֵי יִשְׂרָאֵל

לֵאמֹר הַמַּקְרִיב אֶת־זֶבַח שְׁלָמָיו לַיהוָה יָבִיא אֶת־

ל קָרְבָּנוֹ לַיהוָה מִזֶּבַח שְׁלָמָיו: יָדָיו תְּבִיאֶינָה אֵת אִשֵּׁי

יְהוָה אֶת־הַחֵלֶב עַל־הֶחָזֶה יְבִיאֶנּוּ אֵת הֶחָזֶה לְהָנִיף

לא אֹתוֹ תְּנוּפָה לִפְנֵי יְהוָה: וְהִקְטִיר הַכֹּהֵן אֶת־הַחֵלֶב

Leviticus 7

26–31

the person who eats it shall be cut off from his kin.   **26]** And you must not consume any blood, either of bird or of animal, in any of your settlements.   **27]** Anyone who eats blood shall be cut off from his kin.

28] And the LORD spoke to Moses, saying: **29]** Speak to the Israelite people thus: The offering to the LORD from a sacrifice of well-being must be presented by him who offers his sacrifice of well-being to the LORD: **30]** his own hands shall present the LORD's offerings by fire. He shall present the fat with the breast, the breast to be waved as a wave offering before the LORD;   **31]** the priest shall turn

26–27] On the prohibition of blood, see p. 179.

28–34] The breast and thigh of each *shelamim* sacrifice are to be given to the priest, the first as a *tenufah*, the second as a *terumah*. The old Aramaic translation (Targum) renders these terms as "raising up" and "separation"—presumably meaning that these portions are to be lifted or removed as a special gift. The Greek renders similarly. But the rabbinic sources understood *tenufah* as "waving"; they ruled that the worshiper was to stand before the altar, holding the portions in his hands, and the priest was to move the hands of the sacrificer back and forth horizontally, and then up and down. Hence, the rendering "wave offering" found in most modern versions. But it can hardly be correct. It creates difficulties in chapter 14, verses 12 and 24, where a live lamb is the *tenufah*, and still more in Numbers, chapter 8, verse 11, where the entire tribe of Levi is to be "waved." The root of *tenufah* probably means "to be high"; the term designates either an offering that was literally lifted before the altar—a procedure known from Egyptian religion [5]—or, in a more figurative sense, a special and outstanding gift [6].

There seems to be little, if any, difference in meaning between *tenufah* and *terumah*. The latter also comes from a root meaning "to be high." It is most often rendered "heave offering," sometimes "gift(s)" (e.g., Exod. 25:2). For *terumah* as the technical name for a tax on produce, see Numbers, chapter 18, verses 8ff.

לב הַמִּזְבֵּחָה וְהָיָה הֶחָזֶה לְאַהֲרֹן וּלְבָנָיו: וְאֵת שׁוֹק הַיָּמִין

לג תִּתְּנוּ תְרוּמָה לַכֹּהֵן מִזִּבְחֵי שַׁלְמֵיכֶם: הַמַּקְרִיב אֶת־

דַּם הַשְּׁלָמִים וְאֶת־הַחֵלֶב מִבְּנֵי אַהֲרֹן לוֹ תִהְיֶה שׁוֹק

לד הַיָּמִין לְמָנָה: כִּי אֶת־חֲזֵה הַתְּנוּפָה וְאֵת שׁוֹק

הַתְּרוּמָה לָקַחְתִּי מֵאֵת בְּנֵי־יִשְׂרָאֵל מִזִּבְחֵי שַׁלְמֵיהֶם

וָאֶתֵּן אֹתָם לְאַהֲרֹן הַכֹּהֵן וּלְבָנָיו לְחָק־עוֹלָם מֵאֵת

לה בְּנֵי יִשְׂרָאֵל: זֹאת מִשְׁחַת אַהֲרֹן וּמִשְׁחַת בָּנָיו מֵאִשֵּׁי

לו יְהֹוָה בְּיוֹם הִקְרִיב אֹתָם לְכַהֵן לַיהֹוָה: אֲשֶׁר* צִוָּה

יְהֹוָה לָתֵת לָהֶם בְּיוֹם מָשְׁחוֹ אֹתָם מֵאֵת בְּנֵי יִשְׂרָאֵל

לז חֻקַּת עוֹלָם לְדֹרֹתָם: זֹאת הַתּוֹרָה לָעֹלָה לַמִּנְחָה

* לוֹ סְבִירִין כַּאֲשֶׁר.

Leviticus 7
32–37

the fat into smoke on the altar, and the breast shall go to Aaron and his sons. **32]** And the right thigh from your sacrifices of well-being you shall present to the priest as a gift; **33]** he from among Aaron's sons who offers the blood and the fat of the offering of well-being shall get the right thigh as his portion. **34]** For I have taken the breast of wave offering and the thigh of heave offering from the Israelites, from their sacrifices of well-being, and given them to Aaron the priest and to his sons as their due from the Israelites for all time.

35] Those shall be the perquisites of Aaron and the perquisites of his sons from the LORD's offerings by fire, once they have been inducted to serve the LORD as priests; **36]** these the LORD commanded to be given them, once they had been anointed, as a due from the Israelites for all time throughout the ages.

37] These are the rituals of the burnt offering, the meal offering, the sin offering,

---

35] *Those shall be the perquisites.* Presumably the breast and thigh. But the reference could be to all the portions assigned to the priests throughout these chapters which formally conclude in the ensuing verses.

Perquisites. Literally, "anointment," i.e., accruing from anointment (T.N.).

Inducted. Literally, "brought forward" (T.N.).

לח וְלַחַטָּאת וְלָאָשָׁם וְלַמִּלּוּאִים וּלְזֶבַח הַשְּׁלָמִים: אֲשֶׁר‎

צִוָּה יְהוָה אֶת־מֹשֶׁה בְּהַר סִינָי בְּיוֹם צַוֹּתוֹ אֶת־בְּנֵי‎

יִשְׂרָאֵל לְהַקְרִיב אֶת־קָרְבְּנֵיהֶם לַיהוָה בְּמִדְבַּר‎

סִינָי: פ

* לח סבירין כאשר.

the guilt offering, the offering of ordination, and the sacrifice of well-being,

38] with which the LORD charged Moses on Mount Sinai, when He commanded

that the Israelites present their offerings to the LORD, in the wilderness of Sinai.

37] *The offering of ordination.* This was actually explained in Exodus, chapter 29. But Nachmanides
notes that the ordination ceremonies included all the
types of sacrifices expounded in Leviticus, chapters
1 through 7.

GLEANINGS

Halachah

7:15] *The Flesh of His Thanksgiving Sacrifice . . . Shall Be Eaten on the Day That It Is Offered*

Legally, it could be eaten till dawn of the second day; but the Rabbis forbid eating it after midnight, "to keep man far from sin," i.e., to allow ample margin for error [7]. This principle is also expressed in the aphorism, "Make a fence about the Torah" [8]. In modern terms: Drive ten miles an hour less than the legal limit, to make sure that you don't exceed it.

16] *A Votive or a Freewill Offering*

According to the halachah, the distinction is one of form. "I obligate myself to bring a sacrifice of well-being" is a *neder*, vow. "This sheep shall be a sacrifice of well-being" is a *nedavah*, freewill offering. In the second case, the worshiper was exempt from further obligation if the animal died, was lost, or proved defective. In the case of a vow, he would have to provide a substitute animal [9].

18] *If Any of the Flesh . . . Is Eaten on the Third Day . . . It Is an Offensive Thing [Pigul]*

The Targums render the verse literally; but other rabbinic interpreters [10] depart from the plain sense (as Rashbam states flatly) and explain the law of *pigul* as follows: If the officiating priest, while slaughtering the animal and dashing its blood on the altar, had *the intention* in mind that the flesh should be eaten on the third day, this wrong intention rendered the sacrifice *pigul* from the start.

It is improbable that such a rule obtained during the time of the Second Temple. Most likely it was a refinement of scholars active after 70 C.E. Why did they so radically reinterpret a plain statement? One factor, perhaps, was the question: If a sacrifice was properly performed from the start, how could it be invalidated retroactively? (This argument is raised by Rabbi Akiba in *Sifra*, though he did not consider it conclusive.) It would seem sufficient if the person who ate the food illegally were punished—by being obliged to bring a *chatat* if the act was inadvertent, by being "cut off" if it was deliberate.

A second factor was the language of chapter 19, verse 5, cited by *Sifra* on 7:17, "When you sacrifice an offering of well-being to the LORD, sacrifice it so that it may be accepted in your behalf," which was taken to mean: It must be performed with proper intent from the outset or it will not be accepted. All this is in accord with the great emphasis on intention throughout the halachah [11].

20] *Shall Be Cut Off from His Kin*

This penalty is called in rabbinic texts *karet*, "cutting off," and is the subject of a treatise of the Mishnah and Talmud entitled *Keritot*. There is general agreement that *karet* is a divinely inflicted punishment, but its exact character was debated. The view given in the commentary—that it means premature death—was held by many scholars [12]; others thought it meant that the offender would die childless [13]. Nachmanides [14] distinguished between various degrees of *karet*, depending on the crime and the criminal; the most severe form included annihilation in the world beyond the grave.

Haggadah

7:12] *If He Offers It for Thanksgiving*

"Though all sacrifices may be discontinued in the future (for, in the messianic age, men will be sinless), the offering of thanksgiving will never cease. Though all prayers may be discontinued, the prayer of thanksgiving will never cease" [15].

61

PART II

The Dedication of the Tabernacle
and
The Ordination of the Priests

The Divine Presence in the Sanctuary

At this point, the exposition of the laws is interrupted by a narrative section that tells of the dedication of the Tabernacle and the ordination of Aaron and his sons to the priesthood.

Directions for these rites had been given in Exodus, chapter 29, verses 1 through 37. Now we are told that they were performed by Moses acting temporarily as High Priest. After these ceremonies were conducted for seven days, Aaron and his sons assumed their duties. Their service was crowned by the visible appearance of the Divine Presence, and a miraculous flame consumed the sacrifices on the altar.

This joyous occasion was suddenly disrupted by tragedy. Two of Aaron's sons committed a ceremonial offense; and again a miraculous flame appeared, this time to take the lives of the offenders. Joined to the account of the subsequent mourning are three brief legal sections.

The general intent of these chapters is plain. They emphasize the grandeur and importance of cult and priesthood. Through the sanctuary and the sacrifices, God's nearness to His people is established and maintained. Similarly, at the dedication of Solomon's Temple, the Presence of the LORD is said to have filled the house (I Kings 3:10f.); and one report states that heavenly fire descended and consumed the sacrifices (II Chron. 7:1ff.). The terrible fate of Nadab and Abihu, Aaron's two oldest sons, underscored the need to perform the rituals strictly according to rule and stressed the accountability of the priests for the faithful discharge of their duties. The exact nature of the young men's offense, however, is obscure [1].

The chronology of the events is uncertain. Exodus, chapter 40, verses 2ff., states that Moses had the Tabernacle set up on the first day of the first month in the second year after the Exodus; and, after he had performed the various sacrifices, the Presence of the Lord became manifest. According to Leviticus, chapters 8 and 9, Moses conducted the ceremonies for seven days, but the Divine Presence did not appear until Aaron had officiated on the eighth day—and no definite dates are given. Numbers, chapter 7, moreover, reports that the chieftains of the tribes brought elaborate gifts, including sacrifices, beginning on the day when Moses set up the Tabernacle and continuing for twelve consecutive days. All these passages are from P. Evidently the priests had several traditions on this subject which did not wholly agree. The talmudic authorities felt obligated to harmonize the apparent discrepancies. They explained that the dedication program began on the twenty-third day of the twelfth month. Moses officiated on the last seven days of that month; the eighth day of Leviticus 9:1 was the first day of the first month of Exodus 40:2 when Aaron assumed the priestly duties and the Presence of the Lord appeared. The same day, when "Moses had finished setting up the Tabernacle" (Num. 7:1)—i.e., when he had discharged his responsibilities and Aaron had taken over—the first of the tribal leaders presented his offerings (Num. 7:12) [2].

1. *The Prohibition of Intoxicants*

Chapter 10, verses 8–10 forbid the priests to drink any intoxicant before performing a sacred function. It is doubtful whether there is any connection between this paragraph and its context; but understandably the Rabbis tried to find one, and some of them inferred that Nadab and Abihu had been drinking before they offered the incense [3].

The restriction applied only to times when the priests were on duty. Otherwise, like other Israelites, they were free to make use of wine, which was produced and enjoyed throughout the ancient Near East.

The Bible does speak of individuals called nazirites (*nezirim*, "dedicated ones") who were required to abstain from wine (indeed from anything produced by the grape vine) and to leave their hair uncut. Some persons were lifelong nazirites (Samson, Judg. 13; Samuel, I Sam. 1:1; cf. Amos 2:11f.); they were apparently dedicated by their parents to this special way of life. But the priestly legislation provides that a person of either sex may make a vow to become a nazirite for a specified length of time [4]. At the end of the period, the nazirite cut his hair and

the locks were burned together with the sacrifices that he was required to bring. Thereupon he returned to his secular status (Num. 6). Because of the sacrificial element in this procedure, nazirite vows ceased after the fall of the Second Temple [5].

Aside from this special case, the drinking of wine was considered normal and proper. Wine "cheers the hearts of men" (Ps. 104:15; cf. Judg. 9:13). The Bible indeed contains several warnings against drunkenness; but the tone of these passages suggests that excessive drinking was not considered sinful but rather ugly and degrading, a kind of foolish behavior that may easily lead to impropriety and even immorality (Gen. 9:20 ff.; Prov. 23:29 ff. and 31:4 ff.) The prophets who denounce drunken rulers regard their drinking as the evidence, rather than the cause, of their depravity (Isa. 5:11 ff.; Amos 2:8). The *midrashim* provide sermons to our Leviticus passage expounding the evils of drunkenness in general, without reference to priests; their somewhat jocular tone suggests that the Rabbis were not too seriously concerned about the problem.

Judaism has regularly employed wine in religious ceremonies from the sacrificial libations of the Bible to the traditional rites of Kiddush and Havdalah and the marriage ceremony. Few Jews are total abstainers on principle; yet the incidence of alcoholism among Jews is low, and there is a widespread belief (shared by Jews and non-Jews) that heavy drinking and intoxication are less common among Jews than in the general population. The most intensive study of the subject thus far published suggests that the drinking habits of Jews, in the United States, at least, are more like those of their neighbors than had been supposed. This study does indicate that those Jews who regularly observe the traditional home ceremonials seldom drink to excess, even though they drink frequently; whereas there is a significant increase of intoxication among those Jews who have given up the traditional customs and much of the value system associated with them [6].

2. *Priestly Perquisites*

Chapter 10 verses 12–15 repeat the law (already explained in 6:7–11), concerning the sanctity of the *minchah*, cereal offering, and contrast it with the lesser sanctity of the portions assigned to the priests from sacrifices of well-being, *shelamim*. The latter, it is now made plain, may be eaten in any clean place (according to the halachah of later times, anywhere in Jerusalem), and the women of priestly families may partake of them. This section is connected to the narrative by verse 12 which was perhaps added to supply such a connection.

א וַיְדַבֵּר יְהוָֹה אֶל־מֹשֶׁה לֵּאמֹר: קַח אֶת־אַהֲרֹן וְאֶת־
ב בָּנָיו אִתּוֹ וְאֵת הַבְּגָדִים וְאֵת שֶׁמֶן הַמִּשְׁחָה וְאֵת פַּר
ג הַחַטָּאת וְאֵת שְׁנֵי הָאֵילִים וְאֵת סַל הַמַּצּוֹת: וְאֵת
ד כָּל־הָעֵדָה הַקְהֵל אֶל־פֶּתַח אֹהֶל מוֹעֵד: וַיַּעַשׂ מֹשֶׁה
כַּאֲשֶׁר צִוָּה יְהוָֹה אֹתוֹ וַתִּקָּהֵל הָעֵדָה אֶל־פֶּתַח אֹהֶל
ה מוֹעֵד: וַיֹּאמֶר מֹשֶׁה אֶל־הָעֵדָה זֶה הַדָּבָר אֲשֶׁר־צִוָּה
ו יְהוָֹה לַעֲשׂוֹת: וַיַּקְרֵב מֹשֶׁה אֶת־אַהֲרֹן וְאֶת־בָּנָיו
ז וַיִּרְחַץ אֹתָם בַּמָּיִם: וַיִּתֵּן עָלָיו אֶת־הַכֻּתֹּנֶת וַיַּחְגֹּר
אֹתוֹ בָּאַבְנֵט וַיַּלְבֵּשׁ אֹתוֹ אֶת־הַמְּעִיל וַיִּתֵּן עָלָיו אֶת־
ח הָאֵפֹד וַיַּחְגֹּר אֹתוֹ בְּחֵשֶׁב הָאֵפֹד וַיֶּאְפֹּד לוֹ בּוֹ: וַיָּשֶׂם
עָלָיו אֶת־הַחֹשֶׁן וַיִּתֵּן אֶל־הַחֹשֶׁן אֶת־הָאוּרִים וְאֶת־

1] The LORD spoke to Moses, saying: 2] Take Aaron and his sons with him, the vestments, the anointing oil, the bull of sin offering, the two rams, and the basket of unleavened bread; 3] and assemble the whole community at the entrance of the Tent of Meeting. 4] Moses did as the LORD commanded him. And when the community was assembled at the entrance of the Tent of Meeting, 5] Moses said to the community, "This is what the LORD has commanded to be done."

6] Then Moses brought Aaron and his sons forward and washed them with water. 7] He put the tunic on him, girded him with the sash, clothed him with the robe, and put the *ephod* on him, girding him with the decorated band with which he tied it to him. 8] He put the breastpiece on him, and put into the breast-

---

8:3] *Assemble the whole community.* To give maximum publicity and honor to the new priesthood. Rashi, following the Midrash [7], remarks that the entire community could be accommodated at the entrance of the Tent only by a miracle. More soberly, Ibn Ezra explains that the "whole community" was represented by its leaders. See commentary on 4:13.

68

ט הַתֻּמִּים: וַיָּשֶׂם אֶת־הַמִּצְנֶפֶת עַל־רֹאשׁוֹ וַיָּשֶׂם עַל־
הַמִּצְנֶפֶת אֶל־מוּל פָּנָיו אֵת צִיץ הַזָּהָב נֵזֶר הַקֹּדֶשׁ
י כַּאֲשֶׁר צִוָּה יְהוָֹה אֶת־מֹשֶׁה: וַיִּקַּח מֹשֶׁה אֶת־שֶׁמֶן
הַמִּשְׁחָה וַיִּמְשַׁח אֶת־הַמִּשְׁכָּן וְאֶת־כָּל־אֲשֶׁר־בּוֹ וַיְקַדֵּשׁ
יא אֹתָם: וַיַּז מִמֶּנּוּ עַל־הַמִּזְבֵּחַ שֶׁבַע פְּעָמִים וַיִּמְשַׁח אֶת־
הַמִּזְבֵּחַ וְאֶת־כָּל־כֵּלָיו וְאֶת־הַכִּיֹּר וְאֶת־כַּנּוֹ לְקַדְּשָׁם:
יב וַיִּצֹק מִשֶּׁמֶן הַמִּשְׁחָה עַל רֹאשׁ אַהֲרֹן וַיִּמְשַׁח אֹתוֹ
יג לְקַדְּשׁוֹ: וַיַּקְרֵב מֹשֶׁה אֶת־בְּנֵי אַהֲרֹן וַיַּלְבִּשֵׁם כֻּתֳּנֹת
וַיַּחְגֹּר אֹתָם אַבְנֵט וַיַּחֲבֹשׁ לָהֶם מִגְבָּעוֹת כַּאֲשֶׁר צִוָּה

Leviticus 8
9–13

piece the Urim and Thummim. 9] And he set the headdress on his head; and on the headdress, in front, he put the gold frontlet, the holy diadem—as the LORD had commanded Moses.

10] Moses took the anointing oil and anointed the Tabernacle and all that was in it, thus consecrating them. 11] He sprinkled some of it on the altar seven times, anointing the altar, all its utensils, and the laver with its stand, to consecrate them. 12] He poured some of the anointing oil upon Aaron's head and anointed him, to consecrate him. 13] Moses then brought Aaron's sons forward, clothed them in tunics, girded them with sashes, and wound turbans upon them, as the LORD had commanded Moses.

8] *The Urim and Thummim.* Meaning of these two words uncertain. They designate a kind of oracle. Cf. Num. 27:21 (T.N. at Exod. 28:30).

10] *Moses . . . anointed the Tabernacle. . . .* As commanded in Exod. 29:36, 30:26ff., 40:9f.

13] *Aaron's sons.* Nothing is said here about anointing the sons, though this is mentioned in Exodus 28:41; Leviticus 7:36, 10:7; and elsewhere. Perhaps the sprinkling with oil (8:30) constituted the anointment of the priests, while the High Priest was distinguished by having oil poured on his head (8:12). Otherwise, we must again assume variant traditions. Subsequent to this first ordination, there is no mention of anointment of ordinary priests, as distinguished from the High Priest [8].

יְהֹוָה אֶת־מֹשֶׁה: וַיַּגֵּשׁ אֶת פַּר הַחַטָּאת וַיִּסְמֹךְ אַהֲרֹן

וּבָנָיו אֶת־יְדֵיהֶם עַל־רֹאשׁ פַּר הַחַטָּאת: וַיִּשְׁחָט וַיִּקַּח

מֹשֶׁה אֶת־הַדָּם וַיִּתֵּן עַל־קַרְנוֹת הַמִּזְבֵּחַ סָבִיב

בְּאֶצְבָּעוֹ וַיְחַטֵּא אֶת־הַמִּזְבֵּחַ וְאֶת־הַדָּם יָצַק אֶל־

יְסוֹד הַמִּזְבֵּחַ וַיְקַדְּשֵׁהוּ לְכַפֵּר עָלָיו: וַיִּקַּח אֶת־כָּל־

הַחֵלֶב אֲשֶׁר עַל־הַקֶּרֶב וְאֵת יֹתֶרֶת הַכָּבֵד וְאֶת־שְׁתֵּי

הַכְּלָיֹת וְאֶת־חֶלְבְּהֶן וַיַּקְטֵר מֹשֶׁה הַמִּזְבֵּחָה: וְאֶת־

הַפָּר וְאֶת־עֹרוֹ וְאֶת־בְּשָׂרוֹ וְאֶת־פִּרְשׁוֹ שָׂרַף בָּאֵשׁ

מִחוּץ לַמַּחֲנֶה כַּאֲשֶׁר צִוָּה יְהֹוָה אֶת־מֹשֶׁה: וַיַּקְרֵב

אֵת אֵיל הָעֹלָה וַיִּסְמְכוּ אַהֲרֹן וּבָנָיו אֶת־יְדֵיהֶם עַל־

14] He led forward the bull of sin offering. Aaron and his sons laid their hands upon the head of the bull of sin offering,   15] and it was slaughtered. Moses took the blood and with his finger put some on each of the horns of the altar, cleansing the altar; then he poured out the blood at the base of the altar. Thus he consecrated it and purged it.

16] Moses then took all the fat that was about the entrails, and the protuberance of the liver, and the two kidneys and their fat, and turned them into smoke on the altar.   17] The rest of the bull, its hide, its flesh, and its dung, he put to the fire outside the camp—as the Lord had commanded Moses.

18] Then he brought forward the ram of burnt offering. Aaron and his sons laid

14-17] According to the rule, when the blood of a sin offering was sprinkled inside the sanctuary, the animal was burned outside the camp; if the blood was put only on the horns of the main altar, the meat was eaten by the priests (Lev. 4 and 6:17-23). But in this one case, though the blood was not taken into the sanctuary, the carcass was not eaten but burned. Perhaps this was because Moses was not technically a priest and, therefore, not able to eat a

"most holy" sacrifice; or else special rules applied to this unique occasion.

15] *Thus he consecrated it and purged it.* Future printings of the Torah translation will render this sentence: "Thus he consecrated it for making expiation upon it." That is, the foregoing ritual cleansed the altar of impurity so that henceforth it would be fit for the performance of atonement rites.

ט רֹאשׁ הָאָיִל: וַיִּשְׁחָט וַיִּזְרֹק מֹשֶׁה אֶת־הַדָּם עַל־הַמִּזְבֵּחַ

כ סָבִיב: וְאֶת־הָאַיִל נִתַּח לִנְתָחָיו וַיַּקְטֵר מֹשֶׁה אֶת־

כא הָרֹאשׁ וְאֶת־הַנְּתָחִים וְאֶת־הַפָּדֶר: וְאֶת־הַקֶּרֶב וְאֶת־

הַכְּרָעַיִם רָחַץ בַּמָּיִם וַיַּקְטֵר מֹשֶׁה אֶת־כָּל־הָאַיִל

הַמִּזְבֵּחָה עֹלָה הוּא לְרֵיחַ־נִיחֹחַ אִשֶּׁה הוּא לַיהוָה

כב כַּאֲשֶׁר צִוָּה יְהוָה אֶת־מֹשֶׁה: וַיַּקְרֵב אֶת־הָאַיִל הַשֵּׁנִי

אֵיל הַמִּלֻּאִים וַיִּסְמְכוּ אַהֲרֹן וּבָנָיו אֶת־יְדֵיהֶם עַל־

כג רֹאשׁ הָאָיִל: וַיִּשְׁחָט וַיִּקַּח מֹשֶׁה מִדָּמוֹ וַיִּתֵּן עַל־תְּנוּךְ

Leviticus 8

19–23

their hands upon the ram's head,   19] and it was slaughtered. Moses dashed the blood against all sides of the altar.   20] The ram was cut up into sections and Moses turned the head, the sections, and the suet into smoke—   21] the entrails and the legs having been washed with water. Moses turned all of the ram into smoke on the altar: that was a burnt offering for a pleasing odor, an offering by fire to the LORD—as the LORD had commanded Moses.

22] He brought forward the second ram, the ram of ordination. Aaron and his sons laid their hands upon the ram's head,   23] and it was slaughtered. Moses took some of its blood and put it on the ridge of Aaron's right ear, and on the thumb

22] *Ordination.* Hebrew *milluim,* literally "filling." The full term is "to fill a hand" (e.g., in 8:33). We do not know the exact force of this idiom. Some scholars have offered the guess that during the ordination ceremony the priest was handed some symbol of authority, as kings are handed a scepter during their coronation. But there is no evidence to support the guess.

22–29] The ram of ordination is a sacrifice of well-being, and the worshipers—here Aaron and his sons—eat its flesh. But the ritual procedure described in chapter 8, verses 26 through 29, is different from the usual rules laid down in chapter 7, verses 28 through 33, and does not seem to follow exactly the prescriptions in Exodus, chapter 29, verses 26 and 27.

The ordination, a one-time event, presumably had its special rules. (On "wave," "wave offering," see commentary on 7:28–34.)

23] *On the ridge of Aaron's right ear, on the thumb of his right hand, and on the big toe of his right foot.* Edifying explanations of this procedure have been offered (see Gleanings). But the talmudic sources refrain from moralizing; and a similar procedure was followed in purifying one who had been cured of "leprosy" (see 14:14)—in a situation where nothing "inspirational" was in place. The original intent was probably one of ritual purification; and the extremities served as a kind of summary for the entire body. The priest (or "leper") was to be cleansed of defilement "from top to toe."

Ridge. Or, "lobe" (T.N.).

אֹזֶן־אַהֲרֹן הַיְמָנִית וְעַל־בֹּהֶן יָדוֹ הַיְמָנִית וְעַל־בֹּהֶן

כד רַגְלוֹ הַיְמָנִית: וַיַּקְרֵב אֶת־בְּנֵי אַהֲרֹן וַיִּתֵּן מֹשֶׁה מִן־
הַדָּם עַל־תְּנוּךְ אָזְנָם הַיְמָנִית וְעַל־בֹּהֶן יָדָם הַיְמָנִית
וְעַל־בֹּהֶן רַגְלָם הַיְמָנִית וַיִּזְרֹק מֹשֶׁה אֶת־הַדָּם עַל־

כה הַמִּזְבֵּחַ סָבִיב: וַיִּקַּח אֶת־הַחֵלֶב וְאֶת־הָאַלְיָה וְאֶת־
כָּל־הַחֵלֶב אֲשֶׁר עַל־הַקֶּרֶב וְאֵת יֹתֶרֶת הַכָּבֵד

כו וְאֶת־שְׁתֵּי הַכְּלָיֹת וְאֶת־חֶלְבְּהֶן וְאֵת שׁוֹק הַיָּמִין: וּמִסַּל
הַמַּצּוֹת אֲשֶׁר לִפְנֵי יְהוָה לָקַח חַלַּת מַצָּה אַחַת
וְחַלַּת לֶחֶם שֶׁמֶן אַחַת וְרָקִיק אֶחָד וַיָּשֶׂם עַל־

כז הַחֲלָבִים וְעַל שׁוֹק הַיָּמִין: וַיִּתֵּן אֶת־הַכֹּל עַל כַּפֵּי
אַהֲרֹן וְעַל כַּפֵּי בָנָיו וַיָּנֶף אֹתָם תְּנוּפָה לִפְנֵי יְהוָה:

כח וַיִּקַּח מֹשֶׁה אֹתָם מֵעַל כַּפֵּיהֶם וַיַּקְטֵר הַמִּזְבֵּחָה עַל־
הָעֹלָה מִלֻּאִים הֵם לְרֵיחַ נִיחֹחַ אִשֶּׁה הוּא לַיהוָה:

of his right hand, and on the big toe of his right foot.   24] Moses then brought forward the sons of Aaron, and put some of the blood on the ridges of their right ears, and on the thumbs of their right hands, and on the big toes of their right feet; and the rest of the blood Moses dashed against every side of the altar.   25] He took the fat—the broad tail, all the fat about the entrails, the protuberance of the liver, and the two kidneys and their fat—and the right thigh.   26] From the basket of unleavened bread that was before the LORD, he took one cake of unleavened bread, one cake of oil bread, and one wafer, and placed them on the fat parts and on the right thigh.   27] He placed all these on the palms of Aaron and on the palms of his sons, and waved them as a wave offering before the LORD.   28] Then Moses took them from their hands and turned them into smoke on the altar with the burnt offering. This was an ordination offering for a pleasing odor; it was an offering

כט וַיִּקַּח מֹשֶׁה אֶת־הֶחָזֶה וַיְנִיפֵהוּ תְנוּפָה לִפְנֵי יְהוָה
מֵאֵיל הַמִּלֻּאִים לְמֹשֶׁה הָיָה לְמָנָה כַּאֲשֶׁר צִוָּה יְהוָה
ל אֶת־מֹשֶׁה: וַיִּקַּח מֹשֶׁה מִשֶּׁמֶן הַמִּשְׁחָה וּמִן־הַדָּם אֲשֶׁר
עַל־הַמִּזְבֵּחַ וַיַּז עַל־אַהֲרֹן עַל־בְּגָדָיו וְעַל־בָּנָיו וְעַל־
בִּגְדֵי בָנָיו אִתּוֹ וַיְקַדֵּשׁ אֶת־אַהֲרֹן אֶת־בְּגָדָיו וְאֶת־בָּנָיו
לא וְאֶת־בִּגְדֵי בָנָיו אִתּוֹ: וַיֹּאמֶר מֹשֶׁה אֶל־אַהֲרֹן וְאֶל־
בָּנָיו בַּשְּׁלוּ אֶת־הַבָּשָׂר פֶּתַח אֹהֶל מוֹעֵד וְשָׁם תֹּאכְלוּ
אֹתוֹ וְאֶת־הַלֶּחֶם אֲשֶׁר בְּסַל הַמִּלֻּאִים כַּאֲשֶׁר צִוֵּיתִי
לב לֵאמֹר אַהֲרֹן וּבָנָיו יֹאכְלֻהוּ: וְהַנּוֹתָר בַּבָּשָׂר וּבַלָּחֶם
לג בָּאֵשׁ תִּשְׂרֹפוּ: וּמִפֶּתַח אֹהֶל מוֹעֵד לֹא תֵצְאוּ שִׁבְעַת
יָמִים עַד יוֹם מְלֹאת יְמֵי מִלֻּאֵיכֶם כִּי שִׁבְעַת יָמִים

Leviticus 8

29–33

by fire to the LORD. **29]** Moses took the breast and waved it as a wave offering before the LORD; it was Moses' portion of the ram of ordination—as the LORD had commanded Moses.

30] And Moses took some of the anointing oil and some of the blood that was on the altar and sprinkled it upon Aaron and upon his vestments, and also upon his sons and upon their vestments. Thus he consecrated Aaron and his vestments, and also his sons and their vestments.

31] And Moses said to Aaron and his sons: Boil the flesh at the entrance of the Tent of Meeting and eat it there with the bread that is in the basket of ordination—as I commanded: Aaron and his sons shall eat it; **32]** and what is left over of the flesh and the bread you shall consume in fire. **33]** You shall not go outside the entrance of the Tent of Meeting for seven days, until the day that your period of

31] *As I commanded.* Or, vocalizing *tzuveti,* "I have been commanded"; cf. verse 35 below (T.N.).
31–35] The ritual was to be repeated daily for a week.

33] *You shall not go outside.* The priests were not to absent themselves while the ceremonies were actually in progress (*Sifra*).

לד יְמַלֵּא אֶת־יֶדְכֶם: כַּאֲשֶׁר עָשָׂה בַּיּוֹם הַזֶּה צִוָּה יְהֹוָה

לה לַעֲשֹׂת לְכַפֵּר עֲלֵיכֶם: וּפֶתַח אֹהֶל מוֹעֵד תֵּשְׁבוּ יוֹמָם

וָלַיְלָה שִׁבְעַת יָמִים וּשְׁמַרְתֶּם אֶת־מִשְׁמֶרֶת יְהֹוָה וְלֹא

לו תָמוּתוּ כִּי־כֵן צֻוֵּיתִי: וַיַּעַשׂ אַהֲרֹן וּבָנָיו אֵת כָּל־

הַדְּבָרִים אֲשֶׁר־צִוָּה יְהֹוָה בְּיַד־מֹשֶׁה:

Haftarah Tzav, p. 359

ס   ס   ס

א וַיְהִי בַּיּוֹם הַשְּׁמִינִי קָרָא מֹשֶׁה לְאַהֲרֹן וּלְבָנָיו וּלְזִקְנֵי

ב יִשְׂרָאֵל: וַיֹּאמֶר אֶל־אַהֲרֹן קַח־לְךָ עֵגֶל בֶּן־בָּקָר

לְחַטָּאת וְאַיִל לְעֹלָה תְּמִימִם וְהַקְרֵב לִפְנֵי יְהֹוָה:

ג וְאֶל־בְּנֵי יִשְׂרָאֵל תְּדַבֵּר לֵאמֹר קְחוּ שְׂעִיר־עִזִּים

ד לְחַטָּאת וְעֵגֶל וָכֶבֶשׂ בְּנֵי־שָׁנָה תְּמִימִם לְעֹלָה: וְשׁוֹר

שְׁמִינִי

Shemini

Leviticus 8; 9

34–36; 1–4

ordination is completed. For your ordination will require seven days.   34] Every-thing done today, the LORD has commanded to be done [seven days], to make ex-piation for you.   35] You shall remain at the entrance of the Tent of Meeting day and night for seven days, keeping the LORD's charge—that you may not die—for so I have been commanded.

36] And Aaron and his sons did all the things that the LORD had commanded through Moses.

1] On the eighth day Moses called Aaron and his sons, and the elders of Israel.

2] He said to Aaron: "Take a calf of the herd for a sin offering and a ram for a burnt offering, without blemish, and bring them before the LORD.   3] And speak to the Israelites, saying: Take a he-goat for a sin offering; a calf and a lamb, yearlings with-out blemish, for a burnt offering;   4] and an ox and a ram for an offering of well-

9:1] *On the eighth day.* I.e., of the ordination ceremonies. See pp. 65–66.
Aaron now enters on his priestly duties.

וְאַיִל לִשְׁלָמִים לִזְבֹּחַ לִפְנֵי יְהוָֹה וּמִנְחָה בְּלוּלָה
בַשֶּׁמֶן כִּי הַיּוֹם יְהוָֹה נִרְאָה אֲלֵיכֶם: וַיִּקְחוּ אֵת אֲשֶׁר
צִוָּה מֹשֶׁה אֶל־פְּנֵי אֹהֶל מוֹעֵד וַיִּקְרְבוּ כָּל־הָעֵדָה
וַיַּעַמְדוּ לִפְנֵי יְהוָֹה: וַיֹּאמֶר מֹשֶׁה זֶה הַדָּבָר אֲשֶׁר־
צִוָּה יְהוָֹה תַּעֲשׂוּ וְיֵרָא אֲלֵיכֶם כְּבוֹד יְהוָֹה: וַיֹּאמֶר
מֹשֶׁה אֶל־אַהֲרֹן קְרַב אֶל־הַמִּזְבֵּחַ וַעֲשֵׂה אֶת־חַטָּאתְךָ
וְאֶת־עֹלָתֶךָ וְכַפֵּר בַּעַדְךָ וּבְעַד הָעָם וַעֲשֵׂה אֶת־
קָרְבַּן הָעָם וְכַפֵּר בַּעֲדָם כַּאֲשֶׁר צִוָּה יְהוָֹה: וַיִּקְרַב
אַהֲרֹן אֶל־הַמִּזְבֵּחַ וַיִּשְׁחַט אֶת־עֵגֶל הַחַטָּאת אֲשֶׁר־לוֹ:

being to sacrifice before the LORD; and a meal offering with oil mixed in. For today the LORD will appear to you."

5] They brought to the front of the Tent of Meeting the things that Moses had commanded, and the whole community came forward and stood before the LORD. **6]** Moses said: "This is what the LORD has commanded that you do, that the Presence of the LORD may appear to you." **7]** Then Moses said to Aaron: "Come forward to the altar and sacrifice your sin offering and your burnt offering, making expiation for yourself and for the people; and sacrifice the people's offering and make expiation for them, as the LORD has commanded."

8] Aaron came forward to the altar and slaughtered his calf of sin offering.

6] *The Presence of the Lord.* Hebrew *Kevod Adonai,* formerly translated "the Glory of the LORD." This expression, found chiefly in priestly writings, designates a visible manifestation of the Divine. "The Presence of the LORD appeared . . . as a consuming fire" (Exod. 24:17). It was often accompanied by, or enveloped in, a cloud which perhaps was to protect the people from its overwhelming brilliance or from other destructive effects (Exod. 24:16). See also Ezekiel (especially 1:28), which describes the Presence as having human form, and Isaiah (6:3), "His Presence fills all the earth." Often, as here, the Presence is a

sign of God's favor; but sometimes (e.g., Num. 16:19) it appears in moments of anger and punishment.

The Rabbis speak similarly of the *Shechinah,* the Divine Indwelling, but this is not necessarily something visible to the physical eye [9].

7] *Making expiation for yourself and for the people.* Until Aaron himself had been purified from guilt, he could not intercede for the people. But the Greek version, instead of "for the people," reads "for your household" (cf. 16:11); this may well be correct, since the expiation of the people is treated in the next clause.

ט וַיַּקְרִבוּ בְּנֵי אַהֲרֹן אֶת־הַדָּם אֵלָיו וַיִּטְבֹּל אֶצְבָּעוֹ
בַּדָּם וַיִּתֵּן עַל־קַרְנוֹת הַמִּזְבֵּחַ וְאֶת־הַדָּם יָצַק אֶל־
י יְסוֹד הַמִּזְבֵּחַ: וְאֶת־הַחֵלֶב וְאֶת־הַכְּלָיֹת וְאֶת־הַיֹּתֶרֶת
מִן־הַכָּבֵד מִן־הַחַטָּאת הִקְטִיר הַמִּזְבֵּחָה כַּאֲשֶׁר צִוָּה
יא יְהוָה אֶת־מֹשֶׁה: וְאֶת־הַבָּשָׂר וְאֶת־הָעוֹר שָׂרַף בָּאֵשׁ
יב מִחוּץ לַמַּחֲנֶה: וַיִּשְׁחַט אֶת־הָעֹלָה וַיַּמְצִאוּ בְּנֵי אַהֲרֹן
יג אֵלָיו אֶת־הַדָּם וַיִּזְרְקֵהוּ עַל־הַמִּזְבֵּחַ סָבִיב: וְאֶת־
הָעֹלָה הִמְצִיאוּ אֵלָיו לִנְתָחֶיהָ וְאֶת־הָרֹאשׁ וַיַּקְטֵר
יד עַל־הַמִּזְבֵּחַ: וַיִּרְחַץ אֶת־הַקֶּרֶב וְאֶת־הַכְּרָעָיִם וַיַּקְטֵר
טו עַל־הָעֹלָה הַמִּזְבֵּחָה: וַיַּקְרֵב אֵת קָרְבַּן הָעָם וַיִּקַּח

9] Aaron's sons brought the blood to him; he dipped his finger in the blood and put it on the horns of the altar; and he poured out the rest of the blood at the base of the altar. **10]** The fat, the kidneys, and the protuberance of the liver from the sin offering he turned into smoke on the altar—as the LORD had commanded Moses; **11]** and the flesh and the skin were consumed in fire outside the camp. **12]** Then he slaughtered the burnt offering. Aaron's sons passed the blood to him, and he dashed it against all sides of the altar. **13]** They passed the burnt offering to him in sections, as well as the head, and he turned it into smoke on the altar. **14]** He washed the entrails and the legs, and turned them into smoke on the altar with the burnt offering.

15] Next he brought forward the people's offering. He took the goat for the

---

10] *Turned into smoke.* This seems to contradict verse 24 which tells that the sacrifices were consumed by a heavenly fire. Rashbam, followed by Luzzatto, understands "turned into smoke" to mean simply "laid the pieces on the altar ready for burning." But

Hoffmann notes that on the previous days the offerings had been consumed by normal fire and that a similar fire could have been kindled on the eighth day before the heavenly fire descended.

אֶת־שְׂעִיר הַחַטָּאת אֲשֶׁר לָעָם וַיִּשְׁחָטֵהוּ וַיְחַטְּאֵהוּ

טז כָּרִאשׁוֹן: וַיַּקְרֵב אֶת־הָעֹלָה וַיַּעֲשֶׂהָ כַּמִּשְׁפָּט: וַיַּקְרֵב

אֶת־הַמִּנְחָה וַיְמַלֵּא כַפּוֹ מִמֶּנָּה וַיַּקְטֵר עַל־הַמִּזְבֵּחַ

יח מִלְּבַד עֹלַת הַבֹּקֶר: וַיִּשְׁחַט אֶת־הַשּׁוֹר וְאֶת־הָאַיִל

זֶבַח הַשְּׁלָמִים אֲשֶׁר לָעָם וַיַּמְצִאוּ בְּנֵי אַהֲרֹן אֶת־הַדָּם

יט אֵלָיו וַיִּזְרְקֵהוּ עַל־הַמִּזְבֵּחַ סָבִיב: וְאֶת־הַחֲלָבִים מִן־

הַשּׁוֹר וּמִן־הָאַיִל הָאַלְיָה וְהַמְכַסֶּה וְהַכְּלָיֹת וְיֹתֶרֶת

כ הַכָּבֵד: וַיָּשִׂימוּ אֶת־הַחֲלָבִים עַל־הֶחָזוֹת וַיַּקְטֵר

כא הַחֲלָבִים הַמִּזְבֵּחָה: וְאֵת הֶחָזוֹת וְאֵת שׁוֹק הַיָּמִין

הֵנִיף אַהֲרֹן תְּנוּפָה לִפְנֵי יְהוָה כַּאֲשֶׁר צִוָּה מֹשֶׁה:

Leviticus 9

16—21

people's sin offering, and slaughtered it, and presented it as a sin offering like the previous one.   16] He brought forward the burnt offering and sacrificed it according to regulation.   17] He then brought forward the meal offering and, taking a handful of it, he turned it into smoke on the altar—in addition to the burnt offering of the morning.   18] He slaughtered the ox and the ram, the people's sacrifice of well-being. Aaron's sons passed the blood to him—which he dashed against every side of the altar—   19] and the fat parts of the ox and the ram: the broad tail, the covering [fat], the kidneys, and the protuberances of the livers.   20] They laid these fat parts over the breasts; and Aaron turned the fat parts into smoke on the altar,   21] and waved the breasts and the right thighs as a wave offering before the LORD—as Moses had commanded.

17] *The burnt offering of the morning.* See Exodus, chapter 29, verses 38 through 46 (T.N.).

20] *Aaron.* This word moved up from verse 21 for

clarity (T.N.).

21] *Waved . . . wave offering.* See commentary on 7:28–34.

כב וַיִּשָּׂא אַהֲרֹן אֶת־יָדָו* אֶל־הָעָם וַיְבָרְכֵם וַיֵּרֶד מֵעֲשֹׂת

כג הַחַטָּאת וְהָעֹלָה וְהַשְּׁלָמִים: וַיָּבֹא מֹשֶׁה וְאַהֲרֹן אֶל־
אֹהֶל מוֹעֵד וַיֵּצְאוּ וַיְבָרְכוּ אֶת־הָעָם וַיֵּרָא כְבוֹד־יְהֹוָה

כד אֶל־כָּל־הָעָם: וַתֵּצֵא אֵשׁ מִלִּפְנֵי יְהֹוָה וַתֹּאכַל עַל־
הַמִּזְבֵּחַ אֶת־הָעֹלָה וְאֶת־הַחֲלָבִים וַיַּרְא כָּל־הָעָם
וַיָּרֹנּוּ וַיִּפְּלוּ עַל־פְּנֵיהֶם:

א וַיִּקְחוּ בְנֵי־אַהֲרֹן נָדָב וַאֲבִיהוּא אִישׁ מַחְתָּתוֹ וַיִּתְּנוּ
בָהֵן אֵשׁ וַיָּשִׂימוּ עָלֶיהָ קְטֹרֶת וַיַּקְרִיבוּ לִפְנֵי יְהֹוָה

* כב ידיו קרי.

Leviticus 9;10
22—24; I

22] Aaron lifted his hands toward the people and blessed them; and he stepped down after offering the sin offering, the burnt offering, and the offering of well-being. **23]** Moses and Aaron then went inside the Tent of Meeting. When they came out, they blessed the people; and the Presence of the LORD appeared to all the people. **24]** Fire came forth from before the LORD and consumed the burnt offering and the fat parts on the altar. And all the people saw, and shouted, and fell on their faces.

1] Now Aaron's sons, Nadab and Abihu, each took his fire pan, put fire in it, and laid incense on it; and they offered before the LORD alien fire, which He had not

---

22] *He stepped down.* From the altar.

23] *Moses and Aaron then went inside the Tent of Meeting.* No reason for this is given by Scripture. *Sifra* offers two plausible explanations: Moses went in with Aaron to show him how to perform the incense offering. Or, they went in together to pray for the speedy manifestation of God's Presence.

24] *Fire came forth from before the Lord.* Either from the Presence, or (Rashbam) from the Holy of Holies.

The first alternative is supported by I Kings, chapter 18, verse 38, and II Chronicles, chapter 7, verse 3.

10:1] *Each took his fire pan.* They were not presenting the regular incense offering of the morning (Exod. 30:7) which would not have required two fire pans. Evidently they were attempting something original.

Alien fire. Not from the divine flame that had descended on the altar.

Which He had not enjoined upon them. The priestly ideal is one of conformity, not of innovation.

ב אֵשׁ זָרָה אֲשֶׁר לֹא צִוָּה אֹתָם: וַתֵּצֵא אֵשׁ מִלִּפְנֵי יְהוָה

ג וַתֹּאכַל אוֹתָם וַיָּמֻתוּ לִפְנֵי יְהוָה: וַיֹּאמֶר מֹשֶׁה אֶל־

אַהֲרֹן הוּא אֲשֶׁר־דִּבֶּר יְהוָה לֵאמֹר בִּקְרֹבַי אֶקָּדֵשׁ

ד וְעַל־פְּנֵי כָל־הָעָם אֶכָּבֵד וַיִּדֹּם אַהֲרֹן: וַיִּקְרָא מֹשֶׁה

אֶל־מִישָׁאֵל וְאֶל אֶלְצָפָן בְּנֵי עֻזִּיאֵל דֹּד אַהֲרֹן וַיֹּאמֶר

Leviticus 10

2–4

enjoined upon them.   2] And fire came forth from the Lord and consumed them;
thus they died at the instance of the Lord.   3] Then Moses said to Aaron, "This is
what the Lord meant when He said: / Through those near to Me I show Myself
holy, / And assert My authority before all the people." / And Aaron was silent.

4] Moses called Mishael and Elzaphan, sons of Uzziel the uncle of Aaron, and

2] *Fire came forth.* See commentary on 9:24. The
wording of chapter 16, verse 2, suggests that they
came too close to the Holy of Holies and the disaster
followed automatically—as might happen if one
touched a high tension electric wire without proper
precautions.

And consumed them. They were not literally reduced to ashes for their bodies were later removed in
their apparently undamaged tunics (10:5).

At the instance of the Lord. Others, "before [the
Lord]" (T.N.). The Hebrew *lifne Adonai* does generally have the latter meaning (e.g., in 1:3). But
commentators have recognized that sometimes it has
a different force. The present translation has rendered
it by such phrases as "by the grace of the Lord"
(Gen. 10:7) and "with the Lord's approval" (Gen.
27:7).

3] *This is what the Lord meant when He said.* When
and in what connection had the Lord said this?
Most likely we should understand that Moses recalls
an utterance, not previously recorded, which he had
heard but not understood till that time. Nachmanides
explains that the reference is not to a literal speech
but to God's intent in decreeing the severe punishment. But other commentators sought elsewhere in

the Torah for an utterance to this effect. Rashi,
following the Talmud [10], cites Exodus, chapter 29,
verse 43; Rashbam refers to Leviticus, chapter 21,
verses 10 through 12, and understands the present
verse also as a command rather than a declaration.

Through those near to Me I show Myself holy. I
manifest My holiness by the strict standards I impose
on those nearest to Me. Those who are called to
leadership, especially religious leadership, are singled
out not for privilege but for responsibility. Ibn Ezra
appropriately cites Amos's challenging words to the
people of Israel: "You alone have I singled out, of all
the families of the earth—that is why I will call you
to account for all your iniquities" (Amos 3:2).

And assert My authority. Or, "I will be glorified."
Cf. Exodus 14:4 (T.N.).

And Aaron was silent. He refrained from weeping
and from complaints against God. In the rabbinic
phrase, he "acknowledged the justice of the decree."

4] *Mishael and Elzaphan.* Their pedigree is given
in Exodus (6:18, 22). Being Levites, they were not
forbidden to defile themselves by contact with the
dead. Aaron, as High Priest, was explicitly forbidden
to do so, whereas ordinary priests were allowed to
defile themselves for near relatives (Lev. 21:2f. and

אֲלֵהֶם קִרְבוּ שְׂאוּ אֶת־אֲחֵיכֶם מֵאֵת פְּנֵי־הַקֹּדֶשׁ אֶל־
ה מִחוּץ לַמַּחֲנֶה: וַיִּקְרְבוּ וַיִּשָּׂאֻם בְּכֻתֳּנֹתָם אֶל־מִחוּץ
ו לַמַּחֲנֶה כַּאֲשֶׁר דִּבֶּר מֹשֶׁה: וַיֹּאמֶר מֹשֶׁה אֶל־אַהֲרֹן
וּלְאֶלְעָזָר וּלְאִיתָמָר בָּנָיו רָאשֵׁיכֶם אַל־תִּפְרָעוּ
וּבִגְדֵיכֶם לֹא־תִפְרֹמוּ וְלֹא תָמֻתוּ וְעַל כָּל־הָעֵדָה
יִקְצֹף וַאֲחֵיכֶם כָּל־בֵּית יִשְׂרָאֵל יִבְכּוּ אֶת־הַשְּׂרֵפָה
ז אֲשֶׁר שָׂרַף יְהוָה: וּמִפֶּתַח אֹהֶל מוֹעֵד לֹא תֵצְאוּ פֶּן־
תָּמֻתוּ כִּי־שֶׁמֶן מִשְׁחַת יְהוָה עֲלֵיכֶם וַיַּעֲשׂוּ כִּדְבַר
מֹשֶׁה:
פ

Leviticus 10 ט וַיְדַבֵּר יְהוָה אֶל־אַהֲרֹן לֵאמֹר: יַיִן וְשֵׁכָר אַל־תֵּשְׁתְּ
5–9 אַתָּה וּבָנֶיךָ אִתָּךְ בְּבֹאֲכֶם אֶל־אֹהֶל מוֹעֵד וְלֹא

said to them, "Come forward and carry your kinsmen away from the front of the sanctuary to a place outside the camp." 5] They came forward and carried them out of the camp by their tunics, as Moses had ordered. 6] And Moses said to Aaron and to his sons, Eleazar and Ithamar, "Do not bare your heads and do not rend your clothes, lest you die and anger strike the whole community. But your kinsmen, all the house of Israel, shall bewail the burning that the LORD has wrought. 7] You must not go outside the entrance of the Tent of Meeting, lest you die, for the LORD's anointing oil is upon you." And they did as Moses had bidden.

8] And the LORD spoke to Aaron, saying: 9] Drink no wine or other intoxicant, you or your sons with you, when you enter the Tent of Meeting, that you may not

10f.). But Eleazar and Ithamar were subject to a more stringent rule because they had received the special privilege of anointment (Rashbam; similarly, Nachmanides).

6] *Do not bare your heads.* . . . Or, "dishevel your hair" (T.N.). Do not observe the customary forms of mourning [11].

9] *Other intoxicant.* Hebrew *shechar*, related to *shikor,* "intoxicated." The word is either a synonym for "wine" or else refers to beer which was prepared by some ancient peoples (notably the Egyptians and Babylonians) from fermented grain. It was not, like modern beer, flavored with hops. Distilled liquors were not known in antiquity.

י תָּמֵתוּ חֻקַּת עוֹלָם לְדֹרֹתֵיכֶם: וּלֲהַבְדִּיל בֵּין הַקֹּדֶשׁ

יא וּבֵין הַחֹל וּבֵין הַטָּמֵא וּבֵין הַטָּהוֹר: וּלְהוֹרֹת אֶת־

בְּנֵי יִשְׂרָאֵל אֵת כָּל־הַחֻקִּים אֲשֶׁר דִּבֶּר יְהֹוָה אֲלֵיהֶם

בְּיַד־מֹשֶׁה: פ

יב וַיְדַבֵּר מֹשֶׁה אֶל־אַהֲרֹן וְאֶל אֶלְעָזָר וְאֶל־אִיתָמָר

בָּנָיו הַנּוֹתָרִים קְחוּ אֶת־הַמִּנְחָה הַנּוֹתֶרֶת מֵאִשֵּׁי יְהֹוָה

וְאִכְלוּהָ מַצּוֹת אֵצֶל הַמִּזְבֵּחַ כִּי קֹדֶשׁ קָדָשִׁים הִוא:

יג וַאֲכַלְתֶּם אֹתָהּ בְּמָקוֹם קָדוֹשׁ כִּי חָקְךָ וְחָק־בָּנֶיךָ הוּא

מֵאִשֵּׁי יְהֹוָה כִּי־כֵן צֻוֵּיתִי: וְאֵת חֲזֵה הַתְּנוּפָה וְאֵת

יד שׁוֹק הַתְּרוּמָה תֹּאכְלוּ בְּמָקוֹם טָהוֹר אַתָּה וּבָנֶיךָ

וּבְנֹתֶיךָ אִתָּךְ כִּי־חָקְךָ וְחָק־בָּנֶיךָ נִתְּנוּ מִזִּבְחֵי שַׁלְמֵי

טו בְּנֵי יִשְׂרָאֵל: שׁוֹק הַתְּרוּמָה וַחֲזֵה הַתְּנוּפָה עַל אִשֵּׁי

Leviticus 10

10–15

die—it is a law for all time throughout the ages. **10]** For you must distinguish between the sacred and the profane, and between the unclean and the clean; **11]** and you must teach the Israelites all the laws which the LORD has imparted to them through Moses.

12] And Moses spoke to Aaron and to his remaining sons, Eleazar and Ithamar: Take the meal offering that is left over from the LORD's offerings by fire and eat it unleavened beside the altar, for it is most holy. **13]** You shall eat it in the sacred precinct, inasmuch as it is your due and that of your children, from the LORD's offerings by fire; for so I have been commanded. **14]** But the breast of wave offering and the thigh of heave offering you, and your sons and daughters with you, may eat in any clean place, for they have been assigned as a due to you and your children from the Israelites' sacrifices of well-being. **15]** Together with the fat of fire-offering,

---

10–11] The priests were not only to perform rites in the sanctuary. They were also to instruct the people in their religious duties—and for this too they had to have clear heads.

הַחֲלָבִים יָבִיאוּ לְהָנִיף תְּנוּפָה לִפְנֵי יְהוָה וְהָיָה לְךָ

טז וּלְבָנֶיךָ אִתְּךָ לְחָק־עוֹלָם כַּאֲשֶׁר צִוָּה יְהוָה: וְאֵת

שְׂעִיר הַחַטָּאת דָּרֹשׁ דָּרַשׁ מֹשֶׁה וְהִנֵּה שֹׂרָף וַיִּקְצֹף

עַל־אֶלְעָזָר וְעַל־אִיתָמָר בְּנֵי אַהֲרֹן הַנּוֹתָרִים לֵאמֹר:

יז מַדּוּעַ לֹא־אֲכַלְתֶּם אֶת־הַחַטָּאת בִּמְקוֹם הַקֹּדֶשׁ כִּי

קֹדֶשׁ קָדָשִׁים הִוא וְאֹתָהּ נָתַן לָכֶם לָשֵׂאת אֶת־עֲוֹן

יח הָעֵדָה לְכַפֵּר עֲלֵיהֶם לִפְנֵי יְהוָה: הֵן לֹא־הוּבָא אֶת־

דָּמָהּ אֶל־הַקֹּדֶשׁ פְּנִימָה אָכוֹל תֹּאכְלוּ אֹתָהּ בַּקֹּדֶשׁ

יט כַּאֲשֶׁר צִוֵּיתִי: וַיְדַבֵּר אַהֲרֹן אֶל־מֹשֶׁה הֵן הַיּוֹם

---

they must present the thigh of heave offering and the breast of wave offering, which are to be waved as a wave offering before the LORD, and which are to be your due and that of your children with you for all time—as the LORD has commanded.

16] Then Moses inquired about the goat of sin offering, and it had already been burned! He was angry with Eleazar and Ithamar, Aaron's remaining sons, and said, **17]** "Why did you not eat the sin offering in the sacred area? For it is most holy, and He has given it to you to remove the guilt of the community and to make expiation for them before the LORD? **18]** Since its blood was not brought inside the sanctuary, you should certainly have eaten it in the sanctuary, as I commanded." **19]** And Aaron spoke to Moses, "See, this day they brought their sin offering and their burnt

---

16–20] This passage presents a legal point in the form of a touching dialogue.

16] *The goat of sin offering.* See commentary on 9:15.

He was angry with Eleazar and Ithamar. The Rabbis rightly note that Moses' criticism was directed equally against Aaron who, in fact, replied to the charge (*Sifra*). Moses spoke only to the sons, either out of compassion for Aaron's grief or respect for his dignity as High Priest.

17] *He has given it to you to remove the guilt of the community.* This indicates that the community's sins were not fully expiated until the priests partook of the meat of the sin offering. See commentary on 6:19.

18] *Since its blood was not brought inside the sanctuary.* As is done in the case of the most solemn offerings; see 4:3–21; 16:11–17 (T.N.).

הַקְרִיבוּ אֶת־חַטָּאתָם וְאֶת־עֹלָתָם לִפְנֵי יְהֹוָה

וַתִּקְרֶאנָה אֹתִי כָּאֵלֶּה וְאָכַלְתִּי חַטָּאת הַיּוֹם הַיִּיטַב

בְּעֵינֵי יְהֹוָה: וַיִּשְׁמַע מֹשֶׁה וַיִּיטַב בְּעֵינָיו: ‎כ Leviticus 10:20

פ

offering before the LORD, and such things have befallen me! Had I eaten sin offering today, would the LORD have approved?" **20]** And when Moses heard this, he approved.

19] *And such things have befallen me!* Clearly I am not in favor with God at present. For me to eat sin offering, implying that my intercession had won forgiveness for the people, would be unsuitable (Luzzatto).

20] *And when Moses heard this, he approved.* He recognized the force of Aaron's argument. This chapter depicts Aaron with a dignity and gentleness he does not display in other narratives of the Torah. In the golden calf incident, his behavior is shabby (Exod. 32); on another occasion, he and Miriam make an unkind attack on Moses (Num. 12). Elsewhere he is the symbol of the high priesthood rather than a flesh and blood character. But here he impresses us by his mild but forthright reply to Moses—his younger brother.

GLEANINGS

Halachah

10:7] *You Must Not Go outside the Entrance of the Tent of Meeting, lest You Die*

From this verse, the general rule was inferred that any priest who leaves the sacred precinct while engaged in a sacrificial rite is guilty of a capital crime [12].

11] *You Must Teach the Israelites All the Laws*

Not only priests but all those who give instruction in matters of religious law are required to observe the prohibition against the use of alcohol. If a teacher is asked a question when he has been drinking, he must wait till the effects of the wine have had time to disappear before he renders an opinion [13].

16] *The Goat of Sin Offering*

The Rabbis held that these events occurred on the first day of the first month (p. 66) and therefore three goats were brought as sin offerings—the goat of the people (Lev. 9:15), the goat presented by Nahshon the chieftain of Judah (Num. 7:16), and the regular sin offering for the new moon (Num. 28:15). The first two *were* eaten, for Aaron considered them exceptional sacrifices of ordination, which should be eaten even by those in mourning. But he held that the regular rule that priests should not eat sacrificial meat when in mourning should apply to the new moon sacrifice, which was to be performed through the ages. Moses thereupon admitted he had overlooked this distinction and publicly proclaimed that Aaron was in the right [14].

Haggadah

8:15] *For Making Expiation upon It [the Altar]*

Some Rabbis understood the phrase to mean "to make expiation *for* it." For, they said, when offerings for the Tabernacle were being collected, some persons may have contributed under pressure, or while they were carried away by the general enthusiasm, without really wanting to make such a gift. It was necessary to make atonement for such a possible deficiency [15].

23] *On the Ridge of Aaron's Right Ear*

"In this figure, he indicated that the fully consecrated must be pure in words and actions and in his whole life; for words are judged by hearing, the hand is the symbol of action, and the foot of the pilgrimage of life" [16].

"The ear was touched with blood, that it may be consecrated to hear the word of God; the hand, to perform the duties of the priesthood; and the foot, to walk in the path of righteousness" [17].

9:7] *Come Forward*

Aaron was uncertain of himself, his conscience troubled over his part in the sin of the golden calf. When he looked at the altar, its horns reminded him of the calf, intensifying his embarrassment. Moses therefore bade him come forward: God would not have assigned him the priestly duties without first forgiving him. Moreover, the calf of sin offering (verse 2) was to atone for the sin of the calf.   SIFRA

8] *Take a Calf*

Moses said to Aaron: "Brother Aaron, even though the Everpresent has forgiven your sins, you still need to put something into the mouth of Satan. Send a gift ahead of you before entering the sanctuary, lest he accuse you when you enter the sanctuary" [18].

22] *Aaron Lifted His Hands . . . and Blessed Them*

For the first time he uttered the threefold benediction of Numbers, chapter 6, verses 22ff. [19].

23] *They Blessed the People*

Moses said, "May it be God's will to cause His Shechinah to rest upon the work of your hands! May the LORD, the God of your fathers, increase your numbers a thousandfold and bless you, as He promised you!" They responded, "May the favor of the Lord be upon us; / let all that we put our hands to prosper, / O prosper the work of our hands" (Ps. 90:17 which is ascribed in verse 1 to Moses).

SIFRA

10:1–3] The cryptic narrative of the death of the two young men fairly cried for amplification by later preachers. Perhaps the Rabbis felt that the punishment was unduly harsh for a ritual infraction committed by inexperienced priests; yet they were sure God never acts unjustly. So they sought to solve the problem in various ways.

Most often they expanded on the sinfulness of the young men. The prohibition of wine in verses 9ff. suggested that Nadab and Abihu had been drinking before they entered the sanctuary [20]. They were also guilty of arrogance and irreverence. From Exodus (24:9ff.), it was inferred that on Sinai Nadab and Abihu had gazed boldly at the Divine Presence—as if eating and drinking!—instead of turning their eyes humbly away, as Moses had done at the burning bush (Exod. 3:6). They had refused to marry and beget children because they deemed no woman good enough for men of their exalted birth. Yet, despite their pride of ancestry, they had no respect for Moses and Aaron. "When will those old fellows die," they said, "that we may take control of the community?" [21] Had they sought the guidance of Moses, they would have avoided disaster; but they were too haughty to ask for advice [22], or even to consult each other [23]. And this list does not exhaust all the crimes with which they were charged!

Some scholars took a different approach. They declared that, except for this one offense, Nadab and Abihu were righteous men. Four times Scripture mentions their death, and each time it specifies the sin of "strange fire" to indicate that they were guilty of nothing else. No taint of corruption attached to them [24]. (The Rabbis made similar comments about the one sin that barred Moses from the promised land [25].) Though the young men employed the wrong means to bring down the Divine Presence, their motives were noble, inspired by love and joy [26]. Their punishment, by its very severity, indicates the high spiritual level they had attained.

That is why God said to them, "I will give you more honor than you gave Me. You brought in impure fire, I will slay you with a pure flame." Two threads of fire then issued from the Holy of Holies; each divided into two which entered the nostrils of the offenders and extinguished their lives. Their clothing (and, according to some, their bodies) remained intact [27]. And God grieved over their death even more than Aaron did [28].

A third approach neither vilified nor exculpated the two but actually glorified them. Philo was the most extreme advocate of this view. Nadab and Abihu, he says, had drawn nigh to God and forsaken mortal life [29]. Therefore the Bible says "They died before the Lord" [30]. They were taken up by a rush of fire unquenchable, by an undying splendor [31].

The Rabbis do not go that far, but they also speak of Nadab and Abihu as righteous men [32]. And one old story introduces the notion—unparalleled in rabbinic literature [33]—that the death of a great man may serve to consecrate a shrine: "Through those near to Me I will be sanctified" (verse 3). Moses came to Aaron and said to him, "Brother Aaron, it was told to me at Sinai: 'I am going to sanctify this House, I will sanctify it through a great man.' I always supposed that the House would be sanctified either through you or through me. Now it appears that your sons were greater than we, since it was through them that the House was sanctified." And in this assurance Aaron found comfort [34].

9] *Drink No Wine or Other Intoxicant*

A pious man had a father whose drunken habits were a source of shame to him. One rainy day the son saw a man lying in the street in a drunken stupor, with water pouring over him and urchins taunting him. And he brought his father to see the repulsive sight, hoping it might have a wholesome effect. But the father merely bent down to ask the drunkard where he could buy such potent wine! [35].

20] *And When Moses Heard This, He Approved*
He sent out a herald to proclaim, "I was mistaken about the law, and my brother Aaron instructed me." (Eleazar and Ithamar also knew the correct ruling, but they remained silent so as not to embarrass Moses.) This was one of three occasions when Moses forgot the correct halachah as a result of losing his temper [36].

PART III

Permitted and Forbidden Foods

The Dietary Laws

Most peoples have some food taboos. Naturally ones does not eat products that promptly cause sickness or discomfort, or that are too tough to chew. But foods accepted in one culture as proper and wholesome may be viewed with loathing by another culture.

Sometimes a food is avoided because people have not discovered that it is edible or because they have not learned how to prepare it. Sometimes a food is mistakenly supposed to be harmful; for a long time the tomato was thought to be poisonous. In certain cases, the rejection of a certain food—whatever its psychological origin—is institutionalized. In the United States there is not only a prejudice against eating horse meat, there are also laws forbidding its sale for human consumption and requiring the proper labeling of dog food containing horse meat. Yet in some countries people eat horse without revulsion and without harmful effects.

In many cases, dietary restrictions have been based upon, or reinforced by, religious beliefs. The Jains and Buddhists avoid the taking of life, and therefore they reject all animal food; similar attitudes were held by some individuals and groups in ancient Greece. The Hindus regard the cow as sacred, and therefore they do not eat beef. But the elaborate system of dietary laws contained in the Torah and further extended by post-biblical teachers is probably unique; certainly nothing similar was to be found in the ancient Near East.

Moreover, the motivations mentioned above do not apply to the biblical laws, which do not regard any food as inherently sacred. An animal designated for sacrifice is thereby set apart and may be eaten only by specified persons under specified circumstances—as we have already seen. Otherwise, biblically prohibited foods fall into two classes: (1) those which are restricted temporarily, such as leavened bread on Passover and untithed produce and (2) foods designated as unclean and prohibited unconditionally except in the direst emergency, to save the life of a sick or starving person.

1. A Few Definitions

Currently, food permissible according to Jewish law is called *kasher* (kosher). The word means "fit," "proper." It appears once in the Bible (Esther 8:5), where it has nothing to do with food. It is found frequently in the Talmud, often with reference to food; in later

89

Jewish literature, it is used chiefly in that connection.

The opposite of *kasher* in current usage is *terefah* (sometimes pronounced *treif*). The word means literally "something torn," and in the Bible it refers to an animal killed by another beast (Exod. 22:30).

The Talmud redefined the word *terefah*: it is an animal or fowl of a permitted species which is suffering from a disease, defect, or injury that would cause its death within a year [1]. An animal of a permitted species killed by another beast is called in talmudic-rabbinic literature not *terefah*, but *nevelah*, literally "carcass," "carrion." The same term is applied to an animal that has died of natural causes or has been improperly slaughtered [2].

But today a perfectly healthy animal, bird, or fish of a nonkosher species might be referred to as *terefah*, though the Bible and traditional literature designate such creatures as *tamé*, "unclean."

This word *tamé* does not mean dirty; and the opposite, *tahor*, "pure," means much more than physically clean. A creature is *tamé* because the Torah forbids its consumption. Similarly, the word *sheketz*, "abomination" (Lev. 11:10ff.), does not mean that the birds or fish in question are "naturally repulsive"; they are to be regarded as repulsive because a divine commandment forbids them.

2. *The Scope of the Dietary Laws*

The permanently forbidden foods are all of animal origin. Most of the prohibitions are listed in this chapter and are repeated in Deuteronomy (14:3–20) with a few omissions and additions [3]. These two passages are almost identical, in language as well as substance. The Torah contains a number of repetitions, but none as extended as this one. Since the passage seems typical of P in content and in style, it is probable that a priestly editor inserted the passage into Deuteronomy [4].

Elsewhere in the Torah there are a few other dietary rules; we have already noted the prohibition of blood and certain portions of fat. All the biblical legislation on the subject was greatly expanded by the talmudic authorities who fully developed the laws of ritual slaughtering and the rules against mixing milk and meat. A brief summary of the dietary laws, as currently practiced by traditional Jews, is given in Appendix I, pp. 317–318.

3. *The Reason for the Dietary Laws*

The Torah plainly states (Lev. 11:44ff.) that the people of Israel is sanctified by avoiding the unclean foods. But it does not explain why those foods have a defiling effect.

The Talmud divides all the commandments into two classes: (1) "those which should have been given had they not been given," i.e., moral and social laws whose value is evident, and (2) "those about which Satan and the Gentiles can raise questions," because they have no rational explanation [5]. The prohibition of pork is included in the second category. Elsewhere we read, "One should not say, 'I can't stand pork!' but rather, 'I would like to eat it, but my Father in heaven has forbidden it, and I have no choice' " [6]. And again, "What difference does it make to God whether an animal is slaughtered by cutting its throat or striking it on the back of the neck? Clearly, the commandments were given to discipline us" [7]. To this day, Orthodox teachers adhere to this position: God has imposed this regimen on us for His own reasons, and we hallow our lives by obeying Him without question [8].

Nevertheless many efforts have been made to supply a reason for these enactments. The earliest attempt we possess at a moralizing

90

explanation is that of Philo of Alexandria. The dietary laws, he states, are intended to teach us to control our bodily appetites. Moses did not demand Spartan self-denial; but, to discourage excessive self-indulgence, he forbade pork, the most delicious of all meats. He further prohibited the eating of carnivorous beasts and birds, in order to teach us gentleness and kindness. Philo finds a symbolic meaning in the permission to eat of animals that chew the cud and have divided hoofs: man grows in wisdom only if he repeats and chews over what he has studied and if he learns to divide and distinguish various concepts [9].

More than a thousand years after Philo, Maimonides proposed a similar view. All the commandments aim at human perfection, he declared, and the dietary laws are intended to inculcate self-control [10]. But to this he added another consideration: the idea that these regulations are also health laws. Such a view had also been propounded a little earlier by the French Bible commentator, Rabbi Samuel ben Meir (Rashbam), citing the opinions of "famous physicians" [11]. Maimonides developed the subject quite fully, with the assurance of an experienced and successful physician. All the forbidden foods, he asserts, are unwholesome [12].

Maimonides did not know that tapeworm and trichina may be transmitted through pork, that rabbits carry tularemia, and that shellfish are prone to infection and spoiling. When these facts were established by modern scientists, many persons became all the more convinced that the Mosaic ordinances were hygienic in purpose. Some of the unwary, influenced by eighteenth-century notions about "priestcraft," assumed that Moses had given religious sanction to these sound health rules in order to ensure compliance with them—deceiving the people for their own good.

One can hardly doubt that some of the dietary laws had salutary *results* in terms of health. But we have no evidence that this was their *intent*. There is no hint of such a motive in the Bible or the Talmud. Not all the prohibited foods are injurious to health; and on the other hand there is no religious sanction against the consumption of any vegetable or mineral products, though many of them are noxious.

An analogous instance is provided by the law (Exod. 30:17ff.) requiring priests to wash their hands before approaching the altar. Some time before the Christian era, the Pharisees sought to give a priestly character to all of Jewish life; they regarded the family table as a kind of altar and required all persons to wash their hands before breaking bread. The intent of this ruling was purely religious, but it must also have had the—unplanned—effect of reducing the spread of communicable disease.

The *rabbinic* laws of slaughtering, however, seem to have been designed to make the death of the animal swift and merciful. The animal is rendered unfit for food if there is a nick in the slaughtering knife or if there is delay or bungling in the slaughtering procedure [13].

Modern scholars have tried to elucidate the dietary laws of the Bible through studies in comparative religion and folklore, but these efforts have not yielded many positive results. Theories that these practices were rooted in totemism seem to be unfounded. Probably no one explanation applies to all the dietary restrictions. Some of them may have had an antipagan character.

4. *The Dietary Laws in Jewish History*

Though the food laws are expounded at length only in the priestly writings (including Deut. 14), they were known to other biblical writers. The old version of the Flood story

(Gen. 7:1ff., from the "J" document) tells that Noah was commanded to bring into the ark seven pairs of each species of clean animal, but only one pair each of the unclean beasts [14]. The same source reports that Israelites do not eat the thigh muscle (Gen. 32:33; see further Judg. 13:4; Ezek. 4:14). Saul displayed great concern when he was informed that the people were eating meat "with the blood." (I Sam. 14:32ff.; Isa. 65:3 and 4 and 66:17 are concerned not so much with violation of the food laws as with an obscene idolatrous cult.)

Thus some at least of the dietary rules go far back in the biblical period, perhaps even to prebiblical times. People probably observed them as a matter of course. It was only in the Hellenistic age that these laws seem to have become a burning issue. At that time, the followers of Greek culture—both Gentiles and Jews—began to sneer at all distinctive Jewish observances, especially those that required control of the appetites. The attack on Judaism by Antiochus Epiphanes was marked, among other things, by orders for the Jews to bring sacrifices of swine (I Macc. 1:47). A famous story tells how the Syrians sought to force an aged man named Eleazar to set a public example of eating pork—or even pretending to do so—and how he refused and died as a martyr (II Macc. 6). It is at this time that the pig appears to have become an object of special abhorrence to Jews. In the Bible it does not seem to be more objectionable than other forbidden animals [15].

Something of the spirit of the martyrs of the Maccabean age remained with the people in succeeding centuries, especially after the commandments of the Torah were subjected to Christian attack.

Jesus of Nazareth is reported to have said, "It is not what enters a man's mouth that defiles him; what defiles a man is what comes out of his mouth" (Matt. 15:11; Mark 7:15). But, in referring to "what enters a man's mouth," he was speaking, not of the dietary laws of the Bible, but of the Pharisaic requirement to wash the hands before eating (p. 91). There is no reason to doubt that Jesus observed the biblical food restrictions, and there is no reason to think that he called for their abrogation [16].

But the new church soon had more gentile than Jewish adherents, and it rapidly adjusted to this situation. The apostle Peter was said to have been shown in a vision that the unclean animals were no longer forbidden (Acts 10:9ff.). At a historic gathering, it was decided that gentile converts to Christianity need refrain only from the meat of idolatrous sacrifices, from blood, and from animals that had been strangled (Acts 15:20). In later centuries, Christian critics of Judaism vehemently attacked the dietary laws, with the result that Jewish resistance stiffened. Many Christians resented the unwillingness of Jews to eat in Christian homes. The desire to break down such barriers was one of the considerations that led the founders of the Reform movement to rethink the question of dietary observance.

5. Some Modern Problems

Those who today continue to observe the dietary laws as a matter of conscience face a number of problems, some of which concern the entire Jewish community in its internal and external relations.

The internal problem stems from the fact that, though it is a religious duty for the Orthodox Jew to avoid nonkosher food, the purveying of kosher food is not a religious function, but a commercial enterprise. To prevent conflict of interest, Jewish communities in the past engaged one or more ritual slaughterers (*shochetim*) who were communal employees and who were responsible to the rabbi. They were required to examine the lungs of each animal they slaughtered and, if they found any evidence that the animal *might* not be kosher, to refer the matter to the rabbi for decision. The *shochet* did not sell meat; the meat dealer was a private entrepreneur. Even so, abuses occurred from time to time. Such difficulties have multiplied in contemporary America, where there is no unified, disciplined Jewish community—often no united Orthodox community. In New York State, it has been found necessary to establish a branch of the Department of Agriculture and Markets to police the kosher meat stores and to prosecute dealers who fraudulently sell nonkosher meat as kosher—an unfortunate obtrusion of the state into what are properly religious matters. There have also been charges of corruption and racketeering in the industry. And, while the extra supervision required should make kosher meat a trifle more expensive than comparable cuts of nonkosher meat, the difference in cost has often been so large as to discourage many persons from maintaining *kashrut* in their homes.

The external problem results from the effort in many countries to outlaw kosher slaughtering as cruel. Such efforts have often been motivated, not by compassion for animals, but by malice toward Jews. Jewish law, as we have seen, requires slaughtering to be done quickly and with a minimum of pain; and a United States federal statute recognizes *shechitah* as a humane method of slaughter.

But there is an unresolved problem, and those concerned about it are not necessarily to be dismissed as anti-Semites. The assembly line methods used in American abattoirs often involve shackling animals and hoisting them off the ground before the *shochet* comes to kill them. This procedure is questionable even from the purely ritual standpoint; it is certainly indefensible because of its cruelty. A more humane restraining device has been invented, and the American Society for the Prevention of Cruelty to Animals has expended considerable sums to make it available to meat packers. But, despite support of this effort by national representative Jewish bodies, the new device has not been widely adopted. In the name of human decency, and for the honor of the Jewish name, the American Jewish community should insist that the improved procedure be used everywhere [17].

6. Reform Judaism and the Dietary Laws

Today the observance of *kashrut* has been made easier in many ways. Vegetable shortenings, soap made with vegetable oil, frozen kosher poultry, and prepared dinners are generally available. Many kosher butchers regularly relieve the housewife of the task of washing, salting, and rinsing meat. Yet probably only a minority of today's Jews observe the dietary laws strictly at home; still fewer observe them away from home. Large groups no longer believe these laws were divinely ordained. In Communist countries official policy makes any kind of religious observance difficult if not impossible. But even in Israel, where most of the available meat is kosher slaughtered, indifference has led to widespread disregard of the dietary laws.

American Conservative Judaism upholds *kashrut*, if not as a divine ordinance, at least as a means of inculcating Jewish distinctiveness and strengthening Jewish unity and loyalty. Its national body, the United Synagogue of America, insists that member congregations observe the dietary laws in their synagogue buildings. But only a fraction of their families maintain strictly kosher homes; and, of these, many eat nonkosher food outside their homes.

The issue of dietary observance was raised in Reform Jewish circles in the 1840s, if not earlier, and was under discussion for some decades. In 1885, a group of distinguished Reform rabbis adopted the famous "Pittsburgh Platform"; it contained the statement: "We hold that all such Mosaic and rabbinical laws as regulate diet, priestly purity, and dress originated in ages and under the influence of ideas entirely foreign to our present mental and spiritual state. They fail to impress the modern Jew with a spirit of priestly holiness; their observance in our days is apt rather to obstruct than to further modern spiritual elevation." However, Isaac M. Wise, the chief organizer of the movement in America, publicly advocated the retention of these laws for hygienic reasons and urged that they not be made the subject of controversy and bitterness [18]. To this day a small minority of Reform Jews maintain kosher homes out of sentiment, or out of respect for Orthodox parents, or to express their solidarity with all Israel. Others avoid eating pork and shellfish, though they do not observe all the rules of *kashrut*.

The spokesmen of Reform Judaism rarely find it necessary either to attack or defend these observances. They do not regard such provisions as the literal word of God; they hold that they are no longer religiously meaningful and therefore need not be followed. But they have no quarrel with those who chose to observe the dietary laws.

Yet conscientious Reform Jews cannot disregard the subject altogether. They must help protect the right of all Jews to live by the dietary laws if they so choose—in the name both of Jewish loyalty and of religious freedom. (The national Reform Jewish bodies participate in such efforts.) They must insist that Jewish communal institutions provide kosher food for those who desire it. And they ought to know something about these laws and their meaning.

In a larger sense, we must rethink the whole question of eating, in view of our frequent statements that Judaism deals with every aspect of human life. Is it true that "a man is what he eats"? In what sense and to what degree? Some Jews of widely varied religious backgrounds have become vegetarians on principle. Perhaps it is time to examine the question: Is it right to kill any living thing for food?

Moreover, the problem of food supply has become urgent and critical everywhere. Millions are always hungry, while others eat too much for their own good. Even in the affluent United States, large numbers are malnourished while others oscillate between gourmet cookery and reducing diets.

Judaism has encouraged the enjoyment of simple pleasures. It is a *mitzvah* to have a good Sabbath dinner, just as it is a *mitzvah* to fast on Yom Kippur. But, on the other hand, the experience of self-control is at least as educational as the experience of the latest "taste thrill." The traditional dietary laws—despite Maimonides—did not automatically generate self-control: one could gorge oneself on kosher food. Yet, in practice, adherence to *kashrut* meant for many people, not merely self-discipline, but real sacrifice. This is not to argue that we should revert to the laws of Leviticus, chapter 11; it means only that there are many religious aspects to the question of what we eat and how much, and of what there is for others to eat.

א וַיְדַבֵּר יְהֹוָה אֶל־מֹשֶׁה וְאֶל־אַהֲרֹן לֵאמֹר אֲלֵהֶם:
ב דַּבְּרוּ אֶל־בְּנֵי יִשְׂרָאֵל לֵאמֹר זֹאת הַחַיָּה אֲשֶׁר
ג תֹּאכְלוּ מִכָּל־הַבְּהֵמָה אֲשֶׁר עַל־הָאָרֶץ: כֹּל
מַפְרֶסֶת פַּרְסָה וְשֹׁסַעַת שֶׁסַע פְּרָסֹת מַעֲלַת גֵּרָה
ד בַּבְּהֵמָה אֹתָהּ תֹּאכֵלוּ: אַךְ אֶת־זֶה לֹא תֹאכְלוּ
מִמַּעֲלֵי הַגֵּרָה וּמִמַּפְרִסֵי הַפַּרְסָה אֶת־הַגָּמָל כִּי־
מַעֲלֵה גֵרָה הוּא וּפַרְסָה אֵינֶנּוּ מַפְרִיס טָמֵא הוּא
ה לָכֶם: וְאֶת־הַשָּׁפָן כִּי־מַעֲלֵה גֵרָה הוּא וּפַרְסָה לֹא
ו יַפְרִיס טָמֵא הוּא לָכֶם: וְאֶת־הָאַרְנֶבֶת כִּי־מַעֲלַת

Leviticus 11
1–6

1] And the LORD spoke to Moses and Aaron, saying to them: 2] Speak to the Israelite people thus:

These are the creatures that you may eat from among all the land animals: 3] any animal that has true hoofs, with clefts through the hoofs, and that chews the cud—such you may eat.   4] The following, however, of those that either chew the cud or have true hoofs, you shall not eat: the camel—although it chews the cud, it has no true hoofs: it is unclean for you;   5] the daman—although it chews the cud, it has no true hoofs: it is unclean for you;   6] the hare—although it chews

11:1] *To Moses and Aaron.* Aaron was included in this revelation, since the priests had the duty of teaching the people to distinguish clean from unclean (10:10).

2] Permissible quadrupeds: only such may be eaten as have divided hoofs and chew the cud. That both features must be present is emphasized by the enumeration of animals that have (or appear to have) one of these characteristics, but not the other.

3] ... *That has true hoofs.* So Ibn Ezra and others. Most interpreters take this phrase to mean "that has cloven hoofs," i.e., that two different expressions are used to emphasize the importance of the divided hoof.

Chews. Literally, "brings up" (T.N.).

4] ... *The camel.* A genuine ruminant that has divided hoofs, but they are joined at the bottom by a pad.

5] ... *The daman.* A small west Asian animal of the hyrax family whose other members are found only in southern Africa. It looks something like a small-eared rabbit, though in fact it is distantly related to the horse and elephant. Earlier translations, "cony" and "rock badger," are misleading; "cony" is an archaic word for rabbit, and the European badger is nothing like the hyrax. This shy animal has small undivided hoofs; it does not chew the cud, but its constant munching movements give the impression that it does. The same is true of the hare (verse 6). The biblical writers were not scientific biologists.

גֵּרָה הוּא וּפַרְסָה לֹא הִפְרִיסָה טְמֵאָה הוּא לָכֶם:
ז וְאֶת־הַחֲזִיר כִּי־מַפְרִיס פַּרְסָה הוּא וְשֹׁסַע שֶׁסַע
פַּרְסָה וְהוּא גֵּרָה לֹא־יִגָּר טָמֵא הוּא לָכֶם: מִבְּשָׂרָם
ח לֹא תֹאכֵלוּ וּבְנִבְלָתָם לֹא תִגָּעוּ טְמֵאִים הֵם לָכֶם:
ט אֶת־זֶה תֹּאכְלוּ מִכֹּל אֲשֶׁר בַּמָּיִם כֹּל אֲשֶׁר־לוֹ סְנַפִּיר
וְקַשְׂקֶשֶׂת בַּמַּיִם בַּיַּמִּים וּבַנְּחָלִים אֹתָם תֹּאכֵלוּ:
י וְכֹל אֲשֶׁר אֵין־לוֹ סְנַפִּיר וְקַשְׂקֶשֶׂת בַּיַּמִּים וּבַנְּחָלִים
מִכֹּל שֶׁרֶץ הַמַּיִם וּמִכֹּל נֶפֶשׁ הַחַיָּה אֲשֶׁר בַּמָּיִם שֶׁקֶץ

יא הֵם לָכֶם: וְשֶׁקֶץ יִהְיוּ לָכֶם מִבְּשָׂרָם לֹא תֹאכֵלוּ
יב וְאֶת־נִבְלָתָם תְּשַׁקֵּצוּ: כֹּל אֲשֶׁר אֵין־לוֹ סְנַפִּיר

the cud, it has no true hoofs: it is unclean for you; 7] and the swine—although it has true hoofs, with the hoofs cleft through, it does not chew the cud: it is unclean for you. 8] You shall not eat of their flesh or touch their carcasses; they are unclean for you.

9] These you may eat of all that live in water: anything in water, whether in the seas or in the streams, that has fins and scales—these you may eat. 10] But anything in the seas or in the streams that has no fins and scales, among all the swarming things of the water and among all the other living creatures that are in the water—they are an abomination for you 11] and an abomination for you they shall remain: you shall not eat of their flesh and you shall abominate their carcasses. 12] Everything in water that has no fins and scales shall be an abomination for you.

8] . . . Or touch their carcasses. The wording seems to prohibit such contact absolutely. But, in view of all the law on the subject (p. 104), the sentence probably means no more than "You cannot touch their carcasses without being ritually defiled" (so Rashbam and others).

9–12] Of water creatures: Only those with fins and scales are permitted. Presumably prohibited are shellfish, amphibians, water mammals, and many fish that do not have clearly defined scales, including sharks, eels, and catfish.

יג וְקַשְׁקֶשֶׂת בַּמַּיִם שֶׁקֶץ הוּא לָכֶם: וְאֶת־אֵלֶּה תְּשַׁקְּצוּ
מִן־הָעוֹף לֹא יֵאָכְלוּ שֶׁקֶץ הֵם אֶת־הַנֶּשֶׁר וְאֶת־הַפֶּרֶס
יד וְאֵת הָעָזְנִיָּה: וְאֶת־הַדָּאָה וְאֶת־הָאַיָּה לְמִינָהּ: אֵת
טו כָּל־עֹרֵב לְמִינוֹ: וְאֵת בַּת הַיַּעֲנָה וְאֶת־הַתַּחְמָס וְאֶת־
טז הַשָּׁחַף וְאֶת־הַנֵּץ לְמִינֵהוּ: וְאֶת־הַכּוֹס וְאֶת־הַשָּׁלָךְ
יז וְאֶת־הַיַּנְשׁוּף: וְאֶת־הַתִּנְשֶׁמֶת וְאֶת־הַקָּאָת וְאֶת־הָרָחָם:
יט וְאֵת הַחֲסִידָה הָאֲנָפָה לְמִינָהּ וְאֶת־הַדּוּכִיפַת וְאֶת־
כ הָעֲטַלֵּף: כֹּל שֶׁרֶץ הָעוֹף הַהֹלֵךְ עַל־אַרְבַּע שֶׁקֶץ

Leviticus 11

13–20

13] The following you shall abominate among the birds—they shall not be eaten, they are an abomination: the eagle, the vulture, and the black vulture;   **14]** the kite, falcons of every variety;   **15]** all varieties of raven;   **16]** the ostrich, the nighthawk, the sea gull; hawks of every variety;   **17]** the little owl, the cormorant, and the great owl;   **18]** the white owl, the pelican, and the bustard;   **19]** the stork; herons of every variety; the hoopoe, and the bat.

20] All winged swarming things, that walk on fours, shall be an abomination

13–19] The Torah does not state the characteristics of clean birds but simply gives a list of those that are forbidden. The Rabbis concluded that all those on the list are predators, and they found several anatomical traits that they have in common. "A number of these cannot be identified with certainty" (T.N.). The bat (verse 19) is, of course, a mammal, even though it flies.

Presumably all birds not included in the list are permitted, but traditional practice is much more restrictive. See Appendix I, pp. 317–318.

20–23] . . . *Winged swarming things.* The Hebrew *sheretz,* "creeping/swarming thing," is a term applied broadly to all kinds of vermin: rodents, reptiles, worms, insects, etc. (cf. verses 29 and 30). The present

verses speak of winged *sheretz,* i.e., winged insects, of which four species are singled out as permitted for eating. Every other variety of *sheretz,* with or without wings, is forbidden. Locusts and grasshoppers, cooked in various ways, are still eaten by some peoples in the Near East. Medieval halachists, uncertain about the identity of the kosher species, forbade the eating of any insects. But Kalisch, writing in the 1870s, reported that the Yemenite Jews still ate locusts [19].

20] . . . *That walk on fours.* The clause is perplexing, for all winged insects have *six* legs. Hoffmann, following Jewish tradition, understands verse 21 to mean "all that have [two additional] legs to leap with, higher than their [other] legs." This fits the

כא הוּא לָכֶם: אַךְ אֶת־זֶה תֹּאכְלוּ מִכֹּל שֶׁרֶץ הָעוֹף
הַהֹלֵךְ עַל־אַרְבַּע אֲשֶׁר־לֹא* כְרָעַיִם מִמַּעַל לְרַגְלָיו
כב לְנַתֵּר בָּהֵן עַל־הָאָרֶץ: אֶת־אֵלֶּה מֵהֶם תֹּאכֵלוּ אֶת־
הָאַרְבֶּה לְמִינוֹ וְאֶת־הַסָּלְעָם לְמִינֵהוּ וְאֶת־הַחַרְגֹּל
כג לְמִינֵהוּ וְאֶת־הֶחָגָב לְמִינֵהוּ: וְכֹל שֶׁרֶץ הָעוֹף אֲשֶׁר־
לוֹ אַרְבַּע רַגְלָיִם שֶׁקֶץ הוּא לָכֶם:

* כא לוֹ קרי.

for you.   21] But these you may eat among all the winged swarming things that walk on fours: all that have, above their feet, jointed legs to leap with on the ground—   22] of these you may eat the following: locusts of every variety; all varieties of bald locust; crickets of every variety; and all varieties of grasshopper. 23] But all other winged swarming things that have four legs shall be an abomination for you.

fact that grasshoppers and locusts have hind legs much longer than the other four, but it hardly fits the Hebrew words of the verse [20].

22] *The following.* A number of these cannot be identified with certainty (T.N.).

GLEANING

Haggadah

11:7] ... *The Swine—Although It Has True Hoofs, with the Hoofs Cleft Through, It Does Not Chew the Cud*

When the pig is resting, he stretches out his legs in front of him, displaying his cleft hoofs. "How kosher I am!" he seems to say, making no mention of the fact that he does not chew the cud. He symbolizes the hypocrite who parades his virtues and conceals his faults [21].

PART IV

Defilement and Purification

Defilement from Animal Carcasses

The first half of chapter 11 designates the quadrupeds, birds, fish, and insects that may and may not be eaten. The second part of the chapter deals with the effects of touching or carrying the carcasses of the forbidden creatures. Thus we come to the subject of ritual defilement and its correction, a topic that will be continued through the next four chapters. We must now examine more fully the concepts of *tamé* and *tahor*, "unclean" and "clean." We have already seen that they are not equivalent to "physically dirty" and "spic and span."

We are dealing with notions that are not peculiar to the Bible. They were common to all ancient peoples, who gave them expression in practices somewhat like those we are to examine now. Some of these ideas still survive in certain cultures, and vestiges of them remain even in our supposedly scientific civilization.

From time beyond memory, it was believed that certain places, substances, and persons carried a sort of "high charge," like an electric wire, and must be approached cautiously, if at all. The "charge" was something supernatural. Often a distinction was made between gods, who were sometimes beneficent, and demons, who were invariably hostile and destructive. The distinction was not always sharp, but it led to a distinction of ritual practice. There was a difference between places and objects that had to be avoided, because they were sacred to a deity, and those that were to be shunned as demonic. The former area is designated in Hebrew by *kadosh*, "holy," the latter by *tamé*, "unclean, impure."

In Leviticus the demonic background of the *tamé* has been all but obliterated; there are only a few allusions to primitive concepts. Generally, the laws of purity and impurity are set forth simply as God's commandments, which must be obeyed because God has ordained them. Such obedience makes Israel a holy people.

These physical concepts of the holy, the impure, and the pure are not the only ones found in Scripture. This very book of Leviticus presents a sublime concept of spiritual holiness, expressed in the noblest standards of ethical living. This advanced understanding of holiness, found also in the Prophets, will be discussed in the introduction to chapter 19. Similarly, many biblical passages assert that defilement is caused by bloodshed, idolatry, sexual immorality, and other forms of unethical behavior (see, e.g., Lev. 18:24 f.;

Jer. 2:7 f.; Ezek. 36:17 f.; Hos. 5:1–5). The contrasting word *tahor*, "pure," is also used in nonritual connections. Unalloyed gold is *tahor* (Exod. 25:31); and the Psalmist prays for a clean heart (Ps. 51:12)—that is, a spirit uncontaminated by sin or guilt.

But the present chapters treat the ritual aspects of clean and unclean. And this complex of ideas includes the notion of contagion. We saw (at 6:11) that ritual "holiness" may be transmitted by contact. The same thing is true of defilement. Both the *tamé* and the *kadosh* emit a sort of energy. But ritual purity is a neutral state and is not transmissible. A bandage is no longer sterile if it falls on the floor, yet it does not transmit its former sterility to the spot on which it falls. As with modern asepsis, so with ancient ritual, positive measures are needed to overcome defilement.

But the analogy between ancient and modern notions of contagion is far from exact. As we now understand it, infection is caused by a microorganism which, if transmitted to a new host, can grow with undiminished vigor. Ritual impurity, however, was felt to be a kind of energy which tended to grow weaker as it passed from the source to other persons or objects. In the rabbinic systematization of these laws, the source (Hebrew *av*, "father") of impurity defiles the first contact, which in turn can defile the second contact; the impurity is not transmitted farther [1].

There is indeed one form of ritual defilement of highest intensity: defilement by a human corpse. This uncleanness is transmitted for an additional stage; and the corpse is therefore called by the Rabbis "the father of fathers of impurity." This subject is mentioned only briefly in Leviticus, chapter 21, and receives full treatment in Numbers, chapter 19. The sources of impurity we shall have to deal with are: the carcasses of some of the forbidden animals (chapter 11); a

woman after childbirth (chapter 12); certain disfiguring skin diseases, as well as strange discolorations on fabrics and on the walls of houses (chapters 13 and 14); a menstruating woman, and all discharges from the human genitals, normal and abnormal (chapter 15).

Such types of defilement are clearly quite different from that discussed in the first part of chapter 11. Partaking of forbidden food is a serious violation of the law—in rabbinic terminology, "a defilement of the sacred." (So is intercourse with a menstruating woman. See 15:24, 18:19, 20:18.) But the cases enumerated in the preceding paragraph are for the most part not avoidable. Ritual impurity comes about through accident, through normal physical processes, through illness, and through actions that are in themselves proper and even commendable. One cannot remove a dead mouse from his dwelling, or tend people suffering from certain illnesses, or bury the dead, without defiling himself. The Rabbis classify such types of impurity as "defilement of the body." In general, it is not sinful to become *tamé* through them, or even to remain unpurified. (Indeed, the performance of certain ritual commands entailed defilement: Lev. 16:26 and 28; Num. 19:7, 8, and 10.) Sin occurred only when the *tamé* was brought into contact with the sacred, the *kadosh*. To enter the sacred area of the Tabernacle/Temple, or to partake of consecrated food, while in a state of impurity—that was sacrilege [2]. The priests were expected to take more stringent measures to prevent their defilement, but even for them there were certain dispensations (Lev. 21).

The laws in these chapters are detailed and technical. They were elaborated and systematized by postbiblical teachers. Not only priests, but also the lay scholars known as the Pharisees occupied themselves with these statutes. Some of the Pharisees undertook to emulate the priesthood in observing the rules of purity. They formed *chavurot*, "societies," whose members were pledged to eat their nonsacred food in the same state of ritual purity required of the priests when they ate sacrificial meat or *terumah* ("heave offering," Num. 18:8ff.).

With the fall of the Temple, most of these laws ceased to be operative; but, in view of the lively expectation that the Temple would be rebuilt, scholars continued to study the laws, and the *chavurot* survived for many decades. The sixth section of the Mishnah, *Seder Tohorot*, containing the laws of defilement and purification, is very bulky. But after the second century C.E. it does not seem to have been studied systematically. Only the treatise *Niddah*, dealing with menstrual defilement, was provided with a *Gemara*.

כד וּלְאֵ֖לֶּה תִּטַּמָּ֑אוּ כָּל־הַנֹּגֵ֥עַ בְּנִבְלָתָ֖ם יִטְמָ֥א עַד־הָעָֽרֶב:

כה וְכָל־הַנֹּשֵׂ֖א מִנִּבְלָתָ֑ם יְכַבֵּ֥ס בְּגָדָ֖יו וְטָמֵ֥א עַד־הָעָֽרֶב:

כו לְֽכָל־הַבְּהֵמָ֡ה אֲשֶׁ֣ר הִוא֩ מַפְרֶ֨סֶת פַּרְסָ֜ה וְשֶׁ֣סַע ׀ אֵינֶ֣נָּה שֹׁסַ֗עַת וְגֵרָה֙ אֵינֶ֣נָּה מַעֲלָ֔ה טְמֵאִ֥ים הֵ֖ם לָכֶ֑ם כָּל־הַנֹּגֵ֥עַ

כז בָּהֶ֖ם יִטְמָֽא: וְכֹ֣ל ׀ הוֹלֵ֣ךְ עַל־כַּפָּ֗יו בְּכָל־הַֽחַיָּה֙ הַהֹלֶ֣כֶת עַל־אַרְבַּ֔ע טְמֵאִ֥ים הֵ֖ם לָכֶ֑ם כָּל־הַנֹּגֵ֥עַ

כח בְּנִבְלָתָ֖ם יִטְמָ֥א עַד־הָעָֽרֶב: וְהַנֹּשֵׂא֙ אֶת־נִבְלָתָ֔ם יְכַבֵּ֥ס בְּגָדָ֖יו וְטָמֵ֥א עַד־הָעָ֑רֶב טְמֵאִ֥ים הֵ֖מָּה לָכֶֽם: ס

24] And the following shall make you unclean—whoever touches their carcasses shall be unclean until evening,   25] and whoever carries the carcasses of any of them shall wash his clothes and be unclean until evening—   26] every animal that has true hoofs but without clefts through the hoofs, or that does not chew the cud. They are unclean for you; whoever touches them shall be unclean.   27] Also all animals that walk on paws, among those that walk on fours, are unclean for you; whoever touches their carcasses shall be unclean until evening.   28] And anyone who carries their carcasses shall wash his clothes and remain unclean until evening. They are unclean for you.

11:24] *Shall make you unclean.* By contact.

Shall be unclean until evening. As the text stands, the defiled person need not purify himself actively; he must simply avoid contact with the holy until sunset, by which time the impurity will be dissipated. That is how some modern scholars understand the passage. But *Sifra* may well be correct in understanding (on the analogy of 11:32, 17:5, and 22:6f.) that the person requires a ritual bath but is not completely purified till sunset.

25] *Whoever carries the carcasses of any of them shall*

wash his clothes. Touching might mean grazing the carcass with a finger; but carrying would bring the defiling object into contact with his body and clothing, thus spreading the contagion. Here too the halachah may be correct in understanding: in addition to bathing, he must also wash his clothes; then at sundown he becomes *tahor.*

27] *That walk on paws [and have no hoofs at all].* The verse is added for the sake of completeness. Legally, the horse and bear are equally forbidden and their carcasses are equally defiling.

כט וְזֶה לָכֶם הַטָּמֵא בַּשֶּׁרֶץ הַשֹּׁרֵץ עַל־הָאָרֶץ הַחֹלֶד
וְהָעַכְבָּר וְהַצָּב לְמִינֵהוּ: וְהָאֲנָקָה וְהַכֹּחַ וְהַלְּטָאָה
לא וְהַחֹמֶט וְהַתִּנְשָׁמֶת: אֵלֶּה הַטְּמֵאִים לָכֶם בְּכָל־הַשָּׁרֶץ
לב כָּל־הַנֹּגֵעַ בָּהֶם בְּמֹתָם יִטְמָא עַד־הָעָרֶב: וְכֹל אֲשֶׁר־
יִפֹּל עָלָיו מֵהֶם בְּמֹתָם יִטְמָא מִכָּל־כְּלִי־עֵץ אוֹ בֶגֶד
אוֹ־עוֹר אוֹ שָׂק כָּל־כְּלִי אֲשֶׁר־יֵעָשֶׂה מְלָאכָה בָּהֶם
לג בַּמַּיִם יוּבָא וְטָמֵא עַד־הָעֶרֶב וְטָהֵר: וְכָל־כְּלִי־חֶרֶשׂ
אֲשֶׁר־יִפֹּל מֵהֶם אֶל־תּוֹכוֹ כֹּל אֲשֶׁר בְּתוֹכוֹ יִטְמָא
לד וְאֹתוֹ תִשְׁבֹּרוּ: מִכָּל־הָאֹכֶל אֲשֶׁר יֵאָכֵל אֲשֶׁר יָבוֹא

Leviticus 11
29–34

29] The following shall be unclean for you from among the things that swarm on the earth: the mole, the mouse, and great lizards of every variety;   **30]** the gecko, the land crocodile, the lizard, the sand lizard, and the chameleon.   **31]** Those are for you the unclean among all the swarming things; whoever touches them when they are dead shall be unclean until evening.   **32]** And anything on which one of them falls when dead shall be unclean: be it any article of wood, or a cloth, or a skin, or a sack—any such article that can be put to use shall be dipped in water, and it shall remain unclean until evening; then it shall be clean.   **33]** And if any of those falls into an earthen vessel, everything inside it shall be unclean and [the vessel] itself you shall break.   **34]** As to any food that might be eaten, it shall be-

29–38] Defilement by the bodies of certain "creeping things." For the meaning of *sheretz*, see commentary on 11:20–23.

29] *The following.* A number of these cannot be identified with certainty (T.N.).

31] *Shall be unclean.* See commentary on 11:24.

32–38] The uncleanness of the carcass can be transmitted to various objects which can, in turn, defile still other substances, such as food.

32] *A sack.* A piece of sackcloth, a rough material, worn as a sign of mourning.

Shall be dipped in water. The chief means of ceremonial purification (see Lev. 11:25, 36, 14:5f.; Num. 19:8, 14ff., and elsewhere).

33] *An earthen vessel . . . you shall break.* Cf. 6:21, where the pottery must be broken because it has been made *kadosh.*

עָלָיו מַיִם יִטְמָא וְכָל־מַשְׁקֶה אֲשֶׁר יִשָּׁתֶה בְּכָל־כְּלִי
לה יִטְמָא: וְכֹל אֲשֶׁר־יִפֹּל מִנִּבְלָתָם עָלָיו יִטְמָא תַּנּוּר
לו וְכִירַיִם יֻתָּץ טְמֵאִים הֵם וּטְמֵאִים יִהְיוּ לָכֶם: אַךְ
מַעְיָן וּבוֹר מִקְוֵה־מַיִם יִהְיֶה טָהוֹר וְנֹגֵעַ בְּנִבְלָתָם
לז יִטְמָא: וְכִי יִפֹּל מִנִּבְלָתָם עַל־כָּל־זֶרַע זֵרוּעַ אֲשֶׁר
לח יִזָּרֵעַ טָהוֹר הוּא: וְכִי יֻתַּן־מַיִם עַל־זֶרַע וְנָפַל

come unclean if it came in contact with water; as to any liquid that might be drunk, it shall become unclean if it was inside any vessel.   35] Everything on which the carcass of any of them falls shall be unclean: an oven or stove shall be smashed. They are unclean and unclean they shall remain for you.   36] However, a spring or cistern in which water is collected shall be clean, but whoever touches such a carcass in it shall be unclean.   37] If such a carcass falls upon seed grain that is to be sown, it is clean;   38] but if water is put on the seed and any part of a carcass falls upon it, it shall be unclean for you.

34] *In contact with water.* I.e., if the food then came in contact with the carcass of any animal named in verses 29–30 (T.N.). Dry food and seeds (verse 37) are resistant to contagion; but, if they are moistened, they at once become susceptible to it.

Any liquid that might be drunk. Whereas water in springs, wells, rivers, lakes, and seas is not susceptible to ritual defilement, and indeed neutralizes ritual defilement, "drawn water" in a vessel may be defiled by the vessel itself or by some other source of impurity.

Inside any vessel. I.e., a vessel that had become contaminated by such contact (T.N.).

Verses 34 through 38 form the basis of an entire Mishnah treatise called *Machshirin*, "Things that predispose [to impurity]."

35] *Everything.* This refers back to verse 32.

An oven. See commentary on 2:4.

Stove. Hebrew *kirayim* which occurs nowhere else in the Bible. Rabbinic sources [3] describe the *kirah* as an earthenware container inside which fire was made; it had two openings on top on which pots could be placed. Being made of pottery, like the oven, it could not be purified (verse 33). Ehrlich explains the verse to mean: Though a household, which might have many pots, would ordinarily have only one oven or stove, the latter must nevertheless be smashed if it is defiled.

36–38] See commentary on 11:34.

36] *But whoever touches such a carcass in it.* Do not argue: since the spring or cistern purifies one who is already unclean, it will protect him from defilement by the carcass in the water (*Sifra*).

לט מִנִּבְלָתָם עָלָיו טָמֵא הוּא לָכֶם: ס וְכִי־יָמוּת מִן־
הַבְּהֵמָה אֲשֶׁר־הִיא לָכֶם לְאָכְלָה הַנֹּגֵעַ בְּנִבְלָתָהּ

מ יִטְמָא עַד־הָעָרֶב: וְהָאֹכֵל מִנִּבְלָתָהּ יְכַבֵּס בְּגָדָיו
וְטָמֵא עַד־הָעָרֶב וְהַנֹּשֵׂא אֶת־נִבְלָתָהּ יְכַבֵּס בְּגָדָיו

מא וְטָמֵא עַד־הָעָרֶב: וְכָל־הַשֶּׁרֶץ הַשֹּׁרֵץ עַל־הָאָרֶץ

מב שֶׁקֶץ הוּא לֹא יֵאָכֵל: כֹּל הוֹלֵךְ עַל־גָּחוֹן וְכֹל הוֹלֵךְ
עַל־אַרְבַּע עַד כָּל־מַרְבֵּה רַגְלַיִם לְכָל־הַשֶּׁרֶץ הַשֹּׁרֵץ

מג עַל־הָאָרֶץ לֹא תֹאכְלוּם כִּי־שֶׁקֶץ הֵם: אַל־תְּשַׁקְּצוּ
אֶת־נַפְשֹׁתֵיכֶם בְּכָל־הַשֶּׁרֶץ הַשֹּׁרֵץ וְלֹא תִטַּמְּאוּ בָּהֶם

מד וְנִטְמֵתֶם בָּם: כִּי אֲנִי יְהֹוָה אֱלֹהֵיכֶם וְהִתְקַדִּשְׁתֶּם

Leviticus 11
39–44

* מב ו' רבתי והיא חצי התורה באותיות. * מג חסר א'.

39] If an animal that you may eat has died, anyone who touches its carcass shall be unclean until evening; **40]** anyone who eats of its carcass shall wash his clothes and remain unclean until evening; and anyone who carries its carcass shall wash his clothes and remain unclean until evening.

41] All the things that swarm upon the earth are an abomination; they shall not be eaten. **42]** You shall not eat, among all things that swarm upon the earth, anything that crawls on its belly, or anything that walks on fours, or anything that has many legs; for they are an abomination. **43]** You shall not draw abomination upon yourselves through anything that swarms; you shall not make yourselves unclean therewith and thus become unclean. **44]** For I the Lord am your God: you

---

39–40] Not only do the carcasses of forbidden animals defile; if a permitted animal dies, or is improperly slaughtered, its carcass is a source of impurity also.

39] *Shall be unclean until evening....* See commentary on 11:24 and 25.

41–47] Though the eating of "creeping things" was forbidden by implication in the first half of the chapter, this prohibition is now spelled out.

42] *Belly.* Hebrew *gachon.* In Torah manuscripts, the letter *vav* in this word is written extra large, because—it is said—it is the middle letter of the entire Torah. This detail indicates the meticulous care that the scribes gave to the text.

43] *Draw abomination upon yourselves.* Make yourselves disgusting by such defilement.

And thus become unclean. The repetition is for emphasis. But the spelling of the Hebrew word is

וִהְיִיתֶם קְדֹשִׁים כִּי קָדוֹשׁ אָנִי וְלֹא תְטַמְּאוּ אֶת־
נַפְשֹׁתֵיכֶם בְּכָל־הַשֶּׁרֶץ הָרֹמֵשׂ עַל־הָאָרֶץ: כִּי אֲנִי
יְהֹוָה הַמַּעֲלֶה אֶתְכֶם מֵאֶרֶץ מִצְרַיִם לִהְיֹת לָכֶם
לֵאלֹהִים וִהְיִיתֶם קְדֹשִׁים כִּי קָדוֹשׁ אָנִי: זֹאת תּוֹרַת
הַבְּהֵמָה וְהָעוֹף וְכֹל נֶפֶשׁ הַחַיָּה הָרֹמֶשֶׂת בַּמָּיִם
וּלְכָל־נֶפֶשׁ הַשֹּׁרֶצֶת עַל־הָאָרֶץ: לְהַבְדִּיל בֵּין הַטָּמֵא
וּבֵין הַטָּהֹר וּבֵין הַחַיָּה הַנֶּאֱכֶלֶת וּבֵין הַחַיָּה אֲשֶׁר
לֹא תֵאָכֵל:

Leviticus 11
45–47

Haftarah Shemini, p. 365

shall sanctify yourselves and be holy, for I am holy. You shall not make yourselves unclean through any swarming thing that moves upon the earth.   45] For I the LORD am He who brought you up from the land of Egypt to be your God: you shall be holy, for I am holy.

46] These are the instructions concerning animals, birds, all living creatures that move in water, and all creatures that swarm on earth,   47] for distinguishing between the unclean and the clean, between the living things that may be eaten and the living things that may not be eaten.

unusual; Ibn Ezra and some moderns (citing a similar form in Job 18:13) render it "be made stupid" (see Gleanings).

44] *Sanctify yourselves and be holy.* The chapter concludes by appealing to the people to raise themselves to a higher level by observing the laws just expounded. In similar terms, the Torah (Lev. 19:2)

calls on them to sanctify themselves by ethical conduct.

45] Here, as often, the authority of the laws is reinforced by reference to the great historic memory of redemption from bondage.

46–47] These verses form a concluding summary, typical of priestly writing. Cf. 7:37ff.

GLEANINGS

Halachah

11:31] *Those Are for You the Unclean*

From the word "those," *Sifra* infers that all other species of *sheretz*, though forbidden as food (verse 41), are not a source of defilement when dead.

34] *If It Came in Contact with Water*

The following liquids make food and seeds susceptible to uncleanness: dew, water, wine, oil, blood, milk, and honey [4].

Haggadah

11:43] *And Thus Become Unclean*

See commentary. The eating of these abominable foods causes a deterioration of the soul so that it descends from a human to a beastly level.

LUZZATTO

44] *Sanctify Yourselves and Be Holy*

With reference to both ritual and ethics, the Talmud declares: If a man defiles himself a little here below, he will be defiled still more on high, i.e., providence will give him more occasions for wrongdoing. And also: If he sanctifies himself a little here below, he will be sanctified still more on high [5].

In different terms: If one wants to be unclean, he is given the opportunity; if he wants to be clean, he receives divine support [6].

Sanctify yourself through the practice of the commandments and thus you will become holy. Such observance will help you to gain self-control so that your intelligence can govern your appetites. For our intelligence is doubly handicapped in this struggle: We have the appetites from birth, while intelligence develops slowly; and, our environment encourages us to yield to our urges, whereas intelligence is a lonely stranger in the world.   BACHYA

Defilement through Childbirth

Though we now know more about the reproductive processes than any earlier generation, the birth of a baby still appears to us as something awesome, even miraculous. To prescientific man, it was an uncanny happening—especially, perhaps, since he was not well equipped to deal with the dangers that often threatened mother and child. In many cultures, childbirth was associated with the demonic, and various taboos were imposed on women in labor and after their delivery. This widespread feeling is doubtless the background of the regulations in this chapter, which declare the new mother to be ritually unclean and require sacrifices of purification.

The procedures described in this chapter lapsed with the destruction of the Second Temple. They became, however, the basis of a Christian custom, "the churching of women," still practiced in the Roman and Anglican churches. It is not mandatory; but it is considered proper for a priest to perform it on request. In some parts of Britain, there are still persons who will not admit a woman who has had a baby to their homes until she has been churched [1].

The Authorized Daily Prayer Book of the British United Synagogue (Orthodox) contains a brief service of thanksgiving for a woman after childbirth. Abrahams [2] adduces precedents for this ritual going back to fifteenth-century Germany. In American Reform practice, new parents attend a Sabbath service at which their child is publicly named. These customs have nothing to do with the ritual purification of the mother.

תָזְרִיעַ
וַיִּקְרָא יב
א–ה

Tazria

Leviticus 12

1–5

א וַיְדַבֵּ֥ר יְהֹוָ֖ה אֶל־מֹשֶׁ֥ה לֵּאמֹֽר: דַּבֵּ֞ר אֶל־בְּנֵ֤י יִשְׂרָאֵל֙
לֵאמֹ֔ר אִשָּׁה֙ כִּ֣י תַזְרִ֔יעַ וְיָלְדָ֖ה זָכָ֑ר וְטָֽמְאָה֙ שִׁבְעַ֣ת
ג יָמִ֔ים כִּימֵ֛י נִדַּ֥ת דְּוֺתָ֖הּ תִּטְמָֽא: וּבַיּ֖וֹם הַשְּׁמִינִ֑י יִמּ֖וֹל
ד בְּשַׂ֥ר עׇרְלָתֽוֹ: וּשְׁלֹשִׁ֥ים יוֹם֙ וּשְׁלֹ֣שֶׁת יָמִ֔ים תֵּשֵׁ֖ב בִּדְמֵ֣י
טׇהֳרָ֑ה בְּכׇל־קֹ֣דֶשׁ לֹֽא־תִגָּ֗ע וְאֶל־הַמִּקְדָּשׁ֙ לֹ֣א תָבֹ֔א
ה עַד־מְלֹ֖את יְמֵ֥י טׇהֳרָֽהּ: וְאִם־נְקֵבָ֣ה תֵלֵ֔ד וְטָמְאָ֥ה
שְׁבֻעַ֖יִם כְּנִדָּתָ֑הּ וְשִׁשִּׁ֥ים יוֹם֙ וְשֵׁ֣שֶׁת יָמִ֔ים תֵּשֵׁ֖ב עַל־דְּמֵ֥י

1] The LORD spoke to Moses, saying: 2] Speak to the Israelite people thus: When a woman at childbirth bears a male, she shall be unclean seven days; she shall be unclean as at the time of her menstrual infirmity. 3] —On the eighth day the flesh of his foreskin shall be circumcised.— 4] She shall remain in a state of blood purification for thirty-three days: she shall not touch any consecrated thing, nor enter the sanctuary until her period of purification is completed. 5] If she bears a female, she shall be unclean two weeks as during her menstruation, and she shall remain in a state of blood purification for sixty-six days.

12:2] *When a woman at childbirth bears.* Hebrew *tazria‘*, literally, "brings forth seed" (T.N.).

She shall be unclean . . . as at the time of her menstrual infirmity. The same rules apply as during menstruation (see commentary on 15:19–23).

3] *Shall be circumcised.* The remark here is incidental. (Cf. Gen. 17:12.)

4] *In a state of blood purification.* Hebrew unclear (T.N.). Postpartum discharges do not usually continue more than a week. But their cessation does not terminate the woman's defilement, even after she has taken the ritual bath implicitly required in verse 2 (cf. commentary on 15:19); she is still forbidden to enter the sanctuary or touch sacred food.

5] If the baby is a girl, both states of the mother's impurity last twice as long. No reason is given for this rule. One guesses that, while any childbirth was regarded as uncanny and defiling, the birth of a female, who herself would one day menstruate and bear children, was considered doubly defiling. Christian commentators of former generations saw in this rule an allusion to Eve's special guilt for the "fall of man" [3].

י טָהֳרָה׃ וּבִמְלֹאת יְמֵי טָהֳרָהּ לְבֵן אוֹ לְבַת תָּבִיא
כֶּבֶשׂ בֶּן־שְׁנָתוֹ לְעֹלָה וּבֶן־יוֹנָה אוֹ־תֹר לְחַטָּאת אֶל־
פֶּתַח אֹהֶל־מוֹעֵד אֶל־הַכֹּהֵן׃ וְהִקְרִיבוֹ לִפְנֵי יְהֹוָה
וְכִפֶּר עָלֶיהָ וְטָהֲרָה מִמְּקֹר דָּמֶיהָ זֹאת תּוֹרַת הַיֹּלֶדֶת
ח לַזָּכָר אוֹ לַנְּקֵבָה׃ וְאִם־לֹא תִמְצָא יָדָהּ דֵּי שֶׂה
וְלָקְחָה שְׁתֵּי־תֹרִים אוֹ שְׁנֵי בְּנֵי יוֹנָה אֶחָד לְעֹלָה
וְאֶחָד לְחַטָּאת וְכִפֶּר עָלֶיהָ הַכֹּהֵן וְטָהֵרָה׃ פ

Leviticus 12
6–8

6] On the completion of her period of purification, for either son or daughter, she shall bring to the priest, at the entrance of the Tent of Meeting, a lamb in its first year for a burnt offering, and a pigeon or a turtledove for a sin offering. 7] He shall offer it before the LORD and make expiation on her behalf; she shall then be clean from her flow of blood. Such are the rituals concerning her who bears a child, male or female. 8] If, however, her means do not suffice for a sheep, she shall take two turtledoves or two pigeons, one for a burnt offering and the other for a sin offering. The priest shall make expiation on her behalf, and she shall be clean.

6] *At the entrance of the Tent of Meeting.* She cannot go inside until the purification offerings have been made.

6, 7] *Sin offering . . . make expiation.* Obviously, having a baby is not a sin; it is in fact the fulfillment of a divine command (Gen. 1:18). The reference here is to ritual purgation and nothing else. See T.N. at 4:3 (T.N.).

GLEANINGS

Halachah

12:4] *In a State of Blood Purification*

The Karaite sect held that this rule also required the woman and her husband to refrain from marital relations during the entire 33/66 day period. Against this, Maimonides asserted vehemently that the couple was permitted—and indeed should be required—to resume relations after there had been a seven-day cessation of discharge. But many Rabbanite communities followed the more stringent rule [4].

Haggadah

12:6, 7] *Sin Offering. Make Expiation*

Why should the woman bring a sin offering and require expiation? While in the pain of labor, she might have vowed, "I'll never let my husband come near me again!" The offering atoned for this improper thought or word [5].

Defilement from Tzara'at

Chapters 13 and 14 are usually said to deal with leprosy, but that is begging the question. The single subject of this section is called in Hebrew *tzara'at*, a word of uncertain etymology. It designates a variety of skin ailments and is also applied to unusual changes in the appearance of fabrics and of house walls.

The Greek version of the Torah rendered *tzara'at* by *lepra*, meaning "a scaly condition." This word passed into modern languages via the Latin translation of the Bible; and, during the Middle Ages, *lepra* was identified with the disease we now call leprosy. (Formerly it was called "elephantiasis of the Greeks.")

True leprosy is now referred to as Hansen's disease (or Hansenitis), after the nineteenth-century Norwegian physician who identified the microorganism that causes it. It is not highly contagious, and it develops slowly. Among its symptoms are changes of color and growths on the skin and a loss of sensitivity to pain. In advanced cases the nose, jaw, and extremeties may rot away. Modern medicine can arrest, possibly even cure, the disease; but until recent times the leper was doomed to a horrible end.

It was, then, by a mere accident of history that the usual versions of the Bible render *tzara'at* by "leprosy." The Hebrew word must include other ailments than Hansen's disease, since the recovery of the patient is regarded as possible and even likely. The only question is whether *tzara'at* ever means "leprosy." But this question cannot be answered with certainty. Medical men who have studied our chapter have suggested, variously, that it deals with eczema and psoriasis which are not contagious, of impetigo which is highly contagious, of gangrenous infections, and of true leprosy. In other biblical passages, we read of afflicted persons whose skin turned "white as snow." This description suggests an ailment called leucoderma which is disfiguring but not serious.

Such references are frequent in the biblical narratives [1]. One of the signs Moses was to give Pharaoh was to cause *tzara'at* to appear on his own hand and then disappear (Exod. 4:6ff.). Miriam was punished for her unjustified criticism of Moses by a brief attack of the ailment (Num. 12:1of.). A group of "lepers," excluded from the besieged city of Samaria, discovered that the besiegers had fled and brought the good news to the starving people (II Kings 7:3ff.). Elisha cured Naaman, a Syrian general, of *tzara'at* and would take no compensation for the service. When the prophet's follower Gehazi obtained some of the reward by a ruse, Elisha declared that the "leprosy" of Naaman would cling to Gehazi and his descendants forever (II Kings 5) [2]. King Uzziah had the effrontery to offer incense on the inner altar, whereupon *tzara'at* broke out on his forehead; "the LORD had smitten him." Hastily thrust out of the Temple, he had to live out the rest of his days in isolation (II Chron. 26:16ff.).

The present translation of the Torah renders *tzara'at* by such terms as "scales" (Exod. 4:6; Num. 12:10) and "scaly [affection]" (Lev. 13:2). But, in cases where the patient is declared unclean, the terms "leprous," "leprosy," and "leper" have been retained in the effort to convey something of the horror which the Bible attaches to this affliction. For the biblical authors did not regard *tzara'at* as just one disease among others. To them it was a *nega*, "smiting," the manifestation of extreme divine displeasure. Unlike other forms of defilement, it does not merely exclude the defiled person from the sanctuary—it bars that person from all human society. It is likely that the emotional overtones attached to *tzara'at* contributed to the sense of horror and revulsion which the very word "leprosy" evokes in western culture. Hansen's disease is indeed a terrible affliction, but the thought of it upsets people more than that of other diseases just as deadly and far more infectious.

Regarding *tzara'at* as a plague, the expression of God's anger, it was natural to inquire what sin evokes this punishment. The biblical stories mentioned above suggest that it might be brought on by several different sins; and a variety of opinions is recorded by the Rabbis [3]. A favorite device of midrashic preachers was to pun on *metzora*, "leper," and *motzi ra*, "slanderer" [4]. Thus, they utilized the reading of these Torah sections as an occasion to preach against hostile talk and gossip—always an appropriate topic for a sermon.

These chapters are not concerned with medical practice as such. The priest examined suspected patients and made a diagnosis, not for the purpose of treatment, but to distinguish between *tzara'at*, which defiles, and other skin ailments that do not. The person afflicted with *tzara'at* was isolated to prevent the spread of ritual contamination but not to protect public health. Luzzatto properly notes that no provision was made for isolating other, more virulent ailments, such as bubonic plague [5]. That the intent of the laws was not hygienic appears from Leviticus, chapter 14, verse 26, which speaks of symptoms appearing on the walls of a house. Before such a house is inspected by a priest, it is to be emptied of its contents. For should he pronounce the place "unclean," everything inside it would be defiled; but household goods removed in advance remain clean!

In the same spirit, the halachists held that a person or object affected by *tzara'at* is legally unclean only from the moment when the priest makes the positive diagnosis. Therefore a person should not be examined for *tzara'at* on the eve of a festival in order not to miss the joyous celebration, and a bridegroom is permitted to postpone his examination until the marriage week is over [6]. And a gentile "leper" does not cause ritual defilement [7].

A Note on Judaism and Medicine

The role of the priest in these matters is entirely ritualistic; he does not attempt to cure *tzara'at*. In this regard, Judaism differed from some ancient and modern religions. The Greek temples of Asklepios, the god of healing, were centers of medical treatment as well as of religious observance. Among primitive peoples, medicine men have often combined the use of medication with their rites.

The Bible says almost nothing about medical practice. The cures performed by Elijah and Elisha are presented as miracles, and similar wonder stories are told of various postbiblical personalities. In one case, Isaiah directed that an inflammation be treated with a lump of pressed figs (Isa. 38:21); but this was only after he had announced God's promise that the patient would recover. It is told of King Asa, apparently with disapproval, that, when he became ill, he did not seek the Lord but turned to the healers (II Chron. 16:12); but this probably means that he went to pagan medicine men. The Bible nowhere forbids the use of medical aid; and one who injures another physically must pay for the cure (Exod. 21:19).

Ben Sira, writing about two hundred years before the Christian era, pays a warm tribute to the physician. He urges the sick to seek medical care and, at the same time, to pray for divine help, "for from the Most High cometh healing." Indeed, God has appointed the physician for this beneficent task (Ecclus. 38).

The Talmud, which specifically asserts that the practice of medicine is sanctioned by the Torah [8], contains much medical lore [9]. The sour remark that relegates "the best of physicians to hell" [10] should not be taken too seriously; elsewhere the Talmud remarks that one who cures the sick without pay is worth as much as he gets [11].

Medieval and modern Jews have esteemed the medical profession highly. Some of the most notable teachers of Judaism have been distinguished practicing physicians, among them the poet and philosopher Judah Halevi, the philosopher and halachist Moses Maimonides, and Isaac Lampronti of Ferrara (1670–1756), the compiler of a massive talmudic encyclopedia. The contribution of Jews to the advancement of modern medical science has been outstanding.

Chapter 13 of Leviticus is full of uncertainties as to the meaning of words and phrases and as to the nature of the symptoms and the diseases discussed. Rashbam, whose commentary to the Torah was directed entirely to the plain sense of the text, says that in this chapter we cannot rely on simple grammatical exegesis nor on empirical medical knowledge. Here, for once, he is content to rely on the authority of the halachists. An entire treatise of the Mishnah, entitled *Nega'im,* "Plagues," is devoted to this subject.

וַיְדַבֵּר יְהֹוָה אֶל־מֹשֶׁה וְאֶל־אַהֲרֹן לֵאמֹר: אָדָם כִּי־
יִהְיֶה בְעוֹר־בְּשָׂרוֹ שְׂאֵת אוֹ־סַפַּחַת אוֹ בַהֶרֶת וְהָיָה
בְעוֹר־בְּשָׂרוֹ לְנֶגַע צָרָעַת וְהוּבָא אֶל־אַהֲרֹן הַכֹּהֵן אוֹ
אֶל־אַחַד מִבָּנָיו הַכֹּהֲנִים: וְרָאָה הַכֹּהֵן אֶת־הַנֶּגַע
בְּעוֹר־הַבָּשָׂר וְשֵׂעָר בַּנֶּגַע הָפַךְ לָבָן וּמַרְאֵה הַנֶּגַע
עָמֹק מֵעוֹר בְּשָׂרוֹ נֶגַע צָרַעַת הוּא וְרָאָהוּ הַכֹּהֵן
וְטִמֵּא אֹתוֹ: וְאִם־בַּהֶרֶת לְבָנָה הִוא בְּעוֹר בְּשָׂרוֹ
וְעָמֹק אֵין־מַרְאֶהָ מִן־הָעוֹר וּשְׂעָרָה לֹא־הָפַךְ לָבָן

Leviticus 13

1–4

1] The LORD spoke to Moses and Aaron, saying:

2] When a person has on the skin of his body a swelling, a rash, or a discoloration, and it develops into a scaly affection on the skin of his body, it shall be reported to Aaron the priest or to one of his sons, the priests.   3] The priest shall examine the affection on the skin of his body: if hair in the affected patch has turned white and the affection appears to be deeper than the skin of his body, it is a leprous affection; when the priest sees it, he shall pronounce him unclean.   4] But if it is a white discoloration on the skin of his body which does not appear to be deeper than the skin and the hair in it has not turned white, the priest shall isolate the affected per-

13:1] *And Aaron.* Because the priests had to deal with cases of *tzara'at.*

2–8] First type of *tzara'at* (according to Hoffmann, the "discoloration" of verse 2). When an area of the skin of the body changes in appearance, so that it seems to be deeper than the surrounding skin, and especially if hair on this area turns white, the patient is unclean. If the symptoms are inconclusive, the patient is to be isolated for a week and examined again; this procedure may, if necessary, be repeated once more. If the patient is at any stage pronounced clean and thereafter the affection begins to spread, the priest must see him again and pronounce him unclean.

2] *Scaly affection.* Hebrew *nega'* ("plague of") *tzara'at.* The same words are translated "leprous affection" in verse 3. "Hebrew *tzara'at* is used for a variety of diseases. Where a human being is declared unclean by reason of *tzara'at,* the traditional translation 'leprosy' has been retained without regard to modern medical terminology" (T.N.).   See pp. 115–116.

It shall be reported. Or, "he shall be brought" (T.N.).

3] *Deeper than the skin of his body.* This might mean that the affection is not superficial but extends below the skin. The halachah, however, understands: Because of the change in color, the affected area seems to be lower than the rest of the skin.

ה וְהִסְגִּיר הַכֹּהֵן אֶת־הַנֶּגַע שִׁבְעַת יָמִים: וְרָאָהוּ הַכֹּהֵן
בַּיּוֹם הַשְּׁבִיעִי וְהִנֵּה הַנֶּגַע עָמַד בְּעֵינָיו לֹא־פָשָׂה הַנֶּגַע
בָּעוֹר וְהִסְגִּירוֹ הַכֹּהֵן שִׁבְעַת יָמִים שֵׁנִית: וְרָאָה הַכֹּהֵן
אֹתוֹ בַּיּוֹם הַשְּׁבִיעִי שֵׁנִית וְהִנֵּה כֵּהָה הַנֶּגַע וְלֹא־פָשָׂה
הַנֶּגַע בָּעוֹר וְטִהֲרוֹ הַכֹּהֵן מִסְפַּחַת הִוא וְכִבֶּס בְּגָדָיו
וְטָהֵר: וְאִם־פָּשֹׂה תִפְשֶׂה הַמִּסְפַּחַת בָּעוֹר אַחֲרֵי
הֵרָאֹתוֹ אֶל־הַכֹּהֵן לְטָהֳרָתוֹ וְנִרְאָה שֵׁנִית אֶל־הַכֹּהֵן:
וְרָאָה הַכֹּהֵן וְהִנֵּה פָּשְׂתָה הַמִּסְפַּחַת בָּעוֹר וְטִמְּאוֹ
הַכֹּהֵן צָרַעַת הִוא:
פ

נֶגַע צָרַעַת כִּי תִהְיֶה בְּאָדָם וְהוּבָא אֶל־הַכֹּהֵן: וְרָאָה
הַכֹּהֵן וְהִנֵּה שְׂאֵת־לְבָנָה בָּעוֹר וְהִיא הָפְכָה שֵׂעָר לָבָן

Leviticus 13
5–10

son for seven days.   5] On the seventh day the priest shall examine him, and if the affection has remained unchanged in color and the disease has not spread on the skin, the priest shall isolate him for another seven days.   6] On the seventh day the priest shall examine him again: if the affection has faded and has not spread on the skin, the priest shall pronounce him clean. It is a rash; he shall wash his clothes, and he shall be clean.   7] But if the rash should spread on the skin after he has presented himself to the priest and been pronounced clean, he shall present himself again to the priest.   8] And if the priest sees that the rash has spread on the skin, the priest shall pronounce him unclean; it is leprosy.

9] When a person has a scaly affection, it shall be reported to the priest.   10] If the priest finds on the skin a white swelling which has turned some hair white, with

9–17] Second type of tzara'at (according to Hoffmann, the "swelling" of verse 2). Here the diagnostic factor is that an abnormally white area appears on the skin, with some patches of normal color within it. A patient with these symptoms is unclean. Should the white affection spread over the entire body, the patient is clean; but he reverts to the defiled state as soon as a patch of normal skin appears. No convincing explanation of this strange rule has been offered.

9] *It shall be reported.* See T.N. above, verse 2 (T.N.).

יא וּמִחְיַת בָּשָׂר חַי בַּשְׂאֵת: צָרַעַת נוֹשֶׁנֶת הִוא בְּעוֹר

יב בְּשָׂרוֹ וְטִמְּאוֹ הַכֹּהֵן לֹא יַסְגִּרֶנּוּ כִּי טָמֵא הוּא: וְאִם־

פָּרוֹחַ תִּפְרַח הַצָּרַעַת בָּעוֹר וְכִסְּתָה הַצָּרַעַת אֵת

כָּל־עוֹר הַנֶּגַע מֵרֹאשׁוֹ וְעַד־רַגְלָיו לְכָל־מַרְאֵה עֵינֵי

יג הַכֹּהֵן: וְרָאָה הַכֹּהֵן וְהִנֵּה כִסְּתָה הַצָּרַעַת אֶת־כָּל־

בְּשָׂרוֹ וְטִהַר אֶת־הַנָּגַע כֻּלּוֹ הָפַךְ לָבָן טָהוֹר הוּא:

יד וּבְיוֹם הֵרָאוֹת בּוֹ בָּשָׂר חַי יִטְמָא: וְרָאָה הַכֹּהֵן אֶת־
טו

הַבָּשָׂר הַחַי וְטִמְּאוֹ הַבָּשָׂר הַחַי טָמֵא הוּא צָרַעַת

טז הוּא: אוֹ כִי יָשׁוּב הַבָּשָׂר הַחַי וְנֶהְפַּךְ לְלָבָן וּבָא אֶל־

יז הַכֹּהֵן: וְרָאָהוּ הַכֹּהֵן וְהִנֵּה נֶהְפַּךְ הַנֶּגַע לְלָבָן וְטִהַר

הַכֹּהֵן אֶת־הַנֶּגַע טָהוֹר הוּא: פ

a patch of undiscolored flesh in the swelling,   11] it is chronic leprosy on the skin of his body, and the priest shall pronounce him unclean; he need not isolate him, for he is unclean.   12] But if the eruption spreads out over the skin so that it covers all the skin of the affected person from head to foot, wherever the priest can see— 13] if the priest sees that the eruption has covered the whole body—he shall pronounce the affected person clean; he is clean, for he has turned all white.   14] But as soon as undiscolored flesh appears in it, he shall be unclean;   15] when the priest sees the undiscolored flesh, he shall pronounce him unclean. The undiscolored flesh is unclean; it is leprosy.   16] But if the undiscolored flesh again turns white, he shall come to the priest,   17] and the priest shall examine him: if the affection has turned white, the priest shall pronounce the affected person clean; he is clean.

10] *A patch of undiscolored flesh.* Others, "quick raw flesh" (T.N.).

יח וּבָשָׂר כִּי־יִהְיֶה בוֹ־בְעֹרוֹ שְׁחִין וְנִרְפָּא: וְהָיָה בִּמְקוֹם הַשְּׁחִין שְׂאֵת לְבָנָה אוֹ בַהֶרֶת לְבָנָה אֲדַמְדָּמֶת וְנִרְאָה אֶל־הַכֹּהֵן: וְרָאָה הַכֹּהֵן וְהִנֵּה מַרְאֶהָ שָׁפָל מִן־הָעוֹר כ וּשְׂעָרָהּ הָפַךְ לָבָן וְטִמְּאוֹ הַכֹּהֵן נֶגַע־צָרַעַת הִוא בַּשְּׁחִין פָּרָחָה: וְאִם יִרְאֶנָּה הַכֹּהֵן וְהִנֵּה אֵין־בָּהּ כא שֵׂעָר לָבָן וּשְׁפָלָה אֵינֶנָּה מִן־הָעוֹר וְהִיא כֵהָה וְהִסְגִּירוֹ הַכֹּהֵן שִׁבְעַת יָמִים: וְאִם־פָּשֹׂה תִפְשֶׂה בָּעוֹר כב וְטִמֵּא הַכֹּהֵן אֹתוֹ נֶגַע הִוא: וְאִם־תַּחְתֶּיהָ תַּעֲמֹד כג הַבַּהֶרֶת לֹא פָשָׂתָה צָרֶבֶת הַשְּׁחִין הִוא וְטִהֲרוֹ הַכֹּהֵן: ס אוֹ בָשָׂר כִּי־יִהְיֶה בְעֹרוֹ מִכְוַת־אֵשׁ כד

Leviticus 13

18–24

18] When an inflammation appears on the skin of one's body and it heals, 19] and a white swelling or a white discoloration streaked with red develops where the inflammation was, he shall present himself to the priest. 20] If the priest finds that it appears lower than the rest of the skin and that the hair in it has turned white, the priest shall pronounce him unclean; it is a leprous affection that has broken out in the inflammation. 21] But if the priest finds that there is no white hair in it and it is not lower than the rest of the skin, and it is faded, the priest shall isolate him for seven days. 22] If it should spread in the skin, the priest shall pronounce him unclean; it is an affection. 23] But if the discoloration remains stationary, not having spread, it is the scar of the inflammation; the priest shall pronounce him clean.

24] When the skin of one's body sustains a burn by fire, and the patch from the

18–23] Third type of *tzara'at*. A possible *tzara'at* developing in an inflammation, whether spontaneous or the result of an injury. The priest must distinguish between changes that indicate *tzara'at* and those caused by healing and scarring of the area.

24–28] Similar provisions when suspicious symptoms follow a burn.

וְהָיְתָה מִחְיַת הַמִּכְוָה בַּהֶרֶת לְבָנָה אֲדַמְדֶּמֶת אוֹ

לְבָנָה: וְרָאָה אֹתָהּ הַכֹּהֵן וְהִנֵּה נֶהְפַּךְ שֵׂעָר לָבָן **כה**
בַּבַּהֶרֶת וּמַרְאֶהָ עָמֹק מִן־הָעוֹר צָרַעַת הִוא בַּמִּכְוָה

פָּרָחָה וְטִמֵּא אֹתוֹ הַכֹּהֵן נֶגַע צָרַעַת הִוא: וְאִם **כו**
יִרְאֶנָּה הַכֹּהֵן וְהִנֵּה אֵין־בַּבַּהֶרֶת שֵׂעָר לָבָן וּשְׁפָלָה
אֵינֶנָּה מִן־הָעוֹר וְהִוא כֵהָה וְהִסְגִּירוֹ הַכֹּהֵן שִׁבְעַת

יָמִים: וְרָאָהוּ הַכֹּהֵן בַּיּוֹם הַשְּׁבִיעִי אִם־פָּשֹׂה תִפְשֶׂה **כז**
בָעוֹר וְטִמֵּא הַכֹּהֵן אֹתוֹ נֶגַע צָרַעַת הִוא: וְאִם־תַּחְתֶּיהָ **כח**
תַעֲמֹד הַבַּהֶרֶת לֹא־פָשְׂתָה בָעוֹר וְהִוא כֵהָה שְׂאֵת
הַמִּכְוָה הִוא וְטִהֲרוֹ הַכֹּהֵן כִּי־צָרֶבֶת הַמִּכְוָה

הִוא: פ

וְאִישׁ אוֹ אִשָּׁה כִּי־יִהְיֶה בוֹ נָגַע בְּרֹאשׁ אוֹ בְזָקָן: **כט**

Leviticus 13
25–29

burn is a discoloration, either white streaked with red, or white, **25]** the priest shall examine it. If some hair has turned white in the discoloration, which itself appears to go deeper than the skin, it is leprosy that has broken out in the burn. The priest shall pronounce him unclean; it is a leprous affection. **26]** But if the priest finds that there is no white hair in the discoloration, and that it is not lower than the rest of the skin, and it is faded, the priest shall isolate him for seven days. **27]** On the seventh day the priest shall examine him: if it has spread in the skin, the priest shall pronounce him unclean; it is a leprous affection. **28]** But if the discoloration has remained stationary, not having spread on the skin, and it is faded, it is the swelling from the burn. The priest shall pronounce him clean, for it is the scar of the burn.

29] If a man or a woman has an affection on the head or in the beard,

29–39] Fourth type of *tzara'at*. An affection of the scalp or of areas covered by the beard. Here, thin yellow hair is the important diagnostic factor. White hair, which in other cases indicates *tzara'at*, is not

122

לִ וְרָאָה הַכֹּהֵן אֶת־הַנֶּגַע וְהִנֵּה מַרְאֵהוּ עָמֹק מִן־הָעוֹר

וּבוֹ שֵׂעָר צָהֹב דָּק וְטִמֵּא אֹתוֹ הַכֹּהֵן נֶתֶק הוּא צָרַעַת

לֹא הָרֹאשׁ אוֹ הַזָּקָן הוּא: וְכִי־יִרְאֶה הַכֹּהֵן אֶת־נֶגַע הַנֶּתֶק

וְהִנֵּה אֵין־מַרְאֵהוּ עָמֹק מִן־הָעוֹר וְשֵׂעָר שָׁחֹר אֵין בּוֹ

לב וְהִסְגִּיר הַכֹּהֵן אֶת־נֶגַע הַנֶּתֶק שִׁבְעַת יָמִים: וְרָאָה

הַכֹּהֵן אֶת־הַנֶּגַע בַּיּוֹם הַשְּׁבִיעִי וְהִנֵּה לֹא־פָשָׂה הַנֶּתֶק

וְלֹא־הָיָה בוֹ שֵׂעָר צָהֹב וּמַרְאֵה הַנֶּתֶק אֵין עָמֹק מִן־

לג הָעוֹר: וְהִתְגַּלָּח וְאֶת־הַנֶּתֶק לֹא יְגַלֵּחַ וְהִסְגִּיר הַכֹּהֵן

לד אֶת־הַנֶּתֶק שִׁבְעַת יָמִים שֵׁנִית: וְרָאָה הַכֹּהֵן אֶת־הַנֶּתֶק

בַּיּוֹם הַשְּׁבִיעִי וְהִנֵּה לֹא־פָשָׂה הַנֶּתֶק בָּעוֹר וּמַרְאֵהוּ

אֵינֶנּוּ עָמֹק מִן־הָעוֹר וְטִהַר אֹתוֹ הַכֹּהֵן וְכִבֶּס בְּגָדָיו

* לג ג' רבתי.

Leviticus 13

30–34

30] the priest shall examine the affection. If it appears to go deeper than the skin and there is thin yellow hair in it, the priest shall pronounce him unclean; it is a scall, a scaly eruption in the hair or beard.   31] But if the priest finds that the scall affection does not appear to go deeper than the skin, yet there is no black hair in it, the priest shall isolate the person with the scall affection for seven days.   32] On the seventh day the priest shall examine the affection. If the scall has not spread and no yellow hair has appeared in it, and the scall does not appear to go deeper than the skin, 33] the person with the scall shall shave himself, but without shaving the scall; the priest shall isolate him for another seven days.   34] On the seventh day the priest shall examine the scall. If the scall has not spread on the skin, and does not appear to go deeper than the skin, the priest shall pronounce him clean; he shall wash his

considered such an indication here, according to the halachah—no doubt because hair of the head and beard so often turns gray normally.

30] *A scall.* Hebrew *netek*, from a root meaning "tear off," probably referring to the tearing off of scabs by scratching. The word "scall" means "any scaly or scabby disease of the skin."

לה וְטָהֵר: וְאִם־פָּשֹׂה יִפְשֶׂה הַנֶּתֶק בָּעוֹר אַחֲרֵי טָהֳרָתוֹ:

לו וְרָאָהוּ הַכֹּהֵן וְהִנֵּה פָּשָׂה הַנֶּתֶק בָּעוֹר לֹא־יְבַקֵּר

לז הַכֹּהֵן לַשֵּׂעָר הַצָּהֹב טָמֵא הוּא: וְאִם־בְּעֵינָיו עָמַד

הַנֶּתֶק וְשֵׂעָר שָׁחֹר צָמַח־בּוֹ נִרְפָּא הַנֶּתֶק טָהוֹר הוּא

וְטִהֲרוֹ הַכֹּהֵן: ס וְאִישׁ אוֹ־אִשָּׁה כִּי־יִהְיֶה בְעוֹר־

לט בְּשָׂרָם בֶּהָרֹת בֶּהָרֹת לְבָנֹת: וְרָאָה הַכֹּהֵן וְהִנֵּה

בְעוֹר־בְּשָׂרָם בֶּהָרֹת כֵּהוֹת לְבָנֹת בֹּהַק הוּא פָּרַח

מ בָּעוֹר טָהוֹר הוּא: ס וְאִישׁ כִּי יִמָּרֵט רֹאשׁוֹ קֵרֵחַ

מא הוּא טָהוֹר הוּא: וְאִם מִפְּאַת פָּנָיו יִמָּרֵט רֹאשׁוֹ גִּבֵּחַ

מב הוּא טָהוֹר הוּא: וְכִי־יִהְיֶה בַקָּרַחַת אוֹ בַגַּבַּחַת נֶגַע

Leviticus 13

35–42

clothes, and he shall be clean.   35] If, however, the scall should spread on the skin after he has been pronounced clean,   36] the priest shall examine him. If the scall has spread on the skin, the priest need not look for yellow hair: he is unclean. 37] But if the scall has remained unchanged in color, and black hair has grown in it, the scall is healed; he is clean. The priest shall pronounce him clean.

38] If a man or a woman has the skin of the body streaked with white discolorations,   39] and the priest sees that the discolorations on the skin of the body are of a dull white, it is a tetter broken out on the skin; he is clean.

40] If a man loses the hair of his head and becomes bald, he is clean.   41] If he loses the hair on the front part of his head and becomes bald at the forehead, he is clean.   42] But if a white affection streaked with red appears on the bald part in

---

38–39] Harmless discolorations which do not cause defilement.

39] *Tetter* is defined as "any of various skin diseases, as eczema, characterized by itching." The word represents the Hebrew *bohak*, which occurs nowhere else in the Bible, and it probably comes from a root meaning "to be white, bright," found in postbiblical Hebrew and Aramaic.

40–43] Conditions associated with baldness. (Hebrew has two entirely different words for baldness, according to whether it starts at the front or the back of the head.) Normal baldness is not defiling; if symptoms of *tzara'at* appear in an area already bald, the rules applied are those of the second type (verses 9ff.), not those of the fourth type.

לְבָן אֲדַמְדָּם צָרַעַת פֹּרַחַת הִוא בְּקָרַחְתּוֹ אוֹ
בְגַבַּחְתּוֹ: מה וְרָאָה אֹתוֹ הַכֹּהֵן וְהִנֵּה שְׂאֵת־הַנֶּגַע לְבָנָה
אֲדַמְדֶּמֶת בְּקָרַחְתּוֹ אוֹ בְגַבַּחְתּוֹ כְּמַרְאֵה צָרַעַת עוֹר
בָּשָׂר: מד אִישׁ־צָרוּעַ הוּא טָמֵא הוּא יְטַמְּאֶנּוּ הַכֹּהֵן
בְּרֹאשׁוֹ נִגְעוֹ: מה וְהַצָּרוּעַ אֲשֶׁר־בּוֹ הַנֶּגַע בְּגָדָיו יִהְיוּ
פְרֻמִים וְרֹאשׁוֹ יִהְיֶה פָרוּעַ וְעַל־שָׂפָם יַעְטֶה וְטָמֵא
טָמֵא יִקְרָא: מו כָּל־יְמֵי אֲשֶׁר הַנֶּגַע בּוֹ יִטְמָא טָמֵא הוּא
בָּדָד יֵשֵׁב מִחוּץ לַמַּחֲנֶה מוֹשָׁבוֹ: ס

Leviticus 13
43–46

the front or at the back of the head, it is a scaly eruption that is spreading over the bald part in the front or at the back of the head.   43] The priest shall examine him: if the swollen affection on the bald part in the front or at the back of his head is white streaked with red, like the leprosy of body skin in appearance,   44] the man is leprous; he is unclean. The priest shall pronounce him unclean; he has the affection on his head.

45] As for the person with a leprous affection, his clothes shall be rent, his hair shall be left bare, and he shall cover over his upper lip; and he shall call out, "Unclean! Unclean!"   46] He shall be unclean as long as the disease is on him. Being unclean, he shall dwell apart; his dwelling shall be outside the camp.

45] *Left bare.* See T.N. at 10:6 (T.N.).

Cover over his upper lip. He was to let his head-covering hang down over his face as far as his mouth [12].

He shall call out, "Unclean! Unclean!" To warn passers-by that he is a source of defilement. The Targum paraphrases, "Do not defile yourselves!"

45–46] The "leper," adjudged to be under divine displeasure, was completely isolated and had to observe the rules of mourning (see commentary on 10:6). The "leper" had to remain outside the camp, in later times outside the walls of Jerusalem.

GLEANINGS

Halachah

13:3] *Pronounce Him Unclean*

The indispensable duty of the priest was to speak the words, "You are clean" or "You are unclean." If the priest was ignorant, he might be guided in his diagnosis by an informed layman, but it was he who had to speak the official formula.

SIFRA

6] *He Shall Wash His Clothes*

He also must take a ritual bath. Though he was not defiled, the fact that he had to undergo examination and isolation makes the ritual purification appropriate.

SIFRA

30] *A Scall*

Hebrew *netek*. Maimonides held that the falling out of a patch of hair from an area otherwise hairy (as opposed to normal balding, verses 40ff.) is sufficient evidence of *tzara'at*; Nachmanides argued that the diagnosis is not complete unless yellow hair appears. They both agree that *netek* means "falling out of hair" [13].

33] *Shall Shave Himself, without Shaving the Scall*

He is to leave two rows of hairs around the affected area so that at the end of the week it can be readily seen if the affection has spread.

SIFRA

Haggadah

13:9–17] The Rabbis were deeply aware of the paradoxical character of this rule. They represent Korah in his rebellion against the authority of Moses (Num. 16), citing this passage as proof that "the Torah is not from heaven, Moses is not a prophet, nor is Aaron a High Priest" [14].

Tzara'at of Garments

Chapter 13, verses 47–59, may be out of place. The comparable passage about *tzara'at* of houses is found at the end of chapter 14, after the directions for purifying a cured human patient.

In these verses, *tzara'at* is translated "eruptive affection." The reference seems to be to some sort of mildew or fungus; this suggestion was made in the fourteenth century by the scientifically trained Rabbi Levi ben Gershom. But some two hundred years earlier, Judah Halevi had asserted that *tzara'at* of garments and houses was not a natural phenomenon; it appeared by miracle only in the Holy Land as a sign of God's wrath at the indifferent and sinful. And Maimonides and Nachmanides agreed with him [1].

מז וְהַבֶּגֶד כִּי־יִהְיֶה בוֹ נֶגַע צָרָעַת בְּבֶגֶד צֶמֶר אוֹ בְּבֶגֶד
מח פִּשְׁתִּים: אוֹ בִשְׁתִי אוֹ בְעֵרֶב לַפִּשְׁתִּים וְלַצֶּמֶר אוֹ
מט בְעוֹר אוֹ בְּכָל־מְלֶאכֶת עוֹר: וְהָיָה הַנֶּגַע יְרַקְרַק אוֹ
אֲדַמְדָּם בַּבֶּגֶד אוֹ בָעוֹר אוֹ־בַשְּׁתִי אוֹ־בָעֵרֶב אוֹ
בְכָל־כְּלִי־עוֹר נֶגַע צָרַעַת הוּא וְהָרְאָה אֶת־הַכֹּהֵן:
נ וְרָאָה הַכֹּהֵן אֶת הַנָּגַע וְהִסְגִּיר אֶת־הַנֶּגַע שִׁבְעַת יָמִים:
נא וְרָאָה אֶת־הַנֶּגַע בַּיּוֹם הַשְּׁבִיעִי כִּי־פָשָׂה הַנֶּגַע בַּבֶּגֶד
אוֹ־בַשְּׁתִי אוֹ־בָעֵרֶב אוֹ בָעוֹר לְכֹל אֲשֶׁר־יֵעָשֶׂה הָעוֹר
נב לִמְלָאכָה צָרַעַת מַמְאֶרֶת הַנֶּגַע טָמֵא הוּא: וְשָׂרַף
אֶת־הַבֶּגֶד אוֹ אֶת־הַשְּׁתִי אוֹ אֶת־הָעֵרֶב בַּצֶּמֶר אוֹ

Leviticus 13
47–52

47] When an eruptive affection occurs in a cloth of wool or linen fabric, 48] in the warp or in the woof of the linen or the wool, or in a skin or in anything made of skin; 49] if the affection in the cloth or the skin, in the warp or the woof, or in any article of skin, is streaky green or red, it is an eruptive affection. It shall be shown to the priest; 50] and the priest, after examining the affection, shall isolate the affected article for seven days. 51] On the seventh day he shall examine the affection: if the affection has spread in the cloth—whether in the warp or the woof, or in the skin, for whatever purpose the skin may be used—the affection is a malignant eruption; it is unclean. 52] The cloth—whether warp or woof in wool or

---

13:47] *Wool or linen.* The usual fabrics employed in biblical times.

48] *In the warp or in the woof.* "Warp" designates the threads that are set up on the loom; "woof," the threads passed around the warp threads by means of a shuttle. These terms ordinarily correspond to the Hebrew *sheti* and *erev.* But here this rendering is puzzling: How could *tzara'at* appear on the warp

and not on the woof, or vice versa? Talmudic sources offer a possible solution. In talmudic times a thick thread was used for woof and a thinner one for warp [2]. This procedure may also have been followed in the biblical period. Our passage would then refer to yarns of different thickness, before or even after weaving.

49] *Green.* Or, "yellow" (T.N.).

128

בַּפִּשְׁתִּים אוֹ אֶת־כָּל־כְּלִי הָעוֹר אֲשֶׁר־יִהְיֶה בוֹ הַנֶּגַע

נג כִּי־צָרַעַת מַמְאֶרֶת הִוא בָּאֵשׁ תִּשָּׂרֵף: וְאִם יִרְאֶה

הַכֹּהֵן וְהִנֵּה לֹא־פָשָׂה הַנֶּגַע בַּבֶּגֶד אוֹ בַשְּׁתִי אוֹ בָעֵרֶב

נד אוֹ בְּכָל־כְּלִי־עוֹר: וְצִוָּה הַכֹּהֵן וְכִבְּסוּ אֵת אֲשֶׁר־בּוֹ

נה הַנָּגַע וְהִסְגִּירוֹ שִׁבְעַת־יָמִים שֵׁנִית: וְרָאָה הַכֹּהֵן

אַחֲרֵי הֻכַּבֵּס אֶת־הַנֶּגַע וְהִנֵּה לֹא־הָפַךְ הַנֶּגַע אֶת־

עֵינוֹ וְהַנֶּגַע לֹא־פָשָׂה טָמֵא הוּא בָּאֵשׁ תִּשְׂרְפֶנּוּ פְּחֶתֶת

נו הִוא בְּקָרַחְתּוֹ אוֹ בְּגַבַּחְתּוֹ: וְאִם רָאָה הַכֹּהֵן וְהִנֵּה

כֵּהָה הַנֶּגַע אַחֲרֵי הֻכַּבֵּס אֹתוֹ וְקָרַע אֹתוֹ מִן־הַבֶּגֶד

נז אוֹ מִן־הָעוֹר אוֹ מִן־הַשְּׁתִי אוֹ מִן־הָעֵרֶב: וְאִם־תֵּרָאֶה

עוֹד בַּבֶּגֶד אוֹ־בַשְּׁתִי אוֹ־בָעֵרֶב אוֹ בְכָל־כְּלִי־עוֹר

Leviticus 13
53–57

linen, or any article of skin—in which the affection is found, shall be burned, for it is a malignant eruption; it shall be consumed in fire.   **53]** But if the priest sees that the affection in the cloth—whether in warp or in woof, or in any article of skin—has not spread,   **54]** the priest shall order the affected article washed, and he shall isolate it for another seven days.   **55]** And if, after the affected article has been washed, the priest sees that the affection has not changed color and that it has not spread, it is unclean. It shall be consumed in fire; it is a fret, whether on its inner side or on its outer side.   **56]** But if the priest sees that the affected part, after it has been washed, is faded, he shall tear it out from the cloth or skin, whether in the warp or in the woof;   **57]** and if it occurs again in the cloth—whether in warp or

---

54] *Washed.* To see if the discoloration was just an ordinary stain.

55] *Has not changed color.* Neither laundering nor the passing of time has affected it, so it is adjudged unclean even though it has not spread.

A fret. A worn spot. ("Fretfulness" is derived from this original meaning of rubbing, wearing away.) The wearing away of the fabric provided a favorable place for the development of the plague. But meaning of Hebrew *pechetet* uncertain (T.N.).

Inner side or on its outer side. Hebrew means literally "on its back-baldness or front-baldness" (cf. commentary on 13:40–43).

נח פָּרַחַת הִוא בָּאֵשׁ תִּשְׂרְפֶנּוּ אֵת אֲשֶׁר־בּוֹ הַנָּגַע: וְהַבֶּגֶד
אוֹ־הַשְּׁתִי אוֹ־הָעֵרֶב אוֹ־כָל־כְּלִי הָעוֹר אֲשֶׁר תְּכַבֵּס

נט וְסָר מֵהֶם הַנָּגַע וְכֻבַּס שֵׁנִית וְטָהֵר: זֹאת תּוֹרַת נֶגַע־
צָרַעַת בֶּגֶד הַצֶּמֶר אוֹ הַפִּשְׁתִּים אוֹ הַשְּׁתִי אוֹ הָעֵרֶב
אוֹ כָּל־כְּלִי־עוֹר לְטַהֲרוֹ אוֹ לְטַמְּאוֹ:

Haftarah Tazria, p. 374

in woof—or in any article of skin, it is a wild growth; the affected article shall be consumed in fire. **58]** If, however, the affection disappears from the cloth—warp or woof—or from any article of skin that has been washed, it shall be washed again, and it shall be clean.

59] This is the procedure for eruptive affections of cloth, woolen or linen, in warp or in woof, or of any article of skin, for pronouncing it clean or unclean.

58] *It shall be washed again.* This time not a scrubbing to remove the stain, but a ceremonial dipping (so Targums).

Purification from Tzara'at

Once the priest declared the victim of *tzara'at* unclean, he had no further duties toward the patient until recovery. No doubt the latter and the family offered prayers and sacrifices for a cure. Moses prayed for his stricken sister (Num. 12:13).

If the leprous affection healed, the priest was summoned again to examine the patient. And when he had satisfied himself that the "plague" had disappeared, the priest conducted ceremonies to neutralize the ritual defilement—for the patient, though healed, was still *tamé*.

There were two stages to the purification. The first was performed outside the camp; the second was a sacrificial rite in the sanctuary, performed eight days later. The first part of the procedure required the use of two birds. One bird was slaughtered and its blood was utilized—but this ritual was *not* a sacrifice. It had the character of a magical act—the defilement was transferred to the second bird which was allowed to fly away, carrying the defilement with it. The intent of this ritual is something like that of the scapegoat (Lev. 16:7–10, 20ff.), as Nachmanides clearly understood [1].

The ceremony involves the use of several substances to which strong purificatory power was ascribed. Blood and fresh water are already familiar to us in this connection. Here, we encounter also cedar wood, crimson yarn, and hyssop. The reddish wood and crimson-dyed wool suggest both blood and the demonic world with which the color red has been associated through the ages (cf. conventional pictures of "the devil"). Cedar wood is also aromatic; so too is hyssop, if—as is probable—it is to be identified with Syrian marjoram. The Bible mentions it as a small plant that grows out of walls (I Kings 5:13). Perhaps it was used originally as a convenient means of sprinkling (Exod. 12:22), but it seems to have acquired a positive power to purify [2]. The Psalmist prays, "Purge me with hyssop till I am pure" (Ps. 51:9). The language is figurative, referring to moral and spiritual regeneration, but the allusion to the ritual shows that hyssop was regarded as an effective agent of purification.

The rite is then the survival of something archaic and primitive. The text does not mention anything about the demonic—only in the case of the scapegoat is there a brief allusion—and quite possibly such notions had already vanished from the minds of those who wrote down this chapter. Customs often survive after their original motives are forgotten.

Later on, edifying explanations were offered by talmudic and more recent preachers. But the attempt to find in the rite the symbolism of spiritual regeneration is forced. The ceremonies were designed to remove a defilement that was a threat to the entire community.

The sacrifices on the eighth day also present some exceptional features. Like the woman after childbirth, the recovered "leper" must bring an offering of purgation (*chatat*) and a burnt offering. But he is also obligated to present a guilt offering (*asham*). This sacrifice is usually associated with the restitution of property that has been illegally taken (chapters 5 and 7). Its purpose here is not explained, but it is clearly of highest importance. For, whereas a poor person may substitute fowl for lambs in the case of *chatat* and *olah*, he must bring a lamb as the *asham* despite the drain on his purse. There is also a procedural novelty (verse 12).

מצרע
ויקרא יד
א–ז

א וַיְדַבֵּר יְהוָה אֶל־מֹשֶׁה לֵּאמֹר: וְאת תִּהְיֶה תּוֹרַת
ב הַמְּצֹרָע בְּיוֹם טָהֳרָתוֹ וְהוּבָא אֶל־הַכֹּהֵן: וְיָצָא הַכֹּהֵן
ג אֶל־מִחוּץ לַמַּחֲנֶה וְרָאָה הַכֹּהֵן וְהִנֵּה נִרְפָּא נֶגַע־
הַצָּרַעַת מִן־הַצָּרוּעַ: וְצִוָּה הַכֹּהֵן וְלָקַח לַמִּטַּהֵר שְׁתֵּי־
ד צִפֳּרִים חַיּוֹת טְהֹרוֹת וְעֵץ אֶרֶז וּשְׁנִי תוֹלַעַת וְאֵזֹב:
ה וְצִוָּה הַכֹּהֵן וְשָׁחַט אֶת־הַצִּפּוֹר הָאֶחָת אֶל־כְּלִי־חֶרֶשׂ
ו עַל־מַיִם חַיִּים: אֶת־הַצִּפֹּר הַחַיָּה יִקַּח אֹתָהּ וְאֶת־עֵץ
הָאֶרֶז וְאֶת־שְׁנִי הַתּוֹלַעַת וְאֶת־הָאֵזֹב וְטָבַל אוֹתָם
וְאֵת הַצִּפֹּר הַחַיָּה בְּדַם הַצִּפֹּר הַשְּׁחֻטָה עַל הַמַּיִם
ז הַחַיִּים: וְהִזָּה עַל הַמִּטַּהֵר מִן־הַצָּרַעַת שֶׁבַע פְּעָמִים

Metzora

Leviticus 14

1–7

1] The LORD spoke to Moses, saying: **2]** This shall be the ritual for a leper at the time that he is to be cleansed.

When it has been reported to the priest,   **3]** the priest shall go outside the camp. If the priest sees that the leper has been healed of his scaly affection,   **4]** the priest shall order two live clean birds, cedar wood, crimson stuff, and hyssop to be brought for him who is to be cleansed.   **5]** The priest shall order one of the birds slaughtered over fresh water in an earthen vessel;   **6]** and he shall take the live bird, along with the cedar wood, the crimson stuff, and the hyssop, and dip them together with the live bird in the blood of the bird that was slaughtered over the fresh water.   **7]** He shall then sprinkle it seven times on him who is to be cleansed

---

14:2] *Leper.* Hebrew *metzora.* It was on this form that the Rabbis punned to connect the ailment with gossip (see p. 116).

It has been reported. Cf. T.N. at 13:2 (T.N.).

4] *Birds.* Hebrew *tziporim,* a term applied to small birds, such as swallows and sparrows.

5] *Slaughtered. Sifra* calls attention to this word, inferring, probably correctly, that the bird was to be killed by cutting its throat, not by the "pinching" used for sacrifices (1:15).

In an earthen vessel. It was probably broken after this single use (cf. 6:21, 11:33).

וְטִהֲרוֹ וְשִׁלַּח אֶת־הַצִּפֹּר הַחַיָּה עַל־פְּנֵי הַשָּׂדֶה:

ח וְכִבֶּס הַמִּטַּהֵר אֶת־בְּגָדָיו וְגִלַּח אֶת־כָּל־שְׂעָרוֹ וְרָחַץ
בַּמַּיִם וְטָהֵר וְאַחַר יָבוֹא אֶל־הַמַּחֲנֶה וְיָשַׁב מִחוּץ
ט לְאָהֳלוֹ שִׁבְעַת יָמִים: וְהָיָה בַיּוֹם הַשְּׁבִיעִי יְגַלַּח אֶת־
כָּל־שְׂעָרוֹ אֶת־רֹאשׁוֹ וְאֶת־זְקָנוֹ וְאֵת גַּבֹּת עֵינָיו וְאֶת־
כָּל־שְׂעָרוֹ יְגַלֵּחַ וְכִבֶּס אֶת־בְּגָדָיו וְרָחַץ אֶת־בְּשָׂרוֹ
י בַּמַּיִם וְטָהֵר: וּבַיּוֹם הַשְּׁמִינִי יִקַּח שְׁנֵי־כְבָשִׂים תְּמִימִם
וְכַבְשָׂה אַחַת בַּת־שְׁנָתָהּ תְּמִימָה וּשְׁלֹשָׁה עֶשְׂרֹנִים

יא סֹלֶת מִנְחָה בְּלוּלָה בַשֶּׁמֶן וְלֹג אֶחָד שָׁמֶן: וְהֶעֱמִיד
הַכֹּהֵן הַמְטַהֵר אֵת הָאִישׁ הַמִּטַּהֵר וְאֹתָם לִפְנֵי יְהוָה

of the eruption and cleanse him; and he shall set the live bird free in the open country. **8]** The one to be cleansed shall wash his clothes, shave off all his hair, and bathe in water; then he shall be clean. After that he may enter the camp, but he must remain outside his tent seven days. **9]** On the seventh day he shall shave off all his hair—of head, beard and eyebrows. When he has shaved off all his hair, he shall wash his clothes and bathe his body in water; then he shall be clean. **10]** On the eighth day he shall take two male lambs without blemish, one ewe lamb in its first year without blemish, three tenths of a measure of choice flour with oil mixed in for a meal offering, and one *log* of oil. **11]** These shall be presented before the LORD, with the man to be cleansed, at the entrance of the Tent of Meeting, by the priest who performs the cleansing.

8] *Then he shall be clean.* He is permitted to return to the camp/city; but the rites of purification are not finished.

Remain outside his tent. He must refrain from relations with his wife, according to tradition (see Gleanings); but the intent may be literal.

9] *He shall be clean.* But he must wait to enter the sanctuary until the sacrifices have been performed;

therefore he comes only to the entrance of the Tent of Meeting (verse 11). In the days of the Second Temple, the candidate for purification stood at the Nicanor Gate, just outside the holy area.

10] *Log of oil.* Olive oil is a familiar symbol of purity. The log was a liquid measure, probably less than a pint.

יב פֶּתַח אֹהֶל מוֹעֵד: וְלָקַח הַכֹּהֵן אֶת־הַכֶּבֶשׂ הָאֶחָד

וְהִקְרִיב אֹתוֹ לְאָשָׁם וְאֶת־לֹג הַשָּׁמֶן וְהֵנִיף אֹתָם

יג תְּנוּפָה לִפְנֵי יְהוָה: וְשָׁחַט אֶת־הַכֶּבֶשׂ בִּמְקוֹם אֲשֶׁר

יִשְׁחַט אֶת־הַחַטָּאת וְאֶת־הָעֹלָה בִּמְקוֹם הַקֹּדֶשׁ כִּי

יד כַּחַטָּאת הָאָשָׁם הוּא לַכֹּהֵן קֹדֶשׁ קָדָשִׁים הוּא: וְלָקַח

הַכֹּהֵן מִדַּם הָאָשָׁם וְנָתַן הַכֹּהֵן עַל־תְּנוּךְ אֹזֶן הַמִּטַּהֵר

הַיְמָנִית וְעַל־בֹּהֶן יָדוֹ הַיְמָנִית וְעַל־בֹּהֶן רַגְלוֹ הַיְמָנִית:

טו וְלָקַח הַכֹּהֵן מִלֹּג הַשָּׁמֶן וְיָצַק עַל־כַּף הַכֹּהֵן

טז הַשְּׂמָאלִית: וְטָבַל הַכֹּהֵן אֶת־אֶצְבָּעוֹ הַיְמָנִית מִן

הַשֶּׁמֶן אֲשֶׁר עַל־כַּפּוֹ הַשְּׂמָאלִית וְהִזָּה מִן־הַשֶּׁמֶן

יז בְּאֶצְבָּעוֹ שֶׁבַע פְּעָמִים לִפְנֵי יְהוָה: וּמִיֶּתֶר הַשֶּׁמֶן

Leviticus 14

12–17

12] The priest shall take one of the male lambs and offer it with the *log* of oil as a guilt offering, and he shall wave them as a wave offering before the LORD. 13] The lamb shall be slaughtered at the spot in the sacred area where the sin offering and the burnt offering are slaughtered. For the guilt offering, like the sin offering, goes to the priest; it is most holy. 14] The priest shall take some of the blood of the guilt offering, and the priest shall put it on the ridge of the right ear of him who is being cleansed, and on the thumb of his right hand, and on the big toe of his right foot. 15] The priest shall then take some of the *log* of oil and pour it into the palm of his own left hand. 16] And the priest shall dip his right finger in the oil that is in the palm of his left hand and sprinkle some of the oil with his finger seven times before the LORD. 17] Some of the oil left in his palm shall be

---

12] *Shall wave them as a wave offering.* See commentary on 7:28ff. According to Saadia and others [3], the priest simply led the animal around the altar.

13] *Sin offering and the burnt offering are slaughtered.* See 1:11; 4:23 (T.N.).

14-17] The priest puts blood, and later oil, on the ear, thumb, and toe of the man being cleansed. See p. 71. The fact that the same procedure was followed for the consecration of a priest and the cleansing of a "leper" rules out moralizing explanations.

אֲשֶׁר עַל־כַּפּוֹ יִתֵּן הַכֹּהֵן עַל־תְּנוּךְ אֹזֶן הַמִּטַּהֵר
הַיְמָנִית וְעַל־בֹּהֶן יָדוֹ הַיְמָנִית וְעַל־בֹּהֶן רַגְלוֹ הַיְמָנִית

יח עַל דַּם הָאָשָׁם: וְהַנּוֹתָר בַּשֶּׁמֶן אֲשֶׁר עַל־כַּף הַכֹּהֵן
יִתֵּן עַל־רֹאשׁ הַמִּטַּהֵר וְכִפֶּר עָלָיו הַכֹּהֵן לִפְנֵי יְהֹוָה:

יט וְעָשָׂה הַכֹּהֵן אֶת־הַחַטָּאת וְכִפֶּר עַל־הַמִּטַּהֵר

כ מִטֻּמְאָתוֹ וְאַחַר יִשְׁחַט אֶת־הָעֹלָה: וְהֶעֱלָה הַכֹּהֵן
אֶת־הָעֹלָה וְאֶת־הַמִּנְחָה הַמִּזְבֵּחָה וְכִפֶּר עָלָיו הַכֹּהֵן

כא וְטָהֵר: ס וְאִם־דַּל הוּא וְאֵין יָדוֹ מַשֶּׂגֶת וְלָקַח כֶּבֶשׂ
אֶחָד אָשָׁם לִתְנוּפָה לְכַפֵּר עָלָיו וְעִשָּׂרוֹן סֹלֶת אֶחָד

כב בָּלוּל בַּשֶּׁמֶן לְמִנְחָה וְלֹג שָׁמֶן: וּשְׁתֵּי תֹרִים אוֹ שְׁנֵי
בְּנֵי יוֹנָה אֲשֶׁר תַּשִּׂיג יָדוֹ וְהָיָה אֶחָד חַטָּאת וְהָאֶחָד

כג עֹלָה: וְהֵבִיא אֹתָם בַּיּוֹם הַשְּׁמִינִי לְטָהֳרָתוֹ אֶל־הַכֹּהֵן

put by the priest on the ridge of the right ear of the one being cleansed, on the thumb of his right hand, and on the big toe of his right foot—over the blood of the guilt offering.   18] The rest of the oil in his palm the priest shall put on the head of the one being cleansed. Thus the priest shall make expiation for him before the LORD. 19] The priest shall then offer the sin offering and make expiation for the one being cleansed of his uncleanness. Lastly, the burnt offering shall be slaughtered,   20] and the priest shall offer the burnt offering and the meal offering on the altar, and the priest shall make expiation for him. Then he shall be clean.

21] If, however, he is poor and his means are insufficient, he shall take one male lamb for a guilt offering, to be waved in expiation for him, one-tenth of a measure of choice flour with oil mixed in for a meal offering, and a *log* of oil;   22] and two turtledoves or two pigeons, which are within his means, the one to be the sin offering and the other the burnt offering.   23] On the eighth day of his cleansing he

אֶל־פֶּתַח אֹֽהֶל־מוֹעֵד לִפְנֵי יְהוָֽה: וְלָקַח הַכֹּהֵן אֶת־ כד
כֶּבֶשׂ הָֽאָשָׁם וְאֶת־לֹג הַשָּׁמֶן וְהֵנִיף אֹתָם הַכֹּהֵן תְּנוּפָה
לִפְנֵי יְהוָֽה: וְשָׁחַט אֶת־כֶּבֶשׂ הָֽאָשָׁם וְלָקַח הַכֹּהֵן מִדַּם כה
הָֽאָשָׁם וְנָתַן עַל־תְּנוּךְ אֹֽזֶן־הַמִּטַּהֵר הַיְמָנִית וְעַל־בֹּהֶן
יָדוֹ הַיְמָנִית וְעַל־בֹּהֶן רַגְלוֹ הַיְמָנִֽית: וּמִן־הַשֶּׁמֶן יִצֹק כו
הַכֹּהֵן עַל־כַּף הַכֹּהֵן הַשְּׂמָאלִֽית: וְהִזָּה הַכֹּהֵן כז
בְּאֶצְבָּעוֹ הַיְמָנִית מִן־הַשֶּׁמֶן אֲשֶׁר עַל־כַּפּוֹ הַשְּׂמָאלִית
שֶׁבַע פְּעָמִים לִפְנֵי יְהוָֽה: וְנָתַן הַכֹּהֵן מִן־הַשֶּׁמֶן אֲשֶׁר כח
עַל־כַּפּוֹ עַל־תְּנוּךְ אֹזֶן הַמִּטַּהֵר הַיְמָנִית וְעַל־בֹּהֶן יָדוֹ
הַיְמָנִית וְעַל־בֹּהֶן רַגְלוֹ הַיְמָנִית עַל־מְקוֹם דַּם הָאָשָֽׁם:
וְהַנּוֹתָר מִן־הַשֶּׁמֶן אֲשֶׁר עַל־כַּף הַכֹּהֵן יִתֵּן עַל־רֹאשׁ כט
הַמִּטַּהֵר לְכַפֵּר עָלָיו לִפְנֵי יְהוָֽה: וְעָשָׂה אֶת־הָֽאֶחָד ל

shall bring them to the priest at the entrance of the Tent of Meeting, before the
LORD.   24] The priest shall take the lamb of guilt offering and the *log* of oil, and
wave them as a wave offering before the LORD.   25] When the lamb of guilt offering has been slaughtered, the priest shall take some of the blood of the guilt
offering and put it on the ridge of the right ear of the one being cleansed, on the
thumb of his right hand, and on the big toe of his right foot.   26] The priest shall
then pour some of the oil into the palm of his own left hand,   27] and with the
finger of his right hand the priest shall sprinkle some of the oil that is in the palm
of his left hand seven times before the LORD.   28] Some of the oil in his palm shall
be put by the priest on the ridge of the right ear of the one being cleansed, on the
thumb of his right hand, and on the big toe of his right foot, over the same places
as the blood of the guilt offering;   29] and what is left of the oil in his palm the
priest shall put on the head of the one being cleansed, to make expiation for him
before the LORD.   30] He shall then offer one of the turtledoves or pigeons, de-

לא מִן־הַתֹּרִים אוֹ מִן־בְּנֵי הַיּוֹנָה מֵאֲשֶׁר תַּשִּׂיג יָדוֹ: אֶת
אֲשֶׁר־תַּשִּׂיג יָדוֹ אֶת־הָאֶחָד חַטָּאת וְאֶת־הָאֶחָד עֹלָה
עַל־הַמִּנְחָה וְכִפֶּר הַכֹּהֵן עַל הַמִּטַּהֵר לִפְנֵי יְהוָה:

לב זֹאת תּוֹרַת אֲשֶׁר־בּוֹ נֶגַע צָרָעַת אֲשֶׁר לֹא־תַשִּׂיג יָדוֹ
בְּטָהֳרָתוֹ: פ

pending on his means— **31]** whichever he can afford—the one as a sin offering and the other as a burnt offering, together with the meal offering. Thus the priest shall make expiation before the Lord for the one being cleansed. **32]** Such shall be the ritual for him who has a scaly affection and whose means for his cleansing are limited.

GLEANINGS

Halachah

14:5] *Slaughtered*

See commentary. The halachah also required the priest to dig a hole and bury the dead bird as soon as the blood was poured into the vessel thus stressing the nonsacrificial character of the rite (*Sifra*). Because it was not a sacrifice, this rite could be performed even after the Temple was destroyed. Rabbi Tarfon (end of first and beginning of second century c.e.), who was of priestly descent, stated that he conducted the ceremony on three occasions [4]. No later instance seems to be recorded.

7] *In the Open Country [or Field]*

Not in the direction of the sea, of a desert, or of a city. Should the bird later return, it may be eaten.   SIFRA

8] *Remain outside His Tent*

The separation of man and wife is only for this seven-day period of purification. Previously, while the man was still unclean, his wife was allowed to live with him outside the camp [5].

19] *The Meal Offering*

Not an independent *minchah* with frankincense, but simply the meal offering that regularly accompanies animal sacrifice (Num. 28:12 and elsewhere).   SIFRA

Haggadah

14:4] *Birds*

He was smitten because he engaged in gossip (p. 133); therefore his purification is accomplished by small birds that constantly chirp and chatter [6].

Cedar Wood ... Hyssop

Why is the "leper" to be purified through the tallest of trees and the lowliest of plants? He was stricken because he exalted himself like the cedar; but when he abases himself like the hyssop, he will be healed [7].

Tzara'at of Houses

The phenomenon described in this section suggests some sort of fungus growth, such as mildew. It does not seem to have been common in Palestine. An early talmudic statement denies that any case of the sort ever occurred—this passage was included in the Torah only that we may acquire merit by studying it. And the scholars who questioned this assertion could offer only hearsay evidence of houses afflicted by the plague [1].

In ancient Mesopotamia, however, such manifestations were more frequent—or at least were taken more seriously. Preoccupied as they were with methods of forecasting the future, the Babylonians saw omens also in the changed appearance of buildings [2]. It may be that the appearance of *tzara'at* on garments, and even in human beings, was also utilized for divination [3].

Certainly the biblical author was dealing with what he regarded as an actual fact of experience. The law here is more severe than that for the human "leper." The latter might recover after having been declared unclean; but, if remedial measures did not check the spread of the affection in a house, all hope for a cure was abandoned and the house had to be demolished.

If the removal of stones, scraping, and replastering were effective, the house was to be purified by a rite with two birds, virtually identical with that prescribed above for the cured human being. This fact suggests that the sacrificial rites of verses 10ff. may have been an addition to the older procedure.

לג וַיְדַבֵּר יְהוָה אֶל־מֹשֶׁה וְאֶל־אַהֲרֹן לֵאמֹר: כִּי תָבֹאוּ אֶל־אֶרֶץ כְּנַעַן אֲשֶׁר אֲנִי נֹתֵן לָכֶם לַאֲחֻזָּה וְנָתַתִּי נֶגַע

לד צָרַעַת בְּבֵית אֶרֶץ אֲחֻזַּתְכֶם: וּבָא אֲשֶׁר־לוֹ הַבַּיִת

לה וְהִגִּיד לַכֹּהֵן לֵאמֹר כְּנֶגַע נִרְאָה לִי בַּבָּיִת: וְצִוָּה הַכֹּהֵן וּפִנּוּ אֶת־הַבַּיִת בְּטֶרֶם יָבֹא הַכֹּהֵן לִרְאוֹת אֶת־הַנֶּגַע וְלֹא יִטְמָא כָּל־אֲשֶׁר בַּבָּיִת וְאַחַר כֵּן יָבֹא הַכֹּהֵן

לו לִרְאוֹת אֶת־הַבָּיִת: וְרָאָה אֶת־הַנֶּגַע וְהִנֵּה הַנֶּגַע בְּקִירֹת הַבַּיִת שְׁקַעֲרוּרֹת יְרַקְרַקֹּת אוֹ אֲדַמְדַּמֹּת

לז וּמַרְאֵיהֶן שָׁפָל מִן־הַקִּיר: וְיָצָא הַכֹּהֵן מִן־הַבַּיִת אֶל־

33] The LORD spoke to Moses and Aaron, saying:

34] When you enter the land of Canaan which I give you as a possession, and I inflict an eruptive plague upon a house in the land you possess,   35] the owner of the house shall come and tell the priest, saying "Something like a plague has appeared upon my house."   36] The priest shall order the house cleared before the priest enters to examine the plague, so that nothing in the house may become unclean; after that the priest shall enter to examine the house.   37] If, when he examines the plague, the plague in the walls of the house is found to consist of greenish or reddish streaks, which appear to go deep into the wall,   38] the priest shall come out of the house to the entrance of the house, and close up the house for seven

14:34] *When you enter the land.* During the desert wanderings, the Israelites lived in tents or booths, not permanent houses.

An eruptive plague. Hebrew *nega' tzara'at.* See commentary on 13:2.

35] *Something like a plague.* The owner should not attempt a positive diagnosis which must be left to the priest (*Sifra*).

36] *Order the house cleared.* The contents of the house did not become ritually defiled until the priest declared the house infected. The owner may protect himself against loss by removing his belongings in advance of the examination (see p. 116).

37] *Greenish.* Or, "yellowish" (T.N.).

Reddish streaks. Meaning of Hebrew *sheka 'arurot* uncertain (T.N.).

38] *Close up the house.* Order it closed so that people know to avoid it. Verses 46 and 47 imply that it was not literally locked up.

לט פֶּתַח הַבַּיִת וְהִסְגִּיר אֶת־הַבַּיִת שִׁבְעַת יָמִים: וְשָׁב

הַכֹּהֵן בַּיּוֹם הַשְּׁבִיעִי וְרָאָה וְהִנֵּה פָּשָׂה הַנֶּגַע בְּקִירֹת

מ הַבָּיִת: וְצִוָּה הַכֹּהֵן וְחִלְּצוּ אֶת־הָאֲבָנִים אֲשֶׁר בָּהֵן

הַנָּגַע וְהִשְׁלִיכוּ אֶתְהֶן אֶל־מִחוּץ לָעִיר אֶל־מָקוֹם

מא טָמֵא: וְאֶת־הַבַּיִת יַקְצִעַ מִבַּיִת סָבִיב וְשָׁפְכוּ אֶת־

הֶעָפָר אֲשֶׁר הִקְצוּ אֶל־מִחוּץ לָעִיר אֶל־מָקוֹם טָמֵא:

מב וְלָקְחוּ אֲבָנִים אֲחֵרוֹת וְהֵבִיאוּ אֶל־תַּחַת הָאֲבָנִים

מג וְעָפָר אַחֵר יִקַּח וְטָח אֶת־הַבָּיִת: וְאִם־יָשׁוּב הַנֶּגַע

וּפָרַח בַּבַּיִת אַחַר חִלֵּץ אֶת־הָאֲבָנִים וְאַחֲרֵי הִקְצוֹת

מד אֶת־הַבַּיִת וְאַחֲרֵי הִטּוֹחַ: וּבָא הַכֹּהֵן וְרָאָה וְהִנֵּה פָּשָׂה

הַנֶּגַע בַּבָּיִת צָרַעַת מַמְאֶרֶת הִוא בַּבַּיִת טָמֵא הוּא:

Leviticus 14

39–44

days.   39] On the seventh day the priest shall return. If he sees that the plague
has spread on the walls of the house,   40] the priest shall order the stones with
the plague in them to be pulled out and cast outside the city into an unclean place.
41] The house shall be scraped inside all around, and the coating that is scraped off
shall be dumped outside the city in an unclean place.   42] They shall take other
stones and replace those stones with them, and take other coating and plaster the
house.

43] If the plague again breaks out in the house, after the stones have been pulled
out and after the house has been scraped and replastered,   44] the priest shall
come to examine: if the plague has spread in the house, it is a malignant eruption

40] *An unclean place.* Depositing this material would
make the place unclean; but, presumably, it was
left at a regular dump for ritually unclean materials,
which those in a state of ritual purity would avoid.

41] *Coating.* Literally, "dust," "mud" (T.N.).
42] *Plaster the house.* With fresh mud. Lime plaster
was known, but it was used for mortar and for
caulking cisterns rather than to cover stone or wooden
walls.

מה וְנָתַץ אֶת־הַבַּיִת אֶת־אֲבָנָיו וְאֶת־עֵצָיו וְאֵת כָּל־עֲפַר
הַבָּיִת וְהוֹצִיא אֶל־מִחוּץ לָעִיר אֶל־מָקוֹם טָמֵא:

מו וְהַבָּא אֶל־הַבַּיִת כָּל־יְמֵי הִסְגִּיר אֹתוֹ יִטְמָא עַד־
הָעָרֶב: וְהַשֹּׁכֵב בַּבַּיִת יְכַבֵּס אֶת־בְּגָדָיו וְהָאֹכֵל בַּבַּיִת

מח יְכַבֵּס אֶת־בְּגָדָיו: וְאִם־בֹּא יָבֹא הַכֹּהֵן וְרָאָה וְהִנֵּה
לֹא־פָשָׂה הַנֶּגַע בַּבַּיִת אַחֲרֵי הִטֹּחַ אֶת־הַבָּיִת וְטִהַר

מט הַכֹּהֵן אֶת־הַבַּיִת כִּי נִרְפָּא הַנָּגַע: וְלָקַח לְחַטֵּא אֶת־
הַבַּיִת שְׁתֵּי צִפֳּרִים וְעֵץ אֶרֶז וּשְׁנִי תוֹלַעַת וְאֵזֹב:

נ וְשָׁחַט אֶת־הַצִּפֹּר הָאֶחָת אֶל־כְּלִי־חֶרֶשׂ עַל־מַיִם

נא חַיִּים: וְלָקַח אֶת־עֵץ־הָאֶרֶז וְאֶת־הָאֵזֹב וְאֵת שְׁנִי
הַתּוֹלַעַת וְאֵת הַצִּפֹּר הַחַיָּה וְטָבַל אֹתָם בְּדַם הַצִּפֹּר
הַשְּׁחוּטָה וּבַמַּיִם הַחַיִּים וְהִזָּה אֶל־הַבַּיִת שֶׁבַע

נב פְּעָמִים: וְחִטֵּא אֶת־הַבַּיִת בְּדַם הַצִּפֹּר וּבַמַּיִם הַחַיִּים

in the house; it is unclean.   45] The house shall be torn down—its stones and timber
and all the coating on the house—and taken to an unclean place outside the city.

46] Whoever enters the house while it is closed up shall be unclean until evening.   47] Whoever sleeps in the house must wash his clothes, and whoever eats
in the house must wash his clothes.

48] If, however, the priest comes and sees that the plague has not spread in the
house after the house was replastered, the priest shall pronounce the house clean,
for the plague has healed.   49] To purge the house, he shall take two birds, cedar
wood, crimson stuff, and hyssop.   50] He shall slaughter the one bird over fresh
water in an earthen vessel.   51] He shall take the cedar wood, the hyssop, the
crimson stuff, and the live bird, and dip them in the blood of the slaughtered bird
and the fresh water, and sprinkle on the house seven times.   52] Having purged the

---

52, 53] *Purged. Expiation.* Clearly in a ritual sense. A house cannot be redeemed from sin.

וּבַצִּפֹּר הַחַיָּה וּבְעֵץ הָאֶרֶז וּבָאֵזֹב וּבִשְׁנִי הַתּוֹלָעַת:

נג וְשִׁלַּח אֶת־הַצִּפֹּר הַחַיָּה אֶל־מִחוּץ לָעִיר אֶל־פְּנֵי

נד הַשָּׂדֶה וְכִפֶּר עַל־הַבַּיִת וְטָהֵר: זֹאת הַתּוֹרָה לְכָל־

נה נֶגַע הַצָּרַעַת וְלַנָּתֶק: וּלְצָרַעַת הַבֶּגֶד וְלַבָּיִת: וְלַשְׂאֵת

נו

נז וְלַסַּפַּחַת וְלַבֶּהָרֶת: לְהוֹרֹת בְּיוֹם הַטָּמֵא וּבְיוֹם

הַטָּהֹר זֹאת תּוֹרַת הַצָּרָעַת: פ

house with the blood of the bird, the fresh water, the live bird, the cedar wood, the hyssop, and the crimson stuff,   53] he shall set the live bird free outside the city in the open country. Thus he shall make expiation for the house, and it shall be clean.

54] This is the procedure for every eruptive affection—for scalls,   55] for an eruption on a cloth or a house,   56] for swellings, for rashes, or for discolorations—57] to determine when they are unclean and when they are clean.

Such is the procedure concerning eruptions.

54–57] These verses are a formal summary of the contents of chapters 13 and 14.

GLEANINGS

Halachah

14:34] *Upon a House in the Land You Possess*

The law applies only in the Land of Israel and to houses owned by Israelites. SIFRA

46] *Whoever Enters the House*

The defiled person must take a ritual bath. SIFRA

47] *Whoever Sleeps . . . Whoever Eats*

If he enters the building briefly, he must bathe and remain unclean until evening. If he remains long enough to eat a light meal—still more, if he stays long enough to sleep—the defilement is more severe and he must wash his garments as well. SIFRA

Haggadah

14:34] *I Will Inflict*

Hebrew *venatati*, which can also mean "I will give." According to some haggadists, this passage is a promise. The Canaanites hid treasures in the walls of their houses. When Israel enters the land, God will send *tzara'at* upon these houses; they will have to be demolished and the Israelites will obtain the treasures [4].

Other preachers were less indulgent. Some regarded *tzara'at* of houses as a first warning to sinners. If they disregarded the warning, the plague would appear on their garments; and, if they still remained obdurate, it would afflict their bodies [5].

Still others saw this plague as the special punishment of the miser. If a person is asked for the loan of some grain or of an implement and replies meanly,

"I have none," the house of that person will be visited by *tzara'at*. When the dwelling is emptied, everyone will see what the miser owns and the miser's stinginess will be publicly revealed [6].

36] *Order the House Cleared*

To protect the owner from loss. Yet the only loss would be of pottery vessels which would have to be broken; and earthenware is cheap. (For wood and metal vessels could be purified by dipping; food could be consumed while the owner was in a state of impurity.) Now, if the Torah protects a presumed sinner even from minor loss, all the more does it seek to protect the righteous against serious loss!

SIFRA

Defilement by Discharge from the Sex Organs

For ancient man, as we have seen, birth was not only awesome but frightening; it was regarded as a source of ritual impurity (chapter 12). And death was the source of the most intense defilement (Num. 19). The sexual experience, too, was viewed as uncanny and, hence, as a source of ceremonial uncleanness.

The belief that the sex act is defiling was widespread. The Roman maidens who tended the sacred fire of Vesta had to remain permanently in a virgin state. Though celibacy is alien to the Jewish outlook, we read that, immediately before the revelation at Sinai, the Israelites were directed to stay pure by washing their clothes and remaining apart from their wives (Exod. 19:4f.). And the Rabbis assert that, whereas this separation of the sexes lasted only a few days for the people, Moses—who was to be constantly the recipient of revelation—practiced continence for the rest of his life [1].

Among many peoples, warriors refrained from sexual intercourse during a campaign, not merely to conserve their physical strength, but to avoid ritual contamination. This notion is found in various biblical passages. David's soldiers are permitted to eat "holy bread" because they have been apart

from women for three days (I Sam. 21:5ff.). Uriah, called home from the front, will not enter his house and sleep with his wife while his comrades are encamped in the open (II Sam. 11:11). According to the law of Deuteronomy, a soldier who has a nocturnal emission must leave the camp for a day and take a bath; at sundown he may rejoin his fellows (Deut. 23:11) [2].

Our chapter (verses 16–18) treats human semen as a source of defilement. One who has an emission, or a couple who has intercourse, or a person or object coming into contact with semen, all acquire a mild degree of uncleanness. Similar rules, often more stringent, are found among various other peoples.

Far more severe are the regulations concerning women during their monthly periods. Ancient man reacted to the phenomenon of menstruation with a horror that seems to us grotesque and hysterical, and the same is true of primitive man still today. "According to Pliny, the touch of a menstruous woman turned wine to vinegar, blighted crops, killed seedlings, blasted gardens, brought down the fruit from trees, dimmed mirrors, blunted razors, rusted iron and brass (especially at the waning of the moon), killed bees or at least drove them from their hives, caused mares to miscarry, and so forth" [3]. Many peoples went to extreme and even cruel lengths to protect themselves against any contact with menstrual blood. The onset of puberty in females was regarded as especially dangerous, and among many tribes adolescent girls were isolated for long periods [4].

Similar superstitions were current among Jews. A talmudic statement warns against a woman passing between two men or a man passing between two women; and a further comment explains that, if the woman is at the beginning of her period, she might bring about the death of one of the men and, if at the end, she might cause them to quarrel [5]. Nachmanides asserts that animals die if they consume menstrual blood. He further reports as a matter of experience that, if a menstruating woman stares at a mirror of polished iron, drops of blood will appear on it [6].

Our chapter does not explain why blood defiles; it simply states the rules involved. This is not, however, a simple "defilement of the body"; intercourse with a woman during her menses is a "defilement of the sacred" (p. 102) and is unconditionally forbidden; a violation entails the severest punishment (see 18:19 and 20:18).

In comparison with the taboos found in some societies, biblical law on this subject (verses 19-24) appears mild and rational. The woman must remain apart from her husband for seven days from the onset of her period. During this time, her person, her bedding, and anything she sits on convey ritual uncleanness. After the seven days, tradition requires her to take a ritual bath before she and her husband can share the same bed. The biblical text does not mention this immersion, but it is probably taken for granted since the bath is required for the lesser defilement of normal intercourse

(verse 18). We have called these provisions rational. This does not seem an overstatement in view of the physical difficulties many women suffer during menstruation, ranging from sleepiness to intense pain—to say nothing of the emotional tensions that often appear just before the start of the period. The law protects women from the importunities of their husbands at a time when they are not physically and emotionally ready for coitus.

The Talmud ascribed a psychological benefit to this enforced abstinence. It prevents the marital act from becoming routine; reunited after the period of "uncleanness," the couple recaptures something of the honeymoon mood [7].

The ritual bath at the end of the period may be taken either in a "source"—spring, stream, sea—or in an artificial pool known as a *mikveh* (often incorrectly spelled *mikvah*). The laws of the *mikveh* were greatly elaborated by the rabbinic teachers (see Gleanings). They apply to all cases of defilement treated in these chapters, including the "dipping" of polluted objects. The downfall of the Temple made most laws of purity irrelevant; since then the *mikveh* has been used chiefly by married women after menstruation and by brides just before their marriage. It has, however, been regarded as an expression of piety for men to take a ritual bath, especially on the day before Yom Kippur, as a symbol of cleansing from sin.

The term *niddah*, "something to be shunned," "impurity," is applied in the Bible especially to the condition of a menstruating woman, in postbiblical literature to the woman herself. It is also the name of a tractate, in the Mishnah and Talmuds, that expounds the laws in great detail. The established halachah is in fact much more stringent than the rules as set forth in this chapter (see Gleanings).

Throughout the centuries, these laws were

conscientiously observed. A skeptic once said to Rav Kahana, "You permit a man to be alone with his wife during her period: Do you mean to say that fire can approach flax without kindling it?" The rabbi answered (by citing the words from Song of Songs 7:3, "hedged about with lilies"): The words of Torah, which are as tender as lilies, suffice to restrain them [8].

Today, however, it is certain that a large percentage of Jews do not follow the halachah strictly. This is evidenced by the fact that in many American communities there is no *mikveh* and in others the institution is maintained with great difficulty. It is probable that most Jewish couples refrain from intercourse while the wife is menstruating. The same applies, no doubt, to many non-Jewish Americans. The exaggerated fears of ancient men are not shared by all moderns, and it would be a mistake to assume a "natural revulsion." Men are not invariably finicky; and some women not only tolerate intercourse during menstruation but actively desire it [9].

This chapter also deals with defilement resulting when there is an abnormal discharge from the genitals. A man suffering from such a discharge is called *zav*, "one who flows," and the female equivalent is *zavah*. But the similarity is only in nomenclature. The *zavah* is one who continues to bleed beyond the normal period of her menses or who has bleeding at a different time of the month. (Such bleeding can be a symptom of serious ailments.) There is disagreement as to the discharge affecting the *zav*. Some students identify it as gonorrhea; others think it is only an exceptional discharge of mucus—a minor ailment called blennorrhea. The second view is supported by descriptions of the condition in rabbinic sources.

For both sexes, the "flow" entails major defilement. The patients, and anything they sleep, sit, or ride on, are a source of uncleanness until seven consecutive days pass without any discharge. Then, after a ritual bath, sacrifices of purgation must be offered.

The biblical material is not presented in the order followed in this introduction. The rather haphazard arrangement of the chapter is: verses 1–15, the *zav*; verses 16–18, defilement by semen; verses 19–24, the *niddah*; verses 25–30, the *zavah*; verses 31–33, conclusion.

א וַיְדַבֵּר יְהֹוָה אֶל־מֹשֶׁה וְאֶל־אַהֲרֹן לֵאמֹר: דַּבְּרוּ אֶל־

בְּנֵי יִשְׂרָאֵל וַאֲמַרְתֶּם אֲלֵהֶם אִישׁ אִישׁ כִּי יִהְיֶה זָב

ג מִבְּשָׂרוֹ זוֹבוֹ טָמֵא הוּא: וְזֹאת תִּהְיֶה טֻמְאָתוֹ בְּזוֹבוֹ

רָר בְּשָׂרוֹ אֶת־זוֹבוֹ אוֹ־הֶחְתִּים בְּשָׂרוֹ מִזּוֹבוֹ טֻמְאָתוֹ

ד הִוא: כָּל־הַמִּשְׁכָּב אֲשֶׁר יִשְׁכַּב עָלָיו הַזָּב יִטְמָא וְכָל־

ה הַכְּלִי אֲשֶׁר־יֵשֵׁב עָלָיו יִטְמָא: וְאִישׁ אֲשֶׁר יִגַּע

בְּמִשְׁכָּבוֹ יְכַבֵּס בְּגָדָיו וְרָחַץ בַּמַּיִם וְטָמֵא עַד־הָעָרֶב:

ו וְהַיֹּשֵׁב עַל־הַכְּלִי אֲשֶׁר־יֵשֵׁב עָלָיו הַזָּב יְכַבֵּס בְּגָדָיו

ז וְרָחַץ בַּמַּיִם וְטָמֵא עַד־הָעָרֶב: וְהַנֹּגֵעַ בִּבְשַׂר הַזָּב

ח יְכַבֵּס בְּגָדָיו וְרָחַץ בַּמַּיִם וְטָמֵא עַד־הָעָרֶב: וְכִי־יָרֹק

Leviticus 15

1–8

1] The LORD spoke to Moses and Aaron, saying: 2] Speak to the Israelite people and say to them:

When any man has a discharge issuing from his member, he is unclean.   3] The
uncleanness from his discharge shall mean the following—whether his member runs
with the discharge or is stopped up so that there is no discharge, his uncleanness
means this: 4] Any bedding on which the one with the discharge lies shall be unclean, and every object on which he sits shall be unclean.   5] Anyone who touches
his bedding shall wash his clothes, bathe in water, and remain unclean until evening.
6] Whoever sits on an object on which the one with the discharge has sat shall wash
his clothes, bathe in water, and remain unclean until evening.   7] Whoever touches
the body of the one with the discharge shall wash his clothes, bathe in water, and
remain unclean until evening.   8] If one with a discharge spits on one who is clean,

15:1–15] For the probable nature of the discharge,
see p. 149.

2] *Member*. Literally, "flesh" (T.N.).

4–12] The virulent impurity of the *zav* is communicated to anything he touches, especially bedding,
seats, and the like, which are likely to have been in

direct contact with the affected parts and with the
discharge.

8] *Spits on one who is clean*. The halachah, logically
enough, states that the urine and feces of the *zav*
also defile (*Sifra*).

הַזָּב בַּטָּהוֹר וְכִבֶּס בְּגָדָיו וְרָחַץ בַּמַּיִם וְטָמֵא עַד־
הָעָרֶב: ‎9‎ וְכָל־הַמֶּרְכָּב אֲשֶׁר יִרְכַּב עָלָיו הַזָּב יִטְמָא:
וְכָל־הַנֹּגֵעַ בְּכֹל אֲשֶׁר יִהְיֶה תַחְתָּיו יִטְמָא עַד־הָעֶרֶב
וְהַנּוֹשֵׂא אוֹתָם יְכַבֵּס בְּגָדָיו וְרָחַץ בַּמַּיִם וְטָמֵא עַד־
הָעָרֶב: ‎11‎ וְכֹל אֲשֶׁר יִגַּע־בּוֹ הַזָּב וְיָדָיו לֹא־שָׁטַף בַּמַּיִם
וְכִבֶּס בְּגָדָיו וְרָחַץ בַּמַּיִם וְטָמֵא עַד־הָעָרֶב: וּכְלִי־
חֶרֶשׂ אֲשֶׁר־יִגַּע־בּוֹ הַזָּב יִשָּׁבֵר וְכָל־כְּלִי־עֵץ יִשָּׁטֵף
בַּמָּיִם: ‎13‎ וְכִי־יִטְהַר הַזָּב מִזּוֹבוֹ וְסָפַר לוֹ שִׁבְעַת יָמִים
לְטָהֳרָתוֹ וְכִבֶּס בְּגָדָיו וְרָחַץ בְּשָׂרוֹ בְּמַיִם חַיִּים

Leviticus 15
9–13

the latter shall wash his clothes, bathe in water, and remain unclean until evening.
9] Any means for riding which one with a discharge has mounted shall be unclean;
10] whoever touches anything that was under him shall be unclean until evening;
and whoever carries such things shall wash his clothes, bathe in water, and remain
unclean until evening.   11] If one with a discharge, without having rinsed his hands
in water, touches another person, that person shall wash his clothes, bathe in water,
and remain unclean until evening.   12] An earthen vessel which one with a discharge touches shall be broken; and any wooden implement shall be rinsed with
water.

13] When one with a discharge becomes clean of his discharge, he shall count
off seven days for his cleansing, wash his clothes, and bathe his body in fresh water;

9] *Any means for riding.* A saddle, girth, or blanket—
even the wooden pommel of a saddle (*Sifra*).

11] *Without having rinsed his hands in water.* The
sentence is puzzling. It implies that, if the *zav* has
just washed his hands, he may touch another person
without defiling that person—in contradiction to the
severe rules that precede and follow. Nor is there
any indication as to how long this rinsing would

neutralize the impurity of the *zav*. The Rabbis were
compelled to depart from the plain sense of the
words (see Gleanings).

12] See commentary on 6:21f., 11:33ff.

13] *Fresh water.* Literally, "living [i.e., running]
water." The *zav* (alone among the unclean persons
treated here) cannot purify himself in a *mikveh*, but
he must go to a spring, stream, lake, or sea.

יד וְטָהֵר: וּבַיּוֹם הַשְּׁמִינִי יִקַּח־לוֹ שְׁתֵּי תֹרִים אוֹ שְׁנֵי בְּנֵי
יוֹנָה וּבָא לִפְנֵי יְהוָה אֶל־פֶּתַח אֹהֶל מוֹעֵד וּנְתָנָם
טו אֶל־הַכֹּהֵן: וְעָשָׂה אֹתָם הַכֹּהֵן אֶחָד חַטָּאת וְהָאֶחָד
טז עֹלָה וְכִפֶּר עָלָיו הַכֹּהֵן לִפְנֵי יְהוָה מִזּוֹבוֹ: ס וְאִישׁ
כִּי־תֵצֵא מִמֶּנּוּ שִׁכְבַת־זָרַע וְרָחַץ בַּמַּיִם אֶת־כָּל־בְּשָׂרוֹ
יז וְטָמֵא עַד־הָעָרֶב: וְכָל־בֶּגֶד וְכָל־עוֹר אֲשֶׁר־יִהְיֶה
עָלָיו שִׁכְבַת־זָרַע וְכֻבַּס בַּמַּיִם וְטָמֵא עַד־הָעָרֶב:
יח וְאִשָּׁה אֲשֶׁר יִשְׁכַּב אִישׁ אֹתָהּ שִׁכְבַת־זָרַע וְרָחֲצוּ
בַמַּיִם וְטָמְאוּ עַד־הָעָרֶב: פ
יט וְאִשָּׁה כִּי־תִהְיֶה זָבָה דָּם יִהְיֶה זֹבָהּ בִּבְשָׂרָהּ שִׁבְעַת
יָמִים תִּהְיֶה בְנִדָּתָהּ וְכָל־הַנֹּגֵעַ בָּהּ יִטְמָא עַד־הָעָרֶב:

Leviticus 15

14–19

then he shall be clean. **14]** On the eighth day he shall take two turtledoves or two pigeons and come before the LORD at the entrance of the Tent of Meeting and give them to the priest. **15]** The priest shall offer them, the one as a sin offering and the other as a burnt offering. Thus the priest shall make expiation on his behalf, for his discharge, before the LORD.

16] When a man has an emission of semen, he shall bathe his whole body in water and remain unclean until evening. **17]** All cloth or leather on which semen falls shall be washed in water and remain unclean until evening. **18]** And if a man has carnal relations with a woman, they shall bathe in water and remain unclean until evening.

19] When a woman has a discharge, her discharge being blood from her body, she shall remain in her impurity seven days; whoever touches her shall be unclean

16] Cf. Deut. 23:11f.

18] *Carnal relations with a woman.* The English phraseology is an attempt to make passable prose out of a somewhat unusual Hebrew sentence. There is no implication that the woman is not the man's wife or that the marital act is in any way degrading or sinful.

19–24] The impurity of the menstruating woman

כ וְכֹל אֲשֶׁר תִּשְׁכַּב עָלָיו בְּנִדָּתָהּ יִטְמָא וְכֹל אֲשֶׁר־תֵּשֵׁב

עָלָיו יִטְמָא: כא וְכָל־הַנֹּגֵעַ בְּמִשְׁכָּבָהּ יְכַבֵּס בְּגָדָיו וְרָחַץ

בַּמַּיִם וְטָמֵא עַד־הָעָרֶב: כב וְכָל־הַנֹּגֵעַ בְּכָל־כְּלִי אֲשֶׁר־

תֵּשֵׁב עָלָיו יְכַבֵּס בְּגָדָיו וְרָחַץ בַּמַּיִם וְטָמֵא עַד־

הָעָרֶב: כג וְאִם עַל־הַמִּשְׁכָּב הוּא אוֹ עַל־הַכְּלִי אֲשֶׁר־

הִוא יֹשֶׁבֶת־עָלָיו בְּנָגְעוֹ־בוֹ יִטְמָא עַד־הָעָרֶב: כד וְאִם

שָׁכֹב יִשְׁכַּב אִישׁ אֹתָהּ וּתְהִי נִדָּתָהּ עָלָיו וְטָמֵא

שִׁבְעַת יָמִים וְכָל־הַמִּשְׁכָּב אֲשֶׁר־יִשְׁכַּב עָלָיו

יִטְמָא: ס כה וְאִשָּׁה כִּי־יָזוּב זוֹב דָּמָהּ יָמִים רַבִּים

בְּלֹא עֶת־נִדָּתָהּ אוֹ כִי־תָזוּב עַל־נִדָּתָהּ כָּל־יְמֵי זוֹב

until evening. **20]** Anything that she lies on during her impurity shall be unclean; and anything that she sits on shall be unclean. **21]** Anyone who touches her bedding shall wash his clothes, bathe in water, and remain unclean until evening; **22]** and anyone who touches any object on which she has sat shall wash his clothes, bathe in water, and remain unclean until evening. **23]** Be it the bedding or be it the object on which she has sat, on touching it he shall be unclean until evening. **24]** And if a man lies with her, her impurity is communicated to him; he shall be unclean seven days, and any bedding on which he lies shall become unclean.

25] When a woman has had a discharge of blood for many days, not at the time of her impurity, or when she has a discharge beyond her period of impurity, she

---

(*niddah*). Virtually the same rules about the transmission of defilement apply to the *niddah* and the *zav*. No mention is made of a ritual bath after menstruation, but the Rabbis reasonably inferred the requirement from verse 18.

24] This verse deals only with the ritual defilement that results from intercourse with a menstruating woman. The seriousness of the offense and its punishment are stated in 18:19, 20:18.

Seven days. From the time of the contact, not from the beginning of her period (*Sifra*).

153

כּי טֻמְאָתָהּ כִּימֵי נִדָּתָהּ תִּהְיֶה טְמֵאָה הִוא כָּל־הַמִּשְׁכָּב
אֲשֶׁר־תִּשְׁכַּב עָלָיו כָּל־יְמֵי זוֹבָהּ כְּמִשְׁכַּב נִדָּתָהּ יִהְיֶה־
לָהּ וְכָל־הַכְּלִי אֲשֶׁר תֵּשֵׁב עָלָיו טָמֵא יִהְיֶה כְּטֻמְאַת
כּי נִדָּתָהּ: וְכָל־הַנּוֹגֵעַ בָּם יִטְמָא וְכִבֶּס בְּגָדָיו וְרָחַץ
כּה בַּמַּיִם וְטָמֵא עַד־הָעָרֶב: וְאִם־טָהֲרָה מִזּוֹבָהּ וְסָפְרָה
כּט לָהּ שִׁבְעַת יָמִים וְאַחַר תִּטְהָר: וּבַיּוֹם הַשְּׁמִינִי תִּקַּח־
לָהּ שְׁתֵּי תֹרִים אוֹ שְׁנֵי בְּנֵי יוֹנָה וְהֵבִ֯יאָה אוֹתָם אֶל־
ל הַכֹּהֵן אֶל־פֶּתַח אֹהֶל מוֹעֵד: וְעָשָׂה הַכֹּהֵן אֶת־הָאֶחָד
חַטָּאת וְאֶת־הָאֶחָד עֹלָה וְכִפֶּר עָלֶיהָ הַכֹּהֵן לִפְנֵי
לא יְהֹוָה מִזּוֹב טֻמְאָתָהּ: וְהִזַּרְתֶּם אֶת־בְּנֵי־יִשְׂרָאֵל

* כט סלרע.

shall be unclean, as though at the time of her impurity, as long as her discharge
lasts: she shall be unclean.   26] Any bedding on which she lies while her discharge
lasts shall be for her like bedding during her impurity; and any object on which she
sits shall become unclean, as it does during her impurity: 27] whoever touches
them shall be unclean; he shall wash his clothes, bathe in water, and remain unclean
until evening.

28] When she becomes clean of her discharge, she shall count off seven days,
and after that she shall be clean.   29] On the eighth day she shall take two turtledoves or two pigeons, and bring them to the priest at the entrance of the Tent of
Meeting.   30] The priest shall offer the one as a sin offering and the other as a
burnt offering; and the priest shall make expiation on her behalf, for her unclean
discharge, before the LORD.

31] You shall put the Israelites on guard against their uncleanness, lest they

31] *Put the Israelites on guard.* Hebrew *vehizartem,*
from the same root as *nazir,* nazirite, one set apart
for a sacred function. Literally, "You shall set them

apart carefully from their uncleanness."
31–33] These verses conclude the section.

מִטֻּמְאָתָם וְלֹא יָמֻתוּ בְּטֻמְאָתָם בְּטַמְּאָם אֶת־מִשְׁכָּנִי
אֲשֶׁר בְּתוֹכָם: זֹאת תּוֹרַת הַזָּב וַאֲשֶׁר תֵּצֵא מִמֶּנּוּ לב
שִׁכְבַת־זֶרַע לְטֻמְאָה־בָהּ: וְהַדָּוָה בְּנִדָּתָהּ וְהַזָּב אֶת־ לג
זוֹבוֹ לַזָּכָר וְלַנְּקֵבָה וּלְאִישׁ אֲשֶׁר יִשְׁכַּב עִם־טְמֵאָה:

Haftarah Metzora, p. 378

die through their uncleanness by defiling My Tabernacle which is among them.

32] Such is the ritual concerning him who has a discharge: concerning him who has an emission of semen and becomes unclean thereby,   33] and concerning her who is in menstrual infirmity, and concerning anyone, male or female, who has a discharge, and concerning a man who lies with an unclean woman.

GLEANINGS

Halachah

15:4] *Any Bedding*

Even if the bed of the *zav* was covered by several layers of blankets, one who sat upon them would be defiled. SIFRA

5] *Bathe in Water*

The *mikveh*—which could be used for all immersions and dippings except that of the *zav* (verse 13)—was the subject of elaborate technical rules, codified in a treatise of the Mishnah called *Mikvaot*. It must contain a minimum of forty *se'ah* of water, about twenty-four cubic feet [10]. A *mikveh* is not ritually suitable if water is constantly flowing through it [11] —another indication that these laws are not hygienic in intent. The requirements for the *mikveh* are such that an ordinary bathtub or swimming pool cannot be used for ritual purification. That these rules were already known prior to the fall of the Second Temple is indicated by the fact that the *mikveh* discovered in the ruins of Masada conforms to them [12].

11] *Without Having Rinsed His Hands in Water*

See commentary. The Rabbis understand these words to mean, "One who has not yet recovered from the impurity and taken a ritual bath." Why, then, are the hands mentioned? To indicate that, for a valid immersion, the water must cover all external parts of the body, such as the hands, but need not touch inner surfaces. SIFRA

19] *She Shall Remain in Her Impurity Seven Days*

Because the rules of *niddah* are complicated and difficult, and the punishment for intercourse with a menstruant is so severe, the scholars and the pious Jewish women agreed, during the talmudic period, to apply the simpler but more stringent rules of the *zavah* to the *niddah* as well. The biblical law (verses 19ff.) requires abstention for seven days from the *onset* of the menstrual flow. The later regulation required the woman to count seven days from the time of the *cessation* of the flow, without further reappearance of blood, before she could take her bath and rejoin her husband [13]. A final formulation of the halachah added further stringencies, reducing still more the number of days each month when intercourse was permissible [14].

Haggadah

15:31] *Lest They Die through Their Uncleanness by Defiling My Tabernacle Which Is among Them*

Even though they are unclean, the Divine Presence still abides among them. SIFRA

PART V

The Day of Atonement

Yom Kippur

It is impossible to exaggerate the importance of Yom Kippur in the life of the Jewish people. Even the religiously indifferent respond to its call and crowd the synagogues. To the devout it is the climax and crown of the religious year. It has inspired uplifting prayers in prose and poetry and has evoked sublime music, of which the Kol Nidre melody is only the best known example. It has changed lives. Before seeking divine forgiveness, Jews have often settled quarrels and disagreements among themselves. The Catholic Aimé Pallière began his pilgrimage to Judaism as the result of entering a synagogue on Yom Kippur afternoon. In 1913, a brilliant young German Jew named Franz Rosenzweig, who was about to adopt the Christian religion, became one of the noblest teachers and saints of modern Jewry, following a Day of Atonement spent in a small Orthodox synagogue in Berlin.

1. The Message of the Day of Atonement

The message of the day is not one of national or ethnic loyalty. It speaks to each human being and seeks to bring each person into harmony with others and with God. Non-Jews might well participate in the worship of the day without feeling alien and without forsaking their own loyalties. And yet Jews perhaps never feel so deeply Jewish as when they join with their fellow Jews in the prayers of Yom Kippur.

This holy day as we know it was created by the Jewish people in the past two thousand years. The biblical section now before us hardly suggests anything of inwardness or of moral aspiration. One may well feel disappointed when reading in Leviticus, chapter 16, the outline of a complicated sacrificial service performed by the High Priest on behalf of the community, with the people as passive spectators. At the end of the chapter—almost as an afterthought—they are commanded to fast and abstain from work on the sacred day, but nothing is said about inner contrition, self-discipline, or higher standards of conduct. For this reason, the leaders of Reform Judaism replaced this chapter, the traditional Torah reading for Yom Kippur morning, by selections from Deuteronomy, chapters 29 and 30, which they deemed more appropriate.

They retained, however, the traditional Haftarah (Isa. 57:14–58:14) which declares that fasting and formal prayer are valueless unless they lead to moral regeneration and, above all, to the service of the weak and the unfortunate. This powerful sermon may indeed mark the beginning of the process by which the Day of Atonement was gradually transformed [1]. Most appropriate also is the afternoon Haftarah, the Book of Jonah, with its message of God's universal compassion and forgiveness.

But here we are concerned with the beginnings which seem so unpromising.

2. *The origins of Yom Kippur*

The Day of Atonement appears in the Bible only in the priestly writings. Except for an incidental allusion in Exodus (30:10), the present chapter is the first place where it is mentioned. The festival rules in other codes (Exod. 23:14ff. and 34:18–23; Deut. 16) are silent on the subject, and other biblical sources give no hint that such an observance was known. The earlier generations of biblical critics therefore inferred that Yom Kippur was a new creation of the postexilic priesthood. (The cryptic vision in Zech. 3, composed early in the postexilic period, seems to be a symbolic description of an emerging Yom Kippur ritual.)

This view no longer seems tenable, even for those who, like the present writer, believe that P in its present form was edited after the exile (p. xix). So archaic a ritual, especially the scapegoat ceremony, would hardly have been invented by men who had felt the impact of the great prophets and lived through the chastening experience of the Babylonian captivity.

The Babylonians, and probably other Semitic peoples, had an elaborate new year festival which extended over ten days; on the fifth day a ceremony was performed called *kuppuru*, in which a temple was ceremonially cleansed by rubbing its walls with the body of a beheaded ram, after which the head and trunk were thrown into a river [2]. Recent scholars have theorized that there was a similar observance in ancient Israel, and they have found some evidence in the Bible to support their conjectures. If they are correct, we must further suppose that at some date these rites were detached from the new year festival and assigned to a special day, known henceforth as *Yom ha-Kippurim* [3]. This, however, remains theory. What seems sure is that the rites are ancient and that what was at first a ritual only, or primarily, for the priests later became a religious occasion for the entire community.

3. *Azazel*

The most embarrassing feature of the ancient ritual is the sending of the "scapegoat" to Azazel. The latter was probably a demonic being, residing in the desert, whose abode was regarded as a focus of impurity. Various efforts were made to avoid this embarrassment. The old Greek translation takes *azazel* as a common noun meaning "dismissal." Others rendered the word "steep mountain," or "goat that departs," or understood Azazel to be the name of a place [4].

These apologetic efforts are not convincing. For apocryphal Jewish works, composed in the last few centuries before the Christian era, tell of angels who were lured by beautiful women into lust and, ultimately, into rebellion against God. In these writings, Azazel is one of the two leaders of the rebellion. And posttalmudic documents tell a similar story about two rebel angels, Uzza and Azzael—both variations of the name Azazel [5]. These mythological stories, which must have been widely known, seem to confirm the essentially demonic character of the old biblical Azazel.

The more responsible Jewish teachers avoided the mythological notion of rebel angels. The Talmud indeed refers frequently to Satan; but he is not, like the Satan of the New Testament, an enemy of God. He serves God as prosecutor, though at times he is overeager to get convictions. But, as we shall see, the notion of Satan as a hostile power, who must be overcome or appeased, was not entirely absent in talmudic times; and it emerged in much more open and emphatic form among the Kabalists of the Middle Ages [6].

The term "scapegoat" was apparently coined by William Tyndale, the first great English Bible translator. Thereafter, it came to be used for a person, animal, or object to which the impurity or guilt of a community was formally transferred and then removed. This concept, and the practices it inspired, is found among numberless peoples throughout the world [7]. But, in common usage today, a scapegoat is someone whom people blame for their own misfortunes, and even for their faults and sins—though the original notion of a scapegoat included the public acknowledgment by the community of its own transgressions [8].

4. The Hazards of the Yom Kippur Service

The opening verses of chapter 16 make plain that it was dangerous for the High Priest to enter the inner Shrine (Holy of Holies). The Deity was believed to be literally present, or present in a special degree, inside the Shrine, and too close an approach to divinity entailed risks. ("Man may not see Me and live," Exod. 33:20. In Greek myth, Semele was reduced to ashes when she saw Zeus in his full splendor.)

In addition to the danger of looking at God, to which the Torah plainly alludes, tradition found another hazard. Satan, it was believed, was present in the Holy of Holies, to accuse the Jews and their spokesman, the High Priest, before the divine court. This notion, suggested in Zechariah, chapter 3, is plainly expressed in many talmudic passages.

Because of these dangers, the High Priest in the days of the Second Temple would not linger in the inner Shrine so as not to worry the people waiting in the outer courts [9]. And at the close of the day he would give a banquet to his friends to celebrate his safe emergence from peril [10].

These facts serve to illuminate a controversy regarding verses 2, 12, and 13 of this chapter. The Sadducees, the priestly party, held that the High Priest should enter the Shrine carrying a firepan with incense smoking upon it. The Pharisees, the lay scholars, required him to carry the fire pan in one hand and a bowl of incense in the other; only after he had entered the Holy of Holies was he to put the incense on the burning coals. This second explanation fits the language of verses 12 and 13; yet in general it was the Sadducees who held to the literal sense of the Torah and the Pharisees who interpreted the text more freely. On this crucial point the priests must have had an ancient tradition!

This matter was explained brilliantly by Dr. Jacob Z. Lauterbach [11]. The priestly tradition, he held, sought to protect the High Priest by means of a "smoke screen." This would prevent him from seeing the Divine Presence, which could be fatal (verse 2). It would also serve to drive away Satan—in the folklore of many peoples, evil spirits are defeated by the use of smoke. The Pharisees opposed such superstitious beliefs and sent the High Priest into the sanctuary without this supposed protection. The offering of incense inside the Shrine ceased to be a security measure and was no more than one item of a prescribed ritual. But, despite this reform, the old beliefs survived to some extent.

5. Atonement and Return

In Scripture, this holy day is called the Day of the *Kippurim* (Lev. 23:27f., 25:9). The word probably comes from a root meaning "to cover up" [12]. It refers to the process by which guilt or impurity is canceled out, made nonexistent. It may be translated "expiation" which is defined as "the extinguishing of guilt by suffering or penalty." Similar words are found in other modern languages, but English has in addition the unique word, "atonement," from "at one." It designates the means by which a person estranged from God becomes at one with Him again. Though the word is peculiarly English, it expresses a biblical viewpoint. "Your sins have separated you from your God," says the prophet (Isa. 59:2); when the sin is annulled, the relationship to God is restored [13].

Kippurim and the cognate verb forms are applied in the Bible both to the canceling of guilt for moral offenses and to the purging away of ritual uncleanness (see 8:15 and 12:7 where earlier translations spoke of "atonement" for the altar and for a woman who bore a child). At the start, a clear line was not always drawn between ceremonial defilement and what we today would call sin. And, since ceremonial defilement could be corrected by ceremonial means, there was constant danger that men would rely on ritual procedures to annul moral guilt as well.

The prophets insisted that sacrificial rites alone cannot reconcile a human being to God. They held that sins are forgiven only if the sinner experiences a change of heart leading to a change of ways. They constantly urged people to turn back from evil conduct and to return to God (e.g., Ezek. 18:30; Hos. 14:2; Mal. 3:7). This theme was taken up by the talmudic and later Rabbis in their doctrine of *teshuvah*, "return"—roughly equivalent to "repentance," except that "repentance" refers chiefly to emotion while "return" more plainly involves action. In numberless sayings and parables, the Rabbis teach that, if a person makes the slightest attempt to change for the better, it is possible to count on a loving response from God (see Gleanings). In contrast with both biblical and later Judaism, which are concerned with the attitudes and behavior of each individual, the other religions of the ancient Near East imposed the requirements of cultic and moral purity chiefly upon the king.

Jewish literature has relatively little to say about the process of atonement and focuses rather on the turnabout, the fresh start made by a person. It is confidently expected that *teshuvah* will lead, ultimately if not always immediately (see Gleanings), to God's forgiveness. In contrast, generations of Christian theologians worked out elaborate theories of "the Atonement," endeavoring to explain how the death of Jesus operated to redeem humankind from original sin.

It is true that sacrifices were deemed to have expiatory power; but, as we have seen (pp. 27, 37), Leviticus limits this almost entirely to unintentional violations. The Rabbis held that the blood rites of Yom Kippur atoned for unrecognized defilement of the sanctuary and its sacrifices [14]. (Where defilement was known to have occurred, the prescribed sin offering was brought at once.) The sacrifices and the ceremony of the Azazel-goat were, it is true, thought to have genuine atoning power; they were joined to the confession recited by the High Priest. But the effect of these rites was contingent on the *teshuvah* of the worshipers. According to the Mishnah, an offense against a person cannot be wiped out either by ritual or by simple contrition. The sinner must attempt to rectify the wrong and seek the good will of the injured party. Moreover, one who sins with the intention of repenting afterward, or of obtaining pardon through the Yom Kippur rites, will not obtain forgiveness [15]. The Rabbis also held that, even after the fall of the Temple and the discontinuance of the sacrificial rites, Yom Kippur continued to have an atoning effect, when combined with *teshuvah* [16].

Shortly after the destruction, the disciples of Rabban Johanan ben Zakkai were mourning the loss of the altar as a means of atonement; thereupon the master assured them that acts of kindness and charity are equally efficacious [17]. The dictum that "*teshuvah*, prayer, and charity annul the degree of punishment" [18] was inserted into the prayer book (*Union Prayer Book*, II, pp. 256–257). Most remarkable, the lengthy confession recited on Yom Kippur in traditional synagogues (in much briefer form, *Union Prayer Book*, II, pp. 148ff.) enumerates only sins involving breach of the moral law, whereas such basic observances as Sabbath and dietary laws are not specifically mentioned [19]. Thus, the moral and spiritual aspects of the day triumphed over formal ritual.

6. *Some Problems of the Biblical Material*

Leviticus, chapter 16, presents a number of problems. It begins with the mention of the death of Nadab and Abihu and warns Aaron not to enter the Shrine without due preparation. This preparation is now described at length. It could be (and has been) understood as the ritual to be followed whenever the High Priest chooses to enter the inner Shrine. Only much farther on (verses 29f.) do we read that this ritual is to be an annual event on a specific date (the holy day is not given a name in this chapter) and that on the day in question the people must not eat nor work. This sequence of material suggests that the observance was originally for the priesthood alone and later became a public holy day.

The festival calendar in Leviticus, chapter 23, mentions the day by name for the first time; it announces severe punishment for eating or working on the Day of Atonement. But Numbers (29:7–11) gives a list of sacrifices which does not agree with Leviticus, chapter 16. Later authorities had to harmonize the two sources (both from P). During the days of the Second Temple, the High Priest performed, not only the special Yom Kippur rites, but (on this occasion) also the regular morning and evening sacrifices of lambs and incense (Exod. 29:38ff., 30:7f.). The complete order of the day, as fixed by the halachah, is outlined in Appendix II. It became the subject of poetic compositions during the Middle Ages, and these were incorporated into various versions of the prayer book. A reinterpretation of this material appears in the *Union Prayer Book*, II, pp. 265–274.

אחרי מות
ויקרא טז
א–ג

Achare Mot
Leviticus 16
1–3

א וַיְדַבֵּר יְהוָֹה אֶל־מֹשֶׁה אַחֲרֵי מוֹת שְׁנֵי בְּנֵי אַהֲרֹן
ב בְּקָרְבָתָם לִפְנֵי־יְהוָֹה וַיָּמֻתוּ: וַיֹּאמֶר יְהוָֹה אֶל־מֹשֶׁה
דַּבֵּר אֶל־אַהֲרֹן אָחִיךָ וְאַל־יָבֹא בְכָל־עֵת אֶל־הַקֹּדֶשׁ
מִבֵּית לַפָּרֹכֶת אֶל־פְּנֵי הַכַּפֹּרֶת אֲשֶׁר עַל־הָאָרֹן וְלֹא
ג יָמוּת כִּי בֶּעָנָן אֵרָאֶה עַל־הַכַּפֹּרֶת: בְּזֹאת יָבֹא אַהֲרֹן

1] The LORD spoke to Moses after the death of the two sons of Aaron who died when they drew too close to the presence of the LORD.   2] The LORD said to Moses: Tell your brother Aaron that he is not to come at will into the Shrine behind the curtain, in front of the cover that is upon the ark, lest he die; for I appear in the cloud over the cover.   3] Thus only shall Aaron enter the Shrine: with a bull of the herd

---

16:1] *After the death of the two sons of Aaron.* This phrase connects this chapter with chapter 10; the intervening sections on ritual impurity are a separate block of material.

When they drew too close. Went beyond the limits imposed on them. Ibn Ezra, following a few talmudic remarks, infers that Nadab and Abihu entered the Holy of Holies, since Aaron is now warned against doing so without proper preparation. But probably the sentence means simply, "They broke the rules and were punished; don't you break the rules or you will be punished."

2] *Your brother Aaron.* Moses was permitted to enter the Shrine at will to receive the divine revelation (Exod. 25:22; Num. 7:89); but Aaron did not have this privilege, even though he was Moses' brother (Sifra).

At will. Literally, "at any time" (T.N.).

For I appear in the cloud over the cover. This was understood by the Sadducees (p. 161) to mean "I may be looked at only through the cloud of incense." The Pharisees understood the words similarly, though they postponed the placing of the incense on the coals until the High Priest had entered the Shrine [20]. This explanation is preferred by Ibn Ezra and adopted by Nachmanides. Rashi and Rashbam, however, say it refers to a divinely ordained cloud (like the pillar of cloud that led Israel through the wilderness), not to a man-made cloud of smoke.

Cover. Hebrew *kaporet.* We have seen that *kippurim,* "atonement," very likely comes from a root meaning "to cover." The word *kaporet,* presumably from the same root, could mean either "lid" or "place of atonement." The second interpretation, which goes back to the old Greek translation, is more probable [21]. The Authorized Version, following Luther, rendered "mercy seat."

The Shrine. Hebrew *kodesh,* literally, "holiness." Here, as in chapter 4, verse 6, the term designates the innermost Shrine, called "Holy of Holies" in Exodus 23:33 and elsewhere. But sometimes the whole interior of the Tabernacle is called *kodesh* (e.g., Lev. 10:4).

3] *Thus only.* In accordance with the entire ritual to be set forth. The second half of the verse mentions

אֶל־הַקֹּדֶשׁ בְּפַר בֶּן־בָּקָר לְחַטָּאת וְאַיִל לְעֹלָה:

ד כְּתֹנֶת־בַּד קֹדֶשׁ יִלְבָּשׁ וּמִכְנְסֵי־בַד יִהְיוּ עַל־בְּשָׂרוֹ
וּבְאַבְנֵט בַּד יַחְגֹּר וּבְמִצְנֶפֶת בַּד יִצְנֹף בִּגְדֵי־קֹדֶשׁ
ה הֵם וְרָחַץ בַּמַּיִם אֶת־בְּשָׂרוֹ וּלְבֵשָׁם: וּמֵאֵת עֲדַת בְּנֵי
יִשְׂרָאֵל יִקַּח שְׁנֵי־שְׂעִירֵי עִזִּים לְחַטָּאת וְאַיִל אֶחָד
ו לְעֹלָה: וְהִקְרִיב אַהֲרֹן אֶת־פַּר הַחַטָּאת אֲשֶׁר־לוֹ
ז וְכִפֶּר בַּעֲדוֹ וּבְעַד בֵּיתוֹ: וְלָקַח אֶת־שְׁנֵי הַשְּׂעִירִם

Leviticus 16

4–7

for a sin offering and a ram for a burnt offering.— **4]** He shall be dressed in a sacral linen tunic, with linen breeches next to his flesh, and be girt with a linen sash, and he shall wear a linen turban. They are sacral vestments; he shall bathe his body in water and then put them on.— **5]** And from the Israelite community he shall take two he-goats for a sin offering and a ram for a burnt offering.

6] Aaron is to offer his own bull of sin offering, to make expiation for himself and for his household. **7]** Aaron shall take the two he-goats and let them stand

---

only one item; the bull and ram were, of course, not taken into the Shrine. In fact, the ram, as well as the one mentioned in verse 5, was not actually offered until late in the day (see verse 24).

4] *Linen tunic.* . . . Instead of the gorgeous vestments he customarily wore (Exod. 28), the High Priest was on this occasion to wear plain white linen. The Rabbis give many explanations of this rule (see Gleanings). This priestly rule is the source of the custom for men to wear a white robe (*kittel* or *sargenes*) during the Yom Kippur service.

5] *A ram.* The "burnt offering of the people" of verse 24.

6] *His own bull of sin offering.* Before he could make atonement for the people, he had to purge himself of sin. "Improve yourself first; then improve

others" [22]. The actual sacrifice did not, however, take place until later (verse 11); so the Rabbis, reasonably enough, understood the "offering" and "expiation" mentioned here as the confession recited by the High Priest with his hands on the head of the bull [23].

7–10] The designation of the goats for the Lord and for Azazel (see pp. 160–161). According to the Mishnah [24] the goats were stationed in front of the High Priest, one to his right and one to his left. Two disks, inscribed respectively "for the Lord" and "for Azazel," had been placed in an urn. The High Priest put both hands into the urn, picked up one disk in each hand, and placed them on the heads of the goats. It was considered a good omen if the disk for the Lord came up in his right hand.

7] *Aaron.* Moved up from verse 8 for clarity (T.N.).

ח וְהֶעֱמִיד אֹתָם לִפְנֵי יְהוָה פֶּתַח אֹהֶל מוֹעֵד: וְנָתַן

אַהֲרֹן עַל־שְׁנֵי הַשְּׂעִירִם גֹּרָלוֹת גּוֹרָל אֶחָד לַיהוָה

ט וְגוֹרָל אֶחָד לַעֲזָאזֵל: וְהִקְרִיב אַהֲרֹן אֶת־הַשָּׂעִיר

אֲשֶׁר עָלָה עָלָיו הַגּוֹרָל לַיהוָה וְעָשָׂהוּ חַטָּאת:

י וְהַשָּׂעִיר אֲשֶׁר עָלָה עָלָיו הַגּוֹרָל לַעֲזָאזֵל יָעֳמַד־חַי

לִפְנֵי יְהוָה לְכַפֵּר עָלָיו לְשַׁלַּח אֹתוֹ לַעֲזָאזֵל

יא הַמִּדְבָּרָה: וְהִקְרִיב אַהֲרֹן אֶת־פַּר הַחַטָּאת אֲשֶׁר־לוֹ

וְכִפֶּר בַּעֲדוֹ וּבְעַד בֵּיתוֹ וְשָׁחַט אֶת־פַּר הַחַטָּאת

יב אֲשֶׁר־לוֹ: וְלָקַח מְלֹא־הַמַּחְתָּה גַּחֲלֵי־אֵשׁ מֵעַל הַמִּזְבֵּחַ

מִלִּפְנֵי יְהוָה וּמְלֹא חָפְנָיו קְטֹרֶת סַמִּים דַּקָּה וְהֵבִיא

יג מִבֵּית לַפָּרֹכֶת: וְנָתַן אֶת־הַקְּטֹרֶת עַל־הָאֵשׁ לִפְנֵי

Leviticus 16

8–13

before the LORD at the entrance of the Tent of Meeting; 8] and he shall place
lots upon the two goats, one marked for the LORD and the other marked for Azazel.
9] Aaron shall bring forward the goat designated by lot for the LORD, which he is
to offer as a sin offering; 10] while the goat designated by lot for Azazel shall be
left standing alive before the LORD, to make expiation with it and to send it off to
the wilderness for Azazel.

11] Aaron shall then offer his bull of sin offering, to make expiation for himself
and his household. He shall slaughter his bull of sin offering, 12] and he shall take
a panful of glowing coals scooped from the altar before the LORD, and two handfuls
of finely ground aromatic incense, and bring this behind the curtain. 13] He shall

10–22] Sending away the scapegoat.

11] The bull of sin offering was now slaughtered; its
blood was to be sprinkled in the Shrine. But first the
incense rite had to be performed. Accordingly, the
bowl of blood was given to a priest who stirred it
constantly to keep the blood from congealing until

the High Priest was ready to use it [25]

12–13] The incense rite (see p. 161).
12] *Scooped from the altar before the Lord.* I.e., from
the bronze altar of sacrifice at the door of the sanctuary. There was not a constant fire on the small
incense altar.

166

יְהוָה וְכִסָּה עֲנַן הַקְּטֹרֶת אֶת־הַכַּפֹּרֶת אֲשֶׁר עַל־
הָעֵדוּת וְלֹא יָמוּת: וְלָקַח מִדַּם הַפָּר וְהִזָּה בְאֶצְבָּעוֹ
עַל־פְּנֵי הַכַּפֹּרֶת קֵדְמָה וְלִפְנֵי הַכַּפֹּרֶת יַזֶּה שֶׁבַע־
פְּעָמִים מִן־הַדָּם בְּאֶצְבָּעוֹ: וְשָׁחַט אֶת־שְׂעִיר הַחַטָּאת
אֲשֶׁר לָעָם וְהֵבִיא אֶת־דָּמוֹ אֶל־מִבֵּית לַפָּרֹכֶת וְעָשָׂה
אֶת־דָּמוֹ כַּאֲשֶׁר עָשָׂה לְדַם הַפָּר וְהִזָּה אֹתוֹ עַל־
הַכַּפֹּרֶת וְלִפְנֵי הַכַּפֹּרֶת: וְכִפֶּר עַל־הַקֹּדֶשׁ מִטֻּמְאֹת
בְּנֵי יִשְׂרָאֵל וּמִפִּשְׁעֵיהֶם לְכָל־חַטֹּאתָם וְכֵן יַעֲשֶׂה
לְאֹהֶל מוֹעֵד הַשֹּׁכֵן אִתָּם בְּתוֹךְ טֻמְאֹתָם: וְכָל־אָדָם

Leviticus 16

14–17

put the incense on the fire before the LORD, so that the cloud from the incense screens the cover that is over [the Ark of] the Pact, lest he die.   **14]** He shall take some of the blood of the bull and sprinkle it with his finger over the cover on the east side; and in front of the cover he shall sprinkle some of the blood with his finger seven times.   **15]** He shall then slaughter the people's goat of sin offering, bring its blood behind the curtain, and do with its blood as he has done with the blood of the bull: he shall sprinkle it over the cover and in front of the cover.

16] Thus he shall purge the Shrine of the uncleanness and transgression of the Israelites, whatever their sins; and he shall do the same for the Tent of Meeting, which abides with them in the midst of their uncleanness.   **17]** When he goes in

14–19] The blood rites. After offering the incense, the officiant went outside, got the bowl of bull's blood, brought it into the Shrine, and sprinkled some of the blood, once upward, seven times downward toward the ark cover. Then he went out again, the goat "for the Lord" was slaughtered, and he brought its blood into the Shrine and sprinkled it.

16] *Thus he shall purge the Shrine of the uncleanness and transgression.* The primary stress is on ritual purgation. If an individual discovered that he had

entered the sacred area or eaten consecrated food while he was in a state of ritual uncleanness, he immediately brought a sin offering (5:2f.). The Yom Kippur ceremonies neutralized defilement of which no one was aware. The reference to other sins may be a later insertion (see p. 162).

And he shall do the same for the Tent of Meeting. According to the halachah [26], he brought out the bowls of blood and, standing between the incense altar and the entrance of the Shrine, he sprinkled the blood of the bull and then that of the goat toward the curtain that closed the Shrine.

לֹא־יִהְיֶה בְּאֹהֶל מוֹעֵד בְּבֹאוֹ לְכַפֵּר בַּקֹּדֶשׁ עַד־
צֵאתוֹ וְכִפֶּר בַּעֲדוֹ וּבְעַד בֵּיתוֹ וּבְעַד כָּל־קְהַל
יח יִשְׂרָאֵל: וְיָצָא אֶל־הַמִּזְבֵּחַ אֲשֶׁר לִפְנֵי־יְהוָה וְכִפֶּר
עָלָיו וְלָקַח מִדַּם הַפָּר וּמִדַּם הַשָּׂעִיר וְנָתַן עַל־קַרְנוֹת
יט הַמִּזְבֵּחַ סָבִיב: וְהִזָּה עָלָיו מִן־הַדָּם בְּאֶצְבָּעוֹ שֶׁבַע
כ פְּעָמִים וְטִהֲרוֹ וְקִדְּשׁוֹ מִטֻּמְאֹת בְּנֵי יִשְׂרָאֵל: וְכִלָּה
מִכַּפֵּר אֶת־הַקֹּדֶשׁ וְאֶת־אֹהֶל מוֹעֵד וְאֶת־הַמִּזְבֵּחַ
כא וְהִקְרִיב אֶת־הַשָּׂעִיר הֶחָי: וְסָמַךְ אַהֲרֹן אֶת־שְׁתֵּי יָדוֹ*

Leviticus 16

18–21

עַל־רֹאשׁ הַשָּׂעִיר הַחַי וְהִתְוַדָּה עָלָיו אֶת־כָּל־עֲוֺנֹת
בְּנֵי יִשְׂרָאֵל וְאֶת־כָּל־פִּשְׁעֵיהֶם לְכָל־חַטֹּאתָם וְנָתַן

* כא ידיו קרי.

to make expiation in the Shrine, nobody else shall be in the Tent of Meeting until he comes out.

When he has made expiation for himself and his household, and for the whole congregation of Israel,   18] he shall go out to the altar that is before the LORD and purge it: he shall take some of the blood of the bull and of the goat and apply it to each of the horns of the altar;   19] and the rest of the blood he shall sprinkle on it with his finger seven times. Thus he shall cleanse it of the uncleanness of the Israelites and consecrate it.

20] When he has finished purging the Shrine, the Tent of Meeting, and the altar, the live goat shall be brought forward.   21] Aaron shall lay both his hands upon the head of the live goat and confess over it all the iniquities and transgressions of the Israelites, whatever their sins, putting them on the head of the goat; and it shall

18] *To the altar that is before the Lord.* This seems to mean the bronze altar of sacrifice, as in verse 12; so Ibn Ezra. But the talmudic sources (*Sifra* and others) insist that these rites are to be performed on the incense altar.

168

אֹתָם עַל־רֹאשׁ הַשָּׂעִיר וְשִׁלַּח בְּיַד־אִישׁ עִתִּי

כב הַמִּדְבָּרָה: וְנָשָׂא הַשָּׂעִיר עָלָיו אֶת־כָּל־עֲוֺנֹתָם אֶל־

כג אֶרֶץ גְּזֵרָה וְשִׁלַּח אֶת־הַשָּׂעִיר בַּמִּדְבָּר: וּבָא אַהֲרֹן

אֶל־אֹהֶל מוֹעֵד וּפָשַׁט אֶת־בִּגְדֵי הַבָּד אֲשֶׁר לָבַשׁ

כד בְּבֹאוֹ אֶל־הַקֹּדֶשׁ וְהִנִּיחָם שָׁם: וְרָחַץ אֶת־בְּשָׂרוֹ בַמַּיִם

בְּמָקוֹם קָדוֹשׁ וְלָבַשׁ אֶת־בְּגָדָיו וְיָצָא וְעָשָׂה אֶת־עֹלָתוֹ

כה וְאֶת־עֹלַת הָעָם וְכִפֶּר בַּעֲדוֹ וּבְעַד הָעָם: וְאֵת חֵלֶב

Leviticus 16
22–25

be sent off to the wilderness through a designated man.   **22]** Thus the goat shall carry on it all their iniquities to an inaccessible region; and the goat shall be set free in the wilderness.

23] And Aaron shall go into the Tent of Meeting, take off the linen vestments that he put on when he entered the Shrine, and leave them there.   **24]** He shall bathe his body in water in the holy precinct and put on his vestments; then he shall come out and offer his burnt offering and the burnt offering of the people, making expiation for himself and for the people.   **25]** The fat of the sin offering he shall turn into smoke on the altar.

21] *A designated man.* Meaning of Hebrew *'itti* uncertain (T.N.). Rashbam connects *'itti* with *et*, "time," and explains: a man well acquainted with the desert trails and ready to travel them at any time.

22] *Set free.* This was not the practice in the period of the Second Temple, when the goat was toppled over a cliff to its death (see Gleanings).

23] *And leave them there.* This enigmatic passage has troubled the commentators. Surely the white robes were not left lying indefinitely in the sacred area!

Is the "holy precinct" of verse 24 (the Hebrew is literally "in *a* sacred place") identical with the Tent of Meeting? Further, we must assume that other priests accompanied the High Priest to help him bathe and change, but the text mentions only Aaron. The talmudic rabbis dealt with the passage quite radically, but their reconstruction at least makes sense (see Gleanings).

24] *And put on his vestments.* I.e., his usual vestments, called by the Rabbis "the golden garments."

His burnt offering and the burnt offering of the people. A ram (see verses 3 and 5 above).

כו הַחַטָּאת יַקְטִיר הַמִּזְבֵּחָה: וְהַמְשַׁלֵּחַ אֶת־הַשָּׂעִיר
לַעֲזָאזֵל יְכַבֵּס בְּגָדָיו וְרָחַץ אֶת־בְּשָׂרוֹ בַּמָּיִם וְאַחֲרֵי־

כז כֵן יָבוֹא אֶל־הַמַּחֲנֶה: וְאֵת פַּר הַחַטָּאת וְאֵת שְׂעִיר
הַחַטָּאת אֲשֶׁר הוּבָא אֶת־דָּמָם לְכַפֵּר בַּקֹּדֶשׁ יוֹצִיא
אֶל־מִחוּץ לַמַּחֲנֶה וְשָׂרְפוּ בָאֵשׁ אֶת־עֹרֹתָם וְאֶת־

כח בְּשָׂרָם וְאֶת־פִּרְשָׁם: וְהַשֹּׂרֵף אֹתָם יְכַבֵּס בְּגָדָיו וְרָחַץ

כט אֶת־בְּשָׂרוֹ בַּמָּיִם וְאַחֲרֵי־כֵן יָבוֹא אֶל־הַמַּחֲנֶה: וְהָיְתָה
לָכֶם לְחֻקַּת עוֹלָם בַּחֹדֶשׁ הַשְּׁבִיעִי בֶּעָשׂוֹר לַחֹדֶשׁ
תְּעַנּוּ אֶת־נַפְשֹׁתֵיכֶם וְכָל־מְלָאכָה לֹא תַעֲשׂוּ הָאֶזְרָח

ל וְהַגֵּר הַגָּר בְּתוֹכְכֶם: כִּי־בַיּוֹם הַזֶּה יְכַפֵּר עֲלֵיכֶם

26] He who set the Azazel-goat free shall wash his clothes and bathe his body in water; after that he may re-enter the camp.

27] The bull of sin offering and the goat of sin offering whose blood was brought in to purge the Shrine shall be taken outside the camp; and their hides, flesh, and dung shall be consumed in fire. 28] He who burned them shall wash his clothes and bathe his body in water; after that he may re-enter the camp.

29] And this shall be to you a law for all time: In the seventh month, on the tenth day of the month, you shall practice self-denial; and you shall do no manner of work, neither the citizen nor the alien who resides among you. 30] For on this day atone-

---

26–28] Those who deal with the Azazel-goat and those who burn the carcasses of the sin offerings (cf. 4:11, 12, 21; 6:23; 10:18) are ritually defiled by these powerful instruments of "de-sinning" and must purify themselves before returning to the camp.

29–33] Obligations of the people.

29] *Practice self-denial*. Literally, "afflict yourselves." The traditional rendering "afflict your souls" is misleading; this chapter is not concerned with inner contrition. The idea of "return" appears frequently

in the Bible (p. 162), but it is hardly present in this outline of formal observance. Tradition understood this self-denial as fasting, no doubt correctly (cf. Ps. 35:13, "I afflicted myself with fasting" –the new JPS translation renders simply, "I kept a fast"– and Isa. 58:3, where fasting and self-affliction are parallel).

30] This verse, summing up the intent of the observance, is repeated a number of times in the synagogue liturgy for Yom Kippur.

לְטַהֵר אֶתְכֶם מִכֹּל חַטֹּאתֵיכֶם לִפְנֵי יְהוָה תִּטְהָרוּ:

לא שַׁבַּת שַׁבָּתוֹן הִיא לָכֶם וְעִנִּיתֶם אֶת־נַפְשֹׁתֵיכֶם חֻקַּת

לב עוֹלָם: וְכִפֶּר הַכֹּהֵן אֲשֶׁר־יִמְשַׁח אֹתוֹ וַאֲשֶׁר יְמַלֵּא

אֶת־יָדוֹ לְכַהֵן תַּחַת אָבִיו וְלָבַשׁ אֶת־בִּגְדֵי הַבָּד בִּגְדֵי

לג הַקֹּדֶשׁ: וְכִפֶּר אֶת־מִקְדַּשׁ הַקֹּדֶשׁ וְאֶת־אֹהֶל מוֹעֵד

וְאֶת־הַמִּזְבֵּחַ יְכַפֵּר וְעַל הַכֹּהֲנִים וְעַל־כָּל־עַם הַקָּהָל

לד יְכַפֵּר: וְהָיְתָה־זֹּאת לָכֶם לְחֻקַּת עוֹלָם לְכַפֵּר עַל־

בְּנֵי יִשְׂרָאֵל מִכָּל־חַטֹּאתָם אַחַת בַּשָּׁנָה וַיַּעַשׂ כַּאֲשֶׁר

צִוָּה יְהוָה אֶת־מֹשֶׁה: פ

ment shall be made for you to cleanse you of all your sins; you shall be clean before the LORD.   **31]** It shall be a sabbath of complete rest for you, and you shall practice self-denial; it is a law for all time.   **32]** The priest who has been anointed and ordained to serve as priest in place of his father shall make expiation. He shall put on the linen vestments, the sacral vestments.   **33]** He shall purge the innermost Shrine; he shall purge the Tent of Meeting and the altar; and he shall make expiation for the priests and for all the people of the congregation.

34] This shall be to you a law for all time: to make atonement for the Israelites for all their sins once a year.

And Moses did as the LORD had commanded him.

32] *Anointed and ordained.* In the Second Temple there was no ceremony of anointment; the High Priest was inducted into office by clothing him in the "golden vestments."

34] *And Moses did as the Lord had commanded him.* He gave the instructions to Aaron to be carried out when the Day of Atonement came around. The dedication of the Tabernacle and the death of Aaron's sons occurred in the spring (Exod. 40:17).

GLEANINGS

Halachah

16:4] *Linen Tunic*

The High Priest wore the "white vestments" for all the rites specifically connected with Yom Kippur. But for the daily offerings, morning and evening, he wore the usual "golden vestments" [27].

He Shall Bathe His Body in Water

Each time the High Priest changed from the golden to the linen vestments, or the reverse, he had to take a ritual bath. Before and after doing so, he had to wash his hands and feet from the laver. This process occurred five times during the Yom Kippur observance [28].

6] *Sin Offering*

Over his own bull, the High Priest recited this confession: "O LORD, I have sinned, I have transgressed, I have rebelled against You, I and my household. O LORD, pardon the sins, transgressions, and rebellions which I and my household have committed against You; as it is written in the Torah of Your servant Moses: 'For on this day atonement shall be made for you to cleanse you of all your sins; you shall be clean before the LORD.'" The subsequent confessions were in the same form, except that the second confession also mentioned "the sons of Aaron, Your holy people," and the third (over the Azazel-goat) began "Your people Israel have sinned, have transgressed, . . . pardon the sins which Your people Israel have. . . ." In these prayers the High Priest did not address God as *Adonai* ("Lord") but actually pronounced the tetragrammaton YHWH. Each time the people heard the Name uttered (it was spoken only on this occasion), they responded, "Praised be His Name, whose glorious kingdom is forever and ever" [29].

22] *Set Free in the Wilderness*

See commentary. The Mishnah reports: When the lot designated the goat for Azazel, the High Priest tied a piece of crimson yarn on his head. Ten booths were set up between Jerusalem and the cliff which was known as Bet Hadura (or Bet Chadudo). At each of these stations the goat was offered food and water. When the cliff was reached, the man in charge would divide the strip of crimson wool in two: he would tie one part to the goat's horns, the other to the rock. Then he would topple the goat backward over the cliff; before the animal was half-way to the bottom, its body would be crushed [30].

The Palestinian Targum attempted to harmonize the biblical text and the tradition. It states that the man would release the goat, whereupon a violent wind would hurl the beast over the cliff.

23] *And Leave Them There*

See commentary. The Rabbis held that this verb is out of place. Immediately after sending the Azazel-goat away, the High Priest was to don the golden vestments and offer the two burnt offerings of verse 24—according to Nachmanides, also the regular evening burnt offering and incense. Next, he put on the linen robes once more, in order to enter the Shrine and remove the fire pan and incense bowl. Thence, he would go to a chamber in the sacred area, where he had repeatedly bathed and changed during the day, and there he would discard the linen garments. The words "and leave them there" mean merely that the vestments were to be hidden away and not used on a subsequent Yom Kippur.   SIFRA

When the rites of the day were concluded, the High Priest put on regular attire and returned home, accompanied by his friends, for whom he would

172

hold a banquet celebrating the safe completion of his hazardous duties [31]. To this day, in many communities, some festivities are held after the fast is broken. A beautiful custom observed by some of the pious is to do a little work on the sukah, in preparation for the next holiday in the calendar [32].

29] *Practice Self-Denial*

On Yom Kippur one is forbidden to eat, drink, wash, anoint himself with oil, engage in sexual intercourse, or wear sandals [33]. To this day, Orthodox Jews remove their shoes in the synagogue on Yom Kippur, or wear slippers of a material other than leather. The rule of fasting is suspended when necessary for health reasons [34].

Do No Manner of Work

The same stringent laws apply as on the Sabbath, since Yom Kippur is also called Sabbath (Lev. 23:22). On all other holy days, even Rosh Hashanah, the preparation of food is permitted (Exod. 12:16), including such related tasks as lighting a fire.

32] *Anointed and Ordained to Serve in Place of His Father*

This indicates that the High Priest should be succeeded by his son, if the latter is qualified. But, if he is not worthy to hold the post, another priest is to be selected [35].

Haggadah

16:4] *Linen Tunic*

Why does the High Priest wear this simple garb on Yom Kippur, instead of his usual gorgeous vestments? (a) As an expression of humility and contrition [36]. (b) The regular vestments would be unsuitable for a ceremony of atonement, since their gold adornments would recall the sin of the golden calf [37]. (c) On this day the High Priest wears the white linen garb of the angels (Ezek. 9:2). On Yom Kippur, like the angels, we do not eat nor drink [38].

8] *For Azazel*

Nachmanides regards Azazel as representing the power of evil. *We do not offer him anything.* God controls the lot, and it is He who designates the gift for Azazel. It is as if one entertained a lord at a banquet and the lord directed that a certain dish be served to a mighty general that he might be more favorably inclined toward the host. The powers of evil are under God's control and ultimately serve His ends [39].

30] *For on This Day Atonement Shall Be Made*

Rabbi Ishmael said: There are four divisions in the matter of atonement: If one fails to observe a positive command and then repents, he is forgiven on the spot (Jer. 3:22). If he transgresses a negative command and then repents, repentance suspends punishment and Yom Kippur brings atonement

(Lev. 16:30). If he commits a sin punishable by "cutting off" or by the death sentence and then repents, repentance and the Day of Atonement suspend punishment and suffering throughout the year purifies him (Ps. 89:33). But if one deliberately causes the profanation of God's name and repents, this repentance is not enough to suspend punishment nor will the Day of Atonement bring remission; rather, repentance and Yom Kippur atone for a third of the guilt, suffering atones for another third, and death, along with suffering, brings full purification (Isa. 22:14) [40].

This saying of Rabbi Ishmael was never construed as a dogma: the Rabbis generally stressed the constant availability of forgiveness to those who return: "God says to Israel. Open to Me a gate of repentance no bigger than the point of a needle, and I will open to you a gate [of forgiveness] wide enough to drive wagons and carts through" [41]. A king's son had traveled a hundred days' journey from his father. His friends advised him to return home, but he said, "I cannot, the trip is too long." Then his father sent him word, "Come back as far as your strength permits, and I will go to meet you the rest of the way." Thus God says to Israel, "Return to Me, and I will return to you" (Mal. 3:7) [42].

You Shall Be Clean before the Lord

That is, Yom Kippur will cleanse you of sins

committed only before God (irreverence, neglect of prayer, ceremonial duties); but sins committed against a human being are not absolved by the Day of Atonement unless you try to correct the wrong you have done [43].

Rabbi Akiba said, "Happy are you, O Israel! Who purifies you, and before whom do you become clean? Your Father in heaven! . . . As the *mikveh* cleanses the defiled, so the Holy One (blessed be He) cleanses Israel" [44].

PART VI

The Law of Holiness

Further Laws about Sacrifice and Food

This is the first chapter assigned by modern scholars to the Holiness Code (H). It does not have all the characteristic features of that document [1]; it does not, for example, specifically mention the concept of holiness, and it contains no moral injunctions. But it does give reasons for the commandments (verses 5, 11–12), and it contains some of the phraseology typical of H. It seems to have no connection with the rest of the Holiness Code which appears to be not a single, ordered document but a collection of materials all emanating from the same background and holding much the same viewpoint.

1. Secular Slaughtering Prohibited

The first part of this chapter presents a difficult problem of interpretation, even though the language is simple and clear. It demands that cattle, sheep, and goats—beasts of the species used in sacrifice—be slaughtered only at the gate of the Tabernacle so that their blood may be dashed upon the altar and the fat burned ceremonially; in short, that every such animal intended for food be brought as a *shelamim*

sacrifice. If this ritual is omitted, the person responsible is guilty of bloodshed—as if he had murdered a human being!

Now Deuteronomy (12:20ff.) provides that, after Israel has conquered and occupied the land, animals may be killed for food without sacrificial formalities, as long as the carcasses are drained of blood. The simplest explanation of this chapter, then, is that it was a temporary rule for the period of desert wandering; the Israelites were traveling in constant proximity to the Tabernacle and could easily bring their animals there and present them as sacrifices of well-being. But, after they settled in Canaan and spread over the country, frequent trips to a central Shrine (such as Shiloh and later Jerusalem) would have been burdensome; and secular slaughtering was therefore permitted. This explanation was given by Rabbi Ishmael in the second century and was adopted by later legal authorities [2]. It makes excellent sense, on the assumption that the Torah was all given through Moses, that the present chapter dates from the time of the encampment at Sinai and Deuteronomy from the end of the desert period, just before the invasion of the land.

Yet, even on this assumption, the passage presents a difficulty for it declares that "this shall be to them a law for all time" (verse 7). The Orthodox commentators are forced to restrict the application of this sentence to the immediately preceding clause: "That they may offer their sacrifices no more to the goat-demons" [3]. But, if the text is examined without preconceptions, it becomes evident that the entire provision, not just one clause, is "the law for all time" [4].

Further, we must reckon with all the many reasons for considering the Pentateuch a composite, post-Mosaic work. We cannot disregard the strong evidence that Deuteronomy was the basis for the reforms of Josiah in 621 B.C.E., when the local shrines (bamot) were outlawed and sacrifice was restricted to the Jerusalem Temple. This revolutionary change necessitated many adjustments. One of these concerned slaughtering. A meat meal in ancient times was a special occasion and often (or should we say, always?) took the form of a festive sacrifice performed at the local sanctuary. Now that this procedure was forbidden, and Israelites could hardly be required to travel to Jerusalem whenever they wanted meat for dinner, they were allowed to slaughter for food without sacrificial procedures.

This much is accepted by virtually all non-Orthodox scholars. From it follows the necessity of choosing one of two alternatives. Either this chapter is an old document that is explicitly repealed in Deuteronomy (12:20ff.) or it is a later document than Deuteronomy and is intended to repeal the law that permitted secular slaughtering. Both opinions have their learned supporters.

Thus Kaufmann, who regarded P as the oldest component of the Pentateuch, found in this chapter the old rule that prevailed prior to Deuteronomy, which required all slaughtering to take the form of sacrifice. But one may argue that such offerings were made at the local shrines, whereas our chapter speaks of *the* Tent of Meeting, the central sanctuary. To this Kaufmann replied that the Tent of Meeting is a symbol for any one of the local holy places [5]. This seems forced. Although P nowhere attacks the institution of *bamot*, it nowhere hints that such a multiplicity of altars is envisioned, let alone permitted. It consistently takes for granted the principle of a single sanctuary.

A more recent treatment of the subject by Jacob Milgrom [6] finds the basic intent of the law in the statement (verse 11) that blood is life. The opening verses do not state that nonsacrificial slaughter is as bad as murder, they state that it *is* murder. According to Genesis (1:29), man was supposed to be a vegetarian; and, when Noah was given permission to eat animal food, he was warned strictly against consuming blood (Gen. 9:3f.). Leviticus, chapter 17, describes the only way in which meat may be eaten without blood guilt; and it is this provision which Deuteronomy explicitly rejects [7].

This explanation is also unsatisfactory. If all nonsacrificial slaughtering was plain murder and was so regarded from time immemorial, why should the rule be further explained as a precaution against sacrifice to the goat-demons? And in fact the text does not give this as an added reason but as *the* reason for the rule.

Moreover, Genesis 9:4, according to the plain sense, allows the descendants of Noah to perform secular slaughtering as long as they do not eat of the blood—in short to do just what Deuteronomy prescribes. If H is pre-Deuteronomic and if Leviticus 17 is to limit the application of Genesis 9 imposing on Israelites restrictions from which the gentile descendants of Noah are free, one would have expected a clearer statement of the point.

The alternative possibility is that our chapter is post-Deuteronomic and is an attempt to repeal the Deuteronomic rule. This view has been held by many of the earlier critics who regarded P—including H—as exilic or postexilic [8]. The present writer has already indicated his view that these codes preserve much ancient material but were completed in their present form no earlier than the time of the exile [9]. He thinks it probable that this chapter dates from the early post-exilic period, when the Judean community was a small remnant huddled around what was left of Jerusalem. Those who returned from Babylon looked with some distrust on the peasants who had been left on the soil when the others were deported; such people were suspected, perhaps with reason, of clinging to pagan customs. This regulation was intended to discourage those practices; perhaps also it was instituted to increase the prestige and income of the priests at the small shrine which had replaced the grand Temple of Solomon. As the Palestinian community grew in numbers and spread out over the land, this law became impracticable, the Deuteronomic practice was resumed, and our passage was understood as applying only during the desert wanderings.

This explanation appears to be the least difficult of the possibilities that have been suggested; it can hardly be called certain.

2. The Prohibition of Blood

Leviticus, chapter 3, verse 17, forbids the consumption of blood; chapter 7, verse 27, adds that violation of this rule is to be punished by karet. The present chapter (verses 10ff.) restates the prohibition and the penalty in strongest terms and offers an explanation of the law: the life-principle (nefesh, rendered "soul" in earlier translations) is in the blood—or, very probably, is the blood [10]. It is a sin for a human being, himself a nefesh (or possessed of a nefesh), to consume the nefesh even of beasts. Moreover, God has decreed that blood, as nefesh, shall be used on the altar to purge humankind of sin and impurity [11].

The ancients were just as much aware as we are that blood is indispensable for physical life. They thought of blood as a powerful and dangerous agent, endowed with uncanny, supernatural potencies. Many peoples have had taboos against seeing and touching blood, as well as against shedding or consuming it [12]. Yet, the biblical laws on the subject have no real parallel in the records of the ancient Near East. In Mesopotamia, sacrifice was a presentation of food already prepared; there is nothing in the Babylonian ritual texts comparable to the "dashing" of the blood of ordinary sacrifices on the altar or to the special blood rites of the chatat (above, chapters 1, 3, and 4) [13]. And there are only limited parallels in Greco-Roman practice [14]. Nor is there any known rule which resembles the rigorous and consistent prohibition of tasting blood—either as food or in connection with ritual—set forth in the Bible and elaborated by Jewish tradition. Our chapter requires that the blood of wild animals or fowl, which are not used in sacrifice, be drained and covered with earth (verses 13 and 14). This procedure is still followed in kosher slaughtering. Orthodox law, moreover, requires that, before meat is cooked, it must be soaked in water for a half hour, then salted and left standing for an hour, then washed again, so as to draw out all blood from the tissues [15].

That sacrificial blood has expiatory power is stated in verse 11 and is accepted doctrine in the Talmud [16]. This idea was taken up and further developed in Christianity, which taught that atonement is made for mankind through the blood of Jesus.

אֵ וַיְדַבֵּ֥ר יְהוָ֖ה אֶל־מֹשֶׁ֥ה לֵּאמֹֽר: דַּבֵּ֤ר אֶל־אַהֲרֹ֨ן וְאֶל־
בָּנָ֜יו וְאֶ֥ל כָּל־בְּנֵ֣י יִשְׂרָאֵ֗ל וְאָמַרְתָּ֣ אֲלֵיהֶ֔ם זֶ֣ה הַדָּבָ֔ר

ג אֲשֶׁר־צִוָּ֥ה יְהוָ֖ה לֵּאמֹֽר: אִ֥ישׁ אִ֨ישׁ מִבֵּ֣ית יִשְׂרָאֵ֗ל אֲשֶׁ֨ר
יִשְׁחַ֜ט שׁ֥וֹר אוֹ־כֶ֛שֶׂב אוֹ־עֵ֖ז בַּֽמַּחֲנֶ֑ה א֚וֹ אֲשֶׁ֣ר יִשְׁחָ֔ט

ד מִח֖וּץ לַֽמַּחֲנֶֽה: וְאֶל־פֶּ֜תַח אֹ֤הֶל מוֹעֵד֙ לֹ֣א הֱבִיא֔וֹ
לְהַקְרִ֤יב קָרְבָּן֙ לַֽיהוָ֔ה לִפְנֵ֖י מִשְׁכַּ֣ן יְהוָ֑ה דָּ֣ם יֵחָשֵׁ֞ב
לָאִ֤ישׁ הַהוּא֙ דָּ֣ם שָׁפָ֔ךְ וְנִכְרַ֛ת הָאִ֥ישׁ הַה֖וּא מִקֶּ֥רֶב

ה עַמּֽוֹ: לְמַ֩עַן֩ אֲשֶׁ֨ר יָבִ֜יאוּ בְּנֵ֣י יִשְׂרָאֵ֗ל אֶֽת־זִבְחֵיהֶם֮
אֲשֶׁ֣ר הֵ֣ם זֹבְחִים֮ עַל־פְּנֵ֣י הַשָּׂדֶה֒ וֶהֱבִיאֻ֣ם לַֽיהוָ֗ה אֶל־
פֶּ֛תַח אֹ֥הֶל מוֹעֵ֖ד אֶל־הַכֹּהֵ֑ן וְזָ֣בְח֗וּ זִבְחֵ֤י שְׁלָמִים֙

ו לַֽיהוָ֖ה אוֹתָֽם: וְזָרַ֨ק הַכֹּהֵ֤ן אֶת־הַדָּם֙ עַל־מִזְבַּ֣ח יְהוָ֔ה

Leviticus 17

1–6

1] The Lord spoke to Moses, saying:

2] Speak to Aaron and his sons and to all the Israelite people and say to them:

This is what the Lord has commanded: 3] If any man of the house of Israel slaughters an ox or sheep or goat in the camp, or does so outside the camp,   4] and does not bring it to the entrance of the Tent of Meeting to present it as an offering to the Lord, before the Lord's Tabernacle, bloodguilt shall be imputed to that man: he has shed blood; that man shall be cut off from among his people.   5] This is in order that the Israelites may bring the sacrifices which they have been making in the open—that they may bring them before the Lord, to the priest, at the entrance of the Tent of Meeting, and offer them as sacrifices of well-being to the Lord;   6] that the priest may dash the blood against the altar of the Lord at the entrance

17:4] *Bloodguilt shall be imputed to that man.* He is to be deemed as guilty as if he had committed homicide [17].

5] *The sacrifices which they have been making in the open.* Presumably to the goat-demons of verse 7. The

traditional commentators suppose that Israel had picked up this practice in Egypt, along with other idolatrous customs. Grintz sees rather a reference to underground deities who were worshiped by night [18].

פֶּתַח אֹהֶל מוֹעֵד וְהִקְטִיר הַחֵלֶב לְרֵיחַ נִיחֹחַ לַיהוָֹה:

ז וְלֹא־יִזְבְּחוּ עוֹד אֶת־זִבְחֵיהֶם לַשְּׂעִירִם אֲשֶׁר הֵם זֹנִים

אַחֲרֵיהֶם חֻקַּת עוֹלָם תִּהְיֶה־זֹּאת לָהֶם לְדֹרֹתָם:

ח וַאֲלֵהֶם תֹּאמַר אִישׁ אִישׁ מִבֵּית יִשְׂרָאֵל וּמִן־הַגֵּר

ט אֲשֶׁר־יָגוּר בְּתוֹכָם אֲשֶׁר־יַעֲלֶה עֹלָה אוֹ־זָבַח: וְאֶל־

פֶּתַח אֹהֶל מוֹעֵד לֹא יְבִיאֶנּוּ לַעֲשׂוֹת אֹתוֹ לַיהוָֹה

י וְנִכְרַת הָאִישׁ הַהוּא מֵעַמָּיו: וְאִישׁ אִישׁ מִבֵּית יִשְׂרָאֵל

וּמִן־הַגֵּר הַגָּר בְּתוֹכָם אֲשֶׁר יֹאכַל כָּל־דָּם וְנָתַתִּי פָנַי

בַּנֶּפֶשׁ הָאֹכֶלֶת אֶת־הַדָּם וְהִכְרַתִּי אֹתָהּ מִקֶּרֶב עַמָּהּ:

יא כִּי־נֶפֶשׁ הַבָּשָׂר בַּדָּם הִוא וַאֲנִי נְתַתִּיו לָכֶם עַל־

Leviticus 17

7–11

of the Tent of Meeting, and turn the fat into smoke as a pleasing odor to the LORD; **7]** and that they may offer their sacrifices no more to the goat-demons after whom they stray. This shall be to them a law for all time, throughout the ages.

8] Say to them further: If any man of the house of Israel or of the strangers who reside among them offers a burnt offering or a sacrifice,   **9]** and does not bring it to the entrance of the Tent of Meeting to offer it to the LORD, that man shall be cut off from his people.

10] And if any man of the house of Israel or of the strangers who reside among them partakes of any blood, I will set My face against the person who partakes of the blood, and I will cut him off from among his kin.   **11]** For the life of the flesh is in the blood, and I have assigned it to you for making expiation for your lives upon

7] *Goat-demons.* Hebrew *seᶜirim*, which usually means "goats." The root meaning is "hairy." Perhaps these beings were somewhat like the satyrs of Greek mythology.

A law for all time. See p. 178.

8–9] The preceding verses forbade slaughtering,

even without sacrificial rites, except at the Tent of Meeting. These verses prohibit sacrificial ceremonies away from the sanctuary.

8] *Strangers who reside among them.* See commentary on 19:33ff.

10–14] On the prohibition of blood, see p. 179.

הַמִּזְבֵּחַ לְכַפֵּר עַל־נַפְשֹׁתֵיכֶם כִּי־הַדָּם הוּא בַּנֶּפֶשׁ

יב יְכַפֵּר: עַל־כֵּן אָמַרְתִּי לִבְנֵי יִשְׂרָאֵל כָּל־נֶפֶשׁ מִכֶּם

לֹא־תֹאכַל דָּם וְהַגֵּר הַגָּר בְּתוֹכְכֶם לֹא־יֹאכַל דָּם:

יג וְאִישׁ אִישׁ מִבְּנֵי יִשְׂרָאֵל וּמִן־הַגֵּר הַגָּר בְּתוֹכָם אֲשֶׁר

יָצוּד צֵיד חַיָּה אוֹ־עוֹף אֲשֶׁר יֵאָכֵל וְשָׁפַךְ אֶת־דָּמוֹ

יד וְכִסָּהוּ בֶּעָפָר: כִּי־נֶפֶשׁ כָּל־בָּשָׂר דָּמוֹ בְנַפְשׁוֹ הוּא

וָאֹמַר לִבְנֵי יִשְׂרָאֵל דַּם כָּל־בָּשָׂר לֹא תֹאכֵלוּ כִּי נֶפֶשׁ

טו כָּל־בָּשָׂר דָּמוֹ הוּא כָּל־אֹכְלָיו יִכָּרֵת: וְכָל־נֶפֶשׁ אֲשֶׁר

תֹּאכַל נְבֵלָה וּטְרֵפָה בָּאֶזְרָח וּבַגֵּר וְכִבֶּס בְּגָדָיו

טז וְרָחַץ בַּמַּיִם וְטָמֵא עַד־הָעֶרֶב וְטָהֵר: וְאִם לֹא יְכַבֵּס

וּבְשָׂרוֹ לֹא יִרְחָץ וְנָשָׂא עֲוֹנוֹ: פ

the altar; it is the blood, as life, that effects expiation.   12] Therefore I say to the Israelite people: No person among you shall partake of blood, nor shall the stranger who resides among you partake of blood.

13] And if any Israelite or any stranger who resides among them hunts down an animal or a bird that may be eaten, he shall pour out its blood and cover it with earth.   14] For the life of all flesh—its blood is its life. Therefore I say to the Israelite people: You shall not partake of the blood of any flesh, for the life of all flesh is its blood. Anyone who partakes of it shall be cut off.

15] Any person, whether citizen or stranger, who eats what has died or has been torn by beasts, shall wash his clothes, bathe in water, and remain unclean until evening; then he shall be clean.   16] But if he does not wash [his clothes] and bathe his body, he shall bear his guilt.

13] The prohibition of blood applies even in the case of game, whereas the fat of game animals is not forbidden (7:23).

Cover it with earth. This requirement is not found in Deuteronomy 12:24.

15] *Who eats what has died* [*nevelah*] *or has been torn by beasts* [*terefah*] [19]. This passage repeats substantially the content of chapter 11, verses 39f. (see also commentary on 11:24f. and Gleanings).

GLEANINGS

Halachah

17:7] *That They May Offer Their Sacrifices No More to the Goat-Demons*

For the far-reaching inferences drawn by Rabbi Levi and Maimonides from this verse, see p. 7.

15] *Who Eats What Has Died or Has Been Torn by Beasts*

The law had previously declared that defilement results not only from eating but even from touching or carrying such a carcass (11:39f.). Why then this repetition? According to *Sifra*, it refers to fowl of a clean species which have not been correctly slaughtered; eating of them causes defilement, though touching them does not.

Sex Offenses

We come at length to a topic of deep contemporary concern—sexual morality. Not that we shall find in this chapter—or in the parallel section, chapter 20, which should be read with it—a satisfactory answer to our current questions. These chapters, in fact, do not even provide an inclusive account of the biblical views about sex. They simply enumerate certain forms of sexual conduct that are forbidden and condemned.

1. *Biblical Attitudes toward Sex*

To understand and evaluate this material properly, we must consider how sex is treated throughout the Bible. Such an inquiry is the more necessary because many contemporary writers, in attacking laws which derive from the so-called Judeo-Christian tradition, ascribe to the Hebrew Scriptures certain attitudes that are not Jewish at all. It was Christian teachers who identified "the flesh" with sin, glorified celibacy, and regarded marriage as a concession to human frailty (see especially I Corinthians 7:1-9).

All this is alien to the spirit of the Hebrew Bible. At creation, it asserts, mankind was commanded to be fertile and increase (Gen. 1:28). Man is to cling to his wife so that they become one flesh (Gen. 2:24). The Bible deals frankly with many manifestations of the sex drive, licit and illicit, and recognizes its profound influence on one's emotions and behavior. The Song of Songs is a collection of explicitly erotic poems, expressive both of passion and of tenderness. In these lyrics, the man and the woman are equally open in voicing their feelings.

Very different were the attitudes of the neighbors of ancient Israel. Here we see basic differences between pagan and biblical religion. In Canaan and Mesopotamia, and somewhat differently in Egypt, a central religious element was the worship of the Mother Goddess. In the Near East she was called Astarte, Ishtar, Isis, and other names; the Greek goddesses Aphrodite and Demeter had much the same character. The Mother Goddess personified both the fertile earth and the sexual principle. Her marriage to a divine consort, called Baal and also known by various other names, was a prominent feature in both cult and myth. Some peoples celebrated this divine union by sexual orgies at the shrines or in the fields, believing that these rites increased the fertility of the soil.

In some places, male and female prostitutes were attached to the temples, and their earnings went into the temple treasuries. The Torah found it necessary to forbid such practices and to bar the donation of a whore's fee to the House of the Lord (Deut. 23:18).

The God of Israel has no consort and is not identified with any natural force or principle. He is Lord of nature. The reproductive process is His gift, it is not in itself divine. God's purpose is achieved by responsible use of His gift, not by mindless surrender to sensuality. The sexual impulse is not to be repressed, but it is to be controlled.

The normal sexual outlet is in marriage, which in biblical times usually took place at an early age. The forbidden manifestations of sex, as we shall see in these chapters, are adultery, incest, homosexual practices, and intercourse with animals. Moreover, sexual contact with any woman during her menstrual period—even with one's own wife—was prohibited. These laws will be fully discussed below.

Another marked difference between Israel and its neighbors concerned the practice of castration. The gelding of animals to make them more tractable has been common throughout the world. Among many peoples, notably those of the ancient Near East, the eunuch was a familiar figure. In the Phrygian cult of the "Great Mother," candidates for the priesthood castrated themselves during an orgiastic ritual, and this instance was probably not unparalleled. The Torah, however, excludes priests, suffering from any serious physical defect, from taking part in the altar service and similarly forbids the offering of a defective animal as a sacrifice. In these connections, sexual mutilation is specifically mentioned (Lev. 21:20, 22:24). A eunuch may not marry a Jewess (Deut. 23:2). But a compassionate section in a prophetic work reassures eunuchs, who are apparently here of foreign origin: By loyalty to God and His law, they may obtain "in My House / And within My walls, / A monument and a name / Better than sons or daughters" (Isa. 56:5).

From the words, "You shall have no such practices in your land" (Lev. 22:24), the rabbinic teachers concluded that castration is unconditionally forbidden; and they held that the rule applies in all countries, to human beings and to all species of animals [1].

2. Postbiblical Jewish Attitudes

The healthy affirmative attitude toward sex found in the Bible was somewhat modified in the talmudic period. This change may be due in part to Greek influence. For the Greeks were by no means unanimous in glorifying sensual indulgence. Plato, for example, speaks of the body and its functions with a certain contempt, and perhaps he was not the first of the philosophers to do so. The Cynic and Stoic schools were more emphatic in denigrating bodily functions and appetites. The Stoics taught that a sage is guided by cool reason alone; he must suppress even the tender emotions, still more the irrational and explosive passions. The Neo-Platonist thinkers advocated asceticism and may have influenced nascent Christianity.

The talmudic sources reveal such negative views to a limited extent. The Song of Songs was now interpreted as an allegory of the love between God and the people of Israel, and its primary erotic intent was indignantly rejected [2]. There was also a tendency to identify man's "evil inclination" (yetser hara) with the sexual urge—though in fact the term also includes aggressive and other sinful impulses as well. Yet the Rabbis also declared that the evil impulse is in fact "very good" since it leads man to establish a family [3]. And they called upon man to serve God with the evil impulse as well as the good [4].

186

There is a note of suspicion and ambiguity in some of the rabbinical pronouncements on sex. It may have been affected by economic and social conditions that compelled many persons to delay marriage, with resultant tensions [5]. Nevertheless, marriage and the having of children are still deemed a divine command; to remain a bachelor by choice was considered sinful [6]. Married couples have broad freedom in matters of sexual technique [7], and Friday night is deemed a particularly appropriate time for marital relations [8]. According to the traditional understanding of Exodus, chapter 21, verse 10, a married woman is entitled to regular satisfaction of her sexual needs, even if her husband has another wife [9]. The halachah also gave qualified approval to birth control when couples had at least two children [10]. (Of course, reliable methods of contraception were not available in premodern times.)

Medieval Jewish thinkers were more strongly affected by Greek and Christian views. Ibn Ezra (on Lev. 18:20) regards sexual activity as a necessity for physical and mental health; but sex for fun, he adds, is unworthy of an enlightened person. Maimonides adopts Aristotle's opinion that the sense of touch is degrading to our humanity. We should, he says, regard sexual intercourse with contempt and desire it only at rare intervals [11]. According to Maimonides, circumcision weakens the sexual drive and was ordained by the Torah to help man achieve self-mastery [12].

The much more conservative Nachmanides severely criticized Maimonides for adopting the ideas of the "impure Greek." A special treatise on the marital act (significantly entitled *The Letter on Holiness*, attributed to Nachmanides though not certainly by him) asserts that the act is pure and holy when properly performed, at the right time, and with the right intent. God would not have created the genitals if their function had no positive value. But a man must approach his wife with the exalted hope of producing wise and pious offspring; moreover, he should show her great consideration, so that she may fully share the joy of the sacred moment. Yet, this document too deprecates the "recreational" aspect of the sex relationship.

But, despite this modification of attitude, Jewish tradition was still far from accepting the Christian evaluation of the flesh. Characteristically, the medieval Jewish communities considered it their duty to provide dowries for poor girls and to marry them off; in Christendom, such persons were often relegated to convent life, even though they had no inclination for it.

The Jewish teachers regarded human semen as precious and not to be wasted. Nocturnal emission is not sinful, but one should avoid the fantasies that may cause it; and masturbation is strongly condemned [13].

Yet the halachah permits intercourse that will not result in conception, as when the wife is already pregnant or unable to bear children [14].

3. Modesty

Greek men regularly engaged in physical sports in the nude. Gymnasium means "place of nakedness." On some special occasions young women also appeared unclothed in public. Greek sculpture idealized the nude human body.

In contrast, Judaism insisted on modest attire for both sexes. This fact has led to the mistaken notion that Judaism is prudish. It is in fact a question as to whether sexual interest is stimulated more by exposure or by concealment. The Arabs too insist that both men and women be fully covered in public, although their literature betrays strong preoccupation with sex, including the homosexual relation.

The biblical Jewish tradition also calls for reticence in talking about sex. Not that the subject is avoided in Hebrew sources, which are forthright and free from squeamishness. Yet even in the biblical text, euphemisms are often substituted for blunter terms; in our chapter the sexual act is referred to as "uncovering the nakedness" of a person. The highly erotic material in the Song of Songs is clothed in poetic metaphors. The Rabbis likewise called for restraint of language. "Everyone knows why the bride enters the marriage chamber, but one who engages in vulgar talk brings dire punishment upon himself" [15].

Thus, Judaism through the centuries has combined an affirmative attitude toward marriage and a recognition that its physical side is good and desirable, with the acceptance of controls. The results have been highly creditable. There is always a difference between ideal and reality; and no doubt sentimentalists have on occasion exaggerated the beauty of Jewish family life. Yet, the total record is a good one in terms of family stability, child welfare, and the transmission of moral and social standards [16]. In the light of these results, even those who are most critical of traditional rules of sex morality will be well advised to examine them carefully before rejecting them as outmoded.

4. Incest

Some sort of sexual control is found in all human societies. Among the most widespread of these is the prohibition of marriage and sex relations between blood relatives. The extent of such prohibitions varies, but everywhere sexual congress between parent and child is forbidden. In ancient Egypt, marriage of brother and sister was common in the royal family, but otherwise it was prohibited. Something similar existed in ancient Persia.

It is not easy to explain the origin of these taboos. Freudian speculation about the Oedipus complex may not be universally valid, in view of the diverse forms of family structure found in various cultures. The story of Oedipus simply reveals the horror which some societies felt about sex relations between parent and child.

Moreover, the ancient peoples who formulated these rules knew nothing about genetics and did not understand the reasons why inbreeding is biologically imprudent. (The notion, once widely held, that marriage between near relatives is likely to produce mentally defective or deaf offspring, is incorrect. Inbreeding simply intensifies traits already present. But, since genetic weaknesses are common, marriage even between first cousins, which is generally permitted in both religious and secular law, is risky.) In short, we know little about the origin of the laws against incest—etymologically, the word means simply "unchastity"—even though such laws are virtually universal and are rarely violated.

Biblical law forbids not only unions between close blood relatives but also, in certain cases, those between persons connected by marriage. Thus, one may not marry the widow of his father, uncle, or son. Chapter 18 of Leviticus lists the various forbidden degrees of relationship. A similar list in chapter 20 provides that those who violate these laws shall be punished by *karet* ("cutting off") [17]. The two chapters do not really complement each other, they are rather parallel versions of the same material. The biblical prohibitions were extended somewhat by rabbinic law; violation of the "secondary" rules does not, however, entail the penalty of *karet*. A table of the forbidden relationships, as defined by the halachah, is given in Appendix III.

Several items in this list may strike us as strange. One is an omission. The union of father and daughter is not explicitly forbidden. The Rabbis had to infer it from the prohibition of a union between grandfather and granddaughter (18:10). Most likely, this omission is due to a scribal error. But perhaps intentional is the fact that, though marriage of nephew and aunt is forbidden (18:14, 20:19), there is no corresponding objection to marriage between uncle and niece. The Talmud, in fact, considers such a marriage especially meritorious [18].

Another asymmetrical provision, in verse 18 of our chapter, which has serious implications up to the present, is the prohibition of a man from marrying his wife's sister during the lifetime of the wife. This seems to bar both the polygamous marriage of two sisters and marriage to the sister of a divorced wife. Tradition understood it, reasonably enough, to allow a widower to marry his late wife's sister.

Verse 16 seems to rule out unconditionally the marriage of a man to the divorcée or widow of his brother. But Deuteronomy (25:5–10) rules that, if a man dies childless, one of his brothers must marry the widow; and the first son of the union is to be "accounted to the dead brother, that his name may not be blotted out." If the surviving brother refuses to marry his sister-in-law, he must go through a humiliating ceremony (traditionally called *chalitzah*). Thereafter, the widow may marry anyone she chooses.

The Leviticus and Deuteronomy passages are apparently in contradiction; but Jewish tradition resolved the matter without difficulty. In the case of a childless widow, the so-called levirate marriage was mandatory. But, if there were children, such a marriage was forbidden even if both parties desired it. Moreover, later rabbinic law discouraged levirate marriage in nearly all cases preferring to deal with the situation by *chalitzah* [19].

Reform Judaism discarded *chalitzah* and permitted a childless widow to remarry without any precondition [20]. But no Reform body has officially challenged the law of verse 16, in this chapter, which forbids marriage to a deceased husband's brother. Yet many people believe such a marriage proper and desirable precisely if there are young children—the uncle who already knows and loves them is well suited to act as their father. (A similar argument has always been used to justify marriage with a deceased wife's sister.)

The issue came before the Central Conference of American Rabbis (CCAR) in 1925. Several speakers argued that justice and humanity required a Reform rabbi to officiate at the marriage of a woman to her late husband's brother. If, however, a rabbi had moral qualms about performing such a marriage, he ought in consistency to refuse to officiate when a man married his deceased wife's sister—even though the latter union is halachically permissible. The CCAR took no action in this matter; but many Reform rabbis do marry couples in either case.

5. Homosexual Behavior

Far more controversial, from the modern standpoint, is the absolute condemnation of sexual relations between males (18:22)—conduct for which the death penalty is prescribed (20:13) [21]. We have no record of a death sentence for this crime being carried out under Jewish auspices. Apparently, Christian courts executed some persons for sodomy during the Middle Ages. But, up to the present, persons who commit homosexual acts are subject to severe prison sentences in many countries, including the United States—even in the case of consenting adults.

Until recently, homosexuality, especially among males, has been regarded with horror as unnatural, perverted, and degenerate wherever the Jewish-Christian outlook prevailed. The first public change of attitude in the western world was voiced chiefly by psychiatrists who called for greater compassion toward homosexuals. Such persons, it was argued, are not criminal but sick; according to Freud, they are examples of arrested emotional-sexual development. They require treatment rather than punishment.

But, in the last few years, homosexuals have been identifying themselves as such, instead of trying to conceal their "infirmity." They have demanded an end to persecution and discrimination. They have insisted that adults who find homosexual relationships physically and emotionally satisfying have every right to enter into them. In some instances, they have called for legal and religious recognition of homosexual "marriage." In many cases, this homosexual revolt has been associated with other rebellions against the established order, including women's liberation, various racial movements, and some left-wing groups. Some of the "gay" literature seems to imply a claim of superiority, suggesting that homosexuals are more sensitive, creative, and spiritually advanced than heterosexuals.

The summary and rigid condemnation of homosexual conduct found in the Hebrew Bible [22] will leave many modern readers dissatisfied. Whether the time has come, however, for a complete about-face and the public approval of homosexual unions is still debatable. The subject is difficult to deal with both because of the violent emotions it rouses and because our understanding of the matter is far from complete. The following statements, however, are probably reliable:

In many cultures there has been little or no objection to homosexual behavior. The ancient Egyptians condemned it [23], but it was widespread among the Greeks. In the Athens of Pericles and Plato, love affairs between teenage boys and older men were frequent and were even considered beneficial for the intellectual and moral development of the younger party. Even in societies that officially ban such practices, they occur more frequently than former generations supposed—or, at least, admitted. Homosexual behavior has often been noted among lower animals as well. The extent of homosexual activity in a given time or place is conditioned largely by social factors. It is more common where members of the opposite sex are not readily available and where prevailing standards are more permissive.

The reason for this is that most people cannot be sharply separated into two categories. They can respond to either heterosexual or homosexual stimulation. The exclusively heterosexual and the exclusively homosexual represent extremes; but, as a rule, people are predominantly one or the other.

We do not really know why some people have predominantly homosexual personalities. No identifiable glandular disturbance is involved. Homosexuals are not necessarily effeminate in appearance and manner; nor do they display any consistent or significant pattern of abnormality in other respects. The Freudian theory of arrested emotional development seems to fit some cases, but not all. In some instances, homosexuality appears to have resulted from maternal domination and the absence of a vigorous father figure; but some homosexuals insist they were such from earliest childhood. The effort to transform homosexuals into heterosexuals by psychotherapy has had only the most limited success. Most perplexing, shocking, and pathetic are the occasional cases of married men with children who are arrested for molesting little boys.

Our greatest need at present is for more knowledge on the subject, to be sought objectively and without partisanship [24]. The rage that homosexuality evokes in many "straight" people should certainly be avoided. Defenders of the homosexual have argued with cogency that adultery—which our society views with comparative tolerance—has done far more harm than so-called "unnatural" sex. But, though restraint and tolerance seem to be called for, we should not be stampeded into endorsing and approving these practices.

6. Bestiality

Sexual congress between humans and other animals has not been uncommon in rural areas. Such practices, which are unconditionally forbidden (in 18:23, 20:15 and 16), have most often been the resource of the lonely and the frustrated. Yet the theme appears in a number of pagan myths. Usually, it is a case of a woman coupling with a beast or with a god in the guise of a beast. The myth recurs in Robinson Jeffers's poem, *Roan Stallion.* In our urban society, this matter is hardly of major importance.

On adultery, see Exodus 20:13; on intercourse with a menstruant, see commentary on 15:19ff.

7. Molech Worship

Though this chapter is otherwise devoted to the subject of sexual offenses, verse 21 reads: "Do not allow any of your offspring to be offered up to Molech." The parallel in chapter 20, verses 2 through 5, though longer, is no more enlightening; it states the penalty for the offense but does not explain the offense itself.

The "conventional" account of the matter is as follows: Molech was a heathen god to whom infants were sacrificed. His worshipers called him *Melech,* "King," but in the Bible his name was provided with the vowels of *boshet,* "shame."

Human sacrifices did occur in the ancient Near East. The Moabite king, Mesha, is said (II Kings 3:27) to have sacrificed his oldest son at a time of national crisis; the text does not name the deity who received the sacrifice. One passage identifies Molech as the national god of the Ammonites (I Kings 11:7); elsewhere the Ammonite god is called Milcom. But no extrabiblical source speaks clearly of a god named *Melech.*

Deuteronomy, chapter 12, verse 31, states that the Canaanites burned their children as an offering to their gods but does not mention Molech, nor does the name appear in Deuteronomy, chapter 18, verse 10, which forbids the Israelites to make their sons and daughters "pass through the fire." Our Leviticus passages and Jeremiah (32:5) speak of giving or offering children to Molech, but not of the use of fire. Only in II Kings (23:10) are the two elements, Molech and fire, combined.

What we have called the "conventional" view derives from the assumption that all these citations mean the same thing—which is possible but far from certain.

The Talmud offers two explanations. One is that children were made to walk between two fires as a symbol of their dedication to the god. The other is that the children were tossed back and forth over a fire till they were burned [25].

Diodorus of Sicily, a Greek writer of the first century C.E., asserts that children were burned to the god Melkart ("King of the City") in Carthage which was established by colonists from northern Canaan [26]. Human sacrifice persisted for many centuries in the Roman world [27]. Yet Otto Eissfeldt, a contemporary German scholar, has presented evidence that the word *molek* was used by the Carthaginians, not as a proper name, but as the technical term for an offering made in payment of a vow [28].

An interesting, and apparently brand new, suggestion is made by Snaith in his commentary. Chapters 18 and 20 are concerned almost exclusively with sex offenses. It is therefore reasonable to suppose that the Molech passages deal with a similar theme. Snaith thinks they may forbid the dedication of children as cult prostitutes. His guess is plausible but there is no evidence to support it.

All we can say with certainty is that these laws forbid the devotion of children to a pagan cult. How barbarous the form of devotion was is uncertain.

אַ וַיְדַבֵּר יְהוָֹה אֶל־מֹשֶׁה לֵּאמֹר: דַּבֵּר אֶל־בְּנֵי יִשְׂרָאֵל

גַ וְאָמַרְתָּ אֲלֵהֶם אֲנִי יְהוָֹה אֱלֹהֵיכֶם: כְּמַעֲשֵׂה אֶרֶץ־

מִצְרַיִם אֲשֶׁר יְשַׁבְתֶּם־בָּהּ לֹא תַעֲשׂוּ וּכְמַעֲשֵׂה אֶרֶץ־

כְּנַעַן אֲשֶׁר אֲנִי מֵבִיא אֶתְכֶם שָׁמָּה לֹא תַעֲשׂוּ

דַ וּבְחֻקֹּתֵיהֶם לֹא תֵלֵכוּ: אֶת־מִשְׁפָּטַי תַּעֲשׂוּ וְאֶת־חֻקֹּתַי

הַ תִּשְׁמְרוּ לָלֶכֶת בָּהֶם אֲנִי יְהוָֹה אֱלֹהֵיכֶם: וּשְׁמַרְתֶּם

אֶת־חֻקֹּתַי וְאֶת־מִשְׁפָּטַי אֲשֶׁר יַעֲשֶׂה אֹתָם הָאָדָם וָחַי

Leviticus 18

1–5

1] The LORD spoke to Moses, saying: 2] Speak to the Israelite people and say to them:

I the LORD am your God.   3] You shall not copy the practices of the land of Egypt where you dwelt, or of the land of Canaan to which I am taking you; nor shall you follow their laws.   4] My rules alone shall you observe, and faithfully follow My laws: I the LORD am your God.

5] You shall keep My laws and My rules, by the pursuit of which man shall live: I am the LORD.

18:1-5] The legal enactments are introduced by a solemn exhortation to heed the will of God, which forbids the pagan practices of both Egypt and Canaan.

3] *Nor shall you follow their laws.* Jews have always had to struggle with the question: to what extent should they adopt the ideas and practices of the outside world? Such influences are in some measure inescapable. They have affected not only those who welcomed new cultural values, the medieval Jewish philosophers and the modern Reformers for example, but also the spiritual isolationists. The custom of Yahrzeit was borrowed from the Catholics after the massacres that accompanied the First Crusade; present-day Chasidim wear garb that was fashionable among Polish Gentiles two centuries ago! In general, Judaism has been able to absorb values, ideas, and customs that are compatible with its basic outlook, while rejecting what could not be reconciled with the religious and ethical teachings of the Torah.

5] *You shall keep My laws and My rules, by the pursuit of which man shall live.* The Torah affirms life. By obeying God's law, man lives well and meaningfully and he will be rewarded by long life [29]. Nachmanides thinks the phrase refers to such legal sections as in Exodus, chapters 21 through 23, which provide for an orderly and peaceful society. Luzzatto takes it as alluding to the provisions of this chapter, the restrictions of which constitute the basis for stable and happy family life (see Gleanings).

ו בָּהֶם אֲנִי יְהֹוָה: ס אִישׁ אִישׁ אֶל־כָּל־שְׁאֵר בְּשָׂרוֹ

ז לֹא תִקְרְבוּ לְגַלּוֹת עֶרְוָה אֲנִי יְהֹוָה: ס עֶרְוַת

אָבִיךָ וְעֶרְוַת אִמְּךָ לֹא תְגַלֵּה אִמְּךָ הִוא לֹא תְגַלֶּה

ח עֶרְוָתָהּ: ס עֶרְוַת אֵשֶׁת־אָבִיךָ לֹא תְגַלֵּה עֶרְוַת

ט אָבִיךָ הִוא: ס עֶרְוַת אֲחוֹתְךָ בַת־אָבִיךָ אוֹ בַת־

אִמְּךָ מוֹלֶדֶת בַּיִת אוֹ מוֹלֶדֶת חוּץ לֹא תְגַלֶּה עֶרְוָתָן:

י ס עֶרְוַת בַּת־בִּנְךָ אוֹ בַת־בִּתְּךָ לֹא תְגַלֶּה עֶרְוָתָן כִּי

6] None of you shall come near anyone of his own flesh to uncover nakedness: I am the LORD.

7] Your father's nakedness, that is, the nakedness of your mother, you shall not uncover; she is your mother—you shall not uncover her nakedness.

8] Do not uncover the nakedness of your father's wife; it is the nakedness of your father.

9] The nakedness of your sister—your father's daughter or your mother's, whether born into the household or outside—do not uncover their nakedness.

10] The nakedness of your son's daughter, or of your daughter's daughter—do not uncover their nakedness; for their nakedness is yours.

6] *To uncover nakedness.* Here, and whenever this expression is applied to a woman, it means to have sexual intercourse with her. But when applied to a man (verses 7 and 10), it means to have intercourse with his wife. The general statement in this verse is followed by a number of specific rules.

8] *Your father's wife.* Your stepmother. A man and his wife are one flesh (Gen. 2:24), even if he should die or divorce her (T.N.).

9] *Whether born into the household or outside.* The force of this clause is uncertain. The Targums explain: "Even if she is your father's daughter by a different mother, or your mother's daughter by a different father." Rashbam, Ibn Ezra, and Nachmanides interpret: "Whether born in or out of wedlock." Or, says Ibn Ezra, it could mean, "Whether she grew up in the same household or elsewhere."

10] *For their nakedness is yours.* Meaning of verse obscure (T.N.).

יא עֶרְוָתְךָ הֵנָּה: ס עֶרְוַת בַּת־אֵשֶׁת אָבִיךָ מוֹלֶדֶת
יב אָבִיךָ אֲחוֹתְךָ הִיא לֹא תְגַלֶּה עֶרְוָתָהּ: ס עֶרְוַת
יג אֲחוֹת־אָבִיךָ לֹא תְגַלֵּה שְׁאֵר אָבִיךָ הוּא: ס עֶרְוַת
יד אֲחוֹת־אִמְּךָ לֹא תְגַלֵּה כִּי־שְׁאֵר אִמְּךָ הוּא: ס עֶרְוַת
אֲחִי־אָבִיךָ לֹא תְגַלֵּה אֶל־אִשְׁתּוֹ לֹא תִקְרָב דֹּדָתְךָ
טו הוּא: ס עֶרְוַת כַּלָּתְךָ לֹא תְגַלֵּה אֵשֶׁת בִּנְךָ הוּא
טז לֹא תְגַלֵּה עֶרְוָתָהּ: ס עֶרְוַת אֵשֶׁת־אָחִיךָ לֹא תְגַלֵּה
יז עֶרְוַת אָחִיךָ הוּא: ס עֶרְוַת אִשָּׁה וּבִתָּהּ לֹא תְגַלֵּה

Leviticus 18

11–17

11] The nakedness of your father's wife's daughter, who was born into your father's household—she is your sister; do not uncover her nakedness.

12] Do not uncover the nakedness of your father's sister; she is your father's flesh.

13] Do not uncover the nakedness of your mother's sister; for she is your mother's flesh.

14] Do not uncover the nakedness of your father's brother: do not approach his wife; she is your aunt.

15] Do not uncover the nakedness of your daughter-in-law: she is your son's wife; you shall not uncover her nakedness.

16] Do not uncover the nakedness of your brother's wife; it is the nakedness of your brother.

17] Do not uncover the nakedness of a woman and her daughter; nor shall you

---

11] *Who was born into your father's household.* Hebrew *moledet avicha.* There is no word for "household."

The meaning of the clause is obscure. It might mean: She is to be regarded as a descendant of your father, even though she is not so in fact.

אֶת־בַּת־בְּנָהּ וְאֶת־בַּת־בִּתָּהּ לֹא תִקַּח לְגַלּוֹת עֶרְוָתָהּ

יח שַׁאֲרָה הֵנָּה זִמָּה הִוא: וְאִשָּׁה אֶל־אֲחֹתָהּ לֹא תִקָּח

יט לִצְרֹר לְגַלּוֹת עֶרְוָתָהּ עָלֶיהָ בְּחַיֶּיהָ: וְאֶל־אִשָּׁה בְּנִדַּת

כ טֻמְאָתָהּ לֹא תִקְרַב לְגַלּוֹת עֶרְוָתָהּ: וְאֶל־אֵשֶׁת

עֲמִיתְךָ לֹא־תִתֵּן שְׁכָבְתְּךָ לְזָרַע לְטָמְאָה־בָהּ:

כא וּמִזַּרְעֲךָ לֹא־תִתֵּן לְהַעֲבִיר לַמֹּלֶךְ וְלֹא תְחַלֵּל אֶת־

כב שֵׁם אֱלֹהֶיךָ אֲנִי יְהוָה: וְאֶת־זָכָר לֹא תִשְׁכַּב מִשְׁכְּבֵי

כג אִשָּׁה תּוֹעֵבָה הִוא: וּבְכָל־בְּהֵמָה לֹא־תִתֵּן שְׁכָבְתְּךָ

לְטָמְאָה־בָהּ וְאִשָּׁה לֹא־תַעֲמֹד לִפְנֵי בְהֵמָה לְרִבְעָהּ

marry her son's daughter or her daughter's daughter and uncover her nakedness: they are kindred; it is depravity.

18] Do not marry a woman as a rival to her sister and uncover her nakedness in the other's lifetime.

19] Do not come near a woman during her period of uncleanness to uncover her nakedness.

20] Do not have carnal relations with your neighbor's wife and defile yourself with her.

21] Do not allow any of your offspring to be offered up to Molech, and do not profane the name of your God: I am the LORD.

22] Do not lie with a male as one lies with a woman; it is an abhorrence.

23] Do not have carnal relations with any beast and defile yourself thereby; and let no woman lend herself to a beast to mate with it; it is perversion.

18] *Do not marry a woman as a rival to her sister.* Jacob's marriage to the sisters Leah and Rachel occurred prior to the promulgation of this law at Sinai.

21] On Molech, see p. 191. On profanation of God's name, see p. 204.

כד תֵּבֵל הוּא: אַל־תִּטַּמְּאוּ בְּכָל־אֵלֶּה כִּי בְכָל־אֵלֶּה

כה נִטְמְאוּ הַגּוֹיִם אֲשֶׁר־אֲנִי מְשַׁלֵּחַ מִפְּנֵיכֶם: וַתִּטְמָא
הָאָרֶץ וָאֶפְקֹד עֲוֺנָהּ עָלֶיהָ וַתָּקִא הָאָרֶץ אֶת־

כו יֹשְׁבֶיהָ: וּשְׁמַרְתֶּם אַתֶּם אֶת־חֻקֹּתַי וְאֶת־מִשְׁפָּטַי וְלֹא
תַעֲשׂוּ מִכֹּל הַתּוֹעֵבֹת הָאֵלֶּה הָאֶזְרָח וְהַגֵּר הַגָּר

כז בְּתוֹכְכֶם: כִּי אֶת־כָּל־הַתּוֹעֵבֹת הָאֵל* עָשׂוּ אַנְשֵׁי־

כח הָאָרֶץ אֲשֶׁר לִפְנֵיכֶם וַתִּטְמָא הָאָרֶץ: וְלֹא־תָקִיא
הָאָרֶץ אֶתְכֶם בְּטַמַּאֲכֶם אֹתָהּ כַּאֲשֶׁר קָאָה אֶת־הַגּוֹי

כט אֲשֶׁר לִפְנֵיכֶם: כִּי כָּל־אֲשֶׁר יַעֲשֶׂה מִכֹּל הַתּוֹעֵבֹת
הָאֵלֶּה וְנִכְרְתוּ הַנְּפָשׁוֹת הָעֹשֹׂת מִקֶּרֶב עַמָּם:

ל וּשְׁמַרְתֶּם אֶת־מִשְׁמַרְתִּי לְבִלְתִּי עֲשׂוֹת מֵחֻקּוֹת

* כז סבירין האלה.

24] Do not defile yourselves in any of those ways, for it is by such that the nations which I am casting out before you defiled themselves. **25]** Thus the land became defiled; and I called it to account for its iniquity, and the land spewed out its inhabitants. **26]** But you must keep My laws and My rules, and you must not do any of those abhorrent things, neither the citizen nor the stranger who resides among you; **27]** for all those abhorrent things were done by the people who were in the land before you, and the land became defiled. **28]** So let not the land spew you out for defiling it, as it spewed out the nation that came before you. **29]** All who do any of those abhorrent things—such persons shall be cut off from their people. **30]** You shall keep My charge not to engage in any of the abhorrent practices

24] *Do not defile yourselves....* The chapter concludes, as it began, with an exhortation. The Land of Israel is literally the Holy Land and its sanctity would be defiled by the actions forbidden in this section.

הַתּוֹעֵבֹת אֲשֶׁר נַעֲשׂוּ לִפְנֵיכֶם וְלֹא תִטַּמְּאוּ בָּהֶם אֲנִי **וַיְּקְרָא** יח:ל
יְהוָֹה אֱלֹהֵיכֶם:

Leviticus 18:30

Haftarah Achare Mot, p. 383

that were carried on before you, and you shall not defile yourselves through them:
I the LORD am your God.

GLEANINGS

Halachah

18:3] *Nor Shall You Follow Their Laws*

This passage forbids Jews to attend the bloody entertainments of the Roman amphitheater, to practice various superstitious customs of the gentile world, and even to imitate gentile styles of hairdressing [30].

5] *My Laws and My Rules, by the Pursuit of Which Man Shall Live*

Man is to attain life, not death, through the Torah. Therefore, when danger to life is involved, any commandment of the Torah may be disregarded, except the laws forbidding murder, idolatry, and sexual crime. But this applies only to violations in private. Public violation even of a lesser commandment would profane the name of God (see p. 204), and one should suffer martyrdom rather than desecrate God's name [31].

6] *None of You Shall Come near Anyone of His Flesh*

This general statement is followed by a number of specific instances. In such cases, the generalization is not held to contain more than the ensuing specific cases. We should not infer, e.g., that, because a nephew may not marry his uncle's wife (verse 14), an uncle may not marry his nephew's wife [32].

Haggadah

18:5] *My Laws and My Rules, by the Pursuit of Which Man Shall Live*

Obedience to the Torah will be rewarded by life in the world to come. TARGUMS and SIFRA

This passage speaks not of priests, Levites, and Israelites, but of "man." The moral law is valid for all men, and the heathen who obeys the Torah is equal to the High Priest. SIFRA

25] *The Land Became Defiled . . . and Spewed Out Its Inhabitants*

Unlike other lands, which are ruled by an angelic deputy, the Land of Israel is directly under God's providence and so is more sensitive to defilement. That is why the Canaanites were spewed out of the Holy Land whereas the Egyptians, who committed the same defiling sins, were not expelled from their country (Nachmanides).

30] *You Shall Keep My Charge*

Literally, "You shall guard My guarding." The Talmud finds in this verse the injunction to "make a fence about the Torah," i.e., to make additional restrictions which will prevent accidental violations [33] (see Gleanings, Halachah, on 7:15).

The Life of Holiness

We have reached the climactic chapter of the book, the one most often read and quoted. In American Reform practice, it is the Torah reading for Yom Kippur afternoon.

1. *Holiness*

The constant theme here is *holiness*. We have already encountered this concept, chiefly in reflections of its ancient and primitive form. Here, after summarizing such material, we shall move on to more advanced and mature conceptions of holiness, and we shall consider their implications for our own life. It will, moreover, be proper to make use of Hebrew terminology, for the word *kadosh* (plural *kedoshim*) is only roughly, but not exactly, equivalent to the English "holy." The word *kodesh*, "holiness," is often used where an adjective would be employed in English—"My holy name" (20:3) is literally "the name of My holiness." Other derivatives from the same root are: *kiddush*, "sanctification," applied especially to hallowing Sabbath and festivals over a cup of wine—but see below, "2. Sanctifying and Profaning the Name," p. 204; *kedushah*, also meaning holiness or sanctification, used especially for

a series of responses in the synagogue service; and the familiar Aramaic word *kaddish*.

a. *Kadosh* is the adjective regularly applied to divinity and divinities. In the Book of Daniel (4:5f.), the Babylonian king speaks of the "holy gods" (Aramaic *elahin kadishin*). Other biblical writings refer to angelic beings as *kedoshim* (Zech. 14:5; Ps. 9:8; Job 5:11) [1]. The God of Israel is often characterized as *kadosh*, especially by Isaiah.

b. This term, conventionally associated with deity, is also applied to places, times, objects, and procedures connected with deity. A place of worship is called *mikdash*. The innermost Shrine is *Kodesh Kodashim*, "Holy of Holies"—more exactly, "highest level of holiness." All sacrifices are holy, but some are designated as *Kodesh Kodashim*.

As the deity was regarded anciently as set apart and dangerous to approach, so it was often with places and things that were his special possession. In some Bible passages, *kadosh* has the same force as the Polynesian word *taboo* [2]. In such cases, holiness was conceived as a physical force which can pass from one object to another like an electric current with potentially destructive power.

Kodesh does not necessarily indicate an absolute taboo. The sacred places may be approached, sacred food may be eaten, but only if special rules, especially those of ceremonial purity, are strictly observed. Disregard of these rules, intentional or otherwise, is a desecration that may lead to disastrous results.

c. This mechanical concept of "holiness" was embodied in practices treated in the earlier chapters of this book—practices that survived even after the ideas they expressed had been supplanted by a more mature concept of *kedushah*. For *kadosh* gradually came to indicate, not the physical separation of God and man, but the spiritual gap between human inadequacy and divine perfection.

In his consecration vision, Isaiah (6:3) beholds God surrounded by the *seraphim* who chant: "Holy, holy, holy! The LORD of Hosts! His presence fills all the earth!"

His immediate reaction is: "Woe is me; I am lost! / For I am a man of unclean lips / And I live among a people of unclean lips" (Isa. 6:5).

It is sinfulness, present even in speech, which makes him feel an intruder, unworthy to approach God. The prophets characterize God more often in terms of supreme righteousness than in terms of supreme power. It is Isaiah especially who calls God *Kedosh Yisrael*, "the Holy One of Israel" (e.g., 1:4).

Yet, despite the gap between God's perfection and man's limitations, God was not thought of as remote and unapproachable. A later prophet, whose words are included in the latter chapters of Isaiah, represents God as saying: "I dwell on high, in holiness, / Yet with the contrite and the lowly in spirit" (Isa. 57:15).

Most remarkable of all, our chapter summons the Israelites to imitate God and so become holy themselves.

d. This last point requires special stress in view of the great influence exercised on a generation or more of religious thinkers by the book, *The Idea of the Holy* [3]. The author,

Rudolf Otto, a Protestant theologian, was disturbed by the tendency of liberals to reduce religion to ethics. He sought to prove that man's nature has a religious aspect that was originally independent of the ethical. It is that part of us which responds to the mysterious and awesome—to the reality, at once overwhelming and fascinating, that cannot be adequately understood or rationalized. The word "holy" and its equivalents, says Otto, point to the experience of the "numinous," of a divine reality that evokes fear, awe, and submission. This experience, in its cruder and more primitive forms, is that of the uncanny, ghostly, and hair-raising. Later, as concepts of divinity are purified and elevated, ethical elements are introduced into the idea of holiness, and awe is evoked, not only by the frightening mystery, but also by the divine perfection.

It is striking that Otto, a pious Lutheran, made no mention of this chapter of Leviticus in his book. He spoke only of holiness as an emotional experience, not of *kedushah* as aspiration and task to be approached through a disciplined life. In his zeal to give religion a unique character, Otto reduced the ethical component of holiness to a mere "extra." This is not the Jewish view of the subject, as is plain from the text before us, and also from the recurrent declaration in our prayers and benedictions that God "sanctifies us through His commandments." In Judaism, religion and ethics, though not identical, are inseparable [4].

e. Chapters 18 through 20 give a clear account of holiness in life.

The prime emphasis is ethical. And the moral laws of this chapter are not mere injunctions of conformity. They call for just, humane, and sensitive treatment of others. The aged, the handicapped, and the poor are to receive consideration and courtesy. The laborer is to be promptly paid. The stranger is to be accorded the same love we give our fellow citizens. The law is concerned, not only with overt behavior, but also with motive; vengefulness and the bearing of grudges are condemned.

Among ethical duties, that of sexual decency is singled out for particular emphasis. The Torah demands the control, not the suppression of the sexual instinct. Life is sacred. The physical process by which life is generated is to be treated responsibly.

The ethical injunctions of chapter 19 are interspersed with ritual commandments. Some of these are directed against pagan and superstitious practices deemed incompatible with biblical religion. The intent of others is not so plain. To the biblical author, these ceremonial rulings are divine ordinances with the same authority as the ethical commandments. Traditional Judaism regarded them as "royal decrees," to be observed whether or not we comprehend them (p. 90).

The Jewish modernist cannot agree with this. But he can recognize that worship and ceremony, undertaken thoughtfully and reverently, can elevate personal and family life. Though he may reject older views as to the origin and authority of ritual, he may still benefit from the practice of ritual. In holy living, the ethical factor is primary, but it is not the only one. In combining moral and ceremonial commandments, the authors of the Holiness Code displayed sound understanding.

f. Such are the components of the way of life called *kadosh*. Our chapter begins with the startling declaration that by these means we can and should try to be holy like God. The same Torah that stresses the distance between His sublime perfection and our earthy limitations urges us to strive to reduce that distance. The task is endless, but it is infinitely rewarding. Rabbi Tarfon said: "Do not avoid an undertaking that has no limit or a task that cannot be completed.

It is like the case of one who was hired to take water from the sea and pour it out on the land. But, as the sea was not emptied out or the land filled with water, he became downhearted. Then someone said to him, 'Foolish fellow! Why should you be downhearted as long as you receive a dinar of gold every day as your wage?' " [5]. The pursuit of the unattainable can be a means of fulfillment.

g. The Law of Holiness is not addressed to selected individuals. It is addressed to the entire community of Israel. Its objective is not to produce a few saints, withdrawn from the world in contemplative or ascetic practices. Rather, does the Torah aim to create a holy people which displays its consecration to God's service in the normal day-to-day relations of farming, commerce, family living, and community affairs (cf. Exod. 19:6).

h. Characteristic of H is the notion of the holy land [6]. Though God rules the whole world, He is uniquely attached to, and present in, the land of Canaan, which is to be the Land of Israel. Hence, heathen practices that are tolerable elsewhere will lead to expulsion from the Land of Israel (18:24, 28; 20:22ff.). The law of the Sabbath year is imposed not only on the people but on the soil itself; failure to observe the law will have to be made up for through years of desolation (below, 26:34).

The notion that sanctity should attach to a particular geographic area may seem strange to us. Yet many find it natural for Jews to expect more of themselves than of others, to believe that a Jewish community should be a model community, and a Jewish state different from, and better than, other national states.

The idea of holiness implies that what we do and what we make of our lives matters not only to us as individuals, not only to society, but to the entire cosmos. A divine purpose runs through all existence. We can ally ourselves to it or oppose it—or, perhaps worse, we can ignore it. This climactic chapter of the Torah deserves, not only careful reading and study, but continuing reflection on its astonishing implications.

2. Sanctifying and Profaning the Name

We have already noted the statement (18:21) that one who offers his offspring to Molech profanes the name of God. The same expression appears in chapter 19, verse 12, in connection with swearing falsely. In these contexts, the phrase seems to require no explanation. But its fuller meaning emerges elsewhere. To profane the name of God means to impair His reputation in the non-Israelite world.

Thus, Ezekiel (who, we have seen, shows affinity to the Holiness Code) declares that, when the people of Judah brought the punishment of exile upon themselves, they profaned the name of God. For the Gentiles regarded the defeat of Judah as a defeat for Judah's God as well. They supposed the people were in exile because their God was not strong enough to protect them. Therefore, to retrieve His reputation, God would purify and restore Israel. When they were back on their own soil, strong and prosperous, God's name would be "sanctified in the sight of all the peoples"—that is, the nations would recognize His power and understand that the exile was not evidence of His impotence, but of His unswerving justice (Ezek. 36:16ff.).

This concept was transformed in Rabbinic Judaism from a questionable theological proposition into a powerful moral challenge. The prestige of Israel's God among the Gentiles—the Rabbis taught—is not God's worry, it is humankind's responsibility. Jews must so live and act as to win for their God the respect of all mankind. Any behavior that brings public disgrace on Jews and Judaism is *chilul ha-Shem*, profanation of the divine Name; any action that enhances the dignity and honor of Judaism is *kiddush ha-Shem*, sanctification of the Name.

Robbing a Gentile is doubly sinful, since it adds to the sin of robbery the further sin of *chilul ha-Shem* [7]. A Jew should accept martyrdom rather than publicly violate a commandment and thus profane the name of God [8].

Kiddush ha-Shem has no connection with what we now call "public relations." It does not mean currying favor with the Gentiles. It requires us to deserve the approbation of others, whether we actually obtain it or not. The highest act of *kiddush ha-Shem* is to die for one's faith.

3. The Golden Rule

The culmination of this climactic chapter is verse 18: "Love your neighbor as yourself." It is one of several versions of what in modern times has been called "the golden rule." (We do not know when or by whom the phrase was coined.) It appears in various forms, positive and negative; but all of them demand for others the same kind of treatment we want for ourselves.

Our passage is apparently the oldest written version of the principle. When Hillel, at the beginning of the Christian era, was asked to sum up the entire Torah briefly, he replied: "What is hateful to you, do not do to your fellow" [9]. (This negative form of the golden rule was apparently proverbial in Hillel's time for it appears in practically the same words in the apocryphal book of Tobit [10].) Jesus of Nazareth, Hillel's younger contemporary, declared that the commandment of Leviticus (19:13) is second in importance only to the command to love God (Mark 2:28ff.). In the following century, Rabbi Akiba declared it to be "the great principle of the Torah" (*Sifra*).

Confucius is credited with having taught the golden rule in its negative form [11]. A more abstract version of the principle is Kant's categorical imperative: "Act only on that maxim whereby thou canst at the same time will that it should become a universal law" [12].

Some Christian apologetes have argued that the negative form of the golden rule is spiritually inferior to the positive form ascribed to Jesus: "All that you would wish that men should do unto you, do ye also unto them" (Matt. 7:12). In their zeal, they forgot that the positive form occurs first in the Torah! But, actually, there is virtually no difference in meaning between the two versions. The golden rule, it has been remarked [13], is an instrument of criticism. It enables us to judge a proposed course of action, but it does not provide us the means of proposing a course of action; that always requires an effort of creative imagination. Regarded as a standard of judgment, the golden rule is equally effective in negative or positive form.

Some Christians have also tried to show that the saying of Jesus is more truly universal and inclusive than that of Leviticus. They argue that "neighbor" in Leviticus (19:18) means "fellow Israelite" which is true enough; but they apparently overlook the commandment of verse 34 which requires us to show the same love to a foreigner resident in the land. There is no evidence that Jesus had a broader outlook [14].

Such theoretical distinctions would in any case not be important. Our opportunity to practice the golden rule is chiefly in our relations to those who are physically near to us, our literal neighbors. In ancient times, most people had little awareness of events beyond their immediate vicinity. They had no share in major political and economic decisions.

They rarely knew even of major occurrences until the results came upon them in the form of invasion, deportation, new tax demands, and the like. Only in recent centuries, especially in our own, has the average person had the knowledge, the opportunity, and the obligation to apply the golden rule on a global scale. Today, indeed, we must consider what duties we owe to the Vietnamese, the Biafrans, the Bengalis; but that is something new. And it does not make the question of our relationships with those nearer home any less compelling.

A mechanical, though not accurate, translation of the verse might be, "You shall love to (le-) your neighbor as yourself." This circumstance has suggested to various commentators alternative interpretations of the passage. They are not grammatically justifiable, for there are numerous instances in the Bible of this construction of a direct object with le-; but they are interesting in themselves.

Thus, Ibn Ezra, noting that many commentators took "neighbor" as the direct object, preferred to render, "Love the good for your neighbor as you love it for yourself." And the modern German thinkers Hermann Cohen and Martin Buber explained, "Be loving to your fellow man, as to one who is just like you" [15].

Nachmanides held to the traditional, "Love your neighbor as yourself," but regarded the language as rhetorical exaggeration. Our nature is such that we cannot love others as much as ourselves; and the halachah does not obligate us to sacrifice our lives for others. This commandment, Nachmanides asserts, calls on us to love others as we love good for ourselves. We should free ourselves from jealousy and rejoice in our neighbor's good fortune. But we should not tolerate injustice in the name of ill-considered love.

קדשים
ויקרא יט
א-ד

Kedoshim
Leviticus 19
1–4

א וַיְדַבֵּר יְהוָה אֶל־מֹשֶׁה לֵּאמֹר: דַּבֵּר אֶל־כָּל־עֲדַת
בְּנֵי־יִשְׂרָאֵל וְאָמַרְתָּ אֲלֵהֶם קְדשִׁים תִּהְיוּ כִּי קָדוֹשׁ
ג אֲנִי יְהוָה אֱלֹהֵיכֶם: אִישׁ אִמּוֹ וְאָבִיו תִּירָאוּ וְאֶת־
ד שַׁבְּתֹתַי תִּשְׁמֹרוּ אֲנִי יְהוָה אֱלֹהֵיכֶם: אַל־תִּפְנוּ אֶל־
הָאֱלִילִים וֵאלֹהֵי מַסֵּכָה לֹא תַעֲשׂוּ לָכֶם אֲנִי יְהוָה

1] The LORD spoke to Moses, saying: 2] Speak to the whole Israelite community and say to them:

You shall be holy, for I, the LORD your God, am holy.

3] You shall each revere his mother and his father, and keep My sabbaths: I the LORD am your God.

4] Do not turn to idols or make molten gods for yourselves: I the LORD am your God.

19:2] *Speak to the whole Israelite community.* This section was proclaimed publicly because it contains so many basic laws (*Sifra*). Holiness was to be the ideal, not of a priestly caste alone, but of the entire people.

You shall be holy. See the introduction to this chapter. *Sifra* explains: "As I, God, am set apart [*parush*], so you must be set apart [*perushim*]" (this is the word rendered "Pharisees" in other contexts). Perhaps the best rendering here would be the colloquial phrase, "You shall be something special."

3] *You shall each revere his mother and his father.* It was noted already by the Rabbis [16] that the Ten Commandments are all repeated in this section, though not in the order of Exodus, chapter 20. This verse corresponds to the fifth commandment. The complete list in Leviticus, chapter 19, is as follows:

First commandment, "I the LORD am your God" (verse 4, end)

Second commandment, "You shall have no other gods" (4, beginning)

Third commandment, "You shall not swear falsely" (12)

Fourth commandment, "Remember the Sabbath day" (3)

Fifth commandment, "Honor your father and your mother" (3)

Sixth commandment, "You shall not murder" (16)

Seventh commandment, "You shall not commit adultery" (29)

Eighth commandment, "You shall not steal" (11)

Ninth commandment, "You shall not bear false witness" (16)

Tenth commandment, "You shall not covet" (18)

4] *Idols.* Hebrew *elilim.* A variety of words are used in the Hebrew Bible to designate idols. This is one of the most contemptuous of them. Perhaps it was chosen just because it sounds like the legitimate words for "God," *El* and *Elohim.* In other connections, the same word is used for "worthlessness" (Zech. 11:17; Job 13:4).

ה אֱלֹהֵיכֶם: וְכִי תִזְבְּחוּ זֶבַח שְׁלָמִים לַיהוָה לִרְצֹנְכֶם

ו תִּזְבָּחֻהוּ: בְּיוֹם זִבְחֲכֶם יֵאָכֵל וּמִמָּחֳרָת וְהַנּוֹתָר עַד-

ז יוֹם הַשְּׁלִישִׁי בָּאֵשׁ יִשָּׂרֵף: וְאִם הֵאָכֹל יֵאָכֵל בַּיּוֹם

ח הַשְּׁלִישִׁי פִּגּוּל הוּא לֹא יֵרָצֶה: וְאֹכְלָיו עֲוֹנוֹ יִשָּׂא כִּי-

אֶת-קֹדֶשׁ יְהוָה חִלֵּל וְנִכְרְתָה הַנֶּפֶשׁ הַהִוא מֵעַמֶּיהָ:

ט וּבְקֻצְרְכֶם אֶת-קְצִיר אַרְצְכֶם לֹא תְכַלֶּה פְּאַת שָׂדְךָ

י לִקְצֹר וְלֶקֶט קְצִירְךָ לֹא תְלַקֵּט: וְכַרְמְךָ לֹא תְעוֹלֵל

וּפֶרֶט כַּרְמְךָ לֹא תְלַקֵּט לֶעָנִי וְלַגֵּר תַּעֲזֹב אֹתָם אֲנִי

Leviticus 19
5–10

5] When you sacrifice an offering of well-being to the LORD, sacrifice it so that it may be accepted on your behalf.   **6]** It shall be eaten on the day you sacrifice it, or on the day following; but what is left by the third day must be consumed in fire. **7]** If it should be eaten on the third day, it is an offensive thing, it will not be acceptable.   **8]** And he who eats of it shall bear his guilt, for he has profaned what is sacred to the LORD; that person shall be cut off from his kin.

9] When you reap the harvest of your land, you shall not reap all the way to the edges of your field, or gather the gleanings of your harvest.   **10]** You shall not pick your vineyard bare, or gather the fallen fruit of your vineyard; you shall leave them for the poor and the stranger: I the LORD am your God.

5–8] Sacrifices of well-being. See commentary and gleanings on 7:15ff. H does not expound the sacrificial law at length, though it consistently implies the importance of the cult. Perhaps this item was included because it applies to the lay worshiper rather than to the priest.

9–10] The rights of the poor at harvest time. This law appears again in chapter 23, verse 22. Deuteronomy (24:19ff.) repeats the law about the gleaning of fruit and adds that the farmer should not go back to reclaim a forgotten sheaf of grain, but it does not mention the requirement of leaving a corner of the field uncut.

This passage (and the parallels mentioned) is not an appeal to the generosity of the landowner. It confers the right to glean and to harvest the uncut edge on those who have no resources of their own. It is perhaps the oldest declaration that the disadvantaged members of the society have a right to support from that society and should not be dependent on voluntary benevolence alone—though the latter is constantly stressed as well.

Because the specific laws here apply only to an agricultural society, later tradition applied the principle involved to urban conditions (see Gleanings).

יא יְהוָה אֱלֹהֵיכֶם: לֹא תִּגְנֹבוּ וְלֹא־תְכַחֲשׁוּ וְלֹא־תְשַׁקְּרוּ
יב אִישׁ בַּעֲמִיתוֹ: וְלֹא־תִשָּׁבְעוּ בִשְׁמִי לַשָּׁקֶר וְחִלַּלְתָּ
יג אֶת־שֵׁם אֱלֹהֶיךָ אֲנִי יְהוָה: לֹא־תַעֲשֹׁק אֶת־רֵעֲךָ וְלֹא
יד תִגְזֹל לֹא־תָלִין פְּעֻלַּת שָׂכִיר אִתְּךָ עַד־בֹּקֶר: לֹא־
תְקַלֵּל חֵרֵשׁ וְלִפְנֵי עִוֵּר לֹא תִתֵּן מִכְשֹׁל וְיָרֵאתָ
טו מֵאֱלֹהֶיךָ אֲנִי יְהוָה: לֹא־תַעֲשׂוּ עָוֶל בַּמִּשְׁפָּט לֹא־

11] You shall not steal; you shall not deal deceitfully or falsely with one another.

12] You shall not swear falsely by My name, profaning the name of your God: I am the LORD.

13] You shall not defraud your neighbor. You shall not commit robbery. The wages of a laborer shall not remain with you until morning.

14] You shall not insult the deaf, or place a stumbling block before the blind. You shall fear your God: I am the LORD.

15] You shall not render an unfair decision: do not favor the poor or show def-

11] *You shall not deal deceitfully or falsely.* The medieval commentators disagree as to what particular practices are forbidden by the terms "deceitfully" and "falsely." But, according to most opinions, they forbid deceit concerning property entrusted to one's keeping and concerning loans and the making of fraudulent claims.

12] *Profaning the name of your God.* See the introduction to this chapter, "2. Sanctifying and Profaning the Name."

13] *Defraud.* From *ashak*, "to take advantage of, exploit, withhold something due."

Robbery. By force, in contrast to theft (by stealth). In colloquial English, we often disregard the clear legal distinction between "steal" and "rob." But the corresponding Hebrew terms, *ganav* and *gazal*, are not interchanged.

The wages of a laborer shall not remain with you until morning. Similarly Deuteronomy (24:15). *Sifra* regards this as the continuation and conclusion of the preceding sentences. To hold back the laborer's wage is to defraud him by use of superior force.

14] *You shall not insult the deaf.* Two thoughts seem to be involved: do not take advantage of the handicapped, and do not treat another person contemptuously even if you can do it with impunity.

Or place a stumbling block before the blind. Taken literally, the law seems pointless. Why should anyone commit so childish an act of cruelty? *Sifra* therefore understands the commandment figuratively: Do not give self-serving advice to one who is ignorant and inexperienced [17].

But one who sold worthless stock to a widow could argue, "I really believed it was valuable and that I was helping her to get rich." Who could prove he was insincere? Therefore, adds *Sifra*, wherever the law is something "entrusted to the heart," the Torah cautions, "You shall fear your God." He knows what your motives are!

15] *You shall not render an unfair decision.* The Torah repeatedly admonishes judges to uphold justice unswervingly (Exod. 23:2ff.; Deut. 1:16f.; 16:18ff.).

תִּשָּׂא פְנֵי־דָל וְלֹא תֶהְדַּר פְּנֵי גָדוֹל בְּצֶדֶק תִּשְׁפֹּט

עֲמִיתֶךָ: לֹא־תֵלֵךְ רָכִיל בְּעַמֶּיךָ לֹא תַעֲמֹד עַל־דַּם

רֵעֶךָ אֲנִי יְהוָה: לֹא־תִשְׂנָא אֶת־אָחִיךָ בִּלְבָבֶךָ הוֹכֵחַ

תּוֹכִיחַ אֶת־עֲמִיתֶךָ וְלֹא־תִשָּׂא עָלָיו חֵטְא: לֹא־תִקֹּם

וְלֹא־תִטֹּר אֶת־בְּנֵי עַמֶּךָ וְאָהַבְתָּ לְרֵעֲךָ כָּמוֹךָ אֲנִי

erence to the rich; judge your neighbor fairly.   16] Do not deal basely with your fellows. Do not profit by the blood of your neighbor. I am the LORD.

17] You shall not hate your kinsman in your heart. Reprove your neighbor, but incur no guilt because of him.   18] You shall not take vengeance or bear a grudge against your kinsfolk. Love your neighbor as yourself: I am the LORD.

Misguided sympathy should not lead the judge to show favoritism to the poor (Exod. 23:3).

16] *Do not deal basely with your fellows.* Others, "go about as a talebearer"; meaning of Hebrew uncertain (T.N.). This rendering is traditional. It takes the Hebrew word *rachil* as related to *rochel*, "peddler" (see commentary on verse 3, where this sentence is equated with the ninth commandment). But we do not know what *rachil* really means; and Orlinsky aptly remarks [18], "In such passages as Jeremiah 6:28 and Ezekiel 22:9, the wickedness of the people is surely more grievous than talebearing."

Do not profit by the blood of your neighbor. I.e., do not act in such a way that you profit by his death or injury; so Ehrlich. Literally, "Do not stand upon the blood of your neighbor"; precise meaning of Hebrew phrase uncertain (T.N.). Tradition explained: Do not stand by idly while your neighbor's blood is shed, do not abandon him when he is in danger (see Gleanings). Ibn Ezra takes the verse as forbidding us to associate with bloodthirsty men.

17] *You shall not hate your kinsman in your heart.* The Torah, unlike ordinary legal codes, is concerned not

only with actions but also with attitudes. It recognizes how destructive bottled-up resentment can be and cautions us against wrong feelings as well as wrong acts.

Reprove your neighbor, but incur no guilt because of him. If you think you have a justified complaint, do not brood over it but state it forthrightly. Rashi, following a hint in *Sifra*, explains: Rebuke him, but do not shame him publicly.

Or, substituting "and" for "but" (Exact force of *ve-* uncertain. T.N.), we may interpret: By giving vent to your feelings, you may save yourself from the guilt of a violent act. Or again: By pointing out your fellow's misdeeds and thus affording him the chance to make amends, you are discharging your moral obligation to him (cf. Ezek. 3:17–21).

18] *You shall not take vengeance or bear a grudge.* "A" refuses to lend his spade to "B"; "B" later refuses to lend "A" his ax—that is vengeance. But if "B" lends the ax to "A" and says, "See, I let you have it even though you wouldn't lend me your spade"— that is bearing a grudge, and it is also forbidden (*Sifra*).

Love your neighbor as yourself. See the introduction to this chapter, "3. The Golden Rule."

יט יְהֹוָה: אֶת־חֻקֹּתַי תִּשְׁמֹרוּ בְּהֶמְתְּךָ לֹא־תַרְבִּיעַ
כִּלְאַיִם שָׂדְךָ לֹא־תִזְרַע כִּלְאָיִם וּבֶגֶד כִּלְאַיִם שַׁעַטְנֵז
כ לֹא יַעֲלֶה עָלֶיךָ: וְאִישׁ כִּי־יִשְׁכַּב אֶת־אִשָּׁה שִׁכְבַת־
זֶרַע וְהִוא שִׁפְחָה נֶחֱרֶפֶת לְאִישׁ וְהָפְדֵּה לֹא נִפְדָּתָה
אוֹ חֻפְשָׁה לֹא נִתַּן־לָהּ בִּקֹּרֶת תִּהְיֶה לֹא יוּמְתוּ כִּי־לֹא

19] You shall observe My laws.

You shall not let your cattle mate with a different kind; you shall not sow your field with two kinds of seed; you shall not put on cloth from a mixture of two kinds of material.

20] If a man has carnal relations with a woman who is a slave and has been designated for another man, but has not been redeemed or given her freedom, there shall be an indemnity; they shall not, however, be put to death, since she has not

---

19] *My laws.* The Hebrew term for "law" here is *chukah* (elsewhere it frequently appears in the masculine form *chok*). According to the Rabbis, it designates a commandment whose purpose and meaning are not clear to us and which we must perform with simple, unquestioning obedience (p. 203). Such in fact is the character of the provisions in this verse.

The Hebrew word *kilayim*, meaning "of two kinds," appears in each of the three clauses. Similar regulations, using the same technical term, appear in Deuteronomy (22:9–11); in the latter passage nothing is said about breeding hybrid animals, but the yoking of an ox and an ass to the same plow is forbidden. These rules seem to reflect the belief that there is something unnatural about mixing breeds. Nachmanides is quite explicit—all species were fixed at Creation; the attempt to produce a new species is a defiance of God [19]. Such notions are very strange to us who live in the post-Darwinian age.

A mixture. Hebrew *shaatnez,* a word probably of non-Hebraic origin. It is explained in Deuteronomy 22:11 as a mixture of wool and linen.

The law of *kilayim* is elaborated fully in talmudic literature; it occupies an entire treatise of the Mishnah, called *Kilayim.*

20–22] *The slave woman and her lover.* Biblical law prescribes the death penalty for an adulterous couple (20:10). Moreover, a woman was regarded as married —and so liable to the penalty for adultery—from the time she was engaged to a man by his payment of the bride price, even though the marriage was not yet consummated (cf. Deut. 22:23–27). The present case concerns a slave woman who is about to be set free so that she can be married. The prospective husband had not yet "redeemed" her, that is, purchased her freedom from her master; and the latter has not liberated her of his own accord. If at this point she has sex relations with another man, neither of them is subject to the death penalty for she is still a slave and therefore not legally married. Her lover must, however, pay an indemnity (probably to the prospective husband, perhaps to the owner) and then bring a guilt offering. As usual, the guilt offering is valid only after financial restitution is made (cf. 5:20–26).

20] *Indemnity.* Hebrew *bikoret.* This rendering is supported by a related word in Akkadian [20]. The older Jewish Publication Society translation, following the margin of the Revised Version, rendered "inquisition," i.e., inquiry.

כא חֻפָּשָׁה: וְהֵבִיא אֶת־אֲשָׁמוֹ לַיהוָה אֶל־פֶּתַח אֹהֶל
כב מוֹעֵד אֵיל אָשָׁם: וְכִפֶּר עָלָיו הַכֹּהֵן בְּאֵיל הָאָשָׁם
לִפְנֵי יְהוָה עַל־חַטָּאתוֹ אֲשֶׁר חָטָא וְנִסְלַח לוֹ
מֵחַטָּאתוֹ אֲשֶׁר חָטָא: פ
כג וְכִי־תָבֹאוּ אֶל־הָאָרֶץ וּנְטַעְתֶּם כָּל־עֵץ מַאֲכָל
וַעֲרַלְתֶּם עָרְלָתוֹ אֶת־פִּרְיוֹ שָׁלֹשׁ שָׁנִים יִהְיֶה לָכֶם
כד עֲרֵלִים לֹא יֵאָכֵל: וּבַשָּׁנָה הָרְבִיעִת יִהְיֶה כָּל־פִּרְיוֹ
כה קֹדֶשׁ הִלּוּלִים לַיהוָה: וּבַשָּׁנָה הַחֲמִישִׁת תֹּאכְלוּ אֶת־
פִּרְיוֹ לְהוֹסִיף לָכֶם תְּבוּאָתוֹ אֲנִי יְהוָה אֱלֹהֵיכֶם:

Leviticus 19

21–25

been freed.   21] But he must bring to the entrance of the Tent of Meeting, as his
guilt offering to the LORD, a ram of guilt offering.   22] With the ram of guilt offering the priest shall make expiation for him before the LORD for the sin that he
committed; and the sin that he committed will be forgiven him.

    23] When you enter the land and plant any tree for food, you shall regard its
fruit as forbidden. Three years it shall be forbidden for you, not to be eaten.   24] In
the fourth year all its fruit shall be set aside for jubilation before the LORD;   25] and
only in the fifth year may you use its fruit—that its yield to you may be increased:
I the LORD am your God.

23–25] Prohibition of fruit of new trees. For the
first three years after the tree is planted, its fruit
may not be used at all; in the fourth year, the fruit
must be used only for a religious celebration; thereafter, it is completely permitted. This law no doubt
originated in the widespread belief that all new
life—vegetable, animal, or human—belongs to the
deity; giving a part of it as a redemptive offering
makes the remainder available for our use. Other
biblical examples are the laws of the first born
(Exod. 13:2, 11ff.), the first sheaf of grain (Lev.
23:9ff.), and the first fruits (Deut. 26).

23] *Forbidden.* Hebrew root 'rl, commonly "to be
uncircumcised" (T.N.).

24] *Set aside.* Hebrew *kodesh.* On the *jubilation before
the Lord,* see Gleanings.

25] *That its yield to you may be increased.* Presumably
this is the reward for obeying the commandment.
But the ancients knew just as well as we do that
fruit trees bear little or nothing in their first few
years and that stripping off the blossoms during
those years makes the trees more productive later
on. So perhaps these words emanate from the fruit-
grower's experience as much as from the religious
theories of the lawgiver.

כו לֹא תֹאכְלוּ עַל־הַדָּם לֹא תְנַחֲשׁוּ וְלֹא תְעוֹנֵנוּ: לֹא

כז תַקִּפוּ פְּאַת רֹאשְׁכֶם וְלֹא תַשְׁחִית אֵת פְּאַת זְקָנֶךָ: וְשֶׂרֶט

לָנֶפֶשׁ לֹא תִתְּנוּ בִּבְשַׂרְכֶם וּכְתֹבֶת קַעֲקַע לֹא תִתְּנוּ

כט בָּכֶם אֲנִי יְהֹוָה: אַל־תְּחַלֵּל אֶת־בִּתְּךָ לְהַזְנוֹתָהּ וְלֹא־

ל תִזְנֶה הָאָרֶץ וּמָלְאָה הָאָרֶץ זִמָּה: אֶת־שַׁבְּתֹתַי תִּשְׁמֹרוּ

26] You shall not eat anything with its blood. You shall not practice divination or soothsaying. 27] You shall not round off the side-growth on your head, or destroy the side-growth of your beard. 28] You shall not make gashes in your flesh for the dead, or incise any marks on yourselves: I am the LORD.

29] Do not degrade your daughter, and make her a harlot, lest the land fall into harlotry and the land be filled with depravity. 30] You shall keep My sabbaths and venerate My sanctuary: I am the LORD.

26] *You shall not eat anything with its blood.* According to this rendering, we have one more repetition of the commandment not to consume blood (cf. 17:10ff.). But the Hebrew reads literally, "You shall not eat on [or, with] the blood"; and various explanations have been offered.

Nachmanides connects this prohibition with the ensuing laws against divination and other heathen customs. He finds here a reference to a pagan practice in which blood was poured into a pit and people gathered around it to obtain omens for the future. This, he holds, was the sin of eating on (or, with) the blood, which the people committed according to I Sam. 14:32ff. This account is similar to what we know of Greek rites for the underground deities [21].

The Greek translation was apparently based on a different Hebrew text which read, "You shall not eat on the mountains," referring to heathen celebrations condemned by Ezekiel (18:6, 11, and 15).

Divination or soothsaying. See verse 31. (See also Deut. 18:9ff. and Ezek. 21:26). Ancient peoples had a variety of techniques for discovering the future. The Bible does not suggest that they are ineffective or fraudulent, but it bans them as idolatrous. In Israel, knowledge of the future could be sought legitimately only through prophets, through dreams, or through the sacred lot of Urim and Thummim (I Sam. 28:6).

27–28] Other forbidden pagan practices were certain ways of cutting the hair, "destroying" the beard, gashing oneself as a sign of mourning, tattooing (perhaps with heathen emblems). The wearing of side curls (*peot*) by extreme Orthodox Jews is an attempt to carry out strictly the law of verse 27.

29] *Do not degrade your daughter and make her a harlot.* This may allude to the well-attested institution of cult prostitutes whose earnings helped to maintain the temples where they plied their trade. Such practice is outlawed in Deuteronomy (23:18f.).

Lest the land fall into harlotry. That the land itself is defiled by the sins of its inhabitants is frequently stated in H (18:27ff., 20:22ff., 26:43).

לא וּמִקְדָּשַׁי תִּירָאוּ אֲנִי יְהוָה: אַל־תִּפְנוּ אֶל־הָאֹבֹת וְאֶל־
הַיִּדְּעֹנִים אַל־תְּבַקְשׁוּ לְטָמְאָה בָהֶם אֲנִי יְהוָה
לב אֱלֹהֵיכֶם: מִפְּנֵי שֵׂיבָה תָּקוּם וְהָדַרְתָּ פְּנֵי זָקֵן וְיָרֵאתָ
לג מֵאֱלֹהֶיךָ אֲנִי יְהוָה: ס וְכִי־יָגוּר אִתְּךָ גֵּר בְּאַרְצְכֶם

31] Do not turn to ghosts and do not inquire of familiar spirits, to be defiled by them: I the Lord am your God.

32] You shall rise before the aged and show deference to the old; you shall fear your God: I am the Lord.

33] When a stranger resides with you in your land, you shall not wrong him.

31] *Ghosts . . . familiar spirits.* From remote antiquity people have turned for guidance to the spirits of the dead, and mediums still do a thriving business in supposedly civilized countries. Such practices were well known to the ancient Israelites; though banned by the Torah, they had their devotees (I Sam. 28; Isa. 8:19f.). The term "familiar spirit" means what present-day mediums call a "control," that is, a ghost with which they can readily communicate and so make contact with other persons who have died. The Rabbis, however, explain the words here rendered "ghost" and "familiar spirit" as designating different techniques for consulting the dead (*Sifra*).

32] *You shall rise before the aged.* Hebrew *sevah*, "age," "gray hair." Respect for age is demanded and praised in the Bible and in all ancient Oriental wisdom literature.

The old. Hebrew *zaken*, which also means "elder" in the sense of community leader.

Fear your God. See commentary on verse 14.

33] *When a stranger [ger] resides . . . in your land.* The foreigner, resident in the Land of Israel, must not only be protected against molestation but be shown positive love. Many ancient peoples had rules for the protection of aliens, generally on a basis of personal reciprocity. A Roman protected a Greek acquaintance in Rome and vice versa. (That is why Latin and the Romance languages use one word for both "host" and "guest.") But nowhere in ancient literature is there the deep concern with the feelings of the stranger which the Torah imposes on the entire community. Here and elsewhere (e.g., Exod. 22:20), the requirement is connected with the memory of Israel's own experience as aliens in Egypt. Biblical law applies in many cases to both citizen and *ger* (Num. 9:14 and elsewhere). This meant that the alien had equal rights under the law and also that he must refrain from the forbidden practices that would defile the land. But he was not required to participate in the Israelite cult.

In rabbinic sources, *ger* is used in the sense of "proselyte," and these provisions are applied specifically to those who adopt the Jewish faith. This shift reflects the great interest of the rabbinic teachers in converts who, at the beginning of the Christian era, constituted a sizeable element of the community. It does not mean that these rights were denied the unconverted Gentile who is referred to in talmudic writings as "a son of Noah."

You shall not wrong him. By taking advantage of his unfamiliarity with economic conditions and business practices, or even by unkind words (*Sifra*).

לד לֹא תוֹנוּ אֹתוֹ: כְּאֶזְרָח מִכֶּם יִהְיֶה לָכֶם הַגֵּר הַגָּר
אִתְּכֶם וְאָהַבְתָּ לוֹ כָּמוֹךָ כִּי־גֵרִים הֱיִיתֶם בְּאֶרֶץ
לה מִצְרָיִם אֲנִי יְהֹוָה אֱלֹהֵיכֶם: לֹא־תַעֲשׂוּ עָוֶל בַּמִּשְׁפָּט
לו בַּמִּדָּה בַּמִּשְׁקָל וּבַמְּשׂוּרָה: מֹאזְנֵי צֶדֶק אַבְנֵי־צֶדֶק
אֵיפַת צֶדֶק וְהִין צֶדֶק יִהְיֶה לָכֶם אֲנִי יְהֹוָה אֱלֹהֵיכֶם
לז אֲשֶׁר־הוֹצֵאתִי אֶתְכֶם מֵאֶרֶץ מִצְרָיִם: וּשְׁמַרְתֶּם אֶת־
כָּל־חֻקֹּתַי וְאֶת־כָּל־מִשְׁפָּטַי וַעֲשִׂיתֶם אֹתָם אֲנִי
יְהֹוָה: פ

34] The stranger who resides with you shall be to you as one of your citizens; you shall love him as yourself, for you were strangers in the land of Egypt: I the LORD am your God.

35] You shall not falsify measures of length, weight, or capacity. **36]** You shall have an honest balance, honest weights, an honest *ephah*, and an honest *hin*.

I the LORD am your God who freed you from the land of Egypt. **37]** You shall faithfully observe all My laws and all My rules: I am the LORD.

35–36] Honest weights and measures. Integrity in business dealings is one of the components of holiness. The *ephah* was a dry measure, equivalent to about two pecks. The *hin* was a liquid measure roughly equal to an American gallon.

36] *I the Lord am your God who freed you from the land of Egypt.* Almost the same words with which the Ten Commandments begin are set at the end of the Law of Holiness. God's reality and His redemptive works provide the authority for the exacting demands made in this chapter.

GLEANINGS

Halachah

19:3] You Shall Each Revere His Mother and His Father, and Keep My Sabbaths

The second clause teaches that deference to parents does not justify disobedience of the Torah; if they tell us to violate the Sabbath, we must not heed them.　　　　　　　　SIFRA

4] You Shall Not Reap All the Way to the Edges

The halachah understands: One corner of each field, comprising at least one-sixtieth of its area, must be left uncut for the poor [22].

This law is treated in the section of the Mishnah called *Peah* ("corner"), together with other laws governing our obligations to the poor. Included are provisions to meet the needs of the urban poor—needs that arose as economic and social circumstances changed. The law provided for a daily distribution of food for those in immediate need of it, and for a weekly distribution of money for those who required long-term assistance. Every effort was made to preserve the dignity of those who received charity. Regular members of the community were taxed a certain amount for the maintenance of these and other communal institutions; but all were encouraged to supplement this minimum by generous voluntary contributions [23].

11] You Shall Not Steal

To witness a theft and keep silent about it is also theft.　　　　　　　　IBN EZRA

One should not steal back his own property from a thief—so as to avoid even the appearance of wrong action—but make a direct accusation and so recover what is his [24].

13] The Wages of a Laborer Shall Not Remain with You until Morning

The plain sense seems to be: You must pay at nightfall for work done during the day. But the halachah understood the verse to mean: "You shall not hold back the wages of one hired to work [through the night] till the morning." The corresponding rule in Deuteronomy (24:15) was taken to deal with one who worked during daylight hours up to sunset. From the two passages, the conclusion was derived that one who works during the day may be paid any time during the subsequent night, anyone working at night may be paid any time the ensuing day [25]. Though this gives the employer a few more hours to pay than the biblical author seems to have intended, it still requires prompt reimbursement. There are many other provisions in the halachah for the protection of labor [26].

14] Or Place a Stumbling Block before the Blind

This forbids one to act in such a way as to lead the unwary to violate the Torah (*Sifra*). Therefore, one should not strike his grown son, who might be roused to return the blow or to speak disrespectfully, thus violating the injunctions of verse 3 and Exodus (21:15, 17) [27].

16] Do Not Profit by the Blood of Your Neighbor

This was understood to mean: Do not stand by idly when your neighbor's blood is shed. If you see someone in danger of drowning, or being attacked by robbers, or by a wild beast, you are obligated to rescue that person (*Sifra*). Further, you must not withhold testimony in a criminal case, if you have evidence that favors the accused.

SIFRA and TARGUM PSEUDO-JONATHAN

17] Reprove Your Neighbor

If he does not respond to your reproof, Rabbi Eliezer says: Continue to reprove him until he strikes you; Rabbi Joshua says: until he curses you; Ben Azzai says: until he insults you [28].

19] *You Shall Not Let Your Cattle Mate with a Different Kind*

One may not breed hybrid animals (such as mules), but you may keep and use them [29].

You Shall Not Sow Your Field with Two Kinds of Seed

This law likewise prohibits the grafting of trees [30]. (Orthodox authorities have been greatly concerned that no citrons for use at Sukot should come from grafted trees.) On the other hand, it is permissible to sow vegetables between trees [31]. Though it is forbidden to plant two kinds of seeds together in a field, or to keep them growing, their products may be used. A different and more stringent law applies when mixed seeds are planted in a vineyard (Deut. 22:9) [32].

Cloth from a Mixture of Two Kinds of Material

Deuteronomy (22:11) defines *shaatnez* as a mixture of wool and linen; the halachah limits the prohibition to this one mixture. However, wool or linen may be mixed with cotton, silk, and other fibers [33]. The prohibition is only for the wearing of *shaatnez*; combinations of wool and linen may be used for any other purpose but clothing [34].

20] *Indemnity*

The halachah understood *bikoret* as "punishment," specifically, flogging for the woman; the man's punishment, the payment of indemnity and the presentation of an *asham*, is derived from the ensuing verses (*Sifra*). The Rabbis had great difficulty fitting this case into the general framework of the halachah. According to Maimonides it applies only

when half the sum required for the release of the woman has been paid and when the man to whom she has been designated is a Hebrew slave [35].

24] *Set Aside for Jubilation before the Lord*

On the analogy of Deuteronomy, chapter 14, verses 22ff., the owner was required to bring the fruit to Jerusalem, where he and his family were to consume it while in a state of ritual purity [36].

26] *You Shall Not Eat Anything with its Blood*

Literally, "You shall not eat on [or, with] the blood" (see commentary). From this one verse, *Sifra* drew all the following inferences: (a) Meat may not be eaten until all the lifeblood has been drained from the carcass. (b) Sacrificial meat may not be eaten until the blood has been dashed against the altar. (c) The traditional mourner's meal is not served to relatives of one executed for a crime. (d) Judges who impose a death sentence must fast on the day of the execution.

27] *... Destroy the Side-Growth of Your Beard*

"Destroy" was understood to mean shaving with a blade. Most Orthodox authorities permit the removal of facial hair by depilatories, tweezers, scissors, clippers, or electric shavers [37]. The prohibition in this verse applies only to males.

29] *Do Not Degrade Your Daughter*

This verse forbids a father to arrange or permit a liaison for his daughter. According to Rabbi Eliezer, it also forbids the father to give his daughter in marriage to an old man. According to Rabbi Akiba, a father is obligated to arrange a marriage for his daughter when she arrives at a suitable age, so as to protect her from temptation [38].

Haggadah

19:2] *You Shall Be Holy*

The word "holy" is applied in many different connections. The angels, the heavens, the prophets, the righteous, Israel, the Sabbaths, and the sacrifices are all called *kadosh* in Scripture. You might then suppose that their holiness resembles the holiness of Him whose command brought the world into being; therefore Scripture also declares, "There is none so holy as the Lord" (I Sam. 2:2) [39].

3] *You Shall Each Revere His Father and His Mother*

The word translated "revere" also means "fear." A son ordinarily fears his father more than his mother; he honors mother more than father because she cared for him when he was little. Therefore Scripture puts mother first in this verse and puts father first in "honor your father and mother"—to teach that both parents should be revered and honored equally.   SIFRA

Do not say: Just as I have been humiliated, let my fellow be humiliated too; just as I have been cursed at, let my fellow be cursed at too. Said Rabbi Tanchuma: If you act thus, know whom you are humiliating—"He made him in the likeness of God" (Gen. 5:1) [40].

Out of the endless chaos of the world, one nighest thing, his neighbor, is placed before his soul and concerning this one, and well-nigh only concerning this one, he is told: He is like you! "Like you," and thus not "you." You remain You and you are to remain just that. But he is not to remain a He for you and, thus, a mere It for your You. Rather, he is like You, like your You, a You like You, an I—a soul [41].

Punishment of Sex Offenses

This chapter appears to be a different version of the traditions preserved in chapter 18. Aside from the section on Molech-worship (on which see pp. 191–192), this chapter deals with virtually the same material as chapter 18, except that here the punishment of the various offenses is stated specifically. (But the severe tone of the prohibitions in chapter 18 probably implied the heavy penalties for these crimes.) This chapter also repeats (verse 6), with penalty, the prohibition against necromancy found in 19:31, and the death penalty (verse 9) for insulting a parent (stated in Exod. 21:17).

א וַיְדַבֵּר יְהוָה אֶל־מֹשֶׁה לֵּאמֹר: וְאֶל־בְּנֵי יִשְׂרָאֵל

ב תֹּאמַר אִישׁ אִישׁ מִבְּנֵי יִשְׂרָאֵל וּמִן־הַגֵּר הַגָּר

בְּיִשְׂרָאֵל אֲשֶׁר יִתֵּן מִזַּרְעוֹ לַמֹּלֶךְ מוֹת יוּמָת עַם

ג הָאָרֶץ יִרְגְּמֻהוּ בָאָבֶן: וַאֲנִי אֶתֵּן אֶת־פָּנַי בָּאִישׁ

הַהוּא וְהִכְרַתִּי אֹתוֹ מִקֶּרֶב עַמּוֹ כִּי מִזַּרְעוֹ נָתַן לַמֹּלֶךְ

ד לְמַעַן טַמֵּא אֶת־מִקְדָּשִׁי וּלְחַלֵּל אֶת־שֵׁם קָדְשִׁי: וְאִם

הַעְלֵם יַעְלִימוּ עַם הָאָרֶץ אֶת־עֵינֵיהֶם מִן־הָאִישׁ

הַהוּא בְּתִתּוֹ מִזַּרְעוֹ לַמֹּלֶךְ לְבִלְתִּי הָמִית אֹתוֹ:

ה וְשַׂמְתִּי אֲנִי אֶת־פָּנַי בָּאִישׁ הַהוּא וּבְמִשְׁפַּחְתּוֹ וְהִכְרַתִּי

1] And the LORD spoke to Moses: 2] Say further to the Israelite people:

Any man among the Israelites, or among the strangers residing in Israel, who gives any of his offspring to Molech, shall be put to death; the people of the land shall pelt him with stones.   3] And I will set My face against that man and will cut him off from among his people, because he gave of his offspring to Molech and so defiled My sanctuary and profaned My holy name.   4] And if the people of the land should shut their eyes to that man when he gives of his offspring to Molech, and should not put him to death,   5] I Myself will set My face against that man

---

20:2]   *The strangers.* See commentary on 19:33.

Shall pelt him with stones. This seems to envision a mob overwhelming the offender with a shower of rocks. The halachah understands the rule differently (see Gleanings).

3]   *I will set My face against that man.* I will not turn My attention away from him until he is punished.

Cut him off from among his people. See commentary on 7:21.

Defiled My sanctuary. The sanctuary would not be ritually defiled by pagan rites conducted elsewhere. Here the defilement is figurative: the reputation of the sanctuary will be stained by the misconduct of those who sometimes worship there. The meaning is therefore akin to that of "profaned My holy name" (see p. 204). *Sifra,* however, followed by Rashi and Nachmanides, understands *mikdashi* ("My sanctuary") to mean here "My holy people."

4]   *Shut their eyes.* The phrase is in contrast with, "I will set My face against."

אֹתוֹ וְאֵת כָּל־הַזֹּנִים אַחֲרָיו לִזְנוֹת אַחֲרֵי הַמֹּלֶךְ

מִקֶּרֶב עַמָּם: וְהַנֶּפֶשׁ אֲשֶׁר תִּפְנֶה אֶל־הָאֹבֹת וְאֶל־

הַיִּדְּעֹנִים לִזְנוֹת אַחֲרֵיהֶם וְנָתַתִּי אֶת־פָּנַי בַּנֶּפֶשׁ הַהִוא

וְהִכְרַתִּי אֹתוֹ מִקֶּרֶב עַמּוֹ: וְהִתְקַדִּשְׁתֶּם וִהְיִיתֶם

קְדֹשִׁים כִּי אֲנִי יְהוָֹה אֱלֹהֵיכֶם: וּשְׁמַרְתֶּם אֶת־חֻקֹּתַי

וַעֲשִׂיתֶם אֹתָם אֲנִי יְהוָֹה מְקַדִּשְׁכֶם: כִּי־אִישׁ אִישׁ אֲשֶׁר

יְקַלֵּל אֶת־אָבִיו וְאֶת־אִמּוֹ מוֹת יוּמָת אָבִיו וְאִמּוֹ קִלֵּל

דָּמָיו בּוֹ: וְאִישׁ אֲשֶׁר יִנְאַף אֶת־אֵשֶׁת אִישׁ אֲשֶׁר יִנְאַף

Leviticus 20

6–10

and his kin, and will cut off from among their people both him and all who follow him in going astray after Molech.   6] And if any person turns to ghosts and familiar spirits and goes astray after them, I will set My face against that person and cut him off from among his people.

7] You shall sanctify yourselves and be holy, for I the LORD am your God. 8] You shall faithfully observe My laws: I the LORD make you holy.

9] If any man insults his father or his mother, he shall be put to death; he has insulted his father and his mother—his bloodguilt is upon him.

10] If a man commits adultery with a married woman, committing adultery

---

5] *And his kin.* The phrase seems to suggest the notion of "guilt by family relationship," a concept strongly repudiated in Deuteronomy (24:16). The rabbinic commentators explain, perhaps correctly, that the offender would not have dared commit the crime without the encouragement and protection of his family, who have thus involved themselves in his guilt. And the Targum paraphrases, "His supporters."

7] *Sanctify yourselves.* Cf. 11:44, 19:2.

8] *I the Lord make you holy.* The meaning is clarified in verse 26.

9] *If any man insults his father....* See Exodus (21:17). Respect for parents is mentioned here because it strengthens family life, which the offenses next listed destroy (Hoffmann).

His bloodguilt is upon him. Not on those who condemn and execute him. He has only himself to blame.

10–16] On capital punishment, see Gleanings.

אֶת־אֵשֶׁת רֵעֵהוּ מוֹת־יוּמַת הַנֹּאֵף וְהַנֹּאָפֶת: וְאִישׁ אֲשֶׁר

יִשְׁכַּב אֶת־אֵשֶׁת אָבִיו עֶרְוַת אָבִיו גִּלָּה מוֹת־יוּמְתוּ יא

שְׁנֵיהֶם דְּמֵיהֶם בָּם: וְאִישׁ אֲשֶׁר יִשְׁכַּב אֶת־כַּלָּתוֹ מוֹת יב

יוּמְתוּ שְׁנֵיהֶם תֶּבֶל עָשׂוּ דְּמֵיהֶם בָּם: וְאִישׁ אֲשֶׁר יג

יִשְׁכַּב אֶת־זָכָר מִשְׁכְּבֵי אִשָּׁה תּוֹעֵבָה עָשׂוּ שְׁנֵיהֶם מוֹת

יוּמְתוּ דְּמֵיהֶם בָּם: וְאִישׁ אֲשֶׁר יִקַּח אֶת־אִשָּׁה וְאֶת־ יד

אִמָּהּ זִמָּה הִוא בָּאֵשׁ יִשְׂרְפוּ אֹתוֹ וְאֶתְהֶן וְלֹא־תִהְיֶה

זִמָּה בְּתוֹכְכֶם: וְאִישׁ אֲשֶׁר יִתֵּן שְׁכָבְתּוֹ בִּבְהֵמָה מוֹת טו

יוּמָת וְאֶת־הַבְּהֵמָה תַּהֲרֹגוּ: וְאִשָּׁה אֲשֶׁר תִּקְרַב אֶל־ טז

כָּל־בְּהֵמָה לְרִבְעָה אֹתָהּ וְהָרַגְתָּ אֶת־הָאִשָּׁה וְאֶת־

with his neighbor's wife, the adulterer and the adulteress shall be put to death.
11] If a man lies with his father's wife, it is the nakedness of his father that he has
uncovered; the two shall be put to death—their bloodguilt is upon them.   **12]** If a
man lies with his daughter-in-law, both of them shall be put to death; they have
committed incest—their bloodguilt is upon them.   **13]** If a man lies with a male
as one lies with a woman, the two of them have done an abhorrent thing; they shall
be put to death—their bloodguilt is upon them.   **14]** If a man marries a woman
and her mother, it is depravity; both he and they shall be put to the fire, that there
be no depravity among you.   **15]** If a man has carnal relations with a beast, he
shall be put to death; and you shall kill the beast.   **16]** If a woman approaches any
beast to mate with it, you shall kill the woman and the beast; they shall be put to
death—their bloodguilt is upon them.

11–21] On forbidden sexual relations, see chapter 18.

14] *Both he and they shall be put to the fire.* The first wife entered into a completely legitimate union; it was the second, whether mother or daughter of the first, who joined the man in an act of depravity.

The word "they" must mean "the guilty one of the two." This is the view of the Talmud [1].

Put to the fire. For the procedure, see Gleanings.

15] *And you shall kill the beast.* Though it is not morally responsible, it was the unwitting cause of a human life being destroyed.

יז הַבְּהֵמָה מוֹת יוּמָתוּ דְּמֵיהֶם בָּם: וְאִישׁ אֲשֶׁר־יִקַּח
אֶת־אֲחֹתוֹ בַּת־אָבִיו אוֹ־בַת־אִמּוֹ וְרָאָה אֶת־עֶרְוָתָהּ
וְהִיא־תִרְאֶה אֶת־עֶרְוָתוֹ חֶסֶד הוּא וְנִכְרְתוּ לְעֵינֵי בְּנֵי
יח עַמָּם עֶרְוַת אֲחֹתוֹ גִּלָּה עֲוֹנוֹ יִשָּׂא: וְאִישׁ אֲשֶׁר־יִשְׁכַּב
אֶת־אִשָּׁה דָּוָה וְגִלָּה אֶת־עֶרְוָתָהּ אֶת־מְקֹרָהּ הֶעֱרָה
וְהִוא גִּלְּתָה אֶת־מְקוֹר דָּמֶיהָ וְנִכְרְתוּ שְׁנֵיהֶם מִקֶּרֶב
יט עַמָּם: וְעֶרְוַת אֲחוֹת אִמְּךָ וַאֲחוֹת אָבִיךָ לֹא תְגַלֵּה
כ כִּי אֶת־שְׁאֵרוֹ הֶעֱרָה עֲוֹנָם יִשָּׂאוּ: וְאִישׁ אֲשֶׁר יִשְׁכַּב
אֶת־דֹּדָתוֹ עֶרְוַת דֹּדוֹ גִּלָּה חֶטְאָם יִשָּׂאוּ עֲרִירִים
כא יָמֻתוּ: וְאִישׁ אֲשֶׁר יִקַּח אֶת־אֵשֶׁת אָחִיו נִדָּה הִוא עֶרְוַת
כב אָחִיו גִּלָּה עֲרִירִים יִהְיוּ: וּשְׁמַרְתֶּם אֶת־כָּל־חֻקֹּתַי
וְאֶת־כָּל־מִשְׁפָּטַי וַעֲשִׂיתֶם אֹתָם וְלֹא־תָקִיא אֶתְכֶם

Leviticus 20
17—22

17] If a man marries his sister, the daughter of either his father or his mother, so that he sees her nakedness and she sees his nakedness, it is a disgrace; they shall be excommunicated in the sight of their kinsfolk. He has uncovered the nakedness of his sister, he shall bear his guilt.   18] If a man lies with a woman in her infirmity and uncovers her nakedness, he has laid bare her flow and she has exposed her blood flow; both of them shall be cut off from among their people.   19] You shall not uncover the nakedness of your mother's sister or of your father's sister, for that is laying bare one's own flesh; they shall bear their guilt.   20] If a man lies with his uncle's wife, it is his uncle's nakedness that he has uncovered. They shall bear their guilt: they shall die childless.   21] If a man marries the wife of his brother, it is indecency. It is the nakedness of his brother that he has uncovered; they shall remain childless.

22] You shall faithfully observe all My laws and all My regulations, lest the land

---

17] *Excommunicated.* Literally, "cut off" (T.N.). See p. 57.

22–25] Cf. 18:24ff. The passages are much alike, but here (verse 25) the prohibition of unclean meats is

הָאָ֗רֶץ אֲשֶׁ֨ר אֲנִ֜י מֵבִ֧יא אֶתְכֶ֛ם שָׁ֖מָּה לָשֶׁ֥בֶת בָּֽהּ׃

כג וְלֹ֤א תֵֽלְכוּ֙ בְּחֻקֹּ֣ת הַגּ֔וֹי אֲשֶׁר־אֲנִ֥י מְשַׁלֵּ֖חַ מִפְּנֵיכֶ֑ם כִּ֤י

כד אֶת־כָּל־אֵ֨לֶּה֙ עָשׂ֔וּ וָאָקֻ֖ץ בָּֽם׃ וָאֹמַ֣ר לָכֶ֗ם אַתֶּם֮ תִּֽירְשׁ֣וּ אֶת־אַדְמָתָם֒ וַֽאֲנִ֞י אֶתְּנֶ֤נָּה לָכֶם֙ לָרֶ֣שֶׁת אֹתָ֔הּ אֶ֛רֶץ זָבַ֥ת חָלָ֖ב וּדְבָ֑שׁ אֲנִי֙ יְהֹוָ֣ה אֱלֹֽהֵיכֶ֔ם אֲשֶׁר־

כה הִבְדַּ֥לְתִּי אֶתְכֶ֖ם מִן־הָֽעַמִּֽים׃ וְהִבְדַּלְתֶּ֞ם בֵּֽין־הַבְּהֵמָ֤ה הַטְּהֹרָה֙ לַטְּמֵאָ֔ה וּבֵֽין־הָע֥וֹף הַטָּמֵ֖א לַטָּהֹ֑ר וְלֹֽא־תְשַׁקְּצ֨וּ אֶת־נַפְשֹֽׁתֵיכֶ֜ם בַּבְּהֵמָ֣ה וּבָע֗וֹף וּבְכֹל֙ אֲשֶׁ֣ר

כו תִּרְמֹ֣שׂ הָֽאֲדָמָ֔ה אֲשֶׁר־הִבְדַּ֥לְתִּי לָכֶ֖ם לְטַמֵּֽא׃ וִֽהְיִ֤יתֶם לִי֙ קְדֹשִׁ֔ים כִּ֥י קָד֖וֹשׁ אֲנִ֣י יְהֹוָ֑ה וָֽאַבְדִּ֥ל אֶתְכֶ֛ם מִן־

כז הָֽעַמִּ֖ים לִֽהְי֥וֹת לִֽי׃ וְאִ֣ישׁ אֽוֹ־אִשָּׁ֗ה כִּֽי־יִֽהְיֶ֨ה בָהֶ֥ם א֛וֹב א֥וֹ יִדְּעֹנִ֖י מ֣וֹת יוּמָ֑תוּ בָּאֶ֛בֶן יִרְגְּמ֥וּ אֹתָ֖ם דְּמֵיהֶ֥ם בָּֽם׃

Leviticus 20
23–27

Haftarah Kedoshim, p. 391

to which I bring you to settle in spew you out.   23] You shall not follow the practices of the nation that I am driving out before you. For it is because they did all these things that I abhorred them   24] and said to you: You shall possess their land, for I will give it to you to possess, a land flowing with milk and honey. I the LORD am your God who has set you apart from other peoples.   25] So you shall set apart the clean beast from the unclean, the unclean bird from the clean. You shall not draw abomination upon yourselves through beast or bird or anything with which the ground is alive, which I have set apart for you to treat as unclean.
26] You shall be holy to Me, for I the LORD am holy, and I have set you apart from other peoples to be Mine.

27] A man or a woman who has a ghost or a familiar spirit shall be put to death; they shall be pelted with stones—their bloodguilt shall be upon them.

also mentioned. This subject was treated fully in chapter 11, most of which is from P. There is no need to assume that verse 25 was inserted by a P editor.

The author of H does not detail the dietary laws, just as he does not detail the laws of sacrifice; but no doubt he considered both important.

GLEANINGS

Halachah

20:9-16] The Bible prescribes the death penalty for a number of crimes, of two classes: (1) crimes against persons, such as murder and kidnaping, and (2) acts of sacrilege, such as flagrant violation of the Sabbath, blasphemy, and the sexual offenses enumerated here. These sacrilegious acts were believed to endanger the entire community by calling down divine wrath. Never does the Bible call for the death penalty for crimes against property. In contrast, pickpockets were still hanged in England in the eighteenth century.

The talmudic rabbis, with their great concern for the sanctity of human life, were openly opposed to capital punishment. But, since they had to recognize the letter of the Torah law, they sought a variety of means to render these penal laws inoperative. Thus, in some instances, they held that the Torah referred to death by divine intervention, not to death imposed by a court. They further devised a system of technicalities to prevent the conviction of a defendant for a capital crime. This somewhat offhand approach was relatively easy for them, since the Roman government denied Jewish courts jurisdiction over capital cases.

9] *Pelt Him with Stones*
According to the halachah, the procedure for "stoning" was an orderly one. The criminal was thrown off a high platform. If the fall did not kill him, stones were to be dropped on his body till he died [2].

14] *Put to the Fire*
Not, according to the halachah, the slow agony of death at the stake. The victim's mouth was forced open and molten lead poured down his throat, killing him quickly [3].

15] *And You Shall Kill the Beast*
For, if people saw the beast in the market place, they might say, "That is the animal on account of which so-and-so was put to death." But God would not want the memory of the man's shame kept alive [4]. Moreover, the availability of the animal might tempt others to misconduct [5].

Laws concerning the Priests

For ancient man, the essential form of worship was sacrifice. But a sacrifice not properly performed was worse than useless— it might lead to disaster. It was essential that the cult be directed by responsible and well-informed persons.

The priestly officiants served in some communities for a limited term, in others for life. The priesthood among certain peoples was open to any qualified citizen; but, in many cases, including that of Israel, the priesthood was hereditary.

1. *The Priestly Role*

Frequently, sacrifice was conducted by the head of a family or the chieftain of a tribe. In many societies the ruler was also chief priest, or the priest was also the ruler. But it was likewise a widespread practice to entrust the temples and shrines, and the rituals conducted in them, to a specially trained caste or class of priests. These functionaries often wore distinctive dress, had their special pattern of life, and received their support from the temple income. They served as intermediaries between a people and its god; they presented the offerings of the group and of individuals, and in turn they informed their people of the will of the deity. For this purpose they sometimes made use of oracular techniques, and sometimes they drew upon their extensive knowledge of religious lore and tradition.

2. *Israelite Priesthood*

When God gave instructions for the building of the Tabernacle, He selected Aaron and his sons to serve as priests and ordained that their descendants were to inherit this prerogative forever (Exod. 25:1–29:37, especially 29:9). The rest of the tribe of Levi were assigned important tasks in the sanctuary, but in rank and sanctity they were on a lower level than their fellow Levites of Aaron's family; their duties and prerogatives are expounded at length in Numbers (3, 4, 8, and 18).

The books of Ezra, Nehemiah, and Chronicles give us considerable information about the Levites at the end of the biblical period. In the Second Temple, the Levites served as guards and as singers and instrumentalists.

But this sharp distinction between Aaronide priests and Levites of lower rank is found only in the late books just mentioned and in the Priestly Code. It is not found in the other documents of the Pentateuch, or in the historical books of Joshua, Judges, Samuel, or Kings. The priests at Shiloh (I Sam. 2:24ff.), Nob (I Sam. 21ff.), and Jerusalem (I Kings 2:35) are not designated in these sources as descendants of Aaron. Deuteronomy constantly refers to the "levitical priests," literally, "the priests, the Levites." When "priest" or "Levite" is used alone, there is never an implied contrast between two groups. Sometimes (e.g., Deut. 18:6), "Levite" is plainly identical with "priest."

Ezekiel also uses the term "levitical priests." But he makes a distinction between the descendants of Zadok, the first priest of Solomon's Temple, and the other Levites. The latter, he asserts, had compromised with idolatry; henceforth, they are barred from sacrificial duties and, instead, must perform the menial tasks of the sanctuary. Only the loyal Zadokites are to serve at the altar (Ezek. 44:10ff.). Still later we hear for the first time that Zadok was a descendant of Aaron and of his oldest surviving son Eleazar (Ezra 7:2ff.; I Chron. 5:27ff.).

On the basis of these facts, many modern scholars have concluded that there was no distinction between the terms "priest" and "Levite" prior to the reform of King Josiah in 621 B.C.E. [1]. This reform, based on the Book of Deuteronomy, abolished all the local shrines (see Deut. 12; II Kings 22 and 23). The Deuteronomic Code (19:6ff.) promised that the priests who were deprived of office by the reform might become part of the regular Temple priesthood. But, say these scholars, the Zadokite priests, resident in Jerusalem, were able to resist this provision; they retained priestly rank for themselves and assigned a lesser rank to the newcomers. The latter became known as (nonpriestly) Levites; the Zadokite priests eventually claimed to be descendants of Aaron. And the priestly writings asserted that the distinction between priest and Levite went back to the Mosaic age.

This rather plausible theory has been attacked with considerable effectiveness by Yehezkel Kaufmann. But his own reconstruction of the history of the priesthood [2] is likewise open to criticism. In any case, the evolution must have been a long and complicated process [3].

3. *During the Second Temple*

After the return from Babylon and the rebuilding of the Temple, the priests attained greater power and prestige than at any other time before or since. There was no longer a Davidic king, and so the High Priest became the chief representative of the Jews in dealings with the great empires that successively ruled Palestine. In addition to their importance as religious officiants and political leaders, the priests were also recognized as the custodians and teachers of Torah. They constituted an aristocracy, and it was considered a high honor for Israelites to marry into a priestly family.

But qualifications for religious leadership are not always transmitted from father to son; and wealth, position, and power often corrupt those who possess them. In the days of the mad Syrian tyrant Antiochus IV (second century B.C.E.), many priests supported his effort to impose Greek customs and rites upon Jewish life; and the high priesthood fell into the hands of scoundrels who bribed and flattered the king.

But it was also priests who led the revolt against Syrian oppression—the famed Mattathias and his five sons. These Hasmoneans won the devoted support of the people. But, after the victory was won, Simon the Maccabee assumed the high priesthood, though he was not of the high priestly family, and his far from pious successors on the throne also held the office. This greatly troubled loyal spirits. And the later Hasmonean rulers estranged the people still more by their tyranny and their intrigues.

Meantime, a new popular leadership emerged. Laymen who were respected for their learning and fervor began to challenge the spiritual authority of the priests. The laymen constituted a party which came to be known as the Pharisees (Hebrew *perushim*, "separatists," cf. above, p. 206). They interpreted the Torah in a democratic, humane, and often progressive manner. The priestly party came to be known as Sadducees (from their supposed ancestor Zadok/Sadok); their approach to the Torah was conservative and severe.

Not all priests were Sadducees, and not all laymen Pharisees. (In today's America, many working men are conservative and some wealthy people are Communists.) Nor did the Pharisees seek to deny the priests their position and their perquisites; they were, in fact, sticklers about paying tithes. What the Pharisees did challenge was the exclusive prerogative of the priests to interpret the Torah; and so greatly did they win popular support that in the last years of the Second Temple the priests had to perform the cult according to Pharisaic rulings (see p. 161).

4. In Later Centuries

The destruction of the Temple left the priests with little to do. The Sadducean party ceased to exist [4]. But persons of priestly origin continued to cherish the memory of their high descent. They observed many of the restrictive laws contained in our present chapters, and they were accorded certain honors by the community.

Among traditional Jews up to the present, those of priestly and Levitic descent have special rights and obligations. When the Torah is read in the synagogue, the blessing over the first subsection is recited by a *kohen*, "priest," if any such is present. The blessing for the second section is assigned to a *Levi*, "Levite." On holidays, the *kohanim* ascend the pulpit, raise their hands, and bless the congregation, in conformity with Numbers 6:22ff. Before they commence this ceremony, they leave the sanctuary to prepare themselves, and the *Levi'im* attend upon them and pour water over their hands. (Hence the tombstone of a *kohen* often bears the symbol of hands outstretched for blessing; that of a *Levi* shows a pitcher and towel.) The custom of redeeming a firstborn son (*pidyon ha-ben*) requires that a sum equivalent to five shekels of silver be given to a *kohen* by the father of the child (see Exod. 13:13).

The name *kohen* in all its forms (Cohen, Cohn, Kohn, Kagan, and others) is very common among Jews, but not all those who bear the name possess a family tradition that they are *kohanim* in fact. And many *kohanim* have nondistinctive names. The same thing applies in the case of the name Levy (Levi, Lewy, Halevy) [5].

Reform Judaism regards these distinctions, based on birth, as no longer meaningful.

5. The Laws in Chapters 21 and 22

This section includes a number of provisions we have already met elsewhere, here repeated or elaborated. The ancient rabbis were able to derive new legal details from these repetitions; to us, they are rather indications that the editors of Leviticus drew upon a variety of traditions and documents.

The chief new laws are the following:

a. The most severe ritual defilement is that caused by a corpse (p. 102; Num. 19). It is not a sin for the ordinary Jew to defile himself by such contact, which results from the religious duty of burying the dead or visiting the cemetery. But the priests were required to avoid such contamination. To this day, a traditional Jew who is a *kohen* will not enter a cemetery or a house where there is a corpse. The Torah makes an exception in the case of close relatives; but there are no exceptions for the High Priest who may not attend the funeral even of his own parents (21:1–4, 10–12).

b. A *kohen* may not marry a woman of bad reputation or a divorcée even of the best character. (The halachah expands this rule somewhat.) The High Priest is also forbidden to marry a widow (21:7–8, 13–15).

c. The daughter of a priest who commits an immoral act is to be burned to death (21:9). The halachah limits this rule to the case of adultery.

d. A number of physical defects are enumerated which disqualify a priest from officiating at the altar; but such persons are assigned a share of the sacrificial meats and other perquisites (21:16–24).

e. Certain of the sacred donations are explicitly set aside for consumption by priestly males (above, 6:16, 29). The other gifts may be eaten by all the permanent members of a priest's household, including slaves, but not by temporary employees. A priest's daughter who marries a layman may no longer share the sacred food; but, if she is widowed or divorced and has no children, she may resume her former status (22:10–16).

f. The physical defects that render an animal unfit for sacrifice are listed (22:17–25). In this connection, the practice of castration is categorically prohibited (verse 24). No animal is to be sacrificed until it is at least eight days old; an animal and its young are not to be sacrificed on the same day.

The conclusion of this section has been interpreted by tradition as the classic source for the duty of martyrdom.

אמר

ויקרא כא

א–ו

א וַיֹּאמֶר יְהוָֹה אֶל־מֹשֶׁה אֱמֹר אֶל־הַכֹּהֲנִים בְּנֵי אַהֲרֹן

ב וְאָמַרְתָּ אֲלֵהֶם לְנֶפֶשׁ לֹא־יִטַּמָּא בְּעַמָּיו: כִּי אִם־

לִשְׁאֵרוֹ הַקָּרֹב אֵלָיו לְאִמּוֹ וּלְאָבִיו וְלִבְנוֹ וּלְבִתּוֹ

ג וּלְאָחִיו: וְלַאֲחֹתוֹ הַבְּתוּלָה הַקְּרוֹבָה אֵלָיו אֲשֶׁר לֹא־

ד הָיְתָה לְאִישׁ לָהּ יִטַּמָּא: לֹא יִטַּמָּא בַּעַל בְּעַמָּיו

ה לְהֵחַלּוֹ: לֹא־יִקְרְחָה* קָרְחָה בְּרֹאשָׁם וּפְאַת זְקָנָם לֹא

ו יְגַלֵּחוּ וּבִבְשָׂרָם לֹא יִשְׂרְטוּ שָׂרָטֶת: קְדֹשִׁים יִהְיוּ

לֵאלֹהֵיהֶם וְלֹא יְחַלְּלוּ שֵׁם אֱלֹהֵיהֶם כִּי אֶת־אִשֵּׁי

Emor

Leviticus 21

I–6

* ה יקרחו קרי.

1] The LORD said to Moses: Speak to the priests, the sons of Aaron, and say to them:

None shall defile himself for any [dead] person among his kin,   2] except for the relatives that are closest to him: his mother, his father, his son, his daughter, and his brother;   3] also for a virgin sister, close to him because she has not married, for her he may defile himself.   4] But he shall not defile himself as a kinsman by marriage, and so profane himself.

5] They shall not shave smooth any part of their heads, or cut the side-growth of their beards, or make gashes in their flesh.   6] They shall be holy to their God and

---

21:2]   *Relatives*. Heb. *she'ero*, literally, "his flesh."

3]   *May defile himself*. See Gleanings.

4]   *As a kinsman by marriage*. Literally, "as a husband among his kin"; meaning uncertain (T.N.). This rendering suggests: He is to defile himself only for certain blood relations, not for "in-laws." But *baal*, here rendered "husband," can also mean "lord,

ruler"; and the verse could thus mean, "Being a lord (a man of high dignity), he shall not defile himself" [6].

5]   See above, 19:27–28 and Deuteronomy 14:1, where these prohibitions apply to all Israelites. Perhaps the law was originally for priests only and, as the concept of the holy people developed, all Israelites adopted it.

יְהֹוָה לֶחֶם אֱלֹהֵיהֶם הֵם מַקְרִיבִם וְהָיוּ קֹדֶשׁ:

ז אִשָּׁה זֹנָה וַחֲלָלָה לֹא יִקָּחוּ וְאִשָּׁה גְּרוּשָׁה מֵאִישָׁהּ לֹא

ח יִקָּחוּ כִּי־קָדֹשׁ הוּא לֵאלֹהָיו: וְקִדַּשְׁתּוֹ כִּי־אֶת־לֶחֶם

אֱלֹהֶיךָ הוּא מַקְרִיב קָדֹשׁ יִהְיֶה־לָּךְ כִּי קָדוֹשׁ אֲנִי

ט יְהֹוָה מְקַדִּשְׁכֶם: וּבַת אִישׁ כֹּהֵן כִּי תֵחֵל לִזְנוֹת אֶת־

י אָבִיהָ הִיא מְחַלֶּלֶת בָּאֵשׁ תִּשָּׂרֵף: ס וְהַכֹּהֵן הַגָּדוֹל

מֵאֶחָיו אֲשֶׁר־יוּצַק עַל־רֹאשׁוֹ שֶׁמֶן הַמִּשְׁחָה וּמִלֵּא

אֶת־יָדוֹ לִלְבֹּשׁ אֶת־הַבְּגָדִים אֶת־רֹאשׁוֹ לֹא יִפְרָע

not profane the name of their God; for they offer the LORD's offerings by fire, the food of their God, and so must be holy.

7] They shall not marry a woman degraded by harlotry, nor shall they marry one divorced from her husband. For they are holy to their God   8] and you must treat them as holy, since they offer the food of your God; they shall be holy to you, for I the LORD who sanctify you am holy.

9] When the daughter of a priest degrades herself through harlotry, it is her father whom she degrades; she shall be put to the fire.

10] The priest who is exalted above his fellows, on whose head the anointing oil has been poured and who has been ordained to wear the vestments, shall not

---

6] *The food of their God.* The words were hardly meant in a literal sense by the author of Leviticus. But to preclude misunderstanding, the Targum substitutes the word "offerings" for "food."

8] *You must treat them as holy.* Yet this verse also affirms the holiness of all Israel: *I the LORD . . . sanctify you.*

9] *When the daughter of a priest degrades herself through harlotry.* The plain sense is that any act of

unchastity by the daughter of a priest is punishable by a fiery death; other women were subject to death only for adultery and for what were considered perverted acts (above, 20:10-16). But the halachah limited the present rule to cases of adultery; see Gleanings.

10] *The priest who is exalted.* Heb. *gadol,* "great." Occasionally in the Bible, and regularly in postbiblical literature, he is called *Kohen Gadol,* "High Priest."
   Bare his head. See T.N. at 10:6 (T.N.).

יא וּבְגָדָיו לֹא יִפְרֹם׃ וְעַל כָּל־נַפְשֹׁת מֵת לֹא יָבֹא

יב לְאָבִיו וּלְאִמּוֹ לֹא יִטַּמָּא׃ וּמִן־הַמִּקְדָּשׁ לֹא יֵצֵא וְלֹא

יְחַלֵּל אֵת מִקְדַּשׁ אֱלֹהָיו כִּי נֵזֶר שֶׁמֶן מִשְׁחַת אֱלֹהָיו

יג עָלָיו אֲנִי יְהוָה׃ וְהוּא אִשָּׁה בִבְתוּלֶיהָ יִקָּח׃ אַלְמָנָה

וּגְרוּשָׁה וַחֲלָלָה זֹנָה אֶת־אֵלֶּה לֹא יִקָּח כִּי אִם־בְּתוּלָה

טו מֵעַמָּיו יִקַּח אִשָּׁה׃ וְלֹא־יְחַלֵּל זַרְעוֹ בְּעַמָּיו כִּי אֲנִי

טז יְהוָה מְקַדְּשׁוֹ׃ ס וַיְדַבֵּר יְהוָה אֶל־מֹשֶׁה לֵּאמֹר׃

יז דַּבֵּר אֶל־אַהֲרֹן לֵאמֹר אִישׁ מִזַּרְעֲךָ לְדֹרֹתָם אֲשֶׁר

יח יִהְיֶה בוֹ מוּם לֹא יִקְרַב לְהַקְרִיב לֶחֶם אֱלֹהָיו׃ כִּי

כָל־אִישׁ אֲשֶׁר־בּוֹ מוּם לֹא יִקְרַב אִישׁ עִוֵּר אוֹ פִּסֵּחַ

Leviticus 21

11–18

bare his head or rend his vestments.   **11]** He shall not go in where there is any dead body; he shall not defile himself even for his father or mother.   **12]** He shall not go outside the sanctuary and profane the sanctuary of his God, for upon him is the distinction of the anointing oil of his God, Mine the LORD's.   **13]** He may marry only a woman who is a virgin.   **14]** A widow, or a divorced woman, or one who is degraded by harlotry—such he may not marry. Only a virgin of his own kin may he take to wife—   **15]** that he may not profane his offspring among his kin, for I the LORD have sanctified him.

16] The LORD spoke further to Moses: **17]** Speak to Aaron and say: No man of your offspring throughout the ages who has a defect shall be qualified to offer the food of his God;   **18]** no one at all who has a defect shall be qualified: no

---

12]   *He shall not go outside the sanctuary.* To attend a funeral. The High Priest was not a lifelong prisoner in the Temple.

יט אוֹ חָרֻם אוֹ שָׂרוּעַ: אוֹ אִישׁ אֲשֶׁר־יִהְיֶה בוֹ שֶׁבֶר רָגֶל
כ אוֹ שֶׁבֶר יָד: אוֹ־גִבֵּן אוֹ־דַק אוֹ תְּבַלֻּל בְּעֵינוֹ אוֹ גָרָב
כא אוֹ יַלֶּפֶת אוֹ מְרוֹחַ אָשֶׁךְ: כָּל־אִישׁ אֲשֶׁר־בּוֹ מוּם
מִזֶּרַע אַהֲרֹן הַכֹּהֵן לֹא יִגַּשׁ לְהַקְרִיב אֶת־אִשֵּׁי יְהֹוָה
כב מוּם בּוֹ אֵת לֶחֶם אֱלֹהָיו לֹא יִגַּשׁ לְהַקְרִיב: לֶחֶם
כג אֱלֹהָיו מִקָּדְשֵׁי הַקֳּדָשִׁים וּמִן־הַקֳּדָשִׁים יֹאכֵל: אַךְ
אֶל־הַפָּרֹכֶת לֹא יָבֹא וְאֶל־הַמִּזְבֵּחַ לֹא יִגַּשׁ כִּי־מוּם
בּוֹ וְלֹא יְחַלֵּל אֶת־מִקְדָּשַׁי כִּי אֲנִי יְהֹוָה מְקַדְּשָׁם:
כד וַיְדַבֵּר מֹשֶׁה אֶל־אַהֲרֹן וְאֶל־בָּנָיו וְאֶל־כָּל־בְּנֵי
יִשְׂרָאֵל: פ

Leviticus 21

19—24

man who is blind, or lame, or has a limb too short or too long;   **19]** no man who has a broken leg or a broken arm;   **20]** or who is a hunchback, or a dwarf, or who has a growth in his eye, or who has a boil-scar, or scurvy, or crushed testes.   **21]** No man among the offspring of Aaron the priest who has a defect shall be qualified to offer the LORD's offerings by fire; having a defect, he shall not be qualified to offer the food of his God.   **22]** He may eat of the food of his God, of the most holy as well as of the holy;   **23]** but he shall not enter behind the curtain or come near the altar, for he has a defect. He shall not profane these places sacred to Me, for I the LORD have sanctified them.

24] Thus Moses spoke to Aaron and his sons and to all the Israelites.

18] *Has a limb too short.* So Ibn Ezra. But Heb. *charum* is of uncertain meaning. Sifra explains: "flat-nosed" [7].

20] *Hunchback or dwarf.* These renderings, too, are far from certain, though widely adopted. Sifra understands them as referring to abnormal conditions of the eye.

23] *He shall not enter behind the curtain.* Cf. 16:1ff.

א וַיְדַבֵּר יְהֹוָה אֶל־מֹשֶׁה לֵּאמֹר: דַּבֵּר אֶל־אַהֲרֹן וְאֶל־
ב בָּנָיו וְיִנָּזְרוּ מִקָּדְשֵׁי בְנֵי־יִשְׂרָאֵל וְלֹא יְחַלְּלוּ אֶת־שֵׁם
ג קָדְשִׁי אֲשֶׁר הֵם מַקְדִּשִׁים לִי אֲנִי יְהֹוָה: אֱמֹר אֲלֵהֶם
לְדֹרֹתֵיכֶם כָּל־אִישׁ אֲשֶׁר־יִקְרַב מִכָּל־זַרְעֲכֶם אֶל־
הַקֳּדָשִׁים אֲשֶׁר יַקְדִּישׁוּ בְנֵי־יִשְׂרָאֵל לַיהֹוָה וְטֻמְאָתוֹ
ד עָלָיו וְנִכְרְתָה הַנֶּפֶשׁ הַהִוא מִלְּפָנַי אֲנִי יְהֹוָה: אִישׁ
אִישׁ מִזֶּרַע אַהֲרֹן וְהוּא צָרוּעַ אוֹ זָב בַּקֳּדָשִׁים לֹא
יֹאכַל עַד אֲשֶׁר יִטְהָר וְהַנֹּגֵעַ בְּכָל־טְמֵא־נֶפֶשׁ אוֹ
ה אִישׁ אֲשֶׁר־תֵּצֵא מִמֶּנּוּ שִׁכְבַת־זָרַע: אוֹ־אִישׁ אֲשֶׁר יִגַּע
בְּכָל־שֶׁרֶץ אֲשֶׁר יִטְמָא־לוֹ אוֹ בְאָדָם אֲשֶׁר יִטְמָא־לוֹ
ו לְכֹל טֻמְאָתוֹ: נֶפֶשׁ אֲשֶׁר תִּגַּע־בּוֹ וְטָמְאָה עַד־הָעָרֶב

Leviticus 22
1–6

1] The LORD spoke to Moses, saying: **2]** Instruct Aaron and his sons to be scrupulous about the sacred donations that the Israelite people consecrate to Me, lest they profane My holy name, Mine the LORD's.   **3]** Say to them:

Throughout the ages, if any man among your offspring, while in a state of uncleanness, partakes of any sacred donation that the Israelite people may consecrate to the LORD, that person shall be cut off from before Me: I am the LORD. **4]** No man of Aaron's offspring who has an eruption or a discharge shall eat of the sacred donations until he is clean. If one touches anything made unclean by a corpse, or if a man has an emission of semen,   **5]** or if a man touches any swarming thing by which he is made unclean or any human being by whom he is made unclean— whatever his uncleanness—   **6]** the person who touches such shall be unclean until

---

22:2] *Sacred donations.* The portions of sacrifices assigned to the priests, as well as other dues enumerated in Numbers 18:8ff. Meal offerings, sin offerings, and guilt offerings could be eaten only by males of the priestly order (6:11, 22; 7:6); the other sacred donations were shared by their households.

3] *Cut off.* As in 7:20.

4] For laws of uncleanness, see chapters 13, 15 (T.N.).

Touches anything made unclean by a corpse. Or "anyone."

235

וְלֹא יֹאכַל מִן־הַקֳּדָשִׁים כִּי אִם־רָחַץ בְּשָׂרוֹ בַּמָּיִם:

ז וּבָא הַשֶּׁמֶשׁ וְטָהֵר וְאַחַר יֹאכַל מִן־הַקֳּדָשִׁים כִּי

ח לַחְמוֹ הוּא: נְבֵלָה וּטְרֵפָה לֹא יֹאכַל לְטָמְאָה־בָהּ

ט אֲנִי יְהוָה: וְשָׁמְרוּ אֶת־מִשְׁמַרְתִּי וְלֹא־יִשְׂאוּ עָלָיו חֵטְא

י וּמֵתוּ בוֹ כִּי יְחַלְּלֻהוּ אֲנִי יְהוָה מְקַדְּשָׁם: וְכָל־זָר לֹא־

יֹאכַל קֹדֶשׁ תּוֹשַׁב כֹּהֵן וְשָׂכִיר לֹא־יֹאכַל קֹדֶשׁ:

יא וְכֹהֵן כִּי־יִקְנֶה נֶפֶשׁ קִנְיַן כַּסְפּוֹ הוּא יֹאכַל בּוֹ וִילִיד

יב בֵּיתוֹ הֵם יֹאכְלוּ בְלַחְמוֹ: וּבַת־כֹּהֵן כִּי תִהְיֶה לְאִישׁ

יג זָר הִוא בִּתְרוּמַת הַקֳּדָשִׁים לֹא תֹאכֵל: וּבַת־כֹּהֵן

Leviticus 22

7–13

evening and shall not eat of the sacred donations unless he has washed his body in water.   **7]** As soon as the sun sets, he shall be clean; and afterward he may eat of the sacred donations, for they are his food.   **8]** He shall not eat anything that died or was torn by beasts, thereby becoming unclean: I am the LORD.   **9]** They shall keep My charge, lest they incur guilt thereby and die for it, having committed profanation: I the LORD consecrate them.

10] No lay person shall eat of the sacred donations. No bound or hired laborer of a priest shall eat of the sacred donations;   **11]** but a person who is a priest's property by purchase may eat of them; and those that are born into his household may eat of his food.   **12]** If a priest's daughter marries a layman, she may not eat of the sacred gifts;   **13]** but if the priest's daughter is widowed or divorced

---

8]   *Anything that died or was torn by beasts.* Ezekiel 44:31 likewise states this as a rule for priests. But Exodus 22:30 and Deuteronomy 14:21 impose the prohibition on all Israel (cf. Lev. 11:39; 17:15). This is apparently another case where the entire people adopted a rule of holiness originally intended for the priesthood; cf. on 21:5.

10]   *Bound or hired laborer.* The bound laborer (Heb.

toshav, "sojourner") is most probably the "Hebrew slave" of Exodus 21:2ff. See Gleanings. Since the bound and hired laborers are not permanent members of the household, they may not eat of the sacred donations, although an out and out slave, the property of the priest (Lev. 25:44ff.), may do so.

12]   Cf. Numbers 18:19.

כִּי תִהְיֶה אַלְמָנָה וּגְרוּשָׁה וְזֶרַע אֵין לָהּ וְשָׁבָה אֶל־
בֵּית אָבִיהָ כִּנְעוּרֶיהָ מִלֶּחֶם אָבִיהָ תֹּאכֵל וְכָל־זָר
יד לֹא־יֹאכַל בּוֹ: וְאִישׁ כִּי־יֹאכַל קֹדֶשׁ בִּשְׁגָגָה וְיָסַף
טו חֲמִשִׁיתוֹ עָלָיו וְנָתַן לַכֹּהֵן אֶת־הַקֹּדֶשׁ: וְלֹא יְחַלְּלוּ
אֶת־קָדְשֵׁי בְּנֵי יִשְׂרָאֵל אֵת אֲשֶׁר־יָרִימוּ לַיהוָה:
טז וְהִשִּׂיאוּ אוֹתָם עֲוֹן אַשְׁמָה בְּאָכְלָם אֶת־קָדְשֵׁיהֶם כִּי
אֲנִי יְהוָה מְקַדְּשָׁם: פ
יח וַיְדַבֵּר יְהוָה אֶל־מֹשֶׁה לֵּאמֹר: דַּבֵּר אֶל־אַהֲרֹן וְאֶל־
בָּנָיו וְאֶל כָּל־בְּנֵי יִשְׂרָאֵל וְאָמַרְתָּ אֲלֵהֶם אִישׁ אִישׁ
מִבֵּית יִשְׂרָאֵל וּמִן־הַגֵּר בְּיִשְׂרָאֵל אֲשֶׁר יַקְרִיב קָרְבָּנוֹ
לְכָל־נִדְרֵיהֶם וּלְכָל־נִדְבוֹתָם אֲשֶׁר־יַקְרִיבוּ לַיהוָה

*יג מלרע

Leviticus 22

14–18

and without offspring, and is back in her father's house as in her youth, she may eat of her father's food. No lay person may eat of it: 14] but if a man eats of a sacred donation unwittingly, he shall pay the priest for the sacred donation, adding one fifth of its value.   15] But [the priests] must not allow the Israelites to profane the sacred donations which they set aside for the LORD,   16] or to incur guilt requiring a penalty payment, by eating such sacred donations: for it is I the LORD who make them sacred.

17] The LORD spoke to Moses, saying: 18] Speak to Aaron and his sons, and to all the Israelite people, and say to them:

When any man of the house of Israel or of the strangers in Israel presents a burnt offering as his offering for any of the votive or any of the freewill offerings that they

13] *And without offspring.* A child would constitute a tie with her husband's family.

14] *One fifth.* As in 5:14ff.

15] It is a responsibility of the priests to take such precautions as will protect other Israelites from eating the sacred portions forbidden to them.

17–20] As in 1:1–3.

יט לְעֹלָה: לִרְצֹנְכֶם תָּמִים זָכָר בַּבָּקָר בַּכְּשָׂבִים

כ וּבָעִזִּים: כֹּל אֲשֶׁר־בּוֹ מוּם לֹא תַקְרִיבוּ כִּי־לֹא לְרָצוֹן

כא יִהְיֶה לָכֶם: וְאִישׁ כִּי־יַקְרִיב זֶבַח־שְׁלָמִים לַיהוָה

לְפַלֵּא־נֶדֶר אוֹ לִנְדָבָה בַּבָּקָר אוֹ בַצֹּאן תָּמִים יִהְיֶה

כב לְרָצוֹן כָּל־מוּם לֹא יִהְיֶה־בּוֹ: עַוֶּרֶת אוֹ שָׁבוּר אוֹ־

חָרוּץ אוֹ־יַבֶּלֶת אוֹ גָרָב אוֹ יַלֶּפֶת לֹא־תַקְרִיבוּ אֵלֶּה

לַיהוָה וְאִשֶּׁה לֹא־תִתְּנוּ מֵהֶם עַל־הַמִּזְבֵּחַ לַיהוָה:

כג וְשׁוֹר וָשֶׂה שָׂרוּעַ וְקָלוּט נְדָבָה תַּעֲשֶׂה אֹתוֹ וּלְנֶדֶר

כד לֹא יֵרָצֶה: וּמָעוּךְ וְכָתוּת וְנָתוּק וְכָרוּת לֹא תַקְרִיבוּ

offer to the LORD, **19]** it must, to be acceptable in your favor, be a male without blemish, from cattle or sheep or goats. **20]** You shall not offer any that has a defect, for it will not be accepted in your favor.

21] And when a man offers, from the herd or the flock, a sacrifice of well-being to the LORD for an explicit vow or as a freewill offering, it must, to be acceptable, be without blemish: there must be no defect in it. **22]** Anything blind, or injured, or maimed, or with a wen, boil-scar, or scurvy—such you shall not offer to the LORD; you shall not put any of them on the altar as offerings by fire to the LORD. **23]** You may, however, present as a freewill offering an ox or a sheep with a limb extended or contracted; but it will not be accepted for a vow. **24]** You shall not offer to the LORD anything [with its testes] bruised or crushed or torn or cut. You shall have

21] As in 3:1 and 6. In verse 22, the specific defects that disqualify the animal are listed.

Explicit. Or, "unspecified" or "extraordinary"; meaning of Hebrew *lefalé* uncertain (T.N.).

23] This verse permits a slightly deformed animal to be used as a freewill offering, probably (but not certainly) to be offered as a sacrifice [8]. But it is the only exception to the otherwise invariable rule that sacrifices must be unblemished. The explanation given by the Rabbis is therefore not implausible—

that this "freewill offering" is not to be put on the altar, but it is to be sold and the proceeds contributed to the sanctuary (*Sifra*). On vows and freewill offerings, see commentary on 7:16.

24] *You shall have no such practices in your own land.* I.e., mutilations (T.N.). The Hebrew wording is unusually terse; but the traditional interpretation, that the verse categorically forbids castration, is certainly correct.

כה לַיהוָה וּבְאַרְצְכֶם לֹא תַעֲשׂוּ: וּמִיַּד בֶּן־נֵכָר לֹא
תַקְרִיבוּ אֶת־לֶחֶם אֱלֹהֵיכֶם מִכָּל־אֵלֶּה כִּי מָשְׁחָתָם
כו בָּהֶם מוּם בָּם לֹא יֵרָצוּ לָכֶם: ס וַיְדַבֵּר יְהוָה
כז אֶל־מֹשֶׁה לֵּאמֹר: שׁוֹר אוֹ־כֶשֶׂב אוֹ־עֵז כִּי יִוָּלֵד וְהָיָה
שִׁבְעַת יָמִים תַּחַת אִמּוֹ וּמִיּוֹם הַשְּׁמִינִי וָהָלְאָה יֵרָצֶה
כח לְקָרְבַּן אִשֶּׁה לַיהוָה: וְשׁוֹר אוֹ־שֶׂה אֹתוֹ וְאֶת־בְּנוֹ לֹא
כט תִשְׁחֲטוּ בְּיוֹם אֶחָד: וְכִי־תִזְבְּחוּ זֶבַח־תּוֹדָה לַיהוָה
ל לִרְצֹנְכֶם תִּזְבָּחוּ: בַּיּוֹם הַהוּא יֵאָכֵל לֹא־תוֹתִירוּ מִמֶּנּוּ
לא עַד־בֹּקֶר אֲנִי יְהוָה: וּשְׁמַרְתֶּם מִצְוֹתַי וַעֲשִׂיתֶם אֹתָם
לב אֲנִי יְהוָה: וְלֹא תְחַלְּלוּ אֶת־שֵׁם קָדְשִׁי וְנִקְדַּשְׁתִּי

Leviticus 22
25–32

no such practices in your own land,   25] nor shall you accept such [animals]
from a foreigner for offering as food for your God, for they are mutilated, they have
a defect; they shall not be accepted in your favor.

26] The LORD spoke to Moses, saying: 27] When an ox or a sheep or a goat is
born, it shall stay seven days with its mother, and from the eighth day on it shall
be acceptable as an offering by fire to the LORD.   28] However, no animal from
the herd or from the flock shall be slaughtered on the same day with its young.

29] When you sacrifice a thanksgiving offering to the LORD, sacrifice it so that it
may be acceptable in your favor.   30] It shall be eaten on the same day; you shall
not leave any of it until morning: I am the LORD.

31] You shall faithfully observe My commandments: I am the LORD.   32] You
shall not profane My holy name, that I may be sanctified in the midst of the Israelite

26–28] Humane feeling forbids unnecessary cruelty   29–30] As in 7:15.
to animals (on verse 28, cf. Deut. 22:6f.).   32] *You shall not profane My holy name.* See p. 204.

לג בְּתוֹךְ בְּנֵי יִשְׂרָאֵל אֲנִי יְהֹוָה מְקַדִּשְׁכֶם: הַמּוֹצִיא
אֶתְכֶם מֵאֶרֶץ מִצְרַיִם לִהְיוֹת לָכֶם לֵאלֹהִים אֲנִי
יְהֹוָה: פ

Leviticus 22:33

people—I the Lord who sanctify you,　33] I who brought you out of the land of Egypt to be your God, I the Lord.

GLEANINGS

Halachah

21:1] *Among His Kin*

Sifra understands "his" to refer to the dead person. If the man dies among his kin, i.e., his fellow Jews, there will be someone to bury him. If, however, the priest should come upon the corpse of a Jew in a remote spot where no one else can give him proper burial, the priest would be obligated to do so even though he would become ceremonially unclean.

2] *His Relatives*

Hebrew "his flesh." This is taken to mean his wife who is not specifically mentioned in the list.

SIFRA

3] *May Defile Himself*

So Rabbi Ishmael understood. But Rabbi Akiba explained *"must* defile himself"—the priest is not merely permitted but required to take part in the funeral rites for the relatives mentioned. And so the halachah was decided [9].

7] *Degraded by Harlotry*

Hebrew *zonah va-chalalah*, literally, "a harlot and degraded." The *chalalah* is the offspring of one of the marriages forbidden in this verse, who is disqualified ("degraded") from marrying a priest (*Sifra*). *Zonah* is defined in highly technical terms to include women who for a variety of reasons may not marry a priest [10]. Priests are likewise forbidden to marry proselytes and freed slaves, who are permitted to marry other Jews.

One Divorced from Her Husband

Also one who has gone through the ceremony of *chalitzah* (p. 189).

For They Are Holy to Their God

And, if they contract one of these marriages, they become disqualified and lose their holiness.

8] *You Must Treat Them as Holy*

I.e., the community must, if necessary, compel the priests to preserve their status and to refrain from a disqualifying marriage.

9] *She Shall Be Put to the Fire*

See Gleanings to 20:14. Talmudic literature, however, preserved some recollection of a case when a woman was actually burned at the stake [11]. The halachah limited this law to a woman guilty of adultery. Ordinarily both parties to an adulterous union were to be punished by strangulation; but, if the woman was a betrothed virgin, her partner was to be stoned to death. If, in such case, the woman was of priestly birth, she also was to be stoned. If she was married and subject to burning, her paramour was to be strangled [12].

10] *Exalted*

The High Priest should excel his brothers in beauty, wealth, strength, wisdom, and appearance.

SIFRA

12] *He Shall Not Go outside the Sanctuary*

The High Priest may officiate in the Temple while a near relative is dead and not yet buried. Other priests may not do this; but from this verse the Rabbis deduce that no priest may leave the sanctuary without finishing a rite he has begun. If he does so, he deserves the death penalty. SIFRA

22:6–7] This rule applies only to the eating of *terumah*—nonsacrificial gifts of grain, wine, and oil received by the priests (Num. 18:12). Other sacred donations could not be eaten till the following day; and, where necessary (e.g., where 15:14f. applied), the defiled person also had to bring a purificatory offering [13].

10] *Bound [Laborer]*

According to the halachah, the "Hebrew slave" who chooses to remain in the household after his forced service is over (Exod. 21:5f.). SIFRA

23] *Contracted*

Hebrew *kalut*. According to *Sifra*, an animal whose cloven hoofs are fused so that they look like those of a horse.

24] *You Shall Have No Such Practices in Your Own Land*

Castration of men and animals is unconditionally forbidden. The phrase "in your land" does not limit the ban to the land of Israel; it implies "everything in your land," including unclean beasts. SIFRA

Haggadah

22:32] *You Shall Not Profane My Holy Name*

Though the context treats of ritual purity, tradition regarded this passage as the classical source for the law of martyrdom (see p. 204). To prevent public profanation of God's name ("in the midst of the Israelite people"), the Jew should die rather than transgress even a minor commandment. He should offer himself unreservedly, without expectation of a miracle (Dan. 3:16ff.). Julianus and Pappus, two rebels against the Roman tyranny, were captured. The Roman officer who ordered their execution tauntingly asked them, "Why does your God not rescue you as He rescued Shadrach, Meshach, and Abed-nego?" They replied, "The three men were altogether worthy of a miracle and Nebuchadnezzar was a great king who deserved to be the instrument of a miracle. But you are a wicked ruler and do not merit such an honor, and we have incurred death for our sins. If you do not slay us, God has many other agents to punish us—lions and leopards, snakes and scorpions. But, in the end, you will be punished for our death." And the tale reports that, before the execution had taken place, orders arrived from Rome to put that officer to death. SIFRA

The Festival Calendar

An important feature of nearly every culture, and of nearly all religious systems, is a regular cycle of festivals and sacred occasions. These celebrations dramatize the ideals of the community and impart color and joy to its life. To most moderns, such festivals, however important and pleasurable, appear as creations of the group; their dates are fixed by custom or even by convenience. But, for ancient people (and some moderns as well), religious festivals were divinely ordained; it was urgently necessary to observe them exactly according to the god's commands and on the date he had fixed.

Festival observance is treated many times in the Torah. Short holiday calendars appear in Exodus (23:14–18 and 34:18–25) and there is a fuller statement in Deuteronomy (16:1–16). These passages speak only of the three "pilgrim festivals" [1]—Passover/Feast of Unleavened Bread, Feast of Weeks, and Feast of Booths. The present chapter lists also the New Year (though not by name) and the Day of Atonement. It is, then, the most complete biblical account of the holy days. It is supplemented in Numbers (28:1–30:1) by a detailed schedule of the sacrifices to be performed on each occasion. Moreover, Pass-over is discussed at length in Exodus, chapters 12 and 13, and Yom Kippur in Leviticus, chapter 16 [2].

The festivals are still of major importance to the Jews of today. They have, of course, changed greatly since biblical times. Sacrifice, the central feature of ancient worship, has long since disappeared, and many new forms of celebration have been introduced. More holidays have been added—Purim and Chanukah, the lesser occasions of Chamishah Asar Bi-Shevat and Lag Ba-Omer, and a series of fasts, notably the Ninth of Av. Here, however, we limit ourselves to the holy days commanded in the Torah and to the traditional interpretation of the biblical material [3].

1. Calendar Reckoning

Festivals have their place within some orderly reckoning of time periods. Even primitive peoples acquire some knowledge of practical astronomy. In ancient Egypt, and still more in Mesopotamia, astronomical studies were relatively advanced. And the Hebrews doubtlessly learned and borrowed much from their neighbors.

a. *The day*. Hebrew *yom*, like English "day," designates both the daylight hours and also what we call the civil day which includes nighttime [4]. The division of the day into twenty-four equal hours was probably unknown in Bible times; the night was divided into three or four watches. (In Mesopotamia, the day was divided into twelve double hours, varying in length according to the time of year.)

At what point did the civil day begin? There is some evidence that at one time the day was reckoned from sunrise to sunrise [5]. But, before the close of the biblical period, it had become standard to reckon the day from sunset to sunset, and this has been Jewish practice ever since. The Jewish day does not begin at a fixed hour—as, according to our secular practice, the civil day starts at midnight, regardless of the season. In winter, the Jewish day starts and ends earlier; in summer, later.

b. *The week*. Unlike the other units of time we are considering, the week does not clearly correspond to an astronomical phenomenon —though each phase of the moon lasts about seven days. The origin of the week has been the subject of much scholarly discussion, which has not led to many certain conclusions. So far as we know, a regular, uninterrupted cycle of seven-day units first appeared in Israel; but when and why it was introduced remains an unsettled problem. The week is certainly connected with the sacredness of the number seven and with the Sabbath. It came to the western world through Judaism and Christianity.

c. *Months and years*. As an astronomical concept, the year is the length of time in which the earth makes a circuit of the sun— a little over 365 days. Ancient peoples thought the sun moved around the earth, but they could still measure the year in terms of changing seasons, the series of equinoxes and solstices. In a calendar based on this solar year, such as the Gregorian calendar, the month is simply an arbitrary division, corresponding to no astronomical reality.

The true month (as the name, related to "moon," indicates) is the length of time in which the moon makes a circuit around the earth, readily measured from the appearance of one new moon to the next. It is a fraction over twenty-nine days; for practical purposes, therefore, lunar months are reckoned as alternately of twenty-nine and thirty days. Twelve such months add up to 354 days; a pure lunar system falls behind the sun about eleven days each year. In the Moslem calendar, which is such a system, the penitential month of Ramadan may occur at any season.

But the Israelite calendar, though it consists of lunar months, seems never to have had that character. The festivals were firmly anchored to the seasons of the agricultural year, with Passover in the spring and the Feast of Booths in the fall. There was then presumably some provision for adjusting the lunar and solar years to each other.

Centuries before the Christian era, the Babylonians had a lunisolar calendar. A watch was kept for the appearance of each new moon; when it was sighted, the king was notified, and he in turn sent orders to the temples for the proper rites to be performed. The king, moreover, would add an extra month to the year when his experts so advised, to keep the lunar calendar in balance with the solar year. As scientific knowledge advanced, the Babylonian astronomers worked out a scheme for the alternation of both twenty-nine-day and thirty-day months and for the insertion of an extra month seven times in each cyle of nineteen years. According to a recent study, this computed calendar was introduced about 481 B.C.E., after several centuries of experimentation [6].

Jewish procedure during the Second Commonwealth was much like the earlier Babylonian practice. Witnesses appeared before the high court in Jerusalem to testify that they had seen the crescent moon; thereupon the court formally announced that a month had begun, and so it notified communities throughout the land by signal fires, later by messengers. Until such notice was received, people did not know whether the thirtieth day was the last of the old month or the first of the new. Diaspora Jews, who did not receive official notification, began to keep each of the sacred occasions for two days—Yom Kippur excepted—to be sure of observing them on the proper date.

The high court also determined when an extra month was to be added to the year. Their chief concern was: Would the first grain be ripe for cutting at Passover time? (See p. 247.) When necessary to assure this result, a leap year of thirteen months would be proclaimed [7].

In the fourth century c.e., the Palestinian authorities, headed by Hillel II, promulgated a mathematically computed calendar system, virtually identical with that which the Babylonians had adopted some seven centuries earlier [8]. This system, which is accurate to a high degree, is still standard in Jewish use today. It obviated the need for the two-day observance of holidays in the Diaspora; but the communities outside the land, at the advice of the Palestinian authorities, held on to their established practice, which continues among traditional Jews to the present. In the Land of Israel, the only occasion observed for two days is the Festival of the New Year [9]. Reform Judaism follows the one-day biblical rule.

d. *The names of the months.* Three ways of designating the months are found in the Bible. Most frequently, as in the present chapter, they are indicated by number. In this system, the first month is the spring month in which Passover falls.

At one time, however, the months had

Hebrew or Canaanite names. At least four of them have survived. Most often mentioned is Abib (pronounced Aviv); the word means "fresh grain" and eventually acquired the general meaning "spring" (Exod. 13:4; Deut. 16:1; and elsewhere). Three other names in this series—Ziv, Bul, Ethanim—are mentioned in I Kings (6:37, 38 and 8:2).

In the Book of Esther, and sometimes in other late biblical books—Zechariah, Ezra, and Nehemiah—the ancient Babylonian month names are employed. In postbiblical times, this usage became standard and has continued to the present.

e. *Changes and controversies.* Tradition assumed that these changes of nomenclature were no more than that—that, whether the spring month was called Abib, first month, or Nisan, the calendar system was the same. Some modern scholars, too, hold this view. But there are many reasons for thinking that changes occurred also in the calendar system and in the order and character of some of the holidays. To try to trace the history of the calendar through the centuries would, however, be too complicated and hazardous an undertaking for us.

Only a few points may be noted. Our oldest document on the subject is the Gezer calendar, inscribed in old Hebrew letters on a clay tablet and said to date from the tenth century b.c.e. [10]. It is a sort of children's ditty, which does not name the months but indicates what agricultural work is performed in each of them. It starts with the olive harvest (September–October), and this may mean that the year was reckoned as beginning in the fall.

And, in fact, the day known for the last twenty centuries as the "New Year" does come in the fall; but our chapter (verse 24) locates it on the first day of the seventh month. Moreover, Exodus (12:1ff.) declares that the month of the Exodus is to be observed as the first month of the year—and the emphatic language of the passage suggests that this was an innovation [11].

These data, then, suggest a shift from one calendar system to another. But the different possibility that two methods of reckoning existed side by side has also to be considered. Though the Babylonian new year was customarily celebrated in the spring, there are also reports of a similar observance in the autumn [12]. And an interesting argument has been made for the view that, in the northern kingdom the years of a king's reign were reckoned on the basis of a spring-to-spring year, while in the southern kingdom the reckoning was from fall to fall [13].

Some time during the Second Commonwealth, a sectarian group tried to introduce an entirely new—apparently solar—calendar; this attempt is recorded in two apocryphal books, Jubilees and I Enoch. These proposals seem to have influenced the group that produced the Dead Sea Scrolls, but they do not appear to have been put into practice [14].

On the controversy regarding the date of Shavuot, see p. 247.

We should note that, though the calendar system apparently originated in Babylonia, it was adopted and promulgated by the Jewish leaders in Palestine, who claimed to hold exclusive authority in these matters. But persecution and poverty weakened the Palestinian community from the fourth century C.E. on, and the Babylonian schools became predominant in matters of halachah. Despite protests from the Land of Israel, the Babylonian scholars also regulated calendar matters. In the tenth century, a Palestinian leader named Ben Meir proposed certain departures from the usual system. In addition to substantive arguments for his position, he insisted that the regulation of the calendar was the exclusive prerogative of the Palestinian scholars. A violent conflict resulted. But eventually the authority of Babylonia was upheld, largely through the efforts of a rising young scholar, Saadia ben Joseph, who was to become one of the greatest personalities in Jewish history [15]. Henceforth, there was no serious challenge to the accepted system. In his code of the law, Maimonides drew on the best scientific sources of his time to clarify and support the tradition.

f. *Eras.* We take it for granted that years shall be numbered consecutively from some fixed date which is thought to have marked an important starting point in history. Such fixed eras are a comparatively recent innovation. Perhaps the first of these was the Greek custom of counting from the first Olympiad, in 776 B.C.E. In earlier times, years were designated by names (as still in the traditional Chinese calendar), by names of persons who held office in successive years, or by the years of a king's reign. Biblical writers occasionally used the Exodus as a starting point for dates (e.g., I Kings 6:1).

In 312 B.C.E., a Greco-Syrian empire was established by Seleucus, one of the generals of Alexander the Great. That date was adopted throughout the Middle East as the fixed point for numbering years. This Seleucid era—the first instance of this sort—was used by Jews in legal and business documents long after Rome had swallowed up the Hellenistic states; and it was employed much later by some Oriental Jews, almost to the present.

Meantime, another scheme of chronology was developing—an attempt to date events from the creation of the world. Indications of this reckoning are found in rabbinic literature but it seems to have been accepted generally only in the tenth century C.E. This is the era presently used for Jewish religious purposes. It fixes the date of Creation as 3760 B.C.E. But, even from the Orthodox standpoint, no one is obligated to accept that date as literally correct. The universe, we agree, is immeasurably older than such figures imply; but it is worth noting that urban civilization and recorded history did begin about four thousand years before the Christian era.

2. The Biblical Holy Days

a. *Sabbath.* See Exodus 20:8ff.

b. *Passover/Feast of Unleavened Bread.* See Exodus, chapters 12 and 13.

c. *The offering of the omer.* The Feast of Unleavened Bread was timed to coincide with the start of the grain harvest in the Land of Israel. Our chapter provides (verses 9–14) that the first grain to be cut shall be presented as a special offering at the sanctuary, together with an *olah* (the matter is mentioned nowhere else). None of the new crop may be eaten until this *omer* has been offered.

Three aspects of this law are extensively discussed in rabbinic literature. For the ruling that the offering was to be of barley and for the amount and form in which it was to be presented, see Gleanings.

Here, we must consider the heated controversy over the date when the *omer* is to be presented. According to verse 11, it is to be brought "on the day after the Sabbath." What does this mean? Jewish tradition answers: In this passage, *shabbat* means "rest day" and refers to the first day of the Matzot festival mentioned in the preceding verses. This explanation is found not only in talmudic sources but also in the Greek translation of the Torah (which here renders *shabbat* by "the first day"), Philo, and Josephus [16]. Evidently it is quite old.

But nowhere else is the term *"shabbat"* applied to a festival [17]. In this context it might well refer to the Sabbath of Passover week. A third possibility would be to identify it with the last day of the holiday.

The clarification of the point was important for two reasons. It determined when the grain harvest was to begin and especially how soon new grain could be eaten. And it fixed the date of the Feast of Weeks. For, according to verses 15 and 16, that festival was to be on the fiftieth day after the *omer* was brought. It seems that it was this second issue which led to a bitter controversy.

For there were those who insisted that *shabbat* here means the weekly Sabbath and that consequently Shavuot always falls on Sunday. This view is ascribed in talmudic literature to the Boethusians, a sect about which we have only scraps of information; apparently they were a subgroup of the Sadducees, the priestly conservatives. Probably all the Sadducees understood the verse in this way; the Karaites, who consider themselves heirs of the Sadducees, still observe Shavuot on Sunday.

The sectarian Book of Jubilees (p. 246) [18], which proposes that Shavuot be celebrated on Sivan 15, clearly intended the fifty days to be counted from the last day of Passover. This procedure is also indicated in the Syriac translation of the Bible (made early in the Christian era) and is followed to this day in the practice of the Falashas—the black Jews of Ethiopia—who observe their "harvest festival" on the twelfth day of the third month [19].

Against both these interpretations, the Pharisees—the spiritual fathers of modern Judaism—upheld the view that the *shabbat* was the first day of Passover, that the *omer* must be brought the following day, Nisan 16, and that Shavuot need not fall on a Sunday. According to the present mathematical calendar, it always falls on Sivan 6. Prior to the fourth century C.E. (see p. 245), it could fall on either the fifth, sixth, or seventh.

What motives lay behind the heated struggle of the Pharisees and Boethusians? We can only guess. No Saducean or Boethusian documents survive. We know these sects only through their opponents. And the arguments in the Talmud for the Pharisaic position are by no means conclusive. Orthodox scholars have understandably been at great pains to defend the tradition; Hoffmann devotes sixty pages of his commentary to the subject. Other modern scholars have been divided. Some regard the Boethusian exegesis as correct and assume that the Pharisees departed from the plain sense of the text for a purpose not stated; another view is that the Pharisees were preserving an age-old tradition from which the Boethusians tried to deviate for reasons of self-interest [20]. But none of the explanations of the controversy is entirely convincing.

d. *The omer period*. Both Leviticus (23:15ff.) and Deuteronomy (16:9–10) stress the obligation of counting off seven weeks from the formal start of the grain harvest. This biblical injunction is fulfilled literally in traditional Judaism by the ceremony of "counting the *omer*." Each evening an appropriate benediction is pronounced, followed by the statement: "Today is the —— day of the *omer*." This observance is also incorporated in the daily evening service of the synagogue.

The entire period from Pesach to Shavuot is known as the *omer* (or *sefirah*, "counting") period. In the course of centuries it has acquired associations that have no background in biblical law. Traditional Jews do not marry during this period, which is said to be one of mourning for persecutions that occurred in the spring. (But at what season of the year have persecutions not taken place?) Most probably this custom goes back to ancient superstitions. Also rooted in folklore are the more cheerful practices on the thirty-third day, Lag Ba-Omer [21].

e. *The Feast of Weeks (Shavuot)*. This name is found in Exodus (34:22) and Deuteronomy (16:9). Exodus, chapter 23, verse 16, calls the occasion "the Feast of the Harvest," and in our chapter it is not given a name [22]. In the Talmud it is referred to as *Atzeret*, a word rendered "solemn gathering" in Leviticus (23:36) where it refers to the final day of the fall festival [23]. This name has also been explained as "closing feast." The Rabbis no doubt had that explanation in mind when they spoke of Shavuot as "the Atzeret of Pesach" [24]—thereby stressing the connection between the two festivals, one marking the beginning, the other the climax of the grain harvest.

The Bible describes Shavuot only as an agricultural festival. Later tradition regards it as the anniversary of the giving of the Torah at Sinai. According to Exodus, chapter 19, the revelation occurred early in the third month; but an explicit identification of the festival as anniversary of the revelation is not found until well after the beginning of the Christian era [25]. Thereafter, the stress on the historical meaning of the holiday overshadowed the agricultural aspect. The latter survived only in the custom of decorating the synagogue with greens and flowers. The prayers and hymns of Shavuot all glorify the Torah. And the occasion was fittingly chosen by Reform Jews for the ceremony of confirmation, at which the pledge of Sinai is renewed.

f. *Festival of the New Year (Rosh Hashanah)*. For the past two thousand years, Jews have called the first day of the seventh month Rosh Hashanah, literally "the beginning of the year." But that name is not used in the Torah. Numbers (29:1) calls the occasion "the day of *teruah*" (we shall see shortly what that term means). Leviticus (23:24) calls it a "remembrance [or commemoration] of *teruah*." In the prayer book, its usual name is the Day of Remembrance (*Yom ha-Zikaron*) [26].

The expression "*rosh hashanah*" occurs just once in the Bible—in Ezekiel (40:1), followed by the words "on the tenth day of the month" (presumably the seventh month). To avoid the obvious difficulty, the phrase has usually been rendered "at the beginning of the year" rather than "on the new year." But this customary translation is questionable; the Talmud forthrightly asserts that the reference is to a jubilee year which was formally inaugurated on Yom Kippur (Lev. 25:9) [27]. The critical scholar is likely to conclude rather that Ezekiel's festival calendar differed significantly from that of Leviticus.

New year festivals were well known in the ancient Near East. In Babylonia, the new year was celebrated with great pomp and the statues of the gods were carried in procession through the city. On that day the god Marduk and other deities were said to ascend their thrones and to decree the destinies of men for the coming year. A number of modern scholars have attempted to reconstruct an ancient Israelite new year festival on the Babylonian model, citing such passages as Psalms 47, 81, and 98. And, indeed, the prayers of Rosh Hashanah still stress the kingship of God and the idea of a universal judgment. But the attempt to connect all this with prebiblical new year observances is hardly more than ingenious speculation. The Bible itself tells us little about the celebration of the first day of the seventh month.

The word "teruah" means "a loud noise"; it may be a shout (I Sam. 4:5) or it may be a blast of the ram's horn (shofar). A very ancient tradition calls for the blowing of the horn at our festival; accordingly, yom teruah (Num. 29:1) is translated in our version by "a day when the horn is sounded" and zichron teruah (Lev. 23:24) by "commemorated with loud blasts." The two phrases probably mean the same thing, but see Gleanings. In current usage, moreover, teruah denotes a throbbing blast, a kind of trill, in contrast to tekiah, a plain blast, and shevarim, a series of three short notes.

The silence of the older festival calendars about the High Holy Days and the vagueness of the statements about Rosh Hashanah even in Leviticus do not prove that these occasions were unknown before the Babylonian exile. Very probably the Festival of the New Year and the Day of Atonement rites were part of the great fall festival we now call Sukot and were included in the general commandment for that celebration. Later, these ceremonies were detached from the harvest festival and assigned to special days preceding Sukot.

The magnificent prayers and stirring ceremonies of our present new year observance are, like those of Yom Kippur, a creation of the Jewish people over many centuries.

g. *The Day of Atonement.* See chapter 16.

h. *The Feast of Booths (Sukot).* This name is found here and in Deuteronomy, chapter 16. Exodus, chapters 23 and 34, calls the autumn festival the "Feast of Ingathering." In Numbers, chapter 29, it is simply "a festival of the LORD"; and in the Talmud it is called the *Chag,* the festival par excellence [28]. It marked the close of the agricultural year, specifically of the vintage. And on the second day of the festival, ceremonies were performed—they are not mentioned in the Bible, but they were undoubtedly ancient—to evoke plentiful rains in the new agricultural season about to start. The *Chag* was an expression of grateful joy and a plea for continued blessing.

The booth is still to be seen in the Near East in a utilitarian and nonreligious context. It is a shelter built in the fields so that workers can rest, protected from the midday sun, without returning to their homes. At the height of the harvest, workers can also spend the night in the booth so as to speed up their work and finish it before the beginning of the fall rain. The ceremonial use of the sukah seems to have arisen from this custom. Later, the booth was explained as a memorial of the desert period, when the Israelites lived in frail shelters. Interestingly, the first halt that Israel made after leaving Egypt was at a place called Succoth (Exod. 12:37).

Also characteristic of the feast are the four plants that are combined into a sort of bouquet (Lev. 23:40), the *etrog* (citron) and *lulav* (palm branch), myrtle and willow. The Karaites, who rejected talmudic tradition, understood the verse as referring to materials for the construction of the sukah; and historically they may have been right [29]. But the traditional explanation is very old. The citron and palm branch appear on Maccabean coins (about 100 B.C.E.), and so they were evidently a well-known Jewish symbol by that time.

i. *Shemini Atzeret.* The eighth (*shemini*) day of Sukot is singled out for mention in verse 36; but the point is not clear. If *atzeret* means "a solemn gathering," why is the term applied only to the last day and not also to the first day of the festival? The Talmud [30] discusses the question whether this day is a separate feast or only the conclusion of Sukot. In the traditional synagogue, moreover, the day preceding Shemini Atzeret, known as Hoshana Rabbah ("Great Hosanna"), is marked by a return to the penitential mood of Yom Kippur. These facts lend support to the view mentioned above—that the Festival of New Year and the Day of Atonement rites were originally performed at the close of the fall festival. Even after they were transferred to their present place in the calendar, some memories of the original order survived.

Outside Israel, Shemini Atzeret also was observed for two days; and, in Babylonia, the ninth day was celebrated as Simchat Torah, the Feast of Rejoicing over the Law. On this day the annual cycle of Torah reading was completed and begun again. (In Palestine, the reading was completed only once in three years). Simchat Torah eventually became a more meaningful occasion than the biblical Shemini Atzeret, with characteristic and happy customs of its own. Reform Jewish practice has transferred some of these ceremonies to Shemini Atzeret, thus making one festival of Shemini Atzeret and Simchat Torah.

j. *New moon.* The present chapter does not discuss the celebration of the new moon; but the supplementary section enumerates the additional sacrifices for the "New Moon" day (Num. 28:11ff.). At one time, it seems, the new moon was an occasion that ranked in importance with the Sabbath (Isa. 1:13f.; Amos 8:5). Evidently our author considered it a minor occasion. In traditional Judaism, it is marked by extra prayers but not by abstention from work. Further, the advent of the new moon is solemnly announced in the synagogue on the preceding Sabbath; and a benediction is recited when the new crescent is seen.

א וַיְדַבֵּר יְהֹוָה אֶל־מֹשֶׁה לֵּאמֹר: דַּבֵּר אֶל־בְּנֵי יִשְׂרָאֵל
וְאָמַרְתָּ אֲלֵהֶם מוֹעֲדֵי יְהֹוָה אֲשֶׁר־תִּקְרְאוּ אֹתָם
ב מִקְרָאֵי קֹדֶשׁ אֵלֶּה הֵם מוֹעֲדָי: שֵׁשֶׁת יָמִים תֵּעָשֶׂה
מְלָאכָה וּבַיּוֹם הַשְּׁבִיעִי שַׁבַּת שַׁבָּתוֹן מִקְרָא־קֹדֶשׁ
כָּל־מְלָאכָה לֹא תַעֲשׂוּ שַׁבָּת הִוא לַיהֹוָה בְּכֹל
מוֹשְׁבֹתֵיכֶם: פ

Leviticus 23

1–5

ד אֵלֶּה מוֹעֲדֵי יְהֹוָה מִקְרָאֵי קֹדֶשׁ אֲשֶׁר־תִּקְרְאוּ אֹתָם
ה בְּמוֹעֲדָם: בַּחֹדֶשׁ הָרִאשׁוֹן בְּאַרְבָּעָה עָשָׂר לַחֹדֶשׁ

1] The LORD spoke to Moses, saying: 2] Speak to the Israelite people and say to them:

These are My fixed times, the fixed times of the LORD, which you shall proclaim as sacred occasions.

3] On six days work may be done, but on the seventh day there shall be a sabbath of complete rest, a sacred occasion. You shall do no work; it shall be a sabbath of the LORD throughout your settlements.

4] These are the set times of the LORD, the sacred occasions, which you shall celebrate each at its appointed time: 5] In the first month, on the fourteenth day of the month, at twilight, there shall be a passover offering to the LORD,

---

23:2] *To the Israelite people.* In contrast to the two preceding chapters which deal with priestly matters, the festival laws are addressed to the entire people.

Fixed times. Hebrew *moadim. Moed* means "appointment" and can refer either to the time or place set for a meeting. Then it comes to designate the meeting itself, especially a holy-day gathering. It is the broadest term for a religious occasion, including the High Holy Days and the minor festivals, as well as the three "pilgrim feasts" of Passover, Feast of Weeks, and Feast of Booths. (Only the latter are properly called *chagim* or *regalim.*)

3] The brief reference to the Sabbath is included apparently to preclude the notion that it had been overlooked and to stress its importance.

5] *Fourteenth day of the month, at twilight.* Hebrew *bein ha-arbayim,* literally, "between the sunsets" (see Gleanings). The language of verses 5 and 6 suggests that the evening when this sacrifice was performed was considered part of the fourteenth day and that the fifteenth—the Matzah festival—did not begin until the next morning (see p. 244).

Passover offering. Hebrew *pesach,* which in the Bible designates the sacrifice rather than the festival

י בֵּין הָעַרְבַּיִם פֶּסַח לַיהוָה: וּבַחֲמִשָּׁה עָשָׂר יוֹם לַחֹדֶשׁ
הַזֶּה חַג הַמַּצּוֹת לַיהוָה שִׁבְעַת יָמִים מַצּוֹת תֹּאכֵלוּ:
ז בַּיּוֹם הָרִאשׁוֹן מִקְרָא־קֹדֶשׁ יִהְיֶה לָכֶם כָּל־מְלֶאכֶת
ח עֲבֹדָה לֹא תַעֲשׂוּ: וְהִקְרַבְתֶּם אִשֶּׁה לַיהוָה שִׁבְעַת
יָמִים בַּיּוֹם הַשְּׁבִיעִי מִקְרָא־קֹדֶשׁ כָּל־מְלֶאכֶת עֲבֹדָה
לֹא תַעֲשׂוּ: פ

ט וַיְדַבֵּר יְהוָה אֶל־מֹשֶׁה לֵּאמֹר: דַּבֵּר אֶל־בְּנֵי יִשְׂרָאֵל
וְאָמַרְתָּ אֲלֵהֶם כִּי־תָבֹאוּ אֶל־הָאָרֶץ אֲשֶׁר אֲנִי נֹתֵן

Leviticus 23

6–10

6] and on the fifteenth day of that month the LORD's Feast of Unleavened Bread. You shall eat unleavened bread for seven days.   7] The first day shall be for you a sacred occasion: you shall not work at your occupations.   8] Seven days you shall make offerings by fire to the LORD. The seventh day shall be a sacred occasion: you shall not work at your occupations.

9] The LORD spoke to Moses, saying: 10] Speak to the Israelite people and say to them:

When you enter the land which I am giving to you and you reap its harvest, you

(see Exod. 12:11). In talmudic and later times, the entire week was known as Pesach; but the prayer book still uses regularly the term Feast of Unleavened Bread.

6] *You shall eat unleavened bread.* Exodus (13:7) is more stringent: "No leavened bread shall be found with you, and no leaven shall be found in all your territory."

7] *You shall not work at your occupations.* Literally, "You shall do no work of labor." This phrase is used concerning all the festivals, whereas the law for Sabbath and Yom Kippur is a blunt "You shall do no work" (verses 3 and 28). What then is intended by this provision which presumably is not quite so strict? It hardly means that heavy labor is prohibited and light work allowed; buying and selling were surely not permitted. The present rendering, "You

shall not work at your occupations," is likewise not altogether satisfactory; a man was hardly allowed to labor at something other than his regular job. Perhaps Nachmanides is right in referring to Exodus (12:6) which forbids work on Passover but adds, "Only what every person is to eat, that alone may be prepared for you." In short, says Nachmanides, only work involved in preparing food is permitted— as the halachah rules—and any other kind of work is forbidden as "work of labor."

8] *Offerings by fire.* As in 1:9. This general term is used throughout the chapter, and the specific sacrifices for each occasion are detailed in Numbers (28–29).

10] *When you enter the land.* Laws concerning harvest could not be observed in the desert.

לָכֶם וּקְצַרְתֶּם אֶת־קְצִירָהּ וַהֲבֵאתֶם אֶת־עֹמֶר

יא רֵאשִׁית קְצִירְכֶם אֶל־הַכֹּהֵן: וְהֵנִיף אֶת־הָעֹמֶר לִפְנֵי

יְהֹוָה לִרְצֹנְכֶם מִמָּחֳרַת הַשַּׁבָּת יְנִיפֶנּוּ הַכֹּהֵן:

יב וַעֲשִׂיתֶם בְּיוֹם הֲנִיפְכֶם אֶת־הָעֹמֶר כֶּבֶשׂ תָּמִים בֶּן־

יג שְׁנָתוֹ לְעֹלָה לַיהֹוָה: וּמִנְחָתוֹ שְׁנֵי עֶשְׂרֹנִים סֹלֶת

בְּלוּלָה בַשֶּׁמֶן אִשֶּׁה לַיהֹוָה רֵיחַ נִיחֹחַ וְנִסְכֹּה* יַיִן

יד רְבִיעִת הַהִין: וְלֶחֶם וְקָלִי וְכַרְמֶל לֹא תֹאכְלוּ עַד־

עֶצֶם הַיּוֹם הַזֶּה עַד הֲבִיאֲכֶם אֶת־קָרְבַּן אֱלֹהֵיכֶם

חֻקַּת עוֹלָם לְדֹרֹתֵיכֶם בְּכֹל מֹשְׁבֹתֵיכֶם: ס

טו וּסְפַרְתֶּם לָכֶם מִמָּחֳרַת הַשַּׁבָּת מִיּוֹם הֲבִיאֲכֶם אֶת־

Leviticus 23

11–15

* יין ונסכו קרי.

shall bring the first sheaf of your harvest to the priest.   11] He shall wave the sheaf before the LORD for acceptance in your behalf; the priest shall wave it on the day after the sabbath.   12] On the day that you wave the sheaf, you shall offer as a burnt offering to the LORD a lamb of the first year without blemish.   13] The meal offering with it shall be two-tenths of a measure of choice flour with oil mixed in, an offering by fire of pleasing odor to the LORD; and the libation with it shall be of wine, a quarter of a *hin*.   14] Until that very day, until you have brought the offering of your God, you shall eat no bread or parched grain or fresh ears; it is a law for all time throughout the ages in all your settlements.

15] And from the day on which you bring the sheaf of wave offering—the day

First sheaf. Hebrew *omer.* For the traditional explanation, see Gleanings.

11]   *He shall wave.* See commentary on 7:28–34.
   On the day after the sabbath. See p. 247.

13]   *Two-tenths of a measure.* All other such meal offerings consisted of one-tenth; perhaps it was

thought appropriate to "splurge" a bit at the time of the grain harvest. Only the usual amount of wine, however, is prescribed.

14]   *You shall eat no bread or parched grain or fresh ears.* I.e., of the new crop (T.N.). The Talmud [31] reports that merchants would bring in supplies of new grain to be put on sale as soon as the *omer* had been offered.

יט עֹ֣מֶר הַתְּנוּפָ֗ה שֶׁ֤בַע שַׁבָּתוֹת֙ תְּמִימֹ֣ת תִּהְיֶ֔ינָה: עַ֣ד

מִֽמׇּחֳרַ֤ת הַשַּׁבָּת֙ הַשְּׁבִיעִ֔ת תִּסְפְּר֖וּ חֲמִשִּׁ֣ים י֑וֹם

יז וְהִקְרַבְתֶּ֛ם מִנְחָ֥ה חֲדָשָׁ֖ה לַיהוָֽה: מִמּוֹשְׁבֹ֣תֵיכֶ֞ם

תָּבִ֣יאּוּ ׀ לֶ֣חֶם תְּנוּפָ֗ה שְׁתַּ֙יִם֙ שְׁנֵ֣י עֶשְׂרֹנִ֔ים סֹ֣לֶת

יח תִּהְיֶ֔ינָה חָמֵ֖ץ תֵּאָפֶ֑ינָה בִּכּוּרִ֖ים לַֽיהוָֽה: וְהִקְרַבְתֶּ֣ם

עַל־הַלֶּ֗חֶם שִׁבְעַ֤ת כְּבָשִׂים֙ תְּמִימִם֙ בְּנֵ֣י שָׁנָ֔ה וּפַ֧ר בֶּן־

בָּקָ֛ר אֶחָ֖ד וְאֵילִ֣ם שְׁנָ֑יִם יִהְי֤וּ עֹלָה֙ לַֽיהוָ֔ה וּמִנְחָתָם֙

יט וְנִסְכֵּיהֶ֔ם אִשֵּׁ֥ה רֵֽיחַ־נִיחֹ֖חַ לַיהוָֽה: וַעֲשִׂיתֶ֞ם שְׂעִיר־

עִזִּ֥ים אֶחָ֖ד לְחַטָּ֑את וּשְׁנֵ֧י כְבָשִׂ֛ים בְּנֵ֥י שָׁנָ֖ה לְזֶ֥בַח

כ שְׁלָמִֽים: וְהֵנִ֣יף הַכֹּהֵ֣ן ׀ אֹתָ֡ם עַל֩ לֶ֨חֶם הַבִּכֻּרִ֜ים

Leviticus 23

16–20

after the sabbath—you shall count off seven weeks. They must be complete:
16] you must count until the day after the seventh week—fifty days; then you
shall bring an offering of new grain to the LORD.   **17]** You shall bring from your
settlements two loaves of bread as a wave offering; each shall be made of two-tenths
of a measure of choice flour, baked after leavening, as first fruits to the LORD.
18] With the bread you shall present, as burnt offerings to the LORD, seven yearling
lambs without blemish, one bull of the herd, and two rams, with their meal offerings
and libations, an offering by fire of pleasing odor to the LORD.   **19]** You shall also
offer one he-goat as a sin offering and two yearling lambs as a sacrifice of well-being.
20] The priest shall wave these—the two lambs—together with the bread of first

17] *Two loaves of bread.* This explains the *offering of new grain* in verse 16. These loaves, exceptionally, are to be leavened; they are not to be burned on the altar (cf. 2:11, 7:13). Perhaps the loaves were regarded as a thanksgiving offering and therefore leavened like those of chapter 7, verse 13.

18–19] These verses contain the only specific directions for animal sacrifice in this chapter. This list resembles that in Numbers (28:26ff.), but the two do not agree exactly—another instance of variant traditions in P. The halachah (*Sifra* to the verse) does not harmonize but requires both sets of offerings: those in Leviticus to accompany the loaves, those in Numbers as fixed festival sacrifices [32].

20] *The priest shall wave these—the two lambs.* Hebrew obscure (T.N.). But see p. 58.

תְּנוּפָה לִפְנֵי יְהוָֹה עַל־שְׁנֵי כְּבָשִׂים קֹדֶשׁ יִהְיוּ לַיהוָֹה

כא לַכֹּהֵן: וּקְרָאתֶם בְּעֶצֶם הַיּוֹם הַזֶּה מִקְרָא־קֹדֶשׁ

יִהְיֶה לָכֶם כָּל־מְלֶאכֶת עֲבֹדָה לֹא תַעֲשׂוּ חֻקַּת עוֹלָם

כב בְּכָל־מוֹשְׁבֹתֵיכֶם לְדֹרֹתֵיכֶם: וּבְקֻצְרְכֶם אֶת־קְצִיר

אַרְצְכֶם לֹא־תְכַלֶּה פְּאַת שָׂדְךָ בְּקֻצְרֶךָ וְלֶקֶט

קְצִירְךָ לֹא תְלַקֵּט לֶעָנִי וְלַגֵּר תַּעֲזֹב אֹתָם אֲנִי

יְהוָֹה אֱלֹהֵיכֶם: פ

כג וַיְדַבֵּר יְהוָֹה אֶל־מֹשֶׁה לֵּאמֹר: דַּבֵּר אֶל־בְּנֵי יִשְׂרָאֵל

כד לֵאמֹר בַּחֹדֶשׁ הַשְּׁבִיעִי בְּאֶחָד לַחֹדֶשׁ יִהְיֶה לָכֶם

כה שַׁבָּתוֹן זִכְרוֹן תְּרוּעָה מִקְרָא־קֹדֶשׁ: כָּל־מְלֶאכֶת

עֲבֹדָה לֹא תַעֲשׂוּ וְהִקְרַבְתֶּם אִשֶּׁה לַיהוָֹה: ס

Leviticus 23

21–25

fruits as a wave offering before the LORD; they shall be holy to the LORD, for the priest.   **21]** On that same day you shall hold a celebration; it shall be a sacred occasion for you; you shall not work at your occupations. This is a law for all time in all your settlements, throughout the ages.

22] And when you reap the harvest of your land, you shall not reap all the way to the edges of your field, or gather the gleanings of your harvest; you shall leave them for the poor and the stranger: I the LORD am your God.

23] The LORD spoke to Moses, saying: **24]** Speak to the Israelite people thus: In the seventh month, on the first day of the month, you shall observe complete rest, a sacred occasion commemorated with loud blasts.   **25]** You shall not work at your occupations; and you shall bring an offering by fire to the LORD.

22] This verse reproduces 19:9 with minor changes. Its inclusion here reminds the worshiper that he has social as well as ritual obligations.

24] *Commemorated with loud blasts.* Hebrew *zichron teruah,* literally "a remembrance of a loud blast" (see Gleanings).

כו וַיְדַבֵּר יְהֹוָה אֶל־מֹשֶׁה לֵּאמֹר: אַ֣ךְ בֶּעָשׂ֣וֹר לַחֹ֣דֶשׁ
הַשְּׁבִיעִ֣י הַזֶּה֩ י֣וֹם הַכִּפֻּרִ֣ים ה֗וּא מִֽקְרָא־קֹ֙דֶשׁ֙ יִהְיֶ֣ה
לָכֶ֔ם וְעִנִּיתֶ֖ם אֶת־נַפְשֹׁתֵיכֶ֑ם וְהִקְרַבְתֶּ֥ם אִשֶּׁ֖ה לַֽיהֹוָֽה:
כח וְכָל־מְלָאכָה֙ לֹ֣א תַעֲשׂ֔וּ בְּעֶ֖צֶם הַיּ֣וֹם הַזֶּ֑ה כִּ֣י י֤וֹם
כִּפֻּרִים֙ ה֔וּא לְכַפֵּ֣ר עֲלֵיכֶ֔ם לִפְנֵ֖י יְהֹוָ֥ה אֱלֹהֵיכֶֽם:
כט כִּ֤י כָל־הַנֶּ֙פֶשׁ֙ אֲשֶׁ֣ר לֹֽא־תְעֻנֶּ֔ה בְּעֶ֖צֶם הַיּ֣וֹם הַזֶּ֑ה
ל וְנִכְרְתָ֖ה מֵֽעַמֶּֽיהָ: וְכָל־הַנֶּ֗פֶשׁ אֲשֶׁ֤ר תַּֽעֲשֶׂה֙ כָּל־
מְלָאכָ֔ה בְּעֶ֖צֶם הַיּ֣וֹם הַזֶּ֑ה וְהַֽאֲבַדְתִּ֛י אֶת־הַנֶּ֥פֶשׁ הַהִ֖וא
לא מִקֶּ֥רֶב עַמָּֽהּ: כָּל־מְלָאכָ֖ה לֹ֣א תַעֲשׂ֑וּ חֻקַּ֤ת עוֹלָם֙
לב לְדֹרֹ֣תֵיכֶ֔ם בְּכֹ֖ל מֹֽשְׁבֹֽתֵיכֶֽם: שַׁבַּ֨ת שַׁבָּת֜וֹן הוּא֩ לָכֶם֩

26] The LORD spoke to Moses, saying: 27] Mark, the tenth day of this seventh month is the Day of Atonement. It shall be a sacred occasion for you: you shall practice self-denial, and you shall bring an offering by fire to the LORD;   28] you shall do no work throughout that day. For it is a Day of Atonement, on which expiation is made on your behalf before the LORD your God.   29] Indeed, any person who does not practice self-denial throughout that day shall be cut off from his kin; 30] and whoever does any work throughout that day, I will cause that person to perish from among his people.   31] Do no work whatever; it is a law for all time, throughout the ages in all your settlements.   32] It shall be a sabbath of com-

---

27] *Mark.* Hebrew *ach*, literally, "however, only." Luzzatto says this word is used here and in verse 39 to call attention to something unusual—fasting here, the use of *etrog* and *lulav* there.

27–32] On Yom Kippur, see chapter 16.

30] I will *cause that person to perish.* This passage,

says *Sifra*, clarifies the often repeated expression "so-and-so will be cut off from his kin."

32] *On the ninth day of the month at evening.* Here again is a suggestion that the new day began at daybreak rather than sundown. For the traditional explanation, see Gleanings.

וְעִנִּיתֶם אֶת־נַפְשֹׁתֵיכֶם בְּתִשְׁעָה לַחֹדֶשׁ בָּעֶרֶב מֵעֶרֶב
עַד־עֶרֶב תִּשְׁבְּתוּ שַׁבַּתְּכֶם: פ

לג וַיְדַבֵּר יְהוָה אֶל־מֹשֶׁה לֵּאמֹר: דַּבֵּר אֶל־בְּנֵי יִשְׂרָאֵל
לֵאמֹר בַּחֲמִשָּׁה עָשָׂר יוֹם לַחֹדֶשׁ הַשְּׁבִיעִי הַזֶּה חַג
לה הַסֻּכּוֹת שִׁבְעַת יָמִים לַיהוָה: בַּיּוֹם הָרִאשׁוֹן מִקְרָא־
לו קֹדֶשׁ כָּל־מְלֶאכֶת עֲבֹדָה לֹא תַעֲשׂוּ: שִׁבְעַת יָמִים
תַּקְרִיבוּ אִשֶּׁה לַיהוָה בַּיּוֹם הַשְּׁמִינִי מִקְרָא־קֹדֶשׁ יִהְיֶה
לָכֶם וְהִקְרַבְתֶּם אִשֶּׁה לַיהוָה עֲצֶרֶת הִוא כָּל־
לז מְלֶאכֶת עֲבֹדָה לֹא תַעֲשׂוּ: אֵלֶּה מוֹעֲדֵי יְהוָה אֲשֶׁר־
תִּקְרְאוּ אֹתָם מִקְרָאֵי קֹדֶשׁ לְהַקְרִיב אִשֶּׁה לַיהוָה

Leviticus 23
33–37

plete rest for you, and you shall practice self-denial; on the ninth day of the month
at evening, from evening to evening, you shall observe this your sabbath.

33] The LORD spoke to Moses, saying: **34]** Say to the Israelite people:

On the fifteenth day of this seventh month there shall be the Feast of Booths to
the LORD, [to last] seven days.   **35]** The first day shall be a sacred occasion: you
shall not work at your occupations;   **36]** seven days you shall bring offerings by
fire to the LORD. On the eighth day you shall observe a sacred occasion and bring
an offering by fire to the LORD; it is a solemn gathering: you shall not work at your
occupations.

37] Those are the set times of the LORD which you shall celebrate as sacred occasions, bringing offerings by fire to the LORD—burnt offerings, meal offerings,

34] *Booths.* Others, "Tabernacles" (T.N.).
36] *Solemn gathering.* Precise meaning of Hebrew *atzeret* uncertain (T.N.). See p. 250. Ibn Ezra under-stands the root-meaning of the word as "restrain," re-ferring to restraint from work (see also Gleanings).

37] *Those are the set times. . . .* These verses are clearly the conclusion of the festival calendar. The additional section on Sukot in verses 39–43 appears to be from another source. (On votive and freewill offerings, see p. 56.)

עֹלָה וּמִנְחָה זֶבַח וּנְסָכִים דְּבַר־יוֹם בְּיוֹמוֹ: מִלְּבַד לח

שַׁבְּתֹת יְהוָה וּמִלְּבַד מַתְּנוֹתֵיכֶם וּמִלְּבַד כָּל־נִדְרֵיכֶם

וּמִלְּבַד כָּל־נִדְבֹתֵיכֶם אֲשֶׁר תִּתְּנוּ לַיהוָה: אַךְ לט

בַּחֲמִשָּׁה עָשָׂר יוֹם לַחֹדֶשׁ הַשְּׁבִיעִי בְּאָסְפְּכֶם אֶת־

תְּבוּאַת הָאָרֶץ תָּחֹגּוּ אֶת־חַג־יְהוָה שִׁבְעַת יָמִים בַּיּוֹם

הָרִאשׁוֹן שַׁבָּתוֹן וּבַיּוֹם הַשְּׁמִינִי שַׁבָּתוֹן: וּלְקַחְתֶּם לָכֶם מ

בַּיּוֹם הָרִאשׁוֹן פְּרִי עֵץ הָדָר כַּפֹּת תְּמָרִים וַעֲנַף עֵץ־

עָבֹת וְעַרְבֵי־נָחַל וּשְׂמַחְתֶּם לִפְנֵי יְהוָה אֱלֹהֵיכֶם

שִׁבְעַת יָמִים: וְחַגֹּתֶם אֹתוֹ חַג לַיהוָה שִׁבְעַת יָמִים מא

בַּשָּׁנָה חֻקַּת עוֹלָם לְדֹרֹתֵיכֶם בַּחֹדֶשׁ הַשְּׁבִיעִי תָּחֹגּוּ

אֹתוֹ: בַּסֻּכֹּת תֵּשְׁבוּ שִׁבְעַת יָמִים כָּל־הָאֶזְרָח בְּיִשְׂרָאֵל מב

Leviticus 23
38–42

sacrifices, and libations, on each day what is proper to it— 38] apart from the sabbaths of the LORD, and apart from your gifts and from all your votive offerings and from all your freewill offerings that you give to the LORD.

39] Mark, on the fifteenth day of the seventh month, when you have gathered in the yield of your land, you shall observe the festival of the LORD [to last] seven days: a complete rest on the first day, and a complete rest on the eighth day. 40] On the first day you shall take the product of *hadar* trees, branches of palm trees, boughs of leafy trees, and willows of the brook, and you shall rejoice before the LORD your God seven days. 41] You shall observe it as a festival of the LORD for seven days in the year; you shall observe it in the seventh month as a law for all time, throughout the ages. 42] You shall live in booths seven days; all citizens

---

40] *Product of hadar trees.* Others, "goodly"; exact meaning of *hadar* uncertain. Traditionally the product is understood as "citron" (T.N.). See p. 250. All the citrus fruits were native to the Far East. The citron was the first of the family to be brought to western Asia and thence to Europe.

Leafy trees. Meaning of Hebrew *avot* uncertain (T.N.). It was understood by tradition as myrtle, the leaves of which have a "plaited" appearance, completely covering the stems.

42] *You shall live in booths.* This was understood quite

258

מג יֵשְׁבוּ בַּסֻּכֹּת: לְמַעַן יֵדְעוּ דֹרֹתֵיכֶם כִּי בַסֻּכּוֹת הוֹשַׁבְתִּי אֶת־בְּנֵי יִשְׂרָאֵל בְּהוֹצִיאִי אוֹתָם מֵאֶרֶץ מד מִצְרָיִם אֲנִי יְהֹוָה אֱלֹהֵיכֶם: וַיְדַבֵּר מֹשֶׁה אֶת־מֹעֲדֵי יְהֹוָה אֶל־בְּנֵי יִשְׂרָאֵל: פ

in Israel shall live in booths,   43] in order that future generations may know that I made the Israelite people live in booths when I brought them out of the land of Egypt, I the LORD your God.

44] So Moses declared to the Israelites the set times of the LORD.

literally in Jewish tradition. One was to sleep in the sukah for seven nights and take all his regular meals there. Only the circumstances of modern urban living have compelled many observant Orthodox Jews to limit themselves to eating meals in a communal or congregational booth.

43]   *That I made the Israelite people live in booths when I brought them out of the land of Egypt.* This explanation

gave a Jewish historical aspect to an originally agricultural festival. According to Rashbam, the booth reminds us of our humble beginnings, and so it protects us against arrogance.

44]   *So Moses declared to the Israelites the set times of the Lord.* This verse is sung during the evening service of the three major festivals (e.g., *Union Prayer Book*, I, pp. 190–191).

GLEANINGS

Halachah

23:2] *The Fixed Times of the Lord, Which You Shall Proclaim*

This means that the high court, the Sanhedrin, has the right to determine the time of the new moon—thus fixing the dates of the festivals—and to add a month to the year when necessary. Even should the earthly court make an error in these procedures, its decision is still valid and is confirmed on high.

SIFRA

5] *At Twilight*

Hebrew *bein ha-arbayim*. See commentary. The halachah required that the paschal animals be slaughtered as sacrifices in the Temple. But it must have taken hours to provide this service for the thousands of pilgrims present in Jerusalem, even with all available priests on duty. In this case, therefore, *bein ha-arbayim* was taken to mean the entire afternoon of Nisan 14, from noon on.   SIFRA

7] *You Shall Not Work at Your Occupations*

See in the commentary the citation from Nachmanides, who states the halachah.

10] *First Sheaf*

Hebrew *omer*. This word sometimes means a dry measure of about two quarts (Exod. 16:36); the halachah understands it thus here, as defining the amount of grain required for the offering. This *omer* was identified with the "meal offering of first fruits" in Leviticus (2:14); like other *minchahs*, it had to contain a fixed amount. In accordance with chapter 2, verse 14, the *omer* grain was roasted, then pounded into coarse grits before it was offered (*Sifra* on 2:14). This offering, exceptionally, was of barley, not wheat.   SIFRA

How was the cutting of the first grain performed? Representatives of the court would go out on the day before the holy day (i.e., before the first day of Passover) and tie the standing grain into bunches, so that it would be easy to cut. At the end of the holy day, the people of the nearby villages would assemble at the place, so that the harvesting should be conducted with much ceremony. When it was dark, the appointed reaper would ask, "Has the sun gone down?" and the people would reply, "Yes." This question would be asked and answered three times, and so for the following questions: "Shall I use this sickle?" "Shall I put the grain into this box?" "Shall I do it this week?" "Shall I reap?" and they would reply "Reap!" All this formality was directed against the Boethusians who denied that the grain should be cut immediately after the holy day [33].

11] *On the Day after the Sabbath*
See p. 247.

14] *You Shall Eat No Bread*

From the new crop. Though the *omer* ceremony was discontinued after the fall of the Temple, it is still prohibited to eat of new grain until after Nisan 16.

SIFRA

17] *As First Fruits*

Once these communal first fruits had been offered, individuals might bring their own first fruits, in accordance with Deuteronomy, chapter 26 [34].

18] *You Shall Present . . . Seven Yearling Lambs*
See commentary.

260

20] *They Shall Be Holy to the Lord, for the Priest*

The holiness of the loaves consists in their being assigned to the priest for his exclusive consumption [35].

24] *Commemorated with Loud Blasts*

Hebrew *zichron teruah*, literally "a remembrance of loud blasts." During the shofar service in the synagogue, three groups of verses are recited. The first, called *malchuyot*, affirm God's sovereignty; the second, *zichronot*, speak of God's "remembering" past and present events that evoke His mercy; the third, *shofarot*, refer to blasts of the shofar on various occasions (see *Union Prayer Book*, II, pp. 78–82). The second and third sections are indicated in our verse by the words *zichron* and *teruah*. The *malchuyot* are derived from Numbers (10:10)—this passage deals with the blowing of trumpets, it contains the word "reminder" (a different form of *zichron*), and it concludes with "I the LORD am your God."   SIFRA

In traditional synagogues, the shofar is not blown on the Sabbath. In such a case, the holy day is described in the prayers by the words of our verse as "a day of *remembering* the loud blast"; when Rosh Hashanah falls on a weekday, the phrase of Numbers (29:1), *yom teruah*, "a day when the horn is sounded," is used [36].

30] *I Will Cause That Person to Perish*
See commentary.

32] *On the Ninth Day of the Month at Evening*
See commentary. Tradition understood this to

mean: Begin the fast while it is still daylight on the ninth, to make sure that you do not eat on Yom Kippur itself (*Sifra*). Similarly, one does not break his fast till well after dark, to allow margin for error.

36] *Solemn Gathering*

The commandment of the sukah does not apply to this eighth day (verse 42).

40] *Product of Hadar Trees*

The Rabbis offer several proofs that this means the citron, *etrog*. For example: It is the fruit that remains (*ha-dar*) on the tree from year to year.
SIFRA

Branches of Palm Trees

Despite the plural "branches," tradition prescribed a single *lulav*.   SIFRA

Willows of the Brook

But twigs from willows that grow elsewhere are permitted.   SIFRA

You Shall Rejoice

This is taken as a positive commandment. It is a religious obligation to eat and drink well during the festival, and mourning is forbidden throughout the holiday period [37].

42] *All Citizens*

This masculine term exempts women (as well as slaves) from the duty of living in the sukah.
SIFRA

Haggadah

23:11] *He Shall Wave the Sheaf*

Horizontally, to ward off destructive winds; up and down, to ward off harmful dews.   SIFRA

24] *In the Seventh Month, on the First Day of the Month*

Rosh Hashanah, according to a widely accepted tradition, is the anniversary of the creation of the world [38]. "This day marks the beginning of Your works; it is a memorial of the first day" (from the liturgy). It is also understood as the day of universal judgment, when the destinies of all are decided for the coming year; but the decrees are not sealed until Yom Kippur. Thereby humans are given an oppor-

tunity to repent and correct their ways; for "repentance, prayer, and charity avert the evil decree" [39].

Commemorated with Loud Blasts

The shofar is a simple horn of very ancient origin. It was used to warn people of approaching danger (Amos 3:6; Jer. 4:19, 6:1). Its shrill tone was also thought to drive away evil spirits; and Jewish tradition explains the blowing of the shofar on the new year as having the purpose (among others) of "disconcerting Satan." The latter acts as prosecutor before the heavenly court; and the shofar blast disturbs him and prevents him from reading the record of Israel's sins effectively [40].

Another interpretation connected the shofar with the horn of the ram which Abraham sacrificed instead of Isaac (Gen. 22:13). The story of the "binding of Isaac" is the Torah portion for the second day of Rosh Hashanah in traditional synagogues and is read on Rosh Hashanah proper in Reform congregations. The Midrash represents God as saying to Abraham, "When your descendants sin, and they appear before Me for judgment on Rosh Hashanah, let them blow the ram's horn; this will remind Me of the piety of their ancestors and lead Me to forgive them" [41].

"Happy is the people who know the joyful shout" (Ps. 89:16). Said Rabbi Josiah: Do not other peoples know how to sound blasts? How many kinds of horns and trumpets they possess! But the verse means: Happy is the people who know how to evoke the favor of their Creator by means of the blast. For, when they blow the shofar, the Holy One (blessed be He!) arises from the throne of judgment and sits upon the throne of mercy; He is filled with compassion for them and transforms His Quality of Justice into the Quality of Mercy [42].

In contrast to these views, according to which the sound of the shofar has an influence on the demonic world, and even on the purposes of God, the rationalist Maimonides considers the impact of the ceremony on the worshiper: "The blowing of the shofar on Rosh Hashanah is an ordinance of Scripture [and must therefore be obeyed, if only for that reason]. But it also has a deeper meaning. It says to us: Awake, ye slumberers, from your slumber, and rouse yourselves from your deep sleep. Search your deeds and turn ye in repentance. Remember your Creator, ye who forget truth because of the vanity of the hour, who go astray all through the year in pursuit of trifles which can neither profit nor save. Let every one of you forsake his wicked path and his evil purpose" [43].

27] *Mark, the Tenth Day of This Seventh Month Is the Day of Atonement*

The word "*ach*" (here rendered "mark," literally, "however, only") always has a restrictive force. Here it implies that God forgives *only* those who repent.   SIFRA

36] *On the Eighth Day ... Is a Solemn Gathering* [*Atzeret*]

The Rabbis understand *atzeret* as coming from a root meaning "to restrain." A king once invited his children to a seven-day feast. When it was over, he was reluctant to part with them and "restrained" them to celebrate one more day with him [44].

40] *Branches of Palm Trees*

The palm was a widely accepted symbol of victory in ancient times. Apparently, there was a Roman custom for a successful litigant in a law case to leave the courtroom carrying a palm branch. So likewise, say the Rabbis, accusations are made against Israel during the Days of Awe. Have our adversaries prevailed, or have we emerged with the favor of the divine Judge? The fact that we carry the palm branch on Sukot gives the happy answer [45].

Various allegorical explanations are given of all the four plants. This is one of the most attractive: The citron is both fragrant and edible; it symbolizes those Jews who are learned in the Torah and righteous in deed. The date palm provides food, but it has no fragrance; it symbolizes those who are learned but are deficient in good acts. The myrtle is fragrant, but it yields nothing to eat; it typifies those whose conduct is exemplary but who lack knowledge of the Torah. And the willow, which offers neither nourishment nor fragrance, typifies those who are deficient both in learning and in virtue. Let them all, says God, be bound together in fellowship like a well-tied bouquet, so that the merits of each shall benefit all the others [46].

43] *That I Made the Israelite People Live in Booths When I Brought Them Out of the Land of Egypt*

See commentary. According to Rabbi Akiba, the booths in question were clouds of glory which sheltered and accompanied Israel on their desert wanderings. But Rabbi Eliezer held that the Israelites dwelt in literal booths.   SIFRA

Jewish homilists have also stressed the frail and temporary character of the sukah. We are summoned to leave our solid, seemingly permanent dwellings and live for a time in the fragile sukah, that we may become mindful of our own frailty and impermanence and of our need for divine help [47].

Oil, Bread, and the Blasphemer

This chapter consists of a number of short items that do not seem to be connected with one another.

1. Oil for the Temple Lamps

Verses 1 through 4 repeat Exodus, chapter 27, verses 20 and 21, with a few slight changes. Traditional commentators offer various reasons for the repetition. To us it is one more example of the way in which various sources were combined to form the Torah.

2. The Bread of Display

The furniture of the Tabernacle included a table overlaid with gold on which the priests were to set out "bread of display" (Exod. 25:23ff., 40:22f.). Earlier translations used "shewbread" or "showbread" for the Hebrew *lechem panim*, literally "bread of Face/Presence," a term which has been variously explained [1]. The term does not occur in this chapter, which, however, explains the procedure more fully.

There were to be twelve sizeable loaves, arranged in two rows on the table. They were to be accompanied by incense, no doubt

in bowls set on either side of the rows of bread (so *Sifra*). Fresh bread was to be supplied each Sabbath; last week's loaves were to be removed and, after the incense had been burned, were to be eaten by the priests with due regard for their sanctity.

From remote antiquity, one form of offering was to set food before the image of the god, later to remove it for consumption by king or priest (see p. 4). Babylonian ritual also called for an offering of twelve loaves, but sometimes larger and smaller numbers were offered [2]. That the custom was ancient in Israel is attested by the story in I Samuel, chapter 21. When David fled from Saul, he came to the shrine at Nob and asked for bread. The local priest had nothing but "bread of display" which he gave to David when the latter assured him that he and his followers were in a state of ritual purity [3]. This instance from early Israelite history shows that the priestly writings—whatever the date when they were finally edited—contain very old elements.

3. The Blasphemer

Israel had been commanded (Exod. 22:27), "You shall not revile God." Now, in one of the rare narrative passages of Leviticus, we read of a case where this command was violated. No one knew how to deal with the offender; so Moses sought a special revelation and was told that the criminal must die by stoning.

This is one of four episodes in the Torah in which Moses has to make a special inquiry of God before he can give a legal decision. The others are Numbers (9:6ff., 15:32ff., and 27:1ff.). These passages are discussed at length by Philo and the Rabbis who are troubled by Moses' inability to handle these cases on his own [4].

In the present instance the explanation is not difficult. The penalty for blasphemy had not yet been revealed. But the intent of the entire section remains to be explained and various possibilities suggest themselves. Was it simply to stress the sinfulness of misusing the divine name? Was it a warning of the disastrous results that may follow mixed marriage? Was it to make the legal distinction between ordinary blasphemy, punishment for which is left to God, and cases where the name YHWH is pronounced and the court must execute the offender (see verses 15f.)?

Or was it to emphasize the principle that the law applies equally to citizen and resident alien? This suggestion is supported by the presence in this chapter of other penal laws that have nothing to do with blasphemy. The penalties for murder, mayhem, and the killing of animals are repeated here, with the assertion that one standard must be applied to citizen and stranger alike.

א֨ וַיְדַבֵּ֥ר יְהֹוָ֖ה אֶל־מֹשֶׁ֥ה לֵּאמֹֽר׃ צַ֣ו אֶת־בְּנֵ֣י יִשְׂרָאֵ֗ל

וְיִקְח֨וּ אֵלֶ֜יךָ שֶׁ֣מֶן זַ֥יִת זָ֛ךְ כָּתִ֖ית לַמָּא֑וֹר לְהַעֲלֹ֥ת נֵ֖ר

ג֖ תָּמִֽיד׃ מִחוּץ֩ לְפָרֹ֨כֶת הָעֵדֻ֜ת בְּאֹ֣הֶל מוֹעֵ֗ד יַעֲרֹ֩ךְ֩

אֹת֨וֹ אַהֲרֹ֤ן מֵעֶ֙רֶב֙ עַד־בֹּ֣קֶר לִפְנֵ֤י יְהֹוָה֙ תָּמִ֔יד חֻקַּ֥ת

עוֹלָ֖ם לְדֹרֹתֵיכֶֽם׃ עַ֚ל הַמְּנֹרָ֣ה הַטְּהֹרָ֔ה יַעֲרֹ֖ךְ אֶת־

הַנֵּר֑וֹת לִפְנֵ֥י יְהֹוָ֖ה תָּמִֽיד׃ פ

ה֖ וְלָקַחְתָּ֣ סֹ֗לֶת וְאָפִיתָ֤ אֹתָהּ֙ שְׁתֵּ֣ים עֶשְׂרֵ֔ה חַלּ֑וֹת שְׁנֵי֙

עֶשְׂרֹנִ֔ים יִהְיֶ֖ה הַֽחַלָּ֣ה הָאֶחָֽת׃ וְשַׂמְתָּ֥ אוֹתָ֛ם שְׁתַּ֥יִם

מַעֲרָכ֖וֹת שֵׁ֣שׁ הַֽמַּעֲרָ֑כֶת עַ֛ל הַשֻּׁלְחָ֥ן הַטָּהֹ֖ר לִפְנֵ֥י

ז֖ יְהֹוָֽה׃ וְנָתַתָּ֥ עַל־הַֽמַּעֲרֶ֖כֶת לְבֹנָ֣ה זַכָּ֑ה וְהָיְתָ֤ה לַלֶּ֙חֶם֙

ח֖ לְאַזְכָּרָ֔ה אִשֶּׁ֖ה לַֽיהֹוָֽה׃ בְּיוֹם֩ הַשַּׁבָּ֨ת בְּי֤וֹם הַשַּׁבָּת֙

Leviticus 24

1–8

1] The LORD spoke to Moses, saying:

2] Command the Israelite people to bring you clear oil of beaten olives for lighting, to maintain lights regularly.   3] Aaron shall set them up in the Tent of Meeting outside the curtain of the Pact [to burn] from evening to morning before the LORD regularly; it is a law for all time throughout the ages.   4] He shall set up the lamps on the pure lampstand before the LORD [to burn] regularly.

5] You shall take choice flour and bake of it twelve loaves, two-tenths of a measure for each loaf.   6] Place them on the pure table before the LORD in two rows, six to a row.   7] With each row you shall place pure frankincense, which is to be a token offering for the bread, as an offering by fire to the LORD.   8] He shall ar-

---

24:4] *The pure lampstand* [*menorah*]. Either "the lampstand of pure gold" (so T.N. at Exod. 31:8) or "the lampstand that has been cleansed" before the lamps were refilled and replaced (Rashi).

7] In the case of ordinary cereal offerings, a token portion of meal, oil, and frankincense was burned on the altar (above, 2:2). In this case, the token portion was incense alone.

As an offering by fire. Here and in verse 9, the term refers exceptionally to the frankincense. Usually it designates any sacrifice burned on the altar.

יַעַרְכֶנּוּ לִפְנֵי יְהוָה תָּמִיד מֵאֵת בְּנֵי־יִשְׂרָאֵל בְּרִית

ט עוֹלָם: וְהָיְתָה לְאַהֲרֹן וּלְבָנָיו וַאֲכָלֻהוּ בְּמָקוֹם קָדֹשׁ

כִּי קֹדֶשׁ קָדָשִׁים הוּא לוֹ מֵאִשֵּׁי יְהוָה חָק־עוֹלָם: ס

י וַיֵּצֵא בֶּן־אִשָּׁה יִשְׂרְאֵלִית וְהוּא בֶּן־אִישׁ מִצְרִי בְּתוֹךְ

בְּנֵי יִשְׂרָאֵל וַיִּנָּצוּ בַּמַּחֲנֶה בֶּן הַיִּשְׂרְאֵלִית וְאִישׁ

יא הַיִּשְׂרְאֵלִי: וַיִּקֹּב בֶּן־הָאִשָּׁה הַיִּשְׂרְאֵלִית אֶת־הַשֵּׁם

וַיְקַלֵּל וַיָּבִיאוּ אֹתוֹ אֶל־מֹשֶׁה וְשֵׁם אִמּוֹ שְׁלֹמִית בַּת־

יב דִּבְרִי לְמַטֵּה־דָן: וַיַּנִּיחֻהוּ בַּמִּשְׁמָר לִפְרֹשׁ לָהֶם עַל־

פִּי יְהוָה: פ

יג-יד וַיְדַבֵּר יְהוָה אֶל־מֹשֶׁה לֵּאמֹר: הוֹצֵא אֶת־הַמְקַלֵּל

Leviticus 24

9–14

range them before the LORD regularly every sabbath day—it is a commitment for all time on the part of the Israelites.   9] They shall belong to Aaron and his sons, who shall eat them in the sacred precinct; for they are his as most holy things from the LORD's offerings by fire, a due for all time.

10] There came out among the Israelites one whose mother was Israelite and whose father was Egyptian. And a fight broke out in the camp between that half Israelite and a certain Israelite.   11] The son of the Israelite woman pronounced the Name in blasphemy, and he was brought to Moses—now his mother's name was Shelomith daughter of Dibri of the tribe of Dan—   12] and he was placed in custody, until the decision of the LORD should be made clear to them.

13] And the LORD spoke to Moses, saying: 14] Take the blasphemer outside

10] *That half Israelite.* Literally, "the son of an Israelite woman" (T.N.).

12] *In custody.* The Hebrew form suggests that there was a regular detention area outside the camp for accused persons whose cases were pending. Imprisonment as punishment for a crime does not seem to have been a regular practice in ancient Israel [5].

אֶל־מִחוּץ לַמַּחֲנֶה וְסָמְכוּ כָל־הַשֹּׁמְעִים אֶת־יְדֵיהֶם

טו עַל־רֹאשׁוֹ וְרָגְמוּ אֹתוֹ כָּל־הָעֵדָה: וְאֶל־בְּנֵי יִשְׂרָאֵל

תְּדַבֵּר לֵאמֹר אִישׁ אִישׁ כִּי־יְקַלֵּל אֱלֹהָיו וְנָשָׂא חֶטְאוֹ:

טז וְנֹקֵב שֵׁם־יְהוָה מוֹת יוּמָת רָגוֹם יִרְגְּמוּ־בוֹ כָּל־הָעֵדָה

יז כַּגֵּר כָּאֶזְרָח בְּנָקְבוֹ שֵׁם יוּמָת: וְאִישׁ כִּי יַכֶּה כָּל־נֶפֶשׁ

יח אָדָם מוֹת יוּמָת: וּמַכֵּה נֶפֶשׁ־בְּהֵמָה יְשַׁלְּמֶנָּה נֶפֶשׁ

יט תַּחַת נָפֶשׁ: וְאִישׁ כִּי־יִתֵּן מוּם בַּעֲמִיתוֹ כַּאֲשֶׁר עָשָׂה

כ כֵּן יֵעָשֶׂה לּוֹ: שֶׁבֶר תַּחַת שֶׁבֶר עַיִן תַּחַת עַיִן שֵׁן תַּחַת

Leviticus 24

15–20

the camp; and let all who were within hearing lay their hands upon his head, and let the whole community stone him.

15] And to the Israelite people speak thus: Anyone who blasphemes his God shall bear his guilt; **16]** if he also pronounces the name LORD, he shall be put to death. The whole community shall stone him; stranger or citizen, if he has thus pronounced the Name, he shall be put to death.

17] If a man kills any human being, he shall be put to death. **18]** One who kills a beast shall make restitution for it: life for life. **19]** If anyone maims his fellow, as he has done so shall it be done to him: **20]** fracture for fracture, eye for

14] *Outside the camp.* The camp proper was not to be defiled by an execution.

All who were within hearing. When he uttered the blasphemy and consequently testified against him.

Lay their hands upon his head. This gesture is regularly associated with sacrifice; it appears in connection with a criminal execution only here.

17–22] For these laws, see Genesis 9:6; Exodus 21:12–14, 18–25, 35–36; and Deuteronomy 19:21. We suggested above that the repetition here may be intended to indicate that the laws apply equally to aliens. Note, however, that Exodus 21:20–21 limits

the liability of one who causes the death of his slave by excessive beating; but Leviticus 24:17 rules that all homicide is punishable by death (no doubt intentional homicide is meant).

18] *One who kills a beast shall make restitution for it: life for life.* Not that one of the defendant's beasts should be killed in retaliation, but—as verse 21 indicates—that the plaintiff shall be reimbursed for his loss. So the Talmud correctly understood [6].

19] *As he has done, so shall it be done to him.* See Exodus 21:23f. and Deuteronomy 19:21 on the law of "eye for eye." There is strong reason to believe

ויקרא כד
כא–כג

Leviticus 24
21–23

כא שֵׁן כַּאֲשֶׁר יִתֵּן מוּם בָּאָדָם כֵּן יִנָּתֶן בּוֹ: וּמַכֵּה בְהֵמָה
כב יְשַׁלְּמֶנָּה וּמַכֵּה אָדָם יוּמָת: מִשְׁפַּט אֶחָד יִהְיֶה לָכֶם
כג כַּגֵּר כָּאֶזְרָח יִהְיֶה כִּי אֲנִי יְהוָֹה אֱלֹהֵיכֶם: וַיְדַבֵּר
מֹשֶׁה אֶל־בְּנֵי יִשְׂרָאֵל וַיּוֹצִיאוּ אֶת־הַמְקַלֵּל אֶל־מִחוּץ
לַמַּחֲנֶה וַיִּרְגְּמוּ אֹתוֹ אָבֶן וּבְנֵי־יִשְׂרָאֵל עָשׂוּ כַּאֲשֶׁר
צִוָּה יְהוָֹה אֶת־מֹשֶׁה:

Haftarah Emor, p. 396

eye, tooth for tooth. The injury he inflicted on another shall be inflicted on him.

21] He who kills a beast shall make restitution for it; but he who kills a human being shall be put to death. **22]** You shall have one standard for stranger and citizen alike: for I the LORD am your God.

23] Moses spoke thus to the Israelites. And they took the blasphemer outside the camp and pelted him with stones. The Israelites did as the LORD had commanded Moses.

that the biblical law did not envision literal physical retaliation but rather the payment of money damages [7]. Yet the language of this verse certainly seems to refer to the infliction on the guilty party of the injury he had committed. Two facts, however, are clear. There is no record of a single instance where a Jewish court carried out such retaliation; and Jewish tradition all but unanimously understood the language as referring to financial compensation.

GLEANINGS

Haggadah

24:10] *A Fight Broke Out in the Camp*

Because the half-Israelite sneered at the immediately preceding law of the bread of display. Why should week-old bread be on the table "before the LORD," when kings enjoy bread fresh from the oven?

Another view is that the quarrel arose from the ambiguous status of the half-Israelite. He wanted to pitch his tent with his mother's tribe of Dan. But Israel had been bidden to encamp by "fathers' houses" (this is the literal rendering of the phrase given in Numbers, chapter 2, verse 2, as "ancestral houses"). So this man, the son of an Egyptian, found himself without any regular place in the camp; and in frustration he blasphemed [8].

11] *His Mother's Name Was Shelomith Daughter of Dibri*

Her name is mentioned to indicate that she was the only woman in the entire camp who entered into an improper union. Her character was indicated by her name. She said "hello" (*shalom*) to all the men and she was a chatterbox (*dabranit*, punning on Dibri) [9].

18] *Life for Life*

This is "one of the paradoxes of history. On the one hand, Judaism, the so-called religion of 'strict justice,' rejected the literal application of the law of retaliation and knew neither torture in legal procedure nor mutilation as a form of punishment. In Christian lands, on the other hand, mutilation and torture are well-nigh the indispensable accompaniments of justice from the middle of the thirteenth century down to the middle of the eighteenth, and in some countries to the middle of the nineteenth and beyond" (Hertz) [10].

Sabbatical Year and Jubilee

This chapter is a noble expression of social idealism and humanitarian concern. It presents complicated and tantalizing problems to the student of history, but its message for our time rings out with clarity and power.

1. *The Sabbatical Year*

Verses 2 through 7 prescribe that for one year in every seven the soil of the Land of Israel is to be left untilled. This seventh year is a "sabbath of the Lord." As men are to rest on the seventh day, the land is to rest in the seventh year. If the year of rest is not observed, the land will eventually have to "make up" the lost sabbaths by being laid waste (26:34, 43).

This ancient rule, recorded in the "Book of the Covenant" (Exod. 23:10f.), speaks simply of the "seventh" year and does not call it "sabbath." Now, even if the law is obeyed strictly, there will be some produce in the seventh year; grain will sprout from seed dropped during the previous harvest, and the untended vines and fruit trees will continue to bear, even though in lesser amounts. Exodus 23:11 seems to forbid the owner of the land to use such products. He must leave them to the poor and, thereafter, to foraging beasts. Verses 6 and 7 of this chapter, though forbidding the farmer to gather this yield for his exclusive use, permit him to share in it with all the others. In the sabbatical year, the landowner and the landless pauper are to be on an equal footing. This passage appears to clarify rather than contradict the law in Exodus.

An entirely different law for the seventh year is found in Deuteronomy 15:1–10. In that year, it rules, all outstanding debts are to be canceled [1]. (Further, Deut. 31:10ff. ordains that during the Feast of Booths, in the seventh year, the Torah is to be read publicly at the central sanctuary.)

The remission of debts is called *shemitah*, from a root meaning "to let something drop." A verb from the same root is used in Exodus 23:11 for letting the land rest. (There is thus an ancient basis for the talmudic usage of calling the sabbatical year *shemitah*.) But nothing is said in Deuteronomy about letting the land lie fallow, and nothing in Leviticus about canceling debts. It is true, of course, that, in a year when agriculture was at a standstill, debtors would find it hard to meet their obligations [2].

The halachah combined the two laws. All agricultural labor was to stop (generally) thirty days before Rosh Hashanah of the seventh year, not to be resumed until the eighth year had begun [3]; and, at the end of the seventh year, debts were to be canceled [4]. The second provision, however, did not work out in practice; and, shortly before the beginning of the Christian era, Hillel virtually abrogated it by means of a legal device called *prosbul* [5].

But the "sabbath of the land" was observed for many centuries. No information about such observance has come down from the period of the First Temple, but there is ample attestation from the centuries preceding the Common Era and thereafter.

The First Book of Maccabees reports that in a sabbatical year the city of Beth-zur surrendered to the Syrians, being unable to withstand a siege for lack of provisions (6:49). This incident is also mentioned by the historian Josephus, who also provides other references. The most interesting of these tells that Julius Caesar exempted the Palestinian Jews from certain taxes in sabbatical years [6].

The subject is treated extensively in rabbinic sources—chiefly in a treatise of the Mishnah and of the Palestinian Talmud entitled *Shevi'it*, "Seventh Year." The actual cases cited in these works make it plain that the issue was indeed a practical one. The surprising thing is not that the law was sometimes broken—many persons were suspected of trafficking in fruits of the seventh year—but that so many Jews observed it at great cost to themselves. The words, "mighty creatures who do His bidding" (Ps. 103:20), were applied by Rabbi Isaac to those who keep the sabbatical year. Who is more heroic, he asked, than one who looks out on untilled fields and unworked plantations and shares the scanty yield with others? [7]. Two generations earlier, Rabbi Yannai had authorized some agricultural work in the sabbatical year, in order to meet the exactions of Roman rulers less tolerant than Julius Caesar had

been [8]. But this was evidently an emergency measure and was not accepted as a precedent. The law of the seventh year was deemed to remain in force and is still of concern to extreme Orthodox groups in Israel. It was the subject of lively controversy when the first agricultural colonies were established; today, those who regard the law as operative meet the problem by a fictitious sale of their land to a Gentile.

The sabbatical year may have been of practical benefit in preventing exhaustion of the soil, but that was not the intent of the law. It was rather an expression of the Sabbath idea; and, like the weekly Sabbath, it has no parallel in the other cultures of the ancient Near East.

2. *The Jubilee Year*

a. *The law*. Beginning with verse 8, we are commanded to count off seven "weeks of years" and to consecrate the fiftieth year as a "jubilee" by sounding the ram's horn on the Day of Atonement.

The word "jubilee" (Hebrew *yovel*) might have originally meant "ram," with reference to the blast of the horn that ushers in the holy season. The Greek translation, however, rendered *yovel* by a word meaning "release"; and it has been argued that this translation is scientifically correct [9]. The Latin word *jubilum*, "wild shout," from which we get our word "jubilation," has no connection with *yovel*; but it has probably influenced the modern use of jubilee to designate a festive celebration, especially an important anniversary.

The jubilee year is marked by three chief features. First, the land is to lie fallow. According to the plain sense of Leviticus 25:8ff. and to Jewish tradition, the jubilee year follows the seventh sabbatical year—that is, there are to be two consecutive years without agricultural activity.

Second, all landed property which has been sold is to revert to its original owners, the families that received it when the land was apportioned by lot after the conquest (Josh. 13–21).

Third, Hebrew slaves are to receive their liberty.

The intent of these provisions is stated explicitly in the text. The land is God's property which He has made available for the use of His people (verse 23). It is not to be exploited for the enrichment of some individuals to the detriment of others. If need compels a person to dispose of his holding, he cannot deed it away in perpetuity, for it is not his to sell. He can sell only the number of crops to be harvested up to the next jubilee year. Further, he and the members of his family have the right to reacquire ("redeem") the property by paying a price proportionate to the number of years still to elapse before the jubilee. If it is not redeemed earlier, it reverts to the owner-family when the shofar of jubilee is sounded (verses 13–17, 25–28).

This rule did not apply to houses in walled cities, which could be sold outright; the seller had one year from the date of sale to redeem such property, after which the purchaser had an absolute title. Special laws protected the holdings of the Levites (verses 29–34).

The legislation regarding slaves is motivated by the same kind of thinking as the land law: the Israelites are God's servants and therefore should not be enslaved to any other master. If one of them is forced by poverty to accept the slave status, he is not to be treated with the same severity ordinarily suffered by slaves (verses 39ff.). He may be redeemed at any time by a relative—or by himself, if he can find the means—through payment of a sum proportionate to the time still to elapse before the next jubilee [10]. If this does not happen, he goes free in the jubilee year.

This legislation, then, expresses a constructive social purpose, rooted in the religious conviction that all wealth is God's. As a modern interpreter has put it: "Just as the Communist demand is succinctly formulated, 'None shall have property,' so the biblical formulation is 'Everyone shall have property'" [11]. To achieve this end, wealth must be periodically redistributed. The release of Hebrew slaves is part of the process, since they were most probably sold into servitude for the satisfaction of a debt. The cancellation of debts prescribed in Deuteronomy, chapter 15, had the same objective.

b. *Was the law ever practiced?* Was this inspiring proposal ever more than an idealistic vision? According to the talmudic sources, the law is in effect only when all the tribes are resident in their respective territories; it therefore fell into abeyance as soon as the trans-Jordanian tribes of Reuben and Gad were exiled [12]. There is no record that it was ever practiced during the Second Commonwealth.

Indeed, the basic assumption behind the law—namely, that at some time in the past every Israelite family had its own holding, all approximately equal—is, to put it mildly, open to question. Few historians believe that the entire land was conquered in a brief period, then systematically divided up at one time—as the Book of Joshua reports. The conquest was probably a lengthy process; various tribes and tribal coalitions invaded the country from different starting points, and at different times, and took possession of their several areas. The Book of Judges states that substantial sectors of the country remained for generations in the hands of the earlier inhabitants. The tribal territories varied greatly in size and productivity. And it is unlikely that, within the single tribes, each family got the same amount and kind of land as every other. The ideal past, which the jubilee legislation sought to restore, probably never existed.

Our credulity is further strained by the notion that, even once in a half-century, agricultural work should have been suspended for two consecutive years. The "sabbath of the land" entailed serious hardship; two years without cultivation would have meant ruin and famine [13].

Many modern critics have therefore concluded that the jubilee law was the proposal of a high-minded theorist whose notions were admirable, but impracticable. And in fact the Torah includes a number of provisions that have an air of unreality about them; concerning several of them the Rabbis state that they never have been operative and never will be [14].

But while the law of Leviticus, chapter 25, as it stands, was probably never practiced, the Holiness writer did not create it out of nothing. Israelite and other Near Eastern traditions provided him with the material out of which he built his structure.

First, great stress was laid in Israel on the retention of family and tribal holdings. Naboth refused to sell his vineyard to King Ahab, even at a substantial profit, because he deemed it wrong to give up his ancestral heritage (I Kings 21). The obligation to redeem family property is stressed in Ruth, chapter 4. And the Torah rules that, if women inherit family property in the absence of male heirs, they must marry men of their own tribe—so that the holding is not detached from the tribal territory (Num. 36).

Second, the prophets had bitterly attacked the trend toward the concentration of landed wealth in the hands of a few (Isa. 5:8ff.; Mic. 2:2). (But it is significant that these prophets do not mention the jubilee law or complain of its violation.)

Third, we should take note of the word *deror*, "release" (verse 10). Older translations render it "liberty." The Babylonians had a

term, *duraru*, also *anduraru*, which resembles *deror* both in sound and meaning. (The Babylonians got the concept from their predecessors, the Sumerians.) *Duraru* was sometimes a release of freemen who had been enslaved, sometimes the restoration of real property to its original owners, sometimes a cancellation of debts—or a combination of these [15]. So striking a parallel can hardly be accidental. The Babylonian *duraru* was not, indeed, a regularly recurring procedure. It was an exceptional act of grace on the part of a ruler. Sometimes it marked the accession of a new king. Professor Matitiahu Tsevat has suggested that, in a somewhat similar way, the sabbatical and jubilee years in Israel celebrated the renewal of the covenant between the divine King and His people [16].

At least, then, the biblical author drew on ancient traditions and memories when he formulated his proposals for economic and social reform. Beyond this statement all assertions seem speculative and unsafe. Recent years have seen a number of attempts to assert the historicity of the jubilee as an institution. But they all involve a good deal of theorizing, and they all require some departure from the plain sense of our passage (at the very least, the assumption that when our author wrote "fiftieth year," in verse 10, he meant "forty-ninth") [17].

We may note further that among various peoples the god was deemed the sole owner of the land; but the consequence was generally drawn that, for practical purposes, the land belonged to the god's earthly representative, the king, or to the priests [18]. Only the jubilee law gives a democratic application of the principle. Further, there seems to be no significant resemblance between the various procedures for the redistribution of land in former times and more recent agrarian reform, on the one hand, and the jubilee legislation on the other [19].

c. *The Book of Jubilees.* We possess a lengthy work, composed in Hebrew at some time during the Second Commonwealth, which is most often referred to as the Book of Jubilees (it was also called the Lesser Genesis) [20]. It retells the Bible story from Creation to the arrival at Mount Sinai with many changes and embellishments. The author proposed an apparently new calendar system. He also has his own scheme of biblical chronology. He divided the whole course of history into "jubilee" periods of forty-nine years each, and he dated each of the biblical incidents in such-and-such a year of such-and-such a jubilee. It is from this fact that the customary name of the book is derived. But it does not deal at all with the jubilee law. The Book of Jubilees is of great value for students of the history of the Second Commonwealth, especially of the religious ferment and sectarian conflicts of that period; but it sheds no light on this chapter of Leviticus.

d. *The influence of the jubilee law.* An Armenian code of the twelfth century put some bits of the jubilee law into practice: the rule that urban property could be redeemed only within one year after it was sold, while property outside city walls was subject to redemption for seven years—a very considerable modification [21]. Otherwise, the law as such has not been carried out; yet, it has had an enduring impact on the minds and consciences of men. It has been the inspiration of many efforts for agrarian reform and social justice.

Henry George, the American social reformer (1839–1897), whose eloquent book, *Progress and Poverty*, launched the single tax movement, acknowledged his indebtedness in a famous lecture on Moses (see Gleanings). George sought to eliminate profit from the mere ownership of land, without abolishing private enterprise. Though his system as a whole has never been put into operation, it

has influenced individual legislative acts; and his passion for justice has continued to inspire those who will not accept the inequities of our present economic system as necessary and unchangeable.

It was, however, reserved for Jews to find a practical means of realizing the ideals of the biblical document. In 1897, Professor Herman Schapira proposed to the Zionist Congress that a Jewish National Fund be established for the acquisition of land in Palestine, to be operated on principles in the spirit of our chapter. The proposal was finally adopted in 1901, after Schapira's death. The Jewish National Fund (*Keren Kayemet L'Yisrael*) collected funds from Jews all over the world and began to buy land which became the inalienable property of the Jewish people. These lands were then made available for settlement by individuals and communes, for use but not for profit. Tenants may remain on the soil as long as they cultivate it properly, but they may not sell or mortgage their holdings. The fund has reclaimed much desert and swampland and has provided sites for public buildings and industrial development. Thus, a substantial fraction of the real estate of Israel was withdrawn from the speculative market; social utility was put ahead of individual aggrandizement. By its insistence on soil conservation and proper management, the Jewish National Fund was among the earliest agencies to deal seriously with the protection of natural resources.

Today we are all keenly aware of the evils and dangers inherent in a society where unconscionable wealth and unbearable poverty exist side by side and where the urge for immediate profit threatens the destruction of the environment. Thus, this chapter is of major importance to us, if not for the solutions it offers, certainly by its challenge to us to seek our own solutions to the perennial problems of poverty and injustice.

3. Slavery

The biblical legislation on slavery is not wholly consistent. There are discrepancies between the rules in this chapter and those in Exodus, chapter 21; doubtless these variations are the result of social and economic changes. The biblical writers felt a certain uneasiness about the subject (see Exod. 21). Slavery was a universal institution in the ancient world, and no one had yet proposed abolishing it. Yet some consciences in Israel were troubled by it. Nowhere in the Bible is there a reasoned defense of slavery as an institution comparable to Aristotle's detailed argument on the subject [22]. There were, it seems, some Greeks who had at least theoretical objections to slavery; but by far the strongest extant statement on the subject comes from the Jew Philo who asserted bluntly, "Servants are free by nature, no man being naturally a slave" [23]—a statement foreshadowed by Job's passionate outcry, "Did not He that made me in the womb make him?" (Job 31:15).

It is in this spirit that the Ten Commandments give the slave the right to rest on Sabbath equally with his master (Exod. 20:10; Deut. 5:14). Moreover, the Torah penalizes the slaveowner for grossly mistreating his slaves (Exod. 21:20ff.; Deut. 23:16f.). These provisions—which contrast sharply with the law of most ancient peoples that gave the master absolute power of life and death over his slaves—apply, according to the halachah, to slaves of gentile origin [24].

If the slave is of Israelite birth [25], his rights are much broader and the master's power still more restricted. The law of the "Hebrew slave" in Leviticus, chapter 25, however, is apparently in contradiction to that found in Exodus 21:1ff. and Deuter-

onomy 15:12ff. and cited in Jeremiah 34:14. These passages state that the Hebrew slave is to serve six years from the time of his enslavement; then he is to receive full liberty. Our passage simply states that the Hebrew slave is to be set free in the jubilee year, if he has not been redeemed or has not found means to buy his own freedom at an earlier date. (It also requires that the slave be treated as an employee and not as a chattel, with full regard for his dignity.)

Jewish tradition attempted to reconcile the discrepancies. It held, first, that in a jubilee year all Hebrew slaves went free at once, the remainder of their six-year term being canceled. Second, the law of Exodus and Deuteronomy gave the Hebrew slave the option of remaining permanently in his master's household, as a slave in perpetuity (le*olam, Exod. 21:6; *eved olam, Deut. 15:17). The Rabbis, however, took these phrases to mean "till the jubilee," when a new era (olam) would start.

Gentile slaves, on the other hand, serve for life and pass by inheritance from parents to children (verses 44ff.). The practice of manumitting slaves, however, was not uncommon among ancient peoples, and it was practiced among Jews as well. The Rabbis are reported on occasion to have freed a slave in order to provide the tenth man for a religious quorum (minyan). Yet surprisingly, Rabbi Akiba, known as a great humanitarian, understood verse 46 to forbid the freeing of gentile slaves [26].

It is remarkable that the halachah required a master who acquired a slave of non-Jewish stock to try to convert him to Judaism. But he was not to be forcibly circumcised; if, after the lapse of a year, he still did not wish to adopt the Jewish religion, he was to be resold [27].

276

א וַיְדַבֵּר יְהֹוָה אֶל־מֹשֶׁה בְּהַר סִינַי לֵאמֹר: דַּבֵּר אֶל־
בְּנֵי יִשְׂרָאֵל וְאָמַרְתָּ אֲלֵהֶם כִּי תָבֹאוּ אֶל־הָאָרֶץ אֲשֶׁר
ג אֲנִי נֹתֵן לָכֶם וְשָׁבְתָה הָאָרֶץ שַׁבָּת לַיהֹוָה: שֵׁשׁ שָׁנִים
תִּזְרַע שָׂדֶךָ וְשֵׁשׁ שָׁנִים תִּזְמֹר כַּרְמֶךָ וְאָסַפְתָּ אֶת־
ד תְּבוּאָתָהּ: וּבַשָּׁנָה הַשְּׁבִיעִת שַׁבַּת שַׁבָּתוֹן יִהְיֶה לָאָרֶץ
שַׁבָּת לַיהֹוָה שָׂדְךָ לֹא תִזְרָע וְכַרְמְךָ לֹא תִזְמֹר:
ה אֵת סְפִיחַ קְצִירְךָ לֹא תִקְצוֹר וְאֶת־עִנְּבֵי נְזִירֶךָ לֹא
י תִבְצֹר שְׁנַת שַׁבָּתוֹן יִהְיֶה לָאָרֶץ: וְהָיְתָה שַׁבַּת הָאָרֶץ
לָכֶם לְאָכְלָה לְךָ וּלְעַבְדְּךָ וְלַאֲמָתֶךָ וְלִשְׂכִירְךָ

1] The LORD spoke to Moses on Mount Sinai: 2] Speak to the Israelite people and say to them:

When you enter the land that I give you, the land shall observe a sabbath of the LORD. 3] Six years you may sow your field and six years you may prune your vineyard and gather in the yield. 4] But in the seventh year the land shall have a sabbath of complete rest, a sabbath of the LORD: you shall not sow your field or prune your vineyard. 5] You shall not reap the aftergrowth of your harvest or gather the grapes of your untrimmed vines; it shall be a year of complete rest for the land. 6] But you may eat whatever the land during its sabbath will produce—you, your male and female slaves, the hired and bound laborers who live with you,

25:1] *On Mount Sinai.* These words are a surprise; most of the laws in Leviticus were revealed in the Tent of Meeting (1:1 and elsewhere). Tradition dealt with such anomalies by the maxim, "There is no strict chronological order in the Torah" [28]. The law, presumably, was given to Moses at Sinai and, for some reason, written down in a later passage.

2] Note the parallel between the weekly Sabbath and the "sabbath of the land."

5] *Aftergrowth.* Grain that grew from seed accidentally dropped during the harvest.

Grapes of your untrimmed vines. Failure to prune vines (and trees) may reduce the yield, but fruit will still be available.

6] The owner may not harvest, store, or sell the yield, but he may share with others in consuming it (see p. 271).

ז וּלְתוֹשָׁבְךָ הַגָּרִים עִמָּךְ: וְלִבְהֶמְתְּךָ וְלַחַיָּה אֲשֶׁר
ח בְּאַרְצֶךָ תִּהְיֶה כָל־תְּבוּאָתָהּ לֶאֱכֹל: ס וְסָפַרְתָּ
לְךָ שֶׁבַע שַׁבְּתֹת שָׁנִים שֶׁבַע שָׁנִים שֶׁבַע פְּעָמִים וְהָיוּ
לְךָ יְמֵי שֶׁבַע שַׁבְּתֹת הַשָּׁנִים תֵּשַׁע וְאַרְבָּעִים שָׁנָה:
ט וְהַעֲבַרְתָּ שׁוֹפַר תְּרוּעָה בַּחֹדֶשׁ הַשְּׁבִעִי בֶּעָשׂוֹר
לַחֹדֶשׁ בְּיוֹם הַכִּפֻּרִים תַּעֲבִירוּ שׁוֹפָר בְּכָל־אַרְצְכֶם:
י וְקִדַּשְׁתֶּם אֵת שְׁנַת הַחֲמִשִּׁים שָׁנָה וּקְרָאתֶם דְּרוֹר
בָּאָרֶץ לְכָל־יֹשְׁבֶיהָ יוֹבֵל הִוא תִּהְיֶה לָכֶם וְשַׁבְתֶּם
יא אִישׁ אֶל־אֲחֻזָּתוֹ וְאִישׁ אֶל־מִשְׁפַּחְתּוֹ תָּשֻׁבוּ: יוֹבֵל הִוא
שְׁנַת הַחֲמִשִּׁים שָׁנָה תִּהְיֶה לָכֶם לֹא תִזְרָעוּ וְלֹא

7] and your cattle and the beasts in your land may eat all its yield.

8] You shall count off seven weeks of years—seven times seven years—so that the period of seven weeks of years gives you a total of forty-nine years. 9] Then you shall sound the horn loud; in the seventh month, on the tenth day of the month—the Day of Atonement—you shall have the horn sounded throughout your land 10] and you shall hallow the fiftieth year. You shall proclaim release throughout the land for all its inhabitants. It shall be a jubilee for you: each of you shall return to his holding and each of you shall return to his family. 11] That fiftieth year shall be a jubilee for you: you shall not sow, neither shall you reap the

9] *The Day of Atonement.* The jubilee year begins at Rosh Hashanah, but the release goes into effect only when the shofar is sounded on Yom Kippur.

10] *You shall proclaim release.* Hebrew *deror.* This is the verse traditionally rendered, "Proclaim liberty throughout the land." But the term "release" is more precise and closer to the meaning of *duraru*

(p. 274). Moreover, the fact that this verse was inscribed on the "Liberty Bell," which announced the signing of the Declaration of Independence, might suggest to the modern reader that "liberty" here refers to national autonomy or to civil rights—neither of which was in the author's mind.

Jubilee. Hebrew *yobel,* "ram" or "ram's horn' (T.N.).

יב תִּקְצְרוּ אֶת־סְפִיחֶיהָ וְלֹא תִבְצְרוּ אֶת־נְזִרֶיהָ: כִּי יוֹבֵל
הוּא קֹדֶשׁ תִּהְיֶה לָכֶם מִן־הַשָּׂדֶה תֹּאכְלוּ אֶת־
יג תְּבוּאָתָהּ: בִּשְׁנַת הַיּוֹבֵל הַזֹּאת תָּשֻׁבוּ אִישׁ אֶל־אֲחֻזָּתוֹ:
יד וְכִי־תִמְכְּרוּ מִמְכָּר לַעֲמִיתֶךָ אוֹ קָנֹה מִיַּד עֲמִיתֶךָ
טו אַל־תּוֹנוּ אִישׁ אֶת־אָחִיו: בְּמִסְפַּר שָׁנִים אַחַר הַיּוֹבֵל
תִּקְנֶה מֵאֵת עֲמִיתֶךָ בְּמִסְפַּר שְׁנֵי־תְבוּאֹת יִמְכָּר־לָךְ:
טז לְפִי רֹב הַשָּׁנִים תַּרְבֶּה מִקְנָתוֹ וּלְפִי מְעֹט הַשָּׁנִים
תַּמְעִיט מִקְנָתוֹ כִּי מִסְפַּר תְּבוּאֹת הוּא מֹכֵר לָךְ:
יז וְלֹא תוֹנוּ אִישׁ אֶת־עֲמִיתוֹ וְיָרֵאתָ מֵאֱלֹהֶיךָ כִּי אֲנִי
יח יְהוָה אֱלֹהֵיכֶם: וַעֲשִׂיתֶם אֶת־חֻקֹּתַי וְאֶת־מִשְׁפָּטַי
תִּשְׁמְרוּ וַעֲשִׂיתֶם אֹתָם וִישַׁבְתֶּם עַל־הָאָרֶץ לָבֶטַח:
יט וְנָתְנָה הָאָרֶץ פִּרְיָהּ וַאֲכַלְתֶּם לָשֹׂבַע וִישַׁבְתֶּם לָבֶטַח

Leviticus 25

12–19

aftergrowth or harvest the untrimmed vines,   12] for it is a jubilee. It shall be holy to you: you may only eat the growth direct from the field.

   13] In this year of jubilee, each of you shall return to his holding.   14] When you sell property to your neighbor, or buy any from your neighbor, you shall not wrong one another.   15] In buying from your neighbor, you shall deduct only for the number of years since the jubilee; and in selling to you, he shall charge you only for the remaining crop years: 16] the more such years, the higher the price you pay; the fewer such years, the lower the price; for what he is selling you is a number of harvests.   17] Do not wrong one another, but fear your God; for I the LORD am your God.

   18] You shall observe My laws and faithfully keep My rules, that you may live upon the land in security;   19] the land shall yield its fruit and you shall eat your

---

14] *Your neighbor.* I.e., fellow Israelite; see verse 46 (T.N.)

You shall not wrong one another. By demanding excessive payment.

כ עָלֶיהָ: וְכִי תֹאמְרוּ מַה־נֹּאכַל בַּשָּׁנָה הַשְּׁבִיעִת הֵן לֹא

כא נִזְרָע וְלֹא נֶאֱסֹף אֶת־תְּבוּאָתֵנוּ: וְצִוִּיתִי אֶת־בִּרְכָתִי לָכֶם בַּשָּׁנָה הַשִּׁשִּׁית וְעָשָׂת אֶת־הַתְּבוּאָה לִשְׁלֹשׁ

כב הַשָּׁנִים: וּזְרַעְתֶּם אֵת הַשָּׁנָה הַשְּׁמִינִת וַאֲכַלְתֶּם מִן־הַתְּבוּאָה יָשָׁן עַד הַשָּׁנָה הַתְּשִׁיעִת עַד־בּוֹא תְּבוּאָתָהּ

כג תֹּאכְלוּ יָשָׁן: וְהָאָרֶץ לֹא תִמָּכֵר לִצְמִתֻת כִּי־לִי

כד הָאָרֶץ כִּי־גֵרִים וְתוֹשָׁבִים אַתֶּם עִמָּדִי: וּבְכֹל אֶרֶץ

כה אֲחֻזַּתְכֶם גְּאֻלָּה תִּתְּנוּ לָאָרֶץ: ס כִּי־יָמוּךְ אָחִיךָ וּמָכַר מֵאֲחֻזָּתוֹ וּבָא גֹאֲלוֹ הַקָּרֹב אֵלָיו וְגָאַל אֵת

כו מִמְכַּר אָחִיו: וְאִישׁ כִּי לֹא יִהְיֶה־לּוֹ גֹּאֵל וְהִשִּׂיגָה יָדוֹ

Leviticus 25
20–26

fill, and you shall live upon it in security.   **20]** And should you ask, "What are we to eat in the seventh year, if we may neither sow nor gather in our crops?"   **21]** I will ordain My blessing for you in the sixth year, so that it shall yield a crop sufficient for three years.   **22]** When you sow in the eighth year, you will still be eating old grain of that crop; you will be eating the old until the ninth year, until its crops come in.

23] But the land must not be sold beyond reclaim, for the land is Mine; you are but strangers resident with Me.   **24]** Throughout the land that you hold, you must provide for the redemption of the land.

25] If your brother is in straits and has to sell part of his holding, his nearest redeemer shall come and redeem what his brother has sold.   **26]** If a man has no

---

21–22] It is not quite clear whether this passage refers to the sabbatical or the jubilee year. In any case, the point is that obedience to the law will be rewarded by bumper crops (see the introduction to the next chapter).

25] *Redeemer.* Hebrew *go'el.* I.e., the closest relative able to redeem the land (T.N.). The close relative had the moral obligation to buy back the family holding (cf. Ruth 3:12–4:6). Originally he was also obligated to avenge the murder of a member of the family and, in this situation, was called "*go'el* of the blood" ("blood-avenger," Deut. 19:6). Similarly, God is called the *Go'el* of Israel (Isa. 44:6; cf. Exod. 6:6).

כז וּמָצָא כְּדֵי גְאֻלָּתוֹ: וְחִשַּׁב אֶת־שְׁנֵי מִמְכָּרוֹ וְהֵשִׁיב אֶת־

כח הָעֹדֵף לָאִישׁ אֲשֶׁר מָכַר־לוֹ וְשָׁב לַאֲחֻזָּתוֹ: וְאִם לֹא־

מָצְאָה יָדוֹ דֵּי הָשִׁיב לוֹ וְהָיָה מִמְכָּרוֹ בְּיַד הַקֹּנֶה אֹתוֹ

כט עַד שְׁנַת הַיּוֹבֵל וְיָצָא בַּיֹּבֵל וְשָׁב לַאֲחֻזָּתוֹ: ס וְאִישׁ

כִּי־יִמְכֹּר בֵּית־מוֹשַׁב עִיר חוֹמָה וְהָיְתָה גְאֻלָּתוֹ עַד־

ל תֹּם שְׁנַת מִמְכָּרוֹ יָמִים תִּהְיֶה גְאֻלָּתוֹ: וְאִם לֹא־יִגָּאֵל

עַד־מְלֹאת לוֹ שָׁנָה תְמִימָה וְקָם הַבַּיִת אֲשֶׁר־בָּעִיר

אֲשֶׁר־לֹא* חֹמָה לַצְּמִיתֻת לַקֹּנֶה אֹתוֹ לְדֹרֹתָיו לֹא יֵצֵא

לא בַּיֹּבֵל: וּבָתֵּי הַחֲצֵרִים אֲשֶׁר אֵין־לָהֶם חֹמָה סָבִיב

עַל־שְׂדֵה הָאָרֶץ יֵחָשֵׁב גְּאֻלָּה תִּהְיֶה־לּוֹ וּבַיֹּבֵל יֵצֵא:

לב וְעָרֵי הַלְוִיִּם בָּתֵּי עָרֵי אֲחֻזָּתָם גְּאֻלַּת עוֹלָם תִּהְיֶה

Leviticus 25

27–32

* ל לוֹ קרי.

one to redeem for him, but prospers and acquires enough to redeem with, **27]** he shall compute the years since its sale, refund the difference to the man to whom he sold it, and return to his holding. **28]** If he lacks sufficient means to recover it, what he sold shall remain with the purchaser until the jubilee; in the jubilee year it shall be released, and he shall return to his holding.

29] If a man sells a dwelling house in a walled city, it may be redeemed until a year has elapsed since its sale; the redemption period shall be a year. **30]** If it is not redeemed before a full year has elapsed, the house in the walled city shall pass to the purchaser beyond reclaim throughout the ages; it shall not be released in the jubilee. **31]** But houses in villages that have no encircling walls shall be classed as open country: they may be redeemed, and they shall be released through the jubilee. **32]** As for the cities of the Levites, the houses in the cities they hold—the

29] *A dwelling house in a walled city.* This was not considered tribal territory in the same sense as farm land, and therefore it might be sold in perpetuity.

32-34] *Levites.* On their status, see Numbers, chapters 3 and 4. This is the only place where Leviticus mentions the Levites!

לג לַלְוִיִּם: וַאֲשֶׁר יִגְאַל מִן־הַלְוִיִּם וְיָצָא מִמְכַּר־בַּיִת וְעִיר אֲחֻזָּתוֹ בַּיֹּבֵל כִּי בָתֵּי עָרֵי הַלְוִיִּם הוּא אֲחֻזָּתָם בְּתוֹךְ

לד בְּנֵי יִשְׂרָאֵל: וּשְׂדֵה מִגְרַשׁ עָרֵיהֶם לֹא יִמָּכֵר כִּי־אֲחֻזַּת

לה עוֹלָם הוּא לָהֶם: ס וְכִי־יָמוּךְ אָחִיךָ וּמָטָה יָדוֹ

לו עִמָּךְ וְהֶחֱזַקְתָּ בּוֹ גֵּר וְתוֹשָׁב וָחַי עִמָּךְ: אַל־תִּקַּח מֵאִתּוֹ נֶשֶׁךְ וְתַרְבִּית וְיָרֵאתָ מֵאֱלֹהֶיךָ וְחֵי אָחִיךָ עִמָּךְ:

לז אֶת־כַּסְפְּךָ לֹא־תִתֵּן לוֹ בְּנֶשֶׁךְ וּבְמַרְבִּית לֹא־תִתֵּן

לח אָכְלֶךָ: אֲנִי יְהוָה אֱלֹהֵיכֶם אֲשֶׁר־הוֹצֵאתִי אֶתְכֶם מֵאֶרֶץ מִצְרָיִם לָתֵת לָכֶם אֶת־אֶרֶץ כְּנַעַן לִהְיוֹת

Leviticus 25

33–38

Levites shall forever have the right of redemption. **33]** Such property as may be redeemed from the Levites—houses sold in a city they hold—shall be released through the jubilee; for the houses in the cities of the Levites are their holding among the Israelites. **34]** But the unenclosed land about their cities cannot be sold, for that is their holding for all time.

35] If your brother, being in straits, comes under your authority, and you hold him as though a resident alien, let him live by your side: **36]** do not exact from him advance or accrued interest, but fear your God. Let him live by your side as your brother. **37]** Do not lend him money at advance interest, or give him your food at accrued interest. **38]** I the LORD am your God, who brought you out of the land of Egypt, to give you the land of Canaan, to be your God.

33] First half of verse obscure (T.N.). *Sifra* understands: The right of redemption applies even if the Levite sells his property to another Levite, and not only if he sells it to an ordinary Israelite.

35] Earlier translators understood the verse to mean, "If your brother is in straits and his means fail with you, you shall uphold him: he shall live by your side as a resident alien." The present rendering

follows suggestions first made by Ehrlich, now supported by parallels from Mesopotamia [29].

36] *Advance or accrued interest.* The usual word for "interest" is *neshech*, from the root "to bite"— apparently meaning the "bite" taken in advance from the total sum, as notes are commonly discounted today. This word is rendered here as "advance [interest]." "Accrued interest" is the rendering

לט לָכֶם לֵאלֹהִים: ס וְכִי־יָמוּךְ אָחִיךָ עִמָּךְ וְנִמְכַּר־

מ לָךְ לֹא־תַעֲבֹד בּוֹ עֲבֹדַת עָבֶד: כְּשָׂכִיר כְּתוֹשָׁב יִהְיֶה

עִמָּךְ עַד־שְׁנַת הַיֹּבֵל יַעֲבֹד עִמָּךְ: וְיָצָא מֵעִמָּךְ הוּא

וּבָנָיו עִמּוֹ וְשָׁב אֶל־מִשְׁפַּחְתּוֹ וְאֶל־אֲחֻזַּת אֲבֹתָיו יָשׁוּב:

מב כִּי־עֲבָדַי הֵם אֲשֶׁר־הוֹצֵאתִי אֹתָם מֵאֶרֶץ מִצְרָיִם לֹא

מג יִמָּכְרוּ מִמְכֶּרֶת עָבֶד: לֹא־תִרְדֶּה בוֹ בְּפָרֶךְ וְיָרֵאתָ

מד מֵאֱלֹהֶיךָ: וְעַבְדְּךָ וַאֲמָתְךָ אֲשֶׁר יִהְיוּ־לָךְ מֵאֵת הַגּוֹיִם

מה אֲשֶׁר סְבִיבֹתֵיכֶם מֵהֶם תִּקְנוּ עֶבֶד וְאָמָה: וְגַם מִבְּנֵי

הַתּוֹשָׁבִים הַגָּרִים עִמָּכֶם מֵהֶם תִּקְנוּ וּמִמִּשְׁפַּחְתָּם

אֲשֶׁר עִמָּכֶם אֲשֶׁר הוֹלִידוּ בְּאַרְצְכֶם וְהָיוּ לָכֶם

מו לַאֲחֻזָּה: וְהִתְנַחַלְתֶּם אֹתָם לִבְנֵיכֶם אַחֲרֵיכֶם לָרֶשֶׁת

Leviticus 25
39–46

39] If your brother under you continues in straits and must give himself over to you, do not subject him to the treatment of a slave.   40] He shall remain under you as a hired or bound laborer; he shall serve with you only until the jubilee year. 41] Then he and his children with him shall be free of your authority; he shall go back to his family and return to his ancestral holding.—   42] For they are My servants, whom I freed from the land of Egypt; they may not give themselves over into servitude.—   43] You shall not rule over him ruthlessly; you shall fear your God.   44] Such male and female slaves as you may have—it is from the nations round about you that you may acquire male and female slaves.   45] You may also buy them from among the children of aliens resident with you, or from their families that are among you, whom they begot in your land. These shall become your property: 46] you may keep them as a possession for your children after you, for

of *marbit*, "increase." It is the additional sum to be added to the principal at the time of payment. Earlier translations employed the word "usury" which was formerly synonymous with "interest" and only later came to mean exorbitant interest. The

Torah forbids taking interest in any amount from a fellow Israelite (see further on Deut. 23:21).

43] *You shall fear your God.* See commentary on 19:14.

אַחֻזָּה לְעֹלָם בָּהֶם תַּעֲבֹדוּ וּבְאַחֵיכֶם בְּנֵי־יִשְׂרָאֵל

מז אִישׁ בְּאָחִיו לֹא־תִרְדֶּה בוֹ בְּפָרֶךְ: ס וְכִי תַשִּׂיג יַד

גֵּר וְתוֹשָׁב עִמָּךְ וּמָךְ אָחִיךָ עִמּוֹ וְנִמְכַּר לְגֵר תּוֹשָׁב

מח עִמָּךְ אוֹ לְעֵקֶר מִשְׁפַּחַת גֵּר: אַחֲרֵי נִמְכַּר גְּאֻלָּה

מט תִּהְיֶה־לּוֹ אֶחָד מֵאֶחָיו יִגְאָלֶנּוּ: אוֹ־דֹדוֹ אוֹ בֶן־דֹּדוֹ

יִגְאָלֶנּוּ אוֹ־מִשְׁאֵר בְּשָׂרוֹ מִמִּשְׁפַּחְתּוֹ יִגְאָלֶנּוּ אוֹ־הִשִּׂיגָה

נ יָדוֹ וְנִגְאָל: וְחִשַּׁב עִם־קֹנֵהוּ מִשְּׁנַת הִמָּכְרוֹ לוֹ עַד שְׁנַת

הַיֹּבֵל וְהָיָה כֶּסֶף מִמְכָּרוֹ בְּמִסְפַּר שָׁנִים כִּימֵי שָׂכִיר

נא יִהְיֶה עִמּוֹ: אִם־עוֹד רַבּוֹת בַּשָּׁנִים לְפִיהֶן יָשִׁיב גְּאֻלָּתוֹ

נב מִכֶּסֶף מִקְנָתוֹ: וְאִם־מְעַט נִשְׁאַר בַּשָּׁנִים עַד־שְׁנַת

them to inherit as property for all time. Such you may treat as slaves. But as for your Israelite brothers, no one shall rule ruthlessly over the other.

47] If a resident alien among you has prospered, and your brother, being in straits, comes under his authority and gives himself over to the resident alien among you, or to an offshoot of an alien's family,   48] he shall have the right of redemption even after he has given himself over. One of his brothers shall redeem him, 49] or his uncle or his uncle's son shall redeem him, or anyone of his family who is of his own flesh shall redeem him; or, if he prospers, he may redeem himself. 50] He shall compute with his purchaser the total from the year he gave himself over to him until the jubilee year; the price of his sale shall be applied to the number of years, as though it were for a term as a hired laborer under the other's authority.   51] If many years remain, he shall pay back for his redemption in proportion to his purchase price;   52] and if few years remain until the jubilee

---

48] *He shall have the right of redemption.* If he can furnish the proper sum of money, the owner cannot refuse it and keep him in servitude.

One of his brothers shall redeem him. Cf. commentary on verse 25.

נג הַיֹּבֵל וְחִשַּׁב־לוֹ כְּפִי שָׁנָיו יָשִׁיב אֶת־גְּאֻלָּתוֹ: כִּשְׂכִיר
שָׁנָה בְּשָׁנָה יִהְיֶה עִמּוֹ לֹא־יִרְדֶּנּוּ בְּפֶרֶךְ לְעֵינֶיךָ:
נד וְאִם־לֹא יִגָּאֵל בְּאֵלֶּה וְיָצָא בִּשְׁנַת הַיֹּבֵל הוּא וּבָנָיו
נה עִמּוֹ: כִּי־לִי בְנֵי־יִשְׂרָאֵל עֲבָדִים עֲבָדַי הֵם אֲשֶׁר־
הוֹצֵאתִי אוֹתָם מֵאֶרֶץ מִצְרָיִם אֲנִי יְהֹוָה אֱלֹהֵיכֶם:

year, he shall so compute: he shall make payment for his redemption according to the years involved.   53] He shall be under his authority as a laborer hired by the year; he shall not rule ruthlessly over him in your sight.   54] If he has not been redeemed in any of those ways, he and his children with him shall go free in the jubilee year.   55] For it is to Me that the Israelites are servants: they are My servants, whom I freed from the land of Egypt, I the LORD your God.

GLEANINGS

Halachah

25:8] *You Shall Count Off*

The priests are to count off the years in a formal ceremony, just as each year the days of the *omer* are counted off (see commentary on 23:15).   SIFRA

14] *You Shall Not Wrong One Another*

This rule applies not only to the present case but to all transactions. An overcharge (or underpayment) of more than one-sixth of the fair value of an article constitutes "wrong" (*ona'ah*) and may justify voiding the transaction [30].

17] *Do Not Wrong One Another*

This repetition has a purpose—it forbids *ona'ah* by words: one must not remind a penitent sinner of his former misdeeds or a convert of his heathen ancestry; one should not inquire the price of an article he does not intend to buy.   SIFRA

25–28] Redemption of property. Once he has sold it, the seller must wait a minimum of two years before attempting to redeem it.   SIFRA

29] *A Dwelling House in a Walled City*

This law applies only to cities which were in existence and had walls when Joshua conquered the country, even though the walls have since vanished. It does not apply to more recently established cities, even though they are walled now.   SIFRA

36] *Advance or Accrued Interest*

See commentary. In their treatment of the biblical material, the Rabbis make no distinction between *neshech* and *marbit*. But they apply the word *ribit* (virtually identical with *marbit*) to profit from trading in futures, which is forbidden by rabbinical ordinance [31].

39] *Do Not Subject Him to the Treatment of a Slave*

He must not be made to stand on the auction block; when sold, he must not be required to perform demeaning services for his master.   SIFRA

53] *He Shall Not Rule over Him Ruthlessly in Your Sight*

You shall not allow him to mistreat a Hebrew slave, if you observe him doing so; but you are not required to enter his house to see if he is treating the slave properly.   SIFRA

Haggadah

"Trace to its roots the cause that is thus producing want in the midst of plenty, ignorance in the midst of intelligence, aristocracy in democracy, weakness in strength—that is giving to our civilization a one-sided and unstable development, and you will find it something which this Hebrew statesman three thousand years ago perceived and guarded against. Moses saw that the real cause of the enslavement of the masses of Egypt was what has everywhere produced enslavement, the possession by a class of the land upon which and from which the whole people must live. He saw that to permit in land the same unqualified private ownership that by natural right attaches to things produced by labor would be inevitably to separate the people into the very rich and the very poor, inevitably to enslave labor. . . .

"And, with the foresight of the philosophic states-man who legislates not for the need of a day but for all the future, he sought, in ways suited to his times and conditions, to guard against this error. Every-where in the Mosaic institutions is the land treated as the gift of the Creator to His common creatures, which no one has the right to monopolize. Every-where it is, not your estate, or your property, not the land which you bought, or the land which you conquered, but 'the land which the Lord thy God giveth thee'—'the land which the Lord lendeth thee.' And by practical legislation, by regulations to which he gave the highest sanctions, he tried to guard against the wrong that converted ancient civiliza-tions into despotisms . . . the wrong that is already filling American cities with idle men and our virgin states with tramps. . . .

"I do not say that these institutions were for their ultimate purpose the very best that might even then have been devised, for Moses had to work, as all great constructive statesmen have to work, with the tools that came to his hand and upon materials as he found them. Still less do I mean to say that forms suitable for that time and people are suitable for every time and people. I ask not veneration of the form but recognition of the spirit.

"Yet how common it is to venerate the form and to deny the spirit! There are many who believe that the Mosaic institutions were literally dictated by the Almighty, yet who would denounce as irreligious and 'communistic' any application of their spirit to the present day" (Henry George) [32].

25:40] *He Shall Remain under You as a Hired or Bound Laborer*
But though you should treat him with respect, he should regard himself humbly as a slave.   SIFRA

42] *For They Are My Servants*
And so should not be subject to any of My other subjects.   SIFRA

44–46] Although the Torah does not specifically command us to treat the gentile slave humanely, we should always treat him with decency and kind-ness (Maimonides) [33].

Blessings and Curses

Since chapter 27 takes the form of an appendix, Leviticus actually concludes with chapter 26.

1. *Tochechah*

This is the term used to describe terrible punishment or "reproof." Leviticus, chapter 26, concludes with a fervent appeal for obedience to the laws, promising bliss for the nation if they are observed and threatening terrible punishment if they are violated. The word *tochechah* is also applied to a similar exhortation in Deuteronomy, chapter 28. A shorter and less frightening homily appears in Exodus 23:20ff. In all three cases, an extensive legal section is followed by promises and threats.

This is an ancient pattern. The Babylonian Code of Hammurabi and the still older Sumerian Code of Lipit-Ishtar [1] begin by telling how the laws were promulgated; and the legal section proper is followed by the promise of blessings for those who obey these laws and by curses on those who falsify the text or violate its provisions. Just so, the various legal documents of the Torah are each introduced by an account of the Exodus and the revelation at Sinai and conclude with a *tochechah*.

In recent years, scholars have noted a similar pattern in another category of Near Eastern documents—the treaties made by powerful rulers with the vassal kings whom they "protected." Such documents promulgated by Hittite conquerors begin by reciting the benefits which the great potentate has conferred on his vassal; then the terms of the treaty are stated, followed by threats of punishment if the weaker party should violate the agreement [2].

A still more remarkable parallel is furnished by the vassal treaties of the Assyrian conqueror Esarhaddon. In view of the agreements both in the order of the curses and the language in which they are expressed, it seems certain that the author of Deuteronomy chapter 28 borrowed from these documents [3]. Even here, the extraordinary resemblances are combined with some differences. Deuteronomy, chapter 28, begins with a promise of blessings for obedience, to which nothing in the Assyrian treaties corresponds. And, though some of the striking and vivid phrases of the *tochechah* are now revealed to be conventional curses (see commentary on 26:19 and 29), the biblical author adds psychological touches (Deut. 28:65ff.) and religious references (Deut. 28:45ff. and 58ff.) to which the Assyrian documents offer no parallel [4].

Our chapter does not present such close parallels to any known document from the Near East [5], though it too contains some of the stereotyped language of the treaty curses. But here the material is worked up in a much more rhetorical fashion—and it ends with a glimmering of hope.

A review of the related biblical passages is instructive. The Exodus section (23:20ff.), which all agree is very early, is made up mostly of promises and contains few threats. Deuteronomy, chapter 28, the longest and most gruesome of these sections, ends in a mood of utter despair. (Chapters 29 and 30 of Deuteronomy contain still another *tochechah*, the most eloquent of all, in which there is an explicit promise of the spiritual renewal and then the political restoration of Israel.) Leviticus, chapter 26, concludes with a picture of ruin and dispersion, which may well reflect the actual conditions of the exilic period, yet voices the assurance that God will not abandon His people forever (see below "3. Sources of Hope").

The public reading of these threatening passages caused great uneasiness to former generations. Ordinarily it is an honor to be "called up" to recite the Torah benedictions, and those who receive this honor frequently make a gift to the synagogue in appreciation. But people avoided the privilege of being called up on the Sabbaths when the curses were read from Leviticus and Deuteronomy. The seven subsections into which the weekly Torah portion is divided, and for each of which a worshiper comes forward in the traditional synagogue to pronounce the blessings, are usually of about equal length; they rarely extend over more than twenty-five verses. But the curses in Leviticus (26:10–46) and Deuteronomy (28:7–69) are traditionally read without interruption. This arrangement served a double purpose: the disturbing passage could be completed as quickly as possible and only one reluctant worshiper had to be persuaded to say the benedictions [6].

2. The Problem of Retribution

The modern reader will likewise be stirred by the gloomy eloquence of our chapter; but his reaction will probably be quite different from that of his forebears. Almost automatically he will question the basic assumption of the chapter—that virtue and piety are requited with material benefits and wickedness with material punishment. The doctrine of earthly rewards and punishments is asserted many times in the Bible with vigor and eloquence. It was challenged irresistibly in the Book of Job and elsewhere; still, people continued to believe it because they wanted to believe it. But it cannot be rationally defended.

Let us examine the matter more closely. In Babylonian thought, the welfare of the nation was regarded as dependent on the behavior of the king. If he pleased the gods, his entire people would benefit, and, if he did not please the gods, the entire people would suffer [7]. In Israel, a more "democratic" outlook prevailed. The entire nation must assume responsibility. If it is loyal to God, it will prosper; if it is faithless, it will fall. That is the viewpoint of the present chapter and of many other biblical passages. In some cases, it is even asserted that the misdeeds of a single citizen may bring disaster on the whole community (Josh. 7).

The idea of collective responsibility was gradually modified as prophets and psalmists recognized more fully the religious importance of the individual. This new insight led the prophet Ezekiel to an extreme and untenable version of the concept of retribution. He retained the doctrine of material rewards and punishments, and he applied it to the fate of each individual. The righteous man, he asserted, is blessed with long life and prosperity, whereas the wicked man comes to an early and evil end (Ezek. 18). He even implied (9:44ff.) that every person who died during the storming of Jerusalem deserved his fate because of prior sins! This opinion is echoed in other biblical books, notably Proverbs.

And indeed such a view appeared as the logical inference from the belief in one righteous God. One might have thought that the pagan would find less difficulty (at least in theory) with the fact of suffering, even undeserved suffering. For the many gods of paganism were deemed unstable and capricious, and some were downright hostile to man. Misfortune could then be explained as due to the malice of evil spirits or hostile godlings, to the working of inexorable fate, or (as we saw above) to the guilt of the king. Yet in fact we possess a number of Egyptian, Sumerian, and Akkadian texts which lament the misery, seemingly undeserved, that sometimes comes upon men [8]. And, if these dark realities were a difficult problem for the pagan mind, they were an even more urgent challenge to those who believed in one, all-good, creative God.

As long as people thought in terms of collective responsibility, the problem could somehow be managed. For, if a nation was predominantly righteous and therefore prosperous, even the undeserving citizens might share its good fortunes. And, if national wickedness entailed national disaster, some of the virtuous minority might get hurt in the general crash.

This form of the doctrine, moreover, contains a measure of truth. The stability of a nation depends largely on the honesty of its citizens and the justness of its institutions; moral decline can bring on political disintegration. But morality is not the only condition for national survival, perhaps not even the decisive condition. Peaceable and culturally productive peoples have been subjugated or exterminated by nations inferior to them in everything but military potential and ferocity. Who dare say that the four centuries of expropriation and genocide endured by the American Indians, the liquidation of the Baltic states by Soviet Russia, or the horrors of Auschwitz were punishments which the victims deserved?

Still less acceptable is the application of the doctrine to individual experience, as taught by Ezekiel. It can be upheld only by stubborn disregard of facts. Immoral and criminal persons may enjoy years of health, success, and honor; saintly men and women may have to bear endless agony and sorrow. The passionate eloquence with which the author of Job insisted on these realities is unanswerable. The book finally asserts that the problem of suffering is beyond human understanding. Yet at the end of the work God himself declares that Job has spoken rightly; God's reputation is not to be defended by distorting the truth (Job 42:8).

The theory of mechanical retribution, moreover, is not only mistaken but actually immoral. For, if sin is regularly followed by punishment, it follows that every misfortune is a condemnation. Job poignantly complains of the cruelty of his friends. Instead of giving him sympathy and affection in his misery, they lecture him on the need to reform his conduct (Job 19:1–21).

A few centuries after this masterpiece was written, Jewish teachers affirmed the belief in immortality and thereby provided a new approach to the problem of retribution. In an existence beyond the grave, they taught, true justice will be meted out to righteous and wicked alike; retribution will be spiritual rather than physical. In one form or another, this has been the conviction of most Jews through the ages [9]. It is an assertion of faith which can hardly be proved or disproved.

But, concerning those realities that we can appraise here and now, at least this much may be confidently stated:

First, there is no necessary relation between a man's merits and his fortunes. A person of noblest character may be lucky or he may be miserable; a depraved individual may be lucky or he may be miserable. It is untrue to say that it always pays to be good, and it is equally untrue to say that it never pays. An honest and dependable person is usually respected and trusted; kindness to others often evokes a similar response from them. National righteousness contributes to national stability. But such results are only possibilities; they are not guaranteed.

Second, the consequences of our conduct can rarely be limited to ourselves. For good or for bad, what we do affects the lives of others, in the present and future. We cannot foresee all the effects of our decisions; we can only try to choose wisely and responsibly. Foolish and evil men have caused untold disaster; intelligent and good people have benefited all mankind. The question "Why did God let Hitler do what he did?" cannot be separated from the question "Why did God let Pasteur do what he did?"

Third, it may be that only a world like ours—a world in which we are never sure whether we will be rewarded or punished for our actions—gives us the possibility of leading a truly moral life. For the ethical decision is the decision to do the right because it is right and not for any other advantage.

3. The Sources of Hope

Our chapter, be it noted, deals not only with physical rewards and punishments but also with spiritual concerns. It alludes to the calm assurance that comes with rectitude and to the mindless terror that in moments of adversity grips those who are not sustained by a clear conscience and by the sense of God's nearness.

Toward the end of the chapter, hope is held out even for the sinful and scattered people. They must take the first step toward their redemption, by confessing their wrongdoings and turning back to God (verses 39f.). This is one of the classic passages about teshuvah, "return," "repentance" (see p. 162). Once this step is taken, God will recall and fulfill His promise to the patriarchs that their posterity shall be numerous and shall possess the land of Canaan. For Abraham, Isaac, and Jacob lived up to their side of the covenant with God; and so He is bound to keep His promise, even though the descendants of the patriarchs are not worthy.

This notion is developed in talmudic literature into the concept of zechut avot, "the merit of the fathers." The rabbinic version stresses not so much the obligation of God to keep His word as the great piety of the patriarchs and the love it evoked from God. The merits of the fathers, so to speak, are credited to the delinquent account of the offspring. The Rabbis utilized this doctrine with delicate tact, so as to encourage the people in times of crisis and tragedy, without undermining their own sense of moral responsibility [10].

Finally, our chapter voices a conviction that cannot be fully rationalized—God is for ever the God of Israel (verse 44). And so there is always hope.

א לֹא־תַעֲשׂוּ לָכֶם אֱלִילִם וּפֶסֶל וּמַצֵּבָה לֹא־תָקִימוּ
לָכֶם וְאֶבֶן מַשְׂכִּית לֹא תִתְּנוּ בְּאַרְצְכֶם לְהִשְׁתַּחֲוֺת
ב עָלֶיהָ כִּי אֲנִי יְהֹוָה אֱלֹהֵיכֶם: אֶת־שַׁבְּתֹתַי תִּשְׁמֹרוּ
וּמִקְדָּשִׁי תִּירָאוּ אֲנִי יְהֹוָה:

Haftarah Behar, p. 401

פ   פ   פ

ג אִם־בְּחֻקֹּתַי תֵּלֵכוּ וְאֶת־מִצְוֺתַי תִּשְׁמְרוּ וַעֲשִׂיתֶם אֹתָם:
ד וְנָתַתִּי גִשְׁמֵיכֶם בְּעִתָּם וְנָתְנָה הָאָרֶץ יְבוּלָהּ וְעֵץ
ה הַשָּׂדֶה יִתֵּן פִּרְיוֹ: וְהִשִּׂיג לָכֶם דַּיִשׁ אֶת־בָּצִיר וּבָצִיר
יַשִּׂיג אֶת־זָרַע וַאֲכַלְתֶּם לַחְמְכֶם לָשֹׂבַע וִישַׁבְתֶּם
ו לָבֶטַח בְּאַרְצְכֶם: וְנָתַתִּי שָׁלוֹם בָּאָרֶץ וּשְׁכַבְתֶּם וְאֵין

בחקתי

Bechukotai

Leviticus 26

1–6

1] You shall not make idols for yourselves, or set up for yourselves carved images or pillars, or place figured stones in your land to worship upon, for I the LORD am your God.   2] You shall keep My sabbaths and venerate My sanctuary, Mine, the LORD's.

3] If you follow My laws and faithfully observe My commandments,   4] I will grant your rains in their season, so that the earth shall yield its produce and the trees of the field their fruit.   5] Your threshing shall overtake the vintage, and your vintage shall overtake the sowing; you shall eat your fill of bread and dwell securely in your land.

6] I will grant peace in the land, and you shall lie down untroubled by anyone;

26:1] *Figured stones.* Meaning of Hebrew *maskit* uncertain (T.N.).

4] *Rains in their season.* Especially the early rain (*yoreh*), in the autumn, and the late rain (*malkosh*) shortly before harvest time in the spring.

5] *Your threshing shall overtake the vintage.* The grain harvest in the spring will be so abundant that you will be busy threshing until vintage-time at the end of the summer; and the vintage will occupy you until time for the fall sowing.

מַחֲרִיד וְהִשְׁבַּתִּי חַיָּה רָעָה מִן־הָאָרֶץ וְחֶרֶב לֹא־
תַעֲבֹר בְּאַרְצְכֶם: וּרְדַפְתֶּם אֶת־אֹיְבֵיכֶם וְנָפְלוּ
לִפְנֵיכֶם לֶחָרֶב: וְרָדְפוּ מִכֶּם חֲמִשָּׁה מֵאָה וּמֵאָה
מִכֶּם רְבָבָה יִרְדֹּפוּ וְנָפְלוּ אֹיְבֵיכֶם לִפְנֵיכֶם לֶחָרֶב:
וּפָנִיתִי אֲלֵיכֶם וְהִפְרֵיתִי אֶתְכֶם וְהִרְבֵּיתִי אֶתְכֶם
וַהֲקִימֹתִי אֶת־בְּרִיתִי אִתְּכֶם: וַאֲכַלְתֶּם יָשָׁן נוֹשָׁן וְיָשָׁן
מִפְּנֵי חָדָשׁ תּוֹצִיאוּ: וְנָתַתִּי מִשְׁכָּנִי בְּתוֹכְכֶם וְלֹא־
תִגְעַל נַפְשִׁי אֶתְכֶם: וְהִתְהַלַּכְתִּי בְּתוֹכְכֶם וְהָיִיתִי
לָכֶם לֵאלֹהִים וְאַתֶּם תִּהְיוּ־לִי לְעָם: אֲנִי יְהֹוָה
אֱלֹהֵיכֶם אֲשֶׁר הוֹצֵאתִי אֶתְכֶם מֵאֶרֶץ מִצְרַיִם מִהְיֹת

Leviticus 26

7–13

I will give the land respite from vicious beasts, and no sword shall cross your land.
7] You shall give chase to your enemies, and they shall fall before you by the sword.
8] Five of you shall give chase to a hundred, and a hundred of you shall give chase to ten thousand; your enemies shall fall before you by the sword.

9] I will look with favor upon you, and make you fertile and multiply you; and I will maintain My covenant with you.   10] You shall eat old grain long stored, and you shall have to clear out the old to make room for the new.

11] I will establish My abode in your midst, and I will not spurn you.   12] I will be ever present in your midst: I will be your God, and you shall be My people.

13] I the LORD am your God who brought you out from the land of the Egyptians

8] *Five of you shall give chase to a hundred.* With God on your side, a few of you will be able to rout many enemies. Hebrew style often uses round numbers which are not to be taken exactly (see commentary on verse 14).

9] *I will look with favor upon you.* Literally, "I will turn toward you"—like a king who turns from other affairs to reward a diligent servant (*Sifra*).

10] *You shall eat old grain long stored.* Though long stored, it will not deteriorate. Yet you will have to move some of it out of the granaries, to make room for the new crop.

11] *And I will not spurn you.* Coming after many positive blessings, this negative clause is strangely anticlimactic. If God will not spurn Israel even after they have sinned and been exiled (verse 44), why should there be need for such an assurance to those who obey the laws? Nachmanides therefore conjectured that some secret doctrine was hinted at here.

לָהֶם עֲבָדִים וָאֶשְׁבֹּר מֹטֹת עֻלְּכֶם וָאוֹלֵךְ אֶתְכֶם
קוֹמְמִיּוּת: פ

יד וְאִם־לֹא תִשְׁמְעוּ לִי וְלֹא תַעֲשׂוּ אֵת כָּל־הַמִּצְוֹת
טו הָאֵלֶּה: וְאִם־בְּחֻקֹּתַי תִּמְאָסוּ וְאִם אֶת־מִשְׁפָּטַי תִּגְעַל
נַפְשְׁכֶם לְבִלְתִּי עֲשׂוֹת אֶת־כָּל־מִצְוֹתַי לְהַפְרְכֶם אֶת־
טז בְּרִיתִי: אַף־אֲנִי אֶעֱשֶׂה־זֹּאת לָכֶם וְהִפְקַדְתִּי עֲלֵיכֶם
בֶּהָלָה אֶת־הַשַּׁחֶפֶת וְאֶת־הַקַּדַּחַת מְכַלּוֹת עֵינַיִם
וּמְדִיבֹת נָפֶשׁ וּזְרַעְתֶּם לָרִיק זַרְעֲכֶם וַאֲכָלֻהוּ
יז אֹיְבֵיכֶם: וְנָתַתִּי פָנַי בָּכֶם וְנִגַּפְתֶּם לִפְנֵי אֹיְבֵיכֶם
וְרָדוּ בָכֶם שֹׂנְאֵיכֶם וְנַסְתֶּם וְאֵין־רֹדֵף אֶתְכֶם:

Leviticus 26
14–17

to be their slaves no more, who broke the bars of your yoke and made you **walk erect.**

14] But if you do not obey Me and do not observe all these commandments, **15]** if you reject My laws and spurn My rules, so that you do not observe all My commandments and you break My covenant, **16]** I in turn will do this to you: I will wreak misery upon you—consumption and fever, which cause the eyes to pine and the body to languish; you shall sow your seed to no purpose, for your enemies shall eat it. **17]** I will set My face against you: you shall be routed by your enemies, and your foes shall dominate you. You shall flee though none pursues.

13] *Made you walk erect.* Which you could not do till the yoke was removed.

14–45] The curses. "The empty-headed have declared that the curses are more numerous than the blessings, but they have not spoken truth. The blessings are uttered in broad general terms, while the curses are stated in more detail, to awe and frighten the hearers" (Ibn Ezra).

16] *Consumption and fever.* Precise nature of these ills is uncertain (T.N.). Luzzatto thinks these terms also refer to plant diseases (cf. Deut. 28:22). This view was first mentioned, but not adopted, by Ibn Ezra.

You shall sow your seed to no purpose. It will not grow; but, if it should grow, *your enemies shall eat it* (*Sifra*).

17] *I will set My face against you.* This is the opposite of the promise in verse 9.

You shall flee though none pursues. You will be utterly demoralized.

יח וְאִם־עַד־אֵלֶּה לֹא תִשְׁמְעוּ לִי וְיָסַפְתִּי לְיַסְּרָה אֶתְכֶם

יט שֶׁבַע עַל־חַטֹּאתֵיכֶם: וְשָׁבַרְתִּי אֶת־גְּאוֹן עֻזְּכֶם וְנָתַתִּי

כ אֶת־שְׁמֵיכֶם כַּבַּרְזֶל וְאֶת־אַרְצְכֶם כַּנְּחֻשָׁה: וְתַם לָרִיק

כֹּחֲכֶם וְלֹא־תִתֵּן אַרְצְכֶם אֶת־יְבוּלָהּ וְעֵץ הָאָרֶץ לֹא

כא יִתֵּן פִּרְיוֹ: וְאִם־תֵּלְכוּ עִמִּי קֶרִי וְלֹא תֹאבוּ לִשְׁמֹעַ לִי

כב וְיָסַפְתִּי עֲלֵיכֶם מַכָּה שֶׁבַע כְּחַטֹּאתֵיכֶם: וְהִשְׁלַחְתִּי

בָכֶם אֶת־חַיַּת הַשָּׂדֶה וְשִׁכְּלָה אֶתְכֶם וְהִכְרִיתָה

אֶת־בְּהֶמְתְּכֶם וְהִמְעִיטָה אֶתְכֶם וְנָשַׁמּוּ דַּרְכֵיכֶם:

Leviticus 26

18—22

18] And if, for all that, you do not obey Me, I will go on to discipline you sevenfold for your sins,   19] and I will break your proud glory. I will make your skies like iron and your earth like copper,   20] so that your strength shall be spent to no purpose. Your land shall not yield its produce, nor shall the trees of the land yield their fruit.

21] And if you remain hostile toward Me and refuse to obey Me, I will go on smiting you sevenfold for your sins.   22] I will loose wild beasts against you, and they shall bereave you of your children and wipe out your cattle. They shall decimate you, and your roads shall be deserted.

18] *Sevenfold for your sins.* The expression recurs in verses 21, 24, and 28. It is a characteristic way of saying "many times over" (cf. commentary on verse 8 and see Gleanings).

19] *Skies like iron.* Hot and rainless.
   Earth like copper. Hard and unproductive.
  One of the curses in the treaties of Esarhaddon reads: "May all the gods . . . turn your soil into iron so that no one may cut a furrow in it. Just as rain does not fall from a copper sky, so may there come neither rain nor dew upon your fields [11] (cf. Deut. 28:23).

20] *Your land shall not yield its produce.* It shall not yield as much as the seed you brought for planting (*Sifra*).

21] *Hostile.* Hebrew *keri*, found only in this chapter (see Gleanings).

כג וְאִם־בְּאֵלֶּה לֹא תִוָּסְרוּ לִי וַהֲלַכְתֶּם עִמִּי קֶרִי: וְהָלַכְתִּי
אַף־אֲנִי עִמָּכֶם בְּקֶרִי וְהִכֵּיתִי אֶתְכֶם גַּם־אָנִי שֶׁבַע
כה עַל־חַטֹּאתֵיכֶם: וְהֵבֵאתִי עֲלֵיכֶם חֶרֶב נֹקֶמֶת נְקַם־
בְּרִית וְנֶאֱסַפְתֶּם אֶל־עָרֵיכֶם וְשִׁלַּחְתִּי דֶבֶר בְּתוֹכְכֶם
כו וְנִתַּתֶּם בְּיַד־אוֹיֵב: בְּשִׁבְרִי לָכֶם מַטֵּה־לֶחֶם וְאָפוּ
עֶשֶׂר נָשִׁים לַחְמְכֶם בְּתַנּוּר אֶחָד וְהֵשִׁיבוּ לַחְמְכֶם
כז בַּמִּשְׁקָל וַאֲכַלְתֶּם וְלֹא תִשְׂבָּעוּ: ס וְאִם־בְּזֹאת לֹא
כח תִשְׁמְעוּ לִי וַהֲלַכְתֶּם עִמִּי בְּקֶרִי: וְהָלַכְתִּי עִמָּכֶם
בַּחֲמַת־קֶרִי וְיִסַּרְתִּי אֶתְכֶם אַף־אָנִי שֶׁבַע עַל־
כט חַטֹּאתֵיכֶם: וַאֲכַלְתֶּם בְּשַׂר בְּנֵיכֶם וּבְשַׂר בְּנֹתֵיכֶם

23] And if these things fail to discipline you for Me, and you remain hostile to Me, 24] I too will remain hostile to you: I in turn will smite you sevenfold for your sins. 25] I will bring a sword against you to wreak vengeance for the covenant; and if you withdraw into your cities, I will send pestilence among you, and you shall be delivered into enemy hands. 26] When I break your staff of bread, ten women shall bake your bread in a single oven; they shall dole out your bread by weight, and though you eat, you shall not be satisfied.

27] But if, despite this, you disobey Me and remain hostile to Me, 28] I will act against you in wrathful hostility; I, for My part, will discipline you sevenfold for your sins. 29] You shall eat the flesh of your sons and the flesh of your daughters.

25] *Vengeance for the covenant.* Which you broke by disobeying the Torah.

You shall be delivered into enemy hands. Because you will be too weak from illness to resist.

26] *When I break your staff of bread.* As a staff supports one who walks with it, so bread sustains life. The idiom seems to have been familiar (cf. Isa. 3:1).

In a single oven. Because fuel is in short supply (*Sifra*).

Dole out your bread by weight. Rationing will be stringent.

29] *Eat the flesh of your sons....* Doubtless cannibalism has occurred in times of famine; but this seems to have become a literary cliché. It is a recur-

לתֹּאכֵלוּ: וְהִשְׁמַדְתִּי אֶת־בָּמֹתֵיכֶם וְהִכְרַתִּי אֶת־
חַמָּנֵיכֶם וְנָתַתִּי אֶת־פִּגְרֵיכֶם עַל־פִּגְרֵי גִּלּוּלֵיכֶם
לאוְגָעֲלָה נַפְשִׁי אֶתְכֶם: וְנָתַתִּי אֶת־עָרֵיכֶם חָרְבָּה
וַהֲשִׁמּוֹתִי אֶת־מִקְדְּשֵׁיכֶם וְלֹא אָרִיחַ בְּרֵיחַ נִיחֹחֲכֶם:
לבוַהֲשִׁמֹּתִי אֲנִי אֶת־הָאָרֶץ וְשָׁמְמוּ עָלֶיהָ אֹיְבֵיכֶם
הַיֹּשְׁבִים בָּהּ: וְאֶתְכֶם אֱזָרֶה בַגּוֹיִם וַהֲרִיקֹתִי אַחֲרֵיכֶם
לדחָרֶב וְהָיְתָה אַרְצְכֶם שְׁמָמָה וְעָרֵיכֶם יִהְיוּ חָרְבָּה: אָז
תִּרְצֶה הָאָרֶץ אֶת־שַׁבְּתֹתֶיהָ כֹּל יְמֵי הָשַּׁמָּה וְאַתֶּם

30] I will destroy your cult places and cut down your incense stands, and I will heap your carcasses upon your lifeless fetishes.

I will spurn you.   **31]** I will lay your cities in ruin and make your sanctuaries desolate, and I will not savor your pleasing odors.   **32]** I will make the land desolate, so that your enemies who settle in it shall be appalled by it.   **33]** And you I will scatter among the nations, and I will unsheath the sword against you. Your land shall become a desolation and your cities a ruin.

34] Then shall the land make up for its sabbath years throughout the time that

---

rent item in Esarhaddon's vassal treaties [12] and in the Scriptures (Deut. 28:53ff.; II Kings 6:25ff.; and Lam. 4:10).

30] *Your cult places.* The many idolatrous shrines in the country (see p. 178).

Your incense stands. Hebrew *chamanim.* This rendering was established by the unearthing of small altars or stands for offering incense, some of them bearing the word *chaman.* Scholars had previously connected the word with *chamah,* "sun," and supposed them to be some sort of solar image.

Heap your carcasses upon your lifeless fetishes. Literally, "upon the carcasses (*pigre*) of your fetishes." But Hoffmann noted that, in rabbinic Hebrew and Aramaic, the root *pgr* means "break up"; he there-

fore translated, "I will heap your carcasses upon the fragments of your fetishes."

31] *Your sanctuaries.* Cf. verse 30. The plural is the measure of the disloyalty—not "My sanctuary" but "your sanctuaries."

Savor your pleasing odors. Accept your sacrifices (see commentary on 1:9).

32] *Shall be appalled by it.* By the complete devastation.

33] The ultimate punishment is exile; yet even then the Israelites will be pursued by implacable enemies.

34] *Make up for its sabbath years.* This passage and

בְּאֶרֶץ אֹיְבֵיכֶם אָז תִּשְׁבַּת הָאָרֶץ וְהִרְצָת אֶת־

לה שַׁבְּתֹתֶיהָ: כָּל־יְמֵי הָשַּׁמָּה תִּשְׁבֹּת אֵת אֲשֶׁר לֹא־שָׁבְתָה

לו בְּשַׁבְּתֹתֵיכֶם בְּשִׁבְתְּכֶם עָלֶיהָ: וְהַנִּשְׁאָרִים בָּכֶם

וְהֵבֵאתִי מֹרֶךְ בִּלְבָבָם בְּאַרְצֹת אֹיְבֵיהֶם וְרָדַף אֹתָם

קוֹל עָלֶה נִדָּף וְנָסוּ מְנֻסַת־חֶרֶב וְנָפְלוּ וְאֵין רֹדֵף:

לז וְכָשְׁלוּ אִישׁ־בְּאָחִיו כְּמִפְּנֵי־חֶרֶב וְרֹדֵף אָיִן וְלֹא־תִהְיֶה

לח לָכֶם תְּקוּמָה לִפְנֵי אֹיְבֵיכֶם: וַאֲבַדְתֶּם בַּגּוֹיִם וְאָכְלָה

לט אֶתְכֶם אֶרֶץ אֹיְבֵיכֶם: וְהַנִּשְׁאָרִים בָּכֶם יִמַּקּוּ בַּעֲוֹנָם

בְּאַרְצֹת אֹיְבֵיכֶם וְאַף בַּעֲוֹנֹת אֲבֹתָם אִתָּם יִמָּקּוּ:

Leviticus 26
35-39

it is desolate and you are in the land of your enemies; then shall the land rest and make up for its sabbath years. **35]** Throughout the time that it is desolate, it shall observe the rest that it did not observe in your sabbath years while you were dwelling upon it. **36]** As for those of you who survive, I will cast a faintness into their hearts in the land of their enemies. The sound of a driven leaf shall put them to flight. Fleeing as though from the sword, they shall fall though none pursues. **37]** With no one pursuing, they shall stumble over one another as before the sword. You shall not be able to stand your ground before your enemies, **38]** but shall perish among the nations; and the land of your enemies shall consume you.

39] Those of you who survive shall be heartsick over their iniquity in the land of your enemies; more, they shall be heartsick over the iniquities of their fathers;

verse 43 stress the importance of the sabbath year and introduce the notion that the desolation of the land is to make up for sabbath years neglected in the past. A tie is thus established between this chapter and chapter 25. There is no parallel to this idea in Deuteronomy, chapter 28, or elsewhere in the Bible.

35] The exiles will be in such constant terror that the slightest noise will stir them to panic.

38] Though the destiny of the people seems to be complete disintegration, their cause is not entirely hopeless.

39] First source of hope—The survivors acknowledge their guilt and that of their forebears.

מ וְהִתְוַדּוּ אֶת־עֲוֹנָם וְאֶת־עֲוֹן אֲבֹתָם בְּמַעֲלָם אֲשֶׁר
מא מָעֲלוּ־בִי וְאַף אֲשֶׁר־הָלְכוּ עִמִּי בְּקֶרִי: אַף־אֲנִי אֵלֵךְ
עִמָּם בְּקֶרִי וְהֵבֵאתִי אֹתָם בְּאֶרֶץ אֹיְבֵיהֶם אוֹ־אָז
מב יִכָּנַע לְבָבָם הֶעָרֵל וְאָז יִרְצוּ אֶת־עֲוֹנָם: וְזָכַרְתִּי אֶת־
בְּרִיתִי יַעֲקוֹב וְאַף אֶת־בְּרִיתִי יִצְחָק וְאַף אֶת־בְּרִיתִי
מג אַבְרָהָם אֶזְכֹּר וְהָאָרֶץ אֶזְכֹּר: וְהָאָרֶץ תֵּעָזֵב מֵהֶם
וְתִרֶץ אֶת־שַׁבְּתֹתֶיהָ בָּהְשַׁמָּה מֵהֶם וְהֵם יִרְצוּ אֶת־
עֲוֹנָם יַעַן וּבְיַעַן בְּמִשְׁפָּטַי מָאָסוּ וְאֶת־חֻקֹּתַי גָּעֲלָה
מד נַפְשָׁם: וְאַף גַּם־זֹאת בִּהְיוֹתָם בְּאֶרֶץ אֹיְבֵיהֶם לֹא־
מְאַסְתִּים וְלֹא־גְעַלְתִּים לְכַלֹּתָם לְהָפֵר בְּרִיתִי אִתָּם

* סב מלא ו'.

40] and they shall confess their iniquity and the iniquity of their fathers, in that they trespassed against Me, yea, were hostile to Me.   41] When I, in turn, have been hostile to them and have removed them into the land of their enemies, then at last shall their obdurate heart humble itself, and they shall atone for their iniquity. 42] Then will I remember My covenant with Jacob; I will remember also My covenant with Isaac, and also My covenant with Abraham; and I will remember the land.

43] For the land shall be forsaken of them, making up for its sabbath years by being desolate of them, while they atone for their iniquity; for the abundant reason that they rejected My rules and spurned My laws.   44] Yet, even then, when they are in the land of their enemies, I will not reject them or spurn them so as to destroy them, annulling My covenant with them: for I the LORD am their God.

41] *When I, in turn, have been hostile to them.* Or, taking this with what precedes: "They trespassed against Me, yea, were hostile to Me, so that I, in turn, was hostile to them and removed them... enemies. Then at last...." So Ehrlich and Hoffmann.

Obdurate. Others, "uncircumcised"; literally, "blocked" (T.N.).

42] Second source of hope—God will remember His promise to the patriarchs [13].

43] Third source of hope—God is changelessly Israel's God (cf. Mal. 3:6).

מה כִּי אֲנִי יְהוָֹה אֱלֹהֵיהֶם: וְזָכַרְתִּי לָהֶם בְּרִית רִאשֹׁנִים אֲשֶׁר הוֹצֵאתִי־אֹתָם מֵאֶרֶץ מִצְרַיִם לְעֵינֵי הַגּוֹיִם מו לִהְיוֹת לָהֶם לֵאלֹהִים אֲנִי יְהוָֹה: אֵלֶּה הַחֻקִּים וְהַמִּשְׁפָּטִים וְהַתּוֹרֹת אֲשֶׁר נָתַן יְהוָֹה בֵּינוֹ וּבֵין בְּנֵי יִשְׂרָאֵל בְּהַר סִינַי בְּיַד־מֹשֶׁה: פ

45] I will remember in their favor the covenant with the ancients, whom I freed from the land of Egypt in the sight of the nations to be their God: I the Lord.

46] These are the laws, rules, and directions that the Lord established, through Moses on Mount Sinai, between Himself and the Israelite people.

45] *The covenant with the ancients.* At Sinai. The restoration is only foreshadowed here (it is described fully in Deut. 4:29ff. and 30:1ff.).

46] *On Mount Sinai.* This concluding reference provides a connection with the beginning of chapter 25.

Or perhaps we should render "at Mount Sinai" and consider the verse a conclusion to the entire Book of Leviticus, the laws of which were presumably revealed before Israel broke camp at Sinai and set forth through the desert.

GLEANINGS

Haggadah (all from *Sifra*)

26:4] *Rains in Their Season*

On Friday nights, when no one needs to work in the fields.

The Trees of the Field

Even those that do not now bear edible fruit will do so then.

6] *I Will Grant Peace*

For that is equal in value to all the other blessings combined.

7] *No Sword Shall Cross Your Land*

There will be no invasions, nor will an army cross your territory to reach another military objective.

8] *Five of You Shall Give Chase to a Hundred*

See commentary. The Rabbis note the change of ratio (from 5:100 to 100:10,000) and explain: The merit generated when large numbers obey the Torah increases, so to speak, in geometric proportion.

9] *I Will Maintain My Covenant with You*

I will establish a new covenant with you, written on the very hearts of the people (Jer. 31:31ff.).

17] *Your Foes Shall Dominate You*

This second clause refers to internal enemies and civil strife.

18] *Sevenfold for Your Sins*

See commentary. But in each paragraph the Rabbis endeavor to enumerate seven sins and seven corresponding plagues.

19] *Your Proud Glory*

The Temple (cf. Ezek. 24:21).

21] *Hostile*

See commentary. But *Sifra* derives *keri* from the root *krh,* "happen," and explains: If you regard My punishments as mere accidental happenings, I will treat you as of no more than incidental value.

26] *Dole Out Your Bread by Weight*

It will be of such poor quality that the loaves will crumble and the broken pieces will have to be weighed out.

32] *Your Enemies Who Settle in It Shall Be Appalled by It*

This seeming threat really contains a suggestion of hope: foreigners will never be able to settle down comfortably in the Land of Israel; only Jews can be truly at home there.

42] *Then Will I Remember My Covenant with Jacob*

Why are the patriarchs mentioned here in reverse order? To indicate that the merit even of Jacob, the youngest, is sufficient to bring about the redemption; but, if it were not sufficient, the merits of his father Isaac and grandfather Abraham would surely suffice (*Sifra* as elaborated by Rashi).

PART VII

Supplementary Laws

Vows, Gifts, and Dues

This supplementary chapter deals chiefly with gifts to the sanctuary, whether by conditional vows ("if God does such-and-such for me, I will give such-and-such") or by unconditional acts of pious gratitude. A few enigmatic verses at the end treat of certain agricultural dues.

Vows are mentioned frequently in the Bible: in narratives about Jacob (Gen. 28:20ff.), Jephthah (Judg. 11:30ff.), Hannah (I Sam. 1:11), and others; and in the legislation of Leviticus (7:16ff. and 22:17ff.) and Numbers (chapters 6 and 30). Warnings are given against rash and hasty vows (in Deut. 23:22ff. and Eccles. 5:1ff.). The present section presents laws on the subject without discussing their moral and religious implications.

Three types of gifts are treated: (1) the money equivalent of a person, *erech, erkecha*; (2) the dedication of cattle or real property, *hekdesh* [1]—such a gift being subject to redemption if the donor pays its value plus 20 per cent; (3) the irreversible gift, *cherem*.

1. Erech, erkecha

In very ancient times, persons were literally dedicated to a god. This means that they were either sacrificed, as in the case of Jephthah's daughter, or set aside for the service of the sanctuary, as in the case of Samuel. Perhaps our law developed out of the practice of redeeming dedicated persons by a money payment. But the present text indicates no such connection. It deals with a simple vow to contribute a sum equivalent to the valuation—not the value!—of a person who may be the donor, or someone else.

The amount to be contributed was determined by the age and sex of the person "valuated," according to a fixed schedule. Health and earning power were not relevant. If, however, the maker of the vow was unable to pay the fixed tariff, provision was made to give a lesser amount.

Such gifts, as well as those in the two following classes, were to be given "to the LORD." But who received them on His behalf? On this point our chapter is not clear. Verse 21 indicates that in some cases, at least, the recipient was an individual priest [2]. But a different viewpoint emerges from the interesting report in II Kings (12:5ff.).

From this passage we learn that in the days of the monarchy worshipers used to select the priest who received their gifts to the sanctuary, including "the equivalent of persons." The priests as a group were expected, in return, to keep the Temple in repair. But the system did not work well. King Joash therefore decided—and the priests agreed—that thenceforth all donations should go into a separate fund, under the jurisdiction of the chief priest, for the maintenance of the Temple buildings.

The Rabbis interpreted our chapter in the light of this episode, and their interpretation is quite probably correct. According to the halachah, then, vowed sums, as well as the consecrated items discussed below, were applied to the maintenance of the Temple.

Verses 2 through 8 are the basis of a treatise of the Mishnah and Talmud, called *Arachin,* "Valuations."

2. Hekdesh

The second section of the chapter, on the consecration of cattle and real estate, treats of several different circumstances. Common to them all is the rule that, if one declares an item consecrated and later regrets his action, he can recover the property by paying its value, as assessed by a priest, plus 20 per cent.

Though the donor may regain a consecrated animal by a money payment, he cannot do so by substituting another animal, even though the second is more valuable than the first. Were he to attempt this, both animals would be consecrated. This provision (verse 10 and a similar ruling in verse 33) is the biblical basis for another treatise of the Mishnah and Talmud, called *Temurah,* "Substitution."

When the animal consecrated is of a clean species, the donor may designate it for sacrifice. Otherwise, it may be sold and the proceeds put in the fund for building maintenance. This was the regular rule if animals unsuited for the altar were donated. And gifts of real estate were usually applied to the same purpose.

On this subject, the Torah deals separately

with the consecration of a house, of inherited farmland, and of land which the donor had acquired by purchase.

The value of farmland is set arbitrarily according to its area, without regard to the productiveness of the soil—just as the valuation of persons has nothing to do with their actual "sale value." The amount required to redeem such property diminishes with the approach of the jubilee year; and land that the contributor had bought from the original owner is restored to that owner when the jubilee arrives. If, however, one consecrates a field from his own ancestral holding, the law is different—and obscure (see commentary on 27:20–21).

3. Cherem

The third section (verses 28–30) employs the noun *cherem* and related verb forms. These words indicate something forbidden and inviolable. The Arabic word from which our English "harem" is derived is related to the Hebrew *cherem.* A slightly different form of the Arabic term is used for certain holy areas, in Mecca and elsewhere, from which non-Moslems are barred.

In the Bible, *cherem* appears most often in the context of war. It means the extermination of defeated enemies. As regards booty, *cherem* requires that the spoil must either be destroyed or put into a sacred treasury (Exod. 22:19; Num. 21:2f. with footnotes; Deut. 2:34f.; and elsewhere). If anyone appropriates an object that has been declared *cherem,* he himself becomes *cherem* and must be put to death (Deut. 7:25f.; Josh. 7:1ff.). The present Torah translation renders the root most often by "proscribe," a term, derived from Roman practice, which comes fairly close to the meaning of the Hebrew. Sometimes the root is translated "doom," as in Deuteronomy 2:34.

This background, unfortunately, does not

help much in the understanding of verse 28 which speaks of proscribing man or beast or land to the Lord. The traditional expositors held that a gift designated as *cherem* must remain forever sanctuary property—whereas ordinary consecrated gifts (*hekdesh*), if not specifically designated for sacrifice, could be sold by the sanctuary authorities or redeemed by the donor. The man proscribed is explained as a gentile slave who is thereby attached for life to the service of the sanctuary (*Sifra*). I have found no better explanation of the verse.

But the ensuing sentence states that a proscribed human being must be put to death. This cannot possibly refer to someone who was declared *cherem* by the private donor of verse 28. Unlike Roman law, the Torah never granted power of life and death to a father over his children or to a master over his slaves. For some reason, the old fierce law is repeated here: one who converts *cherem* property to his own use becomes *cherem* himself and forfeits his life. (Or perhaps, as Dr. Tsevat has suggested, the verse is a warning against pronouncing a *cherem* upon a person because the consequences would be unbearable.)

It may be noted that, in later Jewish usage, *cherem* came to mean the ban pronounced by the leaders of the community on one who outraged the conscience or flouted the authority of the community. In this sense it is sometimes rendered "excommunication," though "ostracism" would be more accurate.

The end of the chapter (verses 26–27 and 30–33) deals with obligatory dues. These brief passages are largely in conflict with other passages of the Torah and present baffling problems to the student.

In general, it appears that this chapter is a collection of old materials, which, with some later additions, was appended to the Book of Leviticus after the latter was virtually completed, and that the *tochechah* was intended as the original ending of the book.

אַ וַיְדַבֵּר יְהוָֹה אֶל־מֹשֶׁה לֵּאמֹר: דַּבֵּר אֶל־בְּנֵי יִשְׂרָאֵל
וְאָמַרְתָּ אֲלֵהֶם אִישׁ כִּי יַפְלִא נֶדֶר בְּעֶרְכְּךָ נְפָשֹׁת
גַ לַיהוָֹה: וְהָיָה עֶרְכְּךָ הַזָּכָר מִבֶּן עֶשְׂרִים שָׁנָה וְעַד
בֶּן־שִׁשִּׁים שָׁנָה וְהָיָה עֶרְכְּךָ חֲמִשִּׁים שֶׁקֶל כֶּסֶף בְּשֶׁקֶל
דַ הַקֹּדֶשׁ: וְאִם־נְקֵבָה הִוא וְהָיָה עֶרְכְּךָ שְׁלֹשִׁים שָׁקֶל:
הַ וְאִם מִבֶּן־חָמֵשׁ שָׁנִים וְעַד בֶּן־עֶשְׂרִים שָׁנָה וְהָיָה
עֶרְכְּךָ הַזָּכָר עֶשְׂרִים שְׁקָלִים וְלַנְּקֵבָה עֲשֶׂרֶת
וַ שְׁקָלִים: וְאִם מִבֶּן־חֹדֶשׁ וְעַד בֶּן־חָמֵשׁ שָׁנִים וְהָיָה
עֶרְכְּךָ הַזָּכָר חֲמִשָּׁה שְׁקָלִים כֶּסֶף וְלַנְּקֵבָה עֶרְכְּךָ
זַ שְׁלֹשֶׁת שְׁקָלִים כָּסֶף: וְאִם מִבֶּן־שִׁשִּׁים שָׁנָה וָמַעְלָה

Leviticus 27

1–7

1] The LORD spoke to Moses, saying:

2] Speak to the Israelite people and say to them: When a man explicitly vows to the LORD the equivalent for a human being,   **3]** the following scale shall apply: If it is a male from twenty to sixty years of age, the equivalent is fifty shekels of silver by the sanctuary weight;   **4]** if it is a female, the equivalent is thirty shekels. **5]** If the age is from five years to twenty years, the equivalent is twenty shekels for a male and ten shekels for a female.   **6]** If the age is from one month to five years, the equivalent for a male is five shekels of silver, and the equivalent for a female is three shekels of silver.   **7]** If the age is sixty years or over, the equivalent is fifteen

---

27:2]   *Explicitly.* See T.N. at 22:21 (T.N.).

The equivalent for a human being. Hebrew *be'erkecha nefashot.* The ending "cha" ordinarily indicates the possessive "your." Many earlier translations rendered "thy valuation." But the Hebrew construction in this chapter and in chapter 5, verse 15, precludes such a rendering. This was recognized in the Septuagint and Targums, the Talmud, and the classic Jewish commentaries.

3]   *A male from twenty to sixty years of age.* Men became liable for military service when they were twenty years old (Num. 1:3).

6]   *From one month to five years.* Evidently one was not to vow the equivalent of an infant less than a month old. Later Jewish law considered the viability of a child in doubt for the first month.

אִם־זָכָר וְהָיָה עֶרְכְּךָ חֲמִשָּׁה עָשָׂר שָׁקֶל וְלַנְּקֵבָה

עֲשָׂרָה שְׁקָלִים: וְאִם־מָךְ הוּא מֵעֶרְכֶּךָ וְהֶעֱמִידוֹ לִפְנֵי

הַכֹּהֵן וְהֶעֱרִיךְ אֹתוֹ הַכֹּהֵן עַל־פִּי אֲשֶׁר תַּשִּׂיג יַד

הַנֹּדֵר יַעֲרִיכֶנּוּ הַכֹּהֵן: ס וְאִם־בְּהֵמָה אֲשֶׁר יַקְרִיבוּ

מִמֶּנָּה קָרְבָּן לַיהוָה כֹּל אֲשֶׁר יִתֵּן מִמֶּנּוּ לַיהוָה יִהְיֶה־

קֹּדֶשׁ: לֹא יַחֲלִיפֶנּוּ וְלֹא־יָמִיר אֹתוֹ טוֹב בְּרָע אוֹ־רַע

בְּטוֹב וְאִם־הָמֵר יָמִיר בְּהֵמָה בִּבְהֵמָה וְהָיָה־הוּא

וּתְמוּרָתוֹ יִהְיֶה־קֹּדֶשׁ: וְאִם כָּל־בְּהֵמָה טְמֵאָה אֲשֶׁר

לֹא־יַקְרִיבוּ מִמֶּנָּה קָרְבָּן לַיהוָה וְהֶעֱמִיד אֶת־

הַבְּהֵמָה לִפְנֵי הַכֹּהֵן: וְהֶעֱרִיךְ הַכֹּהֵן אֹתָהּ בֵּין טוֹב

ח

ט

י

יא

יב

Leviticus 27

8—12

* ט סבירין סמנה.

shekels in the case of a male and ten shekels for a female. 8] But if one cannot afford the equivalent, he shall be presented before the priest, and the priest shall assess him; the priest shall assess him according to what the vower can afford.

9] If [the vow concerns] any animal that may be brought as an offering to the LORD, any such that may be given to the LORD shall be holy. 10] One may not exchange or substitute another for it, either good for bad, or bad for good; if one does substitute one animal for another, the thing vowed and its substitute shall both be holy. 11] If [the vow concerns] any unclean animal which may not be brought as an offering to the LORD, the animal shall be presented before the priest, 12] and the priest shall assess it. Whether high or low, whatever assessment is set by the

8] *The priest shall assess him according to what the vower can afford.* See commentary on 1:14.

9–13] The law of substitution. See p. 306.

11] *Unclean animal.* E.g., a horse or camel, which could be sold, and the proceeds used for upkeep of the sanctuary.

12] *High or low.* Literally, "good or bad" (T.N.).

יג וּבֵין רַע כְּעֶרְכְּךָ הַכֹּהֵן כֵּן יִהְיֶה: וְאִם־גָּאֹל יִגְאָלֶנָּה

יד וְיָסַף חֲמִישִׁתוֹ עַל־עֶרְכֶּךָ: וְאִישׁ כִּי־יַקְדִּשׁ אֶת־בֵּיתוֹ

קֹדֶשׁ לַיהֹוָה וְהֶעֱרִיכוֹ הַכֹּהֵן בֵּין טוֹב וּבֵין רָע כַּאֲשֶׁר

טו יַעֲרִיךְ אֹתוֹ הַכֹּהֵן כֵּן יָקוּם: וְאִם־הַמַּקְדִּישׁ יִגְאַל אֶת־

טז בֵּיתוֹ וְיָסַף חֲמִישִׁית כֶּסֶף־עֶרְכְּךָ עָלָיו וְהָיָה לּוֹ: וְאִם

מִשְּׂדֵה אֲחֻזָּתוֹ יַקְדִּישׁ אִישׁ לַיהֹוָה וְהָיָה עֶרְכְּךָ לְפִי

יז זַרְעוֹ זֶרַע חֹמֶר שְׂעֹרִים בַּחֲמִשִּׁים שֶׁקֶל כָּסֶף: אִם־

יח מִשְּׁנַת הַיֹּבֵל יַקְדִּישׁ שָׂדֵהוּ כְּעֶרְכְּךָ יָקוּם: וְאִם־אַחַר

הַיֹּבֵל יַקְדִּישׁ שָׂדֵהוּ וְחִשַּׁב־לוֹ הַכֹּהֵן אֶת־הַכֶּסֶף עַל־

פִּי הַשָּׁנִים הַנּוֹתָרֹת עַל שְׁנַת הַיֹּבֵל וְנִגְרַע מֵעֶרְכֶּךָ:

יט וְאִם־גָּאֹל יִגְאַל אֶת־הַשָּׂדֶה הַמַּקְדִּישׁ אֹתוֹ וְיָסַף

Leviticus 27
13–19

priest shall stand;   13] and if he wishes to redeem it, he must add one-fifth to its assessment.

14] If a man consecrates his house to the LORD, the priest shall assess it. Whether high or low, as the priest assesses it, so it shall stand;   15] and if he who has consecrated his house wishes to redeem it, he must add one-fifth to the sum at which it was assessed, and it shall be his.

16] If a man consecrates to the LORD any land that he holds, its assessment shall be in accordance with its seed requirement: fifty shekels of silver to a *homer* of barley seed.   17] If he consecrates his land as of the jubilee year, its assessment stands. 18] But if he consecrates his land after the jubilee, the priest shall compute the price according to the years that are left until the jubilee year, and its assessment shall be so reduced;   19] and if he who consecrated the land wishes to redeem it, he

16–21] Dedication of farm property. As with the valuation of persons, assessment is arbitrary. An area which requires a *homer* of barley to sow it is valued at fifty shekels of silver, regardless of the quality of the soil.

17] *Its assessment stands.* The rate just mentioned applies.

כ חֲמִשִׁית כֶּסֶף־עֶרְכְּךָ עָלָיו וְקָם לוֹ: וְאִם־לֹא יִגְאַל

אֶת־הַשָּׂדֶה וְאִם־מָכַר אֶת־הַשָּׂדֶה לְאִישׁ אַחֵר לֹא־

כא יִגָּאֵל עוֹד: וְהָיָה הַשָּׂדֶה בְּצֵאתוֹ בַיֹּבֵל קֹדֶשׁ לַיהֹוָה

כב כִּשְׂדֵה הַחֵרֶם לַכֹּהֵן תִּהְיֶה אֲחֻזָּתוֹ: וְאִם אֶת־שְׂדֵה

מִקְנָתוֹ אֲשֶׁר לֹא מִשְּׂדֵה אֲחֻזָּתוֹ יַקְדִּישׁ לַיהֹוָה:

כג וְחִשַּׁב־לוֹ הַכֹּהֵן אֵת מִכְסַת הָעֶרְכְּךָ עַד שְׁנַת הַיֹּבֵל

Leviticus 27
20–23

must add one-fifth to the sum at which it was assessed, and it shall pass to him. **20]** But if he does not redeem the land, and the land is sold to another, it shall no longer be redeemable: **21]** when it is released in the jubilee, the land shall be holy to the Lord, as land proscribed; it becomes the priest's holding.

   22] If he consecrates to the Lord land that he purchased, which is not land of his holding,   **23]** the priest shall compute for him the proportionate assessment

---

20–21] *Sifra* explains: If the donor fails to redeem his family holding and the land is sold by the Temple treasurer, it does not revert to the original owners—the donor or his heirs—in the jubilee but shall remain holy "as land proscribed." It does not, however, become the permanent property of the sanctuary but of the priests who are on duty on Yom Kippur, when the jubilee formally commences ("it becomes the priest's holding").

   This explanation presents at least two difficulties. First, no indication is given as to how much time the donor has to redeem his land—for, if the Temple authorities may sell it at any time, his right of redemption is illusory. (The Bible does not mention a Temple treasurer, but verse 27 implies that someone was empowered to sell sanctuary property.) Second, the clause "and the land is sold to another" could also be rendered "and he [i.e., the donor] sells it to another." This is how Luzzatto understood the clause: if the donor consecrates the property, then sells it to someone else, the latter retains possession

till the jubilee; but, because of his duplicity, the donor can never regain it. But the brief and matter-of-fact language of the verse does not suggest any such illegal, not to say immoral, action on the part of the donor. Nor does the text in any way state that the purchaser may retain the property; and indeed why should he be allowed to enjoy the use of consecrated land until the jubilee? M. Noth (*Leviticus*, English translation, p. 206) likewise understands "he sells it to another" with dishonest intent; but he finds no statement in the text as to the consequences of this sale for the buyer.

   Thus the rendering in our translation, which agrees with the tradition, is at least as good as any, though it too leaves several questions unanswered.

22–24] These verses simply spell out the implications of chapter 25, verses 14ff. Since the donor had by his purchase acquired only the right to a number of harvests, he donates only the equivalent of those harvests.

311

כד וְנָתַן אֶת־הָעֶרְכְּךָ בַּיּוֹם הַהוּא קֹדֶשׁ לַיהֹוָה: בִּשְׁנַת
הַיּוֹבֵל יָשׁוּב הַשָּׂדֶה לַאֲשֶׁר קָנָהוּ מֵאִתּוֹ לַאֲשֶׁר־לוֹ
כה אֲחֻזַּת הָאָרֶץ: וְכָל־עֶרְכְּךָ יִהְיֶה בְּשֶׁקֶל הַקֹּדֶשׁ
כו עֶשְׂרִים גֵּרָה יִהְיֶה הַשָּׁקֶל: אַךְ־בְּכוֹר אֲשֶׁר יְבֻכַּר
לַיהֹוָה בִּבְהֵמָה לֹא־יַקְדִּישׁ אִישׁ אֹתוֹ אִם־שׁוֹר אִם־שֶׂה
כז לַיהֹוָה הוּא: וְאִם בַּבְּהֵמָה הַטְּמֵאָה וּפָדָה בְעֶרְכֶּךָ
וְיָסַף חֲמִשִׁתוֹ עָלָיו וְאִם־לֹא יִגָּאֵל וְנִמְכַּר בְּעֶרְכֶּךָ:
כח אַךְ כָּל־חֵרֶם אֲשֶׁר יַחֲרִם אִישׁ לַיהֹוָה מִכָּל־אֲשֶׁר־לוֹ

up to the jubilee year, and he shall pay the assessment as of that day, a sacred dona-tion to the LORD.   24] In the jubilee year the land shall revert to him from whom it was bought, whose holding the land is.   25] All assessments shall be by the sanctuary weight, the shekel being twenty *gerahs*.

26] A firstling of animals, however, which—as a firstling—is the LORD's, cannot be consecrated by anybody; whether ox or sheep, it is the LORD's.   27] But if it is of unclean animals, it may be ransomed at its assessment, with one-fifth added; if it is not redeemed, it shall be sold at its assessment.

28] But of all that a man owns, be it man or beast or land of his holding, nothing

25] *By the sanctuary weight.* These laws antedate the introduction of coinage. The biblical shekel is a weight of metal, not a stamped coin.

26–27] *Firstling.* Verse 26 states, reasonably enough, that a firstborn animal cannot be the object of a special vow since it already belongs to God. But verse 27 is a problem. For Exodus 13:13 requires that the firstling of an ass must be redeemed with a lamb; by implication, other "unclean" animals are not subject to the law of firstlings at all. Moreover, according to Jewish tradition, the firstborn animal and the redemption lamb of Exodus (13:13), as well as the redemption money for a firstborn son, are

to be given to an individual priest chosen by the donor, whereas the present verse implies that the firstling belongs to the sanctuary. The traditional expositors therefore held that verse 27 is not con-nected with verse 26 and does not refer to firstlings; it concerns animals consecrated so that the proceeds of their sale may go to the sanctuary (cf. com-mentary on verse 11). But verses 26 and 27 certainly seem to belong together; from our modern stand-point, they may be a fragment of a different law about firstlings, which eventually did not prevail.

28–29] On "proscription," see p. 305.

מֵאָדָם וּבְהֵמָה וּמִשְּׂדֵה אֲחֻזָּתוֹ לֹא יִמָּכֵר וְלֹא יִגָּאֵל

כט כָּל־חֵרֶם קֹדֶשׁ־קָדָשִׁים הוּא לַיהוָה: כָּל־חֵרֶם אֲשֶׁר

ל יָחֳרַם מִן־הָאָדָם לֹא יִפָּדֶה מוֹת יוּמָת: וְכָל־מַעְשַׂר

הָאָרֶץ מִזֶּרַע הָאָרֶץ מִפְּרִי הָעֵץ לַיהוָה הוּא קֹדֶשׁ

לא לַיהוָה: וְאִם־גָּאֹל יִגְאַל אִישׁ מִמַּעַשְׂרוֹ חֲמִשִׁיתוֹ יֹסֵף

לב עָלָיו: וְכָל־מַעְשַׂר בָּקָר וָצֹאן כֹּל אֲשֶׁר־יַעֲבֹר תַּחַת

לג הַשָּׁבֶט הָעֲשִׂירִי יִהְיֶה־קֹדֶשׁ לַיהוָה: לֹא יְבַקֵּר בֵּין־

Leviticus 27

29–33

that he has proscribed for the LORD may be sold or redeemed; every proscribed thing is totally consecrated to the LORD. **29]** No human being who has been proscribed can be ransomed: he shall be put to death.

30] All tithes from the land, whether seed from the ground or fruit from the tree, are the LORD's; they are holy to the LORD. **31]** If a man wishes to redeem any of his tithes, he must add one-fifth to them. **32]** All tithes of the herd or flock—of all that passes under the shepherd's staff, every tenth one—shall be holy to the LORD. **33]** He must not look out for good as against bad, or make substitu-

30–33] These verses are baffling.

30] *All tithes ... are the Lord's; they are holy to the Lord.* In this chapter, "holy to the LORD" means that something belongs either to the sanctuary or to a priest. But the extended law in Numbers (18:21ff.) assigns the tithe to the Levites. Once the latter have given a tithe of their tithe to the priests, the remainder is their property and may be consumed without any of the restrictions applicable to sacred donations! Tradition therefore identified the tithe of this verse with the tithe described in Deuteronomy (14:22ff.), known in later times as the "second tithe." This tithe remained two years out of three in the possession of the farmer, who was required to take it to Jerusalem where he, his family, and guests were to use it for a festive celebration. The identification

is dubious. Deuteronomy permits the worshiper who lives far from Jerusalem, and for whom it would be a hardship to transport the produce, to substitute money for the tithe and expend the sum on the sacred meal in Jerusalem. Nothing is said there about the additional 20 per cent specified in Leviticus 27:31.

Further, verses 32 and 33 call for a tithe of animals, which is mentioned nowhere else in the Torah! According to the Rabbis, these animals too remain in the possession of the owner and were to be consumed in a festive meal—not a sacrifice. But II Chronicles (31:6) tells of an occasion when the tithe of cattle was presented at the Temple as a sacred donation.

These laws appear to represent an entirely divergent tithe system—either a fragment of an old tradition otherwise discarded or an attempt at reform that did not succeed.

טוֹב לָרַע וְלֹא יְמִירֶנּוּ וְאִם־הָמֵר יְמִירֶנּוּ וְהָיָה־הוּא
לד וּתְמוּרָתוֹ יִהְיֶה־קֹּדֶשׁ לֹא יִגָּאֵל: אֵלֶּה הַמִּצְוֺת אֲשֶׁר
צִוָּה יְהוָה אֶת־מֹשֶׁה אֶל־בְּנֵי יִשְׂרָאֵל בְּהַר סִינָי:

Haftarah Bechukotai, p. 407

tion for it. If he does make substitution for it, then it and its substitute shall both be holy: it cannot be redeemed.

34] These are the commandments that the LORD gave Moses for the Israelite people on Mount Sinai.

34] *These are the commandments.* Cf. 26:46. When this chapter was added on to Leviticus, the need was apparently felt to attach a new concluding verse.

GLEANINGS

Haggadah

27:7] *Fifteen Shekels in the Case of a Male and Ten Shekels for a Female*

At lower age levels, a female is assessed at either three-fifths or one-half the value of a male; but, in the upper age bracket, the woman has two-thirds the value of the man. In old age the usefulness of a man decreases more than that of a woman. "An old man in the house is a snare [nuisance], an old woman in the house is a treasure" [3].

8] *The Priest Shall Assess Him according to What the Vower Can Afford*

The maker of the vow must pay as much of the commitment as he can by the sale of his possessions; but he is not required to give up his dwelling, tools, and necessary household goods.   SIFRA

11] *Unclean Animal*

See commentary. But *Sifra* explains: an animal rendered "unclean" for sacrifice through some defect.

32] *All That Passes under the Shepherd's Staff*

For counting. The animals born in a given year were to be penned and then driven out through a narrow gate. As they moved out, the owner was to count them, marking each tenth animal with a bit of red paint on the end of his staff [4].

34] *These Are the Commandments*

Emphasizing the word "these," *Sifra* declares, "Henceforth, no prophet may introduce anything new."

Yet, fortunately, the men who were responsible for this statement found the means, by interpretation and even by legislation, of developing Jewish law and thought and to keep them responsive to the needs and circumstances of each generation.

The Dietary Laws

Appendix I (to Chapter 11)

The following is an outline of dietary practices as currently observed by traditional Jews.

1. Vegetable Products

Still regarded as in force are (1) the prohibition of grain from the new crop prior to the second day of Passover (see commentary on Lev. 23:9ff.); (2) the prohibition of fruit from trees during their first four years (19:23ff.—this rule is generally held to apply only in the Holy Land); (3) the prohibition during Passover of leavened food and cereals which have not been specially protected from leavening (for details, see Exod., chapter 12); (4) the prohibition of wine and brandy not made under Jewish supervision, for fear that some may have been used for libation to a heathen god. This law does not apply to beer and grain spirits.

2. Meat

The laws of Leviticus, chapter 11, and Deuteronomy, chapter 14, permit the meat of only those mammals that are horned ruminants. This essentially means beef, veal, and lamb, since goat's meat and kosher-slaughtered venison are not normally available. Of these permitted animals, the hind quarter may be eaten only if certain tendons and nerves are removed by a technique called "porging" (see commentary on Gen. 32:33).

In the United States qualified experts in this procedure are not available; the hind quarters of kosher-slaughtered animals are therefore regularly sold to nonkosher meat markets. To be fit for the use of the observant, the animal must be slaughtered in accordance with the traditional rules—by cutting the throat with a sharp knife, severing windpipe, esophagus, and jugular vein so that the blood quickly drains from the carcass.

For centuries, any Jew, man or woman, was permitted to slaughter; later, this right was restricted to qualified slaughterers (shochetim), licensed and supervised by the rabbinate of the community. The shochet, after slaughtering an animal, must inspect the lungs of the carcass, rejecting it if there is evidence of disease or if faulty slaughtering has rendered it nevelah. If he observes certain other injuries or blemishes in other places than the lungs, the animal must be rejected as terefah. Doubtful cases are referred to the rabbi.

3. Poultry

Leviticus and Deuteronomy list a number of birds, many of them predators, which may not be eaten; by implication, all other birds are permitted. But already in the talmudic period it had become the rule to eat only such birds as were certified as kosher by a specific and reliable tradition.

Today only chicken, ducks, geese, turkeys, and pigeons are regarded as proper for a kosher diet. Fowls too must be ritually slaughtered. The rules are slightly different from those for quadrupeds. Certain blemishes may render them *terefah*. But such defects are usually discovered by the housewife. The *shochet* does not inspect the fowl he has killed.

4. *Salting*

Because of the strict prohibition of blood, all meat, whether of quadrupeds or fowl, must be prepared in the following fashion: it is soaked in water for about half an hour, then it is thickly salted. The salt must remain on the meat for about an hour, then the meat is washed thoroughly to remove the salt—and with it any remaining blood. This process may be omitted when meat is broiled over a flame. Liver may be "koshered" only by broiling, after it has been scored with a knife and slightly salted. An egg containing a drop of "blood" must be thrown away.

5. *Fish*

Biblical law permits the eating of only such fish as have both fins and scales. Excluded are eels, sharks, catfish, and sturgeon among others, as well as all kinds of shellfish. The blood of fish must be washed away. Fish may be cooked with milk, but not with meat. Amphibians (e.g., frogs), reptiles, and insects are forbidden—even though the Bible permits certain species of locusts.

6. *Animal Products*

The eggs of forbidden fowl and the milk of forbidden mammals are likewise forbidden. For this reason, formerly, Jews would buy milk from a Gentile only if they saw him milk the animal. This refinement is nowadays observed by only a few. But Orthodox authorities still uphold the talmudic objection to cheese produced under non-Jewish auspices; for many kinds of cheeses are prepared with rennet which might come from an animal not ritually fit.

7. *Milk and Meat*

The commandment, "You shall not boil a kid in its mother's milk" (Exod. 23:19 and 34:26; Deut. 14:21), was understood by tradition to forbid the mixing, cooking, or eating of milk and milk products with meat and meat products. This rule was applied to the meat of poultry as well as to that of mammals but not to fish. Food containing meat is referred to as *fleischig* (or *fleischdig*); food containing milk is *milchig* (or *milchdig*); neutral foods, which may be eaten with either milk or meat, are designated *pareve* (or *minnig*).

Talmudic law requires separate utensils for milk and meat if the containers are of porous material, such as unglazed pottery or wood. (Utensils of other materials, e.g., metal, can be "koshered" and then used for either milk or meat.) Accepted custom, however, is much stricter. Though glass is admittedly nonporous and as such could be used for both milk and meat—and the same would apply to glazed china as long as it is uncracked—it is nevertheless customary to have separate dishes, tableware, and cooking utensils for *milchig* and *fleischig* foods. Two additional sets, further, are needed for Passover use.

After one has eaten meat, he is expected to wait a considerable time before eating dairy foods. This waiting period varies in different communities from one to six hours.

Order of Service for the High Priest on the Day of Atonement

Appendix II (to Chapter 16)

The following account is based on Maimonides, *Hilchot Avodat Yom ha-Kippurim*; other medieval authorities differ as to a few details.

The High Priest performed some parts of the service wearing his customary regalia (the "golden garments"); for other parts, he wore the white linen garments specified in Leviticus 16:4. For each change of costume, he had to wash his hands and feet, remove the garments he was wearing, immerse himself in a ritual bath, dry himself, don the other set of garments, and again wash his hands and feet.

1. *In Golden Garments*

Slaughter the morning *tamid* (Exod. 29:39), receive the blood, and dash it against the altar. Offer incense and tend lamps of the lampstand (Exod. 30:7). Present the parts of the *tamid* with meal offering and libation (Exod. 29:40). Sacrifice the additional offerings—a bull and seven lambs (Num. 29:8; the ram mentioned in this verse was identified by tradition with that of Lev. 16:5).

2. *In White Garments*

Confession over the bull (Lev. 16:6). Cast lots over the goats (Lev. 16:8). Second confession over the bull which is now slaughtered and the blood collected in a bowl (Lev. 16:11). Fill fire pan with coals from the altar (Lev. 16:12). Put incense into a vessel and bring the vessel and fire pan into the Holy of Holies where the incense is spread over the burning coals (Lev. 16:12–13). Recite a short prayer (Yoma 5:1). Go out, get the bowl of bull's blood, return to the Holy of Holies, and sprinkle the blood (Lev. 16:14). Go out, slaughter the goat designated "for the LORD" (known as the people's goat), receive the blood, bring it into the Holy of Holies, and sprinkle it there (Lev. 16:15). Sprinkle the blood of the bull toward the curtain (Yoma 5:4). Combine the blood of the goat and that of the bull in one bowl and use this to purge the altar of incense (Lev. 16:18–19). Make confession over the scapegoat and send it away (Lev. 16:21). Rend the carcasses of the bull and goat and remove the inner parts to be offered later (Mishnah Yoma 6:7 with commentary by Bertinoro). (The carcasses were burned outside the city. Lev. 16:27.) Read aloud, from a scroll, chapter 16 of Leviticus. Recite by heart Numbers, chapter 29, verses 7–11. Recite eight benedictions (Mishnah Yoma 7:1).

3. *In Golden Garments*

Offer the ram of the High Priest (Lev. 16:3), that of the people (Lev. 16:5), the additional goat of sin offering (Num. 29:11), and the inner parts of the bull and goat (Mishnah Yoma 7:3 with commentary by Bertinoro). Offer the evening *tamid* (Exod. 29:41).

4. *In White Garments*

Remove the fire pan and incense vessel from the Holy of Holies (connected by tradition with Lev. 16:23).

5. *In Golden Garments*

Offer the evening incense and tend the lamps (Exod. 30:8).

Prohibited Degrees of Relationship for Marriage

Appendix III (to Chapter 18)

BIBLICAL PROHIBITIONS	TALMUDICAL EXTENSIONS

A. CONSANGUINITY

a. IN THE ASCENDING LINE

1. Mother	Grandmother (paternal as well as maternal)

b. IN THE DESCENDING LINE

2. Daughter (implied in granddaughter)	
3. Granddaughter (son's or daughter's daughter)	Son's or daughter's granddaughter

c. COLLATERAL CONSANGUINITY

4. Sister and half-sister (either born in wedlock or not)	
5. Father's sister	Grandfather's sister
6. Mother's sister	Grandmother's sister

B. AFFINITY

a. THROUGH ONE'S OWN MARRIAGE

7. Wife's mother	Wife's grandmother Wife's stepmother not strictly prohibited but objectionable
8. Wife's daughter (stepdaughter)	
9. Wife's granddaughter	
10. Wife's sister (during the lifetime of the divorced wife)	

b. THROUGH MARRIAGE OF NEAR BLOOD RELATION

11. Father's wife (stepmother)	Father's or mother's stepmother
12. Father's brother's wife	Mother's brother's wife; father's uterine brother's wife
13. Son's wife	Grandson's or great-grandson's wife
14. Brother's wife (except in the case of levirate)	

(From M. Mielziner, *The Jewish Law of Marriage and Divorce*)

NOTES

REFERENCE NOTES

BIBLIOGRAPHY

Notes and Reference Notes

Part I *Laws of Sacrifice*

1. This section is based on R. K. Yerkes, *Sacrifice in Greek and Roman Religions and in Early Judaism* (New York: Allenson, 1952), pp. 1–7.

2. James B. Pritchard, ed., *Ancient Near Eastern Texts*, 3rd ed. (Princeton: Princeton University Press, 1969), p. 207d. [Hereafter cited as *ANET*.]

3. *Ibid.*, p. 208c.

4. *Ibid.*, p. 338 f.

5. *Ibid.*, p. 95a.

6. See Ps. 50:12–13 (cited above); 40:7; 51:19; and the prophetic selections on p. 5.

7. W. W. Hallo and W. K. Simpson, *The Ancient Near East: A History* (New York: Harcourt Brace Jovanovich, 1971), pp. 158 ff.

8. For Babylonian practice, see A. Leo Oppenheim, *Ancient Mesopotamia* (Chicago: University of Chicago Press, 1964), pp. 181 ff. For the more democratic trends, see below, pp. 14 f., 21 ff., and Yerkes, *Sacrifice*, pp. 92 ff.

9. Pritchard, *ANET*, pp. 325, 331 ff.

10. Num. 10:10; Amos 5:23; Ps. 81:2 f.; 92:2 f.; etc. In the Second Temple there was a choir and orchestra composed of Levites.

11. The Passover legislation of J—Exod. 12:21 ff.— is hardly an exception.

12. Exod. 29:38 ff.; Num. 28–29.

13. On the possibility that sacrifices were offered for a time at the site of the ruined Temple, see A. Guttmann, "The End of the Jewish Sacrificial Cult," *Hebrew Union College Annual*, Vol. 38 (1967), pp. 137–148 [hereafter cited as *HUCA*] and the Hebrew note published in A. Rothkoff, *Bernard Revel* (Philadelphia: JPS, 1972), pp. 323 ff.

14. Lev. R. 7:3. According to Meg. 31b and Ta'an. 27b, God gave this assurance to Abraham. See L. Ginzberg, *The Legends of the Jews* (Philadelphia: JPS, 1909–1938), Vol. 5, p. 228, n. 111. [Hereafter cited as Ginzberg, *Legends*.]

15. Ber. 17a.

16. Hag. 12b.

17. Avot de-R. Nathan 4.

18. Midrash Samuel 1:7.

19. Lev. R. 22:8; see pp. 177 ff.

20. D. Hoffmann, *Das Buch Leviticus* (Berlin: M. Poppelauer, 1905), Vol. I, pp. 81 ff., denies that the Midrash supports Maimonides and notes correctly that the version of the Midrash cited by Abarbanel is corrupt. But M. Friedlander, *The Guide of the Perplexed of Maimonides* (reprint, New York: Hebrew Publishing Co., n.d.), Part III, p. 151, n. 2, and M. Margulies, in his notes to Lev. R., agree that R. Levi anticipated the view of Maimonides.

21. Maimonides, *Guide of the Perplexed*, Part III, ch. 32.

22. *Ibid.*, ch. 46.

23. Judah Halevi, *Kuzari*, Part II, par. 25 ff.

24. Some hints of Jewish opposition to sacrifice at the beginning of the Christian era are collected by A. J. Heschel, *Torah min Hashamayim* (London: Soncino Press, 1965), Vol. 2, pp. 115 f.

25. See *Catholic Encyclopedia* (New York: Encyclopedia Press, 1913), Vol. 13, pp. 315 ff., "Christian Sacrifice," and Vol. 10, pp. 6 ff., "Mass, Sacrifice of the."

26. The daily offerings, Exod. 29:38 ff.; offerings of purification, Lev. 12:6 ff.; 14:1–32, 49–53; 15:14, 15, 28–30; Yom Kippur, ch. 16; defective animals, 22:17 ff.; Shavuot sacrifices, 23:18, 19; offerings of the nazirite, Num. 6:13 ff.; meal and wine to accompany animal sacrifices, 15:1–16; expiatory sacrifices, 15:22–29; the red cow, ch. 19; complete annual schedule, chs. 28–29. On the paschal sacrifice, see also Exod. 12:1–27 and 43–49; 23:18; 34:25; Num. 9:1 ff.; Deut. 16:1 ff. The most recent treatment of Jewish sacrifice in depth is B. A. Levine, *In the Presence of the Lord: A Study of Cult and Some Cultic Terms in Ancient Israel* (Leiden, Holland: E. J. Brill, 1974).

The Olah—Burnt Offering LEV. 1:1–17

1. Yerkes, *Sacrifice*, p. 53.
2. Sifra, *ad loc.*
3. Yoma 5a. Cf. p. 27. For a more general account of the significance of blood, see p. 179.
4. Carl H. Kraeling, "The Synagogue," Plate LXII, from *The Excavations at Dura-Europos* (New Haven: Yale University Press, 1956). Though the Dura paintings were executed under Jewish direction in the third century C.E., the painters utilized much older Hellenistic models.
5. Yerkes, *Sacrifice*, pp. 137 f.
6. In II Chron. 35:11, the flaying is done by Levites. See Yoma 26b.

7. Pritchard, *ANET*, p. 656. The tariff may have been sent to Marseilles from Carthage and probably dates from the second or third century B.C.E.
8. Mishnah Zeb. 6:5 prescribes that the entrails be removed with the crop.
9. Zeb. 65a, bottom.
10. Maimonides, Hilch. Ma'aseh Korbanot 3:2.
11. Mishnah Men. 9:8, Bavli 93a–b.
12. Lev. R. 7:3, citing Job 1:5.
13. Kid. 40a.
14. Lev. R. 3:5.

The Minchah—Meal Offering LEV. 2:1–16

1. This development was apparently suggested by I Kings 18:29 which speaks of a *minchah* to be presented after midday; cf. II Kings 16:15 and Ps. 141:2 which speak of an evening *minchah*.
2. Other mandatory grain offerings are treated in 6:12 ff.; 23:13; Num. 5:15. The two loaves of Lev. 23:17 were also classified by the rabbis as a *minchah*, though no part of them was burned on the altar.
3. This is clear also from other talmudic passages, e.g., "When you sift, the *kemach* is underneath [the sieve], the *solet* is above": Yerushalmi Sab. 7, 10b and 20, 17c. The meaning of *solet* was correctly under-

stood by many medieval and modern scholars; see R. David Kimchi, *Sefer Hashorashim* (Berlin: Bethge, 1847), s.v. *solet*; Hoffmann, Vol. I, p. 146, citing S. R. Hirsch; G. Dalman, *Arbeit und Sitte in Palästina* (Gütersloh: C. Bertelsmann, 1928–1942), Vol. 3, pp. 291 ff. Some moderns, led astray by the translation "fine flour," have been baffled by the saying in Avot.
4. Lev. R. 3:5; cf. the similar story of "The Widow's Mites," Mark 12:41 ff.
5. Cited by Rashi and Bachya to the verse.

Zevach Shelamim—Sacrifice of Well-Being LEV. 3:1–17

1. The word *mizbe'ach*, "altar," comes from the same root.
2. So the Septuagint; Josephus, *The Jewish Antiquities*, III:228; Mishnah Tamid 4:3; and various authorities cited by Hoffmann, Vol. I, p. 165.

3. S. Lieberman, *Hellenism in Jewish Palestine* (New York: Jewish Theological Seminary, 1950), p. 153, citing Herodotus, *Persian Wars*, III:113, and Mishnah Sab. 5:4.
4. Hul. 49b.

The Chatat—Sin Offering LEV. 4:1–35

1. Jacob Milgrom, "A Sin-Offering or Purification-Offering," *Vetus Testamentum* (Leiden, Holland: E. J. Brill, April 1971), Vol. 21, pp. 237 ff.
2. See Judg. 20:16; Prov. 19:2; W. G. Plaut, *The*

Book of Proverbs (New York: Union of American Hebrew Congregations, 1961), p. 202.
3. Scholars who regard P as entirely post-exilic have argued that in pre-exilic writings *chatat* always

means sin, not sin offering. Outside P, they say, the latter sense is found only in Ezekiel, Ezra, and Chronicles. They conclude that the *chatat* and the *asham* (treated in ch. 5) were first introduced when the fall of Jerusalem generated a new mood of guilt. But in fact *chatat* and *asham* are both mentioned in II Kings 12:17, which gives every evidence of being early and authentic (cf. I Sam. 3:14). Moreover, the basic character of the *chatat*, which corrects ritual impurity as well as moral guilt, suggests a very ancient origin.

4. For another view, see Hoffmann, Vol. I, p. 182.

5. Yoma 85b–86a. For inadvertent acts of idolatry, special sacrifices were prescribed: Num. 15:22–29 and see Sifre on Num., 111 ff.

6. Midrash Hagadol, Lev., p. 61.

7. *Ibid.*, p. 80. The homily is based on Isa. 64:4.

Chatat—Sin Offering; Asham—Guilt Offering LEV. 5:1–26

1. Samuel David Luzzatto also cites the suggestion of one of his students that someone might become culpable by touching another person—thus transmitting the defilement to him—without informing him of the uncleanness.

2. H. M. Orlinsky, *Notes on the New Translation of the Torah* (Philadelphia: JPS, 1969), pp. 208 f. [Hereafter cited as JPS *Notes.*]

3. Hoffmann's attempt (I, pp. 210 ff.) to show that the halachah agrees with the plain sense is not convincing.

4. Pesikta Rabbati 23(24), p. 121a.

5. Midrash Hagadol, pp. 108 f.

Laws of Sacrifice—Olah, Minchah, Chatat LEV. 6:1–23

1. But Rashbam, here and at Exod. 29:37 and 30:29, understands the sentence as a command: "Whoever touches these must be in a state of ritual purity."

2. For a similar reason, Orthodox practice forbids the preparation or serving of dairy products in pottery dishes that have been used for meat, and vice versa. Further, non-kosher pottery dishes may not be ritually cleansed for the reception of kosher food; and pottery dishes which have contained leavened food may not be cleansed for Passover use. American Orthodox and Conservative custom extends these prohibitions even to perfectly glazed dishes, though the halachah generally applies only to unglazed or imperfectly glazed pottery (*Shulchan Aruch*, Orach Chayim 451:23, and note of R. Moses Isserles).

3. Mishnah Tamid 1:2 ff.

4. *Ibid.*, 1:4; 2:1.

5. *Ibid.*, 2:2.

6. Sifra to 6:19; 7:7, 32 ff.

7. Lev. R. 7:5.

8. Yoma 21b.

Laws of Sacrifice—Zevach Shelamim LEV. 7:1–38

1. The sources of ritual defilement are treated in Lev. 11:24–15:23 and Num. 19.

2. See Gen. 17:14; Exod. 12:15, 19; 30:33, 38; 31:14.

3. The first view is expressed, e.g., by Bruno Baentsch, *Exodus-Leviticus-Numeri* (Göttingen: Vandenhoeck und Ruprecht, 1903), to the verse; the second in Brown-Driver-Briggs, *A Hebrew and English Lexicon* (Boston and N. Y.: Houghton Mifflin, 1907), p. 504a. [Hereafter cited as *Lexicon*.]

4. J. Morgenstern, *HUCA*, Vols. 8–9 (1931–1932), pp. 33 ff.; M. Tsevat, *HUCA*, Vol. 32 (1961), pp. 191 ff. Tsevat argues that, while our expression is found only in P, H, and Ezekiel, the concept is ancient and underlies the narrative of I Sam. 2:27–36.

5. J. Milgrom, "The Alleged Wave-Offering in Israel and in the Ancient Near East," *Israel Exploration Journal*, Vol. 22, pp. 33 ff.

6. G. R. Driver, "Three Technical Terms in the

Pentateuch," *Journal of Semitic Studies* (Manchester, England: Manchester University Press), Vol. 1, pp. 100 ff. Also N. H. Snaith, *Leviticus and Numbers,* Century Bible, new edition (London: Nelson, 1967), on Num. 8:11; so already A. B. Ehrlich, *Mikra Kifeshuto* (reprint, New York: Ktav, 1969), on Lev. 8:27.

7. Mishnah Ber. 1:1.

8. Avot 1:1.

9. Mishnah Kinnim 1:1.

10. Mishnah Zeb. 2:2; Bavli 28a ff.

11. See M. Higger, *Intention in Jewish Law* (New York, 1927) which, however, does not discuss *pigul.* Of course, other legal systems also stress the concept of intention.

12. M.K. 28a.

13. Yeb. 55a. These citations and others are given in H. E. Goldin, *Hebrew Criminal Law and Procedure* (New York: Twayne Publishers, 1952), pp. 40 f.

14. Nachmanides on 18:29, followed by Bachya. There is precedent for this view in earlier sources: Goldin, *loc. cit.*

15. Lev. R. 9:7.

The Divine Presence in the Sanctuary LEV. 8:1–10:20

1. F. M. Cross, *Canaanite Myth and Hebrew Epic* (Cambridge: Harvard University Press, 1973) argues that the story reflects a power struggle between rival priestly clans.

2. Sifra on 8:33; Seder Olam Rabah, ch. 7. A divergent view, found in some rabbinic sources, is cited by Hoffmann, I, p. 274.

3. Lev. R. 12:1, near end.

4. According to Mishnah Nazir 1:3, the nazirite vow is for 30 days unless a longer period is specified in the vow.

5. Jer. 35 tells of a group descended from Jehonadab son of Rechab (II Kings 10:15 ff.), who followed an ordinance of their ancestor not to drink wine. Apparently this was part of a program to maintain the nomad life style without change for these "Rechabites" also refused to establish permanent homes and to till the soil.

6. Charles R. Snyder, *Alcohol and the Jews* (Glencoe: Free Press, 1958). The study was based on data obtained from Jews residing permanently or temporarily in New Haven. One wonders whether the sample studied was representative of American Jewry, let alone world Jewry. There is also some reason to think that drinking habits of Jews have changed significantly since the study was made.

7. Lev. R. 10:9.

8. A few rabbinic sources state specifically that the sons of Aaron were anointed. See Hoffmann, I, pp. 276 f.

9. According to Rashbam, Ibn Ezra, and Luzzatto, the fire that consumed the sacrifices was itself the manifestation of God's presence. But as Hoffmann, I, p. 291, points out, II Chron. 7:3 clearly distinguishes between the heavenly fire and the Presence.

10. Zeb. 115a.

11. According to the halachah, a priest on Temple duty was required to have his hair trimmed every thirty days, the High Priest every Friday: Ta'an. 17a. But contrast Num. 6:5, 9, 18 and the story of Samson, Judg. 13:14; 16:4 ff., where long hair is a mark of consecration.

12. Sifra on 10:7.

13. Erub. 64b.

14. Sifra to the v.

15. Sifra and Targum Pseudo-Jonathan to the v.

16. Philo, *On the Life of Moses,* II:150.

17. J. H. Hertz, ed., *The Pentateuch and Haftorahs* (Oxford: Oxford University Press, 1929–1936) on Exod. 29:20. To the present v. he cites the Christian commentator Dillmann to similar effect.

18. Sifra to 9:2. The reading "accuse you" is given by Nachmanides on 9:7.

19. Sifra; Sotah 38a.

20. See n. 3, above.

21. Lev. R. 20:10.

22. Sifra.

23. *Ibid.*; Lev. R. 20:8.

24. Lev. R. 20:8.

25. Sifre to Deut. 26.

26. Sifra (ed., I. H. Weiss, p. 45c).

27. *Ibid.*

28. Lev. R. 20:10.

29. Philo, *Allegorical Interpretation of the Laws,* II:58.

30. Philo, *Concerning Flight* 59.

31. Philo, *Concerning Dreams,* II:67.

32. Lev. R. 20, end.

33. Cf. the Roman Catholic custom of preserving the relics of martyrs in churches.

34. Sifra. On this passage, see Ginzberg, *Legends*, Vol. 6, p. 75, n. 385.

35. Tanch. Shemini 11.

36. Lev. R. 13:1.

The Dietary Laws LEV. 11:1–23

1. Hul. 42a ff.; Maimonides, Hilch. Ma'achalot Asurot 4:6.

2. Maimonides, Hilch. Ma'achalot Asurot 4:1 ff.

3. Deut. 14:21 is from a different source.

4. See p. XVIII.

5. Yoma 67b.

6. Sifra on 20:26.

7. Gen. R. 44:1.

8. See Luzzatto on Lev. 11:1, rejecting the hygienic explanation.

9. Philo, *The Special Laws*, IV:97 ff.

10. Maimonides, *Guide of the Perplexed*, III, ch. 33.

11. Rashbam, Lev. 11:3. But Rashbam was mistaken in ascribing this view to the Talmud. The passages to which he alludes—Sab. 86b; A.Z. 31b; Nid. 34b—do not clearly state that the forbidden foods are physically harmful; and the second passage even asserts that the non-kosher diet makes Gentiles less susceptible to the effects of snake venom!

12. Maimonides, *Guide*, III, ch. 48.

13. *Shulchan Aruch*, Yoreh Deah 6:1; 18:1 ff. Prof. Alexander Guttmann, in a private communication, agrees that the humanitarian explanation of the dietary laws is generally appropriate. But he points out that an animal slaughtered with a dull knife is still kosher if the knife has no nick and the slaughterer does not interrupt the process: *ibid.*, 8:7.

14. P's version of the story (v. 15) does not make this distinction, since according to P the dietary laws were not instituted until Sinai.

15. E. Wiesenberg, "Related Prohibitions: Swine Breeding and the Study of Greek," *HUCA*, Vol. 27 (1956), pp. 213 ff.

16. The comment, "Thus he declared all foods clean" (Mark 7:19), is a later addition. For when the disciples debated whether gentile converts to Christianity were required to keep the dietary laws, no saying of Jesus was quoted (Acts 15). Had any such saying been known, it would surely have been mentioned.

17. I. Lewin, *In the Struggle against Discrimination* (New York: Bloch Publishing Co., 1957), cites many gentile physiologists, veterinarians, and others who defend Jewish ritual slaughtering as humane; but he does not mention the problem of shackling and hoisting.

18. James G. Heller, *Isaac M. Wise* (New York: UAHC, 1965), pp. 572 f. Oddly, Wise argued that oysters are permitted according to Bible and Talmud: D. Wilansky, *Sinai to Cincinnati* (New York: Renaissance Book Co., 1937), pp. 237 ff.

19. Hoffmann, Vol. I, p. 338.

20. Baentsch had already given the same explanation but eliminated the words "that walk on all fours" from vv. 20 and 23 as due to a scribal error. M. M. Kalisch, *A Critical and Historical Commentary on the Old Testament: Leviticus* (London: Longmans Green, 1867–1872), gives an ingenious but questionable explanation of how the confusion originated.

21. Lev. R. 13:5 (Margulies, p. 291).

Defilement from Animal Carcasses LEV. 11:24–47

1. This statement applies only to unconsecrated food (*chulin*). In the case of "heave offering" (*terumah*, Num. 18:11 ff.) there is a third degree of uncleanness, and in the case of sacrificial foods (*kodashim*) there is a fourth.

2. More exactly: The leper had to remain outside the camp/city of Jerusalem (13:46); those defiled by menstruation, "issues," or childbirth had to remain outside the "camp of the Levites/Temple Mount (Mishnah Kelim 1:8); for other types of defilement, persons were excluded only from the Sanctuary proper.

3. Mishnah Sab. 3:1 and commentaries.

4. Mishnah Machshirin 6:4.

5. Yoma 39a.

6. *Ibid.*, 38b.

Defilement through Childbirth LEV. 12:1–8

1. Snaith, *Leviticus and Numbers*, p. 90.
2. I. Abrahams, *A Companion to the Authorized Daily Prayer Book* (London: Eyre and Spottiswoode, 1922), pp. ccxxxiii f.
3. Cited by Kalisch, II, p. 122.

4. Hoffmann, I, pp. 360 f., citing Maimonides, Hilch. Issure Biah 11:15. See further Nid. 31b; Midrash Hagadol, Lev., p. 273.
5. Nid. 31b.

Defilement from Tzara'at LEV. 13:1–46

1. Deut. 24:8 f., a legal passage, simply enjoins obedience to priestly direction in this matter.
2. We should not suppose that Elisha refused the gifts out of fear of contagion and that Gehazi was infected by natural contact. Elisha had displayed the power of Israel's God to the heathen Naaman; Gehazi was punished for trying to profit by the miracle.
3. Ginzberg, *Legends*, Vol. 3, pp. 213 f.
4. Short for *motzi shem ra*.
5. Luzzatto, pp. 409 f. Luzzatto offers a rationalistic explanation.

6. Sifra to 14:36.
7. Mishnah Nega'im 3:1.
8. B.K. 85a, citing Exod. 21:19.
9. Modern studies in talmudic medicine, mostly in German, are listed in H. L. Strack, *Introduction to the Talmud* (Philadelphia: JPS, 1931), pp. 193 f.
10. Mishnah Kid., end.
11. B.K. 85a.
12. Hoffmann, I, p. 387, citing M.K. 24a.
13. Maimonides, Hilch. Tum'at Tzara'at 8:1; Nachmanides to the verse; Hoffmann, I, p. 380.
14. Yerushalmi San. 10, 27d–28a.

Tzara'at of Garments LEV. 13:47–59

1. Judah Halevi, *Kuzari*, Part II, par. 63; Maimonides, Hilch. Tum'at Tzara'at, end; Nachmanides, Lev. 13:47. See also p. 141.

2. Mishnah Nega'im 11:8 with commentaries; Yerushalmi Shek. 6, 50a, top.

Purification from Tzara'at LEV. 14:1–32

1. Nachmanides, Lev. 14:4, end.
2. Defilement from a corpse was purged with the ashes of a red cow, with which cedar wood, crimson yarn, and hyssop were burned: Num. 19.
3. Cited by Luzzatto, Lev. 14:12.

4. Tosefta Nega'im 8:2.
5. Keritut 8b.
6. Arachin 16b.
7. Pesikta de-R. Kahana, "Parah" (Buber 35a, Mandelbaum 62).

Tzara'at of Houses LEV. 14:33–53

1. Tosefta Nega'im 6:1.
2. F. Nötscher, "Haus- und Stadttomina," *Orientalia*, series prior to Vol. 31, 1928. (I owe this reference to Prof. W. W. Hallo but have not been able to examine the work.)

3. See p. 127.
4. Lev. R. 17:6.
5. Tanch. Metzora 4.
6. Lev. R. 17:2.

1. Sab. 87a.

2. The passage also requires the covering up of feces; this is the only biblical passage which treats normal body wastes as ritually defiling.

3. J. G. Frazer, *The Golden Bough* (New York: Macmillan, 1922), p. 606, which mentions similar superstitions still current in Europe.

4. *Ibid.*

5. Pes. 111a. According to Hor. 13b, one who walks between two women may forget all he has learned.

6. Nachmanides, Lev. 18:19.

7. Nid. 31b. It is a fact that Jewish women have a low incidence of uterine cancer in comparison with the general population, both in Europe and America. Felix A. Theilhaber, writing in 1940, regarded this fact as "really extraordinary" and "thus far unexplained." (*Universal Jewish Encyclopedia*, Vol. 5, p. 268, "Health of Jews.") According to the same authority, Jews have an abnormally high rate of

some other forms of cancer. Orthodox writers have asserted that this relative immunity to cancer of the cervix is due to the observance of the laws of "family purity." See J. Smithline, M.D., "Scientific Aspects of Sexual Purification," in *Some Reasons for Jewish Excellence* (New York, n.d.), citing studies made from 1911 to 1919. The claim has not been adequately proved; if true, it would appear to be one more case where a ritual law produces unforeseen hygienic benefits. Cf. p. 91.

8. San. 37a.

9. W. H. Masters and V. E. Johnson, *Human Sexual Response* (Boston: Little, Brown, 1966), pp. 124 ff.

10. Mishnah Mikvaot 1:7.

11. A *mikveh* is a "gathering" of waters (Gen. 1:10); see Maimonides, Hilch. Mikvaot 4:1.

12. Y. Yadin, *Masada* (New York: Random House, 1966), pp. 164 ff.

13. Maimonides, Hilch. Issure Biah 11:2–4.

14. *Shulchan Aruch*, Yoreh Deah 196.

Yom Kippur LEV. 16:1–34

1. This prophecy does not specifically mention the Day of Atonement, and it is at least possible that it was composed for a special fast in time of drought or other disaster.

2. Pritchard, *ANET*, pp. 331 ff., especially 333d. The tablets containing this ritual text date from after 300 B.C.E., when the Torah was already complete; but the ceremonies they describe may well be very ancient.

3. See Morgenstern, "The Three Calendars of Ancient Israel," *HUCA*, Vol. 1 (1924), especially pp. 22 ff. According to Morgenstern, the New Year on the tenth day of the seventh month (Ezek. 40:1) was originally the concluding day of the fall festival, which in its present form and dating we know as Sukot.

4. Sifra, Yoma 67b, Targum Pseudo-Jonathan, Saadia (cited by Ibn Ezra), and Rashi explain the word as "rough ground," "cliff." Ibn Ezra also cites the view that Azazel was a mountain near Sinai. Rashbam takes the phrase *l'azazel midbarah* to mean "to the desert goats." Hertz cites various moderns who follow the Greek and translate "dismissal" or

"complete removal." Nachmanides regards Azazel as a name for the Power of Evil and struggles to reconcile this concept with monotheism (see Gleanings); he etymologizes the name as "the goat is gone." G. R. Driver has argued for the sense "rough ground" ("Three Technical Terms in the Pentateuch," *Journal of Semitic Studies*, Vol. 1, pp. 97 f.); but some of his evidence supports the "mythological" interpretation. For he accepts the identification of Bet Chadudo, the name given the cliff in the Mishnah, with Dudael, the rocky place where the fallen angel Azazel is imprisoned (I Enoch 10:4–6), and with the modern Bet Hudedun, "a rocky terrace in the wilderness ten miles east of Jerusalem."

5. B. J. Bamberger, *Fallen Angels* (Philadelphia: JPS, 1952), chs. 3–5 and 19.

6. *Ibid.*, pp. 154 ff. and chs. 22, 23.

7. Frazer, *The Golden Bough*, chs. 57, 58.

8. T. H. Gaster, *Festivals of the Jewish Year* (New York: Sloane Associates, 1953), pp. 142 f.

9. Mishnah Yoma 5:1.

10. *Ibid.*, 7:14.

11. "A Significant Controversy between the Sad-

ducees and the Pharisees," *HUCA*, Vol. 4 (1927); reprinted in Jacob Z. Lauterbach, *Rabbinic Essays* (Cincinnati: Hebrew Union College Press, 1951).

12. Or it may come from another root meaning "wipe off."

13. *Kippurim* belongs to a class of abstract nouns that have the plural ending. In later Hebrew, the shorter form Yom Kippur is usual; the "middle Hebrew" of the synagogue prayers retains the biblical *Yom Hakippurim*.

14. Sifra on 16:16.

15. Mishnah Yoma, end.

16. See pp. 173 f.

17. Avot de-R. Nathan 4.

18. Pesikta de-R. Kahana, "Shemini 'Atzeret" (Buber 191a, Mandelbaum 425).

19. Hermann Cohen, *Religion of Reason* (translated by Simon Kaplan; New York: Frederick Ungar, 1972), pp. 218 f.

20. Sifra on 16:14; Yerushalmi Yoma 1, 39a–b.

21. So Hoffmann, I, pp. 438 f.; Brown-Driver-Briggs, *Lexicon*, p. 498b.

22. San. 18a.

23. Sifra to the v.

24. Mishnah Yoma 3:9; 4:1.

25. *Ibid.*, 4:3.

26. *Ibid.*, 5:4.

27. *Ibid.*, 3:4.

28. *Ibid.*, 3:3.

29. *Ibid.*, 3:8; 4:2; 6:2.

30. *Ibid.*, 4:2; 6:5, 6.

31. See n. 10.

32. *Shulchan Aruch*, Orach Chayim 624, end.

33. Mishnah Yoma 8:1.

34. *Ibid.*, 8:5.

35. Sifra to the v.

36. Lev. R. 21:10.

37. *Ibid*.

38. *Ibid.*, 21:11; Pirke de-R. Eliezer 46.

39. Nachmanides to the v.

40. Tosefta Kippurim 4(5):6–8. The statement occurs in several other sources with interesting variants, but the substance is much the same. On profaning the name of God, see p. 204.

41. Cant. R. 5:2.

42. Pesikta Rabbati 44, 184b–185a.

43. Sifra to the v. Cf. n. 15.

44. Mishnah Yoma, end.

Further Laws about Sacrifice and Food LEV. 17:1–16

1. See p. XVIII.

2. Hul. 16b. R. Akiba (*ibid.*, 17a) gave a forced and implausible explanation of the passage. Though his opinion usually prevailed over Ishmael's, the Talmud here follows the latter. See Nachmanides to Lev. 17:2; but cf. Maimonides, Hilch. Shechitah 4:17.

3. So Luzzatto and Hoffmann. An ingenious attempt to bolster this position was made by J. M. Grintz, *Tziyon* (Jerusalem: Historical Society of Israel, 1955), Vol. 31, pp. 1 ff.

4. This expression (Hebrew *chukat olam*) is used of a positive command or institution, often a priestly perquisite, in the following passages: Exod. 12:14, 17; 27:21; 28:43; 29:9; Lev. 7:36; 16:29, 31, 34; 19:10, 21; 23:14, 21; 24:3; Num. 15:15; 18:23; 19:10, 21. Only in Lev. 3:17 and 10:9 are these words attached to a simple prohibition. Note also that in Lev. 23:21 and Num. 19:10 the phrase applies to the entire section, not just to the preceding sentence.

5. Yehezkel Kaufmann, *The Religion of Israel*

(Chicago: University of Chicago Press, 1966), pp. 180 ff.

6. Milgrom, "A Prolegomenon to Leviticus 17:11," *Journal of Biblical Literature* [hereafter cited as *JBL*], 1971, pp. 149–156.

7. *Ibid.*, p. 156, n. 32.

8. So, e.g., Baentsch, p. 389; Morgenstern, *HUCA*, 1935, pp. 38 f.; M. Noth, *Leviticus: A Commentary* (translated by J. E. Anderson, Philadelphia: Westminster Press, 1965), pp. 129 f.

9. Above, p. XIX.

10. The second alternative is upheld by Milgrom, *JBL*, 1971, p. 149. For a different view, see B. A. Levine, Prolegomenon to G. B. Gray, *Sacrifice in the Old Testament* (reprint, New York: Ktav, 1971), p. xxvii.

11. Milgrom understands v. 11 in more specific terms: The use of blood on the altar saves you from the penalty of bloodshed.

12. Frazer, *The Golden Bough*, pp. 227 ff.

13. Oppenheim, *Ancient Mesopotamia* (Chicago: Chicago University Press, 1964), pp. 188 ff.

14. Yerkes, *Sacrifice*, pp. 42 ff.

15. *Shulchan Aruch*, Yoreh Deah 69:1.

16. Yoma 5a. B. A. Levine (in G. B. Gray, *Sacrifice*, pp. xxvii f.) holds that originally the blood rite served two purposes. The dashing of blood against the altar in the case of ordinary sacrifices developed from blood-libations to underground deities; it was intended to assuage the wrath of YHWH, should He be displeased with His worshipers. And, in the case of purgation sacrifices, blood was sprinkled in the sanctuary and placed on the horns of the altars to neutralize the demonic forces of impurity, which threatened the Deity as well as his followers! If these theories are correct, they apply to a very early stage in the development of Israelite religion, which was long past when Leviticus acquired its present form.

17. But cf. above nn. 6, 7, 11.

18. See above n. 3.

19. Cf. p. 90.

Sex Offenses LEV. 18:1–30

1. Sifra to Lev. 22:24; *Shulchan Aruch*, Even Ha'ezer 5:11.

2. Mishnah Yad. 3:5; San. 101a. At this period Homer was also expounded allegorically by some Hellenists.

3. Gen. R. 9:7 on 1:31.

4. Mishnah Ber. 9:5.

5. L. Finkelstein, *Akiba* (reprint, Cleveland: World Publishing Co., 1962), p. 22. The Rabbis considered it proper for a man to marry at eighteen: Avot 5:21.

6. Gen. R. 34:14.

7. Ned. 20b. The choice of technique was, however, the husband's prerogative.

8. B.K. 82a.

9. Mech. to Exod. 21:10. The verse is rendered in the new JPS translation in accordance with this view as "conjugal rights." But the rendering in the margin, "ointment," is almost certainly the correct one: S. Paul, "Exod. 21:10—A Threefold Maintenance Clause," *Journal of Near Eastern Studies*, Vol. 28, pp. 48–53.

10. Lauterbach, "Talmudic-Rabbinic View on Birth Control," *Year Book of CCAR*, Vol. 37; reprinted in *Studies in Jewish Law, Custom, and Folklore* (New York: Ktav, 1970). D. M. Feldman, *Birth Control in Jewish Law* (New York: N. Y. U. Press, 1968).

11. Maimonides, *Guide of the Perplexed*, III:49, referring to Aristotle, *Nichomachean Ethics*, III:13.

12. Maimonides, *Guide*, III:49.

13. Nid. 13a.

14. Lauterbach, *Year Book of CCAR*, Vol. 37, pp. 370 f; *Studies*, pp. 210 f.

15. Ket. 8b.

16. This discussion does not include the legal aspects of Jewish marriage which in their development gave the wife an increasing measure of financial security and personal independence.

17. See Lev. 7:21 and commentary.

18. Yeb. 62b, bottom.

19. M. Mielziner, *The Jewish Law of Marriage and Divorce* (Cincinnati: Bloch, 1884), pp. 54 ff.

20. *Ibid.*, pp. 57 f.

21. Lesbianism is not mentioned in the Bible; Jewish traditional literature rarely speaks of it and apparently regards it as a lesser offense than male homosexuality.

22. See further Gen. 19:5 ff.; Judg. 19:22 ff., dealing with attempts at homosexual rape. The first instance gave the name of "sodomy" to homosexual intercourse.

23. Pritchard, *ANET*, pp. 34, 35.

24. M. Duberman, "Homosexual Literature," *New York Times Book Review*, Dec. 10, 1972, surveyed several dozen publications on the subject. The writer, a professed homosexual, concluded that our present knowledge is insufficient to support broad generalizations.

25. San. 64b.

26. Diodorus, *History*, XX:14, cited in *Interpreter's Dictionary of the Bible*, Vol. 4, p. 154a.

27. See Plutarch, "Roman Questions" 83, *Moralia* (translated by F. C. Babbit, London: Heinemann, Loeb Classical Library, 1962), Vol. 4, pp. 15 f. See also Frazer, *The Golden Bough*, pp. 584 ff.

28. *Interpreter's Dictionary of the Bible*, Vol. 4, p. 154a.

29. See the introduction to ch. 26.

30. Sifra, ed. Weiss, p. 86a.

31. Yoma 85b, Yerushalmi Shevi'it 4, 35a.

32. Sifra, p. 86b.

33. Yeb. 21a.

1. Elsewhere the Bible calls the angels "divine beings" (*elohim*)—Gen. 3:5, 32:29, and Ps. 8:6; (*bene elohim*, literally, "sons of god") Gen. 6:2; (*bene elim*) Ps. 29:1.

2. Cf. Lev. 6:11, 20. In Deut. 22:9, the words "may not be used" render the Hebrew *tikdash*. See further Hag. 2:12. In II Sam. 6:1–10, Uzzah dies when he touches the ark, even though his purpose was to keep it from falling off the cart; but in this passage no form of the word *kadosh* is used.

3. Rudolf Otto, *The Idea of the Holy* (translated by J. W. Harvey, New York: Oxford University Press, 1958).

4. Burton M. Leiser, "The Sanctity of the Profane: A Pharisaic Critique of Rudolf Otto," *Judaism*, Winter 1971, pp. 87 ff. The article is perhaps too severe.

5. Avot de-R. Nathan 27 (Schechter ed., p. 84).

6. Though the concept of the Holy Land pervades H (and indeed the entire Bible), the actual expression "holy land" appears first in Zech. 2:16.

7. Tosefta B.K. 10:15.

8. See ch. 18, n. 31; and cf. San. 74a.

9. Sab. 31a.

10. Tobit 4:15; the book is usually dated toward the end of the third century B.C.E.

11. Further references in G. F. Moore, *Judaism in the First Centuries of the Christian Era* (Cambridge: Harvard University Press, 1927–1930), Vol. 2, p. 87; Vol. 3, p. 180.

12. Cited from *Webster's New International Dictionary* (Springfield: G. & C. Merriam, 1935), p. 423a.

13. I believe this remark appears somewhere in the writings of John Dewey, but I have been unable to locate it.

14. Note especially his contemptuous treatment of a gentile woman, Matthew 15:26, to which there is nothing comparable in talmudic literature.

15. See Buber's introduction to H. Cohen, *Der Nächste* (Berlin: Schocken Verlag, 1935), p. 20, and *Gleanings*, p. 217. Ehrlich connects "as yourself" with "neighbor": Love the neighbor who is a citizen like yourself, and love the alien (v. 34) as if he were a citizen like yourself.

16. Lev. R. 24:5. For a modern investigation of the subject, see Morgenstern, "The Decalogue of the Holiness Code," *HUCA*, 1955, pp. 1 ff.

17. In Pes. 22b, the v. is taken to mean "Do not tempt another to sin," e.g., by offering wine to a nazirite.

18. JPS *Notes*, p. 217.

19. Nachmanides follows the talmudic rabbis, who explain these prohibitions as based on "the laws I established at creation" (Yerushalmi Kil. 1, 27b). In Deut. 22:9 a practical reason for not sowing two kinds of seeds together is given: When one crop was ready for harvesting and a first fruit offering would ordinarily free it for general use, the second variety—still unripe—would transmit its taboo to the entire field. But the text is not entirely clear.

20. This explanation was first offered by Winckler, cited in F. Buhl, ed., *Gesenius Hebräische und Aramäische Wörterbuch* (17th ed., Leipzig: F. C. W. Vogel, 1921), s.v. *bikkoret*, and was elaborated by E. A. Speiser in "Leviticus and the Critics," *Yehezkel Kaufmann Jubilee Volume* (edited by M. Haran, Jerusalem: Hebrew University, 1961), pp. 33 ff. Nachmanides recognized the connection between *bikkoret* and talmudic *hevker* (*hefker*), but he drew a different conclusion.

21. See p. 9.

22. Mishnah Peah 1:2.

23. *Ibid.*, 8:7; Yerushalmi Peah 21a; Bavli B.B. 8b ff.

24. Tosefta B.K. 10:38.

25. Mishnah B.M. 9:11 ff.

26. *Ibid.*, 7:1 ff.

27. M.K. 17a.

28. Arachin 16b.

29. Mishnah Kil. 8:1.

30. *Shulchan Aruch*, Yoreh Deah 295:1.

31. *Ibid.*, par. 3.

32. See n. 29.

33. *Shulchan Aruch*, Yoreh Deah 298:1.

34. Mishnah Kil. 8:1, which notes, however, that the priestly vestments contained both wool and linen. Indeed, according to Josephus (who was of priestly descent), *Antiquities*, IV:208, *shaatnez* was reserved for the priests and therefore prohibited to all others.

35. Maimonides, Hilch. Issure Biah 3:13. The problem is complicated by divergent readings in the text of the Talmud; see Hoffmann, II, pp. 47 ff. The understanding of *bikkoret* as "punishment" was adopted by many moderns, e.g., Brown-Driver-Briggs, *Lexicon*.

36. Maimonides, Hilch. Masser Sheni 9:1.
37. *Shulchan Aruch*, Yoreh Deah 181:3.
38. San. 76a.
39. Midrash Hagadol, Lev. 19:1 (p. 469).

40. Gen. R. 24:7.
41. Franz Rosenzweig, *The Star of Redemption* (translated by W. W. Hallo, New York: Holt, Rinehart, & Winston, 1970), p. 240.

Punishment of Sex Offenses LEV. 20:1–37

1. San. 76b. Though R. Ishmael and R. Akiba disagree as to the exact interpretation of the verse, both—according to the Gemara—hold that the first wife is guiltless and not to be executed.

2. Mishnah San. 6:4.
3. *Ibid.*, 7:2; Bavli 52a.
4. Mishnah San. 7:4.
5. Tifereth Israel, *ad loc.*

Laws concerning the Priests LEV. 21:1–22:33

1. Gen. 34 and 49:5–7 seem to hint that at a very early period Levi was a tribe without priestly functions.
2. Kaufmann, *The Religion of Israel*, pp. 193 ff.
3. Excavations at Arad, on the southern border of Judah, have revealed a sacrificial shrine dating from the period of the Kingdom. The inscriptions contain names associated in the Bible with the priesthood, and some scholars find in this fact evidence for the antiquity of the Priestly Code. But scholars are still divided over the interpretation of the finds at Arad.
4. It is unlikely that the Karaite movement, which began in the eighth century C.E., was a direct continuation of Sadduceeism, though the Karaites adopted many opinions previously held by the Sadducees.

5. Persons named Katz are usually of priestly descent, Katz being an acronym for *Kohen Tzedek*, "righteous priest." Similarly, many "Levites" are named Segel (in all its various spellings), the name being an acronym for *Segan Lakehunah*, "adjunct to the priesthood."
6. Hoffmann, II, pp. 85 f. Cf. Ibn Ezra and Ehrlich.
7. Brown-Driver-Briggs, *Lexicon* offers "mutilated" in the face or "too long in a limb."
8. The word "present" renders Hebrew *ta'aseh*, "make," which is frequently used of preparing a sacrifice, e.g., Lev. 9:16.
9. Sotah 3a.
10. *Shulchan Aruch*, Even Ha'ezer 6:8.
11. Mishnah San. 7:2; Tosefta San. 9:11; Bavli 52a.
12. Mishnah San. 7:4; 9:1; 11:1.
13. Yeb. 74b.

The Festival Calendar LEV. 23:1–44

1. On this term, see below, n. 28.
2. A fragmentary and puzzling version of the calendar appears in Ez. 45:10–24.
3. For a full account, the reader may consult the excellent volume, *The Jewish Festivals* by Hayyim Schauss (translated by S. Jaffe, Cincinnati: UAHC, 1938); see also Franz Rosenzweig's highly personal but arresting interpretation in *The Star of Redemption*, pp. 310 ff.; likewise in N. Glatzer, *Franz Rosenzweig* (Philadelphia: JPS, 1953), pp. 307 ff.
4. It also has the general sense of "time"; the

present translation frequently renders *beyom* (literally, "on the day of") by "when."
5. See Morgenstern, "Supplementary Studies in the Calendars of Ancient Israel," *HUCA*, Vol. 10 (1935), pp. 15 ff.
6. B. Z. Wacholder and D. B. Weisberg, "Visibility of the Moon in Cuneiform and Rabbinic Sources," *HUCA*, Vol. 42 (1971), pp. 227 ff., especially p. 239.
7. See San. 11b.
8. This is the generally accepted view, but it is possible that the mathematical calendar was not

introduced till a later time; see Wacholder and Weisberg, *HUCA*, Vol. 42, p. 239 and n. 19.

9. I Sam. 20:24–27 shows plainly that at one time the New Moon was celebrated for two days, though nothing of this appears in the laws of the Torah. There was thus some biblical basis for the statement in Yerushalmi Erub. 3, 21c, that the second day of Rosh Hashanah was instituted by the early prophets. According to some authorities, this custom was discontinued after the calendar was fixed by Hillel II, and only one day of New Year was observed in the Land of Israel until newcomers reintroduced the observance of the second day in the eleventh century. See S. Zeitlin, "The Second Day of the Holidays in the Diaspora," *Jewish Quarterly Review*, new series, Vol. 44, p. 192, citing Zerachiah Halevi.

10. Pritchard, *ANET*, p. 320.

11. Tradition removed any discrepancy by stating that Nisan 1 is the new year for kings (i.e., the second year of a reign is counted from Nisan 1, regardless of the month in which the king ascended the throne), while Tishri 1 is the starting point of civil, sabbatical, and jubilee years (Lev. 25). So Mishnah R.H. 1:1, which also mentions two other "new years": the fiscal year for the tithe of cattle (Lev. 27:32) begins on Elul 1; that for the period during which the fruit of young trees is forbidden (Lev. 19:23 ff.) on Shevat 15.

12. J. Langdon, *Babylonian Menologies* (London: Humphrey Milford, 1934), pp. 28 f. and 51.

13. E. R. Thiele, *The Mysterious Numbers of the Hebrew Kings* (Chicago: University of Chicago Press, 1951), pp. 32 ff.

14. M. Burrows, *The Dead Sea Scrolls* (New York: Viking, 1955), pp. 239 ff., and *More Light from the Dead Sea Scrolls* (1958), pp. 373 ff.

15. H. Malter, *Life and Works of Saadia Gaon* (Philadelphia: JPS, 1942), pp. 69 ff.

16. Sifra; Mishnah Men. 10:3; Bavli 65a; Josephus, *Antiquities*, III:250; Philo, *The Special Laws*, II:162.

17. Lev. 16:31 and 23:32 are no exception: they refer to Yom Kippur which is not a festival and which they describe by the unusual phrase, *Shabbat Shabbaton*; cf. also 23:24.

18. Jubilees 15:1; 44:f.

19. W. Leslau, *Falasha Anthology* (New Haven: Yale University Press, 1951), pp. xxix, xxxi.

20. For the first opinion, see the authorities cited by R. H. Charles to Jubilees 15:1; for the second,

L. Finkelstein, *The Pharisees* (third edition, Philadelphia: JPS, 1962), pp. 641 ff.

21. See L. H. Silberman, "The Sefirah Season," *HUCA*, Vol. 22 (1949), pp. 221 ff., and his article "Lag Ba'omer," *Universal Jewish Encyclopedia*, Vol. 6, pp. 508 f.

22. It is not mentioned in Ez. 45:18 ff., cf. n. 2, above.

23. Josephus, *Antiquities*, III:252, uses the name *Asartha*, the Aramaic equivalent of *'Atzeret*.

24. E.g., Pesikta de-R. Kahana, "Beyom Shemini 'Atzeret" (Buber, 193a, Mandelbaum, 430 f.).

25. Attempts have been made to prove that the identification was known already in pre-Christian times; but the arguments, though plausible, are not conclusive.

26. This name may allude to the prayers that God will remember us for life, and that He will remember the "binding" of Isaac; perhaps it also implies that we should on this day bring to mind the sins for which we seek forgiveness.

27. Arachin 12a.

28. *Chag* means "festival" but often has the special meaning "pilgrimage, pilgrim festival." (The cognate Arabic *hajj* designates the pilgrimage to Mecca.) Later Jewish usage classes Passover, Weeks, and Booths as the three *regalim* (Exod. 23:14—"three times a year," *shalosh regalim bashanah*).

29. Neh. 8:15. The present translation of 23:40 renders *peri* by "product" rather than "fruit." In biblical Hebrew, *peri* sometimes means "branches."

30. Suk. 47a–48a.

31. Men. 67b.

32. Similarly, Lev. 24:12 ff. is understood to deal with the sacrifices that accompany the *omer*, while Num. 28:16 ordains the festival sacrifices of Passover week.

33. Mishnah Men. 10:3.

34. Mishnah Bik. 1:3.

35. R. Akiba, Men. 45b.

36. Lev.R. 29:12; R.H. 29b.

37. Mishnah Suk. 4:1, 8.

38. Lev.R. 29:1, which contains the liturgical sentence cited in our text.

39. Mishnah R.H. 1:2; Bavli 16b; the sentence quoted in the text is from a famous prayer (*Union Prayer Book*, Vol. 2, pp. 256 f.), which in traditional synagogues is recited both on New Year and on the Day of Atonement.

40. R.H. 16a–b.

41. Tanch. (Buber edition) Vayera, end.

42. Lev.R. 29:4.

43. Maimonides, Hilch. Teshuvah 3:4; the English version is from *Union Prayer Book*, Vol. 2, p. 6.

44. Pesikta de-R. Kahana, "Beyom Shemini 'Atzeret" (Buber 193b, Mandelbaum 432 f.), cf. Rashi to the v.

45. *Ibid.*, "Ulekachtem" (Buber 180a–b, Mandelbaum 406f.).

46. *Ibid.* (Buber 185a, Mandelbaum 416).

47. J. D. Eisenstein, *Otzar Dinim Uminhagim* (New York: J. D. Eisenstein, 1917), p. 285a–b.

Oil, Bread, and the Blasphemer LEV. 24:1–23

1. Rashi to Exod. 25:29 derives the name from the shape of the loaves: they had many surfaces. Rashbam to Exod. 25:30 explains it as "bread fit for a great personage"; Ibn Ezra as bread set before God's presence.

2. Pritchard, *ANET*, pp. 335a, 343c.

3. The rabbis offered an excuse for this violation of the law that the sacred bread be eaten only by priests: This was an emergency measure to save the lives of David and his starving men. See Men. 95b–96a.

4. B. J. Bamberger, "Revelations of Torah after Sinai," *HUCA*, Vol. 16 (1941), pp. 104 ff.

5. I Kings 22:27 and Jer. 32:2 are cases of politically motivated detention, not punishment of criminals. The Mishnah (Git. 9:3, 5) makes provision for life imprisonment; but we have no record of a case when the law was put into practice.

6. B.K. 84a.

7. See J. K. Mikliszanski, "The Law of Retaliation and the Pentateuch," *JBL*, Vol. 66 (1947), pp. 295 ff.

8. Lev.R. 32:3.

9. Midrash Hagadol to the v.

10. J. H. Hertz, *The Pentateuch and Haftorahs* on 24:18.

Sabbatical Year and Jubilee LEV. 25:1–55

1. Some scholars believe the Deuteronomic law intended only a moratorium, with the debts becoming collectible again in the eighth year. But Jewish tradition understood it to mean outright cancellation.

2. M. Tsevat, "Inyan Shemitah etzel Har Sinai," *Chafirot Umechkarim* (edited by J. Aharoni, Jerusalem: Carta, 1973), p. 286.

3. Maimonides, Hilch. Shemitah Veyovel 3:1.

4. *Ibid.*, 9:4. The combination of the two laws seems to be indicated already in Neh. 10:32.

5. Mishnah Shevi'it 10:3 ff.

6. Josephus, *Antiquities*, XII:378 (the siege occurred between 164 and 162 B.C.E.); XIV: 202–206. See further, *Antiquities*, XIII:234 (= *War* I:60); XIV:475; XV:7.

7. Lev.R. 1:1.

8. San. 26a; Yerushalmi Shevi'it 4, 35a.

9. R. North, *Sociology of the Biblical Jubilee* (Rome: Pontefício Instituto Biblico, 1954), pp. 96 ff.

10. Lev. 25:39 ff. makes a clear distinction between the Israelite brother and the gentile slave and does not use the term *eved Ivri*, usually rendered "Hebrew slave." For the original meaning of this term, see the commentary on Genesis, p. 140, and on Exod. 21:2. But note that the *eved Ivri* is already identified as the fellow Judean in Jer. 34:9.

11. Kurt Salomon, cited in North, *Sociology*, p. 163.

12. Sifra on 25:10.

13. North (*Sociology*, pp. 109 ff.) argues that the jubilee year was really the forty-ninth—i.e., the seventh sabbatical year—and that "fiftieth year" in vv. 10–11 is an inaccuracy. This view is likewise held by other scholars mentioned by S. Loewenstamm in *Entsiklopedyah Mikra'it*, Vol. 3, p. 578. Attempting to salvage the historicity of the jubilee, they depart from the plain sense of the biblical text. The Book of Jubilees (below, n. 20) also deals in jubilee periods of 49 years. But this is hardly a support for the scholars just cited, for Jubilees is concerned with a novel calendar system, not with the jubilee law.

14. E.g., the penalty of extermination for inhabitants of a city that has lapsed into idolatry, Deut. 13:13 ff., on which see Tosefta San. 14:1; the death penalty for a juvenile delinquent, Deut. 21:18 ff., on which see Bavli San. 71a.

15. M. Tsevat, *Chafirot Umechkarim*, pp. 285 ff.

16. *Ibid.*, p. 287.

17. See above, n. 13. Even more extreme is the view of S. Zeitlin, *The Rise and Fall of the Judean State* (Philadelphia, JPS, 1962), Vol. 1, pp. 216 ff., that the "jubilee" was a period of 49 *days*—a view based on a mistranslation of Lev. 25:8. Loewenstamm, p. 580, argues from the reference to the year of release in Ez. 46:17 that the institution was ancient and well known. But we have offered reasons (above, p. XVIII) for regarding Ezekiel as roughly contemporary with and closely related to H; so he may not be referring to an ancient institution at all. (If the priestly documents are really so much older, how did the conservative priest Ezekiel venture to disagree with them on so many points?) Loewenstamm argues further that the limitation of the law in respect to urban property (vv. 29 ff.) was a concession to changing conditions, whereas utopian legislation need not be adjusted to changing realities. But one can also argue the other way: The idealistic author incorporated an actual contemporary rule into his proposals. This rule was, in fact, practiced in medieval Armenia; see below, n. 21.

18. E. Ginzberg, "Studies in the Economics of the Bible," *Jewish Quarterly Review*, new series, Vol. 22 (1932), pp. 377 ff.

19. *Ibid.*, pp. 396 ff.

20. English translation in *Apocrypha and Pseudepigrapha of the Old Testament* (Oxford: Clarendon Press, 1913), Vol. 2. See above, n. 13. Jubilees was originally written in Hebrew, and fragments of the Hebrew text have been found among the Dead Sea Scrolls. But the work as a whole survives only in an Ethiopic version made from a Greek translation of the original.

21. E. Ginzberg, "Studies," p. 399.

22. Aristotle, *Politics*, I:2.

23. Philo, *On the Special Laws*, II:69. F. H. Colson, commenting on this passage (Loeb Classics ed., Vol. 7, pp. 624 f.) remarks that this is alleged to be a Stoic doctrine, but no extant Stoic writing is so explicit on this point. Aristotle, however, does state that some persons regarded slavery as contrary to nature—a view he finds applicable only to a very limited extent (*Politics*, I:2).

24. Mech. to Exod. 21:26.

25. See above, n. 10.

26. Git. 38b.

27. *Shulchan Aruch*, Yoreh Deah 267:4. See also Maimonides, Hilch. Milah 1 and Hilch. Avadim 8:12.

28. Mech. to Exod. 15:9.

29. Orlinsky, JPS *Notes*, pp. 220 f.

30. Mishnah B.M. 4:3.

31. *Ibid.*, 5:1.

32. Henry George, "Moses: A Lecture," in *The Complete Works of Henry George* (Garden City, N. Y.: Doubleday, Page, & Co., 1911), Vol. 7, where this lecture is paged separately from the rest of the vol. Our selection is on p. 18. The lecture is available in pamphlet form through the Robert Schalkenbach Foundation, 50 E. 69th St., New York, N. Y. 10021.

33. Maimonides, Hilch. Avadim, end.

Blessings and Curses LEV. 26:1–46

1. Pritchard, *ANET*, pp. 159 ff., 163 ff. The Code of Hammurabi dates from early in his reign, which began in 1728 B.C.E. The Sumerian code is about 150 years earlier.

2. *Ibid.*, pp. 203 ff.

3. *Ibid.*, pp. 534 ff. See M. Weinfeld, *Deuteronomy and the Deuteronomic School* (Oxford: Clarendon Press, 1972), pp. 59 ff. and especially 116 ff. The Assyrian treaties are from the seventh century B.C.E. and so are approximately contemporary with Deuteronomy. The Hittite treaties cited in the previous n. are about 600 years earlier.

4. Another obvious difference is that Esar-haddon invokes a long list of gods to witness and enforce the oaths being taken. In Deuteronomy, the one God is also the Sovereign; there are only two parties, God and Israel. In all the vassal treaties, there are three parties—the suzerain, the vassal, and the gods.

5. Weinfeld, *Deuteronomy*, pp. 124 ff., finds resemblances between Lev. 26 and an Aramaic treaty of about 750 B.C.E., *ANET*, pp. 659 ff. But these similarities appear to me slight and superficial, not like the striking parallels between Deuteronomy and the Assyrian treaties.

6. See A. E. Hirshowitz, *Otzar Kol Minhagei Yeshurun* (Lvov, 1930), p. 160. See also the moving tale, "The Marked One," by J. Picard (*The Marked One and*

Other Stories, translated by L. Lewisohn, Philadelphia: JPS, 1956).

7. This kind of thinking also appears in the Bible, e.g., II Sam. 21:1–14 and ch. 24 (=I Chron. 21); II Kings 23:26.

8. See *ANET*, pp. 405 ff., 589 ff., 596–604. But comparison of these texts to the Book of Job should be viewed with caution. They offer occasional parallels of theme and language; but none of these writings displays the bold and trenchant thought of Job, let alone its literary and spiritual grandeur.

9. There is no "official" Jewish formulation on this subject. The prayer book affirms resurrection of the body, but even this was interpreted by some thinkers as merely a figure of speech for spiritual immortality. Descriptions of heaven and hell are

found in various postbiblical writings, and during the Middle Ages the belief in reincarnation was widely accepted. But the medieval dogmatists were justified in holding that retribution was one of the universally accepted doctrines of Judaism.

10. See S. Schechter, *Some Aspects of Rabbinic Theology* (New York: Macmillan, 1923), pp. 170 ff.

11. Pritchard, *ANET*, p. 539.

12. *Ibid.*, pp. 538–540.

13. Ezekiel, whose language and thought are so often similar to that of H, has very different views on this subject. He ascribes the future change of heart entirely to God's grace (Ez. 36:25 f.), not to any impulse of the people to repent; and he rejects completely the notion of the "merit of the fathers" (Ez. 18:20).

Vows, Gifts, and Dues LEV. 27:1–34

1. This noun-form is found in rabbinic but not in biblical writings; our chapter, however, uses related verbs.

2. The obscure phrase in Deut. 18:8 may have a similar intent. The later halachah permits one to

give his first-born animal to any priest he chooses: Maimonides, Hilch. Bechorot 1:15.

3. Arachin 19a.

4. Mishnah Bechorot 9:7.

Abbreviations

Biblical Books

Chron.	Chronicles	Lam.	Lamentations
Deut.	Deuteronomy	Lev.	Leviticus
Eccles.	Ecclesiastes (Koheleth)	Mal.	Malachi
Exod.	Exodus	Neh.	Nehemiah
Ez.	Ezekiel	Num.	Numbers
Gen.	Genesis	Ob.	Obadiah
Hab.	Habakkuk	Prov.	Proverbs
Hos.	Hosea	Ps.	Psalms
Isa.	Isaiah	Sam.	Samuel
Jer.	Jeremiah	Song	Song of Songs
Josh.	Joshua	Zech.	Zechariah
Judg.	Judges	Zeph.	Zephaniah

Treatises of Talmud (*Mishnah and Gemara*)

A.Z.	Avodah Zarah	M.K.	Mo'ed Katan
B.B.	Bava Batra	Men.	Menachot
B.K.	Bava Kamma	Ned.	Nedarim
B.M.	Bava Metzia	Neg.	Nega'im
Ber.	Berachot	Nid.	Niddah
Bik.	Bikkurim	Pes.	Pesachim
Erub.	Eruvin	R.H.	Rosh Hashanah
Git.	Gittin	Sab.	Shabbat
Hag.	Chagigah	San.	Sanhedrin
Hor.	Horayot	Shek.	Shekalim
Hul.	Chullin	Shev.	Shevuot
Ket.	Ketubot	Suk.	Sukkah
Kid.	Kiddushin	Ta'an.	Ta'anit
Kil.	Kilayim	Yad.	Yadayim
Mak.	Makkot	Yeb.	Yevamot
Meg.	Megillah	Zeb.	Zevachim

Other

ANET	Ancient Near Eastern Texts	(Bibliography, H)	
Cant.R.	Canticles Rabba	”	C
Gen.R.	Genesis Rabba	”	”
Hilch.	Hilchot ("laws of")	”	D
HUCA	Hebrew Union College Annual		
JBL	Journal of Biblical Literature		
JPS	Jewish Publication Society of America		
Lev.R.	Leviticus Rabba	(Bibliography, C)	
Mech.	Mechilta	”	”
R.	Rabbi		
Tanch.	Midrash Tanchuma	”	”
UAHC	Union of American Hebrew Congregations		

Bibliography

The ensuing list includes chiefly works frequently cited in this volume. For other books and articles, bibliographical information appears in the notes. An asterisk * before the name of a Hebrew work indicates that it is available in English translation.

A. Old Bible Translations

SEPTUAGINT, Greek, third-second centuries B.C.E.

TARGUM, Aramaic, attributed to Onkelos, second century C.E.

TARGUM PSEUDO-JONATHAN, Aramaic, about eighth century C.E. (ed., D. Rieder. Jerusalem, 1974).

(Both Targums include earlier material.)

B. Apocryphal and Hellenistic Sources

The Apocrypha and Pseudepigrapha of the Old Testament. Edited by R. H. Charles. Oxford: Clarendon Press, 1913. (Vol. 1 contains Tobit and I Maccabees; Vol. 2 contains Jubilees and I Enoch.)

JOSEPHUS, *The Jewish War, The Jewish Antiquities*, cited by book and paragraph. Translated by H. St. John, Thackeray, and others, Loeb Classics Library. London: Heinemann, 1930–1965.

PHILO, cited by treatise and paragraph. Translated by F. H. Colson and G. H. Whittaker, Loeb Classics Library. London: Heinemann, 1929–1932.

C. Rabbinic Sources

*MISHNAH. Cited by treatise, chapter, and paragraph.

TOSEFTA. Edited by S. Zuckermandel. Pasewalk, 1881. Cited by treatise, chapter, and paragraph.

*TALMUD BAVLI. Cited by treatise and page—same in all editions.

TALMUD YERUSHALMI. Cited by treatise, chapter, and page of first edition.

SEDER OLAM. Cited by chapter.

*AVOT DE-R. NATHAN. Edited by S. Schechter. Vienna, 1887. Cited by chapter.

*MECHILTA = Mekilta de-Rabbi Ishmael. Edited and translated by J. Z. Lauterbach. Schiff Library of Jewish Classics. Philadelphia: JPS, 1933. Cited by Bible verse.

SIFRA. Edited by I. H. Weiss. Cited by Bible verse, occasionally by page of Weiss edition. Reprint, New York: Om Publishing Co., 1946.

SIFRE TO DEUTERONOMY. Edited by L. Finkelstein. New York: Jewish Theological Seminary, 1969. Cited by section.

*GENESIS (BERESHIT) RABBA. Edited by J. Theodor and Ch. Albeck. Berlin, 1912–1936. Cited by chapter and paragraph.

*LEVITICUS (VAYIKRA) RABBA. Edited by M. Margulies. Jerusalem, 1953–1960. Cited by chapter and paragraph.

*CANTICLES (SHIR HASHIRIM) RABBA. Cited by Bible verse. Vilna, 1921.

MIDRASH TANCHUMA. Cited by name of *sidra* (Torah portion) and paragraph. Berlin, 1924.

MIDRASH TANCHUMA. Edited by S. Buber. Cited by *sidra* and paragraph. Vilna, 1913.

*PESIKTA DE-RAV KAHANA. Edited by S. Buber, Lyck, 1868. Also by B. Mandelbaum, New York: Jewish Theological Seminary, 1962. Cited by name of section and page in both editions.

PESIKTA RABBATI. Edited by M. Friedmann, Vienna, 1880. Cited by chapter and page.

MIDRASH SAMUEL. Edited by S. Buber. Cracow, 1893. Cited by chapter and paragraph.

*MIDRASH TEHILLIM (PSALMS). Edited by S. Buber. Vilna, 1891. Cited by psalm and paragraph.

*PIRKE DE-RABBI ELIEZER. Edited and translated by G. Friedlander. London: Keegan Paul, 1916. Cited by chapter.

MIDRASH HAGADOL. LEVITICUS. Edited by E. N. Rabinowitz. New York: Jewish Theological Seminary, 1932. Cited by Bible verse, occasionally by page.

D. Codes

*Maimonides (Moses ben Maimon, 1135–1204), MISHNEH TORAH. Vilna, 1900. Cited by section, chapter, and paragraph. E.g., "Maimonides, Hilch. Ma'achalot Asurot 4:6" = the section on Laws of Forbidden Foods, chapter 4, paragraph 6.

Joseph Karo (1488–1575), SHULCHAN ARUCH. Vilna, 1927. Cited by name of volume (*Orach Chayim, Yoreh Deah, Even Ha'ezer*), chapter, and paragraph.

E. Philosophic Works

*Judah Halevi (c. 1080–1145), THE KUZARI. English translation by Hartwig Hirschfeld. Reprint, New York: Schocken Books, 1964.

*Maimonides, THE GUIDE OF THE PERPLEXED. English translation by M. Friedlander. Reprint, New York: Hebrew Publishing Co., no date.

F. Hebrew Commentaries to the Torah

*Rashi (Rabbi *Shelomoh Itzchaki*), France, 1040–1105.

Rashbam (Rabbi *Shemuel ben* Meir), France, c. 1085–1158. Edited by D. Rosin. Breslau: S. Schottlaender, 1881.

Ibn Ezra (Abraham), Spain, 1092–1169.

*Nachmanides (Rabbi Moses ben Nachman), Spain, 1194–1270. Edited by C. Chavel. Jerusalem: Mosad Harav Kook, 1960.

Bachya ben Asher, Spain, died 1340. Edited by C. Chavel. Jerusalem: Mosad Harav Kook, 1967.

Samuel David Luzzatto, Italy, 1800–1865. New edition, Tel Aviv: Devir, 1965.

Arnold B. Ehrlich, Europe and United States, 1848–1920. *Mikra Kifeshuto*. Reprint, New York: Ktav, 1969.

G. Modern Commentaries

Baentsch, Bruno. *Exodus-Leviticus-Numeri*. Nowack's *Handkommentar*. Göttingen: Vandenhoeck und Ruprecht, 1903.

Elliger, K. *Leviticus*. Tübingen: Mohr, 1966.

Hertz, Joseph H., ed. *The Pentateuch and Haftorahs*. Oxford: Oxford University Press, 1929–1936.

Hoffmann, David. *Das Buch Leviticus*, 2 vols. Berlin: M. Poppelauer, 1905. Usually cited by vol. and page.

[JPS Notes] Orlinsky, H. M., ed. *Notes on the New Translation of the Torah*. Philadelphia: JPS, 1969.

Kalisch, M. M. *A Critical and Historical Commentary on the Old Testament: Leviticus*, 2 vols. London: Longmans Green, 1867–1872.

Noth, M. *Leviticus*, translated by J. E. Anderson. Philadelphia: Westminster Press, 1965.

Snaith, N. H. *Leviticus and Numbers*, The Century Bible, new edition. London: Nelson, 1967.

H. Reference Works

Brown, F.; Driver, S. R.; Briggs, C. A. *A Hebrew and English Lexicon of the Old Testament*. Boston: Houghton Mifflin, 1907.

The Catholic Encyclopedia, 15 vols. New York: The Encyclopedia Press, 1913.

Entsiklopedyah Mikra'it (Hebrew). Jerusalem: Mosad Bialik, 1950–1976.

Ginzberg, L. *The Legends of the Jews*, 7 vols. Philadelphia: JPS, 1909–1938.

The Interpreter's Dictionary of the Bible, 4 vols. New York: Abingdon Press, 1962.

Kimchi, David. France, c. 1162–1230, *Sefer Hashorashim*. Berlin: Bethge, 1847.

[ANET] Pritchard, James B., ed. *Ancient Near Eastern Texts*, 3rd ed. Princeton: Princeton University Press, 1969.

The Universal Jewish Encyclopedia, 12 vols. New York: Ktav, 1939–1943.

I. Other Books Frequently Cited

Frazer, James G. *The Golden Bough.* One-volume edition. New York: Macmillan, 1922.

Kaufmann, Yehezkel. *The Religion of Israel.* Abridged English translation by M. Greenberg. Chicago: University of Chicago Press, 1966.

Rosenzweig, F. *The Star of Redemption.* Translated by W. W. Hallo. New York: Holt, Rinehart, and Winston, 1970.

Yerkes, Royden K. *Sacrifice in Greek and Roman Religions and in Early Judaism.* New York: Allenson, 1952.

הפטרות

HAFTAROT

Haftarah (meaning "conclusion"; plural, *Haftarot*) was originally a special reading from the Prophets which followed the weekly Torah reading and concluded the service. In the following, several *Haftarot* are provided for each Sabbath when Leviticus is read. The first selection for each Sidra is the traditional one; the others are derived from the readings suggested in *Gates of Understanding* (CCAR and UAHC, 1977), pp. 276–277.

The translations of Job and Nehemiah are taken from *The Holy Scriptures*. Philadelphia: Jewish Publication Society, 1917. Those from Psalms are taken from *The Book of Psalms: A New Translation*. Philadelphia: Jewish Publication Society, 1972. All the others are from *The Prophets: A New Translation*. Philadelphia: The Jewish Publication Society, 1978.

וִיקְרָא

FIRST SELECTION

Isaiah

43 : 21 — 44 : 23

Chapter 43

מג

21] The people I formed for Myself
That they might declare My praise.

‏[21 עַם־זוּ יָצַרְתִּי לִי
תְּהִלָּתִי יְסַפֵּרוּ:

22] But you have not worshiped Me, O Jacob,
That you should be weary of Me, O Israel.

‏[22 וְלֹא אֹתִי קָרָאתָ יַעֲקֹב
כִּי יָגַעְתָּ בִּי יִשְׂרָאֵל:

23] You have not brought Me your sheep for burnt
   offerings,
Nor honored Me with your sacrifices.
I have not burdened you with meal offerings,
Nor wearied you about frankincense.

‏[23 לֹא הֵבֵיאתָ לִי שֵׂה עֹלֹתֶיךָ
וּזְבָחֶיךָ לֹא כִבַּדְתָּנִי
לֹא הֶעֱבַדְתִּיךָ בְּמִנְחָה
וְלֹא הוֹגַעְתִּיךָ בִּלְבוֹנָה:

24] You have not bought Me fragrant reed with
   money,
Nor sated Me with the fat of your sacrifices.
Instead, you have burdened Me with your sins,
You have wearied Me with your iniquities.

‏[24 לֹא קָנִיתָ לִּי בַכֶּסֶף קָנֶה
וְחֵלֶב זְבָחֶיךָ לֹא הִרְוִיתָנִי
אַךְ הֶעֱבַדְתַּנִי בְּחַטֹּאותֶיךָ
הוֹגַעְתַּנִי בַּעֲוֹנֹתֶיךָ:

25] It is I, I who—for My own sake*f*—
Wipe your transgressions away
And remember your sins no more.

‏[25 אָנֹכִי אָנֹכִי הוּא מֹחֶה
פְשָׁעֶיךָ לְמַעֲנִי
וְחַטֹּאתֶיךָ לֹא אֶזְכֹּר:

26] Help me remember!
Let us join in argument,
Tell your version,
That you may be vindicated.

‏[26 הַזְכִּירֵנִי
נִשָּׁפְטָה יָחַד
סַפֵּר אַתָּה
לְמַעַן תִּצְדָּק:

---

f I.e., in order to put an end to the profanation of My holy name; cf. 48.9–11

349

27] Your earliest ancestor sinned,
And your spokesmen transgressed against Me.

28] So I profaned ᵍ⁻the holy princes;⁻ᵍ
I abandoned Jacob to proscriptionʰ
And Israel to mockery.

Chapter 44

מד

1] But hear, now, O Jacob My servant,
Israel whom I have chosen!

2] Thus said the LORD, your Maker,
Your Creator who has helped you since birth:
Fear not, My servant Jacob,
Jeshurunᵃ whom I have chosen,

3] Even as I pour water on thirsty soil,
And rain upon dry ground,
So will I pour My spirit on your offspring,
My blessing upon your posterity.

4] And they shall sprout likeᵇ grass,
Like willows by watercourses.

5] One shall say, "I am the LORD's,"
Another shall use the name "Jacob,"
Another shall mark his arm "the LORD's,"ᶜ
And adopt the name "Israel."

6] Thus said the LORD, the King of Israel,
Their Redeemer, the LORD of Hosts:

27] אָבִיךָ הָרִאשׁוֹן חָטָא
וּמְלִיצֶיךָ פָּשְׁעוּ בִי:

28] וַאֲחַלֵּל שָׂרֵי קֹדֶשׁ
וְאֶתְּנָה לַחֵרֶם יַעֲקֹב
וְיִשְׂרָאֵל לְגִדּוּפִים:

מד

1] וְעַתָּה שְׁמַע יַעֲקֹב עַבְדִּי
וְיִשְׂרָאֵל בָּחַרְתִּי בוֹ:

2] כֹּה אָמַר יְהוָה עֹשֶׂךָ
וְיֹצֶרְךָ מִבֶּטֶן יַעְזְרֶךָ
אַל תִּירָא עַבְדִּי יַעֲקֹב
וִישֻׁרוּן בָּחַרְתִּי בוֹ:

3] כִּי אֶצָּק־מַיִם עַל צָמֵא
וְנֹזְלִים עַל יַבָּשָׁה
אֶצֹּק רוּחִי עַל זַרְעֶךָ
וּבִרְכָתִי עַל צֶאֱצָאֶיךָ:

4] וְצָמְחוּ בְּבֵין חָצִיר
כַּעֲרָבִים עַל יִבְלֵי־מָיִם:

5] זֶה יֹאמַר לַיהוָה אָנִי
וְזֶה יִקְרָא בְשֵׁם יַעֲקֹב
וְזֶה יִכְתֹּב יָדוֹ לַיהוָה
וּבְשֵׁם יִשְׂרָאֵל יְכַנֶּה:

6] כֹּה אָמַר יְהוָה מֶלֶךְ יִשְׂרָאֵל
וְגֹאֲלוֹ יְהוָה צְבָאוֹת:

ᵍ⁻ᵍ *Emendation yields "My holy name"; see preceding note*
ʰ *Emendation yields "insult"*

ᵃ *A name for Israel; see note on Num. 23.10; cf. Deut. 32.15; 33.5, 26*
ᵇ *Lit. "in among"*
ᶜ *It was customary to mark a slave with the owner's name*

I am the first and I am the last,
And there is no god but Me.

7] ^dWho like Me can announce,
Can foretell it—and match Me thereby?
Even as I told the future to an ancient people,
So let him foretell coming events to them.

8] Do not be frightened, do not be shaken!
Have I not from of old predicted to you?
I foretold, and you are My witnesses.
Is there any god, then, but Me?
"There is no other rock; I know none!"

9] The makers of idols
All work to no purpose;
And the things they treasure
Can do no good,
As they themselves can testify.
They neither look nor think,
And so they shall be shamed.

10] Who would fashion a god
Or cast a statue
That can do no good?

11] Lo, all its adherents shall be shamed;
They are craftsmen, are merely human.
Let them all assemble and stand up!
They shall be cowed, and they shall be shamed.

12] ^eThe craftsman in iron, with his tools,
Works it^f over charcoal

אֲנִי רִאשׁוֹן וַאֲנִי אַחֲרוֹן

וּמִבַּלְעָדַי אֵין אֱלֹהִים:

7] וּמִי כָמוֹנִי יִקְרָא

וְיַגִּידֶהָ וְיַעְרְכֶהָ לִי

מִשּׂוּמִי עַם עוֹלָם וְאֹתִיּוֹת

וַאֲשֶׁר תָּבֹאנָה יַגִּידוּ לָמוֹ:

8] אַל תִּפְחֲדוּ וְאַל תִּרְהוּ

הֲלֹא מֵאָז הִשְׁמַעְתִּיךָ

וְהִגַּדְתִּי וְאַתֶּם עֵדָי

הֲיֵשׁ אֱלוֹהַּ מִבַּלְעָדַי

וְאֵין צוּר בַּל יָדָעְתִּי:

9] יֹצְרֵי פֶסֶל

כֻּלָּם תֹּהוּ

וַחֲמוּדֵיהֶם

בַּל יוֹעִילוּ

וְעֵדֵיהֶם הֵמָּה

בַּל יִרְאוּ וּבַל יֵדְעוּ

לְמַעַן יֵבֹשׁוּ:

10] מִי יָצַר אֵל

וּפֶסֶל נָסָךְ

לְבִלְתִּי הוֹעִיל:

11] הֵן כָּל־חֲבֵרָיו יֵבֹשׁוּ

וְחָרָשִׁים הֵמָּה מֵאָדָם

יִתְקַבְּצוּ כֻלָּם יַעֲמֹדוּ

יִפְחֲדוּ יֵבֹשׁוּ יָחַד:

12] חָרַשׁ בַּרְזֶל מַעֲצָד

וּפָעַל בַּפֶּחָם

^d Meaning of verse uncertain

^e The meaning of parts of vv. 12–13 is uncertain

^f I.e., the image he is making

And fashions it by hammering,
Working with the strength of his arm.
Should he go hungry, his strength would ebb;
Should he drink no water, he would grow faint.

13] The craftsman in wood measures with a line
And marks out a shape with a stylus;
He forms it with scraping tools,
Marking it out with a compass.
He gives it a human form,
The beauty of a man, to dwell in a shrine.

14] For his use he cuts down cedars;
He chooses plane trees and oaks.
He sets aside trees of the forest;
Or plants firs, and the rain makes them grow.

15] All this serves man for fuel:
He takes some to warm himself,
And he builds a fire and bakes bread.
He also makes a god of it and worships it,
Fashions an idol and bows down to it!

16] Part of it he burns in a fire:
On that part he roasts⁹ meat,
He eats⁹ the roast and is sated;
He also warms himself and cries, "Ah,
I am warm! I can feel ʰ the heat!"

17] Of the rest he makes a god—his own carving!
He bows down to it, worships it;
He prays to it and cries,
"Save me, for you are my god!"

וּבַמַּקָּבוֹת יִצְּרֵהוּ

וַיִּפְעָלֵהוּ בִּזְרוֹעַ כֹּחוֹ

גַּם רָעֵב וְאֵין כֹּחַ

לֹא־שָׁתָה מַיִם וַיִּיעָף׃

13] חָרַשׁ עֵצִים נָטָה קָו

יְתָאֲרֵהוּ בַּשֶּׂרֶד

יַעֲשֵׂהוּ בַּמַּקְצֻעוֹת

וּבַמְּחוּגָה יְתָאֳרֵהוּ

וַיַּעֲשֵׂהוּ כְּתַבְנִית אִישׁ

כְּתִפְאֶרֶת אָדָם לָשֶׁבֶת בָּיִת׃

14] לִכְרָת־לוֹ אֲרָזִים

וַיִּקַּח תִּרְזָה וְאַלּוֹן

וַיְאַמֶּץ־לוֹ בַּעֲצֵי־יָעַר

נָטַע אֹרֶן וְגֶשֶׁם יְגַדֵּל׃

15] וְהָיָה לְאָדָם לְבָעֵר

וַיִּקַּח מֵהֶם וַיָּחָם

אַף־יַשִּׂיק וְאָפָה לָחֶם

אַף־יִפְעַל־אֵל וַיִּשְׁתָּחוּ

עָשָׂהוּ פֶסֶל וַיִּסְגָּד־לָמוֹ׃

16] חֶצְיוֹ שָׂרַף בְּמוֹ־אֵשׁ

עַל־חֶצְיוֹ בָּשָׂר יֹאכֵל

יִצְלֶה צָלִי וְיִשְׂבָּע

אַף־יָחֹם וְיֹאמַר הֶאָח

חַמּוֹתִי רָאִיתִי אוּר׃

17] וּשְׁאֵרִיתוֹ לְאֵל עָשָׂה לְפִסְלוֹ

יִסְגָּד־לוֹ וְיִשְׁתָּחוּ

וְיִתְפַּלֵּל אֵלָיו וְיֹאמַר

הַצִּילֵנִי כִּי אֵלִי אָתָּה׃

---

⁹ *Transposing the Heb. verbs for clarity*   ʰ Lit. "*see*"

18] They have no wit or judgment:
Their eyes are besmeared, and they see not;
Their minds, and they cannot think.

19] They do not give thought,
They lack the wit and judgment to say:
"Part of it I burned in a fire;
I also baked bread on the coals,
I roasted meat and ate it—
Should I make the rest an abhorrence?
Should I bow to a block of wood?"

20] He pursues ashes!^i
A deluded mind has led him astray,
Ane he cannot save himself;
He never says to himself,
"The thing in my hand is a fraud!"

21] Remember these things, O Jacob,
For you, O Israel, are My servant:
I fashioned you, you are My servant—
O Israel, never forget Me.^j

22] I wipe away your sins like a cloud,
Your transgressions like mist—
Come back to Me, for I redeem you.

23] Shout, O heavens, for the LORD has acted;
Shout aloud, O depths of the earth!
Shout for joy, O mountains,
O forests with all your trees!
For the LORD has redeemed Jacob,
Has glorified Himself through Israel.

18]לֹא יָדְעוּ וְלֹא יָבִינוּ
כִּי טַח מֵרְאוֹת עֵינֵיהֶם
מֵהַשְׂכִּיל לִבֹּתָם:

19]וְלֹא יָשִׁיב אֶל לִבּוֹ
וְלֹא דַעַת וְלֹא תְבוּנָה לֵאמֹר
חֶצְיוֹ שָׂרַפְתִּי בְמוֹ־אֵשׁ
וְאַף אָפִיתִי עַל גֶּחָלָיו לֶחֶם
אֶצְלֶה בָשָׂר וְאֹכֵל
וְיִתְרוֹ לְתוֹעֵבָה אֶעֱשֶׂה
לְבוּל עֵץ אֶסְגּוֹד:

20]רֹעֶה אֵפֶר
לֵב הוּתַל הִטָּהוּ
וְלֹא יַצִּיל אֶת־נַפְשׁוֹ
וְלֹא יֹאמַר
הֲלוֹא שֶׁקֶר בִּימִינִי:

21]זְכָר־אֵלֶּה יַעֲקֹב
וְיִשְׂרָאֵל כִּי עַבְדִּי־אָתָּה
יְצַרְתִּיךָ עֶבֶד לִי אַתָּה
יִשְׂרָאֵל לֹא תִנָּשֵׁנִי:

22]מָחִיתִי כָעָב פְּשָׁעֶיךָ
וְכֶעָנָן חַטֹּאותֶיךָ
שׁוּבָה אֵלַי כִּי גְאַלְתִּיךָ:

23]רָנּוּ שָׁמַיִם כִּי עָשָׂה יְהוָה
הָרִיעוּ תַּחְתִּיּוֹת אָרֶץ
פִּצְחוּ הָרִים רִנָּה
יַעַר וְכָל־עֵץ בּוֹ
כִּי גָאַל יְהוָה יַעֲקֹב
וּבְיִשְׂרָאֵל יִתְפָּאָר:

---

^i Lit. "He shepherds ashes"   ^j Emendation yields "them," these things

Isaiah

1 : 10 – 20, 27

Chapter 1

א

10] Hear the word of the LORD,   [10 שִׁמְעוּ דְבַר־יְהֹוָה

You chieftains of Sodom;   קְצִינֵי סְדֹם

Give ear to our God's instruction,   הַאֲזִינוּ תּוֹרַת אֱלֹהֵינוּ

You folk of Gomorrah!   עַם עֲמֹרָה:

11] "What need have I of all your sacrifices?"   [11 לָמָּה־לִּי רֹב־זִבְחֵיכֶם

Says the LORD.   יֹאמַר יְהֹוָה

"I am sated with burnt offerings of rams,   שָׂבַעְתִּי עֹלוֹת אֵילִים

And suet of fatlings,   וְחֵלֶב מְרִיאִים

And blood of bulls;   וְדַם פָּרִים

And I have no delight   וּכְבָשִׂים וְעַתּוּדִים

In lambs and he-goats.   לֹא חָפָצְתִּי:

12] That you come to appear before Me—   [12 כִּי תָבֹאוּ לֵרָאוֹת פָּנָי

Who asked that ᶜ‾of you?   מִי בִקֵּשׁ זֹאת מִיֶּדְכֶם

Trample My courts   רְמֹס חֲצֵרָי:

13]   no more;   [13 לֹא תוֹסִיפוּ

Bringing oblations is futile,‾ᶜ   הָבִיא מִנְחַת־שָׁוְא

Incense is offensive to Me.   קְטֹרֶת תּוֹעֵבָה הִיא לִי

New moon and sabbath,   חֹדֶשׁ וְשַׁבָּת

Proclaiming of solemnities,   קְרֹא מִקְרָא

ᵈ‾Assemblies with iniquity,‾ᵈ   לֹא־אוּכַל אָוֶן וַעֲצָרָה:

I cannot abide.

ᶜ‾ᶜ *Others "of you, to trample My courts? | 13] Bring no more vain oblations"*
ᵈ‾ᵈ *Septuagint "Fast and assembly"; cf. Joel 1.14*

14] Your new moons and fixed seasons
Fill Me with loathing;
They are become a burden to Me,
I cannot endure them.

15] And when you lift up your hands,
I will turn My eyes away from you;
Though you pray at length,
I will not listen.
Your hands are stained with crime—

16] Wash yourselves clean;
Put your evil doings
Away from My sight.
Cease to do evil;

17] Learn to do good.
Devote yourselves to justice;
ᵉ‑Aid the wronged.‑ᵉ
Uphold the rights of the orphan;
Defend the cause of the widow.

18] "Come, ᵉ‑let us reach an understanding‑ᵉ
            —says the Lord.
Be your sins like crimson,
They can turn snow-white;
Be they red as dyed wool,
They can become like fleece."

19] If, then, you agree and give heed,
You will eat the good things of the earth;

20] But if you refuse and disobey,

ᵉ‑ᵉ Meaning of Heb. uncertain

חָדְשֵׁיכֶם וּמוֹעֲדֵיכֶם [14
שָׂנְאָה נַפְשִׁי
הָיוּ עָלַי לָטֹרַח
נִלְאֵיתִי נְשֹׂא:

וּבְפָרִשְׂכֶם כַּפֵּיכֶם [15
אַעְלִים עֵינַי מִכֶּם
גַּם כִּי תַרְבּוּ תְפִלָּה
אֵינֶנִּי שֹׁמֵעַ
יְדֵיכֶם דָּמִים מָלֵאוּ:

רַחֲצוּ הִזַּכּוּ [16
הָסִירוּ רֹעַ מַעַלְלֵיכֶם
מִנֶּגֶד עֵינָי
חִדְלוּ הָרֵעַ:

לִמְדוּ הֵיטֵב [17
דִּרְשׁוּ מִשְׁפָּט
אַשְּׁרוּ חָמוֹץ
שִׁפְטוּ יָתוֹם
רִיבוּ אַלְמָנָה:

לְכוּ־נָא וְנִוָּכְחָה [18
יֹאמַר יְהֹוָה
אִם יִהְיוּ חֲטָאֵיכֶם כַּשָּׁנִים
כַּשֶּׁלֶג יַלְבִּינוּ
אִם יַאְדִּימוּ כַתּוֹלָע
כַּצֶּמֶר יִהְיוּ:

אִם תֹּאבוּ וּשְׁמַעְתֶּם [19
טוּב הָאָרֶץ תֹּאכֵלוּ:

וְאִם תְּמָאֲנוּ וּמְרִיתֶם [20

*ꞟ*You will be devoured [by] the sword.*ꞟ*—
For it was the LORD who spoke.

. . .

חֶרֶב תְּאֻכְּלוּ
כִּי פִּי יְהוָה דִּבֵּר:

. . .

27] *ⁱ*Zion shall be saved in the judgment;
Her repentant ones, in the retribution.*ⁱ*

27] צִיּוֹן בְּמִשְׁפָּט תִּפָּדֶה
וְשָׁבֶיהָ בִּצְדָקָה:

THIRD SELECTION

Psalms

50 : 1-23

Psalm 50

נ

1] A psalm of Asaph.
*ᵃ*God, the LORD God*⁻ᵃ* spoke
and summoned the world from east to west.

1] מִזְמוֹר לְאָסָף
אֵל אֱלֹהִים יְהוָה דִּבֵּר
וַיִּקְרָא־אָרֶץ מִמִּזְרַח־שֶׁמֶשׁ עַד מְבֹאוֹ:

2] From Zion, perfect in beauty,
God appeared

2] מִצִּיּוֹן מִכְלַל־יֹפִי
אֱלֹהִים הוֹפִיעַ:

3] —let our God come and not fail to act!
Devouring fire preceded Him;
it stormed around Him fiercely.

3] יָבֹא אֱלֹהֵינוּ וְאַל יֶחֱרַשׁ
אֵשׁ לְפָנָיו תֹּאכֵל
וּסְבִיבָיו נִשְׂעֲרָה מְאֹד:

4] He summoned the heavens above,
and the earth, for the trial of His people.

4] יִקְרָא אֶל הַשָּׁמַיִם מֵעָל
וְאֶל הָאָרֶץ לָדִין עַמּוֹ:

5] "Bring in My devotees,
who made a covenant with Me over sacrifice!"

5] אִסְפוּ־לִי חֲסִידָי
כֹּרְתֵי בְרִיתִי עֲלֵי־זָבַח:

6] Then the heavens proclaimed His righteousness,
for He is a God who judges.   *Selah*

6] וַיַּגִּידוּ שָׁמַיִם צִדְקוֹ
כִּי אֱלֹהִים שֹׁפֵט הוּא סֶלָה:

ꞟ-ꞟ Or "You will be fed the sword"
ⁱ Others "Zion shall be saved by justice, | Her repentant ones by righteousness"
ʲ For this meaning cf. 5.16; 10.22

ᵃ⁻ᵃ Heb. 'El 'Elohim YHWH

356

7] "Pay heed, My people, and I will speak,
O Israel, and I will arraign you.
I am God, your God.

8] I censure you not for your sacrifices,
and your burnt offerings, made to Me daily;

9] I claim no bull from your estate,
no he-goats from your pens.

10] For Mine is every animal of the forest,
the beasts on [b-]a thousand mountains.[-b]

11] I know every bird of the mountains,
the creatures of the field are subject to Me.

12] Were I hungry, I would not tell you,
for Mine is the world and all it holds.

13] Do I eat the flesh of bulls,
or drink the blood of he-goats?

14] Sacrifice a thank offering to God,
and pay your vows to the Most High.

15] Call upon Me in time of trouble;
I will rescue you, and you shall honor Me."

16] And to the wicked, God said,
"Who are you to recite My laws,
and mouth the terms of My covenant,

17] seeing that you spurn My discipline,
and brush My words aside?

18] When you see a thief, you fall in with him,
and throw in your lot with adulterers;

19] you devote your mouth to evil,
and yoke your tongue to deceit;

[7 שִׁמְעָה עַמִּי וַאֲדַבֵּרָה

יִשְׂרָאֵל וְאָעִידָה בָּךְ

אֱלֹהִים אֱלֹהֶיךָ אָנֹכִי:

8] לֹא עַל זְבָחֶיךָ אוֹכִיחֶךָ

וְעוֹלֹתֶיךָ לְנֶגְדִּי תָמִיד:

9] לֹא אֶקַּח מִבֵּיתְךָ פָר

מִמִּכְלְאֹתֶיךָ עַתּוּדִים:

10] כִּי לִי כָל־חַיְתוֹ־יָעַר

בְּהֵמוֹת בְּהַרְרֵי־אָלֶף:

11] יָדַעְתִּי כָּל־עוֹף הָרִים

וְזִיז שָׂדַי עִמָּדִי:

12] אִם אֶרְעַב לֹא־אֹמַר לָךְ

כִּי־לִי תֵבֵל וּמְלֹאָהּ:

13] הַאוֹכַל בְּשַׂר אַבִּירִים

וְדַם עַתּוּדִים אֶשְׁתֶּה:

14] זְבַח לֵאלֹהִים תּוֹדָה

וְשַׁלֵּם לְעֶלְיוֹן נְדָרֶיךָ:

15] וּקְרָאֵנִי בְּיוֹם צָרָה

אֲחַלֶּצְךָ וּתְכַבְּדֵנִי:

16] וְלָרָשָׁע אָמַר אֱלֹהִים

מַה־לְּךָ לְסַפֵּר חֻקָּי

וַתִּשָּׂא בְרִיתִי עֲלֵי־פִיךָ:

17] וְאַתָּה שָׂנֵאתָ מוּסָר

וַתַּשְׁלֵךְ דְּבָרַי אַחֲרֶיךָ:

18] אִם רָאִיתָ גַנָּב וַתִּרֶץ עִמּוֹ

וְעִם מְנָאֲפִים חֶלְקֶךָ:

19] פִּיךָ שָׁלַחְתָּ בְרָעָה

וּלְשׁוֹנְךָ תַּצְמִיד מִרְמָה:

[b-b] Meaning of Heb. uncertain

357

20] you are busy maligning your brother,
defaming the son of your mother.

21] If I failed to act when you did these things,
you would fancy that I were like you;
so I censure you and confront you with charges.

22] Mark this, you who are unmindful of God,
lest I tear you apart and no one save you.

23] He who sacrifices a thank offering honors Me,
*b-*and to him who improves his way*-b*
I will show the salvation of God."

תֵּשֵׁב בְּאָחִיךָ תְדַבֵּר [20
בְּבֶן־אִמְּךָ תִּתֶּן־דֹּפִי:
אֵלֶּה עָשִׂיתָ וְהֶחֱרַשְׁתִּי [21
דִּמִּיתָ הֱיוֹת־אֶהְיֶה כָמוֹךָ
אוֹכִיחֲךָ וְאֶעֶרְכָה לְעֵינֶיךָ:
בִּינוּ־נָא זֹאת שֹׁכְחֵי אֱלוֹהַּ [22
פֶּן־אֶטְרֹף וְאֵין מַצִּיל:
זֹבֵחַ תּוֹדָה יְכַבְּדָנְנִי [23
וְשָׂם דֶּרֶךְ
אַרְאֶנּוּ בְּיֵשַׁע אֱלֹהִים:

---

b-b Meaning of Heb. uncertain

צו

FIRST SELECTION

Jeremiah

7 : 21 – 8 : 3; 9 : 22 - 23

ז

Chapter 7

21] Thus said the LORD of Hosts, the God of Israel: Add your burnt offerings to your other sacrifices and eat the meat!

22] For when I freed your fathers from the land of Egypt, I did not speak with them or command them concerning burnt offerings or sacrifice.

23] But this is what I commanded them: Do My bidding, that I may be your God and you may be My people; walk only in the way that I enjoin upon you, that it may go well with you.

24] Yet they did not listen or give ear; they followed their own counsels, the willfulness of their evil hearts. They have gone backward, not forward,

25] from the day your fathers left the land of Egypt until today. And though I kept sending all My servants, the prophets, to them[d] daily and persistently,

26] they would not listen to Me or give ear. They stiffened their necks, they acted worse than their fathers.

27] You shall say all these things to them, but they will not listen to you; you shall call to them, but they will not respond to you.

28] Then say to them: This is the nation that

[21] כֹּה אָמַר יְהֹוָה צְבָאוֹת אֱלֹהֵי יִשְׂרָאֵל
עֹלוֹתֵיכֶם סְפוּ עַל זִבְחֵיכֶם וְאִכְלוּ בָשָׂר:
[22] כִּי לֹא דִבַּרְתִּי אֶת־אֲבוֹתֵיכֶם וְלֹא צִוִּיתִים
בְּיוֹם הוֹצִיאִי אוֹתָם מֵאֶרֶץ מִצְרָיִם עַל דִּבְרֵי
עוֹלָה וָזָבַח: [23] כִּי אִם אֶת־הַדָּבָר הַזֶּה
צִוִּיתִי אוֹתָם לֵאמֹר שִׁמְעוּ בְקוֹלִי וְהָיִיתִי
לָכֶם לֵאלֹהִים וְאַתֶּם תִּהְיוּ־לִי לְעָם וַהֲלַכְתֶּם
בְּכָל־הַדֶּרֶךְ אֲשֶׁר אֲצַוֶּה אֶתְכֶם לְמַעַן יִיטַב
לָכֶם: [24] וְלֹא שָׁמְעוּ וְלֹא הִטּוּ אֶת־אָזְנָם
וַיֵּלְכוּ בְּמֹעֵצוֹת בִּשְׁרִרוּת לִבָּם הָרָע וַיִּהְיוּ
לְאָחוֹר וְלֹא לְפָנִים: [25] לְמִן הַיּוֹם אֲשֶׁר
יָצְאוּ אֲבוֹתֵיכֶם מֵאֶרֶץ מִצְרַיִם עַד הַיּוֹם
הַזֶּה וָאֶשְׁלַח אֲלֵיכֶם אֶת־כָּל־עֲבָדַי הַנְּבִיאִים
יוֹם הַשְׁכֵּם וְשָׁלֹחַ: [26] וְלוֹא שָׁמְעוּ אֵלַי וְלֹא
הִטּוּ אֶת־אָזְנָם וַיַּקְשׁוּ אֶת־עָרְפָּם הֵרֵעוּ
מֵאֲבוֹתָם:
[27] וְדִבַּרְתָּ אֲלֵיהֶם אֶת־כָּל־הַדְּבָרִים הָאֵלֶּה
וְלֹא יִשְׁמְעוּ אֵלֶיךָ וְקָרָאתָ אֲלֵיהֶם וְלֹא יַעֲנוּכָה:
[28] וְאָמַרְתָּ אֲלֵיהֶם זֶה הַגּוֹי אֲשֶׁר לוֹא שָׁמְעוּ

[d] Heb. "you"

359

would not obey the LORD their God, that would not accept rebuke. Faithfulness has perished, vanished from their mouths.

29] Shear your locks and cast them away,
Take up a lament on the heights,
For the LORD has spurned and cast off
The brood that provoked His wrath.

30] For the people of Judah have done what displeases Me—declares the LORD. They have set up their abominations in the House which is called by My name, and they have defiled it.
31] And they have built the shrines of Topheth in the Valley of Ben-hinnom to burn their sons and daughters in fire—which I never commanded, which never came to My mind.

32] Assuredly, a time is coming—declares the LORD—when men shall no longer speak of Topheth or the Valley of Ben-hinnom, but of the Valley of Slaughter; and they shall bury in Topheth until no room is left.

33] The carcasses of this people shall be food for the birds of the sky and the beasts of the earth, with none to frighten them off.

34] And I will silence in the towns of Judah and the streets of Jerusalem the sound of mirth and gladness, the voice of bridegroom and bride. For the whole land shall fall to ruin.

Chapter 8

1] At that time—declares the LORD—the bones of the kings of Judah, of its officers, of the priests, of the prophets, and of the inhabitants of Jerusalem shall be taken out of their graves

2] and exposed to the sun, the moon, and all the host of heaven which they loved and served and followed, to which they turned and bowed down. They shall not be gathered for reburial; they shall become dung upon the face of the earth.
3] And death shall be preferable to life for all

בְּקוֹל יְהֹוָה אֱלֹהָיו וְלֹא לָקְחוּ מוּסָר אָבְדָה הָאֱמוּנָה וְנִכְרְתָה מִפִּיהֶם:

29] גָּזִּי נִזְרֵךְ וְהַשְׁלִיכִי
וּשְׂאִי עַל שְׁפָיִם קִינָה
כִּי מָאַס יְהֹוָה וַיִּטֹּשׁ
אֶת־דּוֹר עֶבְרָתוֹ:

30] כִּי עָשׂוּ בְנֵי יְהוּדָה הָרַע בְּעֵינַי נְאֻם יְהֹוָה שָׂמוּ שִׁקּוּצֵיהֶם בַּבַּיִת אֲשֶׁר נִקְרָא שְׁמִי עָלָיו לְטַמְּאוֹ: 31] וּבָנוּ בָּמוֹת הַתֹּפֶת אֲשֶׁר בְּגֵיא בֶן הִנֹּם לִשְׂרֹף אֶת־בְּנֵיהֶם וְאֶת־בְּנֹתֵיהֶם בָּאֵשׁ אֲשֶׁר לֹא צִוִּיתִי וְלֹא עָלְתָה עַל לִבִּי:

32] לָכֵן הִנֵּה יָמִים בָּאִים נְאֻם יְהֹוָה וְלֹא יֵאָמֵר עוֹד הַתֹּפֶת וְגֵיא בֶן הִנֹּם כִּי אִם־גֵּיא הַהֲרֵגָה וְקָבְרוּ בְתֹפֶת מֵאֵין מָקוֹם:

33] וְהָיְתָה נִבְלַת הָעָם הַזֶּה לְמַאֲכָל לְעוֹף הַשָּׁמַיִם וּלְבֶהֱמַת הָאָרֶץ וְאֵין מַחֲרִיד:

34] וְהִשְׁבַּתִּי מֵעָרֵי יְהוּדָה וּמֵחֻצוֹת יְרוּשָׁלַיִם קוֹל שָׂשׂוֹן וְקוֹל שִׂמְחָה קוֹל חָתָן וְקוֹל כַּלָּה כִּי לְחָרְבָּה תִּהְיֶה הָאָרֶץ:

ח

1] בָּעֵת הַהִיא נְאֻם יְהֹוָה יוֹצִיאוּ אֶת־עַצְמוֹת מַלְכֵי יְהוּדָה וְאֶת־עַצְמוֹת שָׂרָיו וְאֶת־עַצְמוֹת הַכֹּהֲנִים וְאֵת עַצְמוֹת הַנְּבִיאִים וְאֵת עַצְמוֹת יוֹשְׁבֵי יְרוּשָׁלָיִם מִקִּבְרֵיהֶם: 2] וּשְׁטָחוּם לַשֶּׁמֶשׁ וְלַיָּרֵחַ וּלְכֹל צְבָא הַשָּׁמַיִם אֲשֶׁר אֲהֵבוּם וַאֲשֶׁר עֲבָדוּם וַאֲשֶׁר הָלְכוּ אַחֲרֵיהֶם וַאֲשֶׁר דְּרָשׁוּם וַאֲשֶׁר הִשְׁתַּחֲווּ לָהֶם לֹא יֵאָסְפוּ וְלֹא יִקָּבֵרוּ לְדֹמֶן עַל פְּנֵי הָאֲדָמָה יִהְיוּ: 3] וְנִבְחַר מָוֶת

that are left of this wicked folk, in all the other places to which I shall banish them—declares the LORD of Hosts.

מְחַיִּים לְכֹל הַשְּׁאֵרִית הַנִּשְׁאָרִים מִן הַמִּשְׁפָּחָה הָרָעָה הַזֹּאת בְּכָל־הַמְּקֹמוֹת הַנִּשְׁאָרִים אֲשֶׁר הִדַּחְתִּים שָׁם נְאֻם יְהֹוָה צְבָאוֹת:

Chapter 9

ט

22] Thus said the LORD:
Let not the wise man glory in his wisdom;
Let not the strong man glory in his strength;
Let not the rich man glory in his riches.

22] כֹּה אָמַר יְהֹוָה
אַל יִתְהַלֵּל חָכָם בְּחָכְמָתוֹ
וְאַל יִתְהַלֵּל הַגִּבּוֹר בִּגְבוּרָתוֹ
אַל יִתְהַלֵּל עָשִׁיר בְּעָשְׁרוֹ:

23] But only in this should one glory:
In his earnest devotion to Me.
For I the LORD act with kindness,
Justice, and equity in the world;
For in these I delight
                          —declares the LORD.

23] כִּי אִם בְּזֹאת יִתְהַלֵּל הַמִּתְהַלֵּל
הַשְׂכֵּל וְיָדֹעַ אוֹתִי
כִּי אֲנִי יְהֹוָה עֹשֶׂה חֶסֶד
מִשְׁפָּט וּצְדָקָה בָּאָרֶץ
כִּי בְאֵלֶּה חָפַצְתִּי
נְאֻם יְהֹוָה:

SECOND SELECTION

Hosea

6 : 1-6

Chapter 6

ו

1] [a]"Come, let us turn back to the LORD:
He attacked, and He can heal us;
He wounded, and He can bind us up.

1] לְכוּ וְנָשׁוּבָה אֶל יְהֹוָה
כִּי הוּא טָרָף וְיִרְפָּאֵנוּ
יַךְ וְיַחְבְּשֵׁנוּ:

2] In two days He will make us whole again;
On the third day He will raise us up,
And we shall be whole by His favor.

2] יְחַיֵּנוּ מִיֹּמָיִם
בַּיּוֹם הַשְּׁלִישִׁי יְקִמֵנוּ
וְנִחְיֶה לְפָנָיו:

[a] As anticipated at the end of chapter 5, Israel seeks the Lord's favor; His answer begins with v. 4

3] Let us pursue obedience to the LORD,
And we shall become obedient.
His appearance is as sure as daybreak,
And He will come to us like rain,
Like latter rain that refreshes[b] the earth."

וְנֵדְעָה נִרְדְּפָה לָדַעַת אֶת־יְהֹוָה [3]

כְּשַׁחַר נָכוֹן מוֹצָאוֹ

וְיָבוֹא כַגֶּשֶׁם לָנוּ

כְּמַלְקוֹשׁ יוֹרֶה אָרֶץ:

4] What can I do for you, Ephraim,
What can I do for you, Judah,[c]
When your goodness is like morning clouds,
Like dew so early gone?

מָה אֶעֱשֶׂה־לְּךָ אֶפְרַיִם [4]

מָה אֶעֱשֶׂה־לְּךָ יְהוּדָה

וְחַסְדְּכֶם כַּעֲנַן־בֹּקֶר

וְכַטַּל מַשְׁכִּים הֹלֵךְ:

5] That is why I have hewn down [d]the prophets,[d]
Have slain them with the words of My mouth:
[e]And the day that dawned [brought on] your
    punishment.[e]

עַל־כֵּן חָצַבְתִּי בַּנְּבִיאִים [5]

הֲרַגְתִּים בְּאִמְרֵי־פִי

וּמִשְׁפָּטֶיךָ אוֹר יֵצֵא:

6] For I desire goodness, not sacrifice;
Obedience to God, rather than burnt offerings.

כִּי חֶסֶד חָפַצְתִּי וְלֹא־זָבַח [6]

וְדַעַת אֱלֹהִים מֵעֹלוֹת:

THIRD SELECTION

Malachi

1 : 6 - 14; 2 : 1 - 7

Chapter 1

ℵ

6] A son should honor his father, and a slave[b]
his master. Now if I am a father, where is the
honor due Me? And if I am a master, where is
the reverence due Me?—said the LORD of Hosts
to you, O priests who scorn My name. But
you ask, "How have we scorned Your name?"

7] You offer defiled food on My altar. But you
ask, "How have we defiled You[c]?" By saying,
"The table of the LORD can be treated with scorn."

בֵּן יְכַבֵּד אָב וְעֶבֶד אֲדֹנָיו וְאִם־אָב אָנִי [6]

אַיֵּה כְבוֹדִי וְאִם אֲדוֹנִים אָנִי אַיֵּה מוֹרָאִי

אָמַר יְהֹוָה צְבָאוֹת לָכֶם הַכֹּהֲנִים בּוֹזֵי שְׁמִי

וַאֲמַרְתֶּם בַּמֶּה בָזִינוּ אֶת־שְׁמֶךָ: [7] מַגִּישִׁים

עַל מִזְבְּחִי לֶחֶם מְגֹאָל וַאֲמַרְתֶּם בַּמֶּה

גֵאַלְנוּךָ בֶּאֱמָרְכֶם שֻׁלְחַן יְהֹוָה נִבְזֶה הוּא:

b Taking yoreh *as equivalent of* yarweh
c Emendation yields "Israel"; cf. "Ephraim . . . Israel" in v. 10
d-d Emendation yields "your children"; cf. 9.13
e-e Cf. v. 3; but meaning of Heb. uncertain

b Septuagint and Targum add "should reverence"; cf. next part of verse
c Septuagint "it"

8] When you present a blind animal for sacrifice—it doesn't matter! When you present a lame or sick one—it doesn't matter! Just offer it to your governor: Will he accept you? Will he show you favor?—said the LORD of Hosts.

9] And now implore the favor of God! Will He be gracious to us? This is what you have done—will He accept any of you?

The LORD of Hosts has said: 10] If only you would lock My doors, and not kindle fire on My altar to no purpose! I take no pleasure in you—said the LORD of Hosts—and I will accept no offering from you.

11] For from where the sun rises to where it sets, My name is honored among the nations, and everywhere incense and pure oblation are offered to My name; for My name is honored among the nations—said the LORD of Hosts.

12] But you profane it when you say, "The table of the LORD is defiled and the meat,[a] the food, can be treated with scorn."

13] You say, "Oh, what a bother!" And so you degrade[a] it—said the LORD of Hosts—and you bring the stolen, the lame, and the sick; and you offer such as an oblation. Will I accept it from you?—said the LORD.

14] A curse on the cheat who has an [unblemished] male in his flock, but for his vow sacrifices a blemished animal to the LORD! For I am a great King—said the LORD of Hosts—and My name is revered among the nations.

Chapter 2

1] And now, O priests, this charge is for you: 2] Unless you obey and unless you lay it to heart, and do honor to My name—said the LORD of Hosts—I will send a curse and turn your blessings into curses. (Indeed, I have turned them into curses, because you do not lay it to heart.) 3] I will [a]put your seed under a ban,[a] and I will strew dung upon your faces, the dung of your festal sacrifices, and you shall be carried out to its [heap].

8] וְכִי־תַגִּשׁוּן עִוֵּר לִזְבֹּחַ אֵין רָע וְכִי תַגִּישׁוּ פִּסֵּחַ וְחֹלֶה אֵין רָע הַקְרִיבֵהוּ נָא לְפֶחָתֶךָ הֲיִרְצְךָ אוֹ הֲיִשָּׂא פָנֶיךָ אָמַר יְהֹוָה צְבָאוֹת:

9] וְעַתָּה חַלּוּ־נָא פְנֵי־אֵל וִיחָנֵּנוּ מִיֶּדְכֶם הָיְתָה זֹּאת הֲיִשָּׂא מִכֶּם פָּנִים אָמַר יְהֹוָה צְבָאוֹת:

10] מִי גַם־בָּכֶם וְיִסְגֹּר דְּלָתַיִם וְלֹא־תָאִירוּ מִזְבְּחִי חִנָּם אֵין לִי חֵפֶץ בָּכֶם אָמַר יְהֹוָה צְבָאוֹת וּמִנְחָה לֹא־אֶרְצֶה מִיֶּדְכֶם: 11] כִּי מִמִּזְרַח־שֶׁמֶשׁ וְעַד־מְבוֹאוֹ גָּדוֹל שְׁמִי בַּגּוֹיִם וּבְכָל־מָקוֹם מֻקְטָר מֻגָּשׁ לִשְׁמִי וּמִנְחָה טְהוֹרָה כִּי־גָדוֹל שְׁמִי בַּגּוֹיִם אָמַר יְהֹוָה צְבָאוֹת:

12] וְאַתֶּם מְחַלְּלִים אוֹתוֹ בֶּאֱמָרְכֶם שֻׁלְחַן אֲדֹנָי מְגֹאָל הוּא וְנִיבוֹ נִבְזֶה אָכְלוֹ:

13] וַאֲמַרְתֶּם הִנֵּה מַתְּלָאָה וְהִפַּחְתֶּם אוֹתוֹ אָמַר יְהֹוָה צְבָאוֹת וַהֲבֵאתֶם גָּזוּל וְאֶת־הַפִּסֵּחַ וְאֶת־הַחוֹלֶה וַהֲבֵאתֶם אֶת־הַמִּנְחָה הַאֶרְצֶה אוֹתָהּ מִיֶּדְכֶם אָמַר יְהֹוָה:

14] וְאָרוּר נוֹכֵל וְיֵשׁ בְּעֶדְרוֹ זָכָר וְנֹדֵר וְזֹבֵחַ מָשְׁחָת לַאדֹנָי כִּי מֶלֶךְ גָּדוֹל אָנִי אָמַר יְהֹוָה צְבָאוֹת וּשְׁמִי נוֹרָא בַגּוֹיִם:

ב

1] וְעַתָּה אֲלֵיכֶם הַמִּצְוָה הַזֹּאת הַכֹּהֲנִים:
2] אִם־לֹא תִשְׁמְעוּ וְאִם־לֹא תָשִׂימוּ עַל־לֵב לָתֵת כָּבוֹד לִשְׁמִי אָמַר יְהֹוָה צְבָאוֹת וְשִׁלַּחְתִּי בָכֶם אֶת־הַמְּאֵרָה וְאָרוֹתִי אֶת־בִּרְכוֹתֵיכֶם וְגַם אָרוֹתִיהָ כִּי אֵינְכֶם שָׂמִים עַל־לֵב: 3] הִנְנִי גֹעֵר לָכֶם אֶת־הַזֶּרַע וְזֵרִיתִי פֶרֶשׁ עַל־פְּנֵיכֶם פֶּרֶשׁ חַגֵּיכֶם וְנָשָׂא אֶתְכֶם אֵלָיו:

---

[a] Meaning of Heb. uncertain   [a-a] Meaning of Heb. uncertain

4] Know, then, that I have sent this charge to you so that My covenant with Levi may endure— said the LORD of Hosts.

5] I had with him a covenant of life and well-being, which I gave to him, and of reverence, which he showed Me. For he stood in awe of My name.

6] *b*Proper rulings were in his mouth,
And nothing perverse was on his lips;
He served Me with complete loyalty
And held the many back from iniquity.

7] *c*For the lips of a priest guard knowledge,
And men seek rulings from his mouth;*c*
For he is a messenger of the LORD of Hosts.

4] וִידַעְתֶּם כִּי שִׁלַּחְתִּי אֲלֵיכֶם אֵת הַמִּצְוָה הַזֹּאת לִהְיוֹת בְּרִיתִי אֶת־לֵוִי אָמַר יְהוָה צְבָאוֹת: 5] בְּרִיתִי הָיְתָה אִתּוֹ הַחַיִּים וְהַשָּׁלוֹם וָאֶתְּנֵם לוֹ מוֹרָא וַיִּירָאֵנִי וּמִפְּנֵי שְׁמִי נִחַת הוּא:

6] תּוֹרַת אֱמֶת הָיְתָה בְּפִיהוּ
וְעַוְלָה לֹא נִמְצָא בִשְׂפָתָיו
בְּשָׁלוֹם וּבְמִישׁוֹר הָלַךְ אִתִּי
וְרַבִּים הֵשִׁיב מֵעָוֹן:

7] כִּי שִׂפְתֵי כֹהֵן יִשְׁמְרוּ דַעַת
וְתוֹרָה יְבַקְשׁוּ מִפִּיהוּ
כִּי מַלְאַךְ יְהוָה צְבָאוֹת הוּא:

---

b See Hag. 2.10–13; cf. Lev. 10.8–11; Deut. 33.8, 10
c-c Or: For the lips of a priest are observed; | Knowledge and ruling are sought from his mouth

שמיני

FIRST SELECTION

Second Samuel

6 : 1 – 7 : 17

Chapter 6

1] David again assembled all the picked men of Israel, thirty thousand strong.

2] ^aThen David and all the troops that were with him set out from Baalim^b of Judah to bring up from there the Ark of God to which the Name was attached, the name LORD of Hosts Enthroned on the Cherubim.

3] They loaded the Ark of God onto a new cart and conveyed it from the house of Abinadab which was on the hill; and Abinadab's sons, Uzzah and Ahio, guided the ^cnew cart.

4] They conveyed it from Abinadab's house on the hill, [Uzzah walking]^d alongside^{-c} the Ark of God and Ahio walking in front of the Ark.

5] Meanwhile, David and all the House of Israel danced before the LORD to ^e[the sound of] all kinds of cypress wood [instruments],^{-e} with lyres, harps, timbrels, sistrums, and cymbals.

ו

1] וַיֹּסֶף עוֹד דָּוִד אֶת־כָּל־בָּחוּר בְּיִשְׂרָאֵל שְׁלֹשִׁים אָלֶף: 2] וַיָּקָם וַיֵּלֶךְ דָּוִד וְכָל־הָעָם אֲשֶׁר אִתּוֹ מִבַּעֲלֵי יְהוּדָה לְהַעֲלוֹת מִשָּׁם אֵת אֲרוֹן הָאֱלֹהִים אֲשֶׁר נִקְרָא שֵׁם שֵׁם יְהוָה צְבָאוֹת יֹשֵׁב הַכְּרֻבִים עָלָיו: 3] וַיַּרְכִּבוּ אֶת־אֲרוֹן הָאֱלֹהִים אֶל עֲגָלָה חֲדָשָׁה וַיִּשָּׂאֻהוּ מִבֵּית אֲבִינָדָב אֲשֶׁר בַּגִּבְעָה וְעֻזָּא וְאַחְיוֹ בְּנֵי אֲבִינָדָב נֹהֲגִים אֶת־הָעֲגָלָה חֲדָשָׁה: 4] וַיִּשָּׂאֻהוּ מִבֵּית אֲבִינָדָב אֲשֶׁר בַּגִּבְעָה עִם אֲרוֹן הָאֱלֹהִים וְאַחְיוֹ הֹלֵךְ לִפְנֵי הָאָרוֹן: 5] וְדָוִד וְכָל־בֵּית יִשְׂרָאֵל מְשַׂחֲקִים לִפְנֵי יְהוָה בְּכֹל עֲצֵי בְרוֹשִׁים וּבְכִנֹּרוֹת וּבִנְבָלִים וּבְתֻפִּים וּבִמְנַעַנְעִים וּבְצֶלְצֶלִים:

^a Vv. 2–12 are found also in I Chron. 13.5–14, with variations

^b Identical with Baalah, another name for Kiriath-jearim, where the Ark had been kept (cf. I Sam. 6.21; I Chron. 13.6; Josh. 15.9)

^{c-c} Septuagint and 4QSam^a read "cart alongside" (4QSam^a=manuscript^a of Samuel found in the fourth cave at Qumran, the site of the caves where the Bible manuscripts were found in 1949–50.)

^d Cf. vv. 6–7

^{e-e} Cf. Kimchi; the parallel passage I Chron. 13.8 reads "with all their might and with songs"

6] But when they came to the threshing floor of Nacon, Uzzah reached out for the Ark of God and grasped it, for the oxen had stumbled.*f*
7] The LORD was incensed at Uzzah. And God struck him down on the spot *g-for his indiscretion,-g* and he died there beside the Ark of God.
8] David was distressed because the LORD had inflicted a breach upon Uzzah; and that place was named Perez-uzzah,*h* as it is still called.

9] David was afraid of the LORD that day; he said, "How can I let the Ark of the LORD come to me?"

10] So David would not bring the Ark to his place in the City of David; instead, he diverted it to the house of Obed-edom the Gittite.
11] The Ark of the LORD remained in the house of Obed-edom the Gittite three months, and the LORD blessed Obed-edom and his whole household.

12] It was reported to King David: "The LORD has blessed Obed-edom's house and all that belongs to him because of the Ark of God." *i*Thereupon David went and brought up the Ark of God from the house of Obed-edom to the City of David, amid rejoicing.

13] When the bearers of the Ark of the LORD had moved forward six paces, he sacrificed *i-an ox and a fatling.-i*
14] David whirled with all his might before the LORD; David was girt with a linen ephod.
15] Thus David and all the House of Israel brought up the Ark of the LORD with shouts and with blasts of the horn.
16] As the Ark of the LORD entered the City of David, Michal daughter of Saul looked out of the window and saw King David leaping and

6 וַיָּבֹאוּ עַד־גֹּרֶן נָכוֹן וַיִּשְׁלַח עֻזָּא אֶל אֲרוֹן הָאֱלֹהִים וַיֹּאחֶז בּוֹ כִּי שָׁמְטוּ הַבָּקָר:
7 וַיִּחַר אַף יְהוָה בְּעֻזָּה וַיַּכֵּהוּ שָׁם הָאֱלֹהִים עַל הַשַּׁל וַיָּמָת שָׁם עִם אֲרוֹן הָאֱלֹהִים:
8 וַיִּחַר לְדָוִד עַל אֲשֶׁר פָּרַץ יְהוָה פֶּרֶץ בְּעֻזָּה וַיִּקְרָא לַמָּקוֹם הַהוּא פֶּרֶץ עֻזָּה עַד הַיּוֹם הַזֶּה:
9 וַיִּרָא דָוִד אֶת־יְהוָה בַּיּוֹם הַהוּא וַיֹּאמֶר אֵיךְ יָבוֹא אֵלַי אֲרוֹן יְהוָה: 10 וְלֹא אָבָה דָוִד לְהָסִיר אֵלָיו אֶת־אֲרוֹן יְהוָה עַל־עִיר דָוִד וַיַּטֵּהוּ דָוִד בֵּית עֹבֵד אֱדוֹם הַגִּתִּי:
11 וַיֵּשֶׁב אֲרוֹן יְהוָה בֵּית עֹבֵד אֱדֹם הַגִּתִּי שְׁלֹשָׁה חֳדָשִׁים וַיְבָרֶךְ יְהוָה אֶת־עֹבֵד אֱדֹם וְאֶת־כָּל־בֵּיתוֹ:
12 וַיֻּגַּד לַמֶּלֶךְ דָוִד לֵאמֹר בֵּרַךְ יְהוָה אֶת־בֵּית עֹבֵד אֱדֹם וְאֶת־כָּל־אֲשֶׁר־לוֹ בַּעֲבוּר אֲרוֹן הָאֱלֹהִים וַיֵּלֶךְ דָוִד וַיַּעַל אֶת־אֲרוֹן הָאֱלֹהִים מִבֵּית עֹבֵד אֱדֹם עִיר דָוִד בְּשִׂמְחָה:
13 וַיְהִי כִּי צָעֲדוּ נֹשְׂאֵי אֲרוֹן יְהוָה שִׁשָּׁה צְעָדִים וַיִּזְבַּח שׁוֹר וּמְרִיא: 14 וְדָוִד מְכַרְכֵּר בְּכָל־עֹז לִפְנֵי יְהוָה וְדָוִד חָגוּר אֵפוֹד בָּד:
15 וְדָוִד וְכָל־בֵּית יִשְׂרָאֵל מַעֲלִים אֶת־אֲרוֹן יְהוָה בִּתְרוּעָה וּבְקוֹל שׁוֹפָר:
16 וְהָיָה אֲרוֹן יְהוָה בָּא עִיר דָוִד וּמִיכַל בַּת שָׁאוּל נִשְׁקְפָה בְּעַד הַחַלּוֹן וַתֵּרֶא אֶת־

---

*f Meaning of Heb. uncertain
*g-g So Targum; I Chron. 13.10 reads "because he had laid a hand on the Ark"
*h I.e., "the Breach of Uzzah"; cf. 5.20 and note
*i Vv. 12b–14 are found, with variations, in I Chron. 15.25–27; vv. 15–19a, with variations, in I Chron. 15.28—16.3; vv. 19b–20a, with variations, in I Chron. 16.43
*i-i 4QSamᵃ reads "seven oxen and seven (rams)"; cf. I Chron. 15.26

whirling before the Lord; and she despised him for it.

17] They brought in the Ark of the Lord and set it up in its place inside the tent which David had pitched for it, and David sacrificed burnt offerings and offerings of well-being before the Lord.

18] When David finished sacrificing the burnt offerings and the offerings of well-being, he blessed the people in the name of the Lord of Hosts.

19] And he distributed among all the people—the entire multitude of Israel, man and woman alike—to each a loaf of bread, *ᶠa cake made in a pan, and a raisin cake.ᶠ* Then all the people left for their homes.

20] David went home to greet his household. And Michal daughter of Saul came out to meet David and said, "Didn't the king of Israel do himself honor today—exposing himself today in the sight of the slavegirls of his subjects, as one of the riffraff might expose himself!"

21] David answered Michal, "It was before the Lord who chose me instead of your father and all his family and appointed me ruler over the Lord's people Israel! I will dance before the Lord

22] and dishonor myself even more, and be low in ᵏ⁻my ownᵏ esteem; but among the slavegirls that you speak of I will be honored."

23] So to her dying day Michal daughter of Saul had no children.

Chapter 7

1] ᵃWhen the king was settled in his palace and the Lord had granted him safety from all the enemies around him,

2] the king said to the prophet Nathan: "Here I am dwelling in a house of cedar, while the Ark of the Lord abides in a tent!"

ᶠ⁻ᶠ *Meaning of Heb. uncertain*
ᵏ⁻ᵏ *Septuagint reads "your"*

ᵃ *This chapter is found, with variations, also in I Chron. 17*

הַמֶּלֶךְ דָּוִד מְפַזֵּז וּמְכַרְכֵּר לִפְנֵי יְהוָה וַתִּבֶז
לוֹ בְּלִבָּהּ:

17 וַיָּבִאוּ אֶת־אֲרוֹן יְהוָה וַיַּצִּגוּ אֹתוֹ בִּמְקוֹמוֹ
בְּתוֹךְ הָאֹהֶל אֲשֶׁר נָטָה לוֹ דָּוִד וַיַּעַל דָּוִד
עֹלוֹת לִפְנֵי יְהוָה וּשְׁלָמִים: 18 וַיְכַל דָּוִד
מֵהַעֲלוֹת הָעוֹלָה וְהַשְּׁלָמִים וַיְבָרֶךְ אֶת־הָעָם
בְּשֵׁם יְהוָה צְבָאוֹת: 19 וַיְחַלֵּק לְכָל־הָעָם
לְכָל־הֲמוֹן יִשְׂרָאֵל לְמֵאִישׁ וְעַד־אִשָּׁה לְאִישׁ
חַלַּת לֶחֶם אַחַת וְאֶשְׁפָּר אֶחָד וַאֲשִׁישָׁה אֶחָת
וַיֵּלֶךְ כָּל־הָעָם אִישׁ לְבֵיתוֹ:

20 וַיָּשָׁב דָּוִד לְבָרֵךְ אֶת־בֵּיתוֹ וַתֵּצֵא מִיכַל
בַּת־שָׁאוּל לִקְרַאת דָּוִד וַתֹּאמֶר מַה־נִּכְבַּד
הַיּוֹם מֶלֶךְ יִשְׂרָאֵל אֲשֶׁר נִגְלָה הַיּוֹם לְעֵינֵי
אַמְהוֹת עֲבָדָיו כְּהִגָּלוֹת נִגְלוֹת אַחַד הָרֵקִים:
21 וַיֹּאמֶר דָּוִד אֶל־מִיכַל לִפְנֵי יְהוָה אֲשֶׁר
בָּחַר־בִּי מֵאָבִיךְ וּמִכָּל־בֵּיתוֹ לְצַוֺּת אֹתִי נָגִיד
עַל־עַם יְהוָה עַל־יִשְׂרָאֵל וְשִׂחַקְתִּי לִפְנֵי יְהוָה:
22 וּנְקַלֹּתִי עוֹד מִזֹּאת וְהָיִיתִי שָׁפָל בְּעֵינָי
וְעִם־הָאֲמָהוֹת אֲשֶׁר אָמַרְתְּ עִמָּם אִכָּבֵדָה:
23 וּלְמִיכַל בַּת־שָׁאוּל לֹא־הָיָה לָהּ יָלֶד עַד
יוֹם מוֹתָהּ:

ז

1 וַיְהִי כִּי־יָשַׁב הַמֶּלֶךְ בְּבֵיתוֹ וַיהוָה הֵנִיחַ־
לוֹ מִסָּבִיב מִכָּל־אֹיְבָיו: 2 וַיֹּאמֶר הַמֶּלֶךְ
אֶל־נָתָן הַנָּבִיא רְאֵה נָא אָנֹכִי יוֹשֵׁב בְּבֵית
אֲרָזִים וַאֲרוֹן הָאֱלֹהִים יֹשֵׁב בְּתוֹךְ הַיְרִיעָה:

3] Nathan said to the king, "Go and do whatever you have in mind, for the LORD is with you."

4] But that same night the word of the LORD came to Nathan:

5] "Go and say to My servant David: Thus said the LORD: Are you the one to build a house for Me to dwell in?

6] From the day that I brought the people of Israel out of Egypt to this day I have not dwelt in a house, but have moved about in Tent and Tabernacle. 7] As I moved about wherever the Israelites went, did I ever reproach any of the tribal leaders[b] whom I appointed to care for My people Israel: Why have you not built Me a house of cedar?

8] "Further, say thus to My servant David: Thus said the LORD of Hosts: I took you from the pasture, from following the flock, to be ruler of My people Israel,

9] and I have been with you wherever you went, and have cut down all your enemies before you. Moreover, I will give you great renown like that of the greatest men on earth.

10] I will establish a home for My people Israel and will plant them firm, so that they shall dwell secure and shall tremble no more. Evil men shall not oppress them any more as in the past, 11] ever since I appointed chieftains over My people Israel. I will give you safety from all your enemies.

"The LORD declares to you that He, the LORD, will establish a house[c] for you.

12] When your days are done and you lie with your fathers, I will raise up your offspring after you, one of your own issue, and I will establish his kingship. 13] He shall build a house for My name, and I will establish his royal throne forever.

3 וַיֹּאמֶר נָתָן אֶל הַמֶּלֶךְ כֹּל אֲשֶׁר בִּלְבָבְךָ לֵךְ עֲשֵׂה כִּי יְהוָה עִמָּךְ:

4 וַיְהִי בַּלַּיְלָה הַהוּא וַיְהִי דְּבַר יְהוָה אֶל נָתָן לֵאמֹר: 5 לֵךְ וְאָמַרְתָּ אֶל עַבְדִּי אֶל דָּוִד כֹּה אָמַר יְהוָה הַאַתָּה תִּבְנֶה לִּי בַיִת לְשִׁבְתִּי: 6 כִּי לֹא יָשַׁבְתִּי בְּבַיִת לְמִיּוֹם הַעֲלֹתִי אֶת בְּנֵי יִשְׂרָאֵל מִמִּצְרַיִם וְעַד הַיּוֹם הַזֶּה וָאֶהְיֶה מִתְהַלֵּךְ בְּאֹהֶל וּבְמִשְׁכָּן: 7 בְּכֹל אֲשֶׁר הִתְהַלַּכְתִּי בְּכָל בְּנֵי יִשְׂרָאֵל הַדָּבָר דִּבַּרְתִּי אֶת אַחַד שִׁבְטֵי יִשְׂרָאֵל אֲשֶׁר צִוִּיתִי לִרְעוֹת אֶת עַמִּי אֶת יִשְׂרָאֵל לֵאמֹר לָמָּה לֹא בְנִיתֶם לִי בֵּית אֲרָזִים:

8 וְעַתָּה כֹּה תֹאמַר לְעַבְדִּי לְדָוִד כֹּה אָמַר יְהוָה צְבָאוֹת אֲנִי לְקַחְתִּיךָ מִן הַנָּוֶה מֵאַחַר הַצֹּאן לִהְיוֹת נָגִיד עַל עַמִּי עַל יִשְׂרָאֵל: 9 וָאֶהְיֶה עִמְּךָ בְּכֹל אֲשֶׁר הָלַכְתָּ וָאַכְרִתָה אֶת כָּל אֹיְבֶיךָ מִפָּנֶיךָ וְעָשִׂתִי לְךָ שֵׁם גָּדוֹל כְּשֵׁם הַגְּדֹלִים אֲשֶׁר בָּאָרֶץ: 10 וְשַׂמְתִּי מָקוֹם לְעַמִּי לְיִשְׂרָאֵל וּנְטַעְתִּיו וְשָׁכַן תַּחְתָּיו וְלֹא יִרְגַּז עוֹד וְלֹא יֹסִיפוּ בְנֵי עַוְלָה לְעַנּוֹתוֹ כַּאֲשֶׁר בָּרִאשׁוֹנָה: 11 וּלְמִן הַיּוֹם אֲשֶׁר צִוִּיתִי שֹׁפְטִים עַל עַמִּי יִשְׂרָאֵל וַהֲנִיחֹתִי לְךָ מִכָּל אֹיְבֶיךָ וְהִגִּיד לְךָ יְהוָה כִּי בַיִת יַעֲשֶׂה לְּךָ יְהוָה: 12 כִּי יִמְלְאוּ יָמֶיךָ וְשָׁכַבְתָּ אֶת אֲבֹתֶיךָ וַהֲקִימֹתִי אֶת זַרְעֲךָ אַחֲרֶיךָ אֲשֶׁר יֵצֵא מִמֵּעֶיךָ וַהֲכִינֹתִי אֶת מַמְלַכְתּוֹ: 13 הוּא יִבְנֶה בַּיִת לִשְׁמִי וְכֹנַנְתִּי אֶת כִּסֵּא מַמְלַכְתּוֹ

[b] *Understanding shibṭe as "scepters"; so Kimchi. I Chron. 17.6 reads "chieftains";* *cf. v. 11*

[c] *I.e., a dynasty; play on "house" (i.e., Temple) in v. 5*

14] I will be
a father to him, and he shall be a son to Me.
When he does wrong, I will chastise him ᵈ⁻with
the rod of men and the affliction of mortals;⁻ᵈ
15] but I will never withdraw My favor from him
as I withdrew it from Saul, whom I removed ᵉ⁻to
make room for you.⁻ᵉ

16] Your house and your
kingship shall ever be secure before you;ᶠ your
throne shall be established forever."

17] Nathan spoke to David in accordance with
all these words and all this prophecy.

עַד עוֹלָם: 14] אֲנִי אֶהְיֶה־לּוֹ לְאָב וְהוּא
יִהְיֶה־לִּי לְבֵן אֲשֶׁר בְּהַעֲוֹתוֹ וְהֹכַחְתִּיו בְּשֵׁבֶט
אֲנָשִׁים וּבְנִגְעֵי בְּנֵי אָדָם: 15] וְחַסְדִּי לֹא יָסוּר
מִמֶּנּוּ כַּאֲשֶׁר הֲסִרֹתִי מֵעִם שָׁאוּל אֲשֶׁר הֲסִרֹתִי
מִלְּפָנֶיךָ: 16] וְנֶאְמַן בֵּיתְךָ וּמַמְלַכְתְּךָ עַד
עוֹלָם לְפָנֶיךָ כִּסְאֲךָ יִהְיֶה נָכוֹן עַד עוֹלָם:
17] כְּכֹל הַדְּבָרִים הָאֵלֶּה וּכְכֹל הַחִזָּיוֹן
הַזֶּה כֵּן דִּבֶּר נָתָן אֶל דָּוִד:

SECOND SELECTION

Isaiah

61 : 1-11

Chapter 61

1] The spirit of the Lord GOD is upon me,
Because the LORD has anointed me;
He has sent me as a herald of joy to the humble,
To bind up the wounded of heart,
To proclaim release to the captives,
Liberation to the imprisoned;

2] To proclaim a year of the LORD's favor
And a day of vindication by our God;
To comfort all who mourn—

3] ᵃ⁻To provide for⁻ᵃ the mourners in Zion—
To give them a turban instead of ashes,

סא

1] רוּחַ אֲדֹנָי יֱהֹוִה עָלָי
יַעַן מָשַׁח יְהֹוָה אֹתִי
לְבַשֵּׂר עֲנָוִים שְׁלָחַנִי
לַחֲבֹשׁ לְנִשְׁבְּרֵי־לֵב
לִקְרֹא לִשְׁבוּיִם דְּרוֹר
וְלַאֲסוּרִים פְּקַח־קוֹחַ:
2] לִקְרֹא שְׁנַת רָצוֹן לַיהֹוָה
וְיוֹם נָקָם לֵאלֹהֵינוּ
לְנַחֵם כָּל־אֲבֵלִים:
3] לָשׂוּם לַאֲבֵלֵי צִיּוֹן
לָתֵת לָהֶם פְּאֵר תַּחַת אֵפֶר

ᵈ⁻ᵈ *I.e., only as a human father would*
ᵉ⁻ᵉ *Lit. "from before you"*
ᶠ *Septuagint reads "before Me," i.e., "by My favor"*

ᵃ⁻ᵃ *Meaning of Heb. uncertain*

Festive ointment instead of mourning,
A garment of splendor instead of a drooping spirit.
They shall be called terebinths of victory,
Planted by the LORD for His glory.

שֶׁמֶן שָׂשׂוֹן תַּחַת אֵבֶל
מַעֲטֵה תְהִלָּה תַּחַת רוּחַ כֵּהָה
וְקֹרָא לָהֶם אֵילֵי הַצֶּדֶק
מַטַּע יְהֹוָה לְהִתְפָּאֵר:

4] And they shall build the ancient ruins,
Raise up the desolations of old,
And renew the ruined cities,
The desolations of many ages.

4] וּבָנוּ חָרְבוֹת עוֹלָם
שֹׁמְמוֹת רִאשֹׁנִים יְקוֹמֵמוּ
וְחִדְּשׁוּ עָרֵי חֹרֶב
שֹׁמְמוֹת דּוֹר וָדוֹר:

5] Strangers shall stand and pasture your flocks,
Aliens shall be your plowmen and vine-trimmers;

5] וְעָמְדוּ זָרִים וְרָעוּ צֹאנְכֶם
וּבְנֵי נֵכָר אִכָּרֵיכֶם וְכֹרְמֵיכֶם:

6] While you shall be called "Priests of the LORD,"
And termed "Servants of our God."
You shall enjoy the wealth of nations
And *revel* in their riches.

6] וְאַתֶּם כֹּהֲנֵי יְהֹוָה תִּקָּרֵאוּ
מְשָׁרְתֵי אֱלֹהֵינוּ יֵאָמֵר לָכֶם
חֵיל גּוֹיִם תֹּאכֵלוּ
וּבִכְבוֹדָם תִּתְיַמָּרוּ:

7] Because your shame was double—
Men cried, "Disgrace is their portion"—
Assuredly,
They shall have a double share in their land,
Joy shall be theirs for all time.

7] תַּחַת בָּשְׁתְּכֶם מִשְׁנֶה
וּכְלִמָּה יָרֹנּוּ חֶלְקָם
לָכֵן בְּאַרְצָם מִשְׁנֶה יִירָשׁוּ
שִׂמְחַת עוֹלָם תִּהְיֶה לָהֶם:

8] For I the LORD love justice,
I hate *robbery with a burnt offering.*
I will pay them their wages faithfully,
And make a covenant with them for all time.

8] כִּי אֲנִי יְהֹוָה אֹהֵב מִשְׁפָּט
שֹׂנֵא גָזֵל בְּעוֹלָה
וְנָתַתִּי פְעֻלָּתָם בֶּאֱמֶת
וּבְרִית עוֹלָם אֶכְרוֹת לָהֶם:

9] Their offspring shall be known among the nations,
Their descendants in the midst of the peoples.
All who see them shall recognize
That they are a stock the LORD has blessed.

9] וְנוֹדַע בַּגּוֹיִם זַרְעָם
וְצֶאֱצָאֵיהֶם בְּתוֹךְ הָעַמִּים
כָּל־רֹאֵיהֶם יַכִּירוּם
כִּי הֵם זֶרַע בֵּרַךְ יְהֹוָה:

---

a-a Meaning of Heb. uncertain
b-b Emendation yields "They inherited disgrace as their portion"
c-c Emendation yields "the robbing of wages"

10] I greatly rejoice in the LORD,
My whole being exults in my God.
For He has clothed me with garments of triumph,
Wrapped me in a robe of victory,
Like a bridegroom adorned with a turban,
Like a bride bedecked with her finery.

11] For as the earth brings forth her growth
And a garden makes the seed shoot up,
So the Lord GOD will make
Victory and renown shoot up
In the presence of all the nations.

10] שׂוֹשׂ אָשִׂישׂ בַּיהֹוָה

תָּגֵל נַפְשִׁי בֵּאלֹהַי

כִּי הִלְבִּישַׁנִי בִּגְדֵי־יֶשַׁע

מְעִיל צְדָקָה יְעָטָנִי

כֶּחָתָן יְכַהֵן פְּאֵר

וְכַכַּלָּה תַּעְדֶּה כֵלֶיהָ:

11] כִּי כָאָרֶץ תּוֹצִיא צִמְחָהּ

וּכְגַנָּה זֵרוּעֶיהָ תַצְמִיחַ

כֵּן אֲדֹנָי יֱהֹוִה

יַצְמִיחַ צְדָקָה וּתְהִלָּה

נֶגֶד כָּל־הַגּוֹיִם:

THIRD SELECTION

Psalms

73 : 1-28

Psalm 73

1] A psalm of Asaph.
God is truly good to Israel,
to those whose heart is pure.

2] As for me, my feet had almost strayed,
my steps were nearly led off course,

3] for I envied the profligate,
I saw the wicked at ease.

4] Death has no pangs for them;
their body is healthy.

5] They have no part in the travail of men;
they are not afflicted like the rest of mankind.

עג

1] מִזְמוֹר לְאָסָף

אַךְ טוֹב לְיִשְׂרָאֵל אֱלֹהִים

לְבָרֵי לֵבָב:

2] וַאֲנִי כִּמְעַט נָטָיוּ רַגְלָי

כְּאַיִן שֻׁפְּכוּ אֲשֻׁרָי:

3] כִּי קִנֵּאתִי בַּהוֹלְלִים

שְׁלוֹם רְשָׁעִים אֶרְאֶה:

4] כִּי אֵין חַרְצֻבּוֹת לְמוֹתָם

וּבָרִיא אוּלָם:

5] בַּעֲמַל אֱנוֹשׁ אֵינֵמוֹ

וְעִם אָדָם לֹא יְנֻגָּעוּ:

371

6] So pride adorns their necks,
lawlessness enwraps them as a mantle.

7] ^{a-}Fat shuts out their eyes;
their fancies are extravagant.^{-a}

8] They scoff and plan evil;
from their eminence they plan wrongdoing.

9] They set their mouths against heaven,
and their tongues range over the earth.

10] ^{a-}So they pound His people again and again,
until they are drained of their very last tear.^{-a}

11] Then they say, "How could God know?
Is there knowledge with the Most High?"

12] Such are the wicked;
ever tranquil, they amass wealth.

13] It was for nothing that I kept my heart pure
and washed my hands in innocence,

14] seeing that I have been constantly afflicted,
that each morning brings new punishments.

15] Had I decided to say these things,
I should have been false to the circle of Your
   disciples.

16] So I applied myself to understand this,
but it seemed a hopeless task

17] till I entered God's sanctuary
and reflected on their fate.

18] You surround them with flattery,
make them fall through blandishments.

19] How suddenly are they ruined,
wholly swept away by terrors.

לָכֵן עֲנָקַתְמוֹ גַאֲוָה 6]
יַעֲטָף־שִׁית חָמָס לָמוֹ:

יָצָא מֵחֵלֶב עֵינֵמוֹ 7]
עָבְרוּ מַשְׂכִּיּוֹת לֵבָב:

יָמִיקוּ וִידַבְּרוּ בְרָע 8]
עֹשֶׁק מִמָּרוֹם יְדַבֵּרוּ:

שַׁתּוּ בַשָּׁמַיִם פִּיהֶם 9]
וּלְשׁוֹנָם תִּהֲלַךְ בָּאָרֶץ:

לָכֵן יָשׁוּב עַמּוֹ הֲלֹם 10]
וּמֵי מָלֵא יִמָּצוּ לָמוֹ:

וְאָמְרוּ אֵיכָה יָדַע אֵל 11]
וְיֵשׁ דֵּעָה בְעֶלְיוֹן:

הִנֵּה־אֵלֶּה רְשָׁעִים 12]
וְשַׁלְוֵי עוֹלָם הִשְׂגּוּ־חָיִל:

אַךְ־רִיק זִכִּיתִי לְבָבִי 13]
וָאֶרְחַץ בְּנִקָּיוֹן כַּפָּי:

וָאֱהִי נָגוּעַ כָּל־הַיּוֹם 14]
וְתוֹכַחְתִּי לַבְּקָרִים:

אִם אָמַרְתִּי אֲסַפְּרָה כְמוֹ 15]
הִנֵּה דוֹר בָּנֶיךָ בָגָדְתִּי:

וָאֲחַשְּׁבָה לָדַעַת זֹאת 16]
עָמָל הוּא בְעֵינָי:

עַד אָבוֹא אֶל מִקְדְּשֵׁי־אֵל 17]
אָבִינָה לְאַחֲרִיתָם:

אַךְ בַּחֲלָקוֹת תָּשִׁית לָמוֹ 18]
הִפַּלְתָּם לְמַשּׁוּאוֹת:

אֵיךְ הָיוּ לְשַׁמָּה כְרָגַע 19]
סָפוּ תַמּוּ מִן בַּלָּהוֹת:

a-a Meaning of Heb. uncertain

20] ^aWhen You are aroused You despise their image,
as one does a dream after waking, O Lord.^a

21] My mind was stripped of its reason,
^bmy feelings were numbed.^b

22] I was a dolt, without knowledge;
I was brutish toward You.

23] Yet I was always with You,
You held my right hand;

24] You guided me by Your counsel
^cand led me toward honor.^c

25] Whom else have I in heaven?
And having You, I want no one on earth.

26] My body and mind fail;
but God is the stay^d of my mind, my portion forever.

27] Those who keep far from You perish;
You annihilate all who are untrue to You.

28] As for me, nearness to God is good;
I have made the Lord GOD my refuge
that I may recount all Your works.

20] כַּחֲלוֹם מֵהָקִיץ אֲדֹנָי
בָּעִיר צַלְמָם תִּבְזֶה:

21] כִּי יִתְחַמֵּץ לְבָבִי
וְכִלְיוֹתַי אֶשְׁתּוֹנָן:

22] וַאֲנִי־בַעַר וְלֹא אֵדָע
בְּהֵמוֹת הָיִיתִי עִמָּךְ:

23] וַאֲנִי תָמִיד עִמָּךְ
אָחַזְתָּ בְּיַד יְמִינִי:

24] בַּעֲצָתְךָ תַנְחֵנִי
וְאַחַר כָּבוֹד תִּקָּחֵנִי:

25] מִי־לִי בַשָּׁמָיִם
וְעִמְּךָ לֹא חָפַצְתִּי בָאָרֶץ:

26] כָּלָה שְׁאֵרִי וּלְבָבִי
צוּר לְבָבִי וְחֶלְקִי אֱלֹהִים לְעוֹלָם:

27] כִּי הִנֵּה רְחֵקֶיךָ יֹאבֵדוּ
הִצְמַתָּה כָּל־זוֹנֶה מִמֶּךָּ:

28] וַאֲנִי קִרֲבַת אֱלֹהִים לִי־טוֹב
שַׁתִּי בַּאדֹנָי יֱהֹוִה מַחְסִי
לְסַפֵּר כָּל־מַלְאֲכוֹתֶיךָ:

^{a-a} Meaning of Heb. uncertain
^{b-b} Lit. "I was pierced through in my kidneys"
^{c-c} Meaning of Heb. uncertain; others "And afterward receive me with glory"
^d Lit. "rock"

תזריע

FIRST SELECTION

Second Kings

4 : 42 — 5 : 19

ד

Chapter 4

42] A man came from Baal-shalishah and he brought the man of God some bread of the first reaping—twenty loaves of barley bread, and some fresh grain *ʲin his sack.ʲ* And [Elisha] said, "Give it to the people and let them eat."

43] His attendant replied, "How can I set this before a hundred men?" But he said, "Give it to the people and let them eat. For thus said the LORD: They shall eat and have some left over."

44] So he set it before them; and when they had eaten, they had some left over, as the LORD had said.

42] וְאִישׁ בָּא מִבַּעַל שָׁלִשָׁה וַיָּבֵא לְאִישׁ הָאֱלֹהִים לֶחֶם בִּכּוּרִים עֶשְׂרִים לֶחֶם שְׂעֹרִים וְכַרְמֶל בְּצִקְלֹנוֹ וַיֹּאמֶר תֵּן לָעָם וְיֹאכֵלוּ׃ 43] וַיֹּאמֶר מְשָׁרְתוֹ מָה אֶתֵּן זֶה לִפְנֵי מֵאָה אִישׁ וַיֹּאמֶר תֵּן לָעָם וְיֹאכֵלוּ כִּי כֹה אָמַר יְהֹוָה אָכֹל וְהוֹתֵר׃ 44] וַיִּתֵּן לִפְנֵיהֶם וַיֹּאכְלוּ וַיּוֹתִרוּ כִּדְבַר יְהֹוָה׃

Chapter 5

ה

1] Naaman, commander of the army of the king of Aram, was important to his lord and high in his favor, for through him the LORD had granted victory to Aram. But the man, though a great warrior, was a leper.[a]

2] Once, when the Arameans were out raiding, they carried off a young girl from the land of Israel, and she became an attendant to Naaman's wife.

3] She said to her mistress, "I wish Master could come before the prophet in Samaria; he would cure him of his leprosy."

4] [Naaman] went and told his lord just what the girl from the land of Israel had said.

1] וְנַעֲמָן שַׂר צְבָא מֶלֶךְ אֲרָם הָיָה אִישׁ גָּדוֹל לִפְנֵי אֲדֹנָיו וּנְשֻׂא פָנִים כִּי־בוֹ נָתַן יְהֹוָה תְּשׁוּעָה לַאֲרָם וְהָאִישׁ הָיָה גִּבּוֹר חַיִל מְצֹרָע׃ 2] וַאֲרָם יָצְאוּ גְדוּדִים וַיִּשְׁבּוּ מֵאֶרֶץ יִשְׂרָאֵל נַעֲרָה קְטַנָּה וַתְּהִי לִפְנֵי אֵשֶׁת נַעֲמָן׃ 3] וַתֹּאמֶר אֶל גְּבִרְתָּהּ אַחֲלֵי אֲדֹנִי לִפְנֵי הַנָּבִיא אֲשֶׁר בְּשֹׁמְרוֹן אָז יֶאֱסֹף אֹתוֹ מִצָּרַעְתּוֹ׃ 4] וַיָּבֹא וַיַּגֵּד לַאדֹנָיו לֵאמֹר כָּזֹאת וְכָזֹאת דִּבְּרָה הַנַּעֲרָה אֲשֶׁר מֵאֶרֶץ יִשְׂרָאֵל׃

ʲ‑ʲ Or "on the stalk"; perhaps connected with Ugaritic bṣql   [a] *Cf. note on Lev. 13.3*

5] And the king of Aram said, "Go to the king of Israel, and I will send along a letter."

He set out, taking with him ten talents of silver, six thousand shekels of gold, and ten changes of clothing. 6] He brought the letter to the king of Israel. It read: "Now, when this letter reaches you, know that I have sent my courtier Naaman to you, that you may cure him of his leprosy."

7] When the king of Israel read the letter, he rent his clothes and cried, "Am I God, to deal death or give life, that this fellow writes to me to cure a man of leprosy? Just see for yourselves that he is seeking a pretext against me!"

8] When Elisha, the man of God, heard that the king of Israel had rent his clothes, he sent a message to the king: "Why have you rent your clothes? Let him come to me, and he will learn that there is a prophet in Israel."

9] So Naaman came with his horses and chariots and halted at the door of Elisha's house. 10] Elisha sent a messenger to say to him, "Go and bathe seven times in the Jordan, and your flesh shall be restored and you shall be clean." 11] But Naaman was angered and walked away. "I thought," he said, "he would surely come out to me, and would stand and invoke the Lord his God by name, and would wave his hand toward the spot, and cure the affected part. 12] Are not the Amanah and the Pharpar, the rivers of Damascus, better than all the waters of Israel? I could bathe in them and be clean!" And he stalked off in a rage.

13] But his servants came forward and spoke to him. "Sir,"[b] they said, "if the prophet told you to do something difficult, would you not do it? How much more when he has only said to you, 'Bathe and be clean.'"

b Lit. "(My) father"

5] וַיֹּאמֶר מֶלֶךְ־אֲרָם לֶךְ־בֹּא וְאֶשְׁלְחָה סֵפֶר אֶל־מֶלֶךְ יִשְׂרָאֵל וַיֵּלֶךְ וַיִּקַּח בְּיָדוֹ עֶשֶׂר כִּכְּרֵי־כֶסֶף וְשֵׁשֶׁת אֲלָפִים זָהָב וְעֶשֶׂר חֲלִיפוֹת בְּגָדִים: 6] וַיָּבֵא הַסֵּפֶר אֶל־מֶלֶךְ יִשְׂרָאֵל לֵאמֹר וְעַתָּה כְּבוֹא הַסֵּפֶר הַזֶּה אֵלֶיךָ הִנֵּה שָׁלַחְתִּי אֵלֶיךָ אֶת־נַעֲמָן עַבְדִּי וַאֲסַפְתּוֹ מִצָּרַעְתּוֹ: 7] וַיְהִי כִּקְרֹא מֶלֶךְ־יִשְׂרָאֵל אֶת־הַסֵּפֶר וַיִּקְרַע בְּגָדָיו וַיֹּאמֶר הַאֱלֹהִים אָנִי לְהָמִית וּלְהַחֲיוֹת כִּי־זֶה שֹׁלֵחַ אֵלַי לֶאֱסֹף אִישׁ מִצָּרַעְתּוֹ כִּי אַךְ־דְּעוּ־נָא וּרְאוּ כִּי־מִתְאַנֶּה הוּא לִי:

8] וַיְהִי כִּשְׁמֹעַ אֱלִישָׁע אִישׁ־הָאֱלֹהִים כִּי־קָרַע מֶלֶךְ־יִשְׂרָאֵל אֶת־בְּגָדָיו וַיִּשְׁלַח אֶל־הַמֶּלֶךְ לֵאמֹר לָמָּה קָרַעְתָּ בְּגָדֶיךָ יָבֹא־נָא אֵלַי וְיֵדַע כִּי יֵשׁ נָבִיא בְּיִשְׂרָאֵל:

9] וַיָּבֹא נַעֲמָן בְּסוּסָיו וּבְרִכְבּוֹ וַיַּעֲמֹד פֶּתַח הַבַּיִת לֶאֱלִישָׁע: 10] וַיִּשְׁלַח אֵלָיו אֱלִישָׁע מַלְאָךְ לֵאמֹר הָלוֹךְ וְרָחַצְתָּ שֶׁבַע פְּעָמִים בַּיַּרְדֵּן וְיָשֹׁב בְּשָׂרְךָ לְךָ וּטְהָר: 11] וַיִּקְצֹף נַעֲמָן וַיֵּלַךְ וַיֹּאמֶר הִנֵּה אָמַרְתִּי אֵלַי יֵצֵא יָצוֹא וְעָמַד וְקָרָא בְּשֵׁם־יְהוָה אֱלֹהָיו וְהֵנִיף יָדוֹ אֶל־הַמָּקוֹם וְאָסַף הַמְּצֹרָע: 12] הֲלֹא טוֹב אֲמָנָה וּפַרְפַּר נַהֲרוֹת דַּמֶּשֶׂק מִכֹּל מֵימֵי יִשְׂרָאֵל הֲלֹא־אֶרְחַץ בָּהֶם וְטָהָרְתִּי וַיִּפֶן וַיֵּלֶךְ בְּחֵמָה:

13] וַיִּגְּשׁוּ עֲבָדָיו וַיְדַבְּרוּ אֵלָיו וַיֹּאמְרוּ אָבִי דָּבָר גָּדוֹל הַנָּבִיא דִּבֶּר אֵלֶיךָ הֲלוֹא תַעֲשֶׂה וְאַף כִּי־אָמַר אֵלֶיךָ רְחַץ וּטְהָר:

14] So he went down and immersed himself in the Jordan seven times, as the man of God had bidden; and his flesh became like a little boy's, and he was clean. 15] Returning with his entire retinue to the man of God, he stood before him and exclaimed, "Now I know that there is no God in the whole world except in Israel! So please accept a gift from your servant."

16] But he replied, "As the LORD lives, whom I serve, I will not accept anything." He pressed him to accept, but he refused. 17] And Naaman said, "Then at least let your servant be given two muleloads of earth; for your servant will never again offer up burnt offering or sacrifice to any god, except the LORD. 18] But may the LORD pardon your servant for this: When my master enters the temple of Rimmon to bow low in worship there, and he is leaning on my arm so that I must bow low in the temple of Rimmon— when I bow low in the temple of Rimmon, may the LORD pardon your servant in this."

19] And he said to him, "Go in peace."

14] וַיֵּרֶד וַיִּטְבֹּל בַּיַּרְדֵּן שֶׁבַע פְּעָמִים כִּדְבַר אִישׁ הָאֱלֹהִים וַיָּשָׁב בְּשָׂרוֹ כִּבְשַׂר נַעַר קָטֹן וַיִּטְהָר: 15] וַיָּשָׁב אֶל־אִישׁ הָאֱלֹהִים הוּא וְכָל־מַחֲנֵהוּ וַיָּבֹא וַיַּעֲמֹד לְפָנָיו וַיֹּאמֶר הִנֵּה־נָא יָדַעְתִּי כִּי אֵין אֱלֹהִים בְּכָל־הָאָרֶץ כִּי אִם בְּיִשְׂרָאֵל וְעַתָּה קַח־נָא בְרָכָה מֵאֵת עַבְדֶּךָ: 16] וַיֹּאמֶר חַי יְהוָה אֲשֶׁר עָמַדְתִּי לְפָנָיו אִם אֶקָּח וַיִּפְצַר־בּוֹ לָקַחַת וַיְמָאֵן: 17] וַיֹּאמֶר נַעֲמָן וָלֹא יֻתַּן־נָא לְעַבְדְּךָ מַשָּׂא צֶמֶד פְּרָדִים אֲדָמָה כִּי לוֹא יַעֲשֶׂה עוֹד עַבְדְּךָ עֹלָה וָזֶבַח לֵאלֹהִים אֲחֵרִים כִּי אִם לַיהוָה: 18] לַדָּבָר הַזֶּה יִסְלַח יְהוָה לְעַבְדֶּךָ בְּבוֹא אֲדֹנִי בֵית רִמּוֹן לְהִשְׁתַּחֲוֹת שָׁמָּה וְהוּא נִשְׁעָן עַל יָדִי וְהִשְׁתַּחֲוֵיתִי בֵּית רִמֹּן בְּהִשְׁתַּחֲוָיָתִי בֵּית רִמֹּן יִסְלַח־נָא יְהוָה לְעַבְדְּךָ בַּדָּבָר הַזֶּה: 19] וַיֹּאמֶר לוֹ לֵךְ לְשָׁלוֹם וַיֵּלֶךְ מֵאִתּוֹ כִּבְרַת־אָרֶץ:

v. 18 לֹא קרי

SECOND SELECTION

Job

2 : 1-10

Chapter 2

1] Again it fell upon a day, that the sons of God came to present themselves before the LORD, and Satan came also among them to present himself before the LORD.

2] And the LORD said unto Satan: 'From whence comest thou?' And Satan answered the LORD, and said: 'From going to and fro in the earth, and from walking up and down in it.'

3] And the LORD said unto Satan: 'Hast thou considered My servant Job, that there is none

ב

1] וַיְהִי הַיּוֹם וַיָּבֹאוּ בְּנֵי הָאֱלֹהִים לְהִתְיַצֵּב עַל יְהוָה וַיָּבוֹא גַם הַשָּׂטָן בְּתֹכָם לְהִתְיַצֵּב עַל יְהוָה: 2] וַיֹּאמֶר יְהוָה אֶל הַשָּׂטָן אֵי מִזֶּה תָבֹא וַיַּעַן הַשָּׂטָן אֶת־יְהוָה וַיֹּאמַר מִשֻּׁט בָּאָרֶץ וּמֵהִתְהַלֵּךְ בָּהּ: 3] וַיֹּאמֶר יְהוָה אֶל הַשָּׂטָן הֲשַׂמְתָּ לִבְּךָ אֶל עַבְדִּי אִיּוֹב כִּי אֵין כָּמֹהוּ

376

like him in the earth, a whole-hearted and an upright man, one that feareth God, and shunneth evil? and he still holdeth fast his integrity, although thou didst move Me against him, to destroy him without cause.'

4] And Satan answered the Lord, and said: 'Skin for skin, yea, all that a man hath will he give for his life.

5] But put forth Thy hand now, and touch his bone and his flesh, surely he will blaspheme Thee to Thy face.'
6] And the Lord said unto Satan: 'Behold, he is in thy hand; only spare his life.'

7] So Satan went forth from the presence of the Lord, and smote Job with sore boils from the sole of his foot even unto his crown.

8] And he took him a potsherd to scrape himself therewith; and he sat among the ashes.

9] Then said his wife unto him: 'Dost thou still hold fast thine integrity? blaspheme God, and die.'

10] But he said unto her: 'Thou speakest as one of the impious women speaketh. What? shall we receive good at the hand of God, and shall we not receive evil?' For all this did not Job sin with his lips.

בָּאָרֶץ אִישׁ תָּם וְיָשָׁר יְרֵא אֱלֹהִים וְסָר מֵרָע
וְעֹדֶנּוּ מַחֲזִיק בְּתֻמָּתוֹ וַתְּסִיתֵנִי בוֹ לְבַלְּעוֹ חִנָּם:

4] וַיַּעַן הַשָּׂטָן אֶת־יְהֹוָה וַיֹּאמַר עוֹר בְּעַד־עוֹר
וְכֹל אֲשֶׁר לָאִישׁ יִתֵּן בְּעַד נַפְשׁוֹ: 5] אוּלָם
שְׁלַח־נָא יָדְךָ וְגַע אֶל עַצְמוֹ וְאֶל בְּשָׂרוֹ אִם־
לֹא אֶל פָּנֶיךָ יְבָרְכֶךָּ: 6] וַיֹּאמֶר יְהֹוָה אֶל
הַשָּׂטָן הִנּוֹ בְיָדֶךָ אַךְ אֶת־נַפְשׁוֹ שְׁמֹר:

7] וַיֵּצֵא הַשָּׂטָן מֵאֵת פְּנֵי יְהֹוָה וַיַּךְ אֶת־
אִיּוֹב בִּשְׁחִין רָע מִכַּף רַגְלוֹ עַד קָדְקֳדוֹ:
8] וַיִּקַּח־לוֹ חֶרֶשׂ לְהִתְגָּרֵד בּוֹ וְהוּא יֹשֵׁב בְּתוֹךְ
הָאֵפֶר: 9] וַתֹּאמֶר לוֹ אִשְׁתּוֹ עֹדְךָ מַחֲזִיק
בְּתֻמָּתֶךָ בָּרֵךְ אֱלֹהִים וָמֻת: 10] וַיֹּאמֶר אֵלֶיהָ
כְּדַבֵּר אַחַת הַנְּבָלוֹת תְּדַבֵּרִי גַּם אֶת־הַטּוֹב
נְקַבֵּל מֵאֵת הָאֱלֹהִים וְאֶת־הָרָע לֹא נְקַבֵּל
בְּכָל־זֹאת לֹא־חָטָא אִיּוֹב בִּשְׂפָתָיו:

FIRST SELECTION

Second Kings

7 : 3-20

Chapter 7

ז

3] There were four men, lepers, outside the gate. They said to one another, "Why should we sit here waiting for death?

4] If we decide to go into the town, what with the famine in the town, we shall die there; and if we just sit here, still we die. Come, let us desert to the Aramean camp. If they let us live, we shall live; and if they put us to death, we shall but die."

5] They set out at twilight for the Aramean camp; but when they came to the edge of the Aramean camp, there was no one there.

6] For the LORD had caused the Aramean camp to hear a sound of chariots, a sound of horses—the din of a huge army. They said to one another, "The king of Israel must have hired the kings of the Hittites and the kings of Mizraim[a] to attack us!"

7] And they fled headlong in the twilight, abandoning their tents and horses and asses—the [entire] camp just as it was—as they fled for their lives.

8] When those lepers came to the edge of the camp, they went into one of the tents and ate and drank; then they carried off silver and gold and clothing from there and buried it. They came back

3] וְאַרְבָּעָה אֲנָשִׁים הָיוּ מְצֹרָעִים פֶּתַח הַשַּׁעַר וַיֹּאמְרוּ אִישׁ אֶל רֵעֵהוּ מָה אֲנַחְנוּ יֹשְׁבִים פֹּה עַד־מָתְנוּ: 4] אִם אָמַרְנוּ נָבוֹא הָעִיר וְהָרָעָב בָּעִיר וָמַתְנוּ שָׁם וְאִם יָשַׁבְנוּ פֹה וָמָתְנוּ וְעַתָּה לְכוּ וְנִפְּלָה אֶל מַחֲנֵה אֲרָם אִם יְחַיֻּנוּ נִחְיֶה וְאִם יְמִיתֻנוּ וָמָתְנוּ:

5] וַיָּקוּמוּ בַנֶּשֶׁף לָבוֹא אֶל מַחֲנֵה אֲרָם וַיָּבֹאוּ עַד־קְצֵה מַחֲנֵה אֲרָם וְהִנֵּה אֵין שָׁם אִישׁ: 6] וַאדֹנָי הִשְׁמִיעַ אֶת־מַחֲנֵה אֲרָם קוֹל רֶכֶב קוֹל סוּס קוֹל חַיִל גָּדוֹל וַיֹּאמְרוּ אִישׁ אֶל אָחִיו הִנֵּה שָׂכַר עָלֵינוּ מֶלֶךְ יִשְׂרָאֵל אֶת־מַלְכֵי הַחִתִּים וְאֶת־מַלְכֵי מִצְרַיִם לָבוֹא עָלֵינוּ: 7] וַיָּקוּמוּ וַיָּנוּסוּ בַנֶּשֶׁף וַיַּעַזְבוּ אֶת־אָהֳלֵיהֶם וְאֶת־סוּסֵיהֶם וְאֶת־חֲמֹרֵיהֶם הַמַּחֲנֶה כַּאֲשֶׁר־הִיא וַיָּנֻסוּ אֶל נַפְשָׁם:

8] וַיָּבֹאוּ הַמְצֹרָעִים הָאֵלֶּה עַד קְצֵה הַמַּחֲנֶה וַיָּבֹאוּ אֶל־אֹהֶל אֶחָד וַיֹּאכְלוּ וַיִּשְׁתּוּ וַיִּשְׂאוּ מִשָּׁם כֶּסֶף וְזָהָב וּבְגָדִים וַיֵּלְכוּ וַיַּטְמִנוּ

---

[a] *Cf. I Kings 10.28 and note g there*

378

and went into another tent, and they carried off what was there and buried it.

9] Then they said to one another, "We are not doing right. This is a day of good news, and we are keeping silent! If we wait until the light of morning, we shall incur guilt. Come, let us go and inform the king's palace."

10] They went and called out to the gatekeepers of the city and told them, "We have been to the Aramean camp. There is not a soul there, nor any human sound; but the horses are tethered and the asses are tethered and the tents are undisturbed."

11] The gatekeepers called out, and the news was passed on into the king's palace.

12] The king rose in the night and said to his courtiers, "I will tell you what the Arameans have done to us. They know that we are starving, so they have gone out of camp and hidden in the fields, thinking: When they come out of the town, we will take them alive and get into the town." 13] But one of the courtiers spoke up, "Let a few[b] of the remaining horses that are still here be taken—[c]they are like those that are left here of the whole multitude of Israel, out of the whole multitude of Israel that have perished[c]—and let us send and find out."

14] They took two teams[c] of horses and the king sent them after the Aramean army, saying, "Go and find out."

15] They followed them as far as the Jordan, and found the entire road full of clothing and gear which the Arameans had thrown away in their haste; and the messengers returned and told the king.

16] The people then went out and plundered the Aramean camp. So a *seah* of choice flour sold for a shekel, and two *seahs* of barley for a shekel—as the LORD had spoken.

[b] Lit. *"five"*
[c-c] *Meaning of Heb. uncertain*

וַיֵּשְׁבוּ וַיָּבֹאוּ אֶל־אֹהֶל אַחֵר וַיִּשְׂאוּ מִשָּׁם וַיֵּלְכוּ וַיַּטְמִנוּ: 9 וַיֹּאמְרוּ אִישׁ אֶל רֵעֵהוּ לֹא־כֵן אֲנַחְנוּ עֹשִׂים הַיּוֹם הַזֶּה יוֹם בְּשֹׂרָה הוּא וַאֲנַחְנוּ מַחְשִׁים וְחִכִּינוּ עַד־אוֹר הַבֹּקֶר וּמְצָאָנוּ עָווֹן וְעַתָּה לְכוּ וְנָבֹאָה וְנַגִּידָה בֵּית הַמֶּלֶךְ: 10 וַיָּבֹאוּ וַיִּקְרְאוּ אֶל שֹׁעֵר הָעִיר וַיַּגִּידוּ לָהֶם לֵאמֹר בָּאנוּ אֶל מַחֲנֵה אֲרָם וְהִנֵּה אֵין שָׁם אִישׁ וְקוֹל אָדָם כִּי אִם הַסּוּס אָסוּר וְהַחֲמוֹר אָסוּר וְאֹהָלִים כַּאֲשֶׁר־הֵמָּה: 11 וַיִּקְרָא הַשֹּׁעֲרִים וַיַּגִּידוּ בֵּית הַמֶּלֶךְ פְּנִימָה: 12 וַיָּקָם הַמֶּלֶךְ לַיְלָה וַיֹּאמֶר אֶל עֲבָדָיו אַגִּידָה נָּא לָכֶם אֵת אֲשֶׁר־עָשׂוּ לָנוּ אֲרָם יָדְעוּ כִּי רְעֵבִים אֲנַחְנוּ וַיֵּצְאוּ מִן הַמַּחֲנֶה לְהֵחָבֵה בַשָּׂדֶה לֵאמֹר כִּי יֵצְאוּ מִן הָעִיר וְנִתְפְּשֵׂם חַיִּים וְאֶל הָעִיר נָבֹא: 13 וַיַּעַן אֶחָד מֵעֲבָדָיו וַיֹּאמֶר וְיִקְחוּ־נָא חֲמִשָּׁה מִן הַסּוּסִים הַנִּשְׁאָרִים אֲשֶׁר נִשְׁאֲרוּ־בָהּ הִנָּם כְּכָל־הֲמוֹן יִשְׂרָאֵל אֲשֶׁר נִשְׁאֲרוּ־בָהּ הִנָּם כְּכָל־הֲמוֹן יִשְׂרָאֵל אֲשֶׁר־תָּמּוּ וְנִשְׁלְחָה וְנִרְאֶה: 14 וַיִּקְחוּ שְׁנֵי רֶכֶב סוּסִים וַיִּשְׁלַח הַמֶּלֶךְ אַחֲרֵי מַחֲנֵה אֲרָם לֵאמֹר לְכוּ וּרְאוּ: 15 וַיֵּלְכוּ אַחֲרֵיהֶם עַד הַיַּרְדֵּן וְהִנֵּה כָל־ הַדֶּרֶךְ מְלֵאָה בְגָדִים וְכֵלִים אֲשֶׁר הִשְׁלִיכוּ אֲרָם בְּחָפְזָם וַיָּשֻׁבוּ הַמַּלְאָכִים וַיַּגִּדוּ לַמֶּלֶךְ: 16 וַיֵּצֵא הָעָם וַיָּבֹזּוּ אֵת מַחֲנֵה אֲרָם וַיְהִי סְאָה־סֹלֶת בְּשֶׁקֶל וְסָאתַיִם שְׂעֹרִים בְּשֶׁקֶל כִּדְבַר יְהוָה:

17] Now the king had put the aide on whose arm he leaned in charge of the gate; and he was trampled to death in the gate by the people—just as the man of God had spoken, as he had spoken when the king came down to him.

18] For when the man of God said to the king, "This time tomorrow two *seahs* of barley shall sell at the gate of Samaria for a shekel, and a *seah* of choice flour for a shekel,"

19] the aide answered the man of God and said, "Even if the LORD made windows in the sky, could this come to pass?" And he retorted, "You shall see it with your own eyes, but you shall not eat of it."

20] That is exactly what happened to him: The people trampled him to death in the gate.

17] וְהַמֶּלֶךְ הִפְקִיד אֶת־הַשָּׁלִישׁ אֲשֶׁר נִשְׁעָן עַל יָדוֹ עַל הַשַּׁעַר וַיִּרְמְסֻהוּ הָעָם בַּשַּׁעַר וַיָּמֹת כַּאֲשֶׁר דִּבֶּר אִישׁ הָאֱלֹהִים אֲשֶׁר דִּבֶּר בְּרֶדֶת הַמֶּלֶךְ אֵלָיו: 18] וַיְהִי כְּדַבֵּר אִישׁ הָאֱלֹהִים אֶל הַמֶּלֶךְ לֵאמֹר סָאתַיִם שְׂעֹרִים בְּשֶׁקֶל וּסְאָה־סֹלֶת בְּשֶׁקֶל יִהְיֶה כָּעֵת מָחָר בְּשַׁעַר שֹׁמְרוֹן: 19] וַיַּעַן הַשָּׁלִישׁ אֶת־אִישׁ הָאֱלֹהִים וַיֹּאמַר וְהִנֵּה יְהֹוָה עֹשֶׂה אֲרֻבּוֹת בַּשָּׁמַיִם הֲיִהְיֶה כַּדָּבָר הַזֶּה וַיֹּאמֶר הִנְּךָ רֹאֶה בְּעֵינֶיךָ וּמִשָּׁם לֹא תֹאכֵל: 20] וַיְהִי־לוֹ כֵּן וַיִּרְמְסוּ אֹתוֹ הָעָם בַּשַּׁעַר וַיָּמֹת:

SECOND SELECTION

Psalms

103 : 1 - 22

Psalm 103

1] [A psalm] of David.
Bless the LORD, O my soul,
all my being, His holy name.

2] Bless the LORD, O my soul
and do not forget all His bounties.

3] He forgives all your sins,
heals all your diseases.

4] He redeems your life from the Pit,
surrounds you with steadfast love and mercy.

5] He satisfies you with good things in ᵃ·the prime
of life,·ᵃ
so that your youth is renewed like the eagle's.

קג

1] לְדָוִד
בָּרְכִי נַפְשִׁי אֶת־יְהֹוָה
וְכָל־קְרָבַי אֶת־שֵׁם קָדְשׁוֹ:

2] בָּרְכִי נַפְשִׁי אֶת־יְהֹוָה
וְאַל תִּשְׁכְּחִי כָּל־גְּמוּלָיו:

3] הַסֹּלֵחַ לְכָל־עֲוֺנֵכִי
הָרֹפֵא לְכָל־תַּחֲלֻאָיְכִי:

4] הַגּוֹאֵל מִשַּׁחַת חַיָּיְכִי
הַמְעַטְּרֵכִי חֶסֶד וְרַחֲמִים:

5] הַמַּשְׂבִּיעַ בַּטּוֹב עֶדְיֵךְ
תִּתְחַדֵּשׁ כַּנֶּשֶׁר נְעוּרָיְכִי:

ᵃ·ᵃ *Meaning of Heb. uncertain*

380

6] The LORD executes righteous acts
and judgments for all who are wronged.

7] He made known His ways to Moses,
His deeds to the Children of Israel.

8] The LORD is compassionate and gracious,
slow to anger, abounding in steadfast love.

9] He will not contend forever,
or nurse His anger for all time.

10] He has not dealt with us according to our sins,
nor has He requited us according to our iniquities.

11] For as the heavens are high above the earth,
so great is His steadfast love toward those who
fear Him.

12] As east is far from west,
so far has He removed our sins from us.

13] As a father has compassion for his children,
so the LORD has compassion for those who fear
Him.

14] For He knows how we are formed;
He is mindful that we are dust.

15] Man's days are like grass;
he blooms like a flower of the field;

16] a wind passes by and it is no more,
its own place no longer knows it.

17] But the LORD's steadfast love is for all eternity
toward those who fear Him,
and His beneficence is for the children's children

18] of those who keep His covenant
and remember to observe His precepts.

19] The LORD has established His throne in heaven,
and His sovereign rule is over all.

6] עֹשֵׂה צְדָקוֹת יְהֹוָה
וּמִשְׁפָּטִים לְכָל־עֲשׁוּקִים:

7] יוֹדִיעַ דְּרָכָיו לְמֹשֶׁה
לִבְנֵי יִשְׂרָאֵל עֲלִילוֹתָיו:

8] רַחוּם וְחַנּוּן יְהֹוָה
אֶרֶךְ אַפַּיִם וְרַב־חָסֶד:

9] לֹא לָנֶצַח יָרִיב
וְלֹא לְעוֹלָם יִטּוֹר:

10] לֹא כַחֲטָאֵינוּ עָשָׂה לָנוּ
וְלֹא כַעֲוֹנֹתֵינוּ גָּמַל עָלֵינוּ:

11] כִּי כִגְבֹהַּ שָׁמַיִם עַל הָאָרֶץ
גָּבַר חַסְדּוֹ עַל יְרֵאָיו:

12] כִּרְחֹק מִזְרָח מִמַּעֲרָב
הִרְחִיק מִמֶּנּוּ אֶת־פְּשָׁעֵינוּ:

13] כְּרַחֵם אָב עַל בָּנִים
רִחַם יְהֹוָה עַל יְרֵאָיו:

14] כִּי־הוּא יָדַע יִצְרֵנוּ
זָכוּר כִּי עָפָר אֲנָחְנוּ:

15] אֱנוֹשׁ כֶּחָצִיר יָמָיו
כְּצִיץ הַשָּׂדֶה כֵּן יָצִיץ:

16] כִּי רוּחַ עָבְרָה בּוֹ וְאֵינֶנּוּ
וְלֹא יַכִּירֶנּוּ עוֹד מְקוֹמוֹ:

17] וְחֶסֶד יְהֹוָה | מֵעוֹלָם וְעַד עוֹלָם
עַל יְרֵאָיו
וְצִדְקָתוֹ לִבְנֵי בָנִים:

18] לְשֹׁמְרֵי בְרִיתוֹ
וּלְזֹכְרֵי פִקֻּדָיו לַעֲשׂוֹתָם:

19] יְהֹוָה בַּשָּׁמַיִם הֵכִין כִּסְאוֹ
וּמַלְכוּתוֹ בַּכֹּל מָשָׁלָה:

381

20] Bless the LORD, O His angels,
    mighty creatures who do His bidding,
ever obedient to His bidding;

21] bless the LORD, all His hosts,
His servants who do His will;

22] bless the LORD, all His works,
through the length and breadth of His realm;
bless the LORD, O my soul.

בָּרְכוּ יְהֹוָה מַלְאָכָיו [20

גִּבֹּרֵי כֹחַ עֹשֵׂי דְבָרוֹ

לִשְׁמֹעַ בְּקוֹל דְּבָרוֹ:

בָּרְכוּ יְהֹוָה כָּל־צְבָאָיו [21

מְשָׁרְתָיו עֹשֵׂי רְצוֹנוֹ:

בָּרְכוּ יְהֹוָה כָּל־מַעֲשָׂיו [22

בְּכָל־מְקֹמוֹת מֶמְשַׁלְתּוֹ

בָּרְכִי נַפְשִׁי אֶת־יְהֹוָה:

אַחֲרֵי מוֹת

FIRST SELECTION

Ezekiel

22 : 1-19

Chapter 22

1] The word of the LORD came to me:
2] Further, O mortal, *arraign, arraign*ᵃ the city
of bloodshed; declare to her all her abhorrent
deeds!

3] Say: Thus said the Lord GOD: O city
in whose midst blood is shed, so that your hour is
approaching; within which fetishes are made, so
that you have become unclean!

4] You stand
guilty of the blood you have shed, defiled by the
fetishes you have made. You have brought on your
day; ᵇyou have reached your year.ᵇ Therefore I
will make you the mockery of the nations and the
scorn of all the lands.

5] Both the near and the
far shall scorn you, O besmirched of name, O
laden with iniquity!

6] Every one of the princes of Israel in your
midst used his strength for the shedding of blood.
7] Fathers and mothers have been humiliated
within you; strangers have been cheated in your
midst; orphans and widows have been wronged
within you.

8] You have despised My holy things
and profaned My sabbaths.
9] Baseᶜ men in your midst were intent on
shedding blood; in you they have eaten ᵈupon
the mountains;ᵈ and they have practiced depravity in your midst.

כב

1] וַיְהִי דְבַר־יְהֹוָה אֵלַי לֵאמֹר: 2] וְאַתָּה
בֶן־אָדָם הֲתִשְׁפֹּט הֲתִשְׁפֹּט אֶת־עִיר הַדָּמִים
וְהוֹדַעְתָּהּ אֵת כָּל־תּוֹעֲבוֹתֶיהָ: 3] וְאָמַרְתָּ כֹּה
אָמַר אֲדֹנָי יֱהֹוִה עִיר שֹׁפֶכֶת דָּם בְּתוֹכָהּ
לָבוֹא עִתָּהּ וְעָשְׂתָה גִלּוּלִים עָלֶיהָ לְטָמְאָה:
4] בְּדָמֵךְ אֲשֶׁר־שָׁפַכְתְּ אָשַׁמְתְּ וּבְגִלּוּלַיִךְ אֲשֶׁר־
עָשִׂית טָמֵאת וַתַּקְרִיבִי יָמַיִךְ וַתָּבוֹא עַד־
שְׁנוֹתָיִךְ עַל־כֵּן נְתַתִּיךְ חֶרְפָּה לַגּוֹיִם וְקַלָּסָה
לְכָל־הָאֲרָצוֹת: 5] הַקְּרֹבוֹת וְהָרְחֹקוֹת מִמֵּךְ
יִתְקַלְּסוּ־בָךְ טְמֵאַת הַשֵּׁם רַבַּת הַמְּהוּמָה:
6] הִנֵּה נְשִׂיאֵי יִשְׂרָאֵל אִישׁ לִזְרֹעוֹ הָיוּ בָךְ
לְמַעַן שְׁפָךְ־דָּם: 7] אָב וָאֵם הֵקַלּוּ בָךְ לַגֵּר
עָשׂוּ בַעֹשֶׁק בְּתוֹכֵךְ יָתוֹם וְאַלְמָנָה הוֹנוּ בָךְ:
8] קָדָשַׁי בָּזִית וְאֶת־שַׁבְּתֹתַי חִלָּלְתְּ:
9] אַנְשֵׁי רָכִיל הָיוּ בָךְ לְמַעַן שְׁפָךְ־דָּם
וְאֶל־הֶהָרִים אָכְלוּ בָךְ זִמָּה עָשׂוּ בְתוֹכֵךְ:

ᵃ⁻ᵃ Lit. "will you arraign, arraign"
ᵇ⁻ᵇ *Some Babylonian mss. and ancient versions read "the time of your years has come"*
ᶜ *Meaning of Heb. uncertain*
ᵈ⁻ᵈ *I.e., in idolatry. Emendation yields "with the blood"; cf. Lev. 19.26*

10] In you they have uncovered their fathers' nakedness;[e] in you they have ravished women during their impurity. 11] They have committed abhorrent acts with other men's wives; in their depravity they have defiled their own daughters-in-law; in you they have ravished their own sisters, daughters of their fathers.

12] They have taken bribes within you to shed blood. You have taken advance and accrued interest;[f] you have defrauded your countrymen to your profit. You have forgotten Me—declares the Lord GOD.

13] Lo, I will strike My hands over the ill-gotten gains that you have amassed, and over the bloodshed that has been committed in your midst. 14] Will your courage endure, will your hands remain firm in the days when I deal with you? I the LORD have spoken and I will act.

15] I will scatter you among the nations and disperse you through the lands; I will consume the uncleanness out of you.

16] You shall be dishonored in the sight of nations, and you shall know that I am the LORD.

17] The word of the LORD came to me: 18] O mortal, the House of Israel has become dross to Me; they are all copper, tin, iron, and lead. [e]But in a crucible, the dross shall turn into silver.[e] 19] Assuredly, thus said the Lord GOD: Because you have all become dross, I will gather you into Jerusalem.

עֶרְוַת־אָב גִּלָּה־בָּךְ טְמֵאַת הַנִּדָּה עִנּוּ־בָךְ: [10

וְאִישׁ אֶת־אֵשֶׁת רֵעֵהוּ עָשָׂה תּוֹעֵבָה וְאִישׁ [11
אֶת־כַּלָּתוֹ טִמֵּא בְזִמָּה וְאִישׁ אֶת־אֲחֹתוֹ בַת־
אָבִיו עִנָּה־בָךְ: שֹׁחַד לָקְחוּ בָךְ לְמַעַן [12
שְׁפָךְ־דָּם נֶשֶׁךְ וְתַרְבִּית לָקַחַתְּ וַתְּבַצְּעִי רֵעַיִךְ
בַּעֹשֶׁק וְאֹתִי שָׁכַחַתְּ נְאֻם אֲדֹנָי יֱהוִֹה:

וְהִנֵּה הִכֵּיתִי כַפִּי אֶל־בִּצְעֵךְ אֲשֶׁר [13
עָשִׂית וְעַל דָּמֵךְ אֲשֶׁר הָיוּ בְּתוֹכֵךְ:
הֲיַעֲמֹד לִבֵּךְ אִם תֶּחֱזַקְנָה יָדַיִךְ לַיָּמִים [14
אֲשֶׁר אֲנִי עֹשֶׂה אוֹתָךְ אֲנִי יְהוָה דִּבַּרְתִּי
וְעָשִׂיתִי: וַהֲפִיצוֹתִי אוֹתָךְ בַּגּוֹיִם וְזֵרִיתִיךְ [15
בָּאֲרָצוֹת וַהֲתִמֹּתִי טֻמְאָתֵךְ מִמֵּךְ: וְנִחַלְתְּ [16
בָּךְ לְעֵינֵי גוֹיִם וְיָדַעַתְּ כִּי אֲנִי יְהוָה:

וַיְהִי דְבַר יְהוָה אֵלַי לֵאמֹר: בֶּן [18 [17
אָדָם הָיוּ לִי בֵית יִשְׂרָאֵל לְסִיג כֻּלָּם נְחֹשֶׁת
וּבְדִיל וּבַרְזֶל וְעוֹפֶרֶת בְּתוֹךְ כּוּר סִגִים כֶּסֶף
הָיוּ: לָכֵן כֹּה אָמַר אֲדֹנָי יֱהוִֹה יַעַן הֱיוֹת [19
כֻּלְּכֶם לְסִגִים לָכֵן הִנְנִי קֹבֵץ אֶתְכֶם אֶל־תּוֹךְ
יְרוּשָׁלָ͏ִם:

SECOND SELECTION

Isaiah

58 : 1-14

Chapter 58

1] Cry with full throat, without restraint;
Raise your voice like a ram's horn!
Declare to My people their transgression,
To the House of Jacob their sin.

נח

קְרָא בְגָרוֹן אַל תַּחְשֹׂךְ [1
כַּשּׁוֹפָר הָרֵם קוֹלֶךָ
וְהַגֵּד לְעַמִּי פִּשְׁעָם
וּלְבֵית יַעֲקֹב חַטֹּאתָם:

---

[e] *I.e., have cohabited with a former wife of the father; cf. Lev. 18.7–8*   [f] *Cf. note at 18.8*
[e–e] *Meaning of Heb. uncertain*

2] To be sure, they seek Me daily,
Eager to learn My ways.
Like a nation that does what is right,
That has not abandoned the laws of its God,
They ask Me for the right way,
They are eager for the nearness of God:

[2] וְאוֹתִי יוֹם יוֹם יִדְרֹשׁוּן
וְדַעַת דְּרָכַי יֶחְפָּצוּן
כְּגוֹי אֲשֶׁר צְדָקָה עָשָׂה
וּמִשְׁפַּט אֱלֹהָיו לֹא עָזָב
יִשְׁאָלוּנִי מִשְׁפְּטֵי־צֶדֶק
קִרְבַת אֱלֹהִים יֶחְפָּצוּן:

3] "Why, when we fasted, did You not see?
When we starved our bodies, did You pay no
    heed?"
Because on your fast day
You see to your business
And oppress all your laborers!

[3] לָמָּה צַּמְנוּ וְלֹא רָאִיתָ
עִנִּינוּ נַפְשֵׁנוּ וְלֹא תֵדָע
הֵן בְּיוֹם צֹמְכֶם
תִּמְצְאוּ־חֵפֶץ
וְכָל־עַצְּבֵיכֶם תִּנְגֹּשׂוּ:

4] Because you fast in strife and contention,
And you strike with a wicked fist!
Your fasting today is not such
As to make your voice heard on high.

[4] הֵן לְרִיב וּמַצָּה תָּצוּמוּ
וּלְהַכּוֹת בְּאֶגְרֹף רֶשַׁע
לֹא תָצוּמוּ כַיּוֹם
לְהַשְׁמִיעַ בַּמָּרוֹם קוֹלְכֶם:

5] Is such the fast I desire,
A day for men to starve their bodies?
Is it bowing the head like a bulrush
And lying in sackcloth and ashes?
Do you call that a fast,
A day when the Lord is favorable?

[5] הֲכָזֶה יִהְיֶה צוֹם אֶבְחָרֵהוּ
יוֹם עַנּוֹת אָדָם נַפְשׁוֹ
הֲלָכֹף כְּאַגְמֹן רֹאשׁוֹ
וְשַׂק וָאֵפֶר יַצִּיעַ
הֲלָזֶה תִּקְרָא־צוֹם
וְיוֹם רָצוֹן לַיהוָה:

6] No, this is the fast I desire:
To unlock the fetters of wickedness,
And untie the cords of ᵃ⁻the yoke⁻ᵃ
To let the oppressed go free;
To break off every yoke.

[6] הֲלוֹא זֶה צוֹם אֶבְחָרֵהוּ
פַּתֵּחַ חַרְצֻבּוֹת רֶשַׁע
הַתֵּר אֲגֻדּוֹת מוֹטָה
וְשַׁלַּח רְצוּצִים חָפְשִׁים
וְכָל־מוֹטָה תְּנַתֵּקוּ:

7] It is to share your bread with the hungry,
And to take the wretched poor into your home;

[7] הֲלוֹא פָרֹס לָרָעֵב לַחְמֶךָ
וַעֲנִיִּים מְרוּדִים תָּבִיא בָיִת

ᵃ⁻ᵃ *Change of vocalization yields "lawlessness"; cf.* muṭṭeh, *Ezek. 9.9*

385

When you see the naked, to clothe him,
And not to ignore your own kin.

כִּי־תִרְאֶה עָרֹם וְכִסִּיתוֹ
וּמִבְּשָׂרְךָ לֹא תִתְעַלָּם:

8] Then shall your light burst through like the
    dawn
And your healing spring up quickly;
Your Vindicator shall march before you,
The Presence of the LORD shall be your rear guard.

8] אָז יִבָּקַע כַּשַּׁחַר אוֹרֶךָ
וַאֲרֻכָתְךָ מְהֵרָה תִצְמָח
וְהָלַךְ לְפָנֶיךָ צִדְקֶךָ
כְּבוֹד יְהֹוָה יַאַסְפֶךָ:

9] Then, when you call, the LORD will answer;
When you cry, He will say: Here I am.
If you banish *the yoke* from your midst,
The menacing hand, and evil speech,

9] אָז תִּקְרָא וַיהֹוָה יַעֲנֶה
תְּשַׁוַּע וְיֹאמַר הִנֵּנִי
אִם־תָּסִיר מִתּוֹכְךָ מוֹטָה
שְׁלַח אֶצְבַּע וְדַבֶּר־אָוֶן:

10] And you offer your compassion to the hungry
And satisfy the famished creature—
Then shall your light shine in darkness,
And your gloom shall be like noonday.

10] וְתָפֵק לָרָעֵב נַפְשֶׁךָ
וְנֶפֶשׁ נַעֲנָה תַּשְׂבִּיעַ
וְזָרַח בַּחֹשֶׁךְ אוֹרֶךָ
וַאֲפֵלָתְךָ כַּצָּהֳרָיִם:

11] The LORD will guide you always;
He will slake your thirst in *parched places*
And give strength to your bones.
You shall be like a watered garden,
Like a spring whose waters do not fail.

11] וְנָחֲךָ יְהֹוָה תָּמִיד
וְהִשְׂבִּיעַ בְּצַחְצָחוֹת נַפְשֶׁךָ
וְעַצְמֹתֶיךָ יַחֲלִיץ
וְהָיִיתָ כְּגַן רָוֶה
וּכְמוֹצָא מַיִם אֲשֶׁר לֹא־יְכַזְּבוּ מֵימָיו:

12] Men from your midst shall rebuild ancient
    ruins,
You shall restore foundations laid long ago.
And you shall be called
"Repairer of fallen walls,
Restorer of lanes for habitation."

12] וּבָנוּ מִמְּךָ חָרְבוֹת עוֹלָם
מוֹסְדֵי דוֹר־וָדוֹר תְּקוֹמֵם
וְקֹרָא לְךָ
גֹּדֵר פֶּרֶץ
מְשֹׁבֵב נְתִיבוֹת לָשָׁבֶת:

13] If you *refrain from trampling* the sabbath,
From pursuing your affairs on My holy day;

13] אִם־תָּשִׁיב מִשַּׁבָּת רַגְלֶךָ
עֲשׂוֹת חֲפָצֶיךָ בְּיוֹם קָדְשִׁי

---

a-a Change of vocalization yields "lawlessness"; cf. muṭṭeh, Ezek. 9.9
b-b Lit. "Extending the finger"
c Some Heb. mss. and ancient versions read "bread"
d-d Meaning of Heb. uncertain
e-e Lit. "turn back your foot from"

If you call the sabbath "delight,"
The LORD's holy day "honored";
And if you honor it and go not your ways
Nor look to your affairs, nor strike bargains—

וְקָרָאתָ לַשַּׁבָּת עֹנֶג

לִקְדוֹשׁ יְהוָה מְכֻבָּד

וְכִבַּדְתּוֹ מֵעֲשׂוֹת דְּרָכֶיךָ

מִמְּצוֹא חֶפְצְךָ וְדַבֵּר דָּבָר:

14] Then you ˻can seek the favor of the LORD.˼
I will set you astride the heights of the earth,
And let you enjoy the heritage of your father
    Jacob—
For the mouth of the LORD has spoken.

[14 אָז תִּתְעַנַּג עַל יְהוָה

וְהִרְכַּבְתִּיךָ עַל־בָּמֳתֵי אָרֶץ

וְהַאֲכַלְתִּיךָ נַחֲלַת יַעֲקֹב אָבִיךָ

כִּי פִּי יְהוָה דִּבֵּר:

THIRD SELECTION

Isaiah

59 : 1-21

Chapter 59

1] No, the LORD's arm is not too short to save,
Or His ear too dull to hear;

נט

[1 הֵן לֹא קָצְרָה יַד יְהוָה מֵהוֹשִׁיעַ

וְלֹא כָבְדָה אָזְנוֹ מִשְּׁמוֹעַ:

2] But your iniquities have been a barrier
Between you and your God,
Your sins have made Him turn His face away
And refuse to hear you.

[2 כִּי אִם עֲוֹנֹתֵיכֶם הָיוּ מַבְדִּלִים

בֵּינֵכֶם לְבֵין אֱלֹהֵיכֶם

וְחַטֹּאותֵיכֶם הִסְתִּירוּ פָנִים

מִכֶּם מִשְּׁמוֹעַ:

3] For your hands are defiled with crime[a]
And your fingers with iniquity.
Your lips speak falsehood,
Your tongue utters treachery.

[3 כִּי כַפֵּיכֶם נְגֹאֲלוּ בַדָּם

וְאֶצְבְּעוֹתֵיכֶם בֶּעָוֹן

שִׂפְתוֹתֵיכֶם דִּבְּרוּ־שֶׁקֶר

לְשׁוֹנְכֶם עַוְלָה תֶהְגֶּה:

4] No one sues justly
Or pleads honestly;

[4 אֵין קֹרֵא בְצֶדֶק

וְאֵין נִשְׁפָּט בֶּאֱמוּנָה

˻-˼ Cf. Ps. 37.4; Job 22.26–27; 27.10

[a] Or "blood"

They rely on emptiness and speak falsehood,
Conceiving wrong and begetting evil.

5] They hatch adder's eggs
And weave spider webs;
He who eats of those eggs will die,
And if one is crushed, it hatches out a viper.

6] Their webs will not serve as a garment,
What they make cannot serve as clothing;
Their deeds are deeds of mischief,
Their hands commit lawless acts,

7] Their feet run after evil,
They hasten to shed the blood of the innocent.
Their plans are plans of mischief,
Destructiveness and injury are on their roads.

8] They do not care for the way of integrity,
There is no justice on their paths.
They make their courses crooked,
No one who walks in them cares for integrity.

9] "That is why redress is far from us,
And vindication does not reach us.
We hope for light, and lo! there is darkness;
For a gleam, and we must walk in gloom.

10] We grope, like blind men along a wall;
Like those without eyes we grope.
We stumble at noon, as if in darkness;
b-Among the sturdy, we are-*b* like the dead.

11] We all growl like bears
And moan like doves.

בָּטוֹחַ עַל־תֹּהוּ וְדַבֶּר־שָׁוְא
הָרוֹ עָמָל וְהוֹלֵיד אָוֶן:

5] בֵּיצֵי צִפְעוֹנִי בִּקֵּעוּ
וְקוּרֵי עַכָּבִישׁ יֶאֱרֹגוּ
הָאֹכֵל מִבֵּיצֵיהֶם יָמוּת
וְהַזּוּרֶה תִּבָּקַע אֶפְעֶה:

6] קוּרֵיהֶם לֹא יִהְיוּ לְבֶגֶד
וְלֹא יִתְכַּסּוּ בְּמַעֲשֵׂיהֶם
מַעֲשֵׂיהֶם מַעֲשֵׂי־אָוֶן
וּפֹעַל חָמָס בְּכַפֵּיהֶם:

7] רַגְלֵיהֶם לָרַע יָרֻצוּ
וִימַהֲרוּ לִשְׁפֹּךְ דָּם נָקִי
מַחְשְׁבוֹתֵיהֶם מַחְשְׁבוֹת אָוֶן
שֹׁד וָשֶׁבֶר בִּמְסִלּוֹתָם:

8] דֶּרֶךְ שָׁלוֹם לֹא יָדָעוּ
וְאֵין מִשְׁפָּט בְּמַעְגְּלוֹתָם
נְתִיבוֹתֵיהֶם עִקְּשׁוּ לָהֶם
כֹּל דֹּרֵךְ בָּהּ לֹא יָדַע שָׁלוֹם:

9] עַל־כֵּן רָחַק מִשְׁפָּט מִמֶּנּוּ
וְלֹא תַשִּׂיגֵנוּ צְדָקָה
נְקַוֶּה לָאוֹר וְהִנֵּה־חֹשֶׁךְ
לִנְגֹהוֹת בָּאֲפֵלוֹת נְהַלֵּךְ:

10] נְגַשְׁשָׁה כַעִוְרִים קִיר
וּכְאֵין עֵינַיִם נְגַשֵּׁשָׁה
כָּשַׁלְנוּ בַצָּהֳרַיִם כַּנֶּשֶׁף
בָּאַשְׁמַנִּים כַּמֵּתִים:

11] נֶהֱמֶה כַדֻּבִּים כֻּלָּנוּ
וְכַיּוֹנִים הָגֹה נֶהְגֶּה

b-b Meaning of Heb. uncertain. Emendation yields "In the daytime. . . ."

We hope for redress, and there is none;
For victory, and it is far from us.

12] For our many sins are before You,
Our guilt testifies against us.
We are aware of our sins,
And we know well our iniquities:

13] Rebellion, faithlessness to the LORD,
And turning away from our God,
Planning fraud and treachery,
Conceiving lies and uttering them with the throat.[c]

14] And so redress is turned back
And vindication stays afar,
Because honesty stumbles in the public square
And uprightness cannot enter.

15] Honesty has been lacking,
He who turns away from evil is despoiled."
The LORD saw and was displeased
That there was no redress.

16] He saw that there was no man,
He gazed long, but no one intervened.
Then His own arm won Him triumph,
His victorious right hand[d] supported Him.

17] He donned victory like a coat of mail,
With a helmet of triumph on His head;
He clothed Himself with garments of retribution,
Wrapped Himself in zeal as in a robe.

18] [e-According to their deserts,
So shall He repay-[e] fury to His foes;

נְקַוֶּה לַמִּשְׁפָּט וָאַיִן
לִישׁוּעָה רָחֲקָה מִמֶּנּוּ:

12] כִּי רַבּוּ פְשָׁעֵינוּ נֶגְדֶּךָ
וְחַטֹּאותֵינוּ עָנְתָה בָּנוּ
כִּי פְשָׁעֵינוּ אִתָּנוּ
וַעֲוֹנֹתֵינוּ יְדַעֲנוּם:

13] פָּשֹׁעַ וְכַחֵשׁ בַּיהֹוָה
וְנָסוֹג מֵאַחַר אֱלֹהֵינוּ
דַּבֶּר־עֹשֶׁק וְסָרָה
הֹרוֹ וְהֹגוֹ מִלֵּב דִּבְרֵי־שָׁקֶר:

14] וְהֻסַּג אָחוֹר מִשְׁפָּט
וּצְדָקָה מֵרָחוֹק תַּעֲמֹד
כִּי כָשְׁלָה בָרְחוֹב אֱמֶת
וּנְכֹחָה לֹא תוּכַל לָבוֹא:

15] וַתְּהִי הָאֱמֶת נֶעְדֶּרֶת
וְסָר מֵרָע מִשְׁתּוֹלֵל
וַיַּרְא יְהֹוָה וַיֵּרַע בְּעֵינָיו
כִּי אֵין מִשְׁפָּט:

16] וַיַּרְא כִּי אֵין אִישׁ
וַיִּשְׁתּוֹמֵם כִּי אֵין מַפְגִּיעַ
וַתּוֹשַׁע לוֹ זְרֹעוֹ
וְצִדְקָתוֹ הִיא סְמָכָתְהוּ:

17] וַיִּלְבַּשׁ צְדָקָה כַּשִּׁרְיָן
וְכוֹבַע יְשׁוּעָה בְּרֹאשׁוֹ
וַיִּלְבַּשׁ בִּגְדֵי נָקָם תִּלְבֹּשֶׁת
וַיַּעַט כַּמְעִיל קִנְאָה:

18] כְּעַל גְּמֻלוֹת
כְּעַל יְשַׁלֵּם חֵמָה לְצָרָיו

[c] Lit. "heart"; see note at 33.18 and frequently elsewhere
[d] Cf. Ps. 98.1–2   [e-e] Meaning of Heb. uncertain

389

He shall make requital to His enemies,
Requital to the distant lands.

19] From the west, they shall revere*f* the name of
the Lord,
And from the east, His Presence.
For He shall come like a hemmed-in stream
Which the wind of the Lord drives on;

20] He shall come as redeemer to Zion,
To those in Jacob who turn back from sin
—declares the Lord.

21] And this shall be My covenant with them,
said the Lord: My spirit*g* which is upon you, and
the words which I have placed in your mouth shall
not be absent from your mouth, nor from the
mouth of your children, nor from the mouth of
your children's children—said the Lord—from
now on, for all time.*h*

גְּמוּל לְאֹיְבָיו

לָאִיִּים גְּמוּל יְשַׁלֵּם:

19] וְיִירְאוּ מִמַּעֲרָב אֶת־שֵׁם יְהוָה

וּמִמִּזְרַח־שֶׁמֶשׁ אֶת־כְּבוֹדוֹ

כִּי־יָבוֹא כַנָּהָר צָר

רוּחַ יְהוָה נֹסְסָה בוֹ:

20] וּבָא לְצִיּוֹן גּוֹאֵל

וּלְשָׁבֵי פֶשַׁע בְּיַעֲקֹב

נְאֻם יְהוָה:

21] וַאֲנִי זֹאת בְּרִיתִי אוֹתָם אָמַר יְהוָה

רוּחִי אֲשֶׁר עָלֶיךָ וּדְבָרַי אֲשֶׁר־שַׂמְתִּי בְּפִיךָ

לֹא יָמוּשׁוּ מִפִּיךָ וּמִפִּי זַרְעֲךָ וּמִפִּי זֶרַע זַרְעֲךָ

אָמַר יְהוָה מֵעַתָּה וְעַד־עוֹלָם:

---

f Or (with a number of mss. and editions) "see"
g I.e., the gift of prophecy; cf. 61.1
h Israel is to be a prophet-nation; cf. 51.16

קדשים

FIRST SELECTION

Amos

9 : 7-15

Chapter 9

ט

7] To Me, O Israelites, you are
Just like the Ethiopians
    —declares the Lord.
True, I brought Israel up
From the land of Egypt,
But also the Philistines from Caphtor
And the Arameans from Kir.

7] הֲלוֹא כִבְנֵי כֻשִׁיִּים אַתֶּם לִי

בְּנֵי יִשְׂרָאֵל

נְאֻם יְהֹוָה

הֲלוֹא אֶת־יִשְׂרָאֵל הֶעֱלֵיתִי

מֵאֶרֶץ מִצְרַיִם

וּפְלִשְׁתִּיִּים מִכַּפְתּוֹר

וַאֲרָם מִקִּיר:

8] Behold, the Lord God has His eye
Upon the sinful kingdom:
I will wipe it off
The face of the earth!
But, I will not wholly wipe out
The House of Jacob
    —declares the Lord.

8] הִנֵּה עֵינֵי אֲדֹנָי יֱהֹוִה

בַּמַּמְלָכָה הַחַטָּאָה

וְהִשְׁמַדְתִּי אֹתָהּ

מֵעַל פְּנֵי הָאֲדָמָה

אֶפֶס כִּי לֹא הַשְׁמֵיד אַשְׁמִיד

אֶת־בֵּית יַעֲקֹב

נְאֻם יְהֹוָה:

9] For I will give the order
And shake the House of Israel—
Through all the nations—
As one shakes [sand] in a sieve,[b]
And not a pebble falls to the ground.

9] כִּי הִנֵּה אָנֹכִי מְצַוֶּה

וַהֲנִעוֹתִי בְכָל־הַגּוֹיִם

אֶת־בֵּית יִשְׂרָאֵל

כַּאֲשֶׁר יִנּוֹעַ בַּכְּבָרָה

וְלֹא יִפּוֹל צְרוֹר אָרֶץ:

---

[b] *A coarse sieve used for cleansing grain of straw and stones, or sand of pebbles and shells*

10] All the sinners of My people
Shall perish by the sword,
Who boast,
"Never shall the evil
Overtake us or come near us."

11] In that day,
I will set up again the fallen booth of David:
I will mend its breaches and set up its ruins anew.
I will build it firm as in the days of old,

12] e‑So that they shall possess the rest of Edom
And all the nations once attached to My name‑e
—Declares the LORD who will bring this to pass.

13] A time is coming
                              —declares the LORD—
When the plowman shall meet the reaper,[d]
And the treader of grapes
Him who holds the [bag of] seed;
When the mountains shall drip wine
And all the hills shall wave [with grain].

14] I will restore My people Israel.
They shall rebuild ruined cities and inhabit them;
They shall plant vineyards and drink their wine;
They shall till gardens and eat their fruits.

15] And I will plant them upon their soil,
Nevermore to be uprooted
From the soil I have given them.
                              —said the LORD your God.

10] בַּחֶרֶב יָמוּתוּ

כֹּל חַטָּאֵי עַמִּי

הָאֹמְרִים

לֹא־תַגִּישׁ וְתַקְדִּים בַּעֲדֵינוּ

הָרָעָה:

11] בַּיּוֹם הַהוּא

אָקִים אֶת־סֻכַּת דָּוִיד הַנֹּפֶלֶת

וְגָדַרְתִּי אֶת־פִּרְצֵיהֶן וַהֲרִסֹתָיו אָקִים

וּבְנִיתִיהָ כִּימֵי עוֹלָם:

12] לְמַעַן יִירְשׁוּ אֶת־שְׁאֵרִית אֱדוֹם

וְכָל־הַגּוֹיִם אֲשֶׁר־נִקְרָא שְׁמִי עֲלֵיהֶם

נְאֻם־יְהוָה עֹשֶׂה זֹּאת:

13] הִנֵּה יָמִים בָּאִים

נְאֻם־יְהוָה

וְנִגַּשׁ חוֹרֵשׁ בַּקֹּצֵר

וְדֹרֵךְ עֲנָבִים

בְּמֹשֵׁךְ הַזָּרַע

וְהִטִּיפוּ הֶהָרִים עָסִיס

וְכָל־הַגְּבָעוֹת תִּתְמוֹגַגְנָה:

14] וְשַׁבְתִּי אֶת־שְׁבוּת עַמִּי יִשְׂרָאֵל

וּבָנוּ עָרִים נְשַׁמּוֹת

וְיָשָׁבוּ וְנָטְעוּ כְרָמִים

וְשָׁתוּ אֶת־יֵינָם

וְעָשׂוּ גַנּוֹת וְאָכְלוּ אֶת־פְּרִיהֶם:

15] וּנְטַעְתִּים עַל אַדְמָתָם

וְלֹא יִנָּתְשׁוּ עוֹד

מֵעַל אַדְמָתָם אֲשֶׁר נָתַתִּי לָהֶם

אָמַר יְהוָה אֱלֹהֶיךָ:

e‑e I.e., the House of David shall reestablish its authority over the nations that were ruled by David
d Cf. Lev. 26.5

392

Ezekiel

20 : 2-20

Chapter 20

כ

2] And the word of the LORD came to me:

2] וַיְהִי דְבַר יְהֹוָה אֵלַי לֵאמֹר:

3] O mortal, speak to the elders of Israel and say to them: Thus said the Lord GOD: Have you come to inquire of Me? As I live, I will not respond to your inquiry—declares the Lord GOD.

3] בֶּן אָדָם דַּבֵּר אֶת־זִקְנֵי יִשְׂרָאֵל וְאָמַרְתָּ אֲלֵהֶם כֹּה אָמַר אֲדֹנָי יֱהֹוִה הֲלִדְרֹשׁ אֹתִי אַתֶּם בָּאִים חַי־אָנִי אִם־אִדָּרֵשׁ לָכֶם נְאֻם אֲדֹנָי יֱהֹוִה:

4] ᵃ⁻Arraign, arraign them, O mortal!⁻ᵃ Declare to them the abhorrent deeds of their fathers.

4] הֲתִשְׁפֹּט אֹתָם הֲתִשְׁפּוֹט בֶּן אָדָם אֶת־תּוֹעֲבֹת אֲבוֹתָם הוֹדִיעֵם:

5] Say to them: Thus said the Lord GOD:
On the day that I chose Israel, I ᵇ⁻gave My oath⁻ᵇ to the stock of the House of Jacob; when I made Myself known to them in the land of Egypt, I gave my oath to them. When I said, "I the LORD am your God,"

5] וְאָמַרְתָּ אֲלֵיהֶם כֹּה אָמַר אֲדֹנָי יֱהֹוִה בְּיוֹם בָּחֲרִי בְיִשְׂרָאֵל וָאֶשָּׂא יָדִי לְזֶרַע בֵּית יַעֲקֹב וָאִוָּדַע לָהֶם בְּאֶרֶץ מִצְרָיִם וָאֶשָּׂא יָדִי לָהֶם לֵאמֹר אֲנִי יְהֹוָה אֱלֹהֵיכֶם:

6] that same day I swore to them to take them out of the land of Egypt into a land flowing with milk and honey, a land which I had sought out for them, the fairest of all lands.

6] בַּיּוֹם הַהוּא נָשָׂאתִי יָדִי לָהֶם לְהוֹצִיאָם מֵאֶרֶץ מִצְרָיִם אֶל־אֶרֶץ אֲשֶׁר־תַּרְתִּי לָהֶם זָבַת חָלָב וּדְבַשׁ צְבִי הִיא לְכָל־הָאֲרָצוֹת:

7] I also said to them: Cast away, every one of you, the detestable things ᶜ⁻that you are drawn to,⁻ᶜ and do not defile yourselves with the fetishes of Egypt—I the LORD am your God.

7] וָאֹמַר אֲלֵהֶם אִישׁ שִׁקּוּצֵי עֵינָיו הַשְׁלִיכוּ וּבְגִלּוּלֵי מִצְרַיִם אַל־תִּטַּמָּאוּ אֲנִי יְהֹוָה אֱלֹהֵיכֶם:

8] But they defied Me and refused to listen to Me. They did not cast away the detestable things they were drawn to, nor did they give up the fetishes of Egypt. Then I resolved to pour out My fury upon them, to vent all My anger upon them there, in the land of Egypt.

8] וַיַּמְרוּ־בִי וְלֹא אָבוּ לִשְׁמֹעַ אֵלַי אִישׁ אֶת־שִׁקּוּצֵי עֵינֵיהֶם לֹא הִשְׁלִיכוּ וְאֶת־גִּלּוּלֵי מִצְרַיִם לֹא עָזָבוּ וָאֹמַר לִשְׁפֹּךְ חֲמָתִי עֲלֵיהֶם לְכַלּוֹת אַפִּי בָּהֶם בְּתוֹךְ אֶרֶץ מִצְרָיִם:

ᵃ⁻ᵃ Lit. "Will you arraign them, will you arraign, O mortal?"
ᵇ⁻ᵇ Lit. "raised My hand"
ᶜ⁻ᶜ Lit. "of his eyes"

9] But I acted for the sake of My name, that it might not be profaned in the sight of the nations among whom they were. For it was before their eyes that I had made Myself known to Israel[d] to bring them out of the land of Egypt.

10] I brought them out of the land of Egypt and I led them into the wilderness.

11] I gave them My laws and taught them My rules, by the pursuit of which a man shall live.

12] Moreover, I gave them My sabbaths to serve as a sign between Me and them, that they might know that it is I the LORD who sanctify them.

13] But the House of Israel rebelled against Me in the wilderness; they did not follow My laws and they rejected My rules—by pursuit of which a man shall live—and they grossly desecrated My sabbaths. Then I thought to pour out My fury upon them in the wilderness and to make an end of them;

14] but I acted for the sake of My name, that it might not be profaned in the sight of the nations before whose eyes I had led them out.

15] However, I swore[b] to them in the wilderness that I would not bring them into the land flowing with milk and honey, the fairest of all lands, which I had assigned [to them],

16] for they rejected My rules, disobeyed My laws, and desecrated My sabbaths; their hearts followed after their fetishes.

17] But I had pity on them and did not destroy them; I did not make an end of them in the wilderness.

18] I warned their children in the wilderness: Do not follow the practices of your fathers, do not keep their ways, and do not defile yourselves with their fetishes.

19] I the LORD am your God: Follow My laws and be careful to observe My rules. 20] And hallow My sabbaths, that they may be a sign between Me and you, that you may know that I the LORD am your God.

9] וָאַעַשׂ לְמַעַן שְׁמִי לְבִלְתִּי הֵחֵל לְעֵינֵי הַגּוֹיִם אֲשֶׁר־הֵמָּה בְתוֹכָם אֲשֶׁר נוֹדַעְתִּי אֲלֵיהֶם לְעֵינֵיהֶם לְהוֹצִיאָם מֵאֶרֶץ מִצְרָיִם: 10] וָאוֹצִיאֵם מֵאֶרֶץ מִצְרַיִם וָאֲבִאֵם אֶל הַמִּדְבָּר: 11] וָאֶתֵּן לָהֶם אֶת־חֻקּוֹתַי וְאֶת־מִשְׁפָּטַי הוֹדַעְתִּי אוֹתָם אֲשֶׁר יַעֲשֶׂה אוֹתָם הָאָדָם וָחַי בָּהֶם: 12] וְגַם אֶת־שַׁבְּתוֹתַי נָתַתִּי לָהֶם לִהְיוֹת לְאוֹת בֵּינִי וּבֵינֵיהֶם לָדַעַת כִּי אֲנִי יְהוָה מְקַדְּשָׁם: 13] וַיַּמְרוּ־בִי בֵית יִשְׂרָאֵל בַּמִּדְבָּר בְּחֻקּוֹתַי לֹא הָלָכוּ וְאֶת־מִשְׁפָּטַי מָאָסוּ אֲשֶׁר יַעֲשֶׂה אֹתָם הָאָדָם וָחַי בָּהֶם וְאֶת־שַׁבְּתֹתַי חִלְּלוּ מְאֹד וָאֹמַר לִשְׁפֹּךְ חֲמָתִי עֲלֵיהֶם בַּמִּדְבָּר לְכַלּוֹתָם: 14] וָאֶעֱשֶׂה לְמַעַן שְׁמִי לְבִלְתִּי הֵחֵל לְעֵינֵי הַגּוֹיִם אֲשֶׁר הוֹצֵאתִים לְעֵינֵיהֶם: 15] וְגַם אֲנִי נָשָׂאתִי יָדִי לָהֶם בַּמִּדְבָּר לְבִלְתִּי הָבִיא אוֹתָם אֶל הָאָרֶץ אֲשֶׁר נָתַתִּי זָבַת חָלָב וּדְבַשׁ צְבִי הִיא לְכָל־הָאֲרָצוֹת: 16] יַעַן בְּמִשְׁפָּטַי מָאָסוּ וְאֶת־חֻקּוֹתַי לֹא הָלְכוּ בָהֶם וְאֶת־שַׁבְּתוֹתַי חִלֵּלוּ כִּי אַחֲרֵי גִלּוּלֵיהֶם לִבָּם הֹלֵךְ: 17] וַתָּחָס עֵינִי עֲלֵיהֶם מִשַּׁחֲתָם וְלֹא עָשִׂיתִי אוֹתָם כָּלָה בַּמִּדְבָּר: 18] וָאֹמַר אֶל בְּנֵיהֶם בַּמִּדְבָּר בְּחוּקֵּי אֲבוֹתֵיכֶם אַל תֵּלֵכוּ וְאֶת־מִשְׁפְּטֵיהֶם אַל תִּשְׁמֹרוּ וּבְגִלּוּלֵיהֶם אַל־תִּטַּמָּאוּ: 19] אֲנִי יְהוָה אֱלֹהֵיכֶם בְּחֻקּוֹתַי לֵכוּ וְאֶת־מִשְׁפָּטַי שִׁמְרוּ וַעֲשׂוּ אוֹתָם: 20] וְאֶת־שַׁבְּתוֹתַי קַדֵּשׁוּ וְהָיוּ לְאוֹת בֵּינִי וּבֵינֵיכֶם לָדַעַת כִּי אֲנִי יְהוָה אֱלֹהֵיכֶם:

[b] Lit. "raised My hand"   [d] Lit. "them"

Psalms

15:1-5

Psalm 15

1] A psalm of David.
LORD, who may stay in Your tent,
who may reside on Your holy mountain?

2] He who lives without blame,
who does what is right,
and in his heart acknowledges the truth;

3] *a*‑whose tongue is not given to evil;‑*a*
who has never done harm to his fellow,
or borne reproach for [his acts toward] his
neighbor;

4] for whom a contemptible man is abhorrent,
but who honors those who fear the LORD;
who stands by his oath even to his hurt;

5] who has never lent money at interest,
or accepted a bribe against the innocent;
the man who acts thus shall never be shaken.

טו

1] מִזְמוֹר לְדָוִד
יְהֹוָה מִי יָגוּר בְּאָהֳלֶךָ
מִי יִשְׁכֹּן בְּהַר קָדְשֶׁךָ:

2] הוֹלֵךְ תָּמִים וּפֹעֵל צֶדֶק
וְדֹבֵר אֱמֶת בִּלְבָבוֹ:

3] לֹא רָגַל עַל לְשֹׁנוֹ
לֹא עָשָׂה לְרֵעֵהוּ רָעָה
וְחֶרְפָּה לֹא נָשָׂא עַל קְרֹבוֹ:

4] נִבְזֶה בְּעֵינָיו נִמְאָס
וְאֶת יִרְאֵי יְהֹוָה יְכַבֵּד
נִשְׁבַּע לְהָרַע וְלֹא יָמִר:

5] כַּסְפּוֹ לֹא נָתַן בְּנֶשֶׁךְ
וְשֹׁחַד עַל נָקִי לֹא לָקָח
עֹשֵׂה אֵלֶּה לֹא יִמּוֹט לְעוֹלָם:

---

a‑a Meaning of Heb. uncertain; or "Who has no slander upon his tongue"

אמר

FIRST SELECTION

Ezekiel

44 : 15 - 31

מד

Chapter 44

15] ^cBut the levitical priests descended from Zadok,^{-c} who maintained the service of My sanctuary when the people of Israel went astray from Me—they shall approach Me to minister to Me; they shall stand before Me to offer Me fat and blood—declares the Lord Gᴏᴅ.

16] They alone may enter My sanctuary and they alone shall approach My table to minister to Me; and they shall keep My charge.

17] And when they enter the gates of the inner court, they shall wear linen vestments: they shall have nothing woolen upon them when they minister inside the gates of the inner court.

18] They shall have linen turbans on their heads and linen breeches on their loins; they shall not gird themselves with anything that causes sweat.

19] When they go out to the outer court—the outer court where the people are—they shall remove the vestments in which they minister and shall deposit them in the sacred chambers;^d they shall put on other garments, lest they make the people consecrated^e by [contact with] their vestments.

20] They shall neither shave their heads nor let their hair go untrimmed; they shall keep their hair trimmed.

21] No priest shall drink wine when he enters into the inner court.

15] וְהַכֹּהֲנִים הַלְוִיִּם בְּנֵי צָדוֹק אֲשֶׁר שָׁמְרוּ אֶת־מִשְׁמֶרֶת מִקְדָּשִׁי בִּתְעוֹת בְּנֵי יִשְׂרָאֵל מֵעָלַי הֵמָּה יִקְרְבוּ אֵלַי לְשָׁרְתֵנִי וְעָמְדוּ לְפָנַי לְהַקְרִיב לִי חֵלֶב וָדָם נְאֻם אֲדֹנָי יֱהֹוִה: 16] הֵמָּה יָבֹאוּ אֶל־מִקְדָּשִׁי וְהֵמָּה יִקְרְבוּ אֶל־שֻׁלְחָנִי לְשָׁרְתֵנִי וְשָׁמְרוּ אֶת־מִשְׁמַרְתִּי: 17] וְהָיָה בְּבוֹאָם אֶל־שַׁעֲרֵי הֶחָצֵר הַפְּנִימִית בִּגְדֵי פִשְׁתִּים יִלְבָּשׁוּ וְלֹא־יַעֲלֶה עֲלֵיהֶם צֶמֶר בְּשָׁרְתָם בְּשַׁעֲרֵי הֶחָצֵר הַפְּנִימִית וָבָיְתָה: 18] פַּאֲרֵי פִשְׁתִּים יִהְיוּ עַל־רֹאשָׁם וּמִכְנְסֵי פִשְׁתִּים יִהְיוּ עַל־מָתְנֵיהֶם לֹא יַחְגְּרוּ בַּיָּזַע: 19] וּבְצֵאתָם אֶל־הֶחָצֵר הַחִיצוֹנָה אֶל־הֶחָצֵר הַחִיצוֹנָה אֶל־הָעָם יִפְשְׁטוּ אֶת־בִּגְדֵיהֶם אֲשֶׁר־הֵמָּה מְשָׁרְתִים בָּם וְהִנִּיחוּ אוֹתָם בְּלִשְׁכֹת הַקֹּדֶשׁ וְלָבְשׁוּ בְּגָדִים אֲחֵרִים וְלֹא־יְקַדְּשׁוּ אֶת־הָעָם בְּבִגְדֵיהֶם: 20] וְרֹאשָׁם לֹא יְגַלֵּחוּ וּפֶרַע לֹא יְשַׁלֵּחוּ כָּסוֹם יִכְסְמוּ אֶת־רָאשֵׁיהֶם: 21] וְיַיִן לֹא־יִשְׁתּוּ כָּל־כֹּהֵן בְּבוֹאָם אֶל־הֶחָצֵר

---

^{c-c} *By contrast with the Levite-priests whose demotion has just been announced*

^d *Cf. 42.13–14*

^e *Thereby rendering the people unfit for ordinary activity*

22] They shall not marry widows[f] or divorced women; they may marry only virgins of the stock of the House of Israel, or widows who are widows of priests.

23] They shall declare to My people what is sacred and what is profane, and inform them what is clean and what is unclean.

24] In lawsuits, too, it is they who shall act as judges; they shall decide them in accordance with My rules. They shall preserve My teachings and My laws regarding all My fixed occasions; and they shall maintain the sanctity of My sabbaths.

25] [A priest] shall not defile himself by entering [a house] where there is a dead person. He shall defile himself only for father or mother, son or daughter, brother or unmarried sister.

26] After he has become clean, seven days shall be counted off for him;

27] and on the day that he reenters the inner court of the Sanctuary to minister in the Sanctuary, he shall present his sin offering—declares the Lord GOD.

28] This shall be their portion, for I am their portion; and no holding shall be given them in Israel, for I am their holding.

29] The meal offerings, sin offerings, and guilt offerings shall be consumed by them. Everything proscribed[g] in Israel shall be theirs.

30] All the choice first fruits of every kind, and all the gifts of every kind—of all your contributions—shall go to the priests. You shall further give the first of the yield of your baking[h] to the priest, that a blessing may rest upon your home.

31] Priests shall not eat anything, whether bird or animal, that died or was torn by beasts.

הַפְּנִימִית: 22] וְאַלְמָנָה וּגְרוּשָׁה לֹא יִקְחוּ
לָהֶם לְנָשִׁים כִּי אִם בְּתוּלֹת מִזֶּרַע בֵּית יִשְׂרָאֵל
וְהָאַלְמָנָה אֲשֶׁר תִּהְיֶה אַלְמָנָה מִכֹּהֵן יִקָּחוּ:
23] וְאֶת־עַמִּי יוֹרוּ בֵּין קֹדֶשׁ לְחֹל וּבֵין טָמֵא
לְטָהוֹר יוֹדִעָם: 24] וְעַל־רִיב הֵמָּה יַעַמְדוּ
לְמִשְׁפָּט בְּמִשְׁפָּטַי יִשְׁפְּטוּהוּ וְאֶת־תּוֹרֹתַי וְאֶת־
חֻקֹּתַי בְּכָל־מוֹעֲדַי יִשְׁמֹרוּ וְאֶת־שַׁבְּתוֹתַי יְקַדֵּשׁוּ:
25] וְאֶל־מֵת אָדָם לֹא יָבוֹא לְטָמְאָה כִּי אִם
לְאָב וּלְאֵם וּלְבֵן וּלְבַת לְאָח וּלְאָחוֹת אֲשֶׁר
לֹא הָיְתָה לְאִישׁ יִטַּמָּאוּ: 26] וְאַחֲרֵי טָהֳרָתוֹ
שִׁבְעַת יָמִים יִסְפְּרוּ־לוֹ: 27] וּבְיוֹם בֹּאוֹ אֶל
הַקֹּדֶשׁ אֶל הֶחָצֵר הַפְּנִימִית לְשָׁרֵת בַּקֹּדֶשׁ
יַקְרִיב חַטָּאתוֹ נְאֻם אֲדֹנָי יֱהוִֹה:
28] וְהָיְתָה לָהֶם לְנַחֲלָה אֲנִי נַחֲלָתָם וַאֲחֻזָּה
לֹא תִתְּנוּ לָהֶם בְּיִשְׂרָאֵל אֲנִי אֲחֻזָּתָם:
29] הַמִּנְחָה וְהַחַטָּאת וְהָאָשָׁם הֵמָּה יֹאכְלוּם
וְכָל־חֵרֶם בְּיִשְׂרָאֵל לָהֶם יִהְיֶה: 30] וְרֵאשִׁית
כָּל־בִּכּוּרֵי כֹל וְכָל־תְּרוּמַת כֹּל מִכֹּל
תְּרוּמוֹתֵיכֶם לַכֹּהֲנִים יִהְיֶה וְרֵאשִׁית עֲרִסוֹתֵיכֶם
תִּתְּנוּ לַכֹּהֵן לְהָנִיחַ בְּרָכָה אֶל בֵּיתֶךָ:
31] כָּל־נְבֵלָה וּטְרֵפָה מִן הָעוֹף וּמִן הַבְּהֵמָה
לֹא יֹאכְלוּ הַכֹּהֲנִים:

[f] I.e., of laymen
[g] See Lev. 27.28
[h] See Num. 15.20–21

Isaiah

56 : 1-8

Chapter 56

נו

1] Thus said the LORD:
Observe what is right and do what is just;
For soon My salvation shall come,
And my deliverance be revealed.

[1] כֹּה אָמַר יְהֹוָה

שִׁמְרוּ מִשְׁפָּט וַעֲשׂוּ צְדָקָה

כִּי קְרוֹבָה יְשׁוּעָתִי לָבוֹא

וְצִדְקָתִי לְהִגָּלוֹת:

2] Happy is the man who does this,
The man who holds fast to it:
Who keeps the sabbath and does not profane it,
And stays his hand from doing any evil.

[2] אַשְׁרֵי אֱנוֹשׁ יַעֲשֶׂה־זֹּאת

וּבֶן אָדָם יַחֲזִיק בָּהּ

שֹׁמֵר שַׁבָּת מֵחַלְּלוֹ

וְשֹׁמֵר יָדוֹ מֵעֲשׂוֹת כָּל־רָע:

3] Let not the foreigner say,
Who has attached himself to the LORD,
"The LORD will keep me apart from His people";
And let not the eunuch say,
"I am a withered tree."

[3] וְאַל־יֹאמַר בֶּן־הַנֵּכָר

הַנִּלְוָה אֶל־יְהֹוָה לֵאמֹר

הַבְדֵּל יַבְדִּילַנִי יְהֹוָה מֵעַל עַמּוֹ

וְאַל־יֹאמַר הַסָּרִיס

הֵן אֲנִי עֵץ יָבֵשׁ:

4] For thus said the LORD:
"As regards the eunuchs who keep My sabbaths,
Who have chosen what I desire
And hold fast to My covenant—

[4] כִּי־כֹה אָמַר יְהֹוָה

לַסָּרִיסִים אֲשֶׁר יִשְׁמְרוּ אֶת־שַׁבְּתוֹתַי

וּבָחֲרוּ בַּאֲשֶׁר חָפָצְתִּי

וּמַחֲזִיקִים בִּבְרִיתִי:

5] I will give them, in My House
And within My walls,
A monument and a name
Better than sons or daughters.
I will give them an everlasting name
Which shall not perish.

[5] וְנָתַתִּי לָהֶם בְּבֵיתִי

וּבְחוֹמֹתַי

יָד וָשֵׁם

טוֹב מִבָּנִים וּמִבָּנוֹת

שֵׁם עוֹלָם אֶתֶּן־לוֹ

אֲשֶׁר לֹא יִכָּרֵת:

6] As for the foreigners
Who attach themselves to the LORD,
To minister to Him.
And to love the name of the LORD,
To be His servants—
All who keep the sabbath and do not profane it,
And who hold fast to My covenant—

6] וּבְנֵי הַנֵּכָר
הַנִּלְוִים עַל יְהֹוָה לְשָׁרְתוֹ
וּלְאַהֲבָה אֶת־שֵׁם יְהֹוָה
לִהְיוֹת לוֹ לַעֲבָדִים
כָּל־שֹׁמֵר שַׁבָּת מֵחַלְּלוֹ
וּמַחֲזִיקִים בִּבְרִיתִי:

7] I will bring them to My sacred mount
And let them rejoice in My house of prayer.
Their burnt offerings and sacrifices
Shall be welcome on My altar;
For My House shall be called
A house of prayer for all peoples."

7] וַהֲבִיאוֹתִים אֶל־הַר קָדְשִׁי
וְשִׂמַּחְתִּים בְּבֵית תְּפִלָּתִי
עוֹלֹתֵיהֶם וְזִבְחֵיהֶם
לְרָצוֹן עַל מִזְבְּחִי
כִּי בֵיתִי בֵּית תְּפִלָּה יִקָּרֵא
לְכָל־הָעַמִּים:

8] Thus declares the Lord GOD,
Who gathers the dispersed of Israel:
"I will gather still more to those already gathered."

8] נְאֻם אֲדֹנָי יֱהֹוִה
מְקַבֵּץ נִדְחֵי יִשְׂרָאֵל
עוֹד אֲקַבֵּץ עָלָיו לְנִקְבָּצָיו:

THIRD SELECTION

Ezekiel

36 : 16 – 28

Chapter 36

16] The word of the LORD came to me:
17] O mortal, when the House of Israel dwelt on
their own soil, they defiled it with their ways and
their deeds; their ways were in My sight like the
uncleanness of a menstruous woman.

18] So I
poured out My wrath on them for the blood
which they shed upon their land, and for the
fetishes with which they defiled it.

19] I scat-
tered them among the nations, and they were
dispersed through the countries: I punished them
in accordance with their ways and their deeds.

לו

16] וַיְהִי דְבַר־יְהֹוָה אֵלַי לֵאמֹר: 17] בֶּן־
אָדָם בֵּית יִשְׂרָאֵל יֹשְׁבִים עַל אַדְמָתָם וַיְטַמְּאוּ
אוֹתָהּ בְּדַרְכָּם וּבַעֲלִילוֹתָם כְּטֻמְאַת הַנִּדָּה
הָיְתָה דַרְכָּם לְפָנָי: 18] וָאֶשְׁפֹּךְ חֲמָתִי
עֲלֵיהֶם עַל הַדָּם אֲשֶׁר שָׁפְכוּ עַל הָאָרֶץ
וּבְגִלּוּלֵיהֶם טִמְּאוּהָ: 19] וָאָפִיץ אֹתָם בַּגּוֹיִם
וַיִּזָּרוּ בָּאֲרָצוֹת כְּדַרְכָּם וְכַעֲלִילוֹתָם שְׁפַטְתִּים:

20] But when they came *d-to those nations,-d* they caused My holy name to be profaned,*e* in that it was said of them, "These are the people of the LORD, yet they had to leave His land." 21] Therefore I am concerned for My holy name, which the House of Israel have caused to be profaned among the nations to which they have come.

22] Say to the House of Israel: Thus said the Lord GOD: Not for your sake will I act, O House of Israel, but for My holy name, which you have caused to be profaned among the nations to which you have come. 23] I will sanctify My great name which has been profaned among the nations —among whom you have caused it to be profaned. And the nations shall know that I am the LORD— declares the Lord GOD—when I manifest My holiness before their eyes through you. 24] I will take you from among the nations and gather you from all countries, and I will bring you back to your own land. 25] I will sprinkle clean water upon you, and you shall be clean: I will cleanse you from all your uncleanness and from all your fetishes. 26] And I will give you a new heart and put a new spirit into you: I will remove the heart of stone from your body and give you a heart of flesh; 27] and I will put My spirit into you. Thus I will cause you to follow My laws and faithfully to observe My rules. 28] Then you shall dwell in the land which I gave to your fathers, and you shall be My people and I will be your God.

וַיָּבוֹא אֶל הַגּוֹיִם אֲשֶׁר־בָּאוּ שָׁם וַיְחַלְּלוּ [20
אֶת־שֵׁם קָדְשִׁי בֶּאֱמֹר לָהֶם עַם־יְהֹוָה אֵלֶּה
וּמֵאַרְצוֹ יָצָאוּ: 21] וָאֶחְמֹל עַל־שֵׁם קָדְשִׁי
אֲשֶׁר חִלְּלֻהוּ בֵּית יִשְׂרָאֵל בַּגּוֹיִם אֲשֶׁר־בָּאוּ
שָׁמָּה:

לָכֵן אֱמֹר לְבֵית־יִשְׂרָאֵל כֹּה אָמַר [22
אֲדֹנָי יֱהֹוִה לֹא לְמַעַנְכֶם אֲנִי עֹשֶׂה בֵּית יִשְׂרָאֵל
כִּי אִם־לְשֵׁם־קָדְשִׁי אֲשֶׁר חִלַּלְתֶּם בַּגּוֹיִם אֲשֶׁר־
בָּאתֶם שָׁם: 23] וְקִדַּשְׁתִּי אֶת־שְׁמִי הַגָּדוֹל
הַמְחֻלָּל בַּגּוֹיִם אֲשֶׁר חִלַּלְתֶּם בְּתוֹכָם וְיָדְעוּ
הַגּוֹיִם כִּי־אֲנִי יְהֹוָה נְאֻם אֲדֹנָי יֱהֹוִה בְּהִקָּדְשִׁי
בָכֶם לְעֵינֵיהֶם: 24] וְלָקַחְתִּי אֶתְכֶם מִן־הַגּוֹיִם
וְקִבַּצְתִּי אֶתְכֶם מִכָּל־הָאֲרָצוֹת וְהֵבֵאתִי אֶתְכֶם
אֶל־אַדְמַתְכֶם: 25] וְזָרַקְתִּי עֲלֵיכֶם מַיִם
טְהוֹרִים וּטְהַרְתֶּם מִכֹּל טֻמְאוֹתֵיכֶם וּמִכָּל־
גִּלּוּלֵיכֶם אֲטַהֵר אֶתְכֶם: 26] וְנָתַתִּי לָכֶם לֵב
חָדָשׁ וְרוּחַ חֲדָשָׁה אֶתֵּן בְּקִרְבְּכֶם וַהֲסִרֹתִי אֶת־
לֵב הָאֶבֶן מִבְּשַׂרְכֶם וְנָתַתִּי לָכֶם לֵב בָּשָׂר:
27] וְאֶת־רוּחִי אֶתֵּן בְּקִרְבְּכֶם וְעָשִׂיתִי אֵת
אֲשֶׁר־בְּחֻקַּי תֵּלֵכוּ וּמִשְׁפָּטַי תִּשְׁמְרוּ וַעֲשִׂיתֶם:
28] וִישַׁבְתֶּם בָּאָרֶץ אֲשֶׁר נָתַתִּי לַאֲבֹתֵיכֶם
וִהְיִיתֶם לִי לְעָם וְאָנֹכִי אֶהְיֶה לָכֶם לֵאלֹהִים:

---

d-d Lit. "the nations they came to"
e I.e., the exile of Israel was taken by the nations to be evidence of the LORD'S *weakness*

בהר

FIRST SELECTION

Jeremiah

32 : 6-27

לב

Chapter 32

6] Jeremiah said: The word of the LORD came to me:

7] Hanamel, the son of your uncle Shallum, will come to you and say, "Buy my land in Anathoth, *b*-for you are next in succession to redeem it by purchase."-*b*

8] And just as the LORD had said, my cousin Hanamel came to me in the prison compound and said to me, "Please buy my land in Anathoth, in the territory of Benjamin; for the right of succession is yours, and you have the duty of redemption. Buy it." Then I knew that it was indeed the word of the LORD.

9] So I bought the land in Anathoth from my cousin Hanamel. I weighed out the money to him, seventeen shekels of silver.

10] I wrote a deed, sealed it, and had it witnessed; and I weighed out the silver on a balance.

11] I took the deed of purchase, the sealed text and the open one *c*-according to rule and law,-*c*

12] and gave the deed to Baruch son of Neriah son of Mahseiah in the presence of my kinsman Hanamel, of the witnesses *d*-who were named-*d* in the deed, and

6] וַיֹּאמֶר יִרְמְיָהוּ הָיָה דְבַר־יְהֹוָה אֵלַי לֵאמֹר: 7] הִנֵּה חֲנַמְאֵל בֶּן־שַׁלֻּם דֹּדְךָ בָּא אֵלֶיךָ לֵאמֹר קְנֵה לְךָ אֶת־שָׂדִי אֲשֶׁר בַּעֲנָתוֹת כִּי לְךָ מִשְׁפַּט הַגְּאֻלָּה לִקְנוֹת: 8] וַיָּבֹא אֵלַי חֲנַמְאֵל בֶּן־דֹּדִי כִּדְבַר יְהֹוָה אֶל־חֲצַר הַמַּטָּרָה וַיֹּאמֶר אֵלַי קְנֵה נָא אֶת־שָׂדִי אֲשֶׁר בַּעֲנָתוֹת אֲשֶׁר בְּאֶרֶץ בִּנְיָמִין כִּי־לְךָ מִשְׁפַּט הַיְרֻשָּׁה וּלְךָ הַגְּאֻלָּה קְנֵה־לָךְ וָאֵדַע כִּי דְבַר־יְהֹוָה הוּא:

9] וָאֶקְנֶה אֶת־הַשָּׂדֶה מֵאֵת חֲנַמְאֵל בֶּן־דֹּדִי אֲשֶׁר בַּעֲנָתוֹת וָאֶשְׁקֲלָה־לּוֹ אֶת־הַכֶּסֶף שִׁבְעָה שְׁקָלִים וַעֲשָׂרָה הַכָּסֶף: 10] וָאֶכְתֹּב בַּסֵּפֶר וָאֶחְתֹּם וָאָעֵד עֵדִים וָאֶשְׁקֹל הַכֶּסֶף בְּמֹאזְנָיִם: 11] וָאֶקַּח אֶת־סֵפֶר הַמִּקְנָה אֶת־הֶחָתוּם הַמִּצְוָה וְהַחֻקִּים וְאֶת־הַגָּלוּי: 12] וָאֶתֵּן אֶת־הַסֵּפֶר הַמִּקְנָה אֶל־בָּרוּךְ בֶּן־נֵרִיָּה בֶּן־מַחְסֵיָה לְעֵינֵי חֲנַמְאֵל דֹּדִי וּלְעֵינֵי הָעֵדִים הַכֹּתְבִים בַּסֵּפֶר

b-b Lit. *"for yours is the procedure of redemption by purchase"*

c-c Force of Heb. uncertain

d-d With many mss. and ancient versions; so ancient Near Eastern practice. Other mss. and the editions read "who wrote" all the Judeans who were sitting in the prison compound.

13] In their presence I charged Baruch as follows:

14] Thus said the LORD of Hosts, the God of Israel: "Take these documents, this deed of purchase, the sealed text and the open one, and put them into an earthen jar, so that they may last a long time."

15] For thus said the LORD of Hosts, the God of Israel: "Houses, fields, and vineyards shall again be purchased in this land."

16] But after I had given the deed to Baruch son of Neriah, I prayed to the LORD:

17] "Ah, Lord GOD! You made heaven and earth with Your great might and outstretched arm. Nothing is too wondrous for You!

18] You show kindness to the thousandth generation, but visit the guilt of the fathers upon their children after them. O great and mighty God whose name is LORD of Hosts, 19] wondrous in purpose and mighty in deed, whose eyes observe all the ways of men, so as to repay every man according to his ways, and with the proper fruit of his deeds!

20] You displayed signs and marvels in the land of Egypt ⁻ᵉwith lasting effect,⁻ᵉ and won renown in Israel and among mankind to this very day.

21] You freed Your people Israel from the land of Egypt with signs and marvels, with a strong hand and an outstretched arm, and with great terror.

22] You gave them this land which You had sworn to their fathers to give them, a land flowing with milk and honey,

23] and they came and took possession of it. But they did not listen to You or follow Your Teaching; they did nothing of what You com-

ᵉ⁻ᵉ Lit. "to this day"

הַמִּקְנֶה לְעֵינֵי כָּל־הַיְּהוּדִים הַיֹּשְׁבִים בַּחֲצַר הַמַּטָּרָה: 13 וָאֲצַוֶּה אֶת־בָּרוּךְ לְעֵינֵיהֶם לֵאמֹר: 14 כֹּה אָמַר יְהוָה צְבָאוֹת אֱלֹהֵי יִשְׂרָאֵל לָקוֹחַ אֶת־הַסְּפָרִים הָאֵלֶּה אֵת סֵפֶר הַמִּקְנָה הַזֶּה וְאֵת הֶחָתוּם וְאֵת סֵפֶר הַגָּלוּי הַזֶּה וּנְתַתָּם בִּכְלִי־חָרֶשׂ לְמַעַן יַעַמְדוּ יָמִים רַבִּים: 15 כִּי כֹה אָמַר יְהוָה צְבָאוֹת אֱלֹהֵי יִשְׂרָאֵל עוֹד יִקָּנוּ בָתִּים וְשָׂדוֹת וּכְרָמִים בָּאָרֶץ הַזֹּאת:

16 וָאֶתְפַּלֵּל אֶל־יְהוָה אַחֲרֵי תִתִּי אֶת־סֵפֶר הַמִּקְנָה אֶל־בָּרוּךְ בֶּן־נֵרִיָּה לֵאמֹר: 17 אֲהָהּ אֲדֹנָי יְהוִה הִנֵּה אַתָּה עָשִׂיתָ אֶת־הַשָּׁמַיִם וְאֶת־הָאָרֶץ בְּכֹחֲךָ הַגָּדוֹל וּבִזְרֹעֲךָ הַנְּטוּיָה לֹא יִפָּלֵא מִמְּךָ כָּל־דָּבָר: 18 עֹשֶׂה חֶסֶד לַאֲלָפִים וּמְשַׁלֵּם עֲוֹן אָבוֹת אֶל־חֵיק בְּנֵיהֶם אַחֲרֵיהֶם הָאֵל הַגָּדוֹל הַגִּבּוֹר יְהוָה צְבָאוֹת שְׁמוֹ: 19 גְּדֹל הָעֵצָה וְרַב הָעֲלִילִיָּה אֲשֶׁר עֵינֶיךָ פְקֻחוֹת עַל כָּל־דַּרְכֵי בְּנֵי אָדָם לָתֵת לְאִישׁ כִּדְרָכָיו וְכִפְרִי מַעֲלָלָיו: 20 אֲשֶׁר־שַׂמְתָּ אֹתוֹת וּמֹפְתִים בְּאֶרֶץ מִצְרַיִם עַד הַיּוֹם הַזֶּה וּבְיִשְׂרָאֵל וּבָאָדָם וַתַּעֲשֶׂה־לְּךָ שֵׁם כַּיּוֹם הַזֶּה: 21 וַתֹּצֵא אֶת־עַמְּךָ אֶת־יִשְׂרָאֵל מֵאֶרֶץ מִצְרַיִם בְּאֹתוֹת וּבְמוֹפְתִים וּבְיָד חֲזָקָה וּבְאֶזְרוֹעַ נְטוּיָה וּבְמוֹרָא גָּדוֹל: 22 וַתִּתֵּן לָהֶם אֶת־הָאָרֶץ הַזֹּאת אֲשֶׁר נִשְׁבַּעְתָּ לַאֲבוֹתָם לָתֵת לָהֶם אֶרֶץ זָבַת חָלָב וּדְבָשׁ: 23 וַיָּבֹאוּ וַיִּרְשׁוּ אֹתָהּ וְלֹא שָׁמְעוּ בְקוֹלֶךָ וּבְתוֹרָתְךָ לֹא הָלָכוּ אֵת כָּל־אֲשֶׁר צִוִּיתָה לָהֶם לַעֲשׂוֹת

manded them to do. Therefore You have caused all this misfortune to befall them.

24] Here are the siege-mounds, raised against the city to storm it; and the city, because of sword and famine and pestilence, is at the mercy of the Chaldeans who are attacking it. What You threatened has come to pass—as You see.

25] Yet You, Lord GOD, said to me: Buy the land for money and call in witnesses—when the city is at the mercy of the Chaldeans!"

26] Then the word of the LORD came to Jeremiah:

27] "Behold I am the LORD, the God of all flesh. Is anything too wondrous for Me?

לֹא עָשׂוּ וַתַּקְרֵא אֹתָם אֵת כָּל־הָרָעָה הַזֹּאת:

24] הִנֵּה הַסֹּלְלוֹת בָּאוּ הָעִיר לְלָכְדָהּ וְהָעִיר נִתְּנָה בְּיַד הַכַּשְׂדִּים הַנִּלְחָמִים עָלֶיהָ מִפְּנֵי הַחֶרֶב וְהָרָעָב וְהַדָּבֶר וַאֲשֶׁר דִּבַּרְתָּ הָיָה וְהִנְּךָ רֹאֶה: 25] וְאַתָּה אָמַרְתָּ אֵלַי אֲדֹנָי יֱהֹוִה קְנֵה לְךָ הַשָּׂדֶה בַּכֶּסֶף וְהָעֵד עֵדִים וְהָעִיר נִתְּנָה בְּיַד הַכַּשְׂדִּים:

26] וַיְהִי דְּבַר יְהֹוָה אֶל יִרְמְיָהוּ לֵאמֹר:

27] הִנֵּה אֲנִי יְהֹוָה אֱלֹהֵי כָּל־בָּשָׂר הֲמִמֶּנִּי יִפָּלֵא כָּל־דָּבָר:

SECOND SELECTION

Jeremiah

31 : 1-13

Chapter 31

1] *c*At that time—declares the LORD—I will be God·to all the clans of Israel, and they shall be My people.

2] Thus said the LORD:
The people escaped from the sword,
Found favor in the wilderness;
When Israel was marching homeward,

3] The LORD revealed Himself to me*a* of old.
Eternal love I conceived for you then;
Therefore I continue My grace to you.

לֹא

1] בָּעֵת הַהִיא נְאֻם יְהֹוָה
אֶהְיֶה לֵאלֹהִים לְכֹל מִשְׁפְּחוֹת יִשְׂרָאֵל
וְהֵמָּה יִהְיוּ־לִי לְעָם:

2] כֹּה אָמַר יְהֹוָה
מָצָא חֵן בַּמִּדְבָּר
עַם שְׂרִידֵי חָרֶב
הָלוֹךְ לְהַרְגִּיעוֹ יִשְׂרָאֵל:

3] מֵרָחוֹק יְהֹוָה נִרְאָה לִי
וְאַהֲבַת עוֹלָם אֲהַבְתִּיךְ
עַל־כֵּן מְשַׁכְתִּיךְ חָסֶד:

---

c In some editions, this verse is 30.25
a Emendation yields "him"

403

4] I will build you firmly again,
O Maiden Israel!
Again you shall take up your timbrels
And go forth to the rhythm of the dancers.

5] Again you shall plant vineyards
On the hills of Samaria;
Men shall plant and live to enjoy them.

6] For the day is coming when watchmen
Shall proclaim on the heights of Ephraim:
Come, let us go up to Zion,
To the LORD our God!

7] For thus said the LORD:
Cry out in joy for Jacob,
Shout at the crossroads[b] of the nations!
Sing aloud in praise, and say:
[c-]Save, O LORD, Your people,[-c]
The remnant of Israel.

8] I will bring them in from the northland,
Gather them from the ends of the earth—
The blind and the lame among them,
Those with child and those in labor—
In a vast throng they shall return here.

9] They shall come with weeping,
And with compassion[d] will I guide them.
I will lead them to streams of water,
By a level road where they will not stumble.
For I am ever a Father to Israel,
Ephraim is My firstborn.

עוֹד אֶבְנֵךְ וְנִבְנֵית [4
בְּתוּלַת יִשְׂרָאֵל
עוֹד תַּעְדִּי תֻפַּיִךְ
וְיָצָאת בִּמְחוֹל מְשַׂחֲקִים:

עוֹד תִּטְּעִי כְרָמִים [5
בְּהָרֵי שֹׁמְרוֹן
נָטְעוּ נֹטְעִים וְחִלֵּלוּ:

כִּי יֶשׁ־יוֹם קָרְאוּ נֹצְרִים [6
בְּהַר אֶפְרָיִם
קוּמוּ וְנַעֲלֶה צִיּוֹן
אֶל יְהוָֹה אֱלֹהֵינוּ:

כִּי־כֹה אָמַר יְהוָֹה [7
רָנּוּ לְיַעֲקֹב שִׂמְחָה
וְצַהֲלוּ בְּרֹאשׁ הַגּוֹיִם
הַשְׁמִיעוּ הַלְלוּ וְאִמְרוּ
הוֹשַׁע יְהוָֹה אֶת־עַמְּךָ
אֵת שְׁאֵרִית יִשְׂרָאֵל:

הִנְנִי מֵבִיא אוֹתָם מֵאֶרֶץ צָפוֹן [8
וְקִבַּצְתִּים מִיַּרְכְּתֵי־אָרֶץ
בָּם עִוֵּר וּפִסֵּחַ
הָרָה וְיֹלֶדֶת יַחְדָּו
קָהָל גָּדוֹל יָשׁוּבוּ הֵנָּה:

בִּבְכִי יָבֹאוּ [9
וּבְתַחֲנוּנִים אוֹבִילֵם
אוֹלִיכֵם אֶל־נַחֲלֵי מַיִם
בְּדֶרֶךְ יָשָׁר לֹא יִכָּשְׁלוּ בָּהּ
כִּי־הָיִיתִי לְיִשְׂרָאֵל לְאָב
וְאֶפְרַיִם בְּכֹרִי הוּא:

[b] Lit. "head"   [c-c] Emendation yields "The LORD has saved His people"
[d] For this meaning, cf. Zech. 12.10

10] Hear the word of the LORD, O nations,
And tell it in the coastlands afar.
Say:
He who scattered Israel will gather them,
And will guard them as a shepherd his flock.

11] For the LORD will ransom Jacob,
Redeem him from one too strong for him.

12] They shall come and shout on the heights of
    Zion,
Radiant over the bounty of the LORD—
Over new grain and wine and oil,
And over sheep and cattle.
They shall fare like a watered garden,
They shall never languish again.

13] Then shall maidens dance gaily,
Young men and old alike.
I will turn their mourning to joy,
I will comfort them and cheer them in their grief.

10] שִׁמְעוּ דְבַר יְהֹוָה גּוֹיִם

וְהַגִּידוּ בָאִיִּם מִמֶּרְחָק

וְאִמְרוּ

מְזָרֵה יִשְׂרָאֵל יְקַבְּצֶנּוּ

וּשְׁמָרוֹ כְּרֹעֶה עֶדְרוֹ:

11] כִּי פָדָה יְהֹוָה אֶת־יַעֲקֹב

וּגְאָלוֹ מִיַּד חָזָק מִמֶּנּוּ:

12] וּבָאוּ וְרִנְּנוּ בִמְרוֹם צִיּוֹן

וְנָהֲרוּ אֶל־טוּב יְהֹוָה

עַל דָּגָן וְעַל תִּירשׁ וְעַל יִצְהָר

וְעַל בְּנֵי־צֹאן וּבָקָר

וְהָיְתָה נַפְשָׁם כְּגַן רָוֶה

וְלֹא יוֹסִיפוּ לְדַאֲבָה עוֹד:

13] אָז תִּשְׂמַח בְּתוּלָה בְּמָחוֹל

וּבַחֻרִים וּזְקֵנִים יַחְדָּו

וְהָפַכְתִּי אֶבְלָם לְשָׂשׂוֹן

וְנִחַמְתִּים וְשִׂמַּחְתִּים מִיגוֹנָם:

THIRD SELECTION

Nehemiah

5 : 1-13

Chapter 5

1] Then there arose a great cry of the people
and of their wives against their brethren the Jews.
2] For there were that said: 'We, our sons and our
daughters, are many; let us get for them corn,
that we may eat and live.'

3] Some also there
were that said: 'We are mortgaging our fields, and
our vineyards, and our houses; let us get corn,
because of the dearth.'

ה

1] וַתְּהִי צַעֲקַת הָעָם וּנְשֵׁיהֶם גְּדוֹלָה אֶל

אֲחֵיהֶם הַיְּהוּדִים: 2] וְיֵשׁ אֲשֶׁר אֹמְרִים בָּנֵינוּ

וּבְנֹתֵינוּ אֲנַחְנוּ רַבִּים וְנִקְחָה דָגָן וְנֹאכְלָה

וְנִחְיֶה: 3] וְיֵשׁ אֲשֶׁר אֹמְרִים שְׂדֹתֵינוּ וּכְרָמֵינוּ

וּבָתֵּינוּ אֲנַחְנוּ עֹרְבִים וְנִקְחָה דָגָן בָּרָעָב:

4] There were also that said: 'We have borrowed money for the king's tribute upon our fields and our vineyards. 5] Yet now our flesh is as the flesh of our brethren, our children as their children; and, lo, we bring into bondage our sons and our daughters to be servants, and some of our daughters are brought into bondage already; neither is it in our power to help it; for other men have our fields and our vineyards.'

6] And I was very angry when I heard their cry and these words.

7] Then I consulted with myself, and contended with the nobles and the rulers, and said unto them: 'Ye lend upon pledge, every one to his brother.' And I held a great assembly against them.

8] And I said unto them: 'We after our ability have redeemed our brethren the Jews, that sold themselves unto the heathen; and would ye nevertheless sell your brethren, and should they sell themselves unto us?' Then held they their peace, and found never a word. 9] Also I said: 'The thing that ye do is not good; ought ye not to walk in the fear of our God, because of the reproach of the heathen our enemies?

10] And I likewise, my brethren and my servants, have lent them money and corn. I pray you, let us leave off this exaction. 11] Restore, I pray you, to them, even this day, their fields, their vineyards, their oliveyards, and their houses, also the hundred pieces of silver, and the corn, the wine, and the oil, that ye exact of them.' 12] Then said they: 'We will restore them, and will require nothing of them; so will we do, even as thou sayest.' Then I called the priests, and took an oath of them, that they should do according to this promise.

13] Also I shook out my lap, and said: 'So God shake out every man from his house, and from his labor, that performeth not this promise; even thus be he shaken out, and emptied.' And all the congregation said: 'Amen,' and praised the Lord. And the people did according to this promise.

וְיֵשׁ אֲשֶׁר אֹמְרִים לָוִינוּ כֶסֶף לְמִדַּת הַמֶּלֶךְ [4
שְׂדֹתֵינוּ וּכְרָמֵינוּ: 5] וְעַתָּה כִּבְשַׂר אַחֵינוּ
בְּשָׂרֵנוּ כִּבְנֵיהֶם בָּנֵינוּ וְהִנֵּה אֲנַחְנוּ כֹבְשִׁים
אֶת־בָּנֵינוּ וְאֶת־בְּנֹתֵינוּ לַעֲבָדִים וְיֵשׁ מִבְּנֹתֵינוּ
נִכְבָּשׁוֹת וְאֵין לְאֵל יָדֵנוּ וּשְׂדֹתֵינוּ וּכְרָמֵינוּ
לַאֲחֵרִים:

6] וַיִּחַר לִי מְאֹד כַּאֲשֶׁר שָׁמַעְתִּי אֶת־זַעֲקָתָם
וְאֵת הַדְּבָרִים הָאֵלֶּה: 7] וַיִּמָּלֵךְ לִבִּי עָלַי
וָאָרִיבָה אֶת־הַחֹרִים וְאֶת־הַסְּגָנִים וָאֹמְרָה לָהֶם
מַשָּׁא אִישׁ בְּאָחִיו אַתֶּם נֹשִׁאים וָאֶתֵּן עֲלֵיהֶם
קְהִלָּה גְדוֹלָה: 8] וָאֹמְרָה לָהֶם אֲנַחְנוּ קָנִינוּ
אֶת־אַחֵינוּ הַיְּהוּדִים הַנִּמְכָּרִים לַגּוֹיִם כְּדֵי בָנוּ
וְגַם אַתֶּם תִּמְכְּרוּ אֶת־אֲחֵיכֶם וְנִמְכְּרוּ־לָנוּ
וַיַּחֲרִישׁוּ וְלֹא מָצְאוּ דָּבָר: 9] וָאוֹמַר לֹא־טוֹב
הַדָּבָר אֲשֶׁר אַתֶּם עֹשִׂים הֲלוֹא בְּיִרְאַת אֱלֹהֵינוּ
תֵּלֵכוּ מֵחֶרְפַּת הַגּוֹיִם אוֹיְבֵינוּ: 10] וְגַם אֲנִי
אַחַי וּנְעָרַי נֹשִׁים בָּהֶם כֶּסֶף וְדָגָן נַעַזְבָה־נָּא
אֶת־הַמַּשָּׁא הַזֶּה: 11] הָשִׁיבוּ נָא לָהֶם כְּהַיּוֹם
שְׂדֹתֵיהֶם כַּרְמֵיהֶם זֵיתֵיהֶם וּבָתֵּיהֶם וּמְאַת
הַכֶּסֶף וְהַדָּגָן הַתִּירוֹשׁ וְהַיִּצְהָר אֲשֶׁר אַתֶּם
נֹשִׁים בָּהֶם: 12] וַיֹּאמְרוּ נָשִׁיב וּמֵהֶם לֹא
נְבַקֵּשׁ כֵּן נַעֲשֶׂה כַּאֲשֶׁר אַתָּה אוֹמֵר וָאֶקְרָא
אֶת־הַכֹּהֲנִים וָאַשְׁבִּיעֵם לַעֲשׂוֹת כַּדָּבָר הַזֶּה:

13] גַּם חָצְנִי נָעַרְתִּי וָאֹמְרָה כָּכָה יְנַעֵר הָאֱלֹהִים
אֶת־כָּל־הָאִישׁ אֲשֶׁר לֹא יָקִים אֶת־הַדָּבָר הַזֶּה
מִבֵּיתוֹ וּמִיגִיעוֹ וְכָכָה יִהְיֶה נָעוּר וָרֵק וַיֹּאמְרוּ
כָל־הַקָּהָל אָמֵן וַיְהַלְלוּ אֶת־יְהֹוָה וַיַּעַשׂ הָעָם
כַּדָּבָר הַזֶּה:

בחקתי

FIRST SELECTION

Jeremiah

16 : 19 – 17 : 14

Chapter 16

טז

19] O Lord, my strength and my stronghold,
My refuge in a day of trouble,
To You nations shall come
From the ends of the earth and say:
Our fathers inherited utter delusions,
Things that are futile and worthless.

‫19] יְהֹוָה עֻזִּי וּמָעֻזִּי‬
‫וּמְנוּסִי בְּיוֹם צָרָה‬
‫אֵלֶיךָ גּוֹיִם יָבֹאוּ‬
‫מֵאַפְסֵי־אָרֶץ וְיֹאמְרוּ‬
‫אַךְ־שֶׁקֶר נָחֲלוּ אֲבוֹתֵינוּ‬
‫הֶבֶל וְאֵין בָּם מוֹעִיל׃‬

20] Can a man make gods for himself?
No-gods are they!

‫20] הֲיַעֲשֶׂה־לּוֹ אָדָם אֱלֹהִים‬
‫וְהֵמָּה לֹא אֱלֹהִים׃‬

21] Assuredly, I will teach them,
Once and for all I will teach them
My power and My might.
And they shall learn that My name is Lord.

‫21] לָכֵן הִנְנִי מוֹדִיעָם‬
‫בַּפַּעַם הַזֹּאת אוֹדִיעֵם‬
‫אֶת־יָדִי וְאֶת־גְּבוּרָתִי‬
‫וְיָדְעוּ כִּי־שְׁמִי יְהֹוָה׃‬

Chapter 17

יז

1] The guilt of Judah is inscribed
With a stylus of iron,
Engraved with an adamant point
On the tablet of their hearts,
ᵃ⁻And on the horns of their altars,

‫1] חַטַּאת יְהוּדָה כְּתוּבָה‬
‫בְּעֵט בַּרְזֶל‬
‫בְּצִפֹּרֶן שָׁמִיר חֲרוּשָׁה‬
‫עַל־לוּחַ לִבָּם‬
‫וּלְקַרְנוֹת מִזְבְּחוֹתֵיכֶם׃‬

ᵃ⁻ᵃ *Meaning of Heb. uncertain. Emendation yields "Surely the horns of their altars / Are as a memorial against them"*

407

2] While their children remember‑ᵃ
Their altars and sacred posts,
By verdant trees,
Upon lofty hills.

2] כִּזְכֹּר בְּנֵיהֶם
מִזְבְּחוֹתָם וַאֲשֵׁרֵיהֶם
עַל־עֵץ רַעֲנָן
עַל גְּבָעוֹת הַגְּבֹהוֹת׃

3] ᵇ‑Because of the sin of your shrines
Throughout your borders,
I will make your rampart a heap in the field,
And all your treasures a spoil.‑ᵇ

3] הֲרָרִי בַּשָּׂדֶה חֵילְךָ
כָל־אוֹצְרוֹתֶיךָ לָבַז אֶתֵּן
בָּמֹתֶיךָ בְּחַטָּאת
בְּכָל־גְּבוּלֶיךָ׃

4] ᶜ‑You will forfeit, by your own act,‑ᶜ
The inheritance I have given you;
I will make you a slave to your enemies
In a land you have never known.
For you have kindled the flame of My wrath
Which shall burn for all time.

4] וְשָׁמַטְתָּה וּבְךָ מִנַּחֲלָתְךָ
אֲשֶׁר נָתַתִּי לָךְ
וְהַעֲבַדְתִּיךָ אֶת־אֹיְבֶיךָ
בָּאָרֶץ אֲשֶׁר לֹא־יָדָעְתָּ
כִּי־אֵשׁ קְדַחְתֶּם בְּאַפִּי
עַד־עוֹלָם תּוּקָד׃

5] Thus said the LORD:
Cursed is he who trusts in man,
Who makes mere flesh his strength,
And turns his thoughts from the LORD.

5] כֹּה אָמַר יְהוָה
אָרוּר הַגֶּבֶר אֲשֶׁר יִבְטַח בָּאָדָם
וְשָׂם בָּשָׂר זְרֹעוֹ
וּמִן יְהוָה יָסוּר לִבּוֹ׃

6] He shall be like a bushᵈ in the desert,
Which does not sense the coming of good:
It is set in the scorched places of the wilderness,
In a barren land without inhabitant.

6] וְהָיָה כְּעַרְעָר בָּעֲרָבָה
וְלֹא יִרְאֶה כִּי־יָבוֹא טוֹב
וְשָׁכַן חֲרֵרִים בַּמִּדְבָּר
אֶרֶץ מְלֵחָה וְלֹא תֵשֵׁב׃

7] Blessed is he who trusts in the LORD,
Whose trust is the LORD alone.

7] בָּרוּךְ הַגֶּבֶר אֲשֶׁר יִבְטַח בַּיהוָה
וְהָיָה יְהוָה מִבְטַחוֹ׃

8] He shall be like a tree planted by waters,
Sending forth its roots by a stream:
It does not sense the coming of heat,

8] וְהָיָה כְּעֵץ שָׁתוּל עַל־מַיִם
וְעַל יוּבַל יְשַׁלַּח שָׁרָשָׁיו
וְלֹא יִרְאֶה כִּי־יָבֹא חֹם

ᵇ‑ᵇ Meaning of Heb. uncertain

ᶜ‑ᶜ Meaning of Heb. uncertain. Emendation yields "Your hand must let go"

ᵈ Or "tamarisk"; exact meaning of Heb. uncertain

Its leaves are ever fresh;
It has no care in a year of drought,
It does not cease to yield fruit.

9] Most devious is the heart;
It is perverse—who can fathom it?

10] I the LORD probe the heart,
Search the mind—
To repay every man according to his ways,
With the proper fruit of his deeds.

11] *b-Like a partridge hatching what she did not
    lay,-b*
So is one who amasses wealth by unjust means;
In the middle of his life it will leave him,
And in the end he will be proved a fool.

12] O Throne of Glory exalted from of old,
Our Sacred Shrine!

13] O Hope of Israel! O LORD!
All who forsake You shall be put to shame,
Those in the land who turn from You*e*
Shall be doomed*f* men,
For they have forsaken the LORD,
The Fount of living waters.

14] Heal me, O LORD, and let me be healed;
Save me, and let me be saved;
For You are my glory.

וְהָיָה עָלֵהוּ רַעֲנָן

וּבִשְׁנַת בַּצֹּרֶת לֹא יִדְאָג

וְלֹא יָמִישׁ מֵעֲשׂוֹת פֶּרִי:

9] עָקֹב הַלֵּב מִכֹּל

וְאָנֻשׁ הוּא מִי יֵדָעֶנּוּ:

10] אֲנִי יְהוָה חֹקֵר לֵב

בֹּחֵן כְּלָיוֹת

וְלָתֵת לְאִישׁ כִּדְרָכָיו

כִּפְרִי מַעֲלָלָיו:

11] קֹרֵא דָגַר וְלֹא יָלָד

עֹשֶׂה עֹשֶׁר וְלֹא בְמִשְׁפָּט

בַּחֲצִי יָמָיו יַעַזְבֶנּוּ

וּבְאַחֲרִיתוֹ יִהְיֶה נָבָל:

12] כִּסֵּא כָבוֹד מָרוֹם מֵרִאשׁוֹן

מְקוֹם מִקְדָּשֵׁנוּ:

13] מִקְוֵה יִשְׂרָאֵל יְהוָה

כָּל־עֹזְבֶיךָ יֵבֹשׁוּ

וְסוּרַי בָּאָרֶץ יִכָּתֵבוּ

כִּי עָזְבוּ מְקוֹר מַיִם חַיִּים

אֶת־יְהוָה:

14] רְפָאֵנִי יְהוָה וְאֵרָפֵא

הוֹשִׁיעֵנִי וְאִוָּשֵׁעָה

כִּי תְהִלָּתִי אָתָּה:

---

b-b Meaning of Heb. uncertain

e Lit. "Me"

f Lit. "inscribed"; meaning of line uncertain

Zephaniah

3 : 1-20

Chapter 3

1] Ah, sullied, polluted,
Overbearing[a] city!

2] She has been disobedient,
Has learned no lesson;
She has not trusted in the LORD,
Has not drawn near to her God.

3] The officials within her
Are roaring lions;
Her judges are wolves [b]-of the steppe,
They leave no bone until morning.[-b]

4] Her prophets are reckless,
Faithless fellows;
Her priests profane what is holy,
They give perverse rulings.

5] But the LORD in her midst is righteous,
He does no wrong;
He issues judgment every morning,
As unfailing as the light.
The wrongdoer knows no shame!

6] I wiped out nations:
Their corner towers are desolate;

ג

1] הוֹי מֹרְאָה וְנִגְאָלָה
הָעִיר הַיּוֹנָה׃

2] לֹא שָׁמְעָה בְּקוֹל
לֹא לָקְחָה מוּסָר
בַּיהֹוָה לֹא בָטָחָה
אֶל אֱלֹהֶיהָ לֹא קָרֵבָה׃

3] שָׂרֶיהָ בְקִרְבָּהּ
אֲרָיוֹת שֹׁאֲגִים
שֹׁפְטֶיהָ זְאֵבֵי עֶרֶב
לֹא גָרְמוּ לַבֹּקֶר׃

4] נְבִיאֶיהָ פֹּחֲזִים
אַנְשֵׁי בֹּגְדוֹת
כֹּהֲנֶיהָ חִלְּלוּ־קֹדֶשׁ
חָמְסוּ תּוֹרָה׃

5] יְהֹוָה צַדִּיק בְּקִרְבָּהּ
לֹא יַעֲשֶׂה עַוְלָה
בַּבֹּקֶר בַּבֹּקֶר מִשְׁפָּטוֹ יִתֵּן
לָאוֹר לֹא נֶעְדָּר
וְלֹא יוֹדֵעַ עַוָּל בֹּשֶׁת׃

6] הִכְרַתִּי גוֹיִם
נָשַׁמּוּ פִּנּוֹתָם

---

[a] *Meaning of Heb. uncertain. Emendation yields "harlot"; cf. Isa. 1.21*
[b-b] *Meaning of Heb. uncertain*

410

I turned their thoroughfares into ruins,
With none passing by;
Their towns lie waste without people,
Without inhabitants.

7] And I thought that she[c] would fear Me,
Would learn a lesson,
And that the punishment I brought on them[d]
Would not be [e-lost on her.-e]
Instead, all the more eagerly
They have practiced corruption in all their deeds.

8] But wait for Me—says the LORD—
For the day when I arise as an accuser;[f]
When I decide to gather nations,
To bring kingdoms together,
To pour out My indignation on them,
All My blazing anger.
Indeed, by the fire of My passion
All the earth shall be consumed.

9] For then I will make the peoples pure of speech,
So that they all invoke the LORD by name
And serve Him with one accord.[g]

10] From beyond the rivers of Cush, My suppliants[b]
Shall bring offerings to Me in Fair Puzai.[h]

11] In that day,
You will no longer be shamed for all the deeds

הֶחֱרַבְתִּי חוּצוֹתָם

מִבְּלִי עוֹבֵר

נִצְדּוּ עָרֵיהֶם מִבְּלִי־אִישׁ

מֵאֵין יוֹשֵׁב׃

7] אָמַרְתִּי אַךְ תִּירְאִי אוֹתִי

תִּקְחִי מוּסָר

וְלֹא יִכָּרֵת מְעוֹנָהּ

כֹּל אֲשֶׁר פָּקַדְתִּי עָלֶיהָ

אָכֵן הִשְׁכִּימוּ הִשְׁחִיתוּ

כֹּל עֲלִילוֹתָם׃

8] לָכֵן חַכּוּ־לִי נְאֻם יְהוָה

לְיוֹם קוּמִי לְעַד

כִּי מִשְׁפָּטִי לֶאֱסֹף גּוֹיִם

לְקָבְצִי מַמְלָכוֹת

לִשְׁפֹּךְ עֲלֵיהֶם זַעְמִי

כֹּל חֲרוֹן אַפִּי

כִּי בְּאֵשׁ קִנְאָתִי

תֵּאָכֵל כָּל־הָאָרֶץ׃

9] כִּי־אָז אֶהְפֹּךְ אֶל עַמִּים

שָׂפָה בְרוּרָה

לִקְרֹא כֻלָּם בְּשֵׁם יְהוָה

לְעָבְדוֹ שְׁכֶם אֶחָד׃

10] מֵעֵבֶר לְנַהֲרֵי־כוּשׁ

עֲתָרַי בַּת־פּוּצַי יוֹבִלוּן מִנְחָתִי׃

11] בַּיּוֹם הַהוּא

לֹא תֵבוֹשִׁי מִכֹּל עֲלִילֹתַיִךְ

---

[c] Heb. "you"   [d] Heb. "her"   [e-e] Lit. "cut off [from] her vision"

[f] Understanding 'ad as equivalent to 'ed, with Septuagint and Syriac

[g] Lit. "back," i.e., like beasts of burden

[b] Meaning of Heb. uncertain

[h] Emendation yields "Zion." For the thought, cf. Isa. 18.1, 7

By which you have defied Me.
For then I will remove
The proud and exultant within you,
And you will be haughty no more
On My sacred mount.[i]

אֲשֶׁר פָּשַׁעַתְּ בִּי
כִּי־אָז אָסִיר מִקִּרְבֵּךְ
עַלִּיזֵי גַּאֲוָתֵךְ
וְלֹא תוֹסִפִי לְגָבְהָה עוֹד
בְּהַר קָדְשִׁי:

12] But I will leave within you
A poor, humble folk,
And they shall find refuge
In the name of the LORD.

12] וְהִשְׁאַרְתִּי בְקִרְבֵּךְ
עַם עָנִי וָדָל
וְחָסוּ בְּשֵׁם יְהוָה:

13] The remnant of Israel
Shall do no wrong
And speak no falsehood;
A deceitful tongue
Shall not be in their mouths.
Only such as these shall graze and lie down,
With none to trouble them.

13] שְׁאֵרִית יִשְׂרָאֵל
לֹא יַעֲשׂוּ עַוְלָה
וְלֹא יְדַבְּרוּ כָזָב
וְלֹא יִמָּצֵא בְּפִיהֶם
לְשׁוֹן תַּרְמִית
כִּי־הֵמָּה יִרְעוּ וְרָבְצוּ
וְאֵין מַחֲרִיד:

14] Shout for joy, Fair Zion,
Cry aloud, O Israel!
Rejoice and be glad with all your heart,
Fair Jerusalem!

14] רָנִּי בַּת־צִיּוֹן
הָרִיעוּ יִשְׂרָאֵל
שִׂמְחִי וְעָלְזִי בְּכָל־לֵב
בַּת יְרוּשָׁלָ͏ִם:

15] The LORD has annulled the judgment against you,
He has swept away your foes.
Israel's Sovereign the LORD is within you;
You need fear misfortune no more.

15] הֵסִיר יְהוָה מִשְׁפָּטַיִךְ
פִּנָּה אֹיְבֵךְ
מֶלֶךְ יִשְׂרָאֵל יְהוָה בְּקִרְבֵּךְ
לֹא תִירְאִי רָע עוֹד:

16] In that day,
This shall be said to Jerusalem:
Have no fear, O Zion;
Let not your hands droop!

16] בַּיּוֹם הַהוּא
יֵאָמֵר לִירוּשָׁלַ͏ִם
אַל תִּירָאִי צִיּוֹן
אַל יִרְפּוּ יָדָיִךְ:

17] Your God the LORD is in your midst,
A warrior who brings triumph.

17] יְהוָה אֱלֹהַיִךְ בְּקִרְבֵּךְ
גִּבּוֹר יוֹשִׁיעַ

[i] *I.e., in My holy land; cf. Isa. 11.9; 57.13; 65.25*

He will rejoice over you and be glad,
He will shout over you with jubilation.
He will *i*-soothe with His love

יָשִׂישׂ עָלַיִךְ בְּשִׂמְחָה

יַחֲרִישׁ בְּאַהֲבָתוֹ

יָגִיל עָלַיִךְ בְּרִנָּה:

18] Those long disconsolate.⁻*i*
I will take away from you *b*-the woe
Over which you endured mockery.⁻*b*

18] נוּגֵי מִמּוֹעֵד

אָסַפְתִּי מִמֵּךְ

הָיוּ מַשְׂאֵת עָלֶיהָ חֶרְפָּה:

19] At that time I will make [an end]
Of all who afflicted you.
And I will rescue the lame [sheep]
And gather the strayed;
And I will exchange their disgrace
For fame and renown in all the earth.

19] הִנְנִי עֹשֶׂה אֶת־כָּל־מְעַנַּיִךְ

בָּעֵת הַהִיא

וְהוֹשַׁעְתִּי אֶת־הַצֹּלֵעָה

וְהַנִּדָּחָה אֲקַבֵּץ

וְשַׂמְתִּים לִתְהִלָּה וּלְשֵׁם

בְּכָל־הָאָרֶץ בָּשְׁתָּם:

20] At that time I will gather you,
And at [that] time I will bring you [home];
For I will make you renowned and famous
Among all the peoples on earth,
When I restore your fortunes
Before their*k* very eyes

—said the LORD.

20] בָּעֵת הַהִיא אָבִיא אֶתְכֶם

וּבָעֵת קַבְּצִי אֶתְכֶם

כִּי־אֶתֵּן אֶתְכֶם לְשֵׁם וְלִתְהִלָּה

בְּכֹל עַמֵּי הָאָרֶץ

בְּשׁוּבִי אֶת־שְׁבוּתֵיכֶם לְעֵינֵיכֶם

אָמַר יְהוָה:

---

i⁻i *Meaning of Heb. uncertain. Emendation yields "renew His love / As in the days
of old"*
b⁻b *Meaning of Heb. uncertain*
k Heb. "your"

Psalms

116 : 1-19

Psalm 116

1] *a*I love the LORD
for He hears*a* my voice, my pleas;

2] for He turns His ear to me
whenever I call.

3] The bonds of death encompassed me;
the torments of Sheol overtook me.
I came upon trouble and sorrow

4] and I invoked the name of the LORD,
"O LORD, save my life!"

5] The LORD is gracious and beneficent;
our God is compassionate.

6] The LORD protects the simple;
I was brought low and He saved me.

7] Be at rest, once again, O my soul,
for the LORD has been good to you.

8] You*b* have delivered me from death,
my eyes from tears,
my feet from stumbling.

9] I shall walk before the LORD
in the lands of the living.

10] *c*I trust [in the LORD];
out of great suffering I spoke*c*

קטז

1] אָהַבְתִּי כִּי יִשְׁמַע יְהוָה
אֶת־קוֹלִי תַּחֲנוּנָי:

2] כִּי הִטָּה אָזְנוֹ לִי
וּבְיָמַי אֶקְרָא:

3] אֲפָפוּנִי חֶבְלֵי־מָוֶת
וּמְצָרֵי שְׁאוֹל מְצָאוּנִי
צָרָה וְיָגוֹן אֶמְצָא:

4] וּבְשֵׁם יְהוָה אֶקְרָא
אָנָּא יְהוָה מַלְּטָה נַפְשִׁי:

5] חַנּוּן יְהוָה וְצַדִּיק
וֵאלֹהֵינוּ מְרַחֵם:

6] שֹׁמֵר פְּתָאִים יְהוָה
דַּלּוֹתִי וְלִי יְהוֹשִׁיעַ:

7] שׁוּבִי נַפְשִׁי לִמְנוּחָיְכִי
כִּי יְהוָה גָּמַל עָלָיְכִי:

8] כִּי חִלַּצְתָּ נַפְשִׁי מִמָּוֶת
אֶת־עֵינִי מִן דִּמְעָה
אֶת־רַגְלִי מִדֶּחִי:

9] אֶתְהַלֵּךְ לִפְנֵי יְהוָה
בְּאַרְצוֹת הַחַיִּים:

10] הֶאֱמַנְתִּי כִּי אֲדַבֵּר
אֲנִי עָנִיתִי מְאֹד:

---

a-a Heb. transposed for clarity. Others "I would love that the LORD hear," etc.
b I.e., God   c-c Meaning of Heb. uncertain

11] and said rashly,
"All men are false."

12] How can I repay the LORD
for all His bounties to me?

13] I raise the cup of deliverance
and invoke the name of the LORD.

14] I shall pay my vows to the LORD
in the presence of all His people.

15] The death of His faithful ones
is grievous in the LORD's sight.

16] O LORD,
I am Your servant,
Your servant, the son of Your maidservant;
You have undone the cords that bind me.

17] I will sacrifice a thank offering to You
and invoke the name of the LORD.

18] I will pay my vows to the LORD
in the presence of all His people,

19] in the courts of the house of the LORD,
in the midst of[d] Jerusalem.
Hallelujah.

אֲנִי אָמַרְתִּי בְחָפְזִי [11]
כָּל־הָאָדָם כֹּזֵב:

מָה אָשִׁיב לַיהֹוָה [12]
כָּל־תַּגְמוּלוֹהִי עָלָי:

כּוֹס יְשׁוּעוֹת אֶשָּׂא [13]
וּבְשֵׁם יְהֹוָה אֶקְרָא:

נְדָרַי לַיהֹוָה אֲשַׁלֵּם [14]
נֶגְדָה־נָּא לְכָל־עַמּוֹ:

יָקָר בְּעֵינֵי יְהֹוָה [15]
הַמָּוְתָה לַחֲסִידָיו:

אָנָּה יְהֹוָה [16]
כִּי־אֲנִי עַבְדֶּךָ
אֲנִי־עַבְדְּךָ בֶּן־אֲמָתֶךָ
פִּתַּחְתָּ לְמוֹסֵרָי:

לְךָ־אֶזְבַּח זֶבַח תּוֹדָה [17]
וּבְשֵׁם יְהֹוָה אֶקְרָא:

נְדָרַי לַיהֹוָה אֲשַׁלֵּם [18]
נֶגְדָה־נָּא לְכָל־עַמּוֹ:

בְּחַצְרוֹת בֵּית יְהֹוָה [19]
בְּתוֹכֵכִי יְרוּשָׁלַיִם הַלְלוּיָהּ:

[d] Others "of you"

415

Torah Blessings

Before reading the Torah

בָּרְכוּ אֶת־יְיָ הַמְבֹרָךְ!

בָּרְכוּ יְיָ הַמְבֹרָךְ לְעוֹלָם וָעֶד!

בָּרוּךְ אַתָּה, יְיָ אֱלֹהֵינוּ, מֶלֶךְ הָעוֹלָם, אֲשֶׁר בָּחַר־בָּנוּ
מִכָּל־הָעַמִּים וְנָתַן־לָנוּ אֶת־תּוֹרָתוֹ. בָּרוּךְ אַתָּה, יְיָ,
נוֹתֵן הַתּוֹרָה.

Praise the Lord, to whom our praise is due!

Praised be the Lord, to whom our praise is due, now and
for ever!

Blessed is the Lord our God, Ruler of the universe, who
has chosen us from all peoples by giving us His Torah.
Blessed is the Lord, Giver of the Torah.

♦ ♦

After reading the Torah

בָּרוּךְ אַתָּה, יְיָ אֱלֹהֵינוּ, מֶלֶךְ הָעוֹלָם, אֲשֶׁר נָתַן לָנוּ
תּוֹרַת אֱמֶת וְחַיֵּי עוֹלָם נָטַע בְּתוֹכֵנוּ. בָּרוּךְ אַתָּה, יְיָ,
נוֹתֵן הַתּוֹרָה.

Blessed is the Lord our God, Ruler of the universe, who
has given us a Torah of truth, implanting within us eternal
life. Blessed is the Lord, Giver of the Torah.

Haftarah Blessings

Before reading the Haftarah

בָּרוּךְ אַתָּה, יְיָ אֱלֹהֵינוּ, מֶלֶךְ הָעוֹלָם, אֲשֶׁר בָּחַר
בִּנְבִיאִים טוֹבִים וְרָצָה בְדִבְרֵיהֶם הַנֶּאֱמָרִים בֶּאֱמֶת.
בָּרוּךְ אַתָּה, יְיָ, הַבּוֹחֵר בַּתּוֹרָה וּבְמֹשֶׁה עַבְדּוֹ
וּבְיִשְׂרָאֵל עַמּוֹ וּבִנְבִיאֵי הָאֱמֶת וָצֶדֶק.

Blessed is the Lord our God, Ruler of the universe, who
has chosen faithful prophets to speak words of truth.
Blessed is the Lord, for the revelation of Torah, for Moses
His servant and Israel His people, and for the prophets of
truth and righteousness.

◆ ◆

After reading the Haftarah

בָּרוּךְ אַתָּה, יְיָ אֱלֹהֵינוּ, מֶלֶךְ הָעוֹלָם, צוּר כָּל־
הָעוֹלָמִים, צַדִּיק בְּכָל־הַדּוֹרוֹת, הָאֵל הַנֶּאֱמָן, הָאוֹמֵר
וְעוֹשֶׂה, הַמְדַבֵּר וּמְקַיֵּם, שֶׁכָּל־דְּבָרָיו אֱמֶת וָצֶדֶק.

Blessed is the Lord our God, Ruler of the universe, Rock
of all creation, Righteous One of all generations, the
faithful God whose word is deed, whose every command
is just and true.

עַל־הַתּוֹרָה וְעַל־הָעֲבוֹדָה וְעַל־הַנְּבִיאִים וְעַל־יוֹם
הַשַּׁבָּת הַזֶּה, שֶׁנָּתַתָּ־לָּנוּ, יְיָ אֱלֹהֵינוּ, לִקְדֻשָּׁה וְלִמְנוּחָה,
לְכָבוֹד וּלְתִפְאָרֶת, עַל־הַכֹּל, יְיָ אֱלֹהֵינוּ, אֲנַחְנוּ מוֹדִים
לָךְ, וּמְבָרְכִים אוֹתָךְ. יִתְבָּרַךְ שִׁמְךָ בְּפִי כָּל־חַי תָּמִיד
לְעוֹלָם וָעֶד.

בָּרוּךְ אַתָּה, יְיָ, מְקַדֵּשׁ הַשַּׁבָּת.

For the Torah, for the privilege of worship, for the
prophets, and for this Shabbat that You, O Lord our God,
have given us for holiness and rest, for honor and glory,
we thank and bless You. May Your name be blessed for
ever by every living being.

Blessed is the Lord, for the Sabbath and its holiness.

417